MODERN ART AND THE DEATH OF A CULTURE

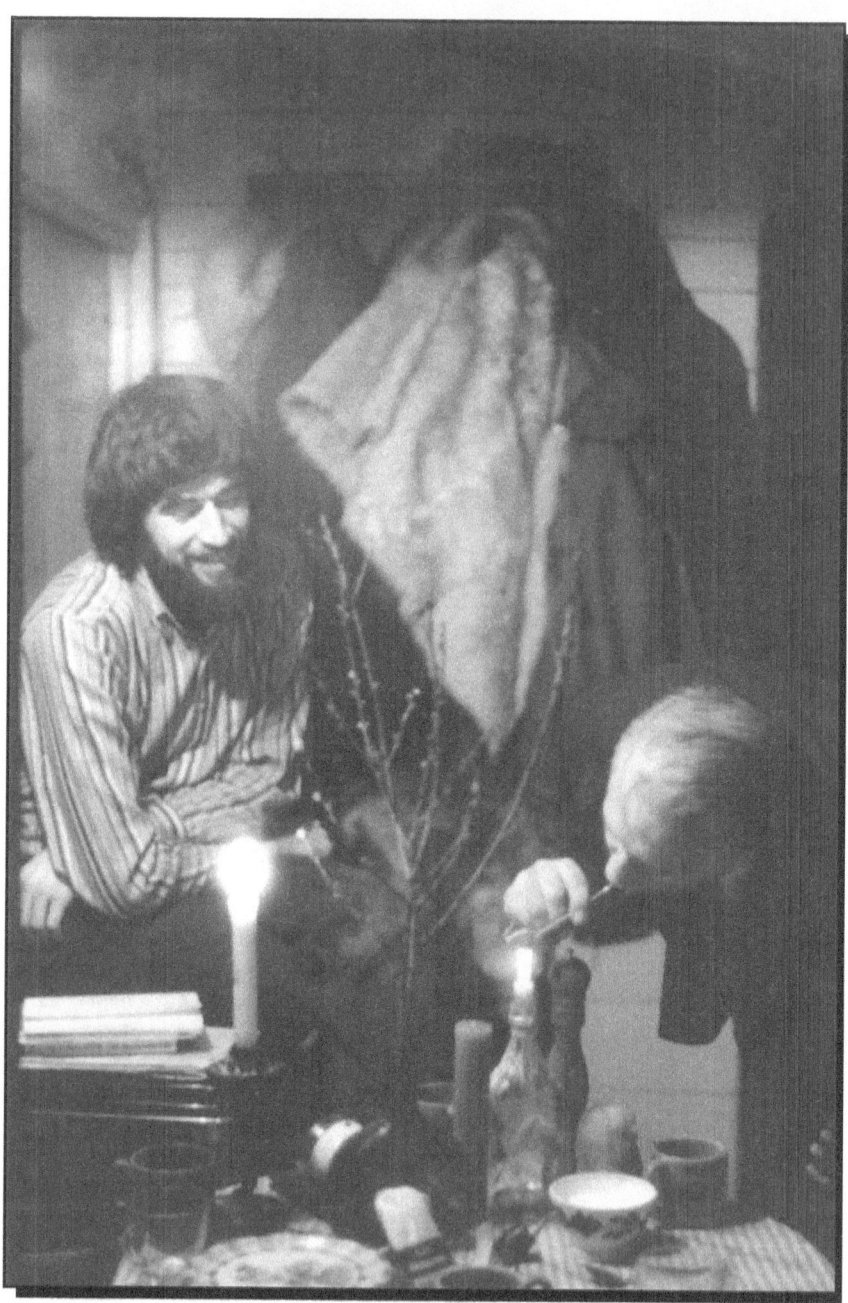

Photograph by Sylvester Jacobs

MODERN ART AND THE DEATH OF A CULTURE

The Complete Works of Hans R. Rookmaaker

Volume 5

Edited by
Marleen Hengelaar-Rookmaaker

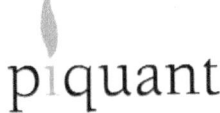

Copyright © 2003 by Marleen Hengelaar-Rookmaaker

This edition copyright © 2021 by Piquant Editions in the UK

Piquant Editions
Website: www.piquanteditions.com

First edition 2003
Paperback edition 2021

ISBN for this volume: 978-1-909281-84-4

The right of Marleen Hengelaar-Rookmaaker to be identified as author of this work has been asserted by her in accordance with the Copyright, Designs and Patents Act, 1988.

All Rights Reserved. No part of this publication may be reproduced, stored in a retrieval system or transmitted, in any form or by any means, electronic, mechanical, photocopying, recording or otherwise, without the prior written permission of the publisher or the Copyright Licensing Agency.

Modern Art and the Death of a Culture, copyright © by H.R. Rookmaaker
(Leicester: Apollos, an imprint of Inter-Varsity Press / Wheaton, Il: Crossway Books, a division of Good News Publishers, 1970, 1973),
copyright © 1994 by Marleen Hengelaar-Rookmaaker and included
in the Complete Works with permission of the publishers
Art and the Public, copyright © by H.R. Rookmaaker (Huémoz-sur-Ollon, Switzerland: L'Abri Fellowship Foundation, 1969, 2nd edn),
copyright © 2000 by Marleen Hengelaar-Rookmaaker
Articles on and reviews of twentieth-century art and artists: copyright © by H.R. Rookmaaker; copyright © 2000 by Marleen Hengelaar-Rookmaaker
Unless otherwise stated or the author's own paraphrase is used,
Scripture quotations are from the HOLY BIBLE, NEW INTERNATIONAL VERSION ® NIV®, copyright © 1973, 1978, 1984 by the International Bible Society.
All rights reserved.

British Library Cataloguing-in-Publication Data
A catalogue record of this book is available in the UK from the British Library.

ISBN 978-1-909281-84-4

Cover art: Marc de Klijn, detail from
Monuments in the (pre)history of modern art (2000)
Cover design: Jonathan Kearney

Piquant Editions actively supports theological dialogue and an author's right to publish but does not necessarily endorse the individual views and opinions set forth here or in works referenced within this publication, nor guarantee technical and grammatical correctness. The publishers do not accept any responsibility or liability to persons or property as a consequence of the reading, use or interpretation of its published content.

Overview Contents for the Six Volumes of the Complete Works of Hans Rookmaaker

The contents of volumes 1 to 6 have been organized partly chronologically and partly thematically. Most of the writings compiled in volumes 1 and 2 date from before 1960, while most of the materials brought together in volumes 3 to 6 were written after 1960. Each of the volumes contains one or more books as well as articles. Two books, previously published in Dutch only, appear in English for the first time: *Jazz, Blues and Spirituals* (1960) and *Art and Entertainment* (1962). In addition, roughly a thousand pages of Dutch articles have been translated into English: exhibition and music reviews; many short articles on art, music, and Christianity and culture written for Christian periodicals; articles that are scholarly and art-historical; and articles that are long and philosophical like the ones for *Philosophia Reformata*. Also included are the lectures given at L'Abri and Westminster Seminary. The two series of lectures, on 'God's Hand in History' and 'Revelation', have been integrated by Colin Duriez into one unit entitled 'God's Hand in History'.

Volume 1: **ART, ARTISTS AND GAUGUIN**

- Foreword by Jeremy Begbie
- Scholarly introduction by Graham Birtwistle
- Gauguin and Nineteenth-Century Art Theory (*Synthetist Art Theories*)
- Rookmaaker as art critic (1949–1956): exhibition reviews

Volume 2: **NEW ORLEANS JAZZ, MAHALIA JACKSON AND THE PHILOSOPHY OF ART**

- Philosophy and aesthetics: articles on style, world view, philosophy of art and education
- *Jazz, Blues and Spirituals*
- Music articles: African-American music, blues, spirituals and gospel, jazz, rock, and classical music

Volume 3: **THE CREATIVE GIFT, DÜRER, DADA AND DESOLATION ROW**

- *Art and Entertainment*
- *The Creative Gift*
- Articles on history, faith and culture, faith and lifestyle, faith and scholarship, and the Westminster discussions on faith, art, culture and lifestyle

Volume 4: **WESTERN ART AND THE MEANDERINGS OF A CULTURE**

- Articles on Western art from the Middle Ages until the nineteenth century: themes and motifs, general reflections on art, plus an unfinished manuscript
- *Art Needs No Justification*
- The Christian and art: articles and letters
- Miscellaneous articles and exhibition reviews

Volume 5: **MODERN ART AND THE DEATH OF A CULTURE**

- *Modern Art and the Death of a Culture*
- *Art and the Public Today*
- Articles on twentieth-century artists and streams, modern art, and the question: Do we need to be modern in order to be contemporary?
- Reviews of books on modern art and reviews of expositions of twentieth-century sculpture

Volume 6: **OUR CALLING AND GOD'S HAND IN HISTORY**

- Biography of Hans Rookmaaker by Laurel Gasque
- Interviews
- 'God's Hand in History' and the L'Abri lectures
- Indexes to all six volumes of the *Complete Works*

Contents of Volume 5

Acknowledgments   x

Part I: Modern Art and the Death of a Culture

Publisher's Foreword to Previous Edition   3
Introduction   5
1 The Message in the Medium   7
> *The icon (7); Beyond history (9); Painting is more than art alone (10); Two landscapes (11); Two world views (14)*

2 The Roots of Contemporary Culture   17
> *Christianity and culture (19); Gnosticism and mysticism (20); A dualism of nature and grace (21); The Reformation attitude (22); Before the Enlightenment (24); Science (26); The Age of Reason (28); 'Man in the box' (31)*

3 The First Step to Modern Art   33
> *Nothing but the facts (33); Landscape and reality (35); The death of themes (36); Naturalistic reality (38); Another initial step to modern art (39); Idealized escapism (40); Christian art? (41); The new naturalism and the bourgeois attitude (46); Reactions to realism (48)*

4 The Second Step to Modern Art   51
> *On from Impressionism (54); The quest for reality (56); The quest for a synthesis (58); A mystic-Romantic reaction (59)*

5 The Last Steps to Modern Art   62
> *Expressionism (62); Developments in Germany (64); Abstraction (67); Cubism (69); The quest for absolutes (72); The decisive step (73); Four reactions (74)*

6 Into the New Era   79
> *A new art for new needs (80); A new art with a new message (82); The irrationality of the rational (83); The Surrealist protest (85); Surreality and Christian reality (89); The real and the horrible (92); A different twentieth-century response (94)*

7 Modern Art and the Twentieth-Century Revolt   96
> *Abstract Expressionism (99); The skeleton of Achilles (100); Two British artists (103); Pop and Op (105); Happenings and hippies (107); Jazz, blues and rock (111)*

8 Protest, Revolution and the Christian Response   116
> *The search for humanity (119); Plastic people (121); Beyond the material (122); Drugs – and religion (126); What is normal? (128); The tragic protest (131); The permissive society (133); Apocalypse (135); Towards a renewal of the church (136)*

9 Faith and Art   140
> *Christianity in art (142); The role of art (143); Questions of aesthetics and morals (145); Norms and structures in art (147); The Christian artist (154); The Christian in a changing world (156)*

Bibliography to Modern Art and the Death of a Culture   162

Part II: Art and the Public Today

Introduction by H.R.R. to the 2nd Edition   167
The Artist as a Prophet?   169
Commitment in Art   188
Appendix: Schematic Summary of the Artistic Revolution   204
> *Protest (204); Teaching (204); Adhered to (205); Promoted by (205); Result (206)*

Part III: Articles and Reviews on Twentieth-Century Art and Artists

Articles on Artists and Art Streams   209
> *New Art: Art Nouveau and Jugendstil (209); Whence do we come? What are we? Where do we go? (210); Angst (217); The art of the twentieth century (219); Pondering four modern drawings (225); Surrealism (231); Rouault (236); This too is our times (239); Wholesome twentieth-century art (245); Aad Veldhoen: contemporary wholesome art (246); Culture and revolution I (247); Culture and revolution II: we live in '1787' (254)*

Reflections on Modern Art   261
> *Why modern art? (261); The function of visual art in our times (279); Form and content of modern art (285); Art or not art? (287)*

Modern Art and Gnosticism   292
> *Shestov (292); Modern art and gnosticism: an open letter to Prof. Dr Jan Aler (296); Is modern art true? (305); Do we need to be modern in order to be contemporary? (311)*

Reviews of Books on Twentieth-Century Art — 336

> J. Stellingwerff: *Werkelijkheid en grondmotief bij Vincent Willem van Gogh* [reality and religious motive and Vincent Willem van Gogh], 1959 (336); H.Redeker: *De dagen der artistieke vertwijfeling* [the days of artistic desperation], 1950 (339); J.M. Prange: *De God Hai-Hai en rabarber* [the god Hai-Hai and rhubarb], 1957 (341); H. Sedlmayr: *Die Revolution der modernen Kunst* ('The revolution of modern art'), 1957 (346); R.W.D. Oxenaar: *De schilderkunst van onze tijd* [the art of painting of our times], 1958 and W. Hess: *Dokumente zum Verständnis der modernen Malerei* ('Documents for the understanding of modern art'), 1957 (350); W.L. Meijer: *Kunst en revolutie* [art and revolution], 1976 (358)

Trouw Reviews of Expositions of Twentieth-Century Sculpture — 361

> Rodin's life's work: Dante's humanism in bronze (361); Henry Moore: creator of dynamic forms (362); Henry Moore searches for a new kind of sculpture (363); Beautiful wood sculptures of high quality: Cor Wijker, spirited and convincing (365); Italian art in Museumpark Rotterdam: an old tradition revived (366); The language of statues – an exhibition in Sonsbeek Park, Arnhem (368); Beauty in stone: the statue as a symbol of our times (370); Biennale of modern sculpture in Middelheim Park, Antwerp (372); Sculptures in park in Groningen (374); Surprises in Arnhem: high-quality Dutch art (376); John Rädecker, artist of great stature: sculpture as a portrayal of an exalted vision of life (377)

Notes to Volume 5 — 381

Acknowledgments

The two books that are taken up in this volume, *Modern Art and the Death of a Culture* and *Art and the Public Today*, were first published in English, though the inaugural speech that was incorporated in the latter had originally been written and delivered in Dutch. Also the open letter to Professor Aler on modern art and gnosticism appeared in print in English, in the *Zeitschrift für Ästhetik und allgemeine Kunstwissenschaft* in 1973. The remainder of the materials in this book, articles and reviews of exhibitions and books on twentieth-century art, were all in Dutch. They were translated by Evelyn Kuntz Hielema and Herbert Donald Morton. I want to express my gratitude for their dedicated work.

Marleen Hengelaar-Rookmaaker
The Netherlands

Part I

MODERN ART AND THE DEATH OF A CULTURE

Note to this edition: The illustrations that accompany the original text have not been included in the *Complete Works* because of copyright restrictions. Most of them, or related works by the same artists, can now be viewed freely on the Internet.

Publisher's Foreword to Previous Edition

When first published in 1970, Malcolm Muggeridge chose *Modern Art and the Death of a Culture* as one of his *Observer* books of the year, and it soon became a bestseller of its type. For its first readers, it was a book that dramatically dealt with 'what is happening now'. As such it brought a brilliant critical perspective to bear on the cultural turmoil of the 'radical sixties', especially as reflected in the art of the time.

But there is a sense in which H.R. Rookmaaker's insights are as timely today as they were a generation ago, and for this reason it is reissued here in this new edition. Rookmaaker indeed would have recognized much of the current art scene today.

The fallacy that the true artist is anarchic, rebellious, a kind of prophet or shaman with mysterious insights into his or her own times, is still largely unchallenged. Rookmaaker would have recognized aspects of postmodernism too. In the 1970s he suggested that the accepted history of modern art might need to be rewritten. We are not faced, he argued, with an inevitable, relentless progress into anarchic forms of anti-war. Perhaps, he suggested, modern art is a kind of gnostic and nihilist cult which is just one movement among many in the twentieth century. Certainly today we can see numerous other movements with a gnostic bent, such as New Age. A new gnosticism may indeed prove to be the common thread running through our postchristian, post-everything culture. He pointed out other contemporary work where a renewed interest in visual language did not mean a rejection of a more ordinary, less bizarre and abnormal view of human experience. Since the mid-1980s it has become obvious that something like this is the case – which Rookmaaker would have been pleased to see

The excitement generated by the book when first published was not simply a product of those times of counter-culture and student revolution. It came also from Rookmaaker's ability to articulate his faith and scholarship in a manner equal to the occasion.

As a young man in wartime Holland, he was interned for distributing anti-Nazi leaflets. During his imprisonment he became a Christian by reading a Bible he had been given and through contacts with imprisoned Dutch Christians. For Rookmaaker there was no conflict between faith and academic study. In the early 1950s he was an art critic for *Trouw*, one of Holland's daily papers. In some circles he was better known for his expertise in early jazz. During that time too his lifelong friendship with Francis Schaeffer and L'Abri developed. With the publication in 1959 of his doctoral thesis on Gauguin, his academic credentials were established, along with his interest in the genesis of the ideas which underpin modern art in the twentieth century.

This, then, is something of the background to Rookmaaker's concern in 1970 – to share with the non-specialist and the church what he had discovered as a Christian in his studies. The book itself grew out of a series of lectures Rookmaaker gave in the late 1960s at art colleges and British and American universities. The popularity of the book lies to a great extent in his ability to move freely and with a sense of urgency between the worlds of High Culture, popular art and music, and matters of faith.

Rookmaaker's death in 1977, in the midst of plans for new works, seemed sudden and untimely. He was exploring biblical principles which illuminated the rise and decline of cultures and civilizations, and also was undertaking pioneering work on biblical symbolism. A periodical at the time commented that 'The Christian world lost one of its most formative thinkers in the postwar era.' It is a privilege, then, as a publisher, to make his most important work available to a new generation.

The Publisher
Spring 1994

Introduction

> Something is happening here
> But you don't know what it is,
> Do you, Mister Jones?[1]

We live at a time of great change, of protest and revolution. We are aware that something radical is happening around us, but it is not always easy to see just what it is.

We are aware too of a tremendous change that has come over the arts in the twentieth century. Why? What are the forces behind the change? What does modern art really mean?

My aim in this book is to show the relationship between the great cultural revolution of our times and the general spirit of the age – an age which, as we shall see, would seem to be drawing to a close. To do so, we must first go back to look at the art of an age before our own began. Then we shall examine the new forces that have made the modern world what it is and see the various decisive steps by which art has developed as it works out these new forces.

Most of my examples are from painting: as an art historian this is the field I know best. But I shall not be excluding the other arts, although they will not be getting the amount of space they deserve. In any case, I feel that the visual arts are in fact the most important today (with an almost religious aura to them), so I will not have by-passed the really significant issues.

This book has also been written with the needs of younger artists in mind, particularly Christian artists. I am very aware that the issues at stake are not just cultural and intellectual but also spiritual. What is involved is a whole way of thinking that leaves out of account, and so largely negates, vital aspects of our humanity and our understanding of reality. Christians today must understand the spirit of the age. They must realize that the protesters and revolutionaries are often fighting against the same evils of society as they are themselves. But they must also see the inadequacy of all answers that do not tackle the root of the problem.

My closing chapter has particularly in mind Christian artists for whom the problems, spiritual and artistic, are often overwhelming. How should we react as Christians to the pressures around us? What does it mean to trust Christ at such a time as our own? In the battle against the spirit of our age, how can we use the weapons that have been given to us, our humanity, our understanding, our emotions, our artistry – and, of course, the written revelation of God?

But whatever our starting point, whether we are Christians or not, artists or not, it is my hope that this book will help us understand the attitudes, problems and concerns of the times in which we live.

H.R.R.

I
The Message in the Medium

> Through art we can know another's
> view of the universe.[2]

The aim of this book is to discuss modern art, its meaning and its relation to the contemporary cultural scene at large. But modern art did not just happen. It came as a result of a deep reversal of spiritual values in the Age of Reason, a movement that in the course of a little more than two centuries changed the world. If we want to understand how new modern art is, and why it carries the sort of message it does, we have to confront it with the art of the period before the great change began.

For that reason I want to go back in this chapter to discuss some specific works of 'old art'. It is not my intention to give a complete historical survey; quite to the contrary. My aim is to analyse briefly some particular works in order to see their meaning, their content, their spiritual message. In doing so, too, a fact emerges which is common to them all, and vital for an understanding of the particular role in society which art, and painting especially, has been called upon to play. I have chosen works that represent the major historical movements that contributed to the culture of the period before the Enlightenment. The works belong to the great tradition that began in the later Middle Ages, and ended during the nineteenth century – the period when the new world emerged and modern art slowly took shape.

The icon

To illustrate what I want to say, I have chosen, first, a Madonna by Duccio.[3] I could have chosen many other paintings of the Madonna. Each would have some particular feature of its own and, of course, the paintings vary in quality. But all of them, or almost all, are alike in the points that I want to discuss.

The painting is on wood and is quite small. As we look at it, we can ask ourselves what the artist meant when he was painting it. Or we can ask what people wanted the artist to create, for he did not stand alone as a creative artist but was closely tied to his community. What does the painting mean?

Is it supposed to be a picture of something that could have been seen at Bethlehem in AD 1, a reconstruction of the sort of photograph that would have been taken if they had had a camera? If we look at the picture – and perhaps even more if we look at representations of other biblical scenes – we shall soon see that this is not the case. Medieval people did not really think that the air in Bethlehem was golden! And they might even have realized that fashion had changed since then. The artist might well depict his Madonna in rich attire even though he knew that she was poor, as the Gospel writers tell us (if he did not read the Bible for himself, the priest would have told him). So it is not AD 1. What is it supposed to be, then? A scene in heaven? But medieval people were theologically well informed, and they would not have tolerated the thought that Christ would still be a baby in heaven. There is nothing to suggest that it is supposed to be set in the future. But neither does it seem to represent a specific scene on earth. So what does it mean?

Well, let us see what the picture itself says. It tells us obviously about the Madonna, called the 'Mother of God' – that alone would be good enough reason to depict Christ as a baby – the Madonna is looking at us, and seems interested in us, even if in rather an aloof way. She is obviously no ordinary person – not even the greatest blasphemer could make a pin-up girl out of her, nor would the picture make an advertisement for childcare. She is more than human, yet still human. This is what the picture tells us. It is a sermon on Mary, if you like. In a deep and truly religious sense, the picture was a 'poster' telling people to 'go to Mary with all your troubles'.

In the Roman Catholic churches that have given Mary an exalted position these pictures are universal. The oldest are from before AD 500, the latest probably from yesterday. They do not tell about a reality of historical importance nor of a historical event – even though the picture is in fact related to an event such as the birth of Christ. No, these pictures talk about a reality claimed for this very moment, a reality that is to be believed and cannot be seen, that Mary, the Mother of God, can help you if you pray to her.

Such pictures we could call icons. They depicted something felt to be of supreme importance, and sometimes even the picture itself was considered holy. They stood for something supernatural, something above and beyond ordinary human experience, and were loaded with religious meaning. The painting was thus much more than a simple picture, a memory of an important event, and very much more than a portrayal of something as humanly important as motherhood. They represented Mary, the Madonna, 'Our Lady'!

But there is more to it than the subject matter alone. The artistic qualities have a part to play. The last thing the painters of these icons did was to take the subject just as an excuse for making a fine composition. Of course, if they were going to paint a picture of the Madonna, they wanted it to be as beautiful as possible: if one loves somebody, one never wants less. But the picture had more to say than just 'Madonna'. One can follow almost all the different stages in Mariology just by looking at these paintings. For instance, in the fourteenth century one sees a new type emerge, the Madonna of Humility, where we see the Madonna sitting on a cushion on the ground, often offering her breast to the child. This is a marked change from the Madonna as Queen that we see in the earlier periods, and specifically in Romanesque times. Later, after the fourteenth century, the portrayal becomes more natural, with more attention to details like the hair, the chair, the background that often becomes a landscape. And in the Baroque period she sits on clouds, high above us mortals, often accompanied by adoring saints – they are setting us an example, the painting tells us. So the important thing is that it is precisely the artistic qualities of the composition that pass on the message – not just what we know or think about the Madonna ourselves.

Beyond history

Though I have begun with a painting of a Madonna, I might just as well have chosen another theme, a Crucifixion, or an Adoration of the Magi, or a Resurrection, for instance. In all these I could equally have stressed that the artist was not concerned with historical events as such and certainly not with archaeological accuracy but with dogma, with a creedal statement in a well-defined, traditional, compositional scheme. The styles might change, and with them the theological overtones, but the basic ideas remain.

Many things did change. The Counter-Reformation came as a Roman Catholic reaction to the Protestant Reformation. The forms of piety, the subjective feelings in worship, the 'propaganda' of the Catholic Church, the points of emphasis, all these changed while retaining the same basic ideas. One thing that was new was an emphasis on the greatness of the martyrs. Rubens, one of the greatest painters within this stream, painted some of the most convincing examples. His *Martyrdom of St Livinus*[4] will illustrate what I mean.

The saint is in the left-hand corner in all his clerical attire, his arms outstretched, calling to God, giving himself to God. Just earlier he had been standing before his judges telling them that he could not recant even if they would otherwise put him to death, for there was an absolute, deeper and higher than anything else, a truth that one may never deny. The judges themselves stood for another absolute, one that gave them the conviction that Livinus was dangerous. He had accepted the condemnation. His tongue was to be cut out. This is what we see. He calls to God, and look, the heavens are open, angels come carrying wreaths to crown the martyr and others bring the sword of God's wrath. But it is not just a vision of a highly exalted mind: the soldiers see it too and flee. The horses stagger. The painting speaks of an open sky, a world that is not closed within itself: God and his hosts are there too. Truth has meaning.

Historical scenes, scenes from the Bible, for instance, were no problem to the medieval person. He meant his picture to be a symbol of a truth deeper than the eye can see. But, with the Renaissance, art began to have greater pictorial realism and this raised a problem. What will the artist depict: what he knows to be true or what the eye would have seen at that particular time and place? Let us take as an example Christ on the way to Emmaus. We know from the biblical story that there were three men on the road, and two of them did not yet know that the third was Christ himself. What must the artist show? What he or she knows or what the casual passer-by might have seen? Either way the artist is at variance with the biblical truth.

This problem is always present in one way or another in the portrayal of biblical narrative. The picture can be made historically exact (as in the nineteenth century), attempting to reconstruct what a camera would have recorded. But that would reduce the event to something of no more than historical interest. Or it can give the true, timeless message, but often only by losing the historical truth of the fact. And true Christianity is firmly based on historical facts. The fact that God led his chosen people out of Egypt is a historical event to which the whole Old Testament refers again and again. It is equally vital for Christianity that the event of the resurrection of Christ is recognized as really having happened in history. Otherwise, says Paul, 'your faith is in vain.'

This dilemma led many seventeenth-century painters in the countries of the Reformation, in Holland for instance, to abandon painting biblical scenes entirely. Only Rembrandt really tried to overcome the problem. His drawing of Christ on the way to Emmaus[5] shows his answer perhaps best of all. When we look at the drawing, at first glance there is nothing special about it. Three men are standing together near a house. Yet we gather that the middle one is most important. Rembrandt has made this apparent by pictorial means, by making the side of the house dark, thus creating a rhythm, man-Christ-man-house, with the downbeat on Christ and the house. He also makes Christ stand out as important by the way he has placed him between the two disciples. Then Rembrandt draws some trees in the distance in such a way that, although there is no halo, yet there is a suggestion of one. In this way the drawing is natural, and yet it is much more than just three men on a road. It brings out the fact which he wanted to get across.

Painting is more than art alone

In discussing the Madonna with which we began, I made it clear that such a painting is much more than just decoration, or a memory of an event, or a didactic statement about the structure of a situation. The painting is loaded with religious meaning. It is crucial that we understand this. For in this way we can understand why in the course of Western European history, painting has very often been much more than just decoration or something that people enjoy looking at. It has often been more loaded than is justified by its being art. It has been taken to be of deeper significance than tapestry, for instance (even when tapestry was pictorial), or ceramics or often even than sculpture. And this was not only because of its subject matter but more often than not simply because it made visible a particular view on life and the world, it expressed deeply-felt values and truths through the way the theme and the subject matter were handled. Modern art cannot be understood if we do not take this into account. Many works would be senseless, real junk, but for the fact that, being art, they are exhibited because they have a message of almost religious importance, interpreting humanity and their world – yes, perhaps even as junk.

We called the Madonnas we were talking about icons. So we may call this extra value that is often found in Western painting its iconic quality. Perhaps the strangeness of modern painting has some connection with this, for the art of painting has been given too high a value, too great a task. Perhaps too that is the reason why many of the so-called 'applied arts' have escaped this type of modernity. Madonna paintings, icons, have something of the quality of idols, and that is perhaps the mistake that has led to this specific problem. But we cannot solve the problem overnight by saying that we feel that painting should be just painting and no more. Even if we do feel that this should be the case, we can do no more than work towards it.

Two landscapes

A landscape by Jan van Goyen, possibly the greatest of all landscape painters, will illustrate how art gives an interpretation of reality. Look at the picture.[6] It is as simple as can be – a calm sea, storm clouds, some boats in the distance, and to the right boats lying alongside the harbour jetties. The furthest point is to the far left, the brightest highlight – it is very far away indeed. How has the painter managed to achieve such depth in the painting? Van Goyen was one of the greatest in this respect.

The cloud formation helps, of course, with its peculiar kind of perspective effect. Then we look at the water: there are light strokes alternating with dark ones. On the dark strip towards the front there is a small boat that makes a kind of silhouette against the lighter strip 'behind' it. Yet we must realize that this 'behind' is achieved precisely by making the dark stand out against the light – an effect called *repoussoir*, a method of helping to make clear the structure of the reality we see by creating depth. Where we see the tone becoming lighter and weaker, where for instance a boat is further away, this is known as aerial perspective.

For it is important to realize that this is no superficial painting. The artist is very much aware of what he is doing. We realize this better when we try to analyse the composition. We read a picture from left to right. (This is probably related to the way we write; Japanese art, for instance, 'reads' from right to left.) So, to use musical terminology, the introduction is in the little rowing boat on the left. Through it we are brought into the first theme: the far distance out to sea. Then there is a bridge passage: the boat that is exactly in the middle of the picture. The second theme, the right half of the painting, could be called 'Boats in a Harbour'. It is, as such, much nearer and more complex than the first theme. The coda is to be found in the walls of the town that can be seen at the extreme right.

It is typical that this composition can be read on the surface in such a musical way. This is not just by chance. Many pictures by van Goyen and by many other painters of the seventeenth century can be 'read' like this. We realize in this way too that the painter has brought together in his picture many different things that belong to the sea, or rather to an inland sea or lake. It gives a concentrated view and analyses the structure of its reality. It is not just a view from a particular point. A study of Jan van Goyen will show that he never painted a view from a particular position. There is no photographic quality in his painting.

Yet we feel that it is so real. The simplicity of the painting is its greatness and artistry. It is so real that many people today by-pass the picture thinking that it simply copies nature. Yet it never does. The paint is laid very thin and in almost only one brownish colour, so that the whole design is realized in fine differences of tone. Note too how the clouds underline the whole two-theme quality of the composition – something that is very different from what is natural. How can it be so real, then? Those who think that a painting must be a copy of nature to be realistic are mistaken: art never copies nature but always portrays reality in a human way. That means that this painting does not copy nature as a camera would, but depicts a human experience, a human understanding, an insight and emotion into what the truth about reality is. It speaks in an artistic way about reality, as have all paintings ever made. This one speaks about clouds, bad weather coming, the sea, water, boats, work and rest. It does not copy, it is about something that is of human relevance. In a way one can say that the painting gives a particular view on reality, a philosophy. But it is of course given not in words, even less in arguments, but in its own artistic way. It is in the same way that the Roman Catholic painter expressed a theological understanding of Mary and her role in religious life.

This painting, then, seems to be so natural that some people (by a most common mistake, a legacy of the nineteenth century as we shall see) think it copies nature as a camera does; but in fact it presents a philosophy of reality that is very true and very deep. Where does this insight come from?

The answer becomes clear when we compare the art of van Goyen, working in Holland, with some of his Belgian (Flemish) contemporaries. Holland was deeply influenced by the Protestant Reformation; Belgium was very much in the Roman Catholic world of the Counter-Reformation. There is no doubt that the two attitudes to reality, to the physical as well as to the spiritual world, were a result of the deep influence of the two faiths on their whole culture and thought patterns.

There is probably nothing more typical of a truly Protestant vision of reality than the painting by van Goyen we have been discussing. What is important is that he was painting out of a culture that had been reorientated according to the Bible. Even if we know that van Goyen was a Catholic himself, and however shallow or deep his own personal faith may have been, yet the fact remains that he was acting and thinking along the lines of a biblical view of nature.

Perhaps this is an illustration of the way in which a biblical Christianity can act as 'salt' in society. It is really a secondary fruit of the gospel. Individuals become Christians by accepting Jesus Christ as their Saviour and Lord. The fact that he comes to indwell them by his Spirit means that they will be bearing the 'fruit' of the Spirit in their lives. This, working in and through the world, leads to the 'secondary' fruits in culture, the consensus of Christian, biblical attitudes to work, to money, to nature, to the whole of reality which deeply influence the whole nation. And it is these which are reflected in the nation's art.

The landscape artists of the classical tradition, humanist in inspiration, depicted quite another world: a more lofty, ideal world, a setting fit for great human deeds, heroic acts, deep thoughts, surpassing the mean, everyday world. Poussin, the great French painter who lived most of his life in Rome, is perhaps the best example of a man with such a vision. Claude Lorraine is another.

A work of Poussin, his picture of the burial of Phocion,[7] will illustrate what I mean. This is a beautifully constructed landscape, with a clear composition. We see a wonderful classical city in the near distance: Athens as Poussin dreamt it might have been. Phocion, a great man, a Stoic like Poussin himself, is being buried. The painting has a nostalgic mood: death is here, even in the classicist's paradise.

Poussin painted a world as it should or might have been: a world inhabited by gods – in a deep sense allegorical figures – or heroes, ideal human beings from a lofty and poetic past. He painted more than the eye can see, he painted a norm, a wish, a vision of humanity. His art is imbued with a philosophy of life and of the cosmos, ordered and well defined, deeply human while yet more than human.

Yet it is not a Christian vision. The difference between this and van Goyen's picture is striking: van Goyen sings his song in praise of the beauty of the world here and now, the world God created, the fullness of reality in which we live – if we only open our eyes. Poussin dreams of an earthly paradise with great men, a high humanity – but, alas, a fragile and easily broken one, as if it is a dream that will never be fulfilled. Van Goyen knows that the world is not without its storm clouds, that it is not unspoilt, but basically he loves the world in which he lives.

Two world views

Jan Steen was van Goyen's son-in-law. His art can be compared with that of Rubens, living not so far away but in a totally different culture: the differences can be understood for the most part only as the differences between their Reformation and Counter-Reformation cultural backgrounds, even though Steen was himself a Catholic.

Look at his *St Nicholas morning*,[8] for instance, which pictures a typical Dutch festival during which the children get presents, presumably from St Nicholas (or 'Santa Claus'), who has sent his servant down the chimney to place the presents in the shoes put out for that purpose. But naughty children get only a brush. Now look at the story Jan Steen paints for us: the mother is asking the little girl what she received; a girl holds up a shoe with the brush her brother was given, teasing him, while his younger brother calls for the mother's attention. Near the fireplace we see an older boy holding a small child and singing a 'thank you' song together with another boy. Father or grandfather sits in the middle of the commotion enjoying the feast, while grandma in the background has something put aside for the boy who was given the brush. Steen has understood life perfectly, the psychology of a grandmother, the commotion and differences in attitude of the members of the family. And he has also not forgotten to give a rich picture of the many different kinds of special dishes belonging to the feast, piled to the left and the right.

Even if you had a quick eye for things, it would have taken time to see and understand all that was going on in a typical Dutch room in the seventeenth century. One simply cannot take it all in at a glance because of all the noise and commotion. Yet Jan Steen has succeeded in producing a very clear picture of it because of his intimate understanding of it, and because of his gift for composition. The scene would have been virtually an impossible one to photograph. The result would have been either a dull line of people sitting side by side or a chaos of quite 'unreadable' forms. Or the people would have had to pose, making the whole thing into a tableau. Yet Steen's picture has nothing forced or artificially posed about it.

Look how he 'makes' space, by placing the people clearly one behind the other, and by the lines that, for instance, go through the heads of the child, the father and the grandmother or that starts at the mother's head and go on through the father and sister. The whole story of the small boy crying as he is teased by the others is brought out by the line that goes straight 'through' this space. And how is the commotion realized? Through lines forming Vs, for example starting at the small shoe in the middle foreground, one line that is indicated by the stick held up by the little boy and another line follows from the handle of the little girl's bucket to her face and that of her sister. And look at the diagonal that follows the arm of the boy by the fireplace, then goes along the head of the mother and the strong orange colour in the little girl's bucket over to the left-hand corner. All these very cleverly interrelated lines 'make' the picture. This is no snapshot. It is a true human understanding of real family life, realized in an artistic way.

One is not normally concerned, when looking at pictures like this one, to think in terms of world views, or philosophies. It all seems so natural, so open and free. And it really is open, free and natural, real in a very deep sense. One more readily raises questions of world view and philosophy when looking at a strange picture, one that seems unnatural. I am reminded, for instance, of the discussions that have centred around El Greco. Yet we must realize that the naturalness, the full humanity of such pictures as Jan Steen's, is not just a chance product. It must be controlled by a true insight into reality, an insight that must have a deep foundation, one that really leads to the opening up of reality. The very normality of the picture is founded in a deep understanding, a 'philosophy'. This understanding comes, as I have said, from the Reformation, which means from the Bible's view of life. It is an understanding that leads life back to the foundation of biblical Christianity, Jesus Christ himself. It is an insight drawn from the well of life, from the Scriptures. Such things do not come cheaply.

We must look at one more picture in this section: Titian's *Venus and Music*.[9] He painted several versions. Titian's world was a Roman Catholic one. His contacts with the king and court of Spain connected him with the Counter-Reformation. Yet, as so often, Roman Catholicism went together with humanism, the third force beside the Reformation and the Counter-Reformation that contributed to the great European civilization of the seventeenth century. Humanism, this basic force that emerged with the Renaissance, took its starting point in humanity. It is human insight, human power, that would rebuild the world. At times it was non-Christian, even antichristian, but as a whole the humanists, because they were not deeply concerned with the church, compromised with the church – which after all could become somewhat dangerous, with its Inquisition. As the Roman Catholic world awakened out of its slumber with the Counter-Reformation, humanism was put in its place – a secondary place: it could cater for worldly activities and insight, not be concerned with religion . . .

So Titian painted both altarpieces and many works with a marked humanist tendency. This painting of *Venus and Music* is one of them. To understand it one must ask oneself: Who is Venus? Nobody worshipped Venus in a religious way, of course, or believed she really existed. No, the old pagan gods of antiquity were revived to be used as allegorical figures, figures through which invisible yet real concepts could be symbolized and visualized by means of painting. Mars stood for war, Hercules often for the human soul, Mercury for trade, and Flora for the world of flowers. Venus was the goddess of love and beauty. The sixteenth- and seventeenth-century conception of the world was in many respects a mixture: it combined the old scholastic philosophy, itself a synthesis of pagan Greek philosophy and Christian theology, with the rediscovery of late Greek and Roman thinking as well as the renewed insights into biblical truth of the Reformation. It was a world in which it was possible to speak of the reality of such concepts as beauty or love. They were realities outside humanity, and people in their life and work had to reflect them, to realize them by working according to them. Love and beauty were not just human feelings and subjective tastes; they were really there: if people did not follow them, hate and ugliness would be the result.

So we must be careful and understand that the woman on the couch in this picture is not a real woman, which would make the picture somewhat strange, if not of questionable propriety! In a way there is no woman in the room with the musician at all. Titian makes it clear through his composition that she is of a different kind, living in a different realm. There is a jump in space between the feet of the Venus and the back of the musician. The organist looks back at her as he draws his inspiration from love and beauty. So the title of the painting is rightly *Venus and Music* as music is inspired by love and beauty. This mixing of allegorical figures with real ones was typical of the Venetian painters of the sixteenth century.

Venus is reclining. We often find reclining nudes in sixteenth- and seventeenth-century painting, and very often their position symbolizes inspiration. In a picture by Rubens, a man looks at a reclining nude: Cimon is being inspired by her beauty and thus changed from rogue to gentleman, a story from Boccaccio with Neoplatonic overtones. We can see her too as Danae in a famous painting by Rembrandt in the Hermitage in Leningrad: the woman is a portrait of his young wife, and he speaks of her as inspiring him – mixing in a peculiar way allegory (in the form of an ancient myth) and reality.

The fact that these pictures show more than the eye sees means that they acquire a meaning that goes beyond photographic representation. They speak of human insight and understanding, of human values and truth – human in the sense that they belong to people, not necessarily in the sense that they are invented by people.

So, from the Madonna on, paintings give a philosophy of the world and of life. They are more than decorations, simply pleasant to look at. They have a message and, what is vital to notice, a message realized by artistic means. The picture gets across what it wants to say, not just through its title but by its own built-in qualities of artistry and method.

2
The Roots of Contemporary Culture

> When Man throws God right out of the window
> It ain't so much a case of
> He don't believe in nothing.
> But more a case that he
> Believes in anything and everything[10]

At this stage in the historical development we have been tracing, there is a picture missing. For our next picture we would naturally have looked to see what the great Christian movement which had its starting-point in the Reformation went on to express in its art. We may acknowledge the deep influence of Calvinist Christianity on the culture and art of the seventeenth century, particularly in Holland. But otherwise we draw a virtual blank. Protestantism as such did not foster the arts. Why?

For the only apparent explanation we must look rather further back. At the time of the beginning of the Reformation the main spiritual and cultural forces in Europe were a Roman Catholicism in decay and the lively and growing humanism of the Renaissance. But, perhaps less obvious but no less important, there was also a mystical stream. The whole cultural scene changed according to the content and strength of the different spiritual streams. The Reformation came as a challenge to the authority of the Roman Catholic Church, which up to that time had forced many to pay at least lip service to its doctrines. Soon we see Roman Catholicism trying to renew and reinforce itself with the Counter-Reformation. Humanism became more openly worldly and secular, though it thereby lost some of its strength and influence on the course of events (in fact, a kind of crisis can be seen here, expressing itself in the Mannerist art of Pontormo, Giulio Romano and Pellegrino Tibaldi). The mystical stream was expressed in the movement loosely labelled Anabaptist, which included a variety of viewpoints, Christian and anarchistic, pacifist and militant.

The sixteenth-century battle between the Reformation and the mystical movements was won, by and large, by the Reformation, but it did not emerge completely unscathed. A secondary stream of mysticism went along with the Reformation, tinging its efforts and thinking, sometimes more strongly, sometimes almost not at all.

This accounts for the differences in the subsequent development within the Reformed camp. Puritanism is not a unified movement. It took from the Reformation its profound reverence for the Scriptures as a base for all theological thinking and daily living. But through mystical streams it was often tinged by a kind of subjectivism and a tendency to look for holiness in a legalistic and spiritualized way in an effort to keep clear of all worldly and fleshly pursuits.

It is hard to give a full picture of the Puritan movement. There was certainly much biblical wisdom, but again and again the mystical undercurrent came to the surface. For instance, Morgan Llwyd is a typical example of one who held radical Puritan views.[11] He combined a scepticism about outward forms of religion, a strong antipathy to dogmatism about church order and ordinances, and a marked tendency to evangelical antinomianism, a false idea of freedom from the law.

This mystical stream often depreciated everything outside the 'spiritual', the 'religious' in the more narrow sense. It must have had a stronger influence than we often assume, as only in this way can we understand why psalm singing, which was originally very lively, cheerful and attractive (Queen Elizabeth once called the psalms 'Geneva gigs'!), was abandoned for a very slow and almost unmusical way of singing – the sort of thing against which Isaac Watts later protested and which was only superseded by the vigorous hymn singing of the Wesleyans.

Yet music was to some extent still acceptable to them. The other arts fared worse. We can only conclude that the Calvinistic and Puritan movement (at least from the seventeenth century on) had virtually no appreciation for the fine arts due to a mystic influence that held that the arts were in themselves worldly, unholy, and that a Christian should never participate in them.

Only in this way can we account for the fact that the real Puritan or Calvinist movement did not produce its own style of painting. As we have seen, Dutch painting in the first half of the seventeenth century was strongly influenced by Calvinist Christian thinking. We mentioned Rembrandt, who was certainly searching to achieve in his art a true portrayal of the biblical message. But can Rembrandt be called either a Calvinist or a Puritan?

In the second half of the seventeenth century in Holland the humanist stream gained in strength, and a humanist-classical style, imported from France and Italy, began to take over. In England before the time of Cromwell, the court art of Van Dyck and kindred spirits made any developments from the side of the more Puritan stream of thought and feeling almost impossible – and later it never had much of a chance.[12] When the chances did come, much later, in the eighteenth century with the revival of faith with the Wesleys or with the nineteenth-century revivals, the Protestant stream was no longer interested in the arts at all.

We cannot say that Christianity had no influence at all. On the contrary, it had a great influence on public morality, concern for the poor and oppressed, and generally speaking on people's way of life. What we shall call the bourgeois mentality in a later section of this book is often in fact a secularized form of Christian ethics, even though morality may have become no more than moralism and legalism. But the fact that most Christians did not take part in the arts and the general trends of culture to any extent allowed those areas to become completely secular, and in the long run even contrary to Christianity. However that may be, it is the reason why in this book we have to deal with developments outside the realm of Christianity if we are to understand what is going on today.

Christianity and culture

Today it is well known that within evangelical Christian circles there is little interest in the arts. As a change becomes apparent, as the younger generation born and raised within these circles comes to understand the importance of the arts, all kinds of problems and tensions arise. Any sort of critical thinking is almost completely lacking. There is no artistic insight, nothing to point to, no answer to the relevant questions of the rising generation. Many want to be artists in a Christian sense but have to find the answers for themselves. How should they go about it? What does it mean? Many have turned away from Christianity or, more tragically, from Christ, as they have come to feel that if this vital aspect of human life is outside religion or faith then something basic must be defective in the faith. In different ways they have to join in spiritual battle against the spirit of the age, which is expressed so very strongly in the arts – and many succumb.

It is only too possible of course to take the same Puritan position today: keep away from the arts, they are worldly, they are secular and unholy. But that is no answer. It misses the point. For one thing, it ignores the fact that the arts are particularly strong protagonists for a new non-Christian way of thinking. It could well be that the arts are indeed 'avant-garde' in the sense that they are ahead of the rest in the quest for a non-Christian way of spirituality. Why? Because for so long Christians have taken no part in artistic discussion or activity.

But this is to anticipate the argument of later chapters. At this stage it may be helpful to show in broad outline the different attitudes there have been in the past to the relationship between Christianity and culture. By 'Christianity' I mean something very general: a cultural and spiritual stream that has historical connections with biblical faith and religion. Christianity is not a normative term but rather a loosely meant framework, to differentiate it from Islam, paganism or the world of Eastern religions.

Christianity and culture can, of course, mean two things: what attitude the Christian should have to the surrounding (non-Christian or secular) culture; or what kind of a culture will be the result of a Christian way of life. The two answers are in practice closely bound together and, as in the following discussion it will be clear what is meant, we have not tried to be systematic in this respect.

Some major diverging answers to the question of the Christian's attitude to culture have been given in history. They were discussed by H. Richard Niebuhr in his *Christ and Culture*[13] whose main approach I follow here.

Gnosticism and mysticism

It was gnosticism that was in many ways the influence behind the mysticism of later ages. It was the view that lay behind some of the letters of John and Paul to the early church, written with the express purpose of warning the Christians against it. Without going into detail, we can say that the gnostics made a synthesis of biblical thought, Neoplatonism and pagan mystery religions. One of the main ideas involved was that the material world is wholly bad. So salvation means escape from this world, getting nearer to God who reigns above this world. And not only is the material world bad but so are all our worldly passions.

The early mystics were akin in many ways. They were concerned not just with mortifying their sinful nature but the body itself, the physical, the material. So, they said, we must flee this world – and they did, with austere asceticism, trying to climb towards God whose reign is in the world of grace, beyond the material, in the spiritual realm.

So the life of faith consists in fleeing sin, living in the spirit, seeking to be holy. These words certainly sound biblical, but gnosticism gave them a very specific tinge. This life is of no value. The material world is sinful. Life is no more than a time of trial, and the true goal can be reached only by those who have worked themselves up towards God by their own holiness, by conquering all fleshly desires.

It is important to understand these basic ideas of mysticism, for our own century and particularly the arts of our century are strongly mystical in spirit. Mysticism has also often been Christian, meaning that Christians have looked in this direction for their way of salvation. But the Bible gives no grounds whatsoever for such a view; quite the contrary, for the apostles fought it strongly in their letters. But as most 'Christian' mystics depreciate the Bible for a more subjective experience this argument often fails to reach them.

In the visual arts in the Middle Ages mystical tendencies can be seen at work in the art of the fourteenth century in Germany, also in the extreme, spiritual, 'fleshless' beauty of the Madonnas and in the extreme portrayal of Christ's suffering on the cross (as in Grünewald, for instance). A more practical and less extreme mysticism was very strong in the Netherlands in the fifteenth century amongst the Brethren of the Common Life, whose major literary work was Thomas à Kempis's *The*

Imitation of Christ. In the visual arts we see its subdued and inward way of expression in the works of Geertgen of St John and other Dutch artists (who were of considerable influence in the formation of the Dutch character).

As I have already shown, mysticism's influence on Calvinism, expressing itself in an extreme, passive, almost fatalistic view of election, was mainly responsible for the lack of real interest in the arts. It introduced a kind of spirituality that often kept Calvinism from realizing one of its main principles, that faith is not just a matter of 'religion', of the soul and its salvation in heaven, but of salvation for the whole person, a way of life and thought affecting all aspects of human life.

A dualism of nature and grace

Another answer to the problem of the relation of Christianity and culture was worked out in the medieval theology, or rather philosophy, of men such as Thomas of Aquinas – what has come to be known as scholasticism. As a complete Roman Catholic system of thought, it was to have a lasting influence on all Christian thinking, and its attitude to the world in which we live is one of the most subtle and dangerous enemies of true biblical thinking, even today.

Basic to it is its dualism: this world is good, but yet has an autonomy of its own. The world of faith, of grace, of religion is the higher one, a world for which we have need of God's revelation. This is where our aims and affections should be set. But the lower world, the human world, the world of 'nature', can be understood by reason and here, in fact, reason reigns. It is as such non-religious, secular. Here there is no difference between the Christian and the non-Christian, as both act according to the natural laws of thought and action.

Being biblical scholars, and trying to find a unity in their original duality, these men often softened their principles in practice. In the Middle Ages, when the Roman Church was overwhelmingly powerful, they tried to get the secular world into their power in order to prevent autonomous 'nature' from becoming non-Christian and truly autonomous, emancipated from Christianity. Yet this is just what did happen in the Renaissance with the birth of humanism.

We often hear people say in discussions about the sciences and the arts that these cannot be Christian – even devout Christians say so sometimes. We must be careful to distinguish what they mean to say. Often they do in fact mean that these realms of 'worldly' pursuit, belonging to our human nature and not sinful as such, are just human, that is, apart, outside of the realm of grace, of God's work and revelation. The only claim God has in this realm of human endeavour is in the field of ethics; so painting is simply painting, whoever does it, but the

Christians must show their Christianity by avoiding immorality of any sort. This raises all sorts of questions about the attitude of Christian artists to their work. But I will forbear from commenting at this stage, as I shall be attempting to formulate a rather different answer in a later chapter.

The Reformation attitude

Christians have sought in all sorts of ways for an answer to the question of how a Christian should live and act in her or his daily life and academic and creative endeavours. Augustine, later Calvin and, in his wake, the Calvinists and Puritans, though sometimes hindered by the mystical influences we have been discussing, looked for the answer in a more directly biblical way.

I used the phrase 'how a Christian should live and act' rather than 'a Christian's attitude to culture' advisedly. For we can easily slip into the mistake of making Christianity and culture two distinct entities, quite separate from each other. Then, if we find we have difficulties in resolving the two, the mistake may well be that we are trying to bring together two different things which we have separated artificially. Culture is the result of human creative activity within God-given structures. So it can never be something apart from our faith. All our work is ultimately directed by our answer to the question of who – or what – our God is, and where for us the ultimate source of all reality and life lies. So our resulting 'culture' can never be something separate from our 'faith'. This is just as true for those who do not acknowledge the true God, the Creator: their cultural activity is coloured by their basic non-Christian faith. For the Christian the problem remains of how we have to deal with the culture around us, often the fruit of a non-Christian point of departure. But then this is dealt with at length and depth in the Bible itself: it is even one of its main concerns, bound up with its teaching on sin, redemption and sanctification.

It is basic to thinking about culture in the tradition of the Calvinist Reformation that there is no duality between a higher and a lower, between grace and nature. This world is God's world. He created it, he sustains it, he is interested in it. He called the work of his hands good in the very beginning. Nothing is excluded. Everything, from the lowest atom or form of animal life to the highest doxology, everything belongs to him. Nothing can exist outside of him, and all things have a meaning only in relation to him.

Yet there is a sharp division – not between a realm that God deals with and another that is more or less autonomous, not between a higher and a lower, but between the kingdom, the rule, the realm of God and the kingdom of darkness. Humanity, in the Fall, brought sin and consequently a curse into the world. And so there is a duality, between good and bad, right and wrong, beautiful and ugly. In their sinfulness people wanted to be like God, to be autonomous. And sin, bringing with it decay, sickness and ultimately death, is still in the world, marring God's wonderful creation. This is the true division. It goes through all humanity, affecting every human being; two opposite ways, one as God wants, the other against his will. So, as Paul said, nothing is sinful, neither eating and drinking nor any kind of activity whatsoever, if done with thanksgiving. But all things are sinful if done in disobedience to God's will and word. The First and Second Commandments express this basic division within humankind. Nobody is excluded. And so too the fact that Jesus Christ died to take upon himself the sin of humanity is not just something for the 'soul'. The whole cosmos is to be redeemed, to be 'bought back', for all things are under the curse of sin and evil. His saving grace, his offer of new life in all its fullness – for he is the Way, the Truth and the Life – excludes no aspect of human reality.

Seen in this way all of life and reality is related to God – and all our thinking, work, action, feeling is in a way 'religion'. Religion in the narrow sense, prayer, the devotional, is only a part of the life of faith. The Bible makes it clear that we should not try to turn all human life into the devotional in the sense that Christians have often made a division between direct, conscious devotion, or worship, and 'natural' life. The Roman Catholic ideas outlined in the last section were not just theory but common practice. Sincere and committed Christians have often struggled with this duality in their desire to bring everything under God's dominion. It led some to become hermits or monks, as they wanted to give their whole life to God. But it is not just the soul, the religious in the narrow sense that belongs to God – it is the fullness of life. Nothing is excluded. That is why we pray 'Thy kingdom come.' We ask for God's rule to be acknowledged and extended in this life, in this world, 'on earth as it is in heaven'.

To make this full relationship with God clear, including both the devotional and all other aspects of daily life, we may use the Old Testament term 'covenant'. As the Old Testament covenant was for the Jewish people, those who were circumcised, so the New Testament covenant is for all those who call on Jesus as their Lord and Saviour, those who are baptized. Within the covenant there is no division between a higher and a lower, no part of life that God would not be interested in. Though we sleep or plough or solve mathematical problems – all activities in which we do not think consciously of God and our 'faith' seems to be non-active – yet we are never outside God's covenant. We can never be out of his world, and he never forsakes us.

We see that God makes this abundantly clear in the Old Testament. He did not want his people to turn everything into 'religion', into 'cult'. So he told the Israelites that they could slaughter everywhere, though it was only in the Temple that it would be done as an offering. He told them they could feast with the offering of thanksgiving in the Temple, though not for more than three days. And he also told them that it was good to put a fence round a roof to stop people from falling off. He was anxious to give them good advice in many matters that were not simply cultic but yet belonged to his dominion. He wanted his people to live, as he was the God of life, life in the full sense, in all human realms. He showed that nothing was excluded, neither stealing nor judging, trading nor property, sexuality nor eating and drinking. His commandments were not simply religious or ethical, they were basic principles of life, though including of course both worship and ethics.

God in his wisdom knew that if his children took to other gods they were not only wrong in their faith and worship but that all of life was in principle threatened: sex, politics, daily happiness. In the Old Testament books and prophets we read about the results of leaving the true God – and in the New Testament too. And if his people were reluctant to listen to the prophets, God told them that he would come with his judgment, which again was not only in matters of faith, salvation or the afterlife, but also in this life, in their political freedom, their possessions and wellbeing.

So without going into more detail, these great biblical principles of the Reformation gave an answer not only to the question of what a Christian's attitude to culture should be, but also to the question of what a Christian's attitude to a non-Christian culture should be, the very practical problem of how we are to live in a world that is full of sin and ungodliness. Where things are loving, good, right and true, where things are according to God's law and his will for creation, there is no problem. The Christian will appreciate and actively enjoy and enter into all the good things God has made. But where they have been spoilt or warped by sin, there the Christian must show by his or her life, words, actions, creativity, what God really intended them to be. Christians have been made new in Christ, have been given a new quality of life which is in harmony with God's original intention for humankind. They have been given the power of God himself by the Holy Spirit, who will help them to work out their new life in the world around them. They are the 'salt of the earth', keeping society from corruption and giving savour to every aspect of life.

Before the Enlightenment

The relation of Christianity to culture can in many respects be seen as what we might call a secondary blessing. Most people, simply by being human, long for true humanity, for righteousness, love and goodness; if Christians are showing these things, the primary fruits of the gospel, in their lives, this will have a great influence in itself. In this way even in a sinful world – even in a world where Christians too are still far from being without sin – a 'consensus' can develop, a general cultural pattern which will include an insight into what is best and right, an understanding of what is truly human. I would call it a 'secondary' blessing of Christianity because it influences not only the true Christians, those who have trusted in Jesus Christ, but also people who do not want to be Christians themselves. In fact even those who are living sinful lives accept the standards of the consensus.

Something like this happened in the seventeenth century. The consensus was to a large extent the fruit of the Reformation. Also it influenced the Roman Catholic Church to review its teaching and (perhaps more important) its practices. Because of this the power of humanism was contained for a time. Though humanism was certainly a contributory factor in the seventeenth-century consensus, it was a minor force and, to a certain extent, christianized.

We must realize that to seventeenth-century people there was no doubt about the reality of the things in Scripture. Even those who were not Christians still acknowledged the facts. Marlowe lived somewhat earlier, but his play *Dr Faustus* is typical. Here is a man who has sold his soul to the Devil; when hell is very near, he cries out: 'See, see where Christ's blood streams in the firmament. One drop would save my soul, half a drop, ah my Christ.' He does not repent and is not saved, but he knew, though an unbeliever, where redemption was to be found. And Marlowe was not a Christian; and he knew. The same sort of thing happens again and again: the philosopher Descartes discovered by his famous 'method' the way for people to find human certainty – which meant that biblical realities were cast out. But after he made his great discovery and formulated his *cogito, ergo sum* he made a pilgrimage to the Virgin Mary to thank her! The world view of seventeenth-century people was a traditionally Christian (and mainly biblical) one, even though many of the people themselves were not Christians.

The greatness and fullness of seventeenth-century culture, its art and science and depth of understanding, its wealth and power, were not the result only of human endeavour – as if Christians made these things their main aim. No, they were by-products of basic Christian attitudes and, in the final analysis, blessings and gifts from God. Jesus himself told us to look first for the kingdom of God and all these things would be given to us. And all these things, the great culture of the seventeenth century, were given after European people returned to God. God promised his people (for instance in Deuteronomy 28) that, if they were willing to walk in his ways, he would make them outstanding among the nations and give them a leading role in the world. And this was not only true for ancient Israel, it is still true today. The blessings listed in that chapter were the natural results of walking in the ways God had designed for individuals and societies to live.

How did seventeenth-century people understand the world around them? Of course there were many interpretations and opinions, but the basic core, the consensus, was something like this. There is a triune God who created heaven and earth, the whole cosmos. In this cosmos there are angels and devils, and there are humans, animals, plants and material things. But there is more, much more than the eye can see. There are principles and norms, or laws, and therefore we can speak of good and evil, right or wrong. The world has a structure, given by God, in which all things are in a specific order. All things have meaning in this structured order of things. Creation is harmonious and good, even if polluted by human sin. Within this ordered universe people too have their specific place: they may be the crown of creation, but they are not the centre of it.

This description is in no way complete, of course. It was a very rich understanding of the world and of humanity and their life. Yet seventeenth-century people were really no better than we are: they were sinful and often stupid. For instance[14] their attitude to 'witches' is the last thing we would want to defend, though it was an attitude possible only within such a world view. And above all seventeenth-century people were no different from the Israelites of the Old Testament: when it came to it they forgot that their wisdom and greatness were gifts from God. They did as Moses said the Jews would do, 'Jeshurun waxed fat, and kicked . . . he forsook God who made him and scoffed at the Rock of his salvation.'[15]

Christianity grew weaker in the same way. There were increasingly people who said they believed in God but no longer acted on his promises. They tried to be moral in their own strength. And they failed. And humanism grew in influence.

This might seem a somewhat negative way of introducing the great movement which has come to be known as the Enlightenment. But it is a crucial point in our story. For the Enlightenment was to change the world. It is a period in which we today are still living, though at its end. Its aims have been fulfilled. The world is different. What started in the philosopher's study is now in the hearts and minds of the whole Western world. It is essential for us to understand it in outline if we are to appreciate either art today or the whole position of people today which our art expresses.

Science

Before discussing the main themes of the Enlightenment in more general terms, we must first concentrate on one key area – science – in which it is essential to compare what was to come with what had already gone before.[16]

When Christianity was preached in Europe, culture and spirituality were changed very deeply. If we realize what the simple conclusion of understanding Genesis 1 means to a person's outlook on reality and one's endeavour to understand it, this will be immediately clear. Genesis says that God created the world and that there is no being that has not been created. This has given people a freedom for research formerly unknown. To the heathen, whether Greek or Germanic, the gods gave order to reality.

Ionian natural philosophy, for instance, began something that might have developed into a scientific philosophy similar to that of the eighteenth century; but there were objections from the majority of the Greeks who were afraid of such impiety.

Take lightning, for instance. What is it? The wrath of the highest god? His tool and weapon? Can we investigate it? We had better not, as that could be sacrilegious – and dangerous. The heathen gods, being part of the cosmos and its regulating principles, made it at the same time impossible to analyse these principles open-mindedly. But as soon as we come to know the true God, who is not part of the cosmos but its Creator, then everything is open for investigation, for everything has been created by him. So only on this basis is there freedom for science.

What is more, in contrast to the ancient scientists who were always in danger of being accused of going against the 'divine' order, this Christian freedom did not need to go against the understanding that God reigns over the cosmos. Science proceeds from the assumption of causality. We ask what made it happen like that when we conduct an experiment. There is no event without a cause, no cause without a result. If we see a stone moving, the question is what made it move. And we always try to find a natural cause, a cause within the created order of reality. But again, this does neither exclude God nor explain him away.

Elijah, for instance, prayed to God for rain. But he knew, as people have always known, that there can be no rain without clouds. So he sends his servant up the hill to see whether the clouds were coming. Praying for rain and understanding the basic rule of causality do not conflict. Why should it be a problem that Jesus walked on the water? If Jesus was God, and so Lord of creation, there is no reason to query whether he could. This is not contradicting science. It keeps the world open to God, who as Creator can work in his creation. This is the basic assumption of all prayer, and it is at the heart of biblical teaching: that God has created *and* sustains the world; that he is interested in his creation and does not let things happen 'by chance'. He looks after humankind, his creatures.

It is a pity that it took a long time before these principles were realized. Perhaps it had been mystical ideas about the relationship of Christianity to the world that had previously kept people from being really interested in matters of science (and historical circumstances such as the barbarian invasions cannot be ignored). So it was only in the sixteenth century, after the Reformation, that science really began its fantastic development. Of course humanism played its part. But it must be said that it capitalized on the freedom in looking at the world which Christianity brought. Many of the scientists of the seventeenth century were in fact devout Christians who never found their scientific activity minimizing their faith.

The Age of Reason

What happened, then, with the eighteenth-century Enlightenment? As with all periods of deep and many-sided changes, it was a time of conflict and contradictory aims and ideas. Yet, as we have seen, it is essential for an insight into what was to follow to understand its basic principles. For they were principles which still very much affect us today.

In a way the Enlightenment was the resurgence of the principles of humanism, gaining new strength as the impetus of true Christianity after the Reformation lost momentum or retreated into a mysticism that left the world to its own devices. The old pseudo-Christian view of the two provinces in human life, faith and nature, which was revived at this time in a neo-scholastic theology among both Catholics and Protestants, made it easier initially for humanism to gain ground. The inevitable result was only apparent later as faith became something set apart from the real problems of culture, something of no more than private importance, with no influence on the things that really matter. And so, in the long run, the place of Christianity became problematical and many lost their faith.

The first principles of this new cultural movement known as the Age of Reason were developed in France and England by philosophers such as Descartes, Hobbes, Locke, Hume, and the French Encyclopedists such as Diderot. The first three wanted to retain their Christianity. Descartes made his pilgrimage to the Virgin Mary. Locke wrote a much-used book in 1695 called *The Reasonableness of Christianity* (for he would accept revelation only so long as it was reasonable). Indeed, their basic starting point was found in reason. I doubt everything, said Descartes, but one thing I know for certain, that I am, because I think. So God was made unnecessary, left out of account. However gently, he was pushed out of the door. For personal life, for heaven and redemption he might be useful, but in the discussion of matters of science, politics, the big issues of the organization of the world, one must start with reason.

We can understand their intention. Reason, or, as they called it in the eighteenth century, common sense, is something that all people have in common. And they all live in the same world and use the same senses. Starting from this, one can get rid of all the seemingly subjective discussions on matters of religion. And, after all – in this they were true humanists – people are good, and in starting from human reason and perception things will go better; a better, more humane world can be made, a world in which people will be tolerant of their neighbours rather than persecute them.

In pushing God out of the door by their reasoning, the result may well have been a radical scepticism of everything. But they avoided this either by sheer humanistic optimism or by keeping detached from the ultimate questions one is inclined to ask.[17] What they did not avoid was an increasing change of emphasis from what was reasonable to what was rational. The rationalist's reason is like an idol; it is like King Midas's fulfilled wish: everything it touches, changes and dies even if it glitters and sparkles. The Reformation had never asked one to accept faith as a leap in the dark: for the Bible itself points to facts. Faith and rationality do not exclude each other. But rationalism is something different: it means that there is nothing more in the world than what the senses can perceive and reason apprehend. There is nothing but scientific fact – or fancy. And God? God is amenable neither to sense-perception nor to reason. So God is left out.

Starting in every human endeavour with people changed virtually everything, though it took a long time before all the consequences were seen or realized – perhaps only today are we beginning to see it in all its depth and breadth. In the older framework, people had their place in a large universe. There were principles, ideas outside humanity, just as there were angels, devils and other forces. In philosophy, human endeavour was placed in the field of ontology, the theory of being: how is the world structured, what is the place of humankind in it? But now the primary problem was that of epistemology, the theory of knowledge: how can we know, how do we get true knowledge? Locke wrote an *Essay concerning Human Understanding*,[18] Hume an *Inquiry concerning Human Understanding*,[19] while Kant made epistemology the cornerstone of his philosophy. Again and again the main point is this: we as people stand before a big 'X' called the universe, and the only way to come to any understanding of it is to use our senses (seeing, hearing, weighing, measuring) and to use our reason to coordinate the sensations or perceptions we have had. So the ideas outside humanity are no longer of any reality nor of any validity as normative principles.

Of course, starting with people and their reason meant that not only God (who is he, an idea too?) but also many other elements were excluded from the human world view. Angels, devils – they are probably only old superstitions. At least one thing is sure, we cannot prove their existence: have you ever *seen* an angel? They did not stop to ask whether many people in biblical times had seen angels either – they were not a common everyday experience in the sense of being frequently seen or heard, but then belief in biblical times was not based solely on statistical evidence.

Then the principles, norms and laws themselves also disappeared. If we have agreed upon the principle that we shall not ask God for guidance nor accept his commandments, and if we say only things experienced or reasonable are true, well then, why not steal? The fact that God gave a commandment is irrelevant. So Hobbes constructed his 'social contract': people in the beginning of history, having found that stealing is a nuisance and a hindrance to all human endeavour, decided that it was reasonable that they should not steal. This is fine, of course, but what if a person (or a group of people) decided by a majority vote, tomorrow, that in the present situation it is now more reasonable to steal? The principle of the Enlightenment excludes the possibility of true norms or basic principles. So good and evil have to be put aside as part of real reality – they can at best be considered subjective human evaluations of behaviour.

But in a way humanity also disappears. Diderot wrote in the famous *Encyclopedia* (1752–1572) under the entry 'Man' that he 'seems to stand above the other animals'. 'Man' is really only an animal – who can *see* any basic difference? If we read on, and appreciate the spirit in which sentences like these were written, it comes down to this: there is no basic difference between people, animals, plants and things. This was a creedal statement, of course avowedly antichristian, but of a faith without any sort of proof. So the sciences were called in to provide the proof and give it a solid base. Science accepted the new task and, with the theory of evolution, would seem to have 'proved' it finally, for in examining the possible mechanism of evolutionary change there would seem no need for a God behind natural reality, no need for a Creator. Science became scientism. Evolution was from its very beginning evolutionism, more than just a scientific theory rather a philosophy with its own antichristian or at least non-Christian dogmas. In this way human existence was equated with natural, biological or physical, reality and the new science tried to give this view a foundation in facts. But they were naturalistic facts alone, from which, following the principle of uniformity, everything beyond the natural, everything which cannot be perceived by the senses, everything beyond the rationalist's reason, is excluded.

So people became 'natural' and lost their particular place in the cosmos. They lost their humanity. What does that mean? If a person is just another animal, for instance, then what is 'love'? After a long development the answer came out loud and clear: libido. Lust. Love is *really* only sex. All that seems to be more is 'in fact' sublimation, a nice kind of façade to hide the real drives. Sex one can see and experience. But love?

We must always be on our guard when we hear the word 'really' used like this. More often than not it means that an essential quality is removed! For the new science, which we should call mechanistic science, became a kind of 'revelation', the only way to get true knowledge. All things are *really* only natural things, animals, plants, non-living matter. There are no basic differences to the scientific eye. Science has become the revelation of the new world, and people cling superstitiously to the word 'scientific' as meaning 'true to reality'. But it is a reduced reality.

The nineteenth century – and our twentieth century too – has laboured to work the new principles out. The result has been a *démasqué* in which many things held sacred or deep are brought down to what they 'really' are: sex, lust, power, the survival of the fittest, an instinct or will to live. Life itself, instead of the varied and deep meaning it had in biblical language – a person's full being, true humanity, work, dreams and aims, so that Christ himself was able to say that he is the Life – life became nothing more than biological life, a beating heart and sexual urges and the quest for food and drink. We can understand the man who, standing at the end of this development, asked recently in one of the underground papers, 'Is there a life before death?'

'Man in the box'

Science had been the way to acquire insight into the structure of reality, the way this world is built, to find out the greatness of God's creation. But now it was elevated by the rationalist into the tool to know all truth, the foundation of all knowledge. The world was no longer open to a transcendent God. It had become a closed box and people were caught in that box. The content of the box was the only true reality allowed by the men of the Age of Reason, the things that can be understood by rationalist reason and mechanistic science, together with the dream of the new world they had begun to build. What we have already called 'scientism' was this faith in reason, with science as a kind of revelation. The world they were building was a fulfilled technocracy, scientistic truth put into practice.

It took a long time before all this was fully worked out. Maybe it never will be, completely and fully, for real reality, that which is more than naturalistic nature, cannot be ignored. It took a long time before the scientific methods that were used with such great success in the natural sciences and technology were applied to other fields of human endeavour, to economics, sociology, and soon too, through Freud and others, to psychology. Then people are really caught in the box, objects determined by natural laws to be studied by science with scientific methods – and nothing more. Scientism was almost a new religion: humans were *really* no different from animals, plants and things. And Darwin seemed to give the final proof, by providing the mechanism of natural selection, of the evolutionary vision of what humanity really are and could become.[20]

The world in which we live is built upon these principles. They still hold people in their grip. Scientism is still the way people hope to make a better world. It is, and will be, a technocratic world, as technocracy, which includes humanity too, is at its heart. People are no longer human beings who buy things: no, they are consumers. They have become a little wheel in the big machine, a unit in social statistics, an electronic oscillation in the computer.

We shall be seeing later what this means when we discuss modern art. But in thinking of the process by which 'man' has become what Marcuse has called 'one-dimensional man', there is one thing we must never forget. People will always remain human, for they cannot change their own basic created being, whatever they think of themselves. They can never get away from their place, which was assigned to them in the fullness of the created universe. This means that people can never be happy with the fact that they are 'caught in the box'. They know that they are *really* more than an atom or a rabbit. And so they want to escape from the box, even if the principles of their own philosophy deny them the possibility of doing so. They can but protest against the dehumanization of present-day society, the establishment.

The existentialists in our century have been the philosophers who have thought deeply about this human condition. And they have told people to jump out of the box – following such great men of the nineteenth century as Kierkegaard, the Romanticists or some of the great artists such as Baudelaire or the Cubist painters. They have said to people: get out of the box, you are more than matter, more than the naturalistic sciences can tell you. You are really human if you transcend your human condition, your fate of being in the box. Of course, this reality is above reality, it has to be irrational, for rationalism is the main principle of the box – and irrational means unreasonable, undiscussable, understood by neither reason nor science.

For many reasons,[21] art has been assigned the role of the revelation of this existential, irrational order which is above technocracy and apart from technocracy. But before showing how this has worked out, we must wait until we have advanced so far in our argument. At this stage we must turn to the development of modern art and the genesis of its basic principles. We must turn from the background, the principles of the Enlightenment, to their consequences.

3
The First Step to Modern Art

> Impaled on my wall my eyes can dimly see
> the pattern of my life and the puzzle that is me.
> From the moment of my birth till the instant of my death
> there are patterns I must follow just as I must breathe each breath
> like a rat in a maze the path before me lies
> and the pattern never alters – until the rat dies.[22]

The Enlightenment may have begun as a philosophical movement, but deep spiritual problems related to religious truth were also very much at stake. Its influence was not only on the minds but also on the hearts of people, it affected their sensitivity and emotions, it really changed their life in all its aspects. The eighteenth century was the beginning of a revolution of life and society that has not yet come to an end. The denial to God of the place that he deserves as Creator and Lawgiver has had many repercussions. And as people's understanding of themselves and their world has changed, so inevitably has their art.

The Enlightenment involved raising the epistemological question: *How can we know* the world and its governing principles? This had considerable implications for art. The problem for the artist was now what to paint, what to see. What could one see, how could one achieve any sort of artistic understanding of the world, of humanity, of what one wanted to paint? In a way intellectual questions came to hinder the artist's vision.

Nothing but the facts

One of the first to appreciate these things deeply was Goya, whom many would call the first modern artist. So deeply in fact did he understand them that he produced an etching with the title *The dream of reason produces monsters*.[23] He has depicted humans, in war, in daily life, as monstrous. He has depicted the irrationality of this seemingly rational world. It must be stressed that he always avoids showing any sort of normative principle at work. People are fighting in the street: it is a fact, people are fighting in the street, but he does not show us heroes fighting for right against cruel oppressors. In one very well-known painting he shows an execution: men are being shot by a firing squad.[24] It is terrible. Yet the modernity of the picture lies precisely in the fact that we do not see heroes who have fought for the liberty of their country giving up their lives, nor revolutionaries rightly condemned by the forces of law and order. No, these are simply men being shot and others doing the shooting. The sky is closed. This is quite different from the martyrdom by Rubens we have already discussed, with angels coming to bring the true confessor of the faith his heavenly reward. No, the sole facts are the things that we can see – the things we see are really the only facts there are. And Goya shows us no more than that.

Goya painted his mistress, the Duchess of Alba, in two versions: a naked and a clothed Maya.[25] She is lying on a couch, following the well-known formula originated by the Venetians of the sixteenth century (which we discussed in connection with *Venus and Music*). Who is the nude on the couch? Venus? No, she is simply a beautiful woman, portrayed from her head down to her feet. There can be no more Venuses, for the old ideas are dead, and Venus was killed in the eighteenth century. There is no longer any such thing as 'ideas' like this, principles external to humanity, as we have seen. Now there is only subjective reasoning from a person's perceptions, from the sensations one has in seeing things. So we can no longer paint a Venus, but we can *see* the beauty of a woman and *experience* desire in looking at her. Venus of course could stand up (we have quite a few paintings of a standing Venus), but could not be clothed. Clothes would make her into a different allegory, the representation of another idea, a Juno or Flora or Diana. Venus's nudity is an attribute by which we recognize her. But a real woman can be clothed, and so we can have a portrait of the same lady as in the nude, Maya, but now clothed. It may have been that Goya made these two companion pictures to show that Venus was dead. The only thing left was his sensibility as a man before his mistress.

Delacroix, the great artist of the first half of the nineteenth century in France, wrestled very consciously with this same problem. We can read about it in his diary. He tells us how he would like to have painted like Rubens or Titian or Rembrandt, but that he despaired of ever being able to do so. The women of Rubens are marvellous, exactly right as Venus or Fame, but how could he ever paint them? He never had such models in his studio. Delacroix could do no more than paint the model, that is, make a portrait of her – as he did of Mademoiselle Rose in a small painting now in the Louvre, a study never intended to be on display. When he was painting his great works, works for exhibition, and wanted them to be meaningful and important, he started from his visual experience in his studies and then stylized, generalized, idealized in order to achieve something that could be compared with the great works of the Baroque painters. He stylized, but without having a true basis for doing so. He had no foundation for his art but the great tradition of painting. Hence there was always the haunting question: How could they do it? How did they achieve it? How can we make something that is more than we can see?

Delacroix's answer in a way was the same as that given by his main supporter, the art critic Baudelaire: it is through imagination that we must do it. It is an answer typical of Romanticism. It is perhaps an affirmation of humanity not fully 'caught in the box'. Romanticism was the first major revolt against the rationalism of the eighteenth century. It exalted the irrational, the strange, the mysterious. It was a movement of more importance in literature than in painting, and I do not intend to spend further time on it now. In any case, my aim is not to try to write a history of art! But I shall be returning to the painting of William Blake in a later section.

Landscape and reality

It was also in the Romantic period that landscape painting became of great importance. The study of landscape was parallel to the observations of science. I say the 'study of landscape', as there is a marked change here from the seventeenth-century type of landscape as created by Jan van Goyen or (perhaps of greater importance for England and France) by his contemporary Claude Lorraine. Constable was the first to make scientific studies in the painting of clouds, and many of his landscapes picture actual places. Turner too began as a 'topographical' watercolour-painter. Later he frequently made precise studies of natural phenomena, such as particular weather conditions. His *Rain, steam and speed*,[26] depicting a train crossing a bridge over the Thames in London, is justly famous as the first rendering of a type of weather condition in this way. Turner painted what he saw.

There is here a certain kind of duality. On the one hand Turner was a Romantic, painting human vision and feelings, free from a slavish, 'scientific' copying of nature, expressing the non-rational and 'spiritual' in humanity. On the other hand he did paint exactly what he saw, nature as it can be experienced by the senses. He wanted to paint like a Claude Lorraine, just as Delacroix was trying to work in the tradition of the great Baroque painters. Yet he is different from the examples he admired so greatly because of this inbuilt tension – what we have come to know as the Romantic. Lorraine painted a lyrical version of a humanist ideal landscape, a vision of the structure of the countryside around Rome. Insofar as it was humanist idealism, dreaming of a greater past, a human possibility, it prefigures the art of men like Turner. But there is this other side to Turner, his naturalism, and the tension between these two sides makes up his Romanticism.

The duality we noted in Delacroix, who made studies from nature in order to be able then to idealize, is also to be found to a certain extent in Constable. His well-known twofold painting of *The haywain*[27] is very typical of this. First he made the rough painting, to keep as close as possible to the direct sensation of nature in all its freshness and colour, its 'light, dews and breezes', as he called it; then he painted the more finished picture, which was much more in line with the great landscape tradition. It is not really relevant to discuss which one is the true Constable, and whether he made the second one only to please the public. Both pictures are truly Constable. They typify the epistemological problem, the question of the true source of knowledge, which the landscape painters were having to face because of the new naturalistic spirit of the age. The sketch is from nature, the second painting tries to retain what made the old art from before the Age of Reason great. The first pointed more to the future, the second to the past. Yet there was good reason why these painters were reluctant to give themselves immediately and wholeheartedly to the directly-from-nature approach. We have no difficulty in understanding it when we see the problems art has run into since. These painters realized the importance of the 'human' in older painting, and were hesitant to lose it. But at the same time they had to start from what they saw directly, from their immediate sensations.

So in many ways these painters still belonged to the great tradition; yet the germs that were to destroy that tradition were already active. The same duality was found in Corot who, in his early days, also painted two pictures of which one was painted directly on the spot and the other idealized according to the principles of Claude Lorraine. That the second is the lesser is understandable: it really simply follows Lorraine, according to the vision of another age that cannot be copied just at random, while the first is more in line with the understanding of nature in the thinking of his own day. Yet we must honour his hesitation.

The death of themes

It was not only in method but also in subject matter that art changed deeply. Even a noted traditionalist, the great painter Ingres, working according to the principle of Raphael, did not paint a reclining Venus but his *Great Odalisque*. An odalisque is the favourite concubine of a great oriental ruler and so what we see is not Venus, an allegory of love and beauty, but a kind of ideal female, even if she is only there for sexual gratification and even if love is understood in the sense of lust. Ingres has placed his ideal woman in a faraway world to make the painting acceptable. Yet, in one sense, she is a real woman and in no way a goddess. In another sense she has already lost something of her humanity and is no more than an object of lust.

The final blow was given by Courbet – the final blow against the old pre-eighteenth-century principles of choosing subject matter. Let us reconsider those basic ideas for a moment. The great facts of history, biblical scenes, myths taken from the Graeco-Roman world were depicted not for their own sake, nor for their special interest as history, but as examples to illustrate (in a deep sense) human truths. Hercules was a kind of allegory of the human soul; the great deeds of a man like Alexander the Great showed the greatness of humankind and their heroism; biblical scenes were chosen to preach Christian truths.

But the old principles were gone. Now, in a rationalist, scientific age, there were no laws, no norms outside of humanity at all. They were 'man-made', inherent in 'man' himself. The neoclassical or Romantic historical pictures already show the loss of meaning: they were often large reconstructions of a scene from so many years ago, a kind of blown-up photograph of what the painter thought it would have been like.

An example of this is David's famous *Battle of the Romans and the Sabines* of 1799. Of course there is no denying its quality, nor the fact that it reveals strong compositional elements. Yet everything is painted with painstaking precision in archaeological detail and, as these classicists erroneously thought that the heroes of those days fought naked, in some ways one cannot escape the feeling that the whole thing is a sort of great, strange nudist camp! True, there was a deeper layer to the picture, in its aim of trying to express the strong contemporary desire for peace: note the Sabine woman trying to separate the two armies. But we do not learn about this from the picture itself; we can only know about it from other sources and then see it in the picture. For the painting itself conveys nothing but a kind of archaeological and rather idealistic understanding of something that happened somewhere in Roman history.

Later historical paintings were to go even further in the same direction. If we look in the catalogues of the Salons, the large annual exhibitions in Paris, or the exhibitions at the Royal Academy in London, we see that the paintings were described in long, precise titles, with a note added about the story that the picture depicted. These had become necessary as the incidents painted were often rather minor and of no consequence whatsoever. Just because they were so 'photographic' their content was often not at all clear. In a seventeenth-century picture the meaning was usually clear even if we do not know the picture's title. (Who could misunderstand a *Susanna and the Elders* despite never having read the apocryphal story?) But now the main general theme and meaning of the picture was often sadly not apparent from the picture itself.

Courbet, as I have said, dealt the final blow to the old idea of choosing subject matter. He faced up to the consequences of the fact that previous principles had become empty and without any sort of basis for the deep appreciation of reality. Instead of trying to cling to a dead tradition as the historical painters did, he said he wanted to paint only what he could see. 'I have never seen an angel,' he said, 'so I shall not paint one.' He painted peasant girls at work,[28] or stonebreakers, or people coming back from the market. And the public was shocked. For he made these pictures just as large as the 'important', 'high', fashionable historical paintings, and people realized that what his work was saying was, 'Look, this is really just as important, perhaps even more true, and surely just as human and deep.'

For us, living so much later, it is often difficult to realize how revolutionary and new his work was. Its message is less in the handling of the artistic tools, the style, as in the subject matter, or rather in the lack of a theme. These are the things one can see, his works cried out, and that is the only thing that can be called true or important.

And so the first step towards modern art was taken. Themes in the old sense had become obsolete. In the art to come they had no further role to play.

Naturalistic reality

There were two other men working in the same direction: Daumier and Manet. With Daumier it was his lithographs rather than his paintings which were crucial. In a series depicting the old Greek and Roman myths, such as Oedipus or Odysseus, he showed what they would have been 'in reality'. Penelope was an old haggard woman, sentimentally looking at a worn portrait of her husband who had been away for many years. Narcissus,[29] who died as his eye was fascinated by his own beauty as he looked at his reflection in the water, what else could he have been but a starving idiot, grinning at his own hollow cheeks? Who could ever paint these themes seriously again? No painter of any merit ever did . . . Manet completed the work of Courbet and Daumier, and in finalizing the first step to modern art prepared the way for the next step. His *Picnic on the grass* and *Olympia* are particularly famous. The former starts from the idyllic beauty of a humanist poem by Giorgione, his *Pastoral concerto* (in the Louvre), in which we see musicians attended by their muse and, to the left, the nymph of the well, lower deities, personifications even: all this Manet has translated into the rather dubious picnic of some men (dressed) and women (nude – or rather, undressed). The latter showed the consequences of the direction already taken by Goya. The painting shows a nude woman on a couch. To Titian she had been Venus, to Goya a mistress. But Manet might have argued, 'What man is going to paint his own mistress and so display her to the world?' Where in reality, that is in the world in which we live, can we see an unclothed woman on a couch otherwise? Surely only in a brothel! And so he painted a prostitute, looking at us out of the picture quite unabashed. And when we realize that she was a character of some notoriety – rather like Christine Keeler a few years ago in Britain – we can understand that the people of the time were shocked. They were shocked not only perhaps because she was who she was – and certainly not because the painting was poor, for as people realized, it was painted magnificently – but because human values were at stake, and Venus was now not only dead but also well and truly buried.

Another initial step to modern art

Modern art is very complex. It is a fruit of the Enlightenment; it expresses the consequences of its basic principles. What is at stake is human insight and knowledge of reality. But we must also account for another aspect of our age, the reaction against rationalism and naturalistic science. It is a reaction, and yet dependent on what it is reacting against: it makes sense only because it does in fact acknowledge the truth (or at least the inevitability) of naturalism and naturalistic science.

This reaction came very early. It was already there in the eighteenth century. In the nineteenth century it soon became a sideline, as it was the art of the Salon (with which we shall deal in a later section) and the development from Goya to Manet we have already discussed which predominated. Only at the end of the century did this movement come to the fore again in the form of symbolism and Art Nouveau.

The rationalist movement of the Enlightenment initially expressed itself mainly in classicism and in a renewed interest in historical painting. In France there was the work of David, while in England there were no really great artists but quite a number of painters and sculptors working in this line, such as Copley, Benjamin West, Flaxman, Haydon. The main artists here in fact were the great portrait painters such as Reynolds and Gainsborough, whose art served the nobility and gentry of England, the ruling class that as such was not yet deeply touched by the new spirit. But they were far less out of touch than the French court, which was less involved with the realities of life and took much less interest in the problems of the majority of the people – and who through their frivolity and lack of real concern added fuel to the fire of the up-and-coming rationalist and revolutionary movement.

Yet it is in this same England that the reaction against the spirit of the Age of Reason found early expression in the works of poets and writers such as Young, Gray, Walpole (*Castle of Otranto*), the novels of terror and other pre- or early Romantic genres. Among the painters were Fuseli and William Blake.

William Blake was a mystic who thought the greatest enemies of his time and his country were reasoning, the philosophy of Locke, and the science of Newton. He was afraid of their systems and, in an almost anarchistic way, looked for human freedom. He related their work to the Industrial Revolution, the deadening effects of which he prophesied in many books. He mourned the fact that the machine would dominate the mind as well as the body, until it makes out of the person at the machine another machine, without intelligence and, finally, no more than an animal. He wrote that 'A Machine is not a Man nor a Work of Art; it is destructive of Humanity and of Art; the world Machination.'[30] He also reacted strongly against the rigid sexual morality, the already growing 'Victorian' bourgeois prudishness that we shall discuss later in this chapter, and preached free love and the virtue of acting on our impulses rather than repressing them.

His own answer to these problems was a kind of mysticism, based on Swedenborg, Neoplatonist and gnostic ideas, that had as its basic teaching the importance of the spiritual – that there are other spiritual beings, and that the world is greater than is acknowledged by the rationalistic or scientific view of reality. He expressed his theories in very involved prophecies, inventing new mythological figures with names like Los, Enitharmon and Golganooza. In fact he is thinking about the realities of the world he lived in in a mythologizing way: Los is the symbol of the age of iron, Enitharmon of textiles, and Golganooza stands for London. Their main concern again and again is that the forces of evil are 'petrifying all the human imagination into rock and sand'. He speaks of Satan, whose work is 'eternal Death with Mills and Ovens and Cauldrons'. Deeply inbuilt into all his work is the 'hatred of reason and restraint, which has no other function than to limit and destroy energy, the only source of good.' People, he says, can only attain salvation by the full development of their impulses, and all restraint on them whether by law, religion or moral code is wrong.[31]

The interesting thing is that Blake printed his own books, writing them and illustrating them in a completely original and new way. His style is wildly imaginative, fantastic and yet real, depicting the great realities that are more than the eye can see or logic can reason about. The curved lines, the letters that turn into plants (such as on the title page of his *Songs of Innocence*[32]) are especially typical, and show graphically his irrational, sweeping way of thinking.

William Blake had a few followers but not many. But in his reaction against rationalism, his search for the spiritual and the mystical, for imagination and liberty, for sexual freedom, he brought together many elements that would and did appeal to young artists in later periods, both in the 1890s and again in our own time with its psychedelic art.

Idealized escapism

There is another art that is called 'Romantic', namely the art of a John Martin and of many other landscape and genre painters. Today they are not valued particularly highly, although, to say the least, many of them were accomplished artists technically who achieved works with a merit, style and atmosphere of their own.

One example here will serve better than a list of names. It is a pastoral scene painted by Klombeck, of the school of the well-known Dutch landscape painter B.C. Koekkoek. What is Romantic in this landscape? There is nothing wild or dangerous, nothing heroic or extravagant. It is, quite to the contrary, peaceful, restful, rustic, with a kind of contentment and almost sentimental poetry. There are the woods, the old oak tree, the stream and little waterfall (you can almost hear the water), the peasant folk with their cattle, and the beauty and golden sunshine of a fine summer's day. There is nothing of the agitation and problems of the larger world with its ever-changing culture, its revolution and counter-revolution. It is the world of contented people living away from the turmoil amidst the beauties of the world that remained untouched by the new industrialization. It is the world 'at its best', in its almost eternal (even if almost secular) bliss.

This vision is the world of the restoration that came over Europe after the turmoil of the French Revolution and the Napoleonic wars. It is a restoration that idealized the 'old world', longed for it and hoped to find it in the simplicity of rural, rustic life. We may call it early Victorian, or Biedermeyer, or simply Romantic. It was a kind of escapism – to use a word coined by the fiercely committed generations of our own times. It looked back and found its inspiration in the art of the past, in seventeenth-century Dutch landscape art (Ruisdael and Hobbema), perhaps too in artists such as George Morland and other minor masters of the late eighteenth century. Where it differs from seventeenth-century art, and resembles the late eighteenth century, is in the idealization, the remoteness from life, the placid dream.

Here we see the bourgeois spirit at its best – and its limitations. We shall be looking in a moment at another rather more negative aspect of the bourgeois spirit. But first we must see how Christian art reacted to the antichristian or non-Christian forces let loose by the Age of Reason.

Christian art?

What happened to 'Christian art', or, better, to art depicting biblical stories or subjects related to the Christian faith, in the aftermath of the Enlightenment? Two facts stand out before any discussion of actual works. First, orthodox evangelical groups are conspicuously absent, in spite of the Great Awakening of the eighteenth and early nineteenth centuries, for the newly revived evangelicalism was often marred by an unbiblical anti-intellectual and anti-cultural outlook (of which we have already seen the background in an earlier chapter). Second, the 'spirit of the age' was not really Christian in a biblical sense at all. Perhaps one of the most tragic aspects of the nineteenth century lies in the fact that so very few Christians really did see the deep dechristianizing influences of the Enlightenment. In Holland there was Groen van Prinsterer, who wrote his *Unbelief and Revolution* in the middle of the century – a book which is still a key one in showing the revolution in its real depth. As a whole people did not wake up to the deep ideas at work before Darwin's *Origin of Species* was published. Many compromised, and others were concerned wholly with doctrinal orthodoxy and evangelism, failing to meet the enemy in its own field.

The main art of that period was to be found in the bourgeois art already briefly referred to, the art exhibited at the Paris Salons, comparable with the art of the Royal Academy in England. Here too in the course of the century we see the old themes lose their meaning, together with the values of a time now irrevocably past. This academic art had the façade of old art, but in reality it was very naturalistic: its historical pieces became increasingly either sentimental stories or rather idealized genre pieces. Kings and other great men were shown in their daily all too common reality. Salon art reflected the bourgeois spirit: it tried to cover up the fact that the old values had lost their hold. At the same time its basic outlook on reality was positivist, painting only what was as photographically precise as the eye can see. In fact there is not really so great a distance between the line of Manet and that of the Salon artists in basic principles; it was the bourgeois spirit of the latter that made the difference.[33]

Christian painting, in the sense indicated above, belonged almost completely to the stream of Salon art. Most of the painters in this line were liberal Roman Catholics (and liberal Protestants in Britain). They took the point of view of the average person of the nineteenth century: they stood in the line of development that started with the Enlightenment, but with the principles mellowed, and professing at the same time a Christianity which was also watered down and not held with any great conviction.

Leys was a painter from Antwerp. Around the middle of the nineteenth century he painted a series of wall paintings in the town hall there very typical of the period. They are very precise renderings of often not very important historical events, and one can very rarely understand them without reading the text that explains what is intended. They are paintings which are more illustrations from a history book than depictions of important human issues. As far as his religious work was concerned, he painted no biblical stories to my knowledge. His picture of people in the sixteenth century praying in front of a crucifix is typical of this type of work.[34] The people are as precisely reconstructed as possible. Considerable study of contemporary fashions and so on was involved. We see people moving from left to right, and a girl kneeling, with as background a particular well-known place near an Antwerp church where there is a large sculpture of a group at the crucifixion. We can see some glimpses of statues of the apostles which stand near the entrance to the little garden in which the sculpture stands, but we do not see the sculpture itself, which stands several yards to the right, outside the picture. We presume it is there, but we do not see it in the picture.

So what do we see? People from a past period, full of faith, reverent, praying – but we do not see the object of faith, the crucified Christ. This is typical. The whole scene is designed to create an atmosphere of the golden times of the past, when people were still full of faith – it is all very beautiful and fine. But the focus is on the faithful men and women, not on the content of their faith. The crucifix, Christ himself, has been left outside the picture-frame.

This was done again and again by nineteenth-century painters. By removing Christ or Mary or other Christian themes from the picture itself, leaving them outside the picture frame, it is as if Christ himself, and the reality of the things Christians believed in, was placed outside the world. We could almost say that we see within the picture frame a part at least of the contemporary view of the world and human being, and as God and Christ were spiritually set aside in the eighteenth century, so were they too in the painting of the time. Yet they were there, not in reality but by implication. To borrow a term from mathematics: Christ was extrapolated. He was put outside the framework (in a double sense) of human endeavour.

There are two more pictures that we must look at: first, one by Ciseri, an Italian painter famous in his time. His large *Ecce homo*[35] is one of the best works of the kind we are discussing. The question is, what does the painting mean? What does it tell us? Is it about Christ's importance, or about his suffering, or his Passion? But Christ is seen half from behind, and is not particularly drawn to our attention. The soldier standing beside him seems more important in a way, even though we cannot say that the painter really meant him to be the real centre of attention. Is it the throne in front, painted so precisely that it looks like a reconstruction? It may seem strange, but when a group of people looks at the picture there is very soon a discussion about whether the reconstruction of the details of the throne and the palace and the city is adequate and true. To some degree it is, but the column, for instance, with the spiral relief on it is an anachronism; it was only around AD 100 that the Romans began to build these, and then only a few, in the great capitals of Rome and Constantinople.

But what *is* important in the picture? Pilate's wife going sadly away? Or Pilate himself? He is standing in the middle, after all. But we see only his back. What can the meaning of the picture be? We are not talking about what you (or your aunt) feels to be important in the Passion, or what one might have felt if present, but what interpretation the artist gives of the scene. Our thoughts, perhaps induced by the picture, are probably sentimental, for there is no 'sermon' in the painting to react to. It gives no more than a photographic record, in which everything has equal weight and validity – shoes, columns, hair, clothes, everything. It does not interpret history, nor can we 'see' human meaning and content. In fact, as figures seen from behind are often used in painting to create a sense of space, and as Pilate has very much this effect in the painting, one is tempted to say that the only real meaning in the picture is space, the space around the figures and things. Is it a Christian picture in a true sense? It would certainly not seem to be: I sometimes even feel that it is doing away with true Christian content, avoiding any idea of 'testimony', recording no more than a historical fact in a naturalistic way.

The problem which we have already discussed in a previous chapter comes to us here in all its force: if we paint events 'as they would have been seen', they may well be interesting as history but lose their true content, for there is no sense of their being things of importance for all history and for all humankind. But if they are not painted as being 'historically true', the factuality on which Christianity is founded is lost for, as we have seen, 'if Christ has not been raised, your faith is in vain.'

The problem lies somewhere in the words 'historically true'. The nineteenth century developed new methods and new aims for historiography: they wanted to know 'how things really were', which means what could have been seen, or measured (the number of people), or described precisely (dates, geography, etc.). People continued to look for truth, but the concept of truth itself had changed. For instance, the genealogy in Matthew 1 could never have been written by a modern historian. It would not seem to be wholly accurate historically when compared with the Old Testament. It looks wrong to modern eyes. But to Matthew and his contemporaries it was true – after all, he had written his Gospel to convince people of the truth of Christ! Their truth was deeper and more comprehensive, and so more truly historical, including all the facts, than that of modern people with their limited understanding of factuality.

This conflict between modern scientific historical method and the way the Bible tells its true story is to be found in the modern 'demythologizing' of the Bible. Bultmann has said that in our modern technological age we cannot believe the things the Bible presents as real. That would mean a sacrifice of intellect. But I would want to say that, on the contrary, we must really listen to the Bible, and look not only at what it says but also at the methods it uses. For the biblical writers were richer and nearer to the fullness of reality than we modern folk are; and not only did they write as people, but their message is God's revelation, and so their approach to 'facts' and 'reality' is normative for us. We have reduced reality, and technological reality is nothing but a box limited by the scientist's approach to reality, leaving out everything that is beyond rationalistic reason and naturalistic nature. Matthew was not just interested in 'what actually happened' in the modern sense, the sense of measurable and rationalistically controllable data. He wanted to show the meaning of history, the deeper spiritual and therefore human relationships in time and in history, the relation between the many relevant facts. And above all he wanted to show that God had something to do with it. He is interpreting history. The names he mentions are significant. Christ was born from a real human lineage in which quite a few strange and far from 'decent' people are found. The numbers of generations too are significant. God acted in history and was preparing for the coming of Christ in this way. Matthew spoke the truth; he did not want to by-pass the facts, but he did not want to see the facts only in their factuality but also in their true meaning. We, in our obsession with tangible facts alone, have become the poorer.

This digression makes it clear that a painting like Ciseri's is not Christian in the biblical sense, even if the subject matter is taken from the Bible. Yet it has content and expresses ideas. The content reflects a new way of understanding, a new idea of truth that has been engendered by the Enlightenment.

Tissot's *Crucifixion* shows how far these painters went. It seems strange at first, but one soon realizes that the crucifixion itself is not shown at all, for we are looking through the eyes of the Crucified to the scene around the cross. Is this not almost too clever a device to get rid of Christ? The painter did not show him; he extrapolated him from the world he painted – and yet he is there, as the painter almost blasphemously makes his own point of view to be that of Christ.

In what way was the Protestant world expressing itself in art? For that we must turn our attention to the Pre-Raphaelite painters, and particularly to Holman Hunt. We are now in a position to understand his *Scapegoat*. What does it mean? He went to paint the picture on the spot, by the Dead Sea, with a gun on his knees (the Bedouin could be dangerous), an umbrella over his head against the sun, trying endlessly to keep the poor animal in position. It took him some months. One cannot say it is not naturalistically true. It is. But is it biblical? Does the painting change at all if we tell each other that the scapegoat was a sacrifice, sent away into the desert yearly bearing the sins of the people of Israel? And look at Hunt's picture of Jesus in his father's workshop.[36] The boy is stretching, and we see his shadow against the wall in the form of a cross. Hunt took pains to paint this on the roof of his house in Jerusalem . . . but is it truly biblical? I am not wanting to criticize it just because the Bible does not mention the story but because the whole feeling of the picture would seem to be no more than sheer sentimentality: our feelings are kindled, but the painter shows us nothing of any depth or importance at all. There is no 'exegesis', no confession, no creedal statement. Here is a fact, of no importance . . . and we are invited to give it meaning, within us, in our feelings (certainly not with our intelligence).

Of course, the work of these Victorian artists is of historical importance and has a quality of its own. But it is particularly important that we should see what they were doing, for almost all 'Christian' art since has followed this line. Think of Bible illustrations or Sunday school pictures or reproductions on the walls of church halls. As a style it became the Christian style, until the Second World War, at least . . . and in some places it is still alive.

For centuries evangelical Christians have steered clear of art, and so lost their critical powers and any real understanding of the arts. It is only in this way that we can explain why Christians took this art to be Christian in spirit and so fit to illustrate our Bibles and teach our children. Christians saw the deficiencies of the liberal reconstructions of the life of Christ of Hall Caine and Renan, but failed to see that the same spirit was at work in these pictures.

Evangelicals have also underestimated the importance of art. They have thought of biblical pictures as being representations of biblical stories. But they did not see that the salt had become tasteless, that there was so much idealization, so much of a sort of pseudo-devotional sentimentality in these pictures that they are very far from the reality the Bible talks about. Could it be that the false ideas many people, non-Christians as well as Christians, have of Christ as a sentimental, rather effeminate man, soft and 'loving', never really of this world, are the result of the preaching inherent in the pictures given to children or hanging on the wall? Their theology, their message, is not that of the Bible but of nineteenth-century liberalism.

The new naturalism and the bourgeois attitude

The prophet Isaiah spoke of people whom God had to address as those who 'draw near me with their mouth, and with their lips do honour me but have removed their heart from me, and their fear towards me is taught by the precept of men'. It was a spirit that the prophets preached against, again and again. But is not that exactly the type of Christianity we have described in the last section? We could call it bourgeois. It is true that it is found at all times in history, the spirit of a Christianity which has lost the true faith and does not really trust its Lord. But in the form in which it appears around us it is really a manifestation of the bourgeois. It is interesting to note that it came into being virtually at the same time as the growth of the influence of the Enlightenment. As we have suggested already, it might even have been one of the sources of the Age of Reason.

What was the bourgeois spirit? 'Well, you know, we Christians are very nice, decent people. Please don't keep on at us with all this talk about sin in the Bible. We are much more civilized now than people were then. And anyway, it's what Christ said in the Sermon on the Mount that really matters (*He* didn't talk about sin, did he?). That's the spirit we want to live in – love and kindness and so on.' They never said so, but what they meant was: 'Please don't remind us of the hard facts of life, don't open our eyes to them, as then it will be impossible for us to live in peace and unity with the establishment of today. You cannot expect us to be haggard prophets, that sort of thing isn't really done. We are too good and moral and righteous . . .'

The bourgeois are people who looked for certainty and security. With their lips they might honour God, but in their hearts they looked for a more 'tangible' kind of foundation. They found it in money, in a career, in status, in their moral uprightness. And so morality became moralism and insurance often took the place of the assurance that God does not forsake one. They wanted their lives to be moral, true and normal, but they had no foundation for it, for true Christianity was rejected and turned into liberalism.

These very nice people lived in the Age of Reason. And of course, they looked with dismay on the new generation who were taking to the principles of the Enlightenment. Morals were going downhill and the old established rules were being challenged. This was bad enough. And when the new thinkers started preaching that people were basically animals, that love was really only sex, then they were shocked. Human beings like animals? . . . No, that could never be. Yet, what could they do? Had they not got desires themselves? Oh no, *we* haven't got them, they told themselves. And so they began to push the fact that a person has a body, and especially sexuality, into the dark, hidden corners of life. Of course lust was beastly and should be suppressed – maybe young people could have their fling in their youth, but that is only passing, and one must not talk about that, even if it means maintaining a double morality.

So towards the end of the eighteenth century the bourgeois world, which often coincided for various historical reasons with the middle class, began to build up the defensive attitude towards sex that later became known as Victorian prudishness.[37] We, living so much later and following that period, can no longer really understand what it was like in pre-Victorian times – when people knew that the fact that they had bodies and sexual urges was because they were human. We can only understand the loss of it. Around 1600, for instance, people had many words for sexual intercourse, but today we can only say that people 'go to bed with each other' or else we have to use more scientific (and therefore neutral) words. We can never fathom the depth of the loss of this, or what it has meant in the lives of many, many men and women.

Out of this grew the notion of romantic love, a love pure and beautiful and eternal, virgin-white and virtually sex-less. It meant the myth of the pure virgin, beautiful and truthful to the very end – but with almost no real passion – married to the ever-faithful husband, loving and caring and never looking for another woman, as his pure heart is unable to do such a thing. Reality, alas, is different: men and women are sinful, and even if one partner wants to remain faithful in marriage, only too often the other is likely to be an easy prey to temptation. Romantic love is a lie and has proved a great deceiver. Biblical marriage is designed for men and women as they really are. It is true that for sinful men and women the Old Testament recognizes something less than the ideal – divorce was allowed 'for the hardness of men's hearts' – but it also shows that those who have been made new in Christ can now realize what marriage was really intended to be, a union of two people become 'one flesh'.

It may seem strange that Christians fell victim to the optimistic, humanistic, 'romantic' vision of love so much so that its last strongholds are probably within Christian circles. Perhaps it was the old ideas of Greek philosophy so popular in medieval times (for medievalism enjoyed a revival in Victorian times) with its mystical exaltation of the spirit over against the lowness or even sinfulness of the flesh, which were the cause of this. Or, more probably, perhaps it was a necessary part of this bourgeois type of moralistic Christianity.

Beside 'lily-white' romantic love there also existed another concept, the romantic concept of true passion – meaning that passionate love was irresistible and could break all barriers, those of social standing, age or even marriage ties. This type of love, popularized in romantic novels, is still very much with us today. It too is a lie, as many have found to their cost. But it is an idea which sinful men and women are only too ready to believe as it gives them an excuse to pander to their desires.

So the Enlightenment changed the world. Its principles were not 'just' philosophy but had their consequences, in sorrow and deception and ruined lives. Sexuality has never been the same again. On the one hand there was Victorian prudishness, on the other the reaction to it, the salaciousness of some of the Romantic writers (probably stronger in France than in England), which only too easily degenerated into pornography. The former naturalness in speaking about these things was completely lost; many passages in books written before the Age of Reason are either unreadable for us today or are read almost as pornography. Who today could do what John Dowland did, write a song to be sung at a wedding, an epithalamium, with the refrain, 'Ride happy, ride happy, happy lovers'?

Reactions to realism

Beside Victorian prudishness and salaciousness the nineteenth century also witnessed the 'positivist' trend that has been discussed in talking about Goya, Delacroix and Manet, who had no intention of being pornographic at all but only of seeing and speaking the simple truth.

It is against this threefold background that we must understand the beginning of censorship in the nineteenth century of all kinds of art that speak about straight 'facts'. Flaubert's book *Madame Bovary* would seem to have been the first to have been brought to court, in 1857, though there had of course already been suppression of true pornography much earlier, but this is not our concern here. When we read this book, it is hard for us to understand what was considered wrong with it. Its heroine is a woman who commits adultery with different men while being married to a bore of a husband. Only in a few passages do we read anything of the sexual pleasures she indulged in, and then never does it go into detail as pornography would. In the court the book was accused of offence against public and religious morality. But the lawyer who defended Flaubert said that the scenes had a fidelity comparable with the daguerreotype (the early form of photography then current). Here we have the real problem. Things and actions were described photographically, with no reference to norms or principles at all, though the narrative did in fact end with the downfall and suicide of the woman. The woman's life was shown photographically, factually. And that was exactly what horrified Flaubert's contemporaries. They felt that human values were at stake, the more so as their own principles were based on a negative defence rather than a positive moral, as we have seen.

This way of writing was called 'realistic'. And it was under the name of Realism that Courbet had exhibited his works and that Manet's pictures of the Picnic and the Olympia had been painted. Yes, they were true to life, if life is no more than factual, no more than the things we can see and experience.

Soon the writers began to talk about 'art for art's sake' – which meant that in creating works of art no moral ideas needed to be considered at all. Art had to depict life 'as it is'. Zola, the great writer who was contemporary with the Impressionists, shocked the world again and again with his 'fidelity' to true life.

Two questions must be asked. First, was this really reality? Second, did this have any influence on reality? There is no need to labour the answer to the first question. It was life only as it was understood by men of the 'avant-garde', a view of life in line with the principles of the Enlightenment or, as we must call it now, of positivism, the philosophy which made everything depend on scientific observation and experiment. Auguste Comte, Herbert Spencer, John Stuart Mill, these were the positivist philosophers who began to apply the spirit and methods of naturalistic science to the humanities, especially to economics and sociology. But even if it was reality as they understood it, was it true reality? We can only refer back to what we have already discussed, for it was really a very impoverished world, the closed world of 'the box' of the Age of Reason. True humanity, being much more than factuality, was left out of account.

The second question is a very important one. It is difficult to prove statistically one way or the other just how much influence the artist has on reality. For there will always be only a small gap between the artist and his public. Both are part of the same culture, which is moving 'forward'. Where to? In this case it was once again to an ever increasing consistency with the principles of the Enlightenment. Realism, or rather naturalism, in books and films today, for example including all the facts of sexuality, was prepared for, and was propelled by, the nineteenth-century type of art we have been discussing. Since the eighteenth century there has been a constant reduction of the 'old' moral principles, a *démasqué* leaving us at the end amidst the ruins of the one-time Christian consensus.

At the same time what we have been describing in this chapter may help us to understand some elements of our times. On the one hand there is this type of realistic, open portrayal of sexual matters, while at the same time in daily life these things are still kept hidden and a Victorian attitude remains, even if in a watered-down form. We still cannot sing Dowland's song at a wedding. And we still have not regained a full understanding of what sexuality means. Only too often it is something strange and shameful or it is a fact, an appetite to be satisfied, something which is no more than animal. Sexuality today has sometimes become almost amoral, something outside morality altogether, catering to drives comparable with those of thirst or hunger.

A final conclusion must be this: we must not be surprised if a section of the youth of today has begun to live according to the principles – or lack of them – found in films, books and theatre. They are often protesting against the bourgeois people, whose Victorian understanding of sexuality is equally a lie, people who still cling to the 'old morality' yet have no true foundation for it.

4
The Second Step to Modern Art

> Through the corridors of sleep past the shadows dark and deep
> my mind dances and leaps in confusion.
> I don't know what is real, I can't touch what I feel
> and I hide behind the shield of my illusion;
> So I continue to continue to pretend
> that my life will never end
> and the flowers never bend with the rainfall.[38]

Goya, Delacroix, Constable, Corot, Courbet, Daumier, Manet had worked towards realizing some of the consequences of the new principles of looking at reality as developed in the Age of Reason – and art had become 'realistic'. This art had at the same time, at least with the later artists, a certain degree of protest inherent in it, protest against the shallowness of Salon painting which, in the course of time, was to become even more shallow and vulgar in the hands of men like Gerôme and Bouguereau.

But, following this naturalistic trend further, how was it possible to develop it? What, in fact, was there left to paint? For the only things that are real and true are the things seen, and the rest is façade, traditional ideas that have been emptied of meaning.

It was here that the Impressionists came in. Monet, Renoir and their friends set out to paint what they saw, what the eye recorded. In the late 1860s Monet painted Paris seen from a high window: houses, water, trees, churches, people walking along the pavements . . . this was Paris. In the early 1870s Renoir painted an open-air dance, with some of his friends sitting in the foreground.[39] Nothing special, though all would admit that the quality of the painting is very high and his brushwork and use of colour superb. Nothing special? Look a bit closer. What are the light spots on the jacket of the man in the foreground? Perhaps he forgot to brush his jacket? Or he has leant against a wall and got some whitewash on it? No, of course! They are simply 'spots' of sunlight dappled by the leaves. And there are 'spots' of light on the faces, too, and, most conspicuous, on the straw hat of the man behind the first group.

We must realize that it is the first time in history that things like this had been painted. Nobody had done it before. Of course in the seventeenth-century paintings of Rembrandt, the church interiors of Emanuel de Witte and many others, spots of light had been included. But they never blurred the vision, they never made the structure of the things depicted unclear. No one ever painted sunshine falling through leaves at random as Renoir did, or light spots on a hat as in Renoir's painting. They would have thought that this falsified reality. Even when we look at a painting of the young Guercino – his *Elijah in the Wilderness* for instance – or a Caravaggio, we may see dark and light passages alternating, and light is truly handled in a fantastic way, but it was done in quite a different way from Renoir's. They were playing with light in an early Baroque way, using it to give a sense of illusion, for instance, or even to make part of the picture apparently obscure (Where *has* that man's leg got to?), but it was never done in the naturalistic way of the Impressionists.

These paintings were just the beginning. Now look at a later Monet from around 1880. We should really look at a reproduction of it in colour or, better still, look at the original. What do we see? Nothing special at first. It is not an important place. Monet just chose a 'corner of nature'. It was not the start of the regatta, or a place where a famous man was drowned, or anything. It is just a certain point of the River Seine near Paris.[40] Subject matter in the old sense has become obsolete.

Here I must go into a problem arising from a basic principle of the Enlightenment. Reality, the cosmos, is an unknown 'X'. And a person can find out what it is like only by using one's eyes and senses and then, with one's brain, find a structure in the sensations coming from outside. Already Hume had pointed to a peculiar problem coming out of this. If I roll a billiard ball over the table against another one, the other one starts to move. Now, how does one know that this is causality? We only see what happens. The interpretation of it is another matter. If I let a knife fall 999 times, how do I know that it will fall the next time I drop it? Are there laws? We know only that it fell so many times, and statistically we may take the chance that it will do so again the next time, but we must admit that we can never be sure. This was a problem which positivism had run into at about the time of Monet's painting. It was in fact an epistemological problem, a question of the source of our knowledge of reality. Monet wrestled with it too, not as a philosopher but as a painter.

So, what do we see in the picture? Monet's brush strokes, recording what he saw? In a way, no. Not *what* he saw. But he recorded what reached his eyes, the light beams that caused a sensation on his retina. The question is whether there is something behind them, a reality of things that caused the light beams. One may conjecture that there is a reality, in the same way as one is likely to take the chance that the knife will fall again, but one never knows for sure.

In the years before 1885 the Impressionist group became restless and nervous. Heated discussions took place. The public were very critical and were asking awkward questions. Everybody who was in contact with this art realized there was something at stake. What is it? they were asking themselves. Where are we heading? Are we losing painting altogether? Are our works simply becoming muddled? Is this art worthy of our galleries? This world we are depicting, is it really reality? Can we go on in this way? What must be the next step? The artists themselves felt unsure, for they realized that there were deep implications. Their public too were aware of it.

Only Monet seemed to be sure of himself. He simply went on, and in 1885 dared to take the great step. The decisive step. The step over the threshold, the second step towards modern art. No, one never knows whether there is a reality behind the sensations we receive. There is no reality. Only the sensations are real.

If we look at his paintings after 1885 we see the difference. He went on in the Impressionist line, more consistently than ever. He did various series of paintings depicting one spot – a row of trees by a river,[41] Rouen Cathedral but in different conditions: in rain and snow, in the morning, in the afternoon. It could not have been more naturalistic. Yet this is not the impression you get when looking at these pictures. They are more like dream pictures, pictures showing a world that is immaterial, ghost-like. The colours are beautiful, and one can sense that there was a world that induced his sensations – the picture has some relationship to a real cathedral, for instance but the reality does not seem so real.

In 1891 Kandinsky saw a painting of a haystack at a large exhibition of French painting in Moscow. He tells us how he looked at it, how magnificent he thought the painting was, the colours brilliant – but that he could not make out what kind of reality was represented. Was there a subject? He saw only colour. Only after he had consulted the catalogue did he see what was meant. A strange picture, he thought. Beautiful, yes but what about the reality depicted? It gave him, some twenty years later, the courage to paint an abstract picture.

Renoir in 1885 tried to steer painting back to the portrayal of reality. He had no desire to follow Monet. He wrestled with a large painting of bathing girls, not Diana and her nymphs, of course, for they were long dead and buried. He tried to do it in the style of Ingres, a pre-Impressionist style: a painting that depicted solid things, a leg that had volume and form; a painting with structure and . . . well, did it have meaning? To his tremendous disappointment, no doubt, Renoir must have realized that his painting had not really succeeded. It seems stiff and awkward. The girls were as it were caught in action, like a still. And their solid forms were more like wood than flesh. It was so, because he did not really believe his own painting. This was not the world as he could understand it.

And so he fell back to a kind of middle way. It is strange, but the works of the later Renoir never have the impact and strength of his earlier ones before 1885. He seems to have lost something. He was never the great painter again. We can understand. Because he did not dare to follow Monet, whose step was consistent and true to principle. Because he did not want to lose hold of reality. Because he was too weak, spiritually. Yet we must understand that his weakness is his greatness. Surely it is greatness if a man stops short of the ultimate consequences of what he is doing when he sees that something of vital importance will be lost; if he takes the risk of losing the strength and consistency of his work in order not to lose something of such importance to people as reality itself? His weakness was his greatness, his greatness his weakness.

On from Impressionism

The year 1885 was one in which many things happened that were of great consequence for the future. In immediate reaction to the Impressionist dilemma some began to think in new directions. In that year the following was written in a letter:

> To me the great artist is defined by his great intelligence, and he has feelings that are very delicate and therefore almost imperceptible translations of his understanding. Observe in the vast natural creation and see whether you cannot find laws to create all human passions in a way that, even if they are not quite equivalent, yet are clear in their effect.[42]

This letter was written by Gauguin. It was written from Copenhagen, where he was staying temporarily, addressed to another painter. In it he expresses his idea that the artist should not copy nature but use particular methods of arranging lines and colours in order to denote particular feelings. These are evoked by reality and represent far more than simply what you see. If you see a rat (or even a spider!) you may well feel fear . . .

We are fortunate that Gauguin, because he happened not to be in Paris, wrote these letters, as they show us how he struggled to find new ways of representing reality in order to include more than the eye can see, in order not to imitate or copy but to create in a truly human way. In this same decisive year of 1885 we see him trying to overcome the extreme naturalism of the Impressionists. He felt that with them the artist had become a slave of nature. Yet it took some years before he was able to realize his new approach to reality, in which the artist expresses his understanding of a human situation by the way he handles his artistic means, his lines and colours on the flat surface of the canvas.

In 1889 he painted one of the first great works that expressed his aims, the *Vision after the sermon*.[43] Women from Brittany, with their simple yet deep faith, have heard a sermon on the fight between Jacob and the Angel: they *see* it in all its reality before their eyes. Yet they are not so stupid as to think that it is a real man fighting the angel there before them – they are human ! – so Gauguin paints the grass red. Yet, to these women, the story of Jacob is as real as their cows; the story took place on the same level of reality as the one on which they themselves lived and so, on the same red grass, we see a real cow. The whole composition is built up by means of planes, with the very decorative effect of the women's hoods forming a linear pattern, and then the flat colours – the red, the brown of the tree, the white of the hoods.

In this sort of way Gauguin tried to give his work a more human touch, expressing feelings and knowledge and human reactions to the realities of life, while at the same time he gained a new freedom for the artist to use colours and design in a free way, overcoming the narrowness of merely copying what the eye registers. In an explicit and definite way he wanted to overcome the positivist approach to reality, with (as Gauguin said himself) its loss of all feeling 'for the mystery and the enigma of the great world in which we live'.

To reach this goal, and as it were to regain humanity in its basic, original form, he went in the 1890s to Tahiti. It was here that he painted his greatest work, the one he intended as the embodiment and legacy of his vision, *Whence? What? Whither?* (commonly called *Where do we come from? What are we? Where do we go to?*). In writing about it to a friend, he said that his work was a philosophical one, with the subject comparable with that of the Gospels. We must 'read' the work, he said, from right to left: Where do we come from? A source, a child. What are we? Man stands questioning. Where are we going? An old woman, a bird of death. In the background mysterious figures, in sad colours, standing near the tree of knowledge – sad as a result of that knowledge.

It is interesting to note that Gauguin painted all these works 'realistically': he did not use the themes of the past, but painted the world we have around us, the world in which we live. But he composed his work in such a way as to show a deeper meaning, a more profound, more general sense.

The art of Gauguin and his followers, as well as of those that we shall deal with later in this chapter, is aimed at synthesis, realizing freedom and humanity in art without losing the realism of the previous generation. It was an unstable equilibrium between human freedom and human ties to natural reality. Gauguin was not able to do much more in the way of painting towards the end of his life, and so his evolution as a painter ends when this synthesis had been realized; but in his writing he goes further, and just after the turn of the century, shortly before his death, he came down unequivocally on the side of freedom. The equilibrium has been broken. The art that belongs to his new formulation was Expressionism, the art of the younger generation, just starting then. He wrote of it as follows:

> So what was necessary, without bypassing all the efforts already made and all the research, even scientific research, was to think in terms of complete liberation: to break windows even at the risk of cutting one's finger. From now on the next generation is independent and free from any fetters: it is up to them to try to resolve the whole problem. I do not say they will do so definitely, for art is limitless and rich in techniques of all kinds, fit to translate

all the emotions of nature and man, from any individual and from any period, in joy and in sorrow.

To achieve this you will have to throw yourself into the battle, body and soul, the battle against all schools, all without distinction, not only by disparaging them, but by something else, insulting not only the official artists (the Salon artists) but also the Impressionists, the Neo-Impressionists, the public old and new. No matter if your wife and children disown you. What does insult matter? What do wretchedness and poverty matter? In our work itself, we need a method of contradiction, we must attack the strongest abstractions, do all that was prohibited, reconstruct art without fear of exaggeration – if necessary with exaggeration; we must learn anew, and, when we have done that, learn all over again; we must conquer all diffidence, whatever ridicule may ensue. Before an easel a painter is no slave, neither of the past, nor of the present, neither of nature, nor of his neighbour. He is himself, himself again, always himself.[44]

The quest for reality

Quite a different way of overcoming the crisis of the Impressionists was taken by Seurat. He tried to find a way of expressing things in a very orderly and organized way, almost scientifically. He applied a very involved colour theory, which led him to the pointillist method, putting little dots of primary colour side by side to give a luminous effect. His compositions were rigid, and very studied in an almost classical way. Yet he never painted the ancient gods or other themes from the past: he depicted the world around him, a Sunday afternoon on a Parisian island, dancing chorus girls,[45] a circus with a clown and a woman on a horse, a model in his studio.

This last painting is very characteristic of his aims. He painted the same woman in three different poses, as if he wanted to show the fullness of the reality of humanity. Just as in previous periods painters would use the nude to represent humanity or universal principles, so Seurat wanted more than the specific and very individual, almost chance, aspect of a particular person.

This latter was more Degas's way. Degas was very close to the Impressionists in his aims. He painted his nudes 'as seen through the keyhole' as he said himself, which means that he tried to come as near to the particular as possible, with no idealizing – just everyday, normal reality. By comparing the work of these two great artists one can see the marked change in direction and aim. However different Seurat's works might have been from Gauguin's in subject matter and style, yet they were quite close in the 'flat' layout of their composition and in their understanding of the emotive and expressive values of lines and colours.

Another painter, and one who knew both Gauguin, with whom he was friendly, and Seurat, whom he met just before he left Paris, was van Gogh. He had arrived in Paris in 1886, just after the decisive events that we have described, followed the discussions and then in 1888 went to the South of France. He solved the problem posed by the Impressionists in his own original way: he did not paint what his eyes saw but expressed his feelings, his experience when confronted with reality. He was not concerned about making an accurate representation of particular trees, rock formations or houses. He painted his own artistic, poetic, emotional reactions, his vision. Trees like flames, mountains like waves of a great sea, everything was painted in strong, bright colours.

Van Gogh believed in reality, but painted only his personal reaction, hoping to reach a deep and general truth and longing to bring joy to ordinary people, for he was strongly attracted to the ideals of socialism, as were most of the Impressionist and Post-Impressionist painters. In this their politics were consistent with the aims of their art: both left-wing socialism and their art were developing on the foundation of the basic ideas of the Enlightenment and, in the case of politics, on from the ideas of the French Revolution.

In some ways, the greatest of this quartet was Cézanne. His aims were most consistent and directly related to the problems we have been dealing with. With great obstinacy he tried to unite the conflicting principles in order to solve the Impressionists' dilemma.

'Monet is only an eye', was Cézanne's critical comment on Impressionism, though he added, 'a magnificent eye'. Cézanne had started as a kind of Romantic painter in the tradition of Delacroix and Daumier, but he soon met the Impressionists. They initiated him into their creed of painting directly from nature, of painting in bright colours, painting nothing but what the eye sees. Yet he always differed from them in that he never sought to represent the fleeting, momentary aspects of reality, but tried to make clear the structure, the lasting elements of the landscape he was representing. And slowly but steadily he worked at the development of his own ideas: our view of nature does not stop at what we see, we must add our understanding. It is as if he said to the Impressionists, 'You have forgotten that the great principle of the Enlightenment is not only that we have to start with our perceptions, but that we have to use our reason in order to make a rational structure out of these perceptions.'

Cézanne was very much aware of the fact that the painter does not copy nature, but that he paints on the flat surface of his canvas an equivalent of reality. And this equivalent must convey a rationalized, human insight into the reality he sees. In this way he tried to make a new impressionistic art worthy of the art gallery, of equal standing with the great masterpieces of the past. Here he was thinking specifically of the great classical landscape painter Poussin, who also aimed for rational and clear structure in his work. Cézanne wanted to restore the great tradition of Poussin, but of course without the classical themes: the first step to modern art had been taken and could not be undone; the second was in his view disastrous and had to be overcome. So, he said, he would do what Poussin did but from nature.

Cézanne wanted, as it were, two things at once: to paint only what the eye sees, and yet to paint the structure of reality as understood by human rationality. This led him to his slow, laborious method: by looking, looking, looking again and again he tried to see the structures, the rationalistic principles 'behind' the thing seen, the universal ideas that ordered what he saw. There is always this feeling of conflict inherent in his art: it is a structure – and yet only a rendering of what the eye registers. Sometimes he did not hesitate to make changes to the actual scene, removing a tree, changing the position of a building, in order to make the structure clear. He never painted the fleeting aspects of nature, outlines blurred by rain, distant hills fading through haze, the lack of clarity of perception resulting from some chance viewpoint.

The quest for a synthesis

In discussing the art of these four great Post-Impressionist painters, I have deliberately left out details more suited to a history of art than to the argument of this book. My aim is to discuss the problems that resulted in the rise of modern painting. In a way, when the second step had been taken, modern art was already born. But these four tried to solve the problem, to regain the ground, to bring humanity and reality back into art.

They had to escape from the principle that there is nothing more than what the eye can see at any given moment, that there is nothing there but the individual, the specific, things just as they can be *seen* – and no more. It was a problem arising from the positivist and Impressionist principle that there are no laws that govern reality, that only experimental facts can be called true and certain. So these four Post-Impressionists tried to depict something that is more than what the momentary, fleeting impression can make us understand. They looked for a way to find something of the true values and the lasting principles of reality, the deeper universal. This is what drove them on to overcome the consistent naturalism of the preceding period and to search for new ways of approaching reality.

So they brought together the two great principles of the modern post-Enlightenment world: the principle of starting from sense-perception in order to gain knowledge of the universe; and the other great principle of human freedom, the search for a humanist humanity. One was the principle of positivism, of science. The other was a reaction against positivism, against the optimistic idea that all nature could be conquered solely by the techniques of the laboratory, that human happiness lay in material wealth. They re-asserted human freedom against the narrowed down naturalistic reality of humanity caught 'in the box', tried to rediscover humanity over against the pressure to make people no more than atoms or animals, but yet they retained their respect for the great achievements of their century.

It was because they achieved this synthesis that their art was probably the fullest and richest the world had seen since the seventeenth century. In bringing together the best of the two opposing streams, the more scientific positivism and the more irrational search for freedom, they remained true to reality without falling into the trap of either depicting only external, irrelevant details or letting the imagination run wild into fantasy or the vaguely mystical. They tried to achieve the synthesis by creating a rational universal out of what can be perceived with the senses.

The harmony they achieved was an unstable one. It was soon to be broken. Neither van Gogh nor Seurat lived long enough to see it. But in the last work of Cézanne, for instance, we already see a tendency towards the abstract, the breaking down of the clear image, the failure to retain the natural in his striving for human, rational expression. And, as I have already shown, in his last writings Gauguin reached a more irrational abstraction in the name of freedom.

A new century was already beginning. But before we see where it led, we must look at a rather different movement – one which in its own way tackled the basic nineteenth-century problem we have been discussing in this chapter.

A mystic-Romantic reaction

All that I have been discussing in this chapter happened in a restricted circle of artists and their friends in France. The art textbooks show the line of development of art as going from Delacroix to Courbet to Manet, then to the Impressionists and the Post-Impressionists, and we can easily get the impression that this is a true account of nineteenth-century art. But it is not. This line, even if of great importance, is not the art nineteenth-century people themselves talked about. The mainstream of art in that period was to be found in the bourgeois art I referred to in the last chapter, the Salon art in France and the art of the Royal Academy in England.

A reaction that emerged in England against this academic sort of art led to a kind of mystic-Romantic art that is called Art Nouveau. In its reaction against such academic, bourgeois shallowness it tried in its own way to solve the artistic problems that were posed by the developments of the nineteenth century. In its time it was more highly rated than the

Post-Impressionists, but in the twentieth century it lost its importance and was swept aside by the 'other' modern art. Yet it did have a deep and lasting influence on the decorative forms of our century, and the design of many household tools had their origins here – even the so-called 'streamlined' forms to be found, for instance, in door handles. Only with the psychedelic art of the 1960s did Art Nouveau become a real artistic source again, and then not so much in gallery art as in posters,[46] graphic design, fabric design and interior decoration.

It was back in August 1827 that William Blake died. In his last years he had started to learn Italian so as to be able to read his beloved Dante in the original. Exactly nine months later, not far from the place where he died, Dante Gabriel Rossetti was born, the son of an Italian refugee who named the child after his favourite poet. Later, in his first year at the Academy, Rosetti obtained, almost by chance and for a very low price, a Blake manuscript that put into his hands the work of a man whose ideas would influence him throughout his whole life.

Yet Rossetti did not become an imitator or a follower of Blake in the narrow sense. Rather, through Rossetti's version of Pre-Raphaelitism, with its wavy lines and emphasis on imagination and poetic subject matter, a more Romantic than 'positivist' kind of art was introduced in England. He took a different path from his original fellow Pre-Raphaelites, from Holman Hunt, who remained a naturalist to the end, and from Millais, who became a society painter. Rossetti's friends and followers William Morris and Burne-Jones defined a style that was to influence the young generation of the 1890s, real aestheticists, enemies of positivism and its dehumanizing science, enemies of the machine age longing for spirituality, beauty and a new way of life.

They looked for help in their quest to the newly discovered Japanese art, to the medieval dream as exemplified by the Faery Queen and her retinue, to ancient mystic philosophies and, of course, to Blake. They turned everything into poems, not only painting but also china, silverware, book design, wallpaper – and so created what has come to be known as Art Nouveau. They were dreaming of a new world, aristocratic and yet anarchistic, a world of freedom without Victorian sexual repression, without the ugliness of machine-produced utility wares, a world in which beauty and not the laboratory would set values and truths. A world, in short, that was characterized perfectly, even if only in its more fashionable aspect, by Gilbert and Sullivan when they described the 'very cultivated, clever young man', who would walk down Piccadilly with a poppy or a lily in his medieval hand:

> If you're anxious for to shine in the high aesthetic line as a man of culture rare,
> You must get up all the germs of the transcendental terms, and plant them everywhere.
> You must lie upon the daisies and discourse in novel phrases of your

> complicated state of mind,
> The meaning doesn't matter if it's only idle chatter of a
> transcendental kind ...[47]

Art nouveau was not confined to England. As its name implies, it was also to be found in France, and soon over the whole of Europe, having centres in Brussels, Vienna, München and Turin. Its masterpieces are not so much the weird and debatable paintings of men like Knopf, or even of Klimt, but rather posters by men like the Beggarstaff brothers, Bradley, Toulouse-Lautrec, Bonnard, Toorop and others, and its most typical works are found in book design, in illustrations such as those by Beardsley, in typography or in the design of furniture, utility ware or small *objets d'art*. It also involved interior design and even architecture, where its products could be strange and extreme at times, as in Gaudi's buildings or Horta's interiors. But yet there are elements in their style that prepared the way for twentieth-century industrial design (look at the handle of an Olivetti typewriter, for example).

Art Nouveau has had its own development and is not restricted only to the 1890s: you can, if you want to, see its principles working until far into the twentieth century, in the architecture of the rather Romantic Amsterdam school, in Mendelsohn's Einstein Tower, even in much of the work of Frank Lloyd Wright and Berlage, and in book illustration right up to the 1930s. Its freakish elements, its extremes, were discarded, but its importance continued in its influence in renewing industrial design and giving beauty to machine products.

In revolutionizing the applied arts, Art Nouveau not only brought them up to date but also swept away the chaos of historical styles of the nineteenth century. It is as if that century had been afraid of applying its own principles. It was always looking nostalgically backwards to the great styles of the past. It is telling that in some ways it was 'engineer's art', the 'style-less' bridges and utility buildings, that prepared the way for these renewals. It was in these that the nineteenth century was honest to itself.[48]

The inner tensions of modern times are grafted onto the history of Art Nouveau and its subsequent development: it began as a revolt against the all-embracing claims made in the name of science and industry, as a search for the spiritual, the truly human; and it ended by having its lasting fruits precisely in the area of industrial design. It helped to prepare the way for the great revolution in art that was to take place after the turn of the century, even though the new art was to take as its point of departure the achievements of the Post-Impressionists. Hence it was to be largely confined to painting and sculpture and to continue in the tradition not of the applied arts but of High Art. In this way it was, too, to take on the tradition that we have followed in this book, that art should be 'loaded' with meaning and express a philosophy. But this is to anticipate the next chapter.

5
The Last Steps to Modern Art

> Like a bird on a wire
> Like a drunk in a midnight choir
> I have tried in my way to be free[49]

It was as if the turn of a century really meant something. The divisions of earlier centuries are no doubt a help to students in remembering the broad outlines of the history of art: the High Renaissance 'began' in 1500, seventeenth-century art began (almost precisely!) in 1600, Rococo more or less in 1700 – and nineteenth-century art in 1800. But no one would claim for the divisions of the centuries any deeper meaning.

But the year 1900 really did mean the start of something new. In 1890 van Gogh and Seurat had already died, Gauguin was beginning to have some influence on younger painters, while Cézanne worked on almost unheeded and unknown, except by a few real connoisseurs and a small group of artists. Yet the new emerging style just after 1900 looked to these for example and inspiration, and almost wholly by-passed the rather ephemeral Art Nouveau, despite the fact that it had set out to renew the face of the world. Perhaps Art Nouveau was too aristocratic, or at least snobbish, in its aestheticism, perhaps the times were not yet ripe for a major revolution in the so-called minor arts.

Expressionism

For the art historian the years around 1900 are of bewildering complexity, and no great artist can be picked out as really typifying them. But around 1905 the eruption came: with Expressionism, with the Fauves in France, with Die Brücke ('The bridge') in Germany, soon too the group in München known from their journal *Der blaue Reiter* ('The blue rider'), and here and there small groups scattered over Europe, all going in the same direction or immediately accepting and passing on the word.

Expressionism – the word that was only coined some years later – had no defined programme, no definite philosophy, no rules, no special publicity. The young men who formed the style, often working close together, had a certain inheritance in common in Art Nouveau – the flat, non-naturalistic, decorative patterns, the concern for the 'spiritual', the imaginative, and the move away from a naturalistic treatment of a simple subject. They were all heavily influenced by the work of Gauguin, Munch (who was in many ways akin to Gauguin), van Gogh and to a lesser extent Seurat. They had learned to use colour freely, and to express by pictorial means human values and feelings, the realities which are more than the eye can see. They had learned that a painting is a flat surface covered with colours and lines, a human creation that surpasses the slavish copying of reality as it is seen in a naturalistic way.

Perhaps Expressionism was born that afternoon when Gauguin gave a lesson to the young Sérusier (who later went off along other lines and did not play a decisive role in the movement again). In the summer of 1888, in Brittany, he had approached Gauguin asking for advice. Gauguin took him to a park. 'How do you see that tree?' Gauguin had asked at a corner of the Bois d'Amour. 'Is it green? Then paint it green, the most beautiful green of your palette. And that shadow? A bit blue? Don't be afraid to paint it as blue as blue can be.' The painting, on the lid of a cigar box, caused a sensation among a group of young painters in Paris. They called it 'the talisman'.

The young painters inherited this attitude. They also inherited the almost passionate disdain for the Salon art of their times. Even Art Nouveau had not been able to overcome this broad stream of bourgeois mediocrity and shallowness that made up the large official exhibitions right up to the First World War, perhaps even later. What we now see as the great stream of art was in fact only a fringe. The revolutionaries were often revolutionary in the political sense, too, and increasingly opposed to the traditionalism and bourgeois taste of the Salon artists. Their hate had been returned, and by 1900 the gulf between them was deep and wide. Yet in a way the Salon artists acted again and again as catalysts to the new movement.

Matisse must have understood that in the art of his day, both in Salon art and in Impressionist naturalism, humanism was already dead. He tried to revive it by searching for new meaningful forms. His *Luxury, Calm and Voluptuousness*[50] of 1906 used the nude in the humanistic way; in many respects it can be compared with the art of such painters as Poussin. Of course, the old humanistic theme was not revived. But it is akin to the ideal world, the dream of a high humanity, conveyed by the metaphor of nudes. In other paintings of this time he used colour much more vehemently, less like Gauguin, more like van Gogh. The forms were new and show the urge to create paintings that show a subjective emotion in the face of reality rather than a naturalistic copy – creating an art that really is art, paint on canvas. It is easy to understand why a critic of those days called these works *fauve*, wild, as there is in these works a wild cry, a desperate attempt to get through to the human and to overcome the defects of the traditions of the nineteenth century.

Yet there is something remarkable in Matisse's development over the next years. The humanist element becomes increasingly smaller. His pictures remain colourful, but become more and more decorative. And in many works there is a stylization that almost chokes the human element; art becomes 'Art', and the means of art are beginning to become autonomous. There is a marked tendency to the abstract, even if Matisse never really reached the point of being a wholly non-figurative artist. Around 1910 he made a series of bronze heads[51] which started from a 'normal' woman's head and then went 'further' in each succeeding work, until the last is still recognizable as being human but has lost any sort of feminine or personal quality. It seems as if Matisse tried to recapture humanity in his art, revive humanism, but lost his track. Maybe he searched for a universal 'humankind' and not 'this particular person' (a problem we will be returning to later when discussing Cubism). But it seems to be the tragedy of much modern art that the artists set out to grasp the fullness of reality and a fullness of humanity, and yet these slip through their fingers, leaving them finally empty-handed.

Developments in Germany

Expressionism is in a way more typical of German art. Matisse and his group may have had an influence on Germany, and probably at some points triggered off the movement, but as a whole the German style has its own character. It is as 'wild' as the French style, if not wilder. There is the desperate search for a new, meaningful art for a humanity that seems to have been lost in the positivist streams of the nineteenth century, for a direct expression of subjectivity, and there is a daring that makes clear how infuriated they were against the deadness of tradition. The art of Gauguin and van Gogh showed an equilibrium between the two opposing tendencies of their times, sticking to reality as it can be experienced by the senses and at the same time looking for human freedom. Now, with the Expressionists, the pendulum swung completely to the side of the freedom of the artist, the human freedom to create, unhampered by the demands of naturalness or what the seventeenth century would have called 'decorum'.

The painters of Die Brücke, a group in Dresden including Kirchner, Pechstein, Schmidt-Rottluff and Heckel, sought a new art, against all tradition, against deadness. Their aims were for a direct expression of personal subjectivity, a new means of representation unhampered by 'truth' in the old sense (naturalness in colour and shape). They wanted a new 'truth', in which colours and shapes speak their own language, in which they have something to say about reality rather than describe it, using a new means which is not easy to define. 'Symbolical' might be misunderstood, as there were no symbols in the old sense. The colours and shapes in themselves were to 'express' the idea, the feeling, the truth about something, by directly artistic means. The work of art is something that stands by itself, and its relation to reality is not direct – 'imitation' – but more in the way of a metaphor.

There was also a strong tendency towards naturalness in a new sense, almost primitive, bypassing the refined veneer of civilization – Rousseau's principles were still very much alive. They lived almost as if they were a primitive tribe, the highlights being the days they passed together in the nude beside a lake – reflected in quite a few paintings from that period, named, for instance, *Girls on the beach*. They were much interested in primitive art, to which they were drawn as to something of a kindred spirit. The violence of it seemed to them genuine and real.

They searched for a new understanding of human being in relation to nature and felt, and therefore often expressed in their work, a conflict between nature and culture. Yet there is a strong urban feeling in their work. Nolde, a true 'natural' man in the peasant sense, was not really one of them; he remained a solitary artist, with a much more lyrical sense of human being and nature. They were striving for what is more than passing, for the deep truth, the essence rather than the fleeting moment, the human truth rather than what the eye can see, namely the exterior alone.

It is not a random result of their new technique that objects, trees, men and women seem to merge into a whole, without any differentiation in colour or texture between, for instance, a human body or a tree, a lake or a mountain. The unity, the totality seems sometimes as it were to consume all differences. Philosophically speaking their work is universalistic, a longing for a universal unity which dispenses with individuality, with the particular a kind of nature-mystique. In this way they looked for a solution to the problem posed by the art of the previous century, which in its search for the naturalness of the particular had exalted the senses and lost all deeper meaning.

The German equivalent to French Impressionism had been a kind of brutal art, in which the ugly, the vulgar, the debased were sought (by Corinth and others); here too one often questions whether there really is a genuine reality behind what is received by the senses (specifically in landscape). In this way German art had made up for backwardness in adhering so long to classicism or Romantic naturalism. The new generation, the Expressionists, took over this heritage but now brought their art into line with what was going on in France. Yet there was no doubt about the fact that their art was German: it was less *charmant*, had less *esprit* and humour, it was more earnest, philosophical and in its own way, romantic.

The group associated with *Der blaue Reiter* magazine in München, was in many ways of kindred spirit to the one in Dresden, though they did not have much contact in this period before the First World War. There was a greater internationalism in München, more direct contact with what was going on in Paris and elsewhere. On the other hand there was less quest for the primitive, the 'natural'. Here the battle was more directly against the older school and its exponents, and with more consciously artistic aims.

Much of what has been said of the Dresden painters applies to those in München, and need not be repeated. But rather more must be said about Marc and Kandinsky, the two greatest exponents of the group. They had a strong antipathy to all naturalism, for, they said, it had not only killed art but also killed the spiritual both in art and in people. 'We must destroy the soulless, materialistic life of the nineteenth century,' said Kandinsky, and 'we must build the life of the soul and the spirit of the twentieth century.' He spoke of the nightmare of materialistic ideas that had degraded life into a monstrous, senseless play. He also commented angrily on the contemporary art in the exhibitions:

> Rooms hung with canvasses, on which elements of 'nature' are represented with paint: animals in light and shadow, standing near the water or lying in the meadow, beside a Crucifixion of Christ painted by an artist who does not believe in Christ; then flower pieces, or human figures, standing, sitting or walking, often nude; lots of nude women, sometimes foreshortened from behind; apples on a silver tray, a portrait of old Mr Such-and-Such, a sunset, flying geese, portrait of Baroness X, flying ducks, a lady in white, cows in the shade with fierce yellow patches of sunlight, a lady in green ...[52]

Why all this? This was his question, and a very right and proper one. He shows it is the end of an era. Art had become senseless, useless.

The principles of the great art in the tradition of which this art claims to stand have become hollow and superseded. As it was formulated in an earlier chapter: Venus is both dead and buried. The great Christian-humanist culture of the time before the Enlightenment has broken down. In the exhibition Kandinsky describes, we are moving amongst the ruins.

How is he going to achieve a new, spiritual, truly human art? First of all by making art into art. He said: 'I have heard a well-known painter saying: When you are painting, take one look at the canvas, half a look at your palette, and ten at the model. It sounded right, but I soon found that I had to proceed quite differently: ten looks at the canvas, one at the palette, half a look at nature.' The artist, he said, must express himself, the times in which he lives, and the 'eternal', namely that which belongs to all times and to all cultures. This, the objective – what I have called the universal – has to be shown by means of the subjective.

In his book, from which I have already quoted, he characterized the art he was looking for as follows (and it must be acknowledged that his works between 1910 and 1914 really fit his aim in a wonderful way): 'The strife of colours, the sense of the balance we have lost, tottering principles, unexpected assaults, great questions, apparently useless striving, storm and tempest, broken chains, oppositions and contradictions – these make up our harmony.'[53]

It is really not difficult to understand that soon after Kandinsky wrote these words he came to abstract painting, an art in which there was no longer any subject matter, what we nowadays call non-figurative art.

Of this he said: 'Abstract painting sheds the skin of nature but not its laws, the cosmic laws.' He was looking for a restoration of art, hoping to regain something that was lost in the nineteenth century, the universal, the deeper structure and law of reality. Art was given a high place in this quest: it is almost the tool and revelation of a new mysticism – or at least it gives form to a new life, a life of the spirit. We know that Kandinsky was highly influenced by the anthroposophy of Rudolf Steiner, a kind of westernized, 'demythologized', eastern way of religious thinking.

I must refrain from going deeper into the art of Kandinsky analysing his pictures and showing his development. Nor can I deal at length with the work of Marc, who started with a kind of impressionistic painting just after the beginning of the century and gradually came to a less naturalistic art in which the general or universal became uppermost over the particular (almost always choosing animals as subject matter), and ending with an almost abstract art, different and yet akin to that of his friend Kandinsky. Marc was much more directly influenced by Cubism, to which we shall have to turn very soon. He tells us:

> I experienced people as ugly – animals are much more beautiful ... but in them too I discovered so much that I felt to be appalling and ugly that my representations of them instinctively, out of inner necessity, became increasingly more schematic, more abstract. Each year trees, flowers, the earth, everything showed me aspects that were more hateful, more repulsive, until I came at last to a full realization of the ugliness, the impurity of nature.

Elsewhere in his letters he says that abstract art meant for him the search to let the world itself speak rather than our soul being moved by the sight of the world. 'The longing for indivisible Being, for liberation from the sense-deception of our ephemeral life, is the main objective of all art.'

Abstraction

So this generation, at the beginning of our century, was looking for a solution to the problem of regaining truth and reality. They had been lost in a development in which the senses were the only source of knowledge, the basic principle of the Enlightenment and of nineteenth-century positivism. They were looking for absolutes, the principles that governed life and art, and perception too, the deep reality of human life, the truth of things behind their appearance. Art, in line with art theory in its long development from the Platonists through the Renaissance and Romanticism, was given the task of revealing this 'eternal truth', which is more than the eye can see. The work of art has to show deep human values, just as a medieval Madonna or, at a later date, a humanistic allegorical painting did. So we can understand Marc when he wrote in a famous article in *Der blaue Reiter* that the true artists were striving 'to create in their work symbols for their time that will belong on the altars of the coming spiritual religion, behind which the technical aspects will disappear'.

This deep-felt reaction against the positivism of the nineteenth century which dissolved all reality, as it were, leaving people with their perceptions alone, searching for true absolutes and distrusting (or even disgusted with) reality, led to a completely new type of art, abstract art, an art that was truly and solely art, and at the same time was spiritual, conceptual and 'absolute'. As such it was parallel to the efforts of the new school of philosophy, that of Husserl's phenomenology (geographically not far from Kandinsky and Marc, even though they probably had no contact with one another). In Husserl's main work, which was published in these same years before World War I, he criticizes the science of his day for having degenerated into an unphilosophical study of mere facts ... positivistic science ... a 'naturalism' incapable of coping with the problems of ultimate truth and validity, as it had no room for ideal entities such as meaning or laws as such.[54]

Husserl wrote in the introduction of his book:[55]

> To get rid of all traditional ways of thinking, to recognize all the spiritual fences that shut off the horizon of our thought and pull them down, to get hold of completely new philosophical problems in the complete freedom of thought that has resulted from the breaking down of all the fences and the opening up of our horizon – all this is hard to achieve. But nothing less is required ... what is necessary is a completely altered approach, different from the natural way of experience and thought.

But these philosophers and artists were trying to overcome the doubtful results of the positivist world view of the Enlightenment without questioning its basic principles. For in starting from the human, from *human* sense-perception, *human* thinking, it automatically closed the world; it shut off any possibility of a transcendental, truly living God. 'God is dead,' Nietzsche had already proclaimed many years before, 'we have killed him, and the stench of his corpse hangs over Europe.' But the tremendous effort involved in attempting to regain true humanity was tragically bound to fail. The strivings and search for renewal in the arts were much more concerned with art for the sake of life than with art for the sake of art. What Holbrook Jackson wrote about the English poet Davidson can equally be applied to these artists: 'The strife of the poet for a new expression, a new poetic value, is too evident, and you lay these ... works down baffled and unconvinced, but reverent before the courage and honesty of a mind valiantly beating itself to destruction against the locked and barred door of an unknown and perhaps nonexistent reality.'[56]

What does it mean 'to get rid of all traditional ways of thinking', to strive for 'a new expression' and 'poetic value', a spirituality beyond the material? We can see what it means simply by looking at one of the great works of Kandinsky in the years immediately before World War I, perhaps his best period, and certainly the work of a genius. But for many people visual art does not communicate as clearly as words do. Certainly poetry can help the understanding of painting, as painting can sometimes make clear the intentions of the poet or, for that matter, the philosopher. So to give some idea of the mood of this striving I should like to quote one of Kandinsky's poems from this period, 'In the Wood' (*Im Walde*) – though it is not so much a poem as soft-spoken prose. It is taken from his anthology published under the title *Klänge* ('Sounds').

> The wood was getting thicker all the time. The red trunks ever closer together. The green crowns ever denser. The air ever darker. The thickets ever more close-set. The mushrooms in ever greater number. Finally there were only mushrooms to tread on. It was more and more difficult for the man to move forward, to push through and not slip. Yet he went on and repeated the same lines over and over again, each time more quickly:
> The healing scars.
> Complementary colours.
> To his left, and slightly behind him, walked a woman. Every time he completed the phrases, she said, convinced and with a strong rolling 'r': verrry prrractical.

Cubism

Around 1906–1907 some of the younger painters in Paris, most of whom had followed in the tracks of the Fauves, the Expressionists, turned in another direction: Cubism. Cézanne's paintings influenced them, and with him they wanted to search for what is more than the eye can see, the principles, the structure of reality. A letter from Cézanne to a young painter, written in 1904, probably summed up his own aims badly, but it suited the young painters very well, for here the carefully sought balance was broken and the place of nature and sense-perception reduced: 'Treat nature by the cylinder, the sphere, the cone, all brought into perspective.' In another letter of the same year he had written: 'You can never be too scrupulous nor too sincere nor too subjected to nature; but you are more or less master of the model, and above all of the means of expression. Penetrate into what you have in front of you, and persevere in expressing yourself as logically as possible.' It was this last piece of advice that meant most to these young painters.

Amongst this group of young painters was Picasso. What influenced him, as well as the others, were, first, Iberian sculpture, blending Greek classical art with a more primitive search for the impersonal and general, and soon, too, African masks and sculptures. The fact that in their reaction against the superficial naturalism of the nineteenth century they 'discovered' the truth and beauty of primitive art (which had previously been the concern only of ethnologists) betrays a deep spiritual similarity in aim and in the understanding of reality. Primitive people feel one with nature and its forces, and in their religion they use masks to lose themselves and become one with the spirit (often an animal one) of the tribe. For modern people, even if in a less mythical way, nature is the only true reality, and human being is basically no more than biological/psychological. The aims of the Cubists, their quest for a new expression, a new art, were in the final analysis the making of a new world view, one that broke away from the age-old humanism of Western society. The personal was lost, for there was no longer a personal God. People, animals, plants, things, they are all basically the same. So there should be no basic difference in the way they are depicted.

The Cubist movement was very complex in its aims. There was the same search for the absolute as we found with the München group of Der Blaue Reiter, the same wish to portray the true reality behind the appearances. It was rather like Plato's search for the basic ideas behind all reality; and it was certainly not by chance that their art was characterized by mathematical, or rather geometrical, forms, just as Plato had said that the geometrical was the deepest idea behind reality. In keeping with the whole of the Western tradition they were rationalistic and intellectual. Yet there was a strange violence, particularly in the works of the first years of Picasso's Cubism, something irrational, overflowing emotions, as if he passionately wanted to break down the old image of humanity, too long revered in a humanist sense as supreme beauty.

Picasso summed up all the conflicting and yet connected ideas of early Cubism in his *Les Demoiselles d'Avignon*, an unsurpassed masterpiece that can at the same time stand as a kind of symbol for all modern art. In this work, painted in 1907, the new era, the new world that even today has not yet been fully realized, was already defined, its world view depicted, its idea of humankind represented in a way that still makes us hold our breath. A friend of Picasso recorded his reactions when shown the painting:

> It contains six huge female nudes: the drawing of them has a rugged accent. For the first time in Picasso's work, the expression of the faces is neither tragic nor passionate. They are masks almost entirely freed from humanity. Yet these people are not gods, nor are they Titans or heroes; not even allegorical or symbolical figures. They are naked problems, white numbers on the blackboard. Thus Picasso has laid down the principle of the picture-as-equation. One of Picasso's friends spontaneously christened the new canvas 'the philosophical brothel' ... Painting, from now on, was becoming a science, and not one of the least austere.[57]

Indeed, as is suggested in the lines just quoted, this picture is completely amoral; it is neither moral or immoral. Morality has nothing to do with it. Even if its starting point was a brothel (hence the name, after Avignon Street in the red-light district of Barcelona), the painting is neither propaganda for this type of sexual activity nor does it show any indignation or say how awful prostitution is. It is simply a picture, as such still in the old humanist tradition, a picture of a number of nude figures, standing in this way for humanity and timeless reality and truth. It is not a question of moral or other standards, but of the quest for the universal. 'Philosophical brothel' is really not so bad a name after all.

What had already struck Picasso's friends at the time was the complete lack of expression in the figures themselves. The figures are taken as objects, their own feelings play no part. The painting treats general structural problems, and looks away from the specific to the general. In this respect we note the geometric, stylized way the figures are rendered. And yet in the raised arms of the central figures, in the exaggerated points that thrust into the surrounding plane, we feel the fierce violence – not of the figures, but of the artistic expression.

Another problem is the use of space. It is clear that 'Renaissance' space, with perspective, depth, foreground and background, has been discarded. This use of space has been called 'acoustic' (using a term from McLuhan), a space that has no depth, nothing in front or behind. Yet, even if there is not much indication of space in the traditional sense in Picasso's painting, it is not flat: not only are there remnants of traditional space rendering (one figure being in front of the other), but a kind of conceptual space is to be seen in the rounded forms of the figures, the curtains and so on. Here a principle of Cézanne was carried to its extreme, and certainly this picture is not so much a depiction of reality, a rendering of what the eye can see, as a building up of a work of art that as such is an independent equation of reality.

The figures represent as it were three aspects of early Cubism or, rather, of early modern art. Perhaps we can discern in this the different stages in the artist's work. But even if we cannot really say just why it was done in this way, it surely has a tale to tell. First we have the Cézanne-type nudes in the middle, though they are simplified and more geometrically rendered than anything Cézanne ever did, including his very late *Baigneuses* ('Bathing women') that are not dissimilar. The mask-like faces show resemblances to Iberian art. The figures are female, but there is nothing feminine about them. Here was expressed the quest for the general, the universal. The violence of it is witness to Picasso's hatred for the trite individualism and superficial naturalism of the previous period.

It was this that drove the painter on to abstraction or near abstraction, just as it did a few years later with Kandinsky and Marc. We can see this on the left-hand side of the picture. The woman's back and the drapery of her clothes (if that is what it is) merge with the curtain, becoming a pattern that has a meaning of its own and losing its descriptive quality. To the right there is yet another aspect: here the figures have mask-like faces, horrible masks, demonic and violent. The friend of Picasso we have already quoted said of them:

Picasso, somewhat deserted, found his true self in the company of the African soothsayers. He composed for himself a palette rich in the colours dear to the old academic painters: ochre, bitumen, sepia ... and painted several formidable grimacing nudes, worthy objects of execration. But with what a singular nobility Picasso invests everything he touches! The monsters of his mind drive us to despair.[58]

The quest for absolutes

So this is an art which is definitely not naturalistic. It seeks the general, the universal. It tends towards abstraction, even towards the demonic. It loses a humanist humanity, and is at the same time both extremely intellectual and irrational. In short, it sums up all aspects of modern art at the very moment that it was born.

The predominant concern following this painting was for the discovery of the universal, the governing principle 'behind' the given visual image. This is what has been called 'analytical Cubism'. The forms that were visually observed were analysed and the underlying geometrical shape, cube or cone or pyramid, was discovered and painted. These figures or objects (a still life with guitars, for instance, or with studio utensils) were placed in a cubistic space. Or Picasso, Braque, Derain or some of their friends would paint landscapes: not of a specific spot, of course, even if a particular place was mentioned in the title of the painting; a house would be a universalized one, not a particular house recognizable from the position of its doors and windows; a tree, too, would be generalized, not a specific one – it was not even possible to tell what the season of the year or the time of day was: it was not the fleeting but the lasting aspects of the subject that were portrayed on the canvas.[59]

This stage of Cubism is rather less fierce and violent than the early start made by Picasso. Its green-ochre colour schemes are very beautiful, and to a certain extent their aims were achieved.

Yet there is always the urge to go further, to let the forms live their own life, to break down the image yet further in a quest for more consistent analysis. When a final stage was reached in about 1909, there was a kind of standstill in the development. For a time the style remained the same. Figures were broken down into a kind of crystalline structure, merging with the background so it becomes hard to tell where the figure ends and the 'space' begins, for there are no contours. It was a kind of supreme, beautiful puzzle. Where is the face? O yes, that must be a hand, that could be a glass, this must be the guitar . . .

The decisive step

It is at this stage that Picasso must have realized that their quest had failed. They had searched for the universal, the general structure of things, that which is more than the strictly individual and specific – and in so doing had lost the personal, the human, the 'real'. It was as if it had been shown to be impossible ever to reach the universal directly, without seeing the absolute through the specific. He who would know love must experience personal, specific love, or there is but a dim abstraction which is no love. Their quest to show what Plato might have called the Idea, or Aristotle the Form, had ended in beautiful pictures that yet presented no more than strange puzzles, enigmatic images in which the real content was virtually lost.

When Picasso realized this, he had to take another step forward. Maybe he hesitated for some time – and this is why the development seemed to have come to a standstill. For the next step was to be a tremendous one. The consequenccs of it could not be foreseen. Slowly it must have entered into Picasso's mind that the step was unavoidable, whatever the results. Only a man of his stature, his talents, his daring, his insight could ever have done it.

And he took the step. He did so when he accepted the failure, and took the consequences. There are no universals. The general, the absolute, is non-existent. And if there are no universal principles, if there are no absolutes, then . . . we can understand his hesitation . . . then this world is absurd, nonsensical, without meaning.

The term absurd here is really an anachronism: it was used only later by Sartre, Camus and the Theatre of the Absurd. But the idea of the absurd had already been there for some years. At the turn of the century there was an absurd play by Jarry, his *Ubu Roi*. The strangeness and absurdity of this world was shown by an art that was not naturalistic, yet was trying to show the truth, a new truth, the truth that there is no truth, that anything may and can happen. This was already true of some nineteenth-century art, the writings of Rimbaud and Mallarmé, Edward Lear's nursery rhymes (and their accompanying illustrations), Grandville's drawings, Odilon Redon's lithographs, even in a work like *Alice in Wonderland*. But the absurdity, often presented in humorous terms (even if we would sometimes want to call it black humour), had been something apart from the main trends . . . now it was to be at the heart of the movement.[60]

We must realize that the men and women who were involved in these new trends of around 1910 were only very few in number. At the most they could not have numbered more than a thousand. But what was happening was finding a response with an ever increasing number of people. Picasso, after some years of preparation, had dared to break through the sound-barrier of reality . . . and the sonic boom was not only heard at the time but the last reverberations are still around us – if we but listen.

The poet Apollinaire, a friend of Picasso, wrote a poem which expressed their spirit and their aim:

> O mouths, mankind is in search of a new form of speech
> With which no grammarian of any language will be able to talk
> And these ancient languages are so close to death
> That it is really sheer habit and laziness
> That allows us to go on using them for poetry
> But they are like invalids who haven't the strength to say no
> Look people would soon get used to being dumb
> Mime is good enough for the cinema
> But we must determine to speak
> To move our tongues
> To splutter and stammer
> We want new sounds new sounds new sounds.[61]

This change in Cubism, taking place in the years 1911–1912, is called in the textbooks of the history of art the change from analytical to synthetic Cubism. The artist felt free to play with the forms that had been invented. The crystalline aspect disappeared, and the colours again became stronger and played a larger part in the composition. A new element appeared: the 'collage', the use of real things in the painting, as a piece of a daily paper, cloth, etc. These things, taken from 'real life', were brought into the painting as an element in the artistic composition, sometimes quite apart from their original utilitarian meaning, sometimes taking their associations with them. They had already incorporated letters, too, into their paintings. In one sense the new art was closer to reality, more recognizable, more direct. But on the other hand the play with reality was more free, more whimsical. But it was precisely this play with natural elements that enhanced the absurdity of the artistic statement – Golding in his book on Cubism uses the word 'satirical' here. And surely, whoever stresses the absurdity of reality laughs at it – or weeps. It was laughter which was predominant at that time: but the cry was there too, and was to be heard again, more loudly, in the years to come.

Four reactions

One group who certainly heard Picasso's 'sonic boom' was a group of young painters then working in Paris. One of them was a Dutchman: Mondrian. He already had a career behind him, first as an Impressionist, then as an Expressionist, but now began to search in the direction of Cubism. He followed analytical Cubism. But when the change came, it is as if he said: No, Picasso, you are going in the wrong direction. You have been doing fine, searching for the true absolute. But now, why . . . why do you forsake us? So Mondrian went off in his own direction. During World War I he was in Holland again and had more contacts with the theosophists; but what was decisive were his discussions with Dr Schoenmaeckers, a mathematician, philosopher and mystic. This man wrote: 'We are now learning to translate reality, by means of our imagination, into constructions which can be controlled by reason, in order to re-form these same constructions again in a "given" natural reality, thus penetrating nature by means of forms that can be seen.'[62] This is exactly what Mondrian tried to do. For Schoenmaeckers as well as Mondrian (and Kandinsky, too, and most of the others involved in the artistic renewal) had a strongly utopian trend in their thinking.

Through this influence and through his contact with young artists like van Doesburg, Mondrian evolved around 1920 his own particular style, the depiction of the absolute, true 'plasticism' as he called it, the creation of absolute form. Pictorial elements were reduced to their simplest and most rigid terms: black horizontal and vertical lines, white, red, yellow and blue colour – and nothing else. But there is no doubt that his art has its own particular kind of beauty, a harmony and inner balance. In a way we can say that he defined twentieth-century style; his influence on architecture, typography and so on has been very great. Going through a modern city we see something of the world that Mondrian dreamed of. Yet whether he achieved what he really wanted, the 'plastic' realization of the absolute, is an open question.

Apart from anything else, Mondrian's art is extremely intellectual (and Neoplatonic). One can readily believe the anecdote told about Mondrian, that he was sitting in front of a white canvas for a whole afternoon without being able to get started with his painting. For even the first little black dot would break the absoluteness of the whiteness, and would create something specific and individual. But, we may ask, what would the cleaner coming in the next day think of the white canvas – or of the white canvas with the little black dot?

There was another group of painters around Picasso and Braque. They saw in Cubism a new style, and some of them had various theories about it: that painting should be in harmony with the universe which is itself an organism, that it should reflect true reality, and so on. In a way their theories were half-truths as far as Picasso's and Braque's art are concerned; yet they are helpful for understanding the spirit of the time. Gleizes and Metzinger wrote in 1912 :

> There is nothing real outside ourselves; there is nothing real except the coincidence of a sensation and an individual mental direction ... we can only have certitude with regard to the images which they produce in the mind ... the only difference between the Impressionists and ourselves is a difference of intensity ... There are as many images of an object as there are eyes which look at it; there are as many essential images of it as there are minds which comprehend it.[63]

Perhaps the fact that they saw in Cubism a kind of renewed and more intellectual Impressionism is their basic misunderstanding and the reason for their failure to be true Cubists.

Delaunay had a better understanding of what Cubism meant, though he used its stylistic means to make a somewhat modernized version of Cézanne: for him Cubism was a new means to represent the modern world. His *Eiffel Tower*[64] shows his method. At this same time the Futurists, an Italian group of artists, had come into contact with those in Paris, and with much noise and enthusiasm inaugurated their own version of modern painting. They were interested in movement, in machines, in power. They had reacted strongly against the naturalistic and romanticized art of late nineteenth-century Italy, and against the burden of Italy's past artistic splendours. We sense the strong influence of Delaunay; and their analysis of movement and of the modern world of crowded streets, racing-cars, sprinting cyclists – again made use of cubist elements to make up a new style.

These efforts to use Cubism as a new means of representing reality, modern reality, were often very interesting. But it is curious to note that most of these painters – one exception is Feininger – sooner or later either went on to paint abstractly or fell back into a more traditional style. Either they searched for the absolute, or for pure beauty and pure art, or they recoiled from the consequences to which their quest might lead them, the absurdity of reality. Only a few dared to go on, but then followed the Surrealism of de Chirico, of whom I shall have more to say later.

Going back to a more traditional style was another answer to Picasso's step, the last and decisive step to modern art. Just as Renoir did not dare nor want to follow Monet, so here again there were artists of whom in one sense it was their weakness, in another their greatness, that they did not want to break with 'real' reality.

Derain, one of Picasso's friends from the early days of Cubism, the man who had introduced Picasso to African sculpture, is one of them. He began to paint in a style that became the landmark of the school of Paris between the two world wars. It was a style that, compared to Impressionism, looked for the more classical and stable elements in reality, human figures, landscapes. But it also sought stylization and decorative qualities.[65] Again and again one senses that there is an inherent weakness in this school – perhaps deep down they felt that the true moderns were really right, but they could not face their revolutionary, terrifying representations. They were perhaps the first to ignore the deep and disquieting aspects of modern art. But they did not like to fight against it, and even tried to minimize the gulf that separated their own works from those of the avant-garde. They were the aestheticists who would carry on maintaining that art is really no more than art, a sensibility, a feeling of artistic appeal, and little – or nothing

– more. In this way disquieting questions about content could be silenced and their own work, with its lack of real depth, defended.

The last group that reacted to Picasso's step was completely positive in their acceptance of it. They accepted the truth of the absurdity of this world and this life. They saw that now all values, norms, forms, traditions, all that belonged to Western culture including its art, had lost their meaning. They looked for a great upheaval, the breakdown of our culture, in the acceptance of nihilism and anarchism. The greatest of the group was Marcel Duchamp, one of the most influential men of the twentieth century, a man of great intellectual ability, a man who could and did dare to risk the consequences of his thinking.

But not even Duchamp could translate principles into practice just like that. It took time, though his development was really surprisingly quick. His first great work, in which he showed the influence of the Cubists, of Delaunay, perhaps too of the Futurists, was his famous *Nude descending a staircase*. One could call it a study in movement. One could also call it a parody of the *Golden stairs* of Burne-Jones; or one could just as well see in it a kind of parody of the Cubists of Delaunay's type. It was a shocking picture – it became the great focal point of the 'Armory Show' in New York in 1913 – not because of the strange immorality which was suggested by a nude woman descending a staircase, but because it was so hard to see the woman at all, and certainly not the tantalizing, titillating elements that both moral and immoral men were looking for.

One of his next works of 1912 (now, with most of his other important works, in the Philadelphia Museum) was *The King and Queen surrounded by their swift nudes*.[66] It could also be called a caricature of Cubism, or a parody of Futurism, but one thing is certain: it shows two towering static built-up forms, in shapes that we would call modern – if we think of cars, or ocean liners or futurist, science-fiction architecture – while between them is a sort of stream made up of moving shapes, resembling metal sheets (developed from the *Nude descending a staircase*). One thing is more than certain: there is no king, no queen, no nudes even. They are anarchistically destroyed in a kind of black humour. And not only is the royalty of the king and queen destroyed; their humanity is dead and gone, too.

'Man is dead' is a theme that is common to much modern art. Human being is dead. People are nothing but machines, very complex machines, absurd machines. The theme of absurdity, already clear in the two works mentioned, was developed further in Duchamp's *Bride*, also in Philadelphia. In another version this painting is called *The change from a virgin to a bride*. Indeed, sexual overtones are always to be found in this type of work, as if this is the only thing that has been left of humanity. What we see (to quote the Philadelphia catalogue) is 'an engine – not with a soul, as one might suspect, but with the clumsy addition of a superimposed human digestive and nervous system'. It is the kind of mechanical contraption you would find in a laboratory, or a sort of absurd apparatus parodying the anatomical drawings in medical textbooks. And, of course, it is hard to find anything of what the title suggested – the title is only a kind of malicious addition, turning the onlookers into voyeurs, soon discovering that it is not the painter but they themselves who have the dirty mind.

Of course there were many more works. The most specific examples of what we are saying are Duchamp's Ready Mades. For instance he takes a bicycle-wheel and puts it on a base; or he takes a comb, a normal everyday comb – and puts his signature on it. Of course these things are absurd as works of art, but their absurdity is willed. Duchamp wanted to kill the idea of High Art standing for high human values. His art is anti-art – and yet lives only by virtue of the fact that there is a tradition of High Art in Western culture, an art that stands for high values. These works stand at the cradle of the Dada movement that came to the fore in the years of the First World War. It was Dada that tried to laugh away all that is of value in our world, a nihilistic, destructive movement of anti-art, anti-philosophy, yet with mystic overtones akin to Zen Buddhism. It could well be seen as a new gnosticism, proclaiming that this world is without meaning or sense, that the world is evil – but with no God to reach out to, as God is also dead by now. In the Philadelphia Museum there is a work by Morton Schamberg from about 1918 called *God:* it is described as 'Mitre-box and plumbing trap, 10 1/2 inches high'.

The Dada movement was founded in Zürich in 1917 by a group of young artists. It used all artforms and tried to break all taboos, all norms for art, all sacred or non-sacred traditions. Dada was a nihilistic creed of disintegration, showing the meaninglessness of all Western thought, art, morals, traditions. It destroyed them by tackling them in an ironic way, with black humour, by showing them in their absurdity, by making them absurd. And this was not just a few men on their own: they were a strong group and were to have considerable influence, determining the form and approach of much that came later, right up to our own time. So the Dada movement was not the whims of a few lunatics at the fringe of our culture: it gave form to at least one side of the spirit of our age.

If we look at the collages of Kurt Schwitters, at the works of many of the Dada artists and those who were working in this line in the Surrealist movement, we discover how much of it came from Cubism, and how important the work of Marcel Duchamp has been. Picasso, in breaking through the barriers of reality, opened a kind of Pandora's box. The spirits took their abode in the minds of men like Duchamp and brought a whirlwind of anarchy, nihilism, and the gospel of absurdity. The wind is still blowing, and is becoming a storm: a storm called revolution.

6
Into the New Era

> Can't you understand what I'm trying to say
> Can't you see the fear that I'm feeling today
> If that button is pushed there is no running away
> There'll be no one to save with a world in a grave
> Take a look around you boy, it's bound to scare you boy,
> And you tell me over and over and over again you don't believe
> We're on the eve of destruction.[67]

If we put on exhibition all the most important works of modern art up to 1920, we would already be able to see almost all the different aspects of twentieth-century art. Expressionism, abstract art, Cubism, Dada, with their new methods of depicting reality, the collages, the particular styles, the use of colour, the search both for the absolute and for absurdity, their negation of all values, their pan-eroticism, we would see all the best and worst features of the art of our century. The years since 1920 have added virtually nothing that has been really new.

But the new spirit spread. While the modern movement was previously the work of a restricted group of artists and their public, it now influenced the minds and way of life of an ever increasing number of people. In fact it is not too much to say that a new era in cultural history was inaugurated. At the start the painters were the real avant-garde, but there were also writers, poets, playwrights, composers, architects, philosophers, and 'ordinary' people taking it up and working towards a new world.

The third step to modern art was like the overture to a new play, a new drama in world history. It was in itself revolutionary, and it was also the starting point of a revolution in which we still live today. For breadth and depth even the Russian revolution cannot stand comparison with it and seems almost old-fashioned in its aims and achievements.

So art played a vital part in giving form to a whole new mentality, a new spirit. It was one of the main agents for spreading the new thinking, the new ideas. Modern art is not neutral (art never was!). Its message is a new age, a new culture, a new world.

But modern art did not come as something inevitable. People, responsible people, with creative talents, human beings, made it what it is and gave it form and content. Yet even if it owes its specific style to particular people, it was still inevitable in the sense that it was the necessary outcome of the long development that we have been tracing from the eighteenth century, or even from as far back as the Renaissance. It is true, and represents the truth, in the sense that it is the expression of a reality: one in which God is dead and so humankind too are dying, losing their humanity, what makes them human, their personality and individuality.

It is striking that in our age there have been many attempts to achieve an impersonal art, an art that does not show the particular individuality of the artist. For modern art is inevitable too in being a reaction against the meaninglessness to which nineteenth-century art had led and, at the same time, against the cult of the artist-prophet-priest of culture, even though modern artists themselves continued to play this role albeit without its aura of Romantic heroism.

So in this sense, modern art is true. But at the same time it is a lie. Its portrayal of reality, of human being, is not a true one. People are not absurd. Reality is beautiful and good not only on the 'spiritual' level, but ever since the very beginning when God said it was good. We may appreciate the efforts, and even admire the greatness, of men who have tried to find the universal, the general 'behind' appearances; yet at the same time their quest was doomed to fail, for all universals break down as soon as the Creator, the One who made human being in his image, is denied or left out of account. It was doomed to fail because people started solely from their senses and their own brains, not accepting any reality beyond that.

This duality, this truth and falseness, must be accepted if we want to understand modern art and the modern age. We must recognize causality, that nothing comes of itself. But we are not slaves of causality, caught in a fatalistic way in the age in which we live. Human freedom implies that we can say 'no', that we do not have to accept the spirit of our age, that we can resist spiritual forces today in the same way as the early Christians were exhorted by Paul to stand firm 'against organizations and powers that are spiritual . . . the unseen power that controls this dark world'.[68]

But if Christians today are to say 'no', we must say so with knowledge and insight, and meet the situation as it really is. We are not free to opt out of the period of history God has placed us in, nor free to opt out of the task he has given us to do as his children here and now. But it is not just Christians who have this responsibility and freedom to say 'no'. Others who are concerned for the future of humankind and society, and who see these forces at work, are just as well able to deny the spirit of the age, even though they may lack the Christian basis for doing so.

A new art for new needs

But our reaction to modern art does not need to be wholly negative. For modern art can also be seen as an answer to new needs and new challenges. The difficulty is that these are deeply interwoven with the deeper issues we have been discussing. It reflects and expresses the new age with its machines, its technological possibilities, its speed, its new means of communication, its deep and wide international connections, its economic and social patterns which require new forms, new ways of expression, a new sensibility and new thought patterns. Modern art as a new spirituality, a new religion (even if a nihilistic one) has often gone to extremes, yet it has created new forms and opened up new possibilities. New ways of expression and new methods of portrayal have been evolved which, when the specific message for which they were made is discarded, and when the highly subjective, esoteric quality has been toned down, could be used to meet new twentieth-century needs.

So alongside modern art as such, the historical stream, the group of artists expressing a more or less common set of basic beliefs, there is an art, or rather a style, which we might call 'twentieth-century'. An example is Cassandre, who around 1920 began to use some of the Cubist stylistic methods for his highly imaginative and effective posters. In fact, in typography, pamphlets, posters and many different forms of visual communication, we find that new stylistic principles are being used, different from those of the last century, different from those still used by people who are now behind the times. They are found in traffic signs, the justly famous signs of the London Underground, in statistics, in magazines, in . . . well, everywhere around us, for they form the visual language of our age and as such can be understood by everybody without having to be learnt. Put Samuel Pepys or Dr Johnson down in the streets of one of our new cities today, and they would feel dazed and mystified: we would have to teach them to understand what was being communicated to them.

Much the same could be said of music or speech or many other aspects of the twentieth century. Yet twentieth-century people, though they may understand all these new ways of expression and communication, still feel estranged in the presence of modern art. However great the artist may be, however honest his or her motives, yet people sense a lie. It is not the method, the pictorial language, the means of communication, for people can appreciate the traffic signs and the toothpaste posters. No, they realize that there is more to modern art. There is the crisis, the absurdity of our age.

After all, there are plenty of good reasons for using new means of expression. It all depends on what you want to say with them. There is a tremendous difference between the wry, anarchistic humour of Duchamp's *King and queen* and the lyric poetry of a Lyonel Feininger, yet both use a Cubist style; or between the cool abstract beauty of a Mondrian picture and the cheerful interior with its primary colours that would never have existed without Mondrian. The Bauhaus, the famous German school of design which was active in the 1920s and which numbered among its teachers some of the greatest modern artists, was a major influence in modernizing the world, and in a double sense: it made modern stylistic forms applicable to twentieth-century life and, at the same time, did much to spread the spirit of true modernism. We can be thankful for the first, even if we would want to criticize it in detail, for as true purists they were sometimes too dogmatic in working out their principles of modern design. But only in this way could they renew architecture, interior design, furniture, lamps, everything that we would nowadays call industrial design, as well as being active in the fields of ballet, drama and much more besides.

A new art with a new message

Modern art is a complex phenomenon. But in the final analysis one thing stands out just as much as with 'old art': each work of art has its own message, its own quality, its own form. And each has to be 'interviewed' for its own individual peculiarity. Some are more extravagant; others use what may seem strange forms while their message is still positive and good; still others may even use rather more traditional forms and yet convey a message of revolution or absurdity; some may have a rather indifferent meaning but yet are beautiful in their colours or their forms, while others again are hideous even if they mean to speak kindly; and then of course some are really deep and important, others shallow and simply boring. To distinguish between them we must understand the forms and means they use.

Too many have by-passed modern art with a shrug of the shoulder, failing to see that it is one of the keys to an understanding of our times. For many of these works, particularly the more extravagant ones, are signs of the crisis of our culture. They embody new ways of thinking. They proclaim the meaninglessness of all we may think sacred. Some of these works may be making a plastic bomb to put under the liberal establishment chair of Western culture in which you may be sitting. Beware. This art forces one to choose. It makes you take a stand – one way or the other.

This art is the work of your neighbours, your contemporaries, human beings who are crying out in despair for the loss of their humanity, their values, their lost absolutes, groping in the dark for answers. It is already late, if not too late, but if we want to help our generation we must hear their cry. We must listen to them as they cry out from their prison, the prison of a universe which is aimless, meaningless, absurd.

Marc sought an art that would form altarpieces for the spiritual religion of tomorrow. Indeed many paintings are such altarpieces. But they are conceived for a nihilistic temple that will never be built, for the echo of Isaiah's words is still heard: 'Don't be so foolish as to bow down before images you have carved yourself.' It is virtually impossible for people now to accept a religion they have invented. In this lie both modern people's real tragedy, their despair, and their understanding of themselves.

Yet Marc did make one of these altarpieces, the large painting now in the art gallery at Basle. It is called *Tierschicksale*[69] and was painted in 1913. We see a rigid structure in Cubist style. If we look closer we discover deer, more deer, till we see that almost the whole picture is made up of deer, running, standing, lying. The fate of the animals: they are bound to cosmic laws which are rigid and leave no room for freedom of any kind. They are bound to die. Humans, Marc said once, are different from the animals insofar as they know that they have to die. On the back of the picture are written the words: 'and all being is flaming agony'.[70] The fact that we are, that we exist, is no cause for joy. It is no more than a question mark or, rather, pain and sorrow. We are bound to being. Bound to die. Here motifs that were to return in existentialism, in Heidegger, for instance, were already alive.

There is a deep pessimism behind Marc's work. Yet we must realize that this is really much deeper and truer to reality than a superficial optimism. It does not by-pass the truth of which the Bible speaks when it says that all creation is groaning in travail, longing to be set free from its bondage to decay.[71] Alas, Marc did not know that there can be a salvation from this death, that creation will be set free.

Beneath the search for the absolute in much modern art, the desire to express what is 'behind' the oppressive appearance of a reality which is almost too naturalistic and too rational, there is an anxiety, a feeling of being lost, of death pervading all. Hence the desperate quest for the real, the positive which lies in the depths, behind, beyond this world. It is a quest for a mystical truth. But it is a truth without God, without any sort of god at all.

The irrationality of the rational

I must repeat once again that I have no intention of giving in this book a complete history of modern art. My aim is simply to point out its main features – and some of its problems. Yet my tale would not be complete if I left it at 1920, even though almost all the modern developments had been achieved already by that time. Some of the great artists of the modern movement took their experiments with the new art further. I want to discuss two of them in particular.

The first is Paul Klee. He had had contacts with the Blaue Reiter group in München before the First World War and created a highly original style and approach of his own. Perhaps the 1920s, while he was teaching at the Bauhaus, were his greatest years. His art was a 'cold romanticism', as he called it himself, a kind of mysticism which sought to depict what is behind, above, beneath the surface of things: the forces of creation, change and destruction, good and evil. It was a sort of cosmological mysticism, or rather cosmogenetical: concerned with the developing, evolving forces behind reality. But they were not sought in any kind of transcendent God – in this sense Klee's mysticism is nihilistic. In many ways he is akin to the Surrealists that I shall be considering in the next section. But there is also another side to his art, his experimentation with pictorial possibilities and the laws of visual communication. In this he is comparable in a way to the logical positivists of that time, who were also very much taken up with the study of the meaning of words.

His influence has been great, especially on some of the Surrealists such as Miró. His enigmatic depth, the frailty yet power of his works (small drawings, watercolours and a few paintings), his wit and his tragic sense, all these made a great impact. His feeling for colour is exceptionally refined. Yet there is a kind of ghostliness in his art, an almost magic force that makes his art modern in a very deep sense, the art of a man who knows about absurdity, chance, alienation and agony – a man who does the same things as Picasso, but in a refined, sophisticated, almost soft way which makes Picasso look brutal and barbaric. The titles of his works are fascinating and enigmatically irrational: they were often given after completion, or rather as the finishing touch to a picture. His work almost always makes its impact through this interplay of title and image.[72]

A friend of Klee and fellow teacher at the Bauhaus was the man we have already discussed for his part in the development of art before 1920. Kandinsky had been in Russia, his native country, during World War I and had even become one of the leaders in artistic matters after the Revolution. Soon however the Communist leaders became hostile to the modern art that was prevalent in the years round 1920, so that Kandinsky and some of the other modern Russian artists had to flee to the West. In Russia he must have been influenced by the Suprematist movement of Malevich and others, a movement parallel to that of Mondrian but freer in its handling of straight lines. Back in Germany his art achieved a very specific geometrical quality, quite different from his earlier, more expressionistic type of abstract art. Yet in depth the meaning was the same. Look at the work reproduced here. There are geometric forms, but they do not seem to be rational. Rationalism had valued geometry very highly, almost as the basis of knowledge, because it seemed so completely rational and at the same time so completely certain and free from subjectivity and the possibility of human error. But time had shown that that certainty was not too certain, and that geometry and mathematics, despite their rationality, induced a problem: the how and why of their 'truths', their origin, the fact that they were so completely 'outside' the human. As Gauguin had put it, 'of course, as everybody has always said, does say and always will say, two and two is four – but that bores me, and deranges much of my reasoning'.[73] It became apparent that rationality itself was irrational. And this is exactly what Kandinsky painted: the irrationality of the rational.[74]

Looking at the picture we see that where once, centuries before, the Madonna had been in the centre of the picture or possibly Christ or a saint, standing for high principles in reality, or later a person pictured allegorically as some ancient god or goddess – now there stands geometry. Geometry is the basic principle of reality, but an irrational, strange and enigmatic geometry, like an esoteric, mysterious rite. And as we look again it seems as if the whole picture is exploding. There is a sort of volcanic, destructive force in this strange geometry. Science threatens human beings, and so is destructive too. So in a new way such a picture is an allegory, a kind of super-ornament that is yet much more than an ornament, a play with forms that yet is loaded with menacing meaning.

The Surrealist protest

The trend in the time between the world wars was in general, however, towards a more acceptable, a less fierce and thoroughgoing modernism, a more human approach. Two styles were predominant: one was a new kind of stylized, generalized, classicist art, with some of the stylistic qualities of Cubism taken over without its deeper intentions. We could mention here the work of Maillol, who was very popular in this period, or the painter Gromaire or, in England, Eric Gill and John Buckland Wright. Some of the more important architectural monuments of this time are the Town Hall in Hilversum by Dudok, the Museum of Modern Art and the new Trocadero in Paris, and London University's Senate House, to name just a few.

The other trend was more expressionistic, and even if the artists involved (such as those who contributed to the Dutch art magazine *Wendingen*) used symbolism in their art, as a whole it can be termed realistic. The sculptor Epstein is a good example of this trend, or we could pick out Stanley Spencer, Permeke, Chabot, and the many artists who belonged to the so-called Paris school which I mentioned in the last chapter. In architecture the works of the Amsterdam school, with de Klerk as its main representative, may be mentioned or Mendelsohn's Einstein Tower in Germany.

As a whole this period liked smooth forms, stylized shapes, predominant horizontals and verticals and the play with cubic volumes, all either in a more classical or in a more expressionistic vein, the whole pervaded with a warm romanticism.

Many adherents of the modern movement felt that its very modernity was thus betrayed and deprived of its real meaning. The modern forms were used out of their own context and became the patterns for fashionable decoration or for pretty pictures, or for the often pompous official or ornamental sculpture attached to new buildings (such as those at the Rockefeller Centre, New York, for instance).

But alongside these movements (and those of De Stijl and Bauhaus which were still going strong) there was another major force: Surrealism. This had its roots in the Dada movement and in some lonely forerunners such as de Chirico. Ideas, feelings and sentiments now came out into the open that had been at work previously, but in a more concealed way. The work of these painters could perhaps be explained by saying that Mondrian and the others were building a beautiful fortress for spiritual humanity, very rational, very formal: but they did so on the very edge of a deep, deep abyss, one into which they did not dare to look. But the Surrealists did look. For them fear, agony, despair and absurdity were the real realities. It was these they wanted to take up and express in their art.

Surrealism was born in the early 1920s in France and it involved writers, visual artists and later also film directors, though perhaps it is the painters who have had the most lasting results. Yet Surrealism is much more than a new style. Surrealism is no easy formula, not even a well-defined theory, and in the final analysis not even an artistic movement; it is a way of life and a direction of one's activity, an attitude of intellectual agony. Surrealism is revolutionary and destructive: the whole of Western culture and its society are thrown away in a battle against all that exists, in a revolt against everything to which a bourgeois world had previously held as firm. They were against nation, God, and reason – particularly the latter. They were against personality, conscience, beauty as an aim, talent, artistry, even the very will to live. Marx, Nietzsche, Freud, Jung were their spiritual leaders, along with men like the Marquis de Sade, Lautréamont, Rimbaud and Apollinaire. They had an interest in long-forgotten mysticisms, gnosticism, the primitive, or the primordial as they called it. One of them wrote about the early years:

> I ... will not soon forget the welcome mood of tonic absurdity, ironic subterfuge, gay as Satie's music, which pervaded them. Their featherweight bombs exploded into golliwogs and tinsel flowers. Surrealism, Dada's firstborn, was tougher, more doctrinaire. The view that the soul (if any) is divided into two compartments, like a Parisian autobus, was gaining acceptance, and the Surrealists, needless to say, staked their all on the dark horse.[75]

Their aim was a liberation of life, in every respect, to free people from this strange world that holds them in a thousand ways; on the basis of Freudianism they wanted to liberate people from convention, culture and society. The third issue of *La Révolution Surréaliste* said: 'Ideas, logic, order, Truth (with a capital T), Reason, all this is given to the nothingness of Death. You do not know how far the hatred we have against logic can lead us.'

This was a truly anarchistic movement. It sought complete freedom. Those involved were never able to work together with the Communists, even if some efforts were made to bring the two revolutionary streams together. They were looking for freedom, complete freedom. Yet their works, full of overt or concealed erotic symbolism, were also full of irrationality, absurdity, alienation, sadism, evil and hell, the horrific, black humour. The basic motifs of their work were human *échec*, human failure to gain true freedom and true humanity, the fact that people are strangers in this absurd reality which they experience as a prison, as frustration, as an obstacle in their way through to themselves. French existentialism found in it one of its roots and gave it a rational, philosophical base: Sartre was in the group in the 1930s, and Camus also had contacts with it.

Surrealism was a movement. As such it was confined and restricted. Its specific forms belonged to this period and to this group. Yet its influence has been great, and it has pervaded much of the expression of our age. Almost all artistic activity since that time has had some sort of surrealistic tinge.

In the wake of Surrealism came, too, the attempt to make a new language as a tool for the expression of new feelings and experiences. The Dada group, as well as the Surrealists themselves, had already worked with strange new irrational ways of verbal expression. The most extreme were the poems by Dadaist Kurt Schwitters, such as the following:

> Bumm bimbimm bamm bimbimm
> Bumm bimbimm bamm bimbimm
> Bumm bimbimm bamm bimbimm
> Bumm bimbimm bamm bimbimm[76]

Quite different and more well known are such writers as James Joyce in his *Ulysses*, Kafka in his story of the man who became a spider or in *The Trial*, Henry Miller in his *Tropic of Cancer*. Many French writers belonged to this movement even if they were never members of the group as such. Amongst the painters were such men as Max Ernst, Miró, Tanguy, Magritte, Dali, Masson, and many others.

What drove them on in this way? Perhaps the best way of expressing it would be to quote at some length from the high point of Miller's *Tropic of Cancer*, where he comes to a mystic ecstasy:

> I see that behind the nobility of (man's) gestures there lurks the spectre of the ridiculousness of it all ... he is not only sublime but absurd. Once I thought that to be human was the highest aim man could have, but I see now that it was meant to destroy me. Today I am proud to say that I am inhuman, that I belong not to men and governments, that I have nothing to do with

creeds and principles. I have nothing to do with the cracking machinery of humanity – I belong to the earth! ... If I'm unhuman it is because my world has slopped over its human bounds, because to be human seems like a poor, sorry, miserable affair, limited by the senses, restricted by moralities and codes, defined by platitudes and isms ... It may be that we are doomed, that there is no hope for us, any of us, but if that is so then let us set up a last agonizing, blood-curdling howl, a screech of defiance, a war-whoop! Away with lamentation! Away with elegies and dirges! Away with biographies and histories, and libraries and museums! Let the dead eat the dead. Let us living ones dance about the rim of the crater, a last expiring dance. But a dance! ... The great incestuous wish is to flow on, one with time, to merge the great image of the beyond with the here and now. A fatuous, suicidal wish that is constipated by words and paralysed by thought.

What has become of people? Miró once painted a picture of a picture. He took a reproduction of a secondary seventeenth-century Dutch picture (it could just as well have been a Vermeer or a Rembrandt) and gave his own reinterpretation. Nothing is more telling. 'Man is dead,' it says. The absurd, the strange, the void, the irrationally horrible is there. The old picture is treated with humour, scorn, black humour and devastating irony until nothing is left. As the image is destroyed, so too is humanity.

In Surrealist painting there are two distinct styles: one abstract, the other concrete. In the latter we are confronted with meticulously precise painted images, 'normal' as far as technique goes: but what is realized is a world that is strange, abnormal, irrational, not so much a nightmare as a horrible daydream. It is as if they put a mirror in front of us and ask us whether we find this strange, whether the world we think is normal is not really just as strange, as irrational, as absurd, as this. This way of painting was started by de Chirico just after 1911: he painted deserted and haunted places, alienated people, as inhuman as puppets, sitting in the middle of boxes with biscuits and the tools of the mathematician, or talking together in a silent dialogue amidst an endless and incongruent space.[77] People become inhuman – or subhuman, if you like – are displaced objects in an estranged world.

Salvador Dali's works, with their more Freudian overtones, were done with a morbid imagination, and with superb draughtsmanship. Magritte and Delvaux have a comparable message. Or there is Max Ernst, whose most typical works are his strange collages: figures made from cuttings out of nineteenth-century illustrated magazines, disorganized, disproportioned, irrational in an irrational world.

All this art showed a world out of order. It brought things together in a haphazard way that gave them as it were a new life, a new absurd and irrational meaning. It is as if we see these things with new eyes. Here we see them 'as they are', 'in themselves', out of any rational or structural context. They get a new life . . . haunt us and dislocate us . . . With the *objet trouvé* or the collage, as well, we find things brought together in a new nonsensical and yet poetical order, and we are confronted with reality in surreality. In the final analysis what we are being confronted with is the material world, the very stuff we are made of – and it appears a phantom, an irrational, meaningless and nevertheless obsessive reality. That they often did achieve this effect shows their artistry, their great imagination, and sometimes Surrealist works can look almost natural. But the title of a landscape I came across recently is very telling: *Abstract vision in form of a Spanish landscape.*[78] This is alienation – what looks real is unreal. Human beings are strangers in God's creation.

The other line was the abstract Surrealism of men such as Masson, Matta and sometimes Miró, Ernst or Yves Tanguy. Here the drawing was often done in a dream-like way, as if the artist was a medium who just drew as it seemed to want to go – like Surrealist writers who sometimes wrote their poetry in this way. Strange, unknown and yet evocative symbols appear, a sort of poetic reality. But this is no ideal spirit-world, no paradise. On the contrary. It is the image of hell, a confrontation with the haunted, the evil, a feeling of 'floating in an empty space', as if being itself collapses and falls to its utter destruction.

Surreality and Christian reality

Buñuel, the Surrealist filmmaker, shows that the human attitude to people is like that of a scorpion to a scorpion: eternal, cruel war. His pictures are like de Sade's *Justine;* even the best intentions always lead to disaster, to sin, pain and putrefaction. Why? He said: 'Because man is not free.' Because there is no justice. Because this world is wrong and rotten ... There is no way out – except perhaps by an anarchist revolution. But one senses that Buñuel does not even believe his own dream at this point.

Surrealism demands that we pause here, for we cannot simply describe it and leave it at that. Perhaps Christians especially are troubled as they hear in it an echo of the Bible's realism about the world, and yet, and yet ... Is Surrealism, is all that is expressed in modern art, really the whole truth?

The picture the Bible gives is in one way certainly even less pleasant. It is not rose-tinted, blindly optimistic. It does not tell us that everything is fine: it says that the universe groans in pain as it looks forward to a future deliverance, that the whole of creation is now in the bondage of corruption.[79] It points not just to the condition of the world but also to the reason for it. As Isaiah put it,

> The earth mourns and withers,
> the world languishes and withers;

> the heavens languish together with the earth.
> The earth lies polluted
> under its inhabitants;
> for they have transgressed the laws,
> violated the statutes,
> broken the everlasting covenant.
> Therefore a curse devours the earth.[80]

So the Bible is very realistic about sorrow, pain, evil, hatred, jealousy, cruelty, unrighteousness and human misery. But the Bible makes it clear that the cause is human sin. It was not only the Old Testament prophets who were scathing in their denunciation of it, it was Christ himself, too, and the early Christians, such as Paul in his devastating analysis of human corruption in the first chapter of his letter to the Romans. There were always those who scoffed at God, as Malachi pointed out in Old Testament times and Peter in the New Testament, for they could not see him at work. But they will know that the wrath of God is kindled against all unrighteousness and that the hills will tremble and that carcasses will be torn in the midst of the streets . . .[81] If God seems to withdraw and let people go their own way – for the time being – in a way this is even more terrible: for the God who hides himself is also the God who will judge. God has given humankind such tremendous possibilities in the creation he has made. Yet people have misused them, wrecked them, turned their backs on the God who has made them. Still, God loves them and because he loves them, because his holiness and his love are absolute, he cannot look on evil . . .

There would seem to be no solution. An anarchist revolution will change nothing, for it will not change sinful peole. There is no solution – but for redemption, for people to be saved from the consequences of their sin by the death of Jesus Christ. For it was to bear the curse on humanity's behalf that Jesus Christ went down into death.

So the Surrealists' view of reality is in a way more akin to the Bible than that of optimistic humanism. But the Bible in which God has revealed himself speaks of a way out. Of those who refuse the way out, those who cry out in anger against the evil of this world but yet see evil as ultimate reality, the psalmist says: 'The fool says in his heart: "There is no God." They are corrupt, they do abominable deeds, there is none that does good.'[82]

Certainly the Surrealists share the realism of the Bible. Buñuel and the others echo the words of the old 'preacher' of Ecclesiastes, who looked at the futility and desperation of life around him, and at the final end of humanity: 'the hearts of men are full of evil, and madness is in their hearts while they live, and after that they go to the dead.' They also share the Bible's standpoint by not accepting death and evil; for Jesus Christ did not accept it either: He was 'deeply moved in spirit and was troubled' when he came to Lazarus' grave, he was angry with the merchants in the Temple because of their sin and greed in fleecing the poor in the name of religion, and he warns us that there will be strife and labour, for he never preached a sentimental peace. Though the Surrealists may hunger and thirst after righteousness, their fear and agony comes precisely from the fact that they cannot see how it can be achieved. For they know nothing of love and beauty and real mercy.

The Bible is not less but more inclined to speak of the evil of this world. Suffering is a reality. When we read the book of Revelation we see something of the world in which we live today – and we hear the repeated message of 'woe' unto the inhabitants of the earth. Yet the Bible is no black book. It is not just pessimistic. Nor does it preach the agony and the absurdity of the Surrealists. Black humour, sick jokes, irony, pulling things down for the sake of it, the erotic as an ultimate value, these are not found in the Bible. For the Bible does not see people as imprisoned in a world in which there can be no love and in which nature is their enemy.

It shows us that at the beginning of all history, God said that his creation was good. Nature itself is to the praise of God, and so clearly does it reveal him that Paul can say in Romans that people have no excuse for not accepting him and for turning instead to what they know to be evil. No, God hates unrighteousness far more than any person ever did. And Christ came for the very purpose of breaking through the reign of evil and sin and suffering. He came to make the world normal. And God must come in judgment because without it this world would be absurd, and love would have no place.

Buñuel and the other Surrealists come to us and say: Protest against evil by doing evil, hate God and your fellow human beings; the world can only be redeemed by revolution, terror and the tearing down of everything that is still standing. Christ comes to us and says: Seek your peace in me, know a new, eternal life which will work itself out in this life in loving your neighbour, showing mercy and humility, hungering and thirsting after righteousness. It is a revolution not of terror but of love.

To the Surrealists in their rejection of the God of the Bible his creation has become a strange prison, irrational, full of agony and fear, a place where they feel they do not belong. They long for a better world in which the absurdity does not exist, not understanding that it is sin and hatred and cruelty that is the real absurdity, alien to the creation as God made it. They long for freedom, but seek it in human being itself by opening their inner selves, their subconsciousness – and so they lose it. Because they have rejected the transcendent God, they are bound to the immanent – and they know it. Again and again God warns people through his prophets not to forget him; now we can see why. There would be truth in the Surrealist affirmation that this world is hell – if there were no God. But it is a lie, for there is a God; it is a lie because there is beauty and truth for whoever wants to see it; it is a lie because people know that love and righteousness are possible and, thank God, belong to the true, real reality.

The real and the horrible

The challenge of Surrealism forces us to react. But its themes are expressed all around us today: it is but one expression of human alienation from reality, this sense of absurdity. Here we must return to Picasso, for his varying styles illustrate the tension of the age.

Picasso's great break through the boundaries of reality took place around 1911. Afterwards he painted absurd humanity, absurd reality; people made up of some planks; the human as non-human. This was what I would call Picasso's first 'horrible' period. But, even so, he was a great man and no mere dogmatist. When he painted the woman he loved, he was free to paint her rather differently. Loved ones cannot be absurd. So in 1915 he painted Olga in a 'normal' way, resembling an Ingres portrait. Even here love breaks through barriers of absurdity and lostness. Again and again in his life we see Picasso returning to a more 'loving' and free expression when he loves a woman. Unfortunately it did not often last very long.

Since 1915 he has had two styles: one more classical, the other more absurd, more Cubist. But even here his expression tones down, and the paintings are more decorative works than statements of absurdity. Yet even his classicist paintings have some disquieting elements for those who look closer. But generally Picasso followed to some extent the trend of his time in a more realistic and less agonizing art.

But in the mid-1920s, influenced by the Dada and Surrealist movements, he again produced pictures in which beauty was lost in the quest for the 'disagreeable form'. Haftmann in his book *Painting in the Twentieth Century* states that the *Tree dancers* (in the Tate Gallery) was the first in this line, near to Surrealism. To describe it he uses words and phrases such as 'convulsive', 'hysterical', new associations that always seek to 'hurt', 'masks', 'crying forms', 'absurdity'. This is the beginning of what I would call Picasso's second 'horrible' period. Its masterpieces are several pictures of bathing girls on the beach. The girl in *Bather* is painted in an almost normal way, as any classicist would have done. But how has she been painted? She is made up of bones (for human being is dead). But she still has sex. She is like a machine, a horrific machine (isn't human being really a machine?). Yet she looks down at us in a superior sort of way – it is an indication of Picasso's greatness that he can achieve this – as if she were saying to the person looking at the picture, 'I'm much greater and more human than you, aren't I?' These pictures depict extremely forcefully the way twentieth-century people look at themselves and understand themselves.

In the 1930s Picasso became more 'friendly' again – and more erotic and sensuous. Once, enraged by the Spanish Civil War, he painted his most human work for many years, *Guernica*. It is a depiction of war, and here agony, distress, evil and sorrow are real, caused by real reality. But there are questions which remain unanswered: Were Picasso's spiritual friends, the Communists and the anarchists, really more friendly themselves and less inclined to use terror as a weapon? And if he is protesting, against whom is he protesting? The fascists? Or against the world as such? Is it not a cry for revenge rather than for repentance? It is Picasso's most human work; but it is enigmatic and its symbolism far from easy to understand.

Around 1940 another 'horrible' period begins. Now a whole gallery of female heads is created, each more absurd than the last, with strange double faces, horrible grimaces.[83] Why? It was Picasso's answer to the critics of his time, who began to accept him by toning down the content, saying that he was just using a new style, a new way of representing, suggesting that the content of his pictures was the same as traditional painting. They explained his forms by saying that he used the Cubist technique in order to show things from different sides at the same time. This of course was seldom if ever true of Picasso (though it might have been the theory behind some of the lesser Cubists). Picasso, hearing his true expression thus deformed and made soft and almost positive, now began, in his disgust and anger, to show what their words really meant. The horrible series of heads are made to fulfil exactly the theories of the critics. This is a face shown from two sides at the same time – Picasso seems to cry out: 'Look, it isn't nice and sweet, it isn't normal reality, look, you fools.'

At about the same time Picasso wrote a play called *How to Catch Wishes up the Tail*. It is one of the most absurd pieces of theatre ever written, more absurd than anything the Theatre of the Absurd has conceived. It was read publicly in 1944; the cast consisted of Simone de Beauvoir, Jean-Paul Sartre, Leiris and others of the group led by Albert Camus – existentialist philosophy and Picassian Surrealism belong together. At this time too Picasso began his series of reinterpretations of old paintings. He took Courbet's *Girls by the Seine* and remade the picture in his own style, not to prove that the critics were right but to show what the picture really meant – or to show what was left of humanity. He took Velasquez's *Las meninas*, a picture of the Spanish royal family (in the Prado, Madrid), and painted both the whole and the details in his own way in a kind of artistic anarchistic murder of the whole royal family and their way of life.

Then there are his series: the bull, Balzac, a girl's head, and others. Each series would begin with a 'normal' drawing, and then he would begin to change it, each picture going further than the previous one. It gets more cubistic, loses more and more of its normal appearance, is reduced to almost nothing. In a film that was once made of Picasso he went on after one such feat, and starting from the last, almost abstract drawing turned it into something else. It was clever, obviously the work of a man of great talent and imagination. But it is more. It shows that he does not stand behind any of his styles. An artist's style expresses his or her personality, views, character, understanding. So normally a person's work will show basically the same style, or at least a consistency before and after a break in the development of a style. But Picasso, being a true nihilist, does not believe in any such view: each different approach is taken up and discarded, changed and then discarded again. He can believe anything, look at things in as many ways as he likes, for everything is possible, even if they are mutually exclusive or contradictory, for there is no one true way.[84]

A different twentieth-century response

Is Picasso really *the* man of our times? History textbooks tend to show us history as pursuing an inevitable course, with artists expressing the spirit of their age. What is often not made clear is that the schematic simplicity of a period as it appears in the textbook shows only the main lines. History is more complex, and any number of different streams can be found side by side. It is important to realize this: it means that people have the freedom to choose, and that they therefore can be held responsible for their actions.

Is Picasso the man of our times? To a certain extent, yes. He brought about the end of a period, the time of the Enlightenment, by breaking through the reality barrier. He was and is the exponent of a trend that has grown increasingly since the beginning of this century, and is becoming (or has become) the main stream. But though Picasso is certainly the man of our times, responding to some of the great questions of our period, and formulating a new way of approach with his answers, that does not mean that there are no other possible answers, or that no other direction of thought and action can be taken.

Georges Rouault is a proof of this. He is of the same generation as Picasso. In his younger years he was influenced by a movement within the Roman Catholic Church that looked to more sincerity, more real faith, less traditional forms, to what we have come to call in our century authenticity. This movement, as is natural for such a Christian endeavour, was very critical of its period. So Rouault began to paint judges, prostitutes, upper-class people and so on in a rather aggressive way. He is a contemporary of the Fauves and the Cubists, but he is different. His prostitutes are not amoral beings, symbolizing the end of morality as such; they are symbols for prostitution, for cheap love for sale, for the depravity of his time. His judges are akin to those of

Daumier: they stand for the corrupt courts of his time. He prophesies against the times in which he lives.

Yet his figures are still symbols in a negative sense. Only in the 1920s does he come to a more humane – not humanistic – point of view; compassion, charity, love come into his work. His greatest achievement was the series of etchings – done with a very intricate special technique – called *Miserere*.[85] Its plates depict war, love, human pride and weakness, suffering and sacrifice, with Christ as Redeemer – in fact, it shows humanity in a variety of aspects that is fantastically rich in comparison with Picasso's *Bathers*, painted at about the same time but showing only human being destroyed, and all the fine nuances and complexities of life missed.

Rouault shows that another kind of art is possible. It is an art which is a positive answer to absurdity and Surrealism and existentialism. Yet it does not show the rosy sentimentality, more humanistic than human, that much so-called Christian art has produced.

Rouault has shown what it means to believe in God and to love people in this age. And we must be thankful. Why did many Christians miss it? And where is the Protestant counterpart of Rouault? Most Protestant artists still worked along traditional lines, either Victorian or impressionistic or following a sweetly symbolistic line.

Why did Christians miss it? Why were they fooled by Salvador Dali when he made his strange, mystic works? Dali's *Last Supper* portrays a very mystical celebration of the sacrament, with a ghost-like Christ (one can look through him). His *Crucifixion of St John of the Cross* was named after a heretical mystic of the sixteenth century who had this strange conception of a cross hanging over the world but not touching it. Did Christ not die for *this* world, for the people of *this* earth, including their material concerns, their daily needs for normal human life, or was his work spiritual in a solely mystical sense, out of this world? It is doubtful whether Dali was ever truly Christian rather than no more than Surrealist. He only introduced mystical elements taken from a heretical (but not biblical) tradition. For mysticism in one way or another was always part of the Surrealist approach, which was as much gnostic as nihilistic. Were Christians misled by Dali's seemingly traditional way of painting which was, superficially speaking, naturalistic? Or were they themselves caught up in an unbiblical mysticism?

So, following the Second World War the modern movement made great headway. Not every young painter went this way, though a great number did. And those who did not were simply considered old-fashioned and out of the game. And in the years since, more and more painters, both those of the older generation and also those of the younger generation who first went in other directions, were won over and became abstract painters of one kind or another. Modern art has won the battle.

7
Modern Art and the Twentieth-Century Revolt

> I do not paint, I hit.
> Painting is destruction.[86]

After half a century of hard and devoted activity, the modern school has won the battle. They have not won cheaply. They have won partly because their opponents have not fought them on proper grounds. Many did not take them seriously or laughed at them, or thought it a passing whim or fashion. Others tried to avoid the real battle, tried to be 'in' and 'with it' (or whatever the current phrase was) without taking issue, even saying that modern art was a new style, a new way of depicting reality. These tried to turn modern art into a new 'normal' art, in the old humanist tradition. But very few really went into the heart of the matter and tried to see what lay behind it.

At the beginning of modern art the public had reacted violently. Kandinsky relates how in 1912 at an exhibition of his work in Berlin people spat at his pictures. Now, he said in 1936, people do not do that any more, they say: 'Isn't that nice?' And, he added, the change does not mean that times have become easier for the artist.

The question is, what had happened? Perhaps the more human, less extravagant trends of modern art in the 1920s had softened people up and made them more susceptible to it. Perhaps they began to realize that at least the modern artists were struggling with problems that were really relevant to the period in which they lived and appropriate to their own cultural situation. More probably they began to understand that the current streams of non-modern art were none too strong and often had no adequate theoretical or 'spiritual' basis. The real creative forces were not there. Humanism had lost its deep grip on people, for its main principles had turned into problems.

Modern art in its more consistent forms puts a question mark behind all values and principles. Its anarchist aims of achieving complete human freedom turn all laws and norms into frustrating and deadening prison walls; the only way to deal with them is to destroy them. Now this principle has a curious side-effect. When we see a work that in its way destroys meaning and says to us that there is no real sense, it not only makes it hard for us to see the value of the reality depicted in this way, but this very message turns against the painting itself. After looking at a Baj painting of a general, it would be hard to have real respect for a general if you met one afterwards, for his office has been downgraded. But the meaning of the picture itself also becomes downgraded and loses its power. So you see people walking through an exhibition of modern art and you would expect them to be enraged, for sometimes things which are quite holy to them are being taken to pieces, but they walk on amused or even hardly interested. For the message itself has no longer any meaning. Anything will do.

Not very long ago the absurd play by Picasso that I have already referred to was staged at St Tropez in the South of France, complete with all its obscenities and worse. For instance, a woman urinates in the middle of the stage, with the sound amplified. But to the dismay of the producers nobody stirred, nobody walked away enraged, nobody seemed shocked. There might have been some snobbishness in this – today everyone has to accept things like that, especially when a big name like Picasso is behind it, but it may well be too that the defiance of all sense of propriety in a completely absurd 'plot' made these actions in themselves senseless and so defeated its own end.

This does not mean that modern art has no influence. Even the well-meaning ignoramus walks through the gallery of modern art with a question mark: Is this art, what does it mean, why do they do it this way? Even such a person is reached, perhaps against his or her will or without even realizing it, by one message: look, these things are works of art, and a thing like this really means just as much as 'your' Rembrandt. Or rather, these may not be works of art but yet they are brought here and considered important: are all the old values really gone and meaningless today? 'Your' Rembrandt speaks of another world that is dead and gone . . . And so even he or she comes out with something destroyed or at least wounded.

There are still people who think they can by-pass these things, can ignore them. Sometimes people are enraged, but in being thus hurt they feel at the same time they are old-fashioned and out of touch with what is going on.

Modern art has won the battle. The galleries of modern art see it as their task to inform people, to educate them, to bring them up to date and, rather idealistically, to promote modern art. Unhappily they side with the modern movement, either out of a deep commitment to its meaning and aims or from an optimistic humanist attitude that this is the new culture, and that humankind must find their way through this crisis; or sometimes they may even do so without realizing what they are really doing. But, whatever their motive, they are all promoting one main stream. Sometimes one even has the feeling that this modern movement has become the official art of today and that some of its products are nothing more than a new Salon art, as superficial and as shallow as that of the last century.

Modern art has won the battle: that means that other streams are sometimes ignored, and that artists who do not follow the trend are by-passed. They have a hard time, even if they are first class. Or, even if they are sometimes shown, their work has lost its force because of the 'side-effect' of the more far-out art I have described.

The fact that modern art has won the battle also means that it is known and available everywhere. For many before the Second World War modern art did not mean very much. Now, and certainly for the younger generation, things are different. The great names of the modern movement are well known, exhibitions all over the world have made their art familiar, books, articles and lectures about the different schools or representatives are in every bookshop. James Joyce's *Ulysses* can be bought as a paperback in every bookstall; even de Sade's works, together with many other 'classics' of pornography, are available without difficulty and for low prices. Films are even made of such works of literature. The great breakthrough has probably only taken place since 1960, and certainly as the result of the renewed and vigorous activity of the modern movement's supporters. If in the wake of this avalanche of modern work of all kinds there is a strong anarchistic trend among the younger generation we must not be surprised. These artists speak about real things that belong to our age and give insight and meaning – even if in a negative sense. The revolution which the great leaders of the modern movement have been dreaming about in the past three quarters of a century is beginning to be realized.

The modern movement has won the battle. It has done so too because many were not alert. Christians have clung to tradition and fought little battles with other Christians. They have only too frequently not understood that art and literature, philosophy and even popular music were the agents of the new spirit of the age, and have left these alone or optimistically assumed they were too remote to exercise influence. Humanists, in a bourgeois mentality, optimistically felt that this gloomy existentialist stream was only a passing whim: the tide will turn, for people are basically good. They too ignored the movement or underestimated its influence.

The only Christians who did not ignore modern art were an intellectual group of liberals, who took side with the new movement, often even claiming modern art as a new religious art.[87] Otherwise Christians of all types and kinds and shades of orthodoxy by-passed the modern movement in art and thought and, what is more serious, did little to solve the problems of our particular times: the problems of mass society, of modern communication, of technology squeezing away human freedom, of the lack of a true foundation for culture. The basic principles of the Enlightenment have proved to be false gods, but there were no new ones with which to replace them. Why, even the true and living God was dead, or so some of the theologians said. Certainly Christians were active in helping people – and in preaching salvation. And, happily, people were sometimes saved, thank God. But the main problems of our culture were not tackled. Yet they were true problems.

Abstract Expressionism

The modern movement won the battle. Now we must see what they had to offer. After the Second World War there was initially a silence, but soon things began to happen, first in Europe. There was a group of young artists from Holland, Denmark and Belgium who called themselves Cobra. Theirs was a new form of Expressionism, wanting to renew art and life by giving free way to creativity. 'Everybody can do it!' 'Create!' And they did create, with childlike non-rational works, direct and uninhibited, free and unashamed. They wanted to be like children, innocent, free from the tarnish of a culture which had become too old. Their works were less aesthetic than those of the Expressionists of the beginning of the twentieth century, and there was a surrealistic tinge here and there. Some Dutch artists, among them Karel Appel, who gained international fame, were of most importance. For the first time such a new movement had a chance to come immediately as it were into the limelight and be officially recognized, in a large exhibition in the Stedelijk Museum of Modern Art in Amsterdam.

In America, after long years of preparation, there was the explosion of a strong modern movement. In it were such different artists as de Kooning, who painted women, sex-bombs without beauty or femininity, utterly horrifying demolitions of the woman image; Guston, Rothko, with his large abstract compositions made up of 'soft' rectangles; Arshile Gorki, whose art was not without Surrealist overtones; and of course the most influential, Jackson Pollock. In the mid-1940s he had come to his 'drippings' – large canvases that were painted 'abstractly' by dripping paint onto them from a can as they lay on the ground, the end of a development in search of a contentless art. De Kooning said of it: 'Every so often, a painter has to destroy painting. Cézanne did it. Picasso did it with Cubism. Then Pollock did it. He busted our idea of a picture all to hell. Then there could be new paintings again.'[88]

Rudi Blesh in his *Modern Art USA* (New York, 1956) relates how it began:

> Everyone had been talking about 'a way to get the explosive moment of creation on the canvas'. (He) had just done it: simply turned the paint loose in the air without a parachute. A violent Duchamps, not gravely accepting the 'laws of chance', but flinging the door open to chaos ... (But) order marshalled itself in all that wilderness. Those violent forces – the whirls, the plunges, the thrusts – began to float in an equilibrium of violence against violence.

Kline, Clifford Still and many others made up this new American school of painting, full of variety, yet one in its modernity. They called it Abstract Expressionism. This title described rather well what most of the artists did. Of course some were different, such as Mark Tobey on the West Coast, who quietly reflected in his art the spirit of Zen Buddhism in his abstract repetitions of little forms – always the same and yet always different, a continuous mystical pattern.

The skeleton of Achilles

In studying these artists and movements one is struck by a paradox. There is a great upsurge against rationality, against the calculated and the finished form. It is a search for the free, direct expression of personality in order to find something more than personal, the mystical all, the ideas behind the discarded 'outward' reality which was deemed unworthy. It is a search for something more, something different from what the rational can encompass – in one word, the irrational. Yet no art has been more philosophical than this art. It was an art by thinkers for thinkers. It involved much discussion by the artists, and even more by the public, or at least the informed and interested public.

In Europe artists from many countries took part in the new movement, many of them working in Paris. Matthieu was elaborating – and somewhat commercializing – the idea of throwing paint onto the canvas in his large abstract signatures; Poliakoff was working more calmly at his abstract coloured canvasses; and we could name many more. Especially important was Dubuffet, whose Art Brut brought together some elements from the Cobra movement with a magic mysticism that looks for the primordial, the not-yet-formed, the just-being-formed, and wandered into the depiction of material itself, confronting us with it in its bare existing self in a way comparable with the abstract Surrealists. Later he made his *hourloupes* – strange, coloured, outlined, interlocking fields that mean nothing and yet irrationally evoke forms of men, men become one with the surrounding fields, a great mystical union in colour and shape, but just the opposite of a quiet *nirvana*, more of a hectic hell, apparently cheerful, but . . .

Sculpture up to the middle of the century had kept to a more or less classical style, with the exception of some modernists such as Zadkine and Lipchitz, some Surrealist abstractionists such as Arp, and some Constructivists who made strictly geometrical shapes that yet seemed free and fantastic. But now, in these years following the middle of the century, a great flood of destruction entered sculpture. Wotroba's lying figures decayed and fell into ruin – or this is how it seems when trying to follow his development. Germaine Richier made her strange 'primordial' figures, *natura naturans*, humanity being a chance product of material just beginning to take shape.

In the later 1950s there was a movement towards 'junk-sculpture', figures welded together from *objets trouvés*, things found at a rubbish dump. Paolozzi made figures like ancient gods, but yet at the same time like discarded pieces of junk, as primordial machines, absurd and yet with a certain kind of primitive sacredness, but very modern and twentieth-century.

In this same period a kind of 'junk-painting' was of importance. Paul Bun, Tapies and others made paintings of sack-cloth with holes in it, with pieces of metal or wood stuck on, like a new kind of collage, in a Neo-Dada style. Perhaps one of the most important artists in this group was Rauschenberg, an American who made large paintings combining real *objets trouvés* with old posters or papers or illustrations with brush strokes superimposed in a way comparable with that of the Abstract Expressionists. He said: 'A pair of socks is no less suitable to make a painting with than wood, nails, turpentine, oil and fabric.' About his *Allegory* Andrew Forge wrote:

> It is one of Rauschenberg's most extreme achievements. What is extraordinary is the way in which such powerful, aggressive forms as the metal, as the umbrella are brought to terms with the picture surface. And yet they remain self-contained, intact. None of the affinities or correspondences I have listed lead to the dominion of one form over another. Things, passages, live side by side as equals, free to expand, to breathe, to display, unassailed by the 'personality' of their neighbours or by some overriding and generalising intention. The calm sun-like frontality of the umbrella is undisturbed by the metal's brittle vigour – although it is not indifferent to it. Nor is the energy of the metal curtailed by the umbrella's stillness. *Allegory* could indeed be an allegory of freedom, of self-determination, of a good city.[89]

Or, I should like to say, of a shabby world in which all things are of equal value, but no great values persist . . . Yet there is some mysticism in this Neo Dada world. Rauschenberg says (in the same catalogue): 'The logical or illogical relationship between one thing and another is no longer a gratifying subject to the artist as the awareness grows that even in his most devastating or heroic moment he is part of the density of an uncensored continuum that neither begins with nor ends with any decision or action of his.'

Neo-Dada was near to a kind of Neo-Surrealism. It exalted the chance product: the artist's jottings or the random throwing of paint onto the canvas, a creative process in the line of the Surrealist writers of the 1920s. In the 1950s it was called 'informal art' or Tachism. A very intelligent German painter, Hans Platschek, has written about it, analysing its sources and meaning. Besides Picasso and the Dada and Surrealist movements he mentions Jackson Pollock, Dubuffet and Wols. He says about the latter's work:

> The 'sick' paintings are yet also signs of a reality that is felt to be rotten and inappropriate, one whose unity is denied. With the destruction of elements of form appears at the same time a destruction of structures and signs of a reality – at least in the painting. The destruction of real objects is not possible, and so their images are questioned.[90]

In all this type of art the onlooker is asked to be active. Viewers have to 'go into the picture', and in a kind of irrational, completely free action get their own meaning out of it. In a way the painting is the catalyst that sets our mind to work, gets us in touch with the irrational forces of reality. And in this way it affects our way of seeing and experiencing reality. And it really does so. Rauschenberg is right when he says, 'If you do not change your mind about something when you confront a picture you have not seen before, you are either a stubborn fool or the painting is not very good.'

In fact, confronting these works of art, we cannot escape the fact that our own view of reality is challenged. Inevitably we are drawn into an argument with modern people about their ideas, about values, norms and ultimate truth, about humanity and our responsibility to help build the future world. These are deep and difficult problems, undoubtedly. But the positive good in this art is that it makes all cheap answers, all worn-out traditions, all ideas that are not firmly based in real truth, pale and useless and senseless.

One thing binds all these groups and arts together: the assertion that reality is at stake, that it has become a question mark, that it seems to be something people cannot be happy with, something that is strange to them. Crisis, alienation, absurdity, it is words like these which describe the artistic situation. There is an underlying 'philosophy', one that can be called a renewed kind of gnosticism, saying that this world is wrong and human beings ill-fated. This is nihilism and at the same time a new kind of mysticism, reaching out for the depth behind appearances, the truth through the squalor and the destruction. Or, to put it another way: we see in this desperate search how right Paul was in his letter to the Romans (see 1:21 ff.).

One has to begin to see that there is truth in it – no person can work without having at least some grounds to start from, some assertion that holds when confronting reality. The old humanist images are faded, and old values generally are often no longer of much use as they do not answer present-day problems. And in the midst of this people are searching for new forms and new answers. Perhaps a new culture is growing that can come into being only when the old civilization is completely destroyed. But if things continue the way they do, the new culture will be neither humanist nor Christian.

The situation can be summed up with Arman's box of shoe-trees. Of course, there is no denying that these *objets trouvés* are arranged in an artistically accepted pattern. There is certainly nothing against the use of unorthodox materials, and I should like to think that the whole is an abstract work of art. But then we should miss the real content of the 'picture'. Shoetrees are junk, and the garbage collector would throw this thing away without any feeling of remorse. Yet this work still belongs to the old Western tradition that art is bound up with the deepest things in life, that it reflects and expresses a particular view on life and its deep, ultimate values. Here we see what is left of the old allegories of Venus and Achilles and the classical figures that have stood for humanist values for so many centuries. Venus and Achilles died in the eighteenth century; they were buried in the middle of the last century. Where are they now? Arman has the answer. He calls his work, very aptly, very consciously, *The skeleton of Achilles*.[91]

Another, perhaps even more final view on the situation is found in the work of Lucio Fontana, one of the first ever actually to make holes in the canvas. For centuries people have made their paintings on a solid base of wood or canvas. The canvas has in fact represented the base and the starting point of the artist's endeavour. It has meant the freedom to create, even if within a set framework, an artistic world, whether it is no more than decorative or is more serious or loaded with meaning. But now people have lost their base. The foundations of the building of our civilization are worn and crumbling. Now it is a fitting allegory of our culture to gash the canvas, to break through the traditional barriers. It is a working out of Gauguin's call to every artist never to set any limit to his or her freedom; to destroy the final ground of all art as it reflects the ground of being itself. Fontana slit the canvas with a razor-blade, jabbed at it in a fierce moment of rage against all limitations, in a moment of despair of ever finding the reason for such a ground at all. He called the work he made in 1964 *The end of God*. First we are left with nothing but the bones of Achilles. Now God himself has been destroyed.

Two British artists

Although there has been a thriving artistic life in Britain since the Second World War, the number of really great names has been small. The scene was made up of groups and movements rather than by great commanding figures. Henry Moore and Francis Bacon have been exceptions – making up for the fact, perhaps, that Britain has played only a secondary role in the upsurge of the modern movement.

Indeed, it seems good to pause a moment to reflect on this phenomenon. Britain has been in many cases the place where the new ideas were born or their consequences thought through most deeply: at the beginning of the Age of Reason, for instance, or in Romanticism or evolutionism or mysticism. Yet the revolutions which have occurred elsewhere have by-passed Britain, where the principles have been worked out with much more restraint. Only one from outside Britain can appreciate fully how much the 'old times' still persist there – certainly outside London. The break-up of society, the alienation of humanity in an all-pervading technocracy, extreme socialism that takes away the individual's freedom, these things are so much less conspicuous there than elsewhere. Maybe this is why existentialism came in later, as something foreign and imported, though the flourishing school of the Theatre of the Absurd in England shows that the soil was fertile. Modern art too came only from elsewhere, and that rather late, even though England had helped to lay its foundations. One reason might be that though the orthodox, evangelical Christian groups did not as such play much part in the intellectual climate, yet their view on life had enough influence, as a salt that had not lost its flavour, to hold up the revolution against the bourgeois spirit. Also, the old consensus may be in ruins in Britain as elsewhere: but the ruins have often been well cared for instead of torn down.

But to return to the artists we have mentioned: Henry Moore of course was no newcomer. He was already doing his sculptures before the Second World War. His main theme has been the reclining figure, which he initially began to develop under the influence of ancient Mexican art. He wanted to make his sculptures look like natural things, like pebbles in the stream or rocks in the sea, worn down through the ages. This gives his sculptures a double impact: on the one hand they are human figures; on the other, rocks with holes in natural forms.

In the 1930s Moore was in close contact with the Surrealist movement, and even much later, in the 1950s, beside the sculptures just mentioned he made strange, absurd figures, mainly small bronzes, related to his other work and yet quite different from it. Just as with Picasso, Moore has different styles. In the course of time, I feel, the Surrealist prevailed, and modernity won over the more humanist elements in his earlier work until finally he was making large bronze abstract works, fantastically refined and strong in shape, and yet like existentialist *chiffres,* symbols for something unnameable, irrational, something deep and mystical almost like primordial products of natural forces.

In this respect he followed the same trend as many other great artists, such as Marino Marini, for instance, another great sculptor whose major theme of 'man on horseback' also got more abstract in the course of the years. It was as if the truth of the initially humanist theme of defeat, 'man' riding on nature without being able to tame it, was so deeply felt that gradually it took over even its means of expression, which began to show increasingly the decay and collapse of all forms and values even in the very piece of sculpture itself.

Francis Bacon is the other great English artist, a man whose images are horrible to look at and haunt the imagination. Images of misery, of despair, of alienation, of decay, of a world in which paralytic, neurotic, leprous schizoids move in cages, human beings become animal and yet remain human, a world in which people, having lost their heads, cry out for help, for reality, and yet are real even if lost in the void. His most famous works were a series of 'portraits', reinterpreting Velasquez's unsurpassed portrait of the pope in the Galleria Doria in Rome – of the pope which is very human, very 'normal', very beautiful and very much the great man (though not in a proud way).[92] Bacon's pictures are like caricatures, not so much of that particular pope as of humankind, not humorous images but great cries of despair for lost values and lost greatness, for a humanity deprived of its freedom, love, rationality, everything that the great humanist painters had celebrated for centuries as they drew on their Christian and classical tradition.

Bacon himself said about his art:

> Also, man now realizes that he is an accident, that he is a completely futile being, that he has to play out the game without reason. I think that even when Velasquez was painting, even when Rembrandt was painting, they were still, whatever their attitude to life, slightly conditioned by certain types of religious possibilities, which man now, you could say, has had cancelled out for him. Man now can only attempt to beguile himself for a time, by prolonging his life – by buying a kind of immortality through the doctors. You see, painting has become – all art has become – a game by which man distracts himself. And you may say that it always has been like that, but now it's entirely a game. What is fascinating is that it's going to become much more difficult for the artist, because he must really deepen the game to be any good at all, so that he can make life a bit more exciting.[93]

Pop and Op

Already in the 1950s, beginning in England, there was a reaction against the Abstract Expressionism that prevailed. This art, even if it celebrated human creativity, even if it demolished the image, even if it exalted the unreasoned, direct stroke, was esoteric, a kind of art for art's sake, works of art made by artists for the artistic few, a snobbish ivory tower. At least, that is what the artists who inaugurated the Pop movement thought.

They reacted by looking for their inspiration to the non-art imagery of our times, the cheap poster, the cartoon, the flag, numbers, illustrations from magazines, preferably the cheap ones. Or they started to copy the commonplace, the obvious, such as a can with brushes on the table in the studio. They exalted the image, accepted it positively, celebrated it, and made an art more real, more truly of this century. They found beauty in the things around us, in the style of the images around us. It was positive and fine. They used all the twentieth-century techniques – the collage, bringing the real thing into the picture, or pasting together popular images like the cinema ad's sex bomb, the bodybuilder, the vacuum cleaner and what not. Girls under showers, highways, the cliché from the cartoon, shelves with rows of Coca-Cola bottles, great American nudes, cars and roses, the American flag and so on were shown life-size, more than life-size, in a cataract of image upon image.

In a way it was positive and happy. Unfortunately our century has taught people to see the absurd in all these things, the commerciality, the cheapness of all the shining chrome, the emptiness and the superficiality. So together with the positive crept in the negative, the critical tone, the downgrading of many things which were not necessarily sacred yet prized or valued emotionally. Pop art has become in this way a kind of recast of Dada and Neo-Dada, a mixture of humour and rage, of smiles and tears, of condescending acceptance and irate rejection, of love and hate or life and death. It is a strange, sometimes fascinating, sometimes boring mixture of positive and negative elements and attitudes.

Pop art has brought the figure back into art, the 'normal' image, the human element that was so obviously lacking in the other modern streams. Maybe precisely because of its 'normality' we feel even more the element of crisis, of the death that has tinged so much of our present-day world. This was the work of Liechtenstein, Wesselman,[94] Rosenquist, Dine, Warhol,[95] Hamilton, Peter Blake, and so many more.

Alongside this has grown Op art. It derives from the Mondrian-type of 'pure' art, the experimentation with the possibilities of the visual in Tachist art, and probably too from the new development in typography, together with some of the elements of the Neo-Dada trend. Its abstract images, more often than not made of geometric forms, straight lines and circles, use all kinds of visual devices to get a static form into movement. It is an art of experimentation with visual means; it makes form configurations that have no other meaning apart from being a form configuration but yet make an impact on the mind and are at least interesting as configurations. As a kind of experiment with the possibilities of optic effects in art it yet makes designs that 'work' and have a frequently irritating effect on the onlooker.

To me it seems to be an art parallel to linguistic analysis. With this philosophy, born out of logical positivism, the idea was to keep away from all problems that are beyond human capabilities and to begin with language itself in order to find a way to come closer to truth. Yet this turning away from all deeper problems is not simply neutral. It is only possible when one does not want to accept not only god or God but anything transcendental. In the same way this almost clinically clean psychological experimentation with optical possibilities has the same deep roots as the other forms of art that engendered it.

Vasarely[96] and Soto are perhaps the best artists in the Op movement. Another is Paolozzi, who has made his name as an important representative of junk-sculpture and later created strange, absurd, Neo-Dada, hard-edge works such as the thing now in the Tate Gallery called *The city of the circle and the square* (1963). But since the 1950s this British artist has also worked in other media – literature, film (a film called *The*

History of Nothing) and graphic work. I quote from a catalogue of his prints exhibited in 1968 at the Amsterdam Stedelijk Museum:

> The series of serigraphs published in 1965 called *As is when* is based on the life and work of Ludwig Wittgenstein. From a collection of weaving-patterns, photographs, architectural drawings and so on were made collages. With the help of these the serigraphs were then made. The result was twelve prints that portray moments out of Wittgenstein's life or of ideas from his works (Paolozzi is equally inspired by Wittgenstein's going to watch a film as by his thoughts on reality and experience). Wittgenstein's ideas about playing with language are consciously expressed in Paolozzi's work. In connection with this playing with language he plays with optical elements, or makes new plays with fragments of existing languages or creates fragments of new languages. It is remarkable that he does not consider it important to give his playing with language any other meaning than the playing itself. The denial of this so-called meaning gives the playing, paradoxically, meaning, and translates it into magic objects.

Titles of his works in this line, graphic designs in strong primary colours, are *Universal electronic vacuum, Moonstrips empire news* and so on.

One inference one could draw from Paolozzi's preoccupation with Wittgenstein is that if we want to understand the deeper sense and meaning of Wittgenstein's work, surely one way of doing so is to use the art of a man like Paolozzi to get into it, to sense the real meaning, its irrational absurdity, its chance element, its magic and loss of meaning.

Happenings and hippies

As we have seen, the movement that was expressed in art was much wider than art. Its expression, too, was wider than the traditional forms of painting or sculpture or theatre. One of its manifestations was in the 'happenings' introduced around 1960. These were created by playwrights and artists, first in New York, then soon all over the world. They find their later development in total theatre. These wholly random happenings were often very much more than simply art: they were at the same time a new form of political demonstration – as with the Provos in Amsterdam in 1966 – and often a new kind of religious rite, or an orgiastic, mystical, atheistic, or rather nihilistic, cult.

Here too we find many kinds of movements and trends coming together: the most important, however, were the Neo-Dada movement and the Surrealist tradition. In the Dutch magazine *Randstad*, in an issue[97] completely devoted to the happening, we find mentioned among the 'precursors' many Surrealist or Dadaist manifestos or publications. Including as it does the political happening, we can safely say that the happening generally is a product of twentieth-century anarchism as this has been fostered and promoted by artistic movements. The anti-art movement was always basically a way of life, an attitude and a cult rather than a new art, even if in some ways it has been creative in forming new artistic means or even a style.

It is remarkable that in this movement we also find again and again the idea of destruction: in Vostell's decollages, for example, in which a TV image is destroyed, or Metzger's ideas, wanting to make a large piece of sculpture that decomposes slowly in the course of a few years. The idea of destruction even brought together an international group for a conference held in London in 1966 called the 'Destruction in Art' Symposium, showing the relationship between anarchistic activity and this type of art, together with the promotion of the obscene and much else. And in 1967 another congress, on the dialectics of revolution, took place in London, and was attended by people such as Ginsberg, Goodman, Laing, Stokeley Carmichael, Marcuse, Eliade and so on.[98] Art and the revolutionary spirit seem increasingly to be one.

What is a happening? It is a kind of instantaneous free play in which all people present participate. It induces a kind of traumatic state of mind, just as in the more static environments, which bring us into an absurd, strange and frustrating situation where our own psychological reaction is a part of the effect. Happenings were prepared for by the Surrealist exhibitions in the 1930s in which Marcel Duchamp played an important role, and his is the presiding influence in this new form of activity. Its impact has been great, not least in its influence on the sort of environmental manipulation of visitors at World Fairs and other exhibitions.

An example from the issue of *Randstad* already quoted will give an idea of what a happening is. It describes one held in 1962 on the island of Ibiza, where many artists came together. It was organized by an American who had participated in New York happenings in 1959:

> Fifty-seven people came together in a small room. We had arranged to play an Ornette Coleman record on a too quick speed, but later in the programme. Somebody, one of the public, put on the record much too soon ... I felt myself swept away, losing all feeling of identity ... Bob, clothed in animal skins, who was doing a bird-dance, was just as surprised as I. We looked each other in the eyes. Then my I stopped being. I was dissolved, washed away in the total energy of the room ... A blue light switched on ... It was just done at random by a girl ... all individual feeling and thinking had disappeared.

One reason for the happenings to emerge was the revolt of artists against the snobbery of the art dealers and their clients. They felt that their works of art which cried out 'absurdity', 'destroy', 'this world is meaningless', 'we are all dead', were hung on the wall, provided with a tag and a lamp, and were then objects of high artistic discussion for people more interested in status, in investment, in novelty and escape from boredom than in anything they said. A happening cannot be tampered with, as it does not happen to remain longer than the thing lasts.

But it turned loose many forces and had a deep impact. It was one more proof that the times were ripe, that the modern movement has won the battle – even though there may still be many who do not belong to it. Many, however, do not dare or do not care to challenge or oppose it. When they do they must carry the burden not only of being called old-fashioned but also of being called authoritarian or not understanding the new quest for freedom.

Freedom, that was at bottom the catchword of the movement. Anarchistic freedom. It was the same spirit which inspired another movement that caught the world's attention: the hippies. It started in San Francisco and then caught on in New York, in England and in many other centres of the world. In a way it was a kind of bohemian life, something that formerly was found only in some circles of artists – loose morals, drugs, a kind of asocial behaviour. It was now offered in a new form and with new slogans: drop out, tune in, turn on. It was an anarchist movement, looking for freedom, for authenticity, for a life that really was life and not a struggle for money and a career. It was a revolutionary movement, even if it was not aggressive. In it, many of the elements brought forward by the modern art movement and the new philosophy were synthesized. Just as it was not by chance that the Provo movement with its happenings started in Amsterdam, the city of the famous Stedelijk Museum of Modern Art, so San Francisco did not just happen to be the first hippie centre, simply because there were many students there. San Francisco was the centre of the new American literature, where many of the so-called beat generation, contemporary with the English Angry Young Men, a kind of existentialist literary movement from the early 1950s, had flocked together. The most important of them were Alan Watts, who had occupied himself with Zen Buddhism and similar concerns, Snyder and Allen Ginsberg. Their creed and protest are epitomized in Ginsberg's famous poem 'Howl':

> I saw the best minds of my generation destroyed by madness,
> starving hysterical naked, ...
> What sphinx of cement and aluminium
> bashed open their skulls and ate up
> their brains and imagination?
> Moloch! Solitude! Filth! Ugliness! ...
> Moloch the incomprehensible prison! ...

It is a long, emotionally loaded poem which sums up all the tears, the disillusionments of a generation that is witnessing the end of our Western civilization, great in its technology, great in its organization, but without an answer to the basic human questions, with God murdered, a generation left to live in a world hopeless, forlorn, desperate, frustrated, full of agony, a world over which Moloch reigns. God is dead and Moloch reigns – this at least implies that the void is still felt, that people are still seeking for answers, that the spiritual is a void. Yet people are crying out for the spiritual, for the true Truth, for the Way, for Life. The hippie question is there in all its despair. Do we have the answer? Or is the answer just another old formula? It is the same question again: Is there a life before death?

It was in this environment of protest and desperate search for meaning and sense, for freedom and real values, that the young hippies moved. Many came from well-to-do homes, from Christian backgrounds, from the classrooms of the better colleges and universities; they came to live an anarchistic and antinomian life. In a way it was like the extreme wing of the old Anabaptist movement again, if not in a Christian form: it was passive, but liable to break out at any time into a war-like activism to conquer the world for a utopian kingdom of God. Free love, nudism, the use of drugs, a new religion looking for a God who is not personal and not interested in the things of this world – why should he be, said these grandchildren of the gnostics of old, abhorring the idea of creed and definitive definitions.

And a new art came with them. An art that was able to express their anti-rationalist yet intellectual mysticism, their trances and unity-with-all, their joys and wavering truth, their humanitarianism and yet revolutionary being-different, their uninhibited sex and love as sublimation.

They found their inspiration in Art Nouveau, another art of protest against rationalism and technology, another art that sought for the mystical and mysterious, for freedom in subjectivity and indulgence in sex. The forms created by William Blake were used again a century and a half later as an expression of the very same basic ideas.

And so the psychedelic forms emerged: posters, patterns on clothes or in body-painting, illustrations in the many underground press magazines. They were influential. The hippie movement may be a subculture, as *Time* called it, but it has influenced the Western world more deeply and widely than many people realize. And with its forms some of its basic philosophy spread, even if tamed or made bourgeois.

This is not the place to go into details, for their art is now a familiar one: endless moving forms, figures and ornamentation fused into a swirling whole, letters like flames or clusters of forms, asymmetry, colours in all shades and kinds but never really loud, and in a way sweet and subdued, the whole making a bizarre effect without being shocking.[99] If it is sometimes shocking, it is in its very free representation of nudity and sex, not in its style. In a way there is a search for beauty, for beautifying the surroundings, rather than the shabbiness of Pop and Neo-Dada.

But hippie art is more than just visual forms. It is music, dance, light-play, a kind of total art that takes the whole person into a kind of magic, mystic whole (even though sometimes aided by drugs), a kind of neo-pagan ritual not excluding its orgiastic aspects. In this there is continuity with the movement of the happenings. But here there is apparent again the quest for a kind of beauty, though an informal, improvised one, rather than the exaltation of the ugly and desperate that made happenings often disgusting.

The music that belongs to this is rock or pop.

Jazz, blues and rock

Any analysis of our times that ignored music would be incomplete, and so I must briefly examine the rise of a musical form that expresses very much the same message as the arts I have been discussing.

At other times, for instance in the seventeenth and eighteenth centuries, before the deep, dissolving effects of the Enlightenment became apparent, there was a unity in the whole culture. As far as music was concerned there were different streams, and certainly different kinds, church music, for instance, or opera, chamber music, dance music, and many more. But there was no break in society. Ordinary churchgoers in Leipzig would listen to Bach's cantatas in church. Even if they did not understand the supreme quality and depth of the music, they could enjoy it. The music was not written for an elite. Nor were the simpler and folksier kinds of music strange to the ears of the cultivated. There was a sense of normality and genuineness about all this music that made it everybody's music. The nineteenth century made music into a kind of refined, cultural, almost pseudo-religious revelation of humanism, composed by the great heroes and prophets of humankind. Everyday music became vulgar and coarse, low and without truly human qualities – with the exception of the waltzes of Strauss and other kinds of simple classical music for the uneducated.

The twentieth century made the split complete, particularly with the advent of modern music with its weird sounds and lack of consonance. So now we have three kinds of music, roughly speaking: widely revered classical music; true modern music, appreciated only by intellectual modernists; and popular entertainment music, apparently of no quality and no cultural import. Perhaps we should add a fourth kind of music: the hymns sung in church and popular choral music, both also remnants of a great musical past and not yet devoid of all its qualities though often artistically poor.

In the first few decades of our century entertainment music (dance music and popular songs) was shallow and devoid of musical interest and power. Into this world burst jazz and blues. They came from quite a different background and from an unpredictable quarter, from the African-American section in the USA, from the freed slaves. Western psalmody and hymnody, the surviving older types of Anglo-Saxon folk music and brass-band marches were interpreted by a poor and uneducated people that had a special gift for music, for rhythm and melody, with only dim recollections of the musical traditions of the Africa of their ancestors. Out of all this grew new kinds of music: the Negro spiritual, a development of the hymns of the Wesleyan type, the folksongs and particularly the completely original blues, and then jazz, born in New Orleans but soon dispersed all over the USA to wherever there was a black ghetto.

Louis Armstrong in 1927 sang,

> I'm not rough, and I don't bite,
> but the woman that gets me, got to squeeze me tight,
> 'cause I'm crazy 'bout my loving,
> and I must have it all the time

in a voice that to a Western ear could only be called rough indeed. This one stanza forms the middle of a record with the strong, seemingly unsophisticated, fierce trumpet playing of Louis himself, the soaring clarinet of Johnny Dodds and the pulsating rhythm of a music that to Western ears could only sound new, exhilarating, uninhibited and filled to the brim with life – all of which was missing in the sweet and dull and unimaginative entertainment music of the day.

So young people took up the music, and loved it, in a revolt against all that was namby-pamby in their own culture, against the shallowness and commerciality that seemed to symbolize their own world. Taking this music, scorned by what we would now call the 'establishment', was in itself an act of protest, even if only a mild one. The result, in the 1930s was the jazz clubs, where the new music was studied, records collected and exchanged. People listened not only to jazz but also soon to the blues that could be heard on many rare collector's items, records from Race series originally released in the black ghettos and now cherished by the happy few who could lay hands on them. What this music meant to the African-Americans themselves is another question. More often than not the real African-American was far out of sight of these youngsters, who nevertheless loved the music and discussed whether any white person would ever be able to make music as good as this. Hot music. Hot jazz. The blues of Bessie Smith and Ma Rainey, or of legendary names like Blind Lemon Jefferson, Kokomo Arnold or Barbecue Bob.

Jazz in the 1930s had a great influence on entertainment music, and African-American musicians such as Fletcher Henderson and others began to shape a new music to be played by whites – the bands with big names and popularity such as Benny Goodman's and Artie Shaw's. They turned this music into a rage, and the new streamlined swing was all over the world. The jazz clubs did not like it at all: their jazz had been stolen from them and turned into another bourgeois music, commercial jazz.

Many of the musicians did not like it either, especially the blacks, who felt that their music had been betrayed and misused and turned into a white gimmick.

Around 1940 there was a reaction. A new music emerged, 'bop' or modern jazz, created by intelligent, well-trained young African-American musicians. It was much influenced by modern music, with the existentialist undertones of protest, rage, agony and despair. It was melancholy, an exaltation of the individual's ability to achieve something difficult. As far as the jazz clubs were concerned this was not the jazz they looked for – it was too far off, too difficult, they were not yet ready to accept the modern sounds and disjointed melodies. But they discovered that the old New Orleans jazz still lived; and they got hold of it and a New Orleans renaissance took place, almost exclusively for white people. Or they got hold of the real folk blues; hearing a man who has been a murderer and a convict sing of his sexual experiences is not exactly soft and sweet – it is the real stuff, strong as life itself, even if it was only a voice of a man on the platform.

Another protest came, this time neither intellectual nor modern. Modern jazz in a way was a sign of acculturation, the African-American coming to grips with the modern movement. The other protest was as black as could be, non-intellectual, very forceful, a music in which all seemingly black elements were exalted, a music that was really too hard for white ears. For years rhythm-and-blues was a music only the African-American people knew and listened to. They enjoyed a music that they knew was not the white man's choice and that could not be stolen. Or could it?

Out of the New Orleans revival came the Dixieland movement. Dixieland was white people trying hard to play the old New Orleans jazz. Some idealists really played it pure, authentic and 'original', and abhorred all compromise. But others turned it into a new kind of entertainment, catering to the dancing crowd. But in this way the lilting, joyful music, strong and intricate, became dulled and tame, and cliché was heaped upon cliché. So jazz again was losing its force and ability to be a symbol and expression of protest.

Therefore a new music emerged, again completely non-intellectual, with a thumping rhythm and shouting voices, each line and each beat full of the angry insult to all Western values, if these could be called values, of music or of culture or of behaviour. Rock-and-roll rolled in – rhythm-and-blues was, about ten years after it began, borrowed by the whites.

In the years after the Second World War some of the US black churches were booming – whether it was really a revival or what it meant precisely is hard to say, though there was certainly much real if utterly non-intellectual Christianity involved. They created a new music, 'gospel', mostly sung by quartets of men or women, or by soloists like Mahalia Jackson. In the groups the responsive pattern was characteristic:

one voice takes the lead, the other voices form a driving, rhythmic, answering refrain.

This device was often taken over by the rhythm-and-blues groups, and so it came into rock-and-roll. Other elements were added. From the folk blues came the harmonica. The rhythm changed. It became a new style, and at least some groups of young people knew it. It was still outlawed by the establishment, and the protest was felt in the roughness and the lack of sophistication.

But it was in the 1960s that things really clicked. It began in England, and was called 'beat'. Everyone knew the Beatles, the Rolling Stones, and all the rest. At first most of the songs were simply stolen from blues, rhythm-and-blues, rock-and-roll and all kinds of black folk songs, heard on the sometimes rare records. But soon new compositions were made. However it happened, 'beat' conquered the world. The new movement of protest and non-Western cultural standards, as such non-humanist, was winning, if not the whole of society, then certainly the younger generation. It was everywhere.

Of course, the bearers of the modern tradition tried to ignore it at first. They had put their stakes on modern music, *musique concrète*, electronic music, the chance music of John Cage, the new sound of Stockhausen. In the same way they by-passed Neo-Art Nouveau, which did not get a showing in modern art galleries and remained a kind of underground art, reaching the new multitudes of the young, the new generation. It would seem almost a tragedy that the very moment the ideas of the modern movement reached a wide audience and gained influence, the older modernists ignored it as they had their own cherished standard of shock and renewal and protest. Yet in 'beat' (with the better groups), as well as with Neo-Art Nouveau hippie art, the old wounds of culture were beginning to heal, the break was covered, the gap closed. A new culture begins to emerge that leaves the old standards far behind, a neo-paganistic primitivism, a new way of life of which this art forms an integral part. Western culture, as built since the Renaissance and the Reformation, slowly undermined since the Enlightenment, is still there, but as a tottering ruin, while the new culture is coming in. The new emerging artforms are still full of the battle-cry and make up the revolution in which we are living. The new culture is only slowly evolving. But its shape is already seen.

Rock groups, protest singers, folk singers, these are the people forming the new art still in the making. Their protest is in their music itself as well as in the words, for those who think that this is all cheap and no more than entertainment have never used their ears. Of course, there are many imitations, many who take advantage of the situation to make money, and there is much that is simply popular music which is borrowing the tricks and forms of the real rock. How could it be otherwise in our Western society? And there are of course plenty of bad groups as well as the good ones – there has always been variety of quality in any style. But in dismissing some of the exponents of the form we cannot afford to dismiss the message, which is heard by millions, often on a subliminal level and therefore subconsciously brainwashing them, from pop radio stations all over the world. We cannot simply stop it, nor is it wise to close our ears. We have to cope with it and at least understand its message.

8
Protest, Revolution and the Christian Response

> Everywhere I hear the sound of marching, charging feet, boy
> 'Cause summer's here and the time is right for fighting in the street, boy[100]

The times in which we live are not a unity, of course, any more than any other period of history has been. Different streams and movements are working side by side. But a period is characterized by the most powerful main movements of the day, powerful either because they have a large number of adherents or because they have, apparently at least, a fitting answer to the problems of the moment.

When we speak of 'our period' we are thinking of Western culture. But we must realize that Western culture has grown, at least geographically, because of its influence on other countries. Modern artists may well be from Argentine or Brazil. Films are made in Japan as well as in the USA or Europe. The cultural situation does not coincide with the economic, though it is closely bound to it. This is not the place to deal with the problem of whether modern technology can be 'exported' without also exporting the basic implications of Western culture. But it would certainly seem that we are exporting with our sciences the crisis of our own culture, undermining the religious and social systems of the non-Western world.[101]

The arts today (thinking particularly now of the visual arts) are diversified. Many artists are still working in the ways of the nineteenth century, their work being impressionistic, or at least naturalistic, using the technical principles of the classical period of the sixteenth to the eighteenth century. Yet one feels that they are increasingly losing ground. They are repeating old formulas and, in keeping the older traditions alive, are standing aside from the main streams of today – certainly from those of the last decade which with revolutionary force are breaking down everything that has no deep roots to stand against them.

Pop art, new forms of caricaturing art, strange new forms of Surrealism, these are the things which are constantly reclaiming our attention. Most of it, to some degree at least, is critical of the world we live in. *Time* magazine, for instance, said this at the end of a review of Westermann's strange 'sculptures': 'His innocence is only a mask for a stilled malice directed against a society he thinks has gone mad . . . His visual jokes are intuitional and may indeed have no rational point. But they end up as a kind of emotional fishhook, snagged in the memory.

They are images not wholly explicable, but impossible to dislodge.'[102]

The modern movement has now emerged from the smaller art dealer's shows or the larger exhibitions in the galleries of modern art. It has come out into the open. Its products can be bought in the large department stores. In Holland, for instance, signed copies of Niki de St Phalle's *Nana* were sold at relatively low prices at the end of 1968. Of these Nanas, Pop-like sculptures of sexy females in glowing colours, it was said: 'They are feasting. One can only feast at the cost of others. Gentlemen, it is at the cost of us that this happens. They kick our bellies, our armies, our morals; they jump our philosophies, they make the grand finale on our nation. Traitoresses.'[103]

Niki is the wife of Tinguely, the man who makes the absurd machines, another anarchist. Together they made the huge image of *Hon*, a sculpture of a nude woman of enormous size which one could enter, through the pudenda of course. It was an exhibit in the Stockholm Museum of Modern Art. Thousands came to see it. Has the modern movement won?

One can also of course make works of art in series, by mechanical reproduction. In this way you can buy a work of modern art at a low price. Op art and 'minimal art' are very suited to this type of work.

Minimal art could be an illustration of something Klee said in his diary in 1915: 'The more horrible this world is, the more abstract art will be, while a happier world brings forth a more realistic (*diesseitige*) art.' Minimal art uses the least possible number of elements. Often it plays with a rhythmic arrangement of the same very simple forms, sometimes it presents a cube as sculpture. In recent years there has grown from this an art that has been called 'hard-edge', that presents forms in simple configurations or 'paintings' with very basic forms in bright colours, all done in a meticulous, technically perfect way, often using new materials. Yet this art has strong emotional overtones that echo what was said in the quotation from *Time* magazine about Westermann above.

The art scene today is made up of strong extremes. It may seem strange that while the visual arts are predominantly abstract and certainly not realistic, the film as an artform is not going in the same direction. It has developed many new techniques, but its main concern is still with reality – the nude that has been considered outmoded on the canvas is here in all its photogenic reality. Yet this does not mean that the film is not touched by the modern movement. Of Bergman, *Time* said that the body of his twenty-nine films 'now amounts to a great literature of heroic despair'.[104] In some films the distinction between 'reality' and imagination is blurred. One no longer knows whether what one sees is what is supposed to be going on in the person's mind, whether it is an aesthetic idea or whether it represents the 'real' story. Yet reality is there. It is sometimes no more than straight, hard reality with no comment. But we must question whether this is really still reality at all or whether it is, in a very different way, just as 'abstract' as the non-figurative visual arts.

Art in a way is dying – as a high human endeavour. It has lost its Romantic high quality; it is coming back to reality. We should not weep because another humanist myth has lost its hold on people. But what has come into its place but anti-art, just as there is anti-philosophy, anti-theatre and so on? It testifies to the fact that art is in a deep crisis at the same time that it is attracting so much attention. Borderline cases can be found, as in minimal art, or the art of Fontana (a canvas with a razor slit, is that really art?) or the music of John Cage which is either noise produced by chance or even complete silence (Cage called his book on music *Silence*). Yet in another way one often feels that art has really become superfluous. After seeing the 'Documenta' exhibition in Kassel in the autumn of 1968, having gone through the Op art section, I felt that Piccadilly Circus or Broadway with their neon advertising are much more fascinating, more fun and more meaningful – even perhaps more artistic.

Maybe the real art of our times, comprising both the aesthetic and the imagination and command of technique, is to be found in advertising, or in magazine layout, or in the graphic design of leaflets or even in scientific drawings. Or there is the often very fine visual means of depicting statistics, and so on. The forms are often strongly influenced by modern High Art, but they have got a meaning, a sense, have become 'normal' and to the point. They have become human and so they live.

Even when abstract forms are used in a brochure or on a book cover they are appropriate to their function, because they have no pretensions to mean something of great depth, but simply evoke a certain feeling or idea. This is the exact opposite of what happens in much minimal art in which, for instance, forms are used that have been inspired by iron tubes in factories or girders in buildings. What often had a fascinating beauty in its own setting, fulfilling a specific task, is strange and almost hallucinatory when emptied of sense and context.

Perhaps too most real art today is in television. There are not only the often very imaginative openings, using drawings, letters, animated figures, photography and so on, but also the representation of many aspects of reality, quite apart from news film and the direct documentary. But maybe it is indeed 'cool communication', suggesting its message through the medium, but never 'reasoning' about it, never defining its value or relating it to an absolute. The message often is hard-core reality, 'facts' themselves, and that is all. TV belongs to the modern world quite as much as the avant-garde cinema. On the screen we can watch with our own eyes the emergence of a new world.

The search for humanity

'When the mode of the music changes, the walls of the city shake,' wrote Tuli Kupferberg.[105] The mode has changed. Are the walls really shaking?

There is a deep dichotomy in our culture, a duality as deep as if there are two different sets of reality. A few years ago there was a cartoon in the *New Yorker* showing a modern box-like building with an abstract wallpainting on it. The caption said: 'The more rational the building, the more irrational the painting.' This sums up the problem and the inherent disharmony of our times.

As we have seen, it all began when people wanted to be autonomous, when they lit the torch of their own reason and resolved to start only from their senses – with the 'enlightenment' of the Age of Reason. And so the sciences have acquired a new meaning of almost religious significance, and reality is equated with what can be seen, weighed, measured, heard. The rest is only secondary reality, not only based on the material and the biological but, in a way, resulting from it: 'struggle for life', 'evolution', 'libido' and 'sublimation' have become the keywords for understanding human reality, and human being is now nothing but a 'naked ape'. This is what I described in an earlier chapter as 'man in the box'. People, being human however, tries again and again to evade the logic of their own position and searches for their true self, their humanity, their freedom, even if they can only do so by means of sheer irrationality or completely unfounded mysticism.

People today are in revolt against the world in which they live, against its dehumanizing tendencies, against slavery under the bosses of the new Galbraith elite, under a computerized bureaucracy, against alienation and the loneliness of the mass person. They search frantically for a new world. They are willing to risk the hardship of revolution. The tragedy is that people have no new principles to offer. All their endeavours result only in a world that is even more consistent with the principles of the Enlightenment, of autonomous humanity – autonomous yet reduced to atoms or rabbits.

In a way this revolt is something to be welcomed. It proves that people are still human, and that deep inside they still know that they cannot be in the box, that they are more than an atom or a rabbit.

'Something is happening here, and you don't know what it is, do you, Mr Jones?' sings Bob Dylan. He points to the fact that many feel and sense that there is something changing, yet they do not see the reasons for the change or the principles behind it, and so they fear it. Some say optimistically it is just a symptom of the third industrial revolution, and all the turmoil today is only a sign that people have not yet adjusted to the new situation in which technology, in a new, even more all-embracing form, is to shape the new world. But then, if this were true, we are even more bedevilled by technology. Is there no way out?

Those who put their faith in a perfected technology have of course some grounds for their optimism, even if they also have their problems. We are living in an advanced world, better equipped than any before to tackle the great problems of humankind: housing, transport, safety, health, home comforts, efficiency. We have better communications, safer systems, more convenient utensils, better organization. Much of our Western society is wealthy, affluent. Economics, by applying the methods of the sciences, has been able to break through old barriers; together with sociology it has been the means of providing for everyone goods and services previously undreamt of. No longer is the world one with a happy few, a small class at the top, and masses of the nameless poor at the bottom. Democracy, leisure and convenience for everyone have been achieved well, but perhaps not quite as well for we are uncomfortably aware of the areas where they have not yet arrived.

Certainly the world is a fast-changing one: air transport is faster and within the reach of an ever increasing number of people. Television, in the course of one or two decades, has changed the habits, knowledge and whole outlook on the world of a large majority of the people. Cars are now a commodity instead of a luxury. More people get better schooling and higher education at university and college level. Books are cheap and within the reach of all. People live longer as a result of the rapidly advancing medical care and research.

All this is true, and many of these things have no doubt led to much greater happiness and satisfaction in life for many. No one wants to undo them or go back to being without them or deny their importance. Nor can it be denied that they all have a deep influence on our lives. Certainly one aspect of the crisis of our age is to be found in the fact that we have not yet completely adjusted to them; we have not yet found the right attitude to them, for we are often still like children completely taken up with a new toy. But the overwhelming ecological problems of today show that we must stop playing at random: our utensils may destroy us, our machines cause the decay of the very earth on which they stand. Perhaps we have bought our affluence at too high a price.

Our world is changing, and we with it. It has become much larger as our horizons have widened; but also much smaller, for we get instant information on problems and events in places far away. We get involved in things we have never even thought of before. So our world has become much more complex, and in our answers to the problems of life we have to cope with far more factors than ever before.

All this means that Christians must go through a period of study, thought and re-evaluation that will take much of our energy. Conflicts will arise within Christian circles, as older people, especially, are not consciously aware of this need for reorientation and therefore think that the old answers are still valid and sufficient. It is not that the foundation has to change or that the basic doctrines have lost their meaning. But the expression and formulation of them sometimes needs rethinking as we listen afresh to God's word and seek to present it to the new world in which we are living.

The whole cultural situation, however, is much more complex than can be dealt with simply by asserting that we have to adjust and rethink. There are many negative elements in the technocracy of today. We must find out what they really are, think through the means of removing them or, at least, of formulating our attitude to them.

We must also learn to react positively to the positive elements of the revolt and protest around us. For it, too, is against the evils of technocracy. We must rejoice in the fact that people are shown to be still human by their protest against the forces that would dehumanize them. We must be alert to see that the lawless and negative revolutionary elements do not obscure the real issues, so that they do not become themselves an obstruction to finding the solution they seek.

Plastic people

Technology is to be welcomed insofar as it offers people new tools and possibilities. But it becomes a real menace to the humanness of people, their freedom and personality, when it becomes an idol, a technocracy. For then a tool is made into an idea, a means into an end, a method into a truth. People become no more than consumers squeezed into the mould of a standardized, dehumanized pseudo-people by the pressures of the advertising industry. As our consumer goods become standardized, so our homes become standardized, *we* become standardized, rolling off the conveyor belt of modern technocracy. Surely we can understand the protest of one of the younger Dutch poets who said: 'What is creativity? A man in Boston, Massachusetts has covered the wall of his drawing room, his study, his bedroom, his closet and his kitchen with sealskins painted white, orange, blue, yellow . . .'

Television is a focus of our standardized homes. Here too, inbuilt in the programmes, is one view, one approach to reality. Sometimes the programmers are consciously trying to convince us of a certain view, but more often they just go on making their programmes without being conscious that they are in fact brainwashing their public. It is their job to be new and up to the minute, which means that they are compelled to follow the latest trends and insights and ideas, often without any attempt to come to grips with their underlying principles. So modern views are constantly 'preached' in a most effective way: effective because it is not intended or overt, so that we are not on our guard against it. The message is there, from pop music up to the most sophisticated 'cultural' programme and the most intellectual lecture.

Indeed, if we want to stand for freedom, human freedom, we have to keep our eyes open for this danger of manipulation. We must point it out wherever it becomes apparent. But we must realize that protests alone do not help. Those who are responsible for it often do not, and cannot, see its consequences. So it is our task to instruct the public, and particularly our own younger generation, that they may see and be aware of this inbuilt scientism, this faith in autonomous humanity that is constantly flung at them. Understanding is the first step against all manipulation, for manipulation can only be effective insofar as it works as a hidden persuader.

There are two results from the view that technocracy is all, that a person is solely determined by economic, sociological, psychological and biological laws, that ideas, religion and everything else which is human are no more than secondary reflexes, sublimation, rationalizations, the result of conditioning. The first is the idea that if things do not go well, the system has to be changed. But a change of system is not going to improve the situation if the spirit underlying the system is not altered. The second result is that people are just plastic.

'Man is plastic' is the very clever formulation given by the Theatre of the Absurd for the human situation. 'Man is plastic' – as dead, as machine-like, as ugly, as open to manipulation, as cheap and as banal as plastic. Plastic, the supreme product of technocracy, the fruit of research, organization, big capital, large factories, clever selling techniques. 'Plastic people' is a phrase that has become almost a slogan.

Our affluent society, our modern science and security and health, our gadgets and luxuries that were beyond even the great, wealthy kings of the past, all these things, none of them evil in themselves, have made people not human and free but manipulated, plastic; for the spirit of the age is in it all. What could have been a blessing has so often become a curse. Instead of making a person free, they enslave him or her. Instead of bringing life, they bring death. It is at this very time, in the face of all these great achievements of humankind, that people are in revolt against the dehumanizing, the alienation, the frustration, the one-dimensionality, the atom-ness and rabbit-ness of being. People are crying out for their humanity, their human-ness. But where is it to be found? For we are really no more than conditioned robots, religion is just another idea of our own, something to give us the tranquillizing thought that we are more than highly complex bundles of atoms evolved in a long history, looking at ourselves . . .

Beyond the material

People want to be human. Caught in technocracy, in computerized bureaucracy, they try to wrestle free. But to get this freedom they must 'jump out of the box', find a freedom outside technocracy, outside the world of naturalistic law and determinism. For modern people understand reality only in terms of scientism. So they have to, it would seem, get out of reality. They become mystics.

There is no age as mystical as ours. Yet it is mysticism with a difference: it is a nihilistic mysticism, for God is dead. Very old ideas are being revived: gnosticism, Neoplatonic ideas of reality emanating from and returning to God, and Eastern religion, a religion with a god that is impersonal and universalist, a god which (not who!) is everything and therefore nothing, with a salvation that is in the end self-annihilation. In the quest for humanity people are even willing to lose their identity, their personality. It is like the creed that the Beatles sing (on their *Sergeant Pepper Lonely Hearts Club Band* record): 'When you've seen beyond yourself . . . the time will come when you see we're all one and life flows on within you and without you.'

We must understand the issue at stake: people search for their humanity and for real reality, reality that is more than the brain can encompass and the eye can see. People search for water – water that is the beauty of the waterfall, the drink offered to the thirsty, also the dirt in the ditch, the rain that beats in our faces, the cold snow as well as the hot bath at home . . . and they hope to find it in a mystic unity, in which water is me and I am water and all is one and all is God! Water that has been reduced to H_2O has been deprived of its reality as water. For every aspect of reality is God – and people today want to experience God. It is not faith or knowledge which is the keyword but experience.

For the same reason they are willing to follow the ways of Zen, in which reality is accepted and yet overcome by being by-passed, and people have become free by being able to transcend the dilemmas of life and thought. Zen has had a great attraction in our times, and many artists have been influenced by it – Mark Tobey, for instance, and the poet Alan Watts, one of the hippie leaders in 1967. Zen seemed to give an answer to the deep questions and offered the wisdom of a long tradition when Western people were just beginning their stumbling search for a new way.

So people in their quest for humanity, in their search for a way of escape from the world of scientism, technocracy and the affluent society, from everything that is rational, become irrational: something ununderstandable, something alien that one cannot talk about in sensible and 'normal' speech, that one cannot discuss and certainly cannot explain. So people have come to live in a twofold world – the rationalist 'box', and the irrational domain of freedom and Being.

In our times this dichotomy has become very deep and radical but it is not new. Ever since the Enlightenment, people have dealt with reality in a double way: reason and Romanticism, positivism and idealism, naturalistic reality and the realm of human freedom in the arts, religion and morals. Kant in his great philosophical synthesis of the many attempts made to evolve a new system based on the principles of the Enlightenment – Descartes, Hobbes, Locke, Hume, Diderot and Rousseau – formulated this duality, this doubleness, in his *Critique of Pure Reason* and his *Critique of Practical Reason*. Kant still dreamt of providing a unity in his answer to the deep problem of the nature of reality. But later Hegel realized that we must accept at the same time the yes and the no, the thesis and the antithesis, for we cannot get hold of the unity. And Kierkegaard understood that therefore faith had to be a jump away from reason. In our own time the existentialists have taken up the theme and highlighted the dilemma humanity are in.

Existentialism is the end of the philosophical tradition that begins with Descartes and was firmly established in the Age of Reason. It is the end, and also the logical conclusion of its premises. William Barrett writes about this as follows:

> As a canny and sagacious Frenchman, he (Descartes) proposed to abide by the customs of his time and place (which included the practice of religion). Hence, when he launched himself into the Doubt, he made certain of securing his lines of communication behind him; he took no chances when he made the descent into the painful night of the void. The next step after the certitude of the *Cogito*, the 'I think', this turns out to be a proof of the existence of God; and with God as guarantee the whole world of nature, the multitude of things with their fixed nature or essences that the mind may now know, is re-established around Descartes. Sartre, however, is the Cartesian doubter at a different place and time: God is dead, and no longer guarantees to this passionate and principled atheist that vast structure of essences, the world, to which his freedom must give assent. As a modern man, Sartre remains in that anguish of nothingness in which Descartes floated before the miraculous light of God shone to lead him out of it. For Sartre there is no unalterable structure of essences or values given prior to man's own existence. That existence has meaning, finally, only as the liberty to say No, and by saying No to create a world. If we remove God from the picture, the liberty which reveals itself in the Cartesian doubt is total and absolute; but thereby also the more anguished, and this anguish is the irreducible destiny and dignity of man. Here Cartesianism has become more heroic – and more demoniacal.[106]

Heidegger, Jaspers, Sartre, Camus, each in his own right and in his own way, speak of the absurdity of humanity, the meaninglessness of their being, of the quest for ultimate experience and for the way people can postulate their essential being by starting from their own existence. Keywords are agony, fear, angst, boredom, becoming, nothingness, the nauseating, ultimate failure. And, of course, freedom, existentialist freedom, 'out of the box', beyond the material.

So people, existential people, try desperately to find some meaning and seek it in some sort of ultimate experience, a kind of irrational, nihilistic experience that will prove their humanity and their freedom to be, a freedom 'out of the box'. It is a freedom that has nothing of the openness and peace that Christian freedom brings. The experience of ultimate reality means that a moment in one's life has to give meaning to the whole of it; it brings no joy, it is no salvation. Human being is after all 'being unto death', *Sein zum Tode*, and death is the ultimate absurdity of being human. For many this is all too remote: they are the ones who sit at the wayside, waiting for Godot (as Beckett put it), waiting for Godot (God? another source of meaning?) ... but Godot never comes!

The artist is the prophet of this search for meaning beyond reality. 'Music is a prayer, a message from God, it is freedom, beyond the material,' said Albert Ayler, a leader of the new wave in jazz of 1965. It is nothing new for art to be given this role. Ever since the beginning of the Enlightenment, art has been separated off from the sciences and assigned the realm of freedom and humanity. Romanticism further elevated art, particularly literature and music, to the highest domains of humanity and gave it the function of revealing the deep realms of truth. Galleries were built as temples of art, for art was to be the great high priest and prophet of humanistic humanity. And so in our own day too, art is given a lofty role. The artist's task is to reveal the deep, irrational secrets of reality, the reality beyond the material, behind the appearances. At the same time artists have the task of interpreting their times, to have a prophetic insight into the important trends and meaning of all that goes on. Today this almost invariably means that artists have to be critical of current values and norms. This last idea is a rather newer one and is the result of the fusion of age-old ideas about the seer-artist with the new notion of an ever changing historical situation.[107]

What I have been saying was well expressed by Finley Eversole in his preface to a collection of essays published under the title *Christian Faith and the Contemporary Arts*.[108] He writes:

> 'The human race,' says Graham Greene, 'is implicated in some terrible aboriginal calamity.' It is this fact, reported and interpreted in the art of our time, which gives the forms of contemporary art the appearance of 'chaos'. It is this fact also which forces upon the artists of the present age their prophetic role. Indeed, it is not the preacher or the sociologist who speak to us most clearly of the 'crisis in civilization' in which we are involved, but the artist. Our art, then, is an art of anguish and guilt, of isolation and emptiness, of doubt and damnation. Contemporary art has rediscovered the irrational – in the depth of the demonic! Yet our art has discovered, as the art of no other generation has, the meaning of freedom, of courage, of inwardness and honesty ... Modern art, with its loss of God and the human image, is the drama of our age. Here we see what *really* is happening to man, to society, and to man's faith in God.

Drugs – and religion

But there is another way of reaching out to the beyond and of experiencing a reality that is outside the realm of common sense, the technological, and the establishment with its capitalism and security: drugs. With drugs, it is said, we can reach a vision of the world transcending anything we experience normally. We can have expanded minds, we can see what 'they' cannot see.

Why the drug? We quote from the *San Francisco Oracle*:[109]

> One of the great mysteries emerging under psychedelic substances is the recognition that the physical self is but a vehicle for the manifestation of soul forces which can be transmitted, transferred and stimulated like rays of Divine Light ... Evocations of your dedication to the nature of the ethic: expose oneself to new forms of energy and find faith in molecular energy released by psychedelic molecules. Not blind faith. But faith in the harmony and wisdom of nature ... Cellular consciousness touches timeless wisdom. Transcendental consciousness – pure energy – the light within – the Void.

Awareness and consciousness are the keywords. And yet all this ignores two objections. First, there is an inbuilt negative in the drug and its effects. This is quite apart from the effect of 'bad trips', people becoming insane or their brains being affected, for these could well be overcome in time with better drugs and do not affect the basic principle. The drugs are made in a factory and, even when they are natural plants or growths, they belong to the material world. The drug experience does not really transcend physical reality. We have expanded minds, and have new experiences, see new things, or rather see well-known things in a new light and yet we are still within the framework of the Enlightenment, for we start from our senses, from our human experience. Faith here is not faith but confidence in a technique to see more than usual, while in principle we are still bound to our human experience.

A different slant on the same fact can be seen in the argument for drugs put forward from the side of 'scientism'. Arthur Koestler in *The Ghost in the Machine* discusses evolution. Incidentally, it is extraordinary how Koestler introduces in a strange and subtle way a kind of immanent thinking element which guides evolution in some way. To Koestler the human being is in a way a mistake of evolution or a transitional phase to something else. But to counteract the wrong element, and perhaps to take human evolution a stage further, we must take drugs. 'Please, chemists, make better drugs in order to save humankind and promote evolution!'

The idea is not a new one. It was already in Huxley's *Brave New World*, in which he describes the technocratic world of the future, the rosy world emerging from a totally successful technological evolution and revolution; yet he introduces a drug, *soma*, which is taken by the supermen to counteract their fears and feelings of meaninglessness. The idea is not new: Huxley not only wrote about it, he used it. Huxley's technological age has already begun.

Thus drugs are both a product of a technological world and a need of a technological world, and so belong wholly to the framework of the world of scientism and technocracy. But this is just what the new generation of hippies and others want to escape from. So in the end it is no good. Drugs are worse than useless. Indeed many of them see this and stop using them, though others continue to advocate them for different reasons. It is not easy to get rid of the demons once they are released.

But there is a second fatal objection to drugs, the fact that they are used to promote a false 'religion'. The aims of drug taking as quoted above are very similar to those of Eastern mystical religions. And indeed, as we have already seen, many turn to these religions. They answer the craving of our times for a religion that is non-Christian, in which one is never asked to believe in any creed, and which is in a way no more than a method, a technique of preparing one's own salvation. It is a way of losing one's identity, one's individuality, and of escaping responsibility for others. It is pseudo-religion.

Modern people long for just such a new myth. They try everything, all kinds of mysticism, the cults, even Devil worship. Human being indeed is more than mechanistic science can account for. People still search for truth, knowing that the world is greater than atoms and rabbits. Their freedom proves it. But it is a freedom that may be used to choose the wrong, the sinful, death and perdition. Paul writes of 'men who by their wickedness suppress the truth'. This is their freedom.

Men and women, human beings, long for true and real reality, true, real life, the fullness of humanity – and the freedom that should go with it. But they have lost it, and continue not to find it so long as they stick to the basic principles of the Enlightenment, of which the first and the last is that people want to be autonomous and do not want to acknowledge God, the God of the Bible, the God and Father of the Lord Jesus Christ.

But who is to blame? Are those of us who are Christians innocent? Can we really say we warned them? Can we really say that we showed them the greatness of the fact that we are indeed new people, new human beings, in the resurrection of Jesus Christ? Have we shown that the world is indeed open, and have we testified not only with words but also in our deeds and in our thinking and our wisdom that we know there is a living God? We must be honest, none of us is free of guilt.

Christians must acknowledge their guilt, too, for allowing their theology to be moulded by the thinking of the age. Too many have swallowed the theology of Bultmann, Tillich and others (especially as popularized by John Robinson), who all accept the picture of reality given by 'scientism': therefore, as Bultmann states, it would mean a *sacrificium intellectum*, a sacrifice of reason, if he were to accept the miracles and the idea of God acting in time-space history as the Bible relates it. Religion belongs to the deeper and higher, to the same realm of the irrational – that which cannot be ascertained by science – as the one in which the existentialists look for humanity, and modern art for meaning. Indeed, there is a great similarity and deep connection between modern mysticism, modern art and modern theology.

What is normal?

What then are people today looking for? What is the force that drives them on, always searching, never satisfied, always up and away again without a moment's peace?

The answer is the fact that the answers are no answers! We can have a drug experience . . . but we come out of it again, and nothing has changed (except for the fact that we may have a hangover). We can have a mystical experience, experience oneness, life that flows within us and without us . . . but one day we see that we were alone after all, and nothing has changed. The world that we wanted to help, to renew, to change . . . remains the same. (Did we really want to change it, in fact, or were we just escaping it?) We can look to the answers of modern art . . . but they tell us that everything is rotten, nothingness, putrid, empty, senseless. But where is beauty, where is truth? We searched for the answer, and they told us: love, love, love. And it was tried, and exhausted we found . . . that love, love, love meant sex, sex, sex, and that nothing had changed.

As we seek life, humanity, the fullness of reality, we must ask: What is this normal human life? There are thousands and thousands of people who do not understand the determinism of scientism, they do not see the fact that they are only rabbits and atoms – copulating atoms, looking at themselves and having problems and worries and frustration. They do not see the real danger of all power being in the hands of big business and industry, manipulating us for profit and making life a lie. They live and work, and think the world goes on as usual, as 'normal'. Modern art is a fake, a hoax and a mistake . . . life goes on, leaving at the roadside the few who cry strange cries. You can try to lift them up and say to them: Why don't you join us? We are making a beautiful world in which everyone will be happy. We can offer money, safety, health and entertainment . . . Of course, there are still some problems left to be solved, poverty, underdeveloped countries, crime and so on, but we'll get these things sorted out in the end. Of course the world will never be perfect, and people will make mistakes or go off the right track, and you've a right to have a fling when you're young . . .

These thousands, millions, live a normal human life. They play it safe. They evade any real problems. They are nice people living a nice life. They have their little melancholies, unfulfilled dreams of youth – but life is like that. They avoid the major sins, for these do not fit into their pattern of life, the pattern of status and the approval of friends and neighbours. So they live their lives fairly happily, even if not exactly adventurously, and look for fulfilment in their career, a nice home, a bit of affluence and some kind words at retirement.

This is of course what is called a middle-class mentality. But the mentality has not so much to do with class or social status. It may be strongest in the middle class. But middle-class people are not necessarily middle class in this sense. It is really the same as what I earlier called bourgeois.

The bourgeois is what the Beatles sing about in their song 'She's leaving home'. She is leaving home, and her parents exclaim when they find that their daughter is dropping out: 'We sacrificed most of our lives, we gave her everything money can buy,' but the verdict is: 'She's leaving home after living alone for so many years.' Alone. For so many years. Yet we gave her everything money can buy.

Is that really real life? Is that what humans were created for? Is that the life Christ died for? Is that Christianity? Heaven forbid! Why is bourgeois life like this? Because it has no foundation. Morality and wisdom and respectability and love, these need a base, a meaning. Or else they atrophy and become like withered leaves or like old faded photographs on the wall. As we have seen, there are good reasons for believing that this type of bourgeois mentality grew in the period of Enlightenment and is related to it. The higher middle-class people of the eighteenth century read about the new view on reality, in their *Spectators*, their *Mercures*, the *Encyclopedia*, and they had no particular answer. They did not have a deep faith, and were not really committed in any way. They accepted the view of the new era – but avoided the consequences. They wanted to play it safe and be nice, respectable people. They were not inclined to face up to the realities of their new view of reality.

So the young generation protests. The protest has already been heard for the whole of the twentieth century. And the preaching of the new ideas of revolution, renewal and change has not remained unheeded and without fruit.

The meaninglessness, the closedness of the world of the bourgeois is made stronger by the new means of communication. The media have to cater to the tastes and ideas of the many. They have to be neutral and avoid taking sides or giving strong verdicts. So they help to build up the image of the complete one-dimensional world. God is no more than an idea of a particular group. Neutrality, the average, means leaving out the basic questions, the basic truths. And so the bourgeois mentality is strengthened.

Many of the films people see, for instance (not the real avant-garde, 'important' films) are good entertainment, and often have a little moral point. Yet they are bad. For they depict as true a world which is limited and superficial, one without God, without the deeper questions in the human heart, without real matters of life and death, for life and death are reduced to sentiment or adventures or crime and violence or cruelty, without any sort of judgment expressed. Most films of this type are good in the bourgeois sense, and they are certainly not meant to be anti-Christian. But they help to close the sky. They leave God out of the picture. Maybe he was an issue in the past, and so he has a part to play in historical pieces, but not in the world of today.

The protest of the new generation is against this lack of commitment, this lack of real values, this lack of 'daring to live'. The shallowness and emptiness are appalling . . .

The new generation begins to look for real humanity, to long for the fullness and openness and freedom of truth and real life. But after a while it finds only the same old thing, the thing it wanted to avoid, to escape, to change, to decry in the first place. Alan Starr expresses the tragedy of degeneration from idealism to a bourgeois mentality as follows:[110]

> Now we have long serious discussions in cafes along the Bayswater Road,
> We see that there is a law of diminishing returns
> Where demos are concerned.
> It's not that I don't admire Jan Palach, of course,
> But I can't help feeling that he's externalising an internal inadequacy –
> The rebel finds the cause; you know what they say about men making God.
> My fiance thinks so. And death's so final, isn't it?
> David left Cambridge last summer – we marry in June.
> We're moving to a house outside Dorking.
> (David says he'll be doing a fair amount of protesting – to Southern Region.)
> But we'll keep in touch:
> I still have my Bob Dylan records,
> And we'll go to the Round House and so on:
> Hear John Peel, maybe.
> David says we'll make friends easily if we join the Conservative Club.
> There are riding stables near our house.
> I've taken out a year's subscription to the Reader's Digest.
> I think we're going to settle down quite well,
> Really.

The tragic protest

And so, inevitably, we have come to protest and the rumblings of revolution. What is wanted is 'relevance and involvement'.[111] The enemies are 'the destructiveness of industrial-age values'.[112] What is meant by this can be best summed up by bringing together what I have called technocracy with the bourgeois mentality. Bourgeois people do not want to be dehumanized and made into little particles of the great industrial – technical – economic machine yet they have no real spiritual misgivings about it, for they have accepted, even if grudgingly, the basic presuppositions of scientism and the naturalistic view of the world. Perhaps deep down they do not accept the devaluation of all norms and values inherent in this view, but they have no deep, committed answer. They have certainly accepted it insofar as technocracy offers leisure, money, pleasure, a certain kind of security and sometimes (if you are at the top) power.

Protest sees through all types of bourgeois values which have no foundation and which try to buy comfort at the expense of a loss of humanity. It begins with the sexual revolution: 'The right of two or more human beings to love one another and to express this love in physical terms.'[113] 'Complete sexual freedom is a number one demand for any student movement. All forms of sexual repression and of puritan "discipline" should be abolished.'[114] A next step was to 'drop out', to leave the establishment and live a kind of bohemian life – indeed, the protest had already begun in the last century with the bohemianism of the artistic circles in France. But now they have seen that they must move on, to quote from the article in *Seed* mentioned above:

> We can escape from these dehumanizing systems. The way ahead will be found by those who are unwilling to be constrained by the apparent all-determining forces and structures of the industrial age. Our freedom and power are determined by our willingness to accept responsibility for the future ... The call is to live the future: let us join together joyfully to celebrate our awareness that we can make our life today the shape of tomorrow's future.

They live in anticipation of a new world, an anarchist world, a world of absolute individual freedom. The French Revolution (at the end of the first period of the new era of the Enlightenment) stood for 'liberty, equality, fraternity': in the revolution of today it is called 'freedom, the end of privilege and license, and love, love, love'.

But just as the French Revolution ended with a dictator, the end of freedom, wars and the end of all the things the revolution stood for, so this could so easily be the case today. Indeed, the revolutionary forces in our society are breaking down real democratic freedom, and the liberal freedom that each person may think for him- or herself. Revolutionary students are asking whether a professor who has particular views on certain issues should be allowed to remain a professor: intellectual freedom is in danger too.

But what if the counter-revolutionary forces take over, defending the establishment and standing for their own bourgeois values? This has happened in Greece and in other countries (and almost happened in the USA). This may sound a better solution, but we must realize that again freedom is lost: totalitarian forces ask for support or else . . . This is the way that leads to the concentration camp. The revolution that starts with anarchism and ends with dictatorship is without any doubt antichristian; but so too could be the counter-revolution, which may well not accept Christians either if they stand for freedom and justice, and hunger and thirst for righteousness. The freedom they stand for is different from that of the anarchists, but in asking for humanity and refusing to bow down to the gods of the totalitarian state they will become marked people nonetheless.

There is a tragedy inherent in revolutionary thought and action today, in the spirit of our age. They are in revolt against forces that are unjustifiable, against a world that is dehumanizing, a system that on many points is wrong, but . . . they have no alternative. Their own world view is basically the same as the one that is responsible for the world they are revolting against. So what will be the result of their revolutionary action? Only a world changed even more in the direction of the world view that has been the driving force ever since the Enlightenment, a completely secularized world, without God, in a closed system, with a duality of rationality and irrationality, naturalistic and mystic at the same time. The last remnants of the older world view, still flavoured with the salt of Christian values – open, knowing of a God, of justice and absolutes – will be done away with. Though many revolutionaries return after a while to bourgeois values of one kind or another in order to be able to live 'a decent life', yet their work will be done, and we must not minimize its importance for the world at large.

So far the revolution has been largely the concern of students or those of student age. But the danger is that the result will be a loss of freedom for all. As *Time* magazine put it:[115] 'Revolution is a serious business, with a terrible but often heroic tradition, and it must be reserved for situations of extreme despair when no other recourse is possible. Playing at it when it is neither possible nor necessary only makes reform harder to achieve and gives revolution a bad name.'

But the revolutionary groups will work on, nevertheless, for they see their work as a historical necessity. They may not be overthrowing governments, and there is no guillotine. But because it is happening in a more unobtrusive way the revolution is achieving more, much more, than most people realize.

The permissive society

Indeed it would seem that the fast-moving cultural scene and the great changes of the last ten years are the result of a revolution. And the end is not yet in sight. Occasional riots, fighting in the streets and on campuses, demonstrations and the like are only the open eruptions, small by comparison with the great volcano on which we are living.

The real revolution is caused by the claim that all values and norms are basically social, and that people are free to live as they wish (provided that there is equality and no one hinders another). So there should be not only no wars, no poverty and no discrimination, but also no barriers, no restraints, no authorities.

Norms have lost their foundation with the Enlightenment: Hobbes, followed later by Rousseau, had looked for a solution in the social contract. Today authority has lost all meaning. One cannot lay down the law for another, it is said; we are each a law only to ourselves, for authority has lost the values on which it depends. The remnants of the dignity of authority in the state, in the family, in the church even, are in danger of being swept away. And yet this only produces agony, frustration and neurosis, not to speak of the lowering of standards or achievement in schools, industry and in many other fields.

For though the new ideas are idealistic and aim for a better world, yet they do not work in practice. Or perhaps we should say that they do work, but in the direction of the breakdown of our society. Statistics are there to prove that moral standards are lower or have collapsed, that there is more crime, more juvenile delinquency, more adultery, more divorces, more homosexuality each year. Some react to this by saying that those things no longer really matter, that traditional moral standards no longer count. There is a cry for free love, for easy ways to divorce, for permissiveness in every way. But when things get so bad that it is clear to all that they are bad, then the structures of society are called into question, and protest and revolution are looked for as a means of making a better world. But these then serve only to quicken the whole process of breakdown.

We see the faults in the underlying principles, in the inner contradictions as well as the contradictory results. To make freedom possible, freedom is quenched. To end violence and war, violence is used. The world must be changed . . . but very few have any real, supposedly workable suggestion about which road to take and what the new world should be like. We must see the tragedy of it as well as the frustrations that result from it.

Playboy magazine, in an article on the hippies in 1967, wrote:

> The rules of habit, tradition and authority are eroded. The threats that kept those rules in force – the punishment of God, pregnancy or disinheritance – have been eliminated by the dimming out of religion, the pill and the

erosion of family structures. One of the dangers of the new youth style is formation of what critic Harold Rosenberg has called 'the herd of independent minds'. The opportunity, however, is to make a new tradition of the tradition of the new.

Indeed, we must realize that the change of manners and morals, showing the speed of the dechristianizing of the Western world, the result of paying no more than lip-service to biblical truth or even to God himself, this is itself the revolution. The permissive society is the result, not the cause. Pornography sold openly; nudity in film, advertising and on stage; free love; experimental marriages and the like are now no longer new. The work of a group of people devoted to change the world, artists, editors such as *Playboy's* Hefner, writers, philosophers and idealists have been successful. For the sake of promoting sales and making money, advertising plays on the fringes of what is and is not acceptable, and so the whole process of breaking down barriers has been speeded up beyond any normal development. The same may be said of films and every kind of mass entertainment. Today things can be shown in films that would have been impossible even five years ago, and in advertising even the most intimate things are blatantly paraded. Here, if ever, the protesters are right when they say that capitalist society is prostituting women for the sake of profit.

An article in *Newsweek* sums up what I have been saying:

> The shattering of taboos on language, fashion and manners generally is part of a larger disintegration of moral consensus in America. Vast numbers of Americans distrust their government. Catholics in increasing numbers simply ignore the church ban on birth control. The family has changed from a breeding ground of common values into a battleground of generations. These dislocations have moved many writers to reach for the strongest language in their arsenal to capture the chaos of their time.[116]

Is this just moralizing? Or exaggeration? Yet there are many others who are seeing the same thing. The artists themselves, the makers and the children of the revolution of today, they see it – in despair, in frustration, or in fits of destructive anger. 'The destruction is more important than the content,' said a rock musician on BBC TV not so long ago.

Martin Esslin (who should know, for he was very much involved) ends his book *The Theatre of the Absurd* as follows:

> Ultimately, a phenomenon like the theatre of the absurd does not reflect despair or a return to dark irrational forces but expresses modern man's endeavour to come to terms with the world in which he lives. It attempts to make him face up to the human condition as it really is ... There are enormous pressures in our world that seek to induce mankind to bear the loss of faith and moral certainties by being drugged into oblivion by mass entertainment, shallow material satisfaction, pseudo-explanations of reality and cheap ideologies. At the end of that road lies Huxley's Brave New World

of senseless euphoric automata. Today ... the need to confront man with the reality of his situation is greater than ever. For the dignity of man lies in his ability to face reality in all its senselessness; to accept it freely, without fear, without illusion and to laugh at it. This is the cause to which ... the dramatists of the Absurd are dedicated.

The question is, what are they really laughing at? We must dig a little deeper.

Apocalypse

When we sense the feeling of our times it may strike us that so much of it seems to echo what is written in the Bible. We see people as it were crying out in their agony, hiding in the caves and among the rocks of the mountains, calling on the mountains and rocks to fall on them and hide them . . . yet, as the book of Revelation has it, 'the rest of mankind, who were not killed by the plagues, did not repent . . . of their murders or their sorceries or their immorality or their thefts.'[117] When we read Paul's second letter to Timothy about 'the last days', we are struck by the fact how true all this is of our day, even more so than a generation ago: 'Men will be lovers of self, lovers of money, proud, arrogant, abusive, disobedient to their parents, ungrateful, unholy, inhuman, implacable, slanderers, profligates, fierce, haters of good, treacherous, reckless, swollen with conceit, lovers of pleasure rather than lovers of God, holding the form of religion but denying the power of it.'

We realize too when reading this how much we ourselves are touched by the spirit of permissiveness: we would scarcely use such strongly critical words today. Paul goes on to speak of people 'who will listen to anybody and can never arrive at a knowledge of the truth.' We too must be aware how near our age is in spirit to that of the 'lawless one' described by Paul in another letter as coming 'with all power and with pretended signs and wonders, and with all wicked deception for those who are to perish, because they refused to love the truth' – and we are wondering whether God is not really sending upon them 'a strong delusion, to make them believe what is false'.[118] We can go on to read 2 Peter 2 or the great preaching of Jesus himself about the last days recorded in Matthew 24.

As we walk through a modern art gallery, do we not see the sky vanished like a scroll that is rolled up, the sun becoming black as sackcloth, the moon becoming like blood, the stars falling down? Even theologians today dare to speak of a God who is dead. 'I hid my face and was angry,' God says through Isaiah. 'They shall go to seek the Lord, but they will not find him; he has withdrawn from them,' says Hosea.[119]

God is not dead, nor is the world a closed system: he, the Creator, the One who loves humankind even to the point of sending his Son to die, he not only came in Old Testament times with his righteous anger and judgment upon people who forgot him and walked in their own sinful ways but will do so in our times too, as Revelation makes clear. The world is open for God: it is the very core of the gospel that he has come in Christ to save the lost. But the other side of the same coin is that there is no love without judgment. There is a God to be feared.

This language is often too hard even for those of us who believe in him. But if we do not listen to it, we shall miss the good news of the gospel as well as the many words of consolation in such books as Revelation itself. And we shall miss the key to our times, which are hard and strange while our culture is breaking down. If any confirmation is needed, go to the films, read the books of today, walk round a modern art gallery, listen to the music of our times – and hear, see, open your eyes and ears to the cries of despair, the cursing, the collapse of this world . . . and see your Lord coming with judgment.

But see too his grace in all this, in wars and rumours of wars, in unsolvable 'world problems', in violence and revolt in the midst of opulence. For it means that he is still concerned for us. History is still in the hands of God. There is nothing happening outside of his knowledge. Did he not send his prophets to foretell these things so that we should not be weak and falter and fall?

But we Christians too must beware. For we must understand that judgment begins with the household of God.

Towards a renewal of the church

> The good Samaritan is dressing,
> getting ready for the show;
> there will be carnival tonight on Desolation Row ...

Bob Dylan's song does not give an exactly flattering picture of the church: Desolation Row! And everyone knows the complaint of the Beatles about Eleanor Rigby and all the lonely people (where do they come from?). The preacher is darning his socks . . . and nobody is saved. For it is easy to say that 'they' are wrong and haters of God. We must realize that in the Bible the people of God too are often depicted in quite dark tones. The prophets thundered at the 'church' of their days, the Jewish people with their Temple . . . Jeremiah was even forbidden to pray for them. We read in Isaiah 1 of the church people whose religion is only lip-service, and who do not really trust in the Lord. No, the situation of a weak, fallen, faithless church is not new. Again and again the people of God have deserted him, looked to other gods, other ways of being saved, other securities and, with the Bible in their hands, have asked of the prophets to speak nothing but peace, peace – yet, says

Jeremiah, there is no peace. Perhaps faith is just a word, a formula, a tradition, and God no more than an idea . . . And God cries out through the prophets in his word, today as ever, 'Where is the love of my people?'

Who were Christ's enemies here on earth? Not the godless and lawless, not the criminals or the 'far-out' people. No, his enemies were the churchmen of his days, the Pharisees with their orthodoxy and knowledge of the Bible, and yet . . . they were seeking for their security in being Jewish, children of Abraham, and in their cleverness in dealing with the Romans. They did not dare to follow God himself, the Son of God amongst men, with the adventure of trusting him, loving in freedom – and of taking up their cross.

In modern terminology this can be described by saying that the churches have become bourgeois. They are moral, even moralistic; they are either deadly orthodox, keeping legalistically to the old creeds, or want to be radical, liberal, modern, and demythologize the Bible, which really means taking out of it a God who is too concrete and too real. A bourgeois Christianity is one in which the salt has lost its flavour, one which is lukewarm and neither hot nor cold – as the Beatles sing on their *Sergeant Pepper* record, 'The love that has gone so cold.'[120]

Certainly, as in Elijah's day, there are still the 'seven thousand' who have not bowed the knee to the gods of today. There are still people who are ready to follow the Lord wherever he leads them. But they are scarce. Would he find faith on earth when he returned? Christ asked. Unless we pray and work (in that order) for true reformation and revival, unless we return to the Lord, there is no future for any church. God himself will throw it away as saltless salt.

We may study the present situation, point to the fact that our culture is collapsing, notwithstanding its technical achievement and great knowledge in many fields . . . yet we must never think that it is just 'they', the haters of God. We must realize that we Christians are also responsible. Much of the protest of today's generation is justifiable. But why did not Christians protest long ago? Why were we not hungering and thirsting for righteousness, helping the oppressed and the poor? To look at modern art is to look at the fruit of the spirit of the avant-garde: it is they who are ahead in building a view of the world with no God, no norms. Yet is this so because Christians long since left the field to the world and, in a kind of mystical retreat from the world, condemned the arts as worldly, almost sinful? Indeed, nowhere is culture more 'unsalted' than precisely in the field of the arts – and that in a time when the arts (in the widest sense) are gaining a stronger influence than ever through mass communications.

Christianity has the answer if it only cares, or dares, to listen for the answer to the problems of our age. But why does it keep silent? Or why does it just say to people who are increasingly estranged from biblical language and thought patterns, 'have faith, have faith', without really answering the chilling questions being cried out in agony. Jesus saves: indeed, but that means not only saving your soul out of the shipwreck of this world! His saving grace redeems us here and now, and gives answers to the problems of today. He is able to redeem us, really and truly, not just 'spiritually', in a narrow sense.

Yet this does not mean that the answer is cheap. It means a call to repent, to trust in the Lord, to be willing to sacrifice. Our culture can be renewed, but if God gave reformation tomorrow, pouring out his Holy Spirit, we would still have to work perhaps a generation or more before the fruit would be ripe, the building mended.

My word is for ever, said Jesus Christ. He does not ask us to jump in the dark, in blind faith. He never asked even his disciples, or others who listened to him in his own time, to accept him only because he said so. There were the 'signs' to back up what he said, and the fulfilment of words spoken in the Old Testament. If Christ was really the one he claimed to be, if God really lives and is Lord of heaven and earth, then it is not so very difficult to believe the things he did. In the same way in the Old Testament, God pointed to things that had happened in history, such as the great deliverance from Egypt, and the way he had spoken to his people from Mount Sinai. He points to the words of the prophets which were fulfilled and sometimes gave miracles. Miracles were not the daily experience of people in Old Testament times – nor just childish fancy as some would have us believe – nor were there angels at every street corner. But, when necessary, God did move and showed his power or presence. So too in the New Testament, Christ showed his power over creation by walking on the water, the very symbol of chaos. He showed the power of his new creation, too, by raising people from the dead, healing, giving new life.

But even signs and miracles will not automatically produce faith. Even at the times when the Jews were shown great signs, when they were brought through the Red Sea and sustained in the desert, there were still people who did not trust in the Lord but grumbled and cursed and rebelled. Today too people can be blind to the work of God and deny with open eyes the things they see. Faith means love and trust. The question is not whether we believe that God exists (even the devils know this) but whether we trust him, love him and are willing to follow him.

But we will never follow a phantom, something beyond our understanding, something vague and above human experience. We cannot understand God fully, nor know his work completely. But we are not asked to accept in blind faith. On the contrary: we are asked to look around us and know that the things he tells us through his Son and his prophets and apostles are true, real and of this world, the cosmos he has made.

Therefore our faith can never be just 'out of the box', irrational. Faith is not a sacrifice of the intellect if we believe in the biblical account of history. For if we accept the view on reality as revealed in Scripture, we know that 'the box is open', that the world is open, that there is a God who can and does act, who answers prayer, who is not hidden away or remote from the factuality of this world. Yes, we can see things happen if we want to. Jesus Christ's promise was not an empty one when he told us that our prayers would be answered if we loved him (during the Last Supper, as recorded in the Gospel of John). Christians can never be rationalists, only accepting things we can prove with our brains, nor naturalists in the sense that only those things are real that can be experienced with our sense-perceptions. Christians are asked to use the brains God gave us, to understand his word, to accept him on the basis of the things he has done in history and in the lives of others and in showing his dominion over the forces of this world.

Unless we understand that a demythologized Bible is a closed Bible, for all the proofs of God's work and acts are taken out of it; unless we understand that a blind faith is no faith and that faith is never irrational, even if it destroys all scientism, the rationalism of the closed naturalistic 'box', knowing that reality is much bigger than the 'box'; unless we understand that we live in an open world and that God has as much to do with the atoms as he has to do with the minds and hearts of people; unless we understand all this, we have no weapon against the spirit of our age. This is the battle of Ephesians 6!

Unless we see that faith means trusting in the Lord, listening to his word, and that therefore a duality of nature and grace is a disgrace to God, robbing him of his authority where he is indeed the Lord; unless we see that there is no higher and lower in the sense of grace and nature, but that the real division is between holy and sinful, true and false, love and hate; unless we see all this, we shall have no answer to the deep agony of the world. Our religion in that case would be just another mystic leap into irrationality, no better and no worse than Eastern religion, modern mysticism or even drugs. Our Christianity then would be no more than pseudo-religion.

But we do understand and see aright when we are really willing to trust and follow Christ in all we do and are; then we must work it out in our lives, in our thinking, in our creativity. In the next chapter we must go on to consider how.

9
Faith and Art

I'm going to live the life I sing about in my song.[121]

How can Christians live out their faith in the culture around them? Or, to put it more widely, how should people go about their life and work in this cosmos, God's creation?

First, they have to act in relation to the given structures of reality. These were given with creation, as possibilities, as open ways, as norms, as a framework in which to work. These of course are nothing like a 'natural law'. There is nothing 'natural' in this sense in the world, for the whole world was created by God, through Christ. 'In the beginning was the Word'; 'through whom also he created the world.'[122]

These norms or structures are 'possibilities'. We could not speak, for instance, unless we had been made with the 'possibility' of speaking. How should we teach, then? By following the given possibilities of teaching and learning, within a given structure. There is no marriage, no economics, no prayer, no art but for the fact that they were made possible by God in his creation: he created the possibility. So these structures are the horizon of human activity. We cannot do anything but within the created order – to be outside this order is to be outside of reality. To this reality belong imagination, fantasy, the discovery of things unheard of and undreamt of – for God gave humankind these things, and imagination is not outside creation's structures.

People can live and act within the structures, and they can do so in love and freedom, with their personality, their subjective humanity, given to them by the Creator of life. This is humanity: to make something of our life; to realize the possibilities God has given us; to realize a good marriage, if that is for us; to do a good job, to enjoy the life one has, the possibilities laid within one's personality. Of course, sin has entered the world. Sin is a would-be freedom from God, but it is no freedom. It makes us captive to the law of sin which dwells in our members: 'for whatever overcomes a man, to that he is enslaved.'[123] And though Christians have been freed from the bondage of their sin by Christ, yet so long as they are in a sinful world they have to do battle against sin, hungering and thirsting after righteousness, seeking peace, helping the oppressed – and fighting against their own sin, too, in order to have the freedom and openness that belong to the fruit of the Spirit: 'love, joy, peace, patience, kindness, goodness, faithfulness, gentleness, self-control'.[124] This is freedom!

Realizing one's possibilities, acting in love and freedom within given structures, fighting against sin and its results, all this is also what creativity means. Artistic creativity is only one of the many creative possibilities.

And if we are creative in this full sense, as new men and women sharing the new resurrection life of Christ,[125] then the fruits of his work will be seen in our lives, which will in turn have results in this world. This will never be perfect, of course. The Christian is no easy idealist, but very much a realist, for the Bible is under no illusions about the realities of human nature. But if we are 'salting salt' at all, then this will do its work in society, making sane and healthy what was crippled and broken. Simply doing the truth and acting according to the will of God will bring life and freedom and love and righteousness. This then is how we can define Christianity's influence in culture: as a fruit of the fruit of the Spirit, as salt in the world.

We are called to be creative in this sense. And we are called to bear the cross that often goes with it, for humankind often prefers darkness to light, enslavement to real freedom.

But are not Christians supposed to be pilgrims and strangers in this dark world? In one sense, no. This creation is God's, and we belong to him, so we are at home in it. We are never frustrated because of the given structures of reality. The gospel is not one of bondage but of freedom. As Paul stressed again and again, Christ came to make us free (see his letter to the Galatians, for example). We have been set free to be what humans were originally intended to be. Beauty, joy, love, all these things are God's gifts to humankind to be entered into and enjoyed.

Yet people have depraved and ruined these things. So in another sense, we are strangers in this world. We are strangers insofar as sin reigns, insofar as corruption is there, unrighteousness, uncleanness, wickedness, greed and ugliness. We realize only too acutely that these things are still in ourselves too, and we weep for the fact and long for the redemption of the body. Blessed are those who weep, those who know that they are not strong in themselves, those who hunger and thirst for righteousness (beginning in their own lives), this is what Christ told us in the Beatitudes.

So if we are called to keep ourselves from sin, keep ourselves clean, it means that we must understand what the world is. If we think we can keep away from the world by living the life of a hermit, we are mistaken: 'For from within, out of the heart of man, come evil thoughts, fornication, theft, murder, adultery, coveting, wickedness.'[126] Nor can walls of legalism, of do's and don'ts, be our fortress, for the Lord must be our fortress; and our enemy is the spiritual powers of wickedness and the spirit of our age. We are certainly not in any position to wash our hands of the whole sinful world, or complacently let it rot, or feel that we are too holy and spiritual to get involved. For we *are* involved: it is *our* sin that has helped to make the world the sinful place it is. We are responsible. If we are not acting as salt, even when we are not involved, or hungering and thirsting for righteousness, we are responsible.

Being a Christian means being clean in an unclean world. It is hopeless to try to be beyond contact with evil. Not only is it within us, it is all around us. Much as we may look forward to 'a new heaven and a new earth', we cannot opt out of the world here and now. It is for us to be not only clean amidst its uncleanness but also joyful and compassionate amidst its sorrows. We must understand it to know what is of God, to know what is good and what is evil. But it is not for us to judge it or write it off; it is for God to judge.

Jesus said, 'You are the salt of the earth.'

Christianity in art

What place should art have in all this? Can there be a Christian art bearing its witness alongside other art? Is there any such thing in fact as Christian art? Can art be used for Christian purposes? Here I must say emphatically: art must never be used to show the validity of Christianity. Rather the validity of art should be shown through Christianity.

In an earlier chapter I discussed the difficulty of portraying biblical themes in art. This does not mean that specifically Christian themes are impossible. It means only that Christian art is not art that uses biblical or other Christian themes. Picasso painted more than one Crucifixion, but they were curses rather than work done in faith. Many biblical themes were handled in a humanist spirit after the Renaissance. And, of course, almost all heresies have found some sort of expression in art.

No, what is Christian in art does not lie in the theme but in the spirit of it, in its wisdom and the understanding of reality it reflects. Just as being a Christian does not mean going round singing hallelujah all day, but showing the renewal of one's life by Christ through true creativity, so a Christian painting is not one in which all the figures have halos and (if we put our ears to the canvas) can be heard singing hallelujahs.

Christian art is nothing special. It is sound, healthy, good art. It is art that is in line with the God-given structures of art, art that has a loving and free view on reality, art that is good and true. In a way there is no specifically Christian art. One can distinguish only between good and bad art, art that is sound or good and that is false or weird in its insight into reality. This is so whether it is painting or drama or music. Christians, however full of faith they may be, can still make bad art. They may be sinful and weak, or they might not have much talent. On the other hand, non-Christians can make a thing of beauty, a joy for ever – provided that they remain within the scope of the norms for art, provided that they work out of the fullness of their humanity and do not glory in the depraved or in iniquity or glorify the Devil.

So a work of art is not good when we know that the artist was a Christian: it is good when we perceive it to be good. Nor is a work bad if we know that the artist was a hater of God. It would be possible to make an exhibition of beautiful Picassos. The exhibition would possibly not do justice to the spirit that drove Picasso on in his creativity, yet it would show us that the man was human. Human beings, even if they do not love God, do not thereby become devils.

This does not mean that art is neutral. Nothing is. Art is a human creation, and as such is closely bound to a particular person's humanity. Therefore it is one's spirit, one's insight, one's feeling and one's sense of beauty, one's imagination and one's subjectivity that the work of art will show.

Is it possible for 'beautiful' art to come out of an unholy, ungodly spirit? History has shown that it can. Yet, in the long run, death must show itself. If we walk through a gallery today, we can see this death. Sometimes art has gone the whole way: with John Cage's music, for example, or Fontana's pierced canvas. Yves Klein showed his 'freedom' by making a painting with a completely blue surface – and nothing else. Whether by showing a void like this we can make art, is another question. In all these cases – often called, by the artists themselves, anti-art – we are dealing with borderline cases. Yet they show that, in the final analysis, with a completely antichristian and anti-humanist spirit, art is finished.

Christianity is about the renewal of life. Therefore it is also about the renewal of art. This is how art can be shown its validity through Christianity. It is an expression of Christian understanding, itself a fruit of the Spirit of God, including the emotion, the feeling, the sense of beauty that is bound up with it. It is for Christians to show what is meant by life and humanity; and to express what it means for them to have been 'made new' in Christ, in every aspect of their being.

The role of art

Art needs no justification. The mistake of many art theorists (and not only of Christian ones) is to try to give art a meaning or a sense by showing that it 'does something'. So art must open people's eyes, or serve as decoration, or prophesy, or praise, or have a social function, or express a particular philosophy. Art needs no such excuse. It has its own meaning that does not need to be explained, just as marriage does not, or human being itself or the existence of a particular bird or flower or mountain or sea or star. These all have meaning because God has made them. Their meaning is that they have been created by God and are sustained by him. So art has a meaning as art because God thought it good to give art and beauty to humanity.

This does not mean that art cannot at times teach, praise, prophesy, decorate and help social relationships. It does so, often, just as a bird can be useful, or even as the life of a particular human being can be fruitful and important. But it would be false to say that art is only good if it promotes Christianity. This would be a perverted kind of utilitarianism. Art and singing can be used to promote worship – indeed, worship without good music is almost unthinkable – and art may be used in evangelism. But art does not need to be justified because it can be useful in this way. We must be careful here: if we are going to use art for these specifically Christian purposes – adorning a church or attracting the unbeliever – then we must see that the art we use is really good. Cheap art means cheap worship or a cheap message. Perhaps I was overstating the case when I said that art should *never* be used to show the validity of Christianity. What I meant was that this is not art's primary function. But if it is going to be used, it must be really good for the purpose and do the job well. But quite apart from the use to which it is put, art has its own validity.

Perhaps one of the main problems of art today has been the result of giving art the wrong function. Formerly art was 'an art', just as we still speak of arts and crafts. Art as a higher function of humankind, the work of the inspired lofty artist, comparable with that of the poet and the prophet, was the outcome of the Renaissance with its Neoplatonic way of thinking. Yet the fatal conclusions were only drawn later: the modern division between the fine arts – drama, poetry, literature, music, painting and sculpture – and the applied arts such as pottery, tapestry and so on, is of fairly recent date. It was the outcome of a development in the theory of art at the end of the seventeenth century in the circles of academics and connoisseurs. It was no accident that this coincided with the beginning of the 'closing of the box', the beginning of the Enlightenment. With the dichotomy of reality, the dualism between the realm of the sciences and the higher realm of human freedom, 'cultural matters' and art were given a new task. Art became Art (with a capital A), a high, exalted, more humanist than human endeavour. Yet precisely in that pseudo-religious function it became almost superfluous, something aside from reality and life, a luxury – fine, refined, but useless.

If we were able to break through this false duality and see art again simply as art, with its own validity, art would regain its freedom as part of human life and acquire a renewed meaning in life. Neither art nor beauty needs to be justified or put on a pedestal. They are to be enjoyed and appreciated and practised, in love and freedom, as a joy for ever, accepted as a great gift of God.

Questions of aesthetics and morals

Some people feel that we ought to define the principle of art solely by the aesthetic. Is not this the core of art, the real heart of it? Is not this its true meaning? Very often in the course of a discussion of modern art, it comes down to saying that its sole meaning is to be found in its lines and forms and colours, the aesthetic element as such.

Personally I have many doubts about this. First of all, this truly abstract art is very rare – much non-figurative art does have a meaning apart from its purely aesthetic appeal. The strange thing is that artists, almost without exception, do strive to express something in their art, and only rarely are happy with the aesthetic element alone. To me this is one of the proofs that any theory that goes too much in this direction is out of touch with real artistic practice. Of course, there exists artistic work done only with an eye to the aesthetic effect: fabrics, ornaments, some types of typography, and so on. But the problem does not really arise with the so-called applied arts. In fact, the beauty often found in good work of this sort is exactly the quality that the modern artists – Pop, Zero and the like – seeks to destroy with their anti-art. Art, it is said, does not need beauty.

The whole argument is full of confusion. In searching for an art that is 'pure', people who stick to this theory tend to do away with everything that is not 'pure', not aesthetic: subject matter, reality, feelings, everything. Certainly this type of pure art would be abstract in its proper sense, because the aesthetic element is indeed an abstraction. But, as I have said, 'pure' art in this sense is very rare. But why should we look for such abstraction? Would it not deprive art of its concrete value and fullness of being? What is love (in a man-woman relationship) if there are not two specific people loving each other? If, as it is said, the most essential element of human being is one's rationality, one's brain, would it not be better to cut a person up and only leave her or his brain? But the person would be dead . . . People who say that money is what matters most in life are not happy with money alone: they want to have the concrete reality that their money can buy.

So in talking about art we are not just discussing aesthetics in an abstract way. We are dealing with the fullness of the phenomenon in the whole of life, in which, even if beauty, the aesthetic, is very important, there are many other elements. The aesthetic can never be realized in its fullness without these other elements, and the other elements only get their artistic meaning because they are brought together in an artistic way. Art is a complex structure (and there is no intention of trying to give a complete analysis of it in this book). As a complex structure, it exists in its realization in concrete works of a reality, a being, a meaning, composed of many elements; and even if it can exist without some of these elements, and sometimes does, yet it is more often than not poorer without them. A man can exist without his legs – but his being is fuller and in a way more meaningful if he has them. 'Pure art' is often poor art, even if it is beautiful.

Another question that is often raised is this. Should art be criticized on two levels, one aesthetic, the other moral? I think not. First, to use the term 'moral' here is too narrow. It is better to speak of content or expression or portrayal of reality. Indeed, real life is complex and through sin, human shortcomings and the fact that all human creations are less than perfect, there will always be inner conflicts. A person may have tremendous insight, deep understanding and a great vision of what one wants to create: but if one is not able to realize it in an adequate form, it will not be a good work of art. Another person may be poor in vision and have almost nothing to say, yet have a superb feeling for colour. He or she paints a picture that is excellent in that respect but poor in content. Well then: the work of art is poor in content and beautiful in colour. When we study the really great works of art of history, we always find that their meaning is a unity: a beautiful idea is expressed and realized in a beautiful way. Each line, each colour, the whole composition is conceived in order to make the idea clear, and the idea would never have been made clearer than precisely by means of that particular composition with its colour scheme and so on. Every brushstroke 'carries' the meaning of the picture.

The question is in fact related to the old philosophical problem of form and content. Without trying to go into it here, I can only say that form can never be without content nor content without form. For, as McLuhan has shown, the meaning is in the medium – that is, in the artistic way of expression itself. So the question poses a false problem. A work of art is much more complex in structure than can be analysed by these two concepts of the aesthetic and the moral: if it is a great work of art, it is a unity in which very many elements can be discovered.

But there may have been another question underlying the old formulation of the problem: Is it possible for a horrible thought to be realized in a beautiful form? The form may not be beautiful, but if the artists have the greatness, the talent and the strength of character they will certainly make a very powerful and clear work that express their thoughts in an overwhelming way. This is true of Picasso, as we have seen. The work may be really horrible: but if it repels us it is because of its high quality. Or, when the form really is beautiful, then the evil expressed by it can make the beauty horrifying. The evil queen in the fairytale should really be ugly; but if she is beautiful, her evil becomes more evil and the whole concept that much more horrifying.[127]

We can ask the same question in another way. Can there be a beautiful work of art that has as subject matter something horrible and ugly? The answer is yes, of course, for there are abundant examples. Does Bach in his Passions portray something attractive and beautiful? The subject matter of Michelangelo's *Last Judgment* or of Rembrandt's etching of the Fall is not exactly sweet and lovely and enjoyable yet they belong to the great works of art. Rubens painted a magnificent *Battle of the Amazons*, Goya made etchings with human depravity as the subject, Kathe Kollwitz made lithos of suffering humankind, works considered to be of the highest quality. And what about Shakespeare's plays or Marlowe's *Dr Faustus* – they talk about sin, crime, pride, all that is evil and ugly. Yet all these works are 'beautiful' – a beauty however which does not mean sweetness and sentimentality, nor a beauty in form or language alone, quite apart from content.

Beauty and truth are closely related. It is precisely in the truth of the portrayal of the demonic as demonic in, for instance, Grünewald's *Temptation of St Anthony*, or of despair as real despair in Rogier van der Weyden's *Last Judgment*, that we appreciate beauty. To truth belongs insight into the greatness and goodness of God's creation, but also the understanding that this world is marred by sin and that apart from God's grace there is also the curse, the terrible inevitability of eternal separation from him. Christ *is* the truth – a fact that is seldom sufficiently considered or appreciated. Truth is more than conceptual truth, for truth in the last analysis is personal. Christ as the truth is the Lamb of God, the agent of God's grace and of the renewal of creation, yet also the one who is to rule all the nations with a rod of iron.[128]

What is the difference between the beauty of these 'horrible' works and the horrible we find in modern art? Again, it is a matter of truth. Modern art often speaks of (or rather swears at) the ugliness of God's creation or of despair without hope or of the meaninglessness of the meaningful: insofar as these things are lies, they are never beautiful. A horrible thought can never be truly beautiful, for a lie is not truth; but truth is beautiful when shown in its depth and fullness. Here we are not dealing with easy formulas or cheap criteria, as already discussed.[129] For the question of truth and beauty is after all as deep and many-sided as real life, and as complex.

Norms and structures in art

If we are going to create a work of art we must follow the norms for art, its structure. How can we compose music, for example, unless we use organized noise (to use the lowest definition possible)? To do a painting we must use the particular qualities of colour and line, realize their potential to represent something in a kind of pictorial language, and put them in a relationship that is pleasing to the eye, powerful and rhythmic and with an aesthetic economy. Then the picture can be 'beautiful' even when it depicts something ugly. It may move us, like van Gogh's *Pair of shoes* or Dürer's wonderful drawing of his old, ugly mother. The subject matter became beautiful in their hands because of their love for it. Love and beauty are closely related, just as love and freedom belong together – a forced love is no love, as many works of literature and poetry (if not life itself) have shown.

But if we are seeking as Christians to understand the structures and norms for art, should we not go to the Bible for them? Certainly, but we will not expect to see them explained in detail. Obviously the modern system of the arts did not exist in biblical times and they were simply not discussed. In the same way we will not find a long discourse in the Bible on the art of shoe-making or of weaving cloth. Of course, people then appreciated beauty; the psalms are superbly beautiful, and elsewhere in the Bible we have descriptions of the beauties of the Temple with its cherubim, pillars of gold and so on. One of the first times the Holy Spirit is mentioned is in relation to a man who was filled 'with the Spirit of God, with ability and intelligence, with knowledge and all craftsmanship, to devise artistic designs'.[130]

But God did not give specific laws concerning the arts, nor for any other cultural element. These things belong to human 'possibilities': God created them, and made and structured people in such a way that they could discover these possibilities, and he gave people the freedom and the task to realize and fulfil them. God left humankind to use all their possibilities in freedom.

This does not mean that there are no norms for art. Some of them are obvious, as the examples we have been discussing. If you are going to paint a sombre picture to express despair, you are not going to use cheerful colours, nor a light rhythmic line. A picture for a specific purpose must be visualized with the specific demands in mind, or else it will fail. If you are an architect designing a private bungalow you will not use heavy masses appropriate to a splendiferous public building. If an artist is not sensitive to this she or he will simply not be a good artist. Of course with less blatant examples I appreciate that this is not always easy. But good art is always the result of hard work. No great art has ever been achieved without the artist not only having talent and imagination but also the character, the energy to keep on working and thinking and toiling in order to achieve his or her aims. It is the artist's character which is really all-important.

The norms for art are in fact basically no different from the norms for the whole of life. Art belongs to human life, is part of it and obeys the same rules. The fact that the artist must keep in mind the specific structures of art is the same as anyone else in other human activities must do: the government has to work within the structures of the state, the motorist within the structures of the way the car works and of the rules of the road. But whether you are an artist, a politician or a motorist you must apply not only the specialized structures of your own field of operations but also the structure of the whole of life, the fact that, being human, people are designed to work in a particular way and that only by being wholly true to humanity will each activity really fulfil its purpose.

The mental attitude involved in being essentially human, expressing the true humanity which Christ came to restore, is summed up by Paul in a passage in his letter to the Philippians (4:8). Paul exhorted his readers to think about whatever is true, honourable, just, pure, lovely, gracious, excellent, worthy of praise. If these are norms for human being, whether Christian or not, they are also norms for the artist. How do they apply?

What does *truth* mean in art? It certainly does not mean that art has to be a copy of reality – in fact, art is never a copy of reality, and cannot be. Art always gives an interpretation of reality, of the thing seen, the relationships, the human reality experienced emotionally, rationally, and in many other human ways. Art always shows what a person – the artist and the group to which she or he belongs, the time in which she or he lives – sees and experiences as relevant, as important, as worthwhile. Otherwise the artist will never try to depict it. For medieval people landscape was not important, even though they lived in it; that is why they never tried to represent it. For the seventeenth-century Dutch, even a silver pitcher could be important or a broken glass, just because of its beauty or the effect of the light as it played over the surface. So for them the still life was important. Of course good artists in other periods might just as well have done the same: but they did not do so, because the ability here is of a 'spiritual' nature. The artist who made the magnificent series of statues in the cathedral at Naumburg with their very individual appearance was certainly able to make portraits, even though the statues were not portraits but representations of important figures who lived long before. Yet neither this artist nor any other at that time made portraits as such for 'spiritually' the times were not yet ripe, and we have to wait about half a century before people slowly and hesitantly made the first portraits. To represent something means that one thinks it to be of importance, and that one is spiritually open and free to do so. Art is always an interpretation, a certain view on reality. To the contemporaries, art sometimes seems to be so true to nature that they think that it is a copy in an almost exact way; but later periods will see the choice, the emphasis, the particular view and understanding. Nineteenth-century naturalism may seem to be almost photographically true – but, as I have shown in an earlier chapter, this type of art belongs to a particular spiritual stream and shows a particular kind of understanding of reality.

Truth in art does not mean doing accurate copies but that the artist's insight is rich and full, that he or she really has a good view of reality, one that does justice to the different elements of the aspect of reality represented. Truth has to do with the fullness of reality, its scope and meaning. So we can find works not only in a naturalistic style but also in the Romanesque style, or Gothic, or Baroque, or expressionistic, that are true, showing in truth at least some aspects of the reality represented.

So for the same reason truth in art does not mean that every detail has to be true in a physical, historical, theological, scientific or any other non-artistic way. It is artistic truth! Hamlet may never have lived – but Shakespeare's Hamlet is true insofar as Shakespeare has been able to make the figure he created true to reality, to human character and potential. If you are going to criticize Hamlet you must show inconsistencies in his character or in the way he is acted. You cannot object that Hamlet was probably never really like this historically. Not only is he no more than a stage figure, acting in keeping with the structure of the play, he is also a figure belonging to Shakespeare's time, not the period in which he is supposed to have lived. So too fairy tales can be true, if they show human action and behaviour in keeping with human character – within the framework of fairy-tale reality.

In our relativistic times it is often said that we cannot speak of truth in art, but that we must speak of honesty. The artist has to be honest. Certainly: this is the minimum requirement. If an artist tries to conceal his or her true intentions or tries to show off, if there is the sort of make-believe (as in many of the Salon pictures) which gives the impression that a work is in the seventeenth-century tradition while, in fact, the values contained in it are dead to the artist, this is dishonesty. These things show in a work of art. Honesty can be called subjective truth. Artists must show their own insight, their own vision, their own understanding. And all good works of art will do this. Picasso gives a clear and consistent statement of his nihilistic view on reality. He is honest to this extent: but does he really show reality in truth? Truth does not mean to be conceptually in accordance with reality – this is a rationalistic view of truth. The Bible speaks of *doing* the truth, acting in love and freedom, according to the relationships God wants for people. So in a way art *does* the truth often more than it *is* true in the sense that it portrays reality according to its conceptual reality. Art does the truth in its own artistic way. Doing the truth in this sense is closely related to the other qualities we must now go on to discuss.

Honour in art suggests to me what was formerly called 'decorum'. A work of art has to be in keeping with the place or occasion for which it is made, or the function it has to fulfil. You are not going to paint Christ on the cross in the style of a cartoon. Indeed, some 'Christian' art is at fault here: certain religious magazines sometimes portray Christ and biblical scenes in a way that is below standard, with a style that is too cheap. What is acceptable in a brochure for a new vacuum cleaner is wrong for such subjects, unless we are going to reduce Christianity to the level of commerciality and profit.

It is almost impossible to judge what is 'honourable' in art without specific examples. For instance, it is possible that some types of jazz could be very suitable as music in church, but we can never give a final evaluation without weighing up factors such as the connotations of jazz for the particular people who will be there. It depends on how people will react to it in a particular situation. The artist must bear this in mind carefully. A biblical figure can be represented in a sculpture of straw or other 'strange' material: but if this means for the person looking (a person of a particular time and culture) that the figure is debased and so of no importance, reducing it to the level of a souvenir, then this cannot be done with 'honour'.

Righteousness in art does not mean that, in fiction or on the stage, for instance, everyone must be upright and good. That would be against truth. Reality is different. The Bible includes plenty of descriptions of wickedness and evil.

To be righteous means to be right to the situation, to give each element its due: to create a right balance, a harmonious whole. Righteous is a biblical term with many overtones, including mercy and grace, and the term never means a hard judgment only with an eye to the letter of the law. It must be seen in the artist's knowledge and insight and right portrayal of reality expressed in his or her painting. So 'righteousness' can be expressed in details of colour, composition, even a brushstroke, as well as in a character in a novel, a situation in a play, even in a modulation in music.

Purity in art is the same as that of which Christ speaks when he said, 'Blessed are the pure in heart'. It is a mentality that cannot stand the evil, the lovelessness that does harm to others. Purity in art means helping those who read or listen or see to have pure thoughts. It does not titillate, does not play on people's wrong desires, it does not seduce. It helps a person to see the good and the beautiful. It shows iniquity, it protests, but in a protest of love against the unjust and the debased and evil.

It is in this framework that I must consider the question of nudity in art. Art does not copy reality, and it is possible to show things in art that cannot be shown in social reality. Nudity is found in the art of every period. In some periods, and among some artists, for instance Rembrandt and (sometimes) Dürer, the nude means a person in his or her nakedness, weakness – quite the opposite of the heroic nude often found in Renaissance art, for instance, where it was a symbol of human greatness. In both cases, however, there was nothing pornographic about it – neither by intention nor in the way it influences the onlooker. In fact, slightly clothed figures are often much more erotic.

The erotic and the sexual have a place in art, as they have in life. As such they are neither dirty nor impure. They are a gift from God and belong to humanity itself. But people have often focused their attention on sex and carnal love in a sinful way. Yet the physical relationship between the sexes can be beautiful when it is an expression of true love. The female body can be beautiful, and this beauty is not a thing to be ashamed of: though in our society a woman is not expected to show her body without clothes, in other cultures this is quite possible without any immorality. Modesty in fact is a moral quality, and its expression is different in different cultures and societies. Even where the body can be shown without clothes one can still speak of modesty and immodesty. Behaviour is the expression of an attitude.

So we cannot simply say that the nude in art is impure. This is against all experience. Look at Jan van Eyck's Eve in his great *Lamb of God* altarpiece in Ghent – there is no purer woman ever painted. And look at the clothed Maya of Goya – she is more immodest than the nude Maya, showing the same woman in the same attitude. Purity is a norm but not an easy rule that can be applied indiscriminately. We have to exercise our human judgment, with all our wisdom, understanding and prudence. For to the artist purity is an intention. It might be appropriate to use the nude in art, whether it is in literature or in the visual arts, and even to speak of intercourse with completely pure motives, while avoiding them does not mean that the intention or the work itself is automatically pure and clean.

Nudity in films and on the stage, permissiveness in books and in fashion and advertising, all this is partly a reaction against Victorian prudishness (itself a sign of an unhealthy view of sex, as we have seen), partly a sign of increasing lawlessness as all conventions and norms are thrown out. As customs change so fast, it is often difficult to know exactly what the intention is in a particular instance of nudity. But it is not always impossible, and we should judge with care rather than hastily. This is even more so when dealing with art from the past or from other cultures. We have to take into account the mores and customs, the prevailing moral rules, if we want to avoid gross mistakes and injustice. However, there is often no need to give a final verdict. As Christians we may often (even must) leave the judgment in God's hands.[131] What is more important is that we can each exercise our own personal responsibility (which may be different for each of us).

In all this it is vital to realize that it is not what goes into us that makes us impure, but what is already within us, or comes out of us, as Jesus showed so trenchantly.[132] It is not when we see or hear or read something that we are wrong and commit sin, but when our thoughts are impure or our imagination adulterous. So each of us must exercise our own Christian responsibility. What one can experience may lead another to sin – and what one cannot stand may not be harmful to another. This is Christian freedom, not a freedom for licence but a Christian responsibility to keep oneself clean from sin. And it is important to be aware of the fact that these things are not only, not even specifically, related to the sexual sphere. What we have been saying applies just as much to other aspects of our daily living.

What is *loveliness* in art? Obviously loveliness and beauty do not just belong to the arts. They belong to life in two ways (leaving the beauty of nature aside). First, beauty and loveliness can be expressed in human character, in inner harmony, in activities that are adequate and good. What we are asked to show and to search for is an inner beauty expressing itself in a 'beautiful' life. This is what Peter meant in his first letter when he said we must keep our tongue from evil and do good. Second, beauty and loveliness should be seen in the things we make and the things we have around us. In the 'applied' arts, for instance, loveliness can be expressed in the design, fitness for purpose and attractiveness of utensils, furniture, in everything we have around us. No people are going to make their environment deliberately ugly, dirty or unpleasant unless they themselves are inwardly ugly or out of keeping with their inner self. I do not mean here that beauty is the final norm or the most important value. If I did, I would be no more than an aestheticist. And I certainly do not mean that we must all possess expensive works of art – taste and a feeling for beauty are not to be bought with money. Loveliness is a norm insofar as it belongs to the whole of life and is held alongside all the other norms.

When thinking of beauty as applied to the arts, many people use the standard of classicism or of artists of the High Renaissance such as Raphael. But the beauty in Raphael's pictures is only a certain type of beauty. Rembrandt often did paintings that would be ugly by this standard – perhaps they are more human and more beautiful for that very reason. And if it is a norm that we should keep our lives clean and pure and beautiful as well as our surroundings, this does not mean that in art nothing that is bad or ugly or negative can be portrayed, as we have seen in our discussion of the 'horrible' in art. Beauty is expressed in line and colour, shape and form, rhythm and sound, rhyme and the relationship of words and composition, unity and diversity. It is through these very things that beauty is realized: it is not found abstractly in them. Truth, honour and purity are made visible by these means, are expressed by them. Without them beauty cannot be realized, yet the means cannot be said to be the end, the aim, the final value. A certain shape that is beautiful and completely right for its particular position within the context of a specific work of art, carrying a particular meaning, can be valueless and even out of place elsewhere.

Excellence and praise in art are again an obvious norm. Which artist would make a work of art that is bad, valueless, disgusting? It is true that today we may often encounter these things, for these are the signs of a strong inner tension, of a crisis, of despair, of revolution, of disgust. But even then their value and effectiveness depend on the fact that the norm is really held to be the norm. They can only break the rules where there are rules. Indeed we can say that if such a work was considered beautiful, or 'normal', it would have lost its meaning, and we should have thrown away the key to understanding it. Dada's black humour can only live in the negation of, or in play with, these norms. The revolt is the anarchy of denial.

So truth, honour, righteousness, loveliness, excellence and praise are as much norms for art as they are for life. And in all of them we feel that to by-pass them is to do wrong to the beholder, to fall short of being truly loving. For basically these norms are all aspects of the great command to love. Love is the great norm, in art as well. Love is to make things that are right and fitting, to help our neighbours, to make this world more beautiful, more harmonious, more suitable for human living, more suitable for expressing that inner beauty and love for which all people are searching – even if, in despair, humankind often breaks it down; even if, in sin, we often destroy beauty and create ugliness. Beauty, as it were, is a by-product of love, of life in its full sense, of life in love and freedom. The artist, with her or his special gifts, has a specific task, a very special and wonderful calling. It is not to play the prophet, nor to be a teacher, nor to be a preacher, nor to evangelize. It is to make life better, more worthwhile, to create the sound, the shape, the tale, the decoration, the environment that is meaningful and lovely and a joy to humankind.

The Christian artist

How is the Christian artist to fulfil this role, and to work out these norms? Can one really create the lovely and beautiful in a loving way for one's neighbours? It is a calling to promote good and to fight evil, ugliness, the negative; to hunger and thirst for righteousness; to search for the right 'finishing touch', the right tone, the right word in the right place.

Christian artists have to create in an open and positive relationship to the structure of the world in which they were created by God; they have to act, on the foundation of Christ as their Lord and Saviour, in love and freedom.

They must have love for the people for whom the work is meant, for the material they use, for the subject they choose, for the truth they are going to express, for the Lord they are serving.

They must know freedom by not being bound wrongly to humanly crafted rules. In their art they are free from the past, the present and the future. They can be traditional if they choose and feel that to be right, they can search for new ways, new materials, new subject matter, new techniques if they feel they need them in order to achieve their goals.

Love and freedom belong closely together, just as sin and slavery belong together. If Christians feel that they have to make all kinds of rules in a legalistic way, even if they do so with the best intentions and aim only to preserve the good, yet they kill freedom, and in the end love is gone and beauty has fled. God gave his children freedom and we should not try to know better. Freedom is only truly possible, as we have seen, within the norms and structures and laws within which God has made us. It is for the Christian to distinguish between a false legalism and a true freedom to be what God intends us to be, for without this freedom art will wither.

Love and freedom are never cheap, and they are weakened by sin, pride, selfishness, greed and hate. Love and freedom belong to normal human life as given by God to people, but now, after the Fall, they are hard to achieve, to create, to realize. Christ came to make them possible. He died in order that we might be truly human, to have love, freedom and beauty and all the good things.

Beauty of course is something given by God as a gift to all to create. It is not limited to Christians. But because Christians have been made new in Christ, they are now in a position to appreciate God's true intention for humankind and the world and to create beauty in art as a result. So we will pray as we work. We will pray to the Lord for help – to open our eyes to the real possibilities, to open our eyes to see how we can achieve the best for our neighbours, to help us in creating according to the best that is in us. Our art, as everything else, must be from him, through him and to him.

When I am walking round an art gallery and see a beautiful painting, it may be good to praise the Lord and to thank him for that great gift. The thing is beautiful, and therefore a joy and spiritually rich, perhaps just because the artist was in tune with reality or because he loved the woman he painted, the landscape she lived in, the people he was working for. It is possible that the artist had prayed to the Lord to help him or her in the work – and then our thanksgiving to God is really thanking God for that answered prayer. We do not usually know. But more than likely it will not even occur to us, for we place the arts out of the context of life, making them something autonomous; or we say that the gift is 'just natural', so opposing nature with grace, forgetting that there is no nature that is out of God's creation. No, let us give praise to God for every manifestation of his gifts. And let Christian artists look to the inspiration of the Holy Spirit and the renewal of their life in Christ, not only to acknowledge the source of the gift they have but also in order to have the love and freedom that will enable them to create the good and the beautiful themselves.

But however much we look to God to help us to remain free, we cannot make art apart from the time in which we live. We must know what is going on and understand our environment if we want to achieve anything of relevance to our times. We must also know the spirit of our times in order to know where it is wrong and should be challenged and fought. We may look for inspiration to the arts of the past – but we may never be slaves of the past. And we can never just follow the past: the battle and the means of creativity were theirs for their own situation. And God, in placing us in another period, has given us our own calling: to be 'salting salt' today, to hunger and thirst for righteousness in the here and now. Our world has changed, for better or for worse. It is for us to find truth and beauty for today, constantly re-applying the truth of God's word to our own times and to our own contemporary situations.

Only if we live in this way shall we be 'salting salt' and the fruit of the Holy Spirit seen in our work. The way will not be easy if we really want to show something of the richness and truth of created reality in our art. We shall soon find that we will have to find a way back to it. It can easily be that our first attempts will be poor and second-rate. I only trust that our fellow Christians who stand beside us and watch our efforts will be helpful and encouraging, so that a new bud will not be frozen by coldness and lack of interest or understanding. The way may be long and hard. And artists are virtually never able to succeed alone. They need a community to back them up: if they fail it may be their fellow Christians who are at fault, failing to give them the positive response they need. But without this creativity we shall not be able to show the real validity of an art and life based on Christ our Lord.

Christian art does not come cheaply and easily. It can never be the first and direct fruit of the work of somebody who is just starting, even if she or he is a real Christian. We have lost so much in our civilization (and we Christians are also responsible for the fact) that the way will be long and tiring. But perhaps we can lay a foundation for the next generation, who may build on what we have done to create something really great and fine. Or perhaps our small evidence of the fruit of the Spirit will have its own influence, helping to stop the rising tide of absurdity and ugly meaninglessness (or even beautiful meaninglessness).

Whether God will give us this or not, whether we shall have time to do it or not, whether as artists we are good or bad, as long as we can stand before him saying that we have fought our battle and followed our calling, we can be confident. We do not need to be afraid, for nothing can separate us from his love.

The Christian in a changing world

What is the Christian's calling in the world of today, which we have seen so clearly reflected in today's art? Can we really take a full part in the arts, plays, literature, philosophy, revolutionary activity? Can we be people of our times in this sense?

The world has changed in the last decades. We have seen the crumbling of a culture. Increasingly we see ourselves living in a world that is postchristian and even post-humanist, a neo-pagan world that which is nihilist or anarchist or mystic. Whatever the signature of the day, however, it must be clear that every day we come nearer to the situation of the early Christians. Every time we read Peter's letters we can understand what he was saying better. For his letters were sent to Christians who were a small minority. We cannot now expect people to follow our rules, our insights, our morals, automatically. We shall be more and more pilgrims and strangers in the world.

What is our calling? Of course each of us has the calling to be a Christian and to live as one. This sometimes, in a world full of all kinds of temptations, in advertising, films, TV and so on, is not so easy. But, in general, if we have the chance of doing something or of saying something because we are in a position to do so, because we are on a committee or have some other responsible position, what should we be doing and saying? What in fact is our calling?

First, we must stand for freedom. Of course the world around us is full of the cry of freedom. But, as Peter writes, they promise them freedom, but they themselves are slaves of corruption. The revolutionaries speak of freedom, yet we find that if you are not for their kind of freedom, you have no right to say so. The revolution is totalitarian. It leads to dictatorship in the name of freedom. Here we are called never to compromise but to fight for true freedom. We must defend the freedom even of those whom we do not like, even of movements we feel to be wrong. We may never be totalitarian in that sense. We shall stand for freedom for many reasons: because humanity is lost if freedom is gone; because love has no place in a world without freedom; and certainly too because in a world without freedom we shall not have the liberty to be Christians, to tell out the good news, to invite others to our meetings. The Bible teaches us to pray for good government, so that we may live in peace and so that others may have the opportunity of hearing the gospel.

We shall stand for freedom. In love, and with responsibility, we must see that in many different ways the people around us are not being deprived of their inner freedom. If young people are ostracized when they do not want to participate in 'free' love, we must fight for their freedom. If people are almost forced to take up the status symbols, we must stand for the freedom to be different. We must stand against the pressures on the person in the crowd towards conformity or bad morals. We must stand against everything that takes away personal freedom of choice. We shall hunger and thirst for righteousness, for we know that sin always takes away freedom and makes men and women into slaves. Where sin is made 'normal' and people are asked to participate or else . . . we always shall stand for freedom against tyranny, against the forces that dehumanize.

Freedom in this sense can never be a simple slogan. It is always something specific. It is never cheap, and always demands responsibility, involvement, loving our neighbour even if that is going to take our time, our energy, even our life.

Of course, we must begin to live freedom ourselves. We must show the inner freedom of those who have been made 'truly free' by Jesus Christ. We must show that we are free from greed, sin, hate, the need to dominate, free to do good, free to fight the evils of the day and to protest in love. Freedom is not just negative, freedom *from* something: on the contrary, freedom opens up possibilities; freedom is *for, towards* something. Christian freedom is positive, dynamic.

But we must not only stand for freedom. We must also stand for humanity. Personality is a great gift, and we shall stand against forces that try to take it away by making people conform or by making people behave 'normally', which means just like everyone else. Humanity is a great asset, a great gift from God, and we shall do all we can to withhold the dehumanizing forces of today which would turn human beings into little cogs in the big machine, into numbers in the computer. Of course, what we ask for may be less efficient or less profitable economically. But efficiency and profitability, though right and important in their place, are not primary values. Humanity comes first. Seek first God's kingdom, Jesus said, 'and all these things shall be yours as well' – yes, perhaps in the long run a stand for humanity will mean more efficiency and more profit, though that is not going to be the reason why we are taking it.

It is for the sake of humanity that we stand against every pressure that would drag women down to the level of objects of lust. For that same reason we are against all kinds of manipulation, in advertising, in the mass communication media, in the policy in the field of the arts that would promote only one stream (however 'contemporary' or 'modern' it may be called). Humanity, involving manhood and womanhood, is something of too great a worth to be deprived of its value and meaning.

Again, humanity is not cheap. It is worth our lives, and it is for us to make something creatively of our lives, to realize the given possibilities, the human potential. And we shall stand for it so that others can enter into the same possibilities if they wish. Here too this means that we must show first of all in our own lives that we have this humanity, that we live openly and creatively; above all, that we show that we are new men and women, a new humanity in Christ.

Our calling is also to be critical of our times. Christians are called to speak prophetically. To hunger and thirst for righteousness means that we shall never just defend the established order of the day. It might be the easiest way; taking new paths, or paths that may be different from the traditional ones, means taking risks and giving energy, time, involvement. But even if defending the establishment is often easy, it cheapens us and leads away from our calling to fight for what is right, for justice, love, beauty, truth. Christians should never be conservative simply for the sake of conformity, of conserving the established order for its own sake. We must be critical.

We may be called to protest, too. Perhaps the strong protest movement of today is a result of the fact that the existing order was too much taken for granted, and was left free to become overconfident and too static. We should have protested before others have shown us the need to do so. Christians should have been aware, not just of the current undermining of sexual morality but also of the wrong sort of prudishness that caused it, the playing down of the fact that the gift of sex is from God and good and to be rejoiced in. We must be constantly aware of any growing lack of freedom, of the authoritarianism of petty bureaucracy that treats people as things, of any forces that dehumanize. We should have protested, and protested in love, not in hate and anarchy, because we care for freedom and humanity and hate all sin and all unrighteousness.

'Protest in love' is just another way of saying that we should always hunger and thirst for righteousness. This means that we shall never compromise, never accept the status quo because that is the easiest thing to do or seems inevitable. For Jesus told us to watch that we do not try to gain the world at the expense of our true selves.

To take this stand, to respond to our calling today means that we shall not be afraid to show that we are Christians; not only in saying that we have been saved by Christ but also in our stand, in our way of life, in our prophetic analysis of the situation. It means to be radical, to go back to the roots, to the very foundation, which is Christ. To be Christian involves all our work and activity, understanding that there is nothing neutral, nothing apart from Christ's reign. Our very humanity, our everyday human life, including both the intellectual and the emotional, is something we shall thank him for, and something that we shall have to defend against the attacks of the spirit of our age, and also something we must develop in a creative way, realizing all our possibilities, our full potential. And we shall not be afraid to be seen and to act as Christians because we know that our Christian life does not depend on ourselves, nor on the fact that we are perfect: 'we have confidence before God; and we receive from him whatever we ask, because we keep his commandments and do what pleases him.'[133]

Our calling is to live in freedom and love, to fight against sin, to stand for freedom and humanity. It is to show love and compassion not only towards those we love and those who love us, but for modern people who have lost the track, who have become enslaved, who cry out for humanity, for love and freedom and truth, without ever finding them. It is not for us to condemn – for God is the judge – but to pray and work for them, meeting them openly and without reproach, accepting their ways and customs in the same way as Paul told us to be both Greek to the Greeks and Jew to the Jews. This means that we will have to study their problems, their ideas, know their language – what words mean to them – in order to be able to communicate. We must realize that the 'world' is not simply something remote – it is more often than not very near to us, in our very beings – but that the 'world' means people, human beings and personalities. We must help them, each of them, in their particular and very specific problems and needs.

As Christians today we realize that we are living in hard times. It is hard to keep to the right path; temptations are legion. And as we look around, it is hard to see a great culture breaking down around us, even though, as we have seen, it is not really based on Christian principles but on those of the Enlightenment.

But for that very reason, these are exciting times. God has called us to bear witness to him at a critical point of history. It is not only exciting and interesting to be a Christian now, it is a great privilege and responsibility. And it is vital.

Perhaps the most fitting conclusion would be to adapt Psalm 136 to express the greatness and wonder of all that we have seen God do in history – and in our own times:

> Give thanks to him who created this great cosmos, this earth, and all the structures that make creative work possible for people in love and freedom,
> *His mercy endures for ever.*
> He did great things in the times of Moses and the beginnings of the written revelation when he spoke to his chosen people from Mount Sinai,
> *His mercy endures for ever.*
> He was great, so great that he inspired the psalmist to sing this psalm in his own time, a time of sorrow and trial, a time of triumph and victory,
> *His mercy endures for ever.*
> He sent his prophets, and they spoke of his mercy; they spoke against a people that walked in their own ways, following strange gods; they warned against wars, droughts and captivity to come – and these came indeed, yet a remnant would remain, for
> *His mercy endures for ever.*
> He sent his Son, who spoke of judgment and mercy, who spoke against those that could see and yet were blind, while opening the blind man's eyes; who said he saw the evil one falling out from heaven; who died for our sin and evil, and rose from the dead, for
> *His mercy endures for ever.*
> And he spoke again, against a church that was lukewarm; He gave great promises for those that would overcome, and showed his servant John all the plagues and wars that were to come, how his people would be sealed with his own seal, and how their prayers would be heard, for
> *His mercy endures for ever.*
> He built and led his church, sent teachers and prophets to warn the church of its complacency and self-sufficiency, sent reformers to lead his church back to the truth, helped his servants and his children, as
> *His mercy endures for ever.*
> He is great in our days, when his hand is heavy on a world that despises him and looks for strange new ideas and new gods, when

the culture once given is crumbling even though people have great technological means at their disposal, when the mode of the music changes, when the times are changing, when things happen and people do not know what they are; when yet many look for humanity, or renewal, or even reformation, for it is still true that he loves us and hears our prayers in order to help his children; so that our song can be,

His mercy endures for ever.

Bibliography to Modern Art and the Death of a Culture

M.H. Abrams, *Natural Supernaturalism: Tradition and Revolution in Romantic Literature.* London: Oxford University Press, 1971.

H.H. Arnason, *A History of Modern Art.* London: Thames and Hudson, 1969.

W. Barclay, *Ethics in a Permissive Society.* London: Fontana, 1972.

W. Barrett, *Irrational Man – A Study in Existential Philosophy.* London: Heinemann, 1961.

H. Blamires, *The Christian Mind.* London: SPCK, 1963.

D.W. Bolam and J.L. Henderson, *Art and Belief.* New York: Schocken Books, 1969.

C. Booker, *The Neophiliacs.* London: Collins, 1969.

D.J. Boorstin, *The Image.* Harmondsworth: Penguin Books, 1963.

H.O.J. Brown, *The Protest of a Troubled Protestant.* Grand Rapids, Michigan: Zondervan, 1970.

H. Dooyeweerd, *In the Twilight of Western Thought.* Philadelphia: Presbyterian and Reformed Publishing Co., 1960.

W.A. Dyrness, *Rouault, a Vision of Suffering and Salvation.* Grand Rapids, Michigan: Eerdmans, 1971.

D.D. Egbert, *Social Radicalism and the Arts: a Cultural History from the French Revolution to 1968.* New York: Knopf, 1970.

M. Esslin, *The Theatre of the Absurd.* New York: Anchor Books, 1961.

R. Etchells, *Unafraid to Be: A Christian Study of Contemporary English Writing.* London: Inter-Varsity Press, 1969.

F. Eversole (ed.), *Christian Faith and the Contemporary Arts.* Nashville: Abingdon Press, 1962.

E.F. Fry, *Cubism.* London: Thames and Hudson, 1966.

P. Gay, *The Enlightenment: An Interpretation* (2 vols). London: Weidenfeld and Nicolson, 1969–1970.

C. Gillett, *The Sound of the City: The Rise of Rock and Roll*. New York: Outerbridge and Dienstfrey, 1970.

B. Griffiths (ed.), *Is Revolution Change?* London: Inter-Varsity Press, 1972.

J.S. Gummer, *The Permissive Society: Fact or Fantasy?* London: Cassell, 1971.

S. Hannema, *Fads, Fakes and Fantasies: the Crisis in the Art Schools and the Crisis in Art*. London: Macdonald, 1970.

K. Harries, *The Meaning of Modern Art: A Philosophical Interpretation*. Evanston: Northwestern University Press, 1968.

W. Hofmann, *The Earthly Paradise, Art in the Nineteenth Century*. London: Faber, London, 1961.

Holbrook Jackson, *The Eighteen Nineties*. Harmondsworth: Penguin Books, 1950 (first edn. 1913).

H.L.C. Jaffé, *De Stijl 1917–1931*. Amsterdam: Meulenhoff, 1956 (English edition, Thames and Hudson, London, 1970).

Kenneth Keniston, *The Uncommitted*. New York: Harvest Books, 1965.

— *Young Radicals*. New York: Harvest Books, 1968.

S. Lövgren, *The Genesis of Modernism* (Seurat, Gauguin, van Gogh and French Symbolism in the 1880s). Stockholm, 1959.

G. Melly, *Revolt into Style – the Pop Arts in Britain*. London, Allen Lane: The Penguin Press, 1970.

H.R. Niebuhr, *Christ and Culture*. London: Faber and Faber, 1952.

V. Packard, *The Hidden Persuaders*. Harmondsworth: Penguin Books, 1960.

— *The Naked Society*. Harmondsworth: Penguin Books, 1964.

M. Praz, *The Romantic Agony*. London: Fontana, 1960.

H. Read, *The Philosophy of Modern Art*. London: Meridian Books, 1955.

J. Rewald, *The History of Impressionism*. New York: Museum of Modern Art, 1946.

— *Post-Impressionism*. New York: Museum of Modern Art, 1956.

H.R. Rookmaaker, *Art and the Public Today*. Huémoz, Switzerland: L'Abri Fellowship, 1968. See part II in this volume of the *Complete Works*.

— *Gauguin and Nineteenth-century Art Theory* (reprint of *Synthetist Art Theories*). Amsterdam: Swets and Zeitlinger, 1972. See *Complete Works* 1.

— 'The Christian and Art'. In *The Encyclopedia of Christianity*, see 'Art'. Wilmington, Delaware, 1964. See *Complete Works* 4, part II.

Th. Roszak, *The Making of a Counter-Culture*. London: Faber, 1970.

S. Rubin, *Do It! Scenarios of the Revolution*. London: Cape, 1970.

Dorothy Sayers, *Christian Letters to a Post-Christian World*. Grand Rapids, Michigan: Eerdmans, 1969.

— *The Mind of the Maker*. New York: Harcourt, 1942.

F.A. Schaeffer, *The Church at the End of the 20th Century*. London: Norfolk Press, 1970.

— *Death in the City*. London: Inter-Varsity Press, 1969.

— *Escape from Reason*. London: Inter-Varsity Press, 1968.

— *The God Who is There*. London: Hodder and Stoughton, 1968.

C. Seerveld, *A Christian Critique of Art and Literature*. Hamilton, Ontario: Guardian Publishing Co., 1968.

A. Shaw, *The Rock Revolution*. New York: Paperback Library, 1971.

F.W. Sypher, *The Loss of Self in Modern Literature and Art*. New York: Random House, 1962.

E.L. Hebdon Taylor, *Reformation or Revolution*. Nutley, N.J.: Craig Press, 1970.

W. Hebdon Taylor, *The Christian Philosophy of Law, Politics and the State*. Nutley, N.J.: Craig Press, 1966.

H.R. van Til, *The Calvinistic Concept of Culture*. Philadelphia: Presbyterian and Reformed Publishing Co., 1959.

A.N. Triton, *Whose World?* London: Inter-Varsity Press, 1970.

A. Willener, *The Action-Image of Society*. London: Tavistock Publications, 1970.

D. Williams, *Trousered Apes: A Study in the Influence of Literature on Contemporary Society*. London: Churchill Press. 1971.

H. Zijlstra, *Testament of Vision*. Grand Rapids, Michigan: Eerdmans, 1961.

Part II

ART AND THE PUBLIC TODAY

Introduction by H.R.R. to the 2nd Edition[134]

On May 28, 1965 the writer delivered the customary inaugural speech marking the assumption of a professorship at a Dutch university, in his case in the History of Art at the Free University at Amsterdam. The English translation of that speech appears here under the title: 'The Artist as a Prophet?'. Some brief additions have been made, one to elucidate more explicitly why Christians cannot accept the old theory that the poet is a prophet, another to clarify the implications for Christian endeavour in the arts. Minor modifications concern only notes or the addition of citations of material that appeared after the address was delivered.

I have also discarded the formal opening and closing words traditionaly addressed to the Trustees of the university, the Faculty, former teachers (in my case Professor Dr J.Q. van Regteren Altena) and colleagues (in my case Professor Dr H. van de Waal, head of the Department of History of Art of the University of Leiden, and the members of that department) and future students. But since the English translation of this speech is now being published by the L'Abri Fellowship Foundation, it seems appropriate to include the words I addressed to the Revd F.A. Schaeffer:

> It seems to me a token, not only of our friendship but also of our spiritual unity, that you have come from Switzerland for this occasion. Since the first time we met, in 1948, we have had many long talks about faith, philosophy, reality, art, the modern world, and their mutual relations. I owe very much to these discussions, which have helped to shape my thoughts on these subjects. I want to express my deep gratitude, and consider it a great honour and joy to be a member of L'Abri Fellowship.

I want to thank the Directors of the Vrije Universiteit [Free University] of Amsterdam for their kindness in providing the funds for the translation of the inaugural speech.

[In this re-publication] we have followed the inaugural speech with another related article, on commitment in art.

Dr H.R. Rookmaaker

The Artist as a Prophet?[135]

I should like to begin by quoting a short American poem:

> VOICE
> If you see a man
> walking down a crowded street
> talking ALOUD to himself
> don't run in the opposite direction
> but run towards him.
> For he is a poet!
> You have nothing to fear
> from the poet
> but the truth![136]

This poem was written by a man named Ted Joans, who belongs to the 'beat' generation, an African-American who is also an Abstract Expressionist painter and trumpet player in the style of Dizzy Gillespie.[137] It says that the poet is not like other people and freely cites Horatius who said, 'Men of sense fear to touch a crazy poet and run away.'[138] In the last lines we are reassured somewhat ironically that the poet speaks only the truth. This brief poem contains the theme I would like to consider here: the artist as prophet, the revealer of truth.

The statement this poem makes is far from original and belongs not only to our times.[139] It is, in fact, a *topos*,[140] namely a very old idea of which the origin lies far back in history. To the Greeks the poet was an inspired man who creates beauty in a divine madness: he examines ideas and reveals the truth. This is the view expressed by Plato in his *Phaidros*,[141] although it must be kept in mind here that some authors hold it is not at all certain that Plato considered art in the same sense we do.[142] But even if this is so, Plato's concepts remain extremely important because of the conclusions drawn from them by later generations.[143] For us, because we are especially concerned with the plastic arts, it is of importance that neither Plato nor his contemporaries considered painting and sculpture as very important and saw them more as technical arts, skills having nothing to do with divine inspiration. Not until the Hellenistic period did painters and sculptors begin to be held in increasing esteem. A more important place in the theory of art was assigned to them in recognition of the honour due to the artists of the fifth and fourth centuries before Christ, artists who were highly admired by the time antiquity drew to a close. For instance, in the first century after Christ a theory of art was ascribed to Phidias in which the plastic arts were seen as the agents of a higher truth; the artist could therefore be mentioned in the same breath as the prophet and the poet.[144]

This theory, however, did not reach its final form until the end of the period, in the third century after Christ, with Plotinus. His influence was indeed so great that even until a fairly recent period it would be more accurate (at least as far as aesthetics are concerned) to speak of Plotinic rather than Platonic philosophy. In Plotinus we find a direct relationship between artistic creativity and mysticism: humankind, alienated from god, see in art, as in a mirror, the reflection of the higher divine being.[145] But, however splendid this theory may have been, it was far from generally accepted with respect to the plastic arts, and had little significance for the appreciation and the social position of the living artist.[146]

With the Renaissance came a revival of Plotinic philosophy in Ficino and Pico della Mirandola.[147] The Plotinic theory of art took hold again and the artist became an *alter deus* ('another God').[148] Kris and Kurz deal very effectively with the point in their important book on the (myth of the) artist: 'The Renaissance thinks of the (plastic) artist as an inspired man; he becomes the pencil of God, and is venerated as divine. The religion, of which he is one of the saints, is the religion of the genius of the modern day.'[149] The antique theory of art, in a new garb, was applied to the living artist. But we cannot entirely escape the impression that the primary concern in this period was to provide the painter and sculptor with a place in the ranks of the important men of culture, poets and scholars, high above the simple artisans of the guilds, rather than to honour them as prophets or to expect of them that they would reveal the truth.[150] This latter concept did not reach full stature until around 1800, at precisely the time when artists began to become more and more alienated from society.

In the art world of the seventeenth and early eighteenth centuries Plotinic concepts were certainly not entirely forgotten or meaningless, but in the classicistic theory of art, with its emphasis on decorum and the belief that art can be taught, there was no mention of divine madness and prophecy. Even though the plastic arts were highly esteemed, they were generally regarded more soberly, more in terms of 'the rules of art'.[151] If artists were asked to paint the passions, this meant more the expression of the feelings and emotions of the figures in the work of art than of those of the artists themselves.[152]

At the end of the eighteenth century, in a violent reaction against, remarkably enough, both academic ideas and the (Baroque) Rococo, the old *topos* was revived once again because of a desire to place art on a very exalted level. The conflict about whether priority was to be given to science or to personality (to the scientistic[153] theories of the Enlightenment or to the ideal of rational and moral humanity) was solved in the idealistic philosophy of Kant and his school by the introduction of a strict separation between them. This necessitated a third principle, in which the two could be related once again in a synthesis. This is the subject treated by Kant in his *Kritik der Urteilskraft*[154] of 1790 which deals with the aesthetic, the beautiful and the sublime. In this volume Kant provided a philosophical basis for a growing and very conscious artistic movement, typified by Goethe and Schiller. It was Schelling who, in the beginning of the nineteenth century, further worked out and gave depth to the idea of the *ästhetische Vernunft*, to arrive finally, once again, at a view of art strongly oriented towards Plotinus, in which art is assigned the exalted task of resolving the conflicts between theoretical and practical philosophy, between nature and freedom.[155]

The artist was seen as prophet, high priest, and in any case as spiritual mentor of humanity.[156] This role was assigned to the genius, the genius as the creative force in human life. In a certain sense the idea of the genius was a secularization of the old concept of the divinely inspired prophet. This is the sense in which Friedrich Schlegel called the artist 'the higher spiritual sense organ of humanity'.[157] The *topos* of divine madness, too, acquired a more secular content: artists are people whose attitudes are not of the real world; their high calling and their nature as geniuses place them in a certain sense above (bourgeois) laws and norms, but also estrange them from the life of the community. In this connection it is interesting to consider another short poem, this one by André Chenier, which at the same time adds an amusing note to Ted Joans's poet talking to himself in the street. This second poem asks of Apollo:

> Give me the mind, glory, genius of a poet,
> everything however except the childlike mania
> of many a person who, possessed by learned breath,
> yet foolish and inept in everything apart from verse,
> ridiculous, driven as a toy by a restless
> spirit, is always a poet and nothing but a poet.[158]

But let us turn back to the lofty theories of art. If art is assigned so high a place, surely that must affect reality. It then becomes hardly surprising that a man like Schiller, who was influenced by both Kant and Goethe, wrote a book called *Über die ästhetische Erziehung des Menschen* ('On the aesthetic education of humankind'),[159] in which he said that art had often been in the service of the spirit of the times and the taste of amateurs; it then renders life more agreeable and drops to the level of humanity. There, however, it is unable to perform its exalted educational task. But from time to time there appears an artist who triumphantly rises above that level. He [or she] comes to purify his own time: 'The subject matter will be taken from the present time, but the form from a loftier period, even better, beyond all time, from the absolute unchangeable unity of his being. Out of the spirit of his demonic[160] nature flows the spring of beauty, undiluted by the rottenness of the generations and the periods.'[161] Therefore, cried

Schiller to the artist, do not attempt to reform the world by direct means, but do it in this way: 'In the secluded stillness of your soul you must bring forth the victorious truth, project it outside of yourself in beauty, so that not only thought praises it, but so that the senses will also accept its appearance in loving caresses.'[162] Schiller's book ends with the expectation that, aroused by the beauty of art, freedom, equality and the brotherhood [and sisterhood] of humanity would at last be realized.[163] It is striking that this aestheticism, in its very attempt to achieve a high place for art, causes art de facto to lose its significance; it is to serve not as art but rather to have a prophetic or educational function in the service of exalted humanistic ideals.

This can also be clearly seen in the remarkable figure of A.J. Langbehn, who at the end of the nineteenth century wished to reform the Germany of Bismarck and Kaiser Wilhelm with its unimaginative worship of science (his ideals indeed closely approached those of Naziism), and to achieve this by means of Rembrandt. The title of his widely read book was *Rembrandt als Erzieher* ('Rembrandt as educator'). For him too the prophet and the artist were closely related: both affect their times and shape the mind of the people.[164]

Schiller's ideals have been developed pedagogically in our times, particularly by Munro and Sir Herbert Read; the humanistic ideals have been retained and the new foundation is found in modern philosophers such as Dewey and in psychology as developed by Freud. The formulation has taken on a strongly secular (*diesseitig*) character, and the masters of education through art are not tempted to speak of artists as divinely inspired prophets. Yes, art as such has even partially disappeared from the horizon and been replaced by creative self-expression. The humanistic ideals, as we have said, are still there; Munro succinctly states his definition: 'the arts as an aid to the balanced harmonious development of personality'.[165]

It is time now for us to ask ourselves whether the exalted ideas of art and beauty entertained by the Romantics had a direct bearing on painting and sculpture. Goethe[166] and Schiller did not forget them; the latter argued, for instance, that the Graeco-Roman works of art held the ideal visibly high in a time of barbaric deterioration.[167] But the painters and the sculptors lagged far behind philosophy and literature. Only after 1800 did they begin to regard themselves in the light of ideas concerning the exalted task and place of their work.[168] It will be sufficient to illustrate this with a quotation from the painter Otto Runge, whose intellectual capacities were indeed stronger than his artistic abilities: 'What you have experienced in your eternal soul is incorruptible; here must spring the source of art if she wants to be eternal . . . we represent symbols of our thoughts about great forces of the world.'[169]

Outside Germany, exalted idealistic-Romantic theories of art took hold more slowly.[170] William Blake, who spoke of 'art's redeeming power', professed and expressed the Plotinic theory of art with the greatest consistency, but he was a strange and exceptional figure and in no sense typical of his times.[171]

The high esteem for the plastic arts – in the first place those of the classical period, in the second place the older art of the nation, and only in the last place contemporary art – is clearly evident in the ideas pertaining to museums as they began to develop after 1800. The starting point was always taken to be the direct influence of art on the soul, however seldom so directly and naïvely as the writer who spoke of 'speaking examples' (*redende Vorbilder*) and who advocated confronting criminals with pictures of torture scenes as a means of impelling confession.[172] A typical representative of this movement is Wilhelm Tischbein, who called the Vatican Museum 'an instructive school for the mind' (*eine lehrreiche Schule für den Geist*), in which painting 'teaches moral behaviour' (*unterrichtet und lehrt sich sittlich zu betragen*)![173] This finally led to the idea that a museum 'is after all not just a building but a temple, a cultic building'.[174]

Thus the plastic arts became completely emancipated. The remarkable fact that the painters and sculptors so obediently followed and remained dependent on the writers (who actually prepared the way for them in all respects) is to be traced to the social position of the former and consequently to the circles from which they originated. The Renaissance had freed them from the guilds but, with the exception of a few illustrious examples, they were (certainly in Germany) far from having reached the level of equality in any practical sense. Furthermore, the young sons of more respectable families seldom became painters or sculptors; such a profession was not considered suitable.[175] Actual equality between the plastic arts and the other fine arts was not achieved until the eighteenth century, and then only by the efforts of art lovers, whose interests led them to construct theories in which the painter and sculptor were included.[176] But this, strangely enough, only widened the divide between the artist and society, which eventually led to the emergence of the bohemian type.[177]

In the nineteenth century the idealistic-Romantic ideas about the plastic arts were worked out further. France, which had originally lagged far behind Germany in this respect, gradually took the lead. There theoretical developments were less philosophical in nature and certainly more closely related to the concrete work of the artist. We might mention Balzac here, and of course Baudelaire, whose influence was so important at the end of the nineteenth century when, in reaction to naturalism in all its forms, art was again seen as the revelation of a spiritual vision. I have discussed this subject in detail elsewhere[178] and will pass over it here to concentrate on our own century.

But before doing so, there is one more question that should be briefly answered: what ideas about art were held in Protestant Christian circles? Not much has been written on this subject, and creative achievements are even more rare. But what was thought about art? We shall limit ourselves to The Netherlands and to the question of whether art was held in esteem. It is not surprising that Bilderdijk advanced a theory of art related to those of the German Romanticists and, in doing so, assigned art a high place.[179] Abraham Kuyper not only wrote on art several times but valued it so highly that he lectured on aesthetics during the early years of the Free University (1880 to about 1900). He gave this definition of art: 'Art is the capacity to oppose the beautiful, the higher world to the baser one, just as the sculptor, with a practised hand, can give a beautiful form to the rough marble block.'[180] Kuyper's followers – in the broadest sense of that word – often said that art was a gift of the Holy Spirit,[181] even if that term was understood in the realm of common grace.[182] This does not mean that art was not frequently compared to prophecy. We read on the first page of a popular history of literature written by Rudolf van Reest: 'Poets are prophets. They prophecy and bear witness to the dominating currents that stir their times.'[183] This same concept, which we will find to be typical of the twentieth century, is also to be found in the following formulation from the preface to a book entitled *Christian Faith and the Contemporary Arts:* 'The artist's sense of his age gives his art revelatory power. In other words, art makes visible those images of society and self that we prefer to keep hidden.'[184]

Before going any further, I wish to stress the fact that it is impossible, except perhaps in a very superficial sense, to christianize the old *topos* of the artist as a prophet, as is done by the writers I have quoted. The word 'prophet' means something entirely different in each of these two concepts. For a Christian, art can have none of the revelatory qualities it possessed in the concepts of the old, originally pagan and later Renaissance, tradition. We must exercise great caution here. To take over the mere wording of the old *topos*, in an attempt to christianize the content by giving a Christian meaning to the word 'prophet', leads to very contradictory statements. A prophet in the Christian biblical framework means a person directly inspired by God with a very specific message, often related to the times he or she lives in, because his or her function is to clarify or expound God's judgment on people's actions. We could even defend the thesis that in the New Testament period all believers were prophets in the sense of knowing God's will. In the Bible the artist as such is never seen in this sense – in contrast to the old *topos* that the artist is the prophet par excellence.

If Christians define the artist as a prophet, they make it impossible for themselves to listen critically to the message of this prophet: either they have to deny a given artist's ability to prophesy if he or she is not a Christian, thus contradicting themselves, or they must accept the artist's message, which must lead them to the acceptance of non-Christian ideas too, which eventually leads to secularization.

We wish to show now that the two quotations given above, found in Christian books, do nothing more than uncritically repeat the *topos* in a contemporary form. But before we go into this we should say a few words about the arts in our century: we live in an age dominated almost completely by technology and an all-levelling democracy.[185] Within this technocracy, people are searching for a way to assert their essential quality as human beings, their real humanity. They seek it in an existential experience, and art – seen in the light of the old *topos* – may be used as a welcome 'revelation' of the irrational, the 'mystic reality', completely separated from technocracy. The realm of the truly human, about which the arts prophesy in their way, is dialectically opposed and yet related to the realm in which the omnipotent sciences and technology reign. Therefore, in our times the importance of art has been magnified as seldom before; it has assumed the task of creating the symbols 'that will belong on the altars of the coming spiritual religion'.[186] And the public, at least the educated public, accepts art as a 'spiritual fetish', which gives the beholder the feeling that transcendental values actually exist.[187] Today art often maintains its position by the authority of the place it presumably once occupied in the past, i.e. as the highest human expression of spiritual values,[188] and it is accepted the more so in this sense because it can be taken as a substitute for the lost function of religion and can be experienced without any commitment whatsoever.

The prophetic significance of art is quite frequently argued with direct reference to Plotinus, or to Schelling, Blake and other Romantic theoreticians.[189] The close relationship between art and mysticism is often expressed more clearly than ever before, whether in the ancient Neoplatonic form[190] or in a more gnostic sense,[191] often with reference to the theories of men like Jung or Klages, or in forms new to the West[192] and taken from Oriental thinking as in theosophy or anthroposophy[193] or more recently even, from Zen Buddhism.[194]

In principle we must not doubt the sincerity of those who endorse these views. But we must also bear in mind that such opinions are often nothing more than quasi-profound philosophizing about works of art that really defy any reasoned appraisal or critical understanding. A recent example of this kind of journalism may be cited:

> One day, the sculpture-architecture of the Brussels Atomium will perhaps signify to our eyes the deep secret of thought, the analysis of the molecular structure of the nervous influx of the brain. That day we will realize that the vision of Scheps anticipated the plastic incarnation of a quality of associative intelligence, and that this architect-surveyor had dreamt of incarnating the Idea within the world of men by reconstructing, beginning with the tree, its dimension of organic relationship.[195]

The artist as prophet, sometimes even defined as the prophet-priest of culture,[196] is thus a very alive concept in the twentieth century. In our times, unlike other centuries, there need be no doubt that the painter and sculptor are included. What is entirely new is the idea that artists express their time, interpret it and are prophets, in that they with their artist's soul sense sooner than others what is essential and can therefore indicate what direction the future will take. In this they are ahead of us who are not artists, and this is why we often do not understand the newest art. Here we see the artist-prophet in a new garb. Or so it is often stated in journalistic writing on art.[197]

This interpretation of the old *topos* is indeed new. In the past, in antiquity and the Renaissance, the prophetic element in art meant that the artist revealed the Idea, in an ontological sense. Even the nineteenth century did not know this new version of the theory. Baudelaire did say that artists see the beauty of their own time and are inspired by it,[198] but however deeply he considered the problem of the relationship between the artist and reality, he never saw a work of art as an interpretation of a time or even as an expression of a period. When the De Goncourts brothers (in 1864) demanded of art that it gives 'the history of contemporary morality' they meant that they wished their work to give a picture of their time, but never in the sense of a deeper interpretation.[189] It is possible that the battle fought at the end of the nineteenth century, especially in the art world, against a positivistic philosophy of life (the artist again being assigned the task, going back to Baudelaire and the Romanticists, of revealing spiritual values[200]) made the artists much aware of the part they had to play in the contemporary cultural scene in the sense of being prophets who reveal spiritual values. Even if we never encounter the idea that the artist is a prophet in the sense that has become almost universal in our own days, we do find in the world of the artists at the beginning of the twentieth century a strong feeling of a renewal of culture, of a new approach to reality in a more spiritual way, borne out of a sense that civilization had become too materialistic and positivistic. Artists are aware of the fact that they play a decisive part in this change. We think here of the Cubist circles in Paris, of the German Expressionists in München and in Dresden, and of the Futurists in Italy.[201]

The twentieth-century formulation of the artist as a prophet is almost entirely a secularization of the Plotinic theory. Artists are bound to their own time and express the spirit animating it. At the same time they are creative and – because they sense the times so distinctly – prophetic. This vision combines the old *topos* and the idea that artists express themselves and thus their view on the world: their work bears a universal character and is therefore truth. We may add that modern revolutionary movements have taken control of art as the expression of their new ideas.

The idea that the work of the artist, as an expression of his or her soul, has a universal character is typically Romantic. We have already come across it in Runge.[202] In Baudelaire it becomes more precise in the sense that the artist expresses his or her own insight into things.[203] Art as self-expression,[204] whether or not tied to the idea that it promulgates a philosophy of life in an artistic form, is one of the most wide-spread concepts of art in our times: it was sharply put, without circumlocutions – and also without proof – by the painter Willy Baumeister as follows: 'Each work of art is the expression of the artist's self . . . the great artists . . . carry their own fundamentals with them;' and he concludes, without clarifying the connection between the two statements: 'It is not the artist as a person who speaks, but primeval forces of the universal life speak through him.'[205]

So these old ideas of the artist as a prophet are still alive, as this quotation proves. But, generally speaking, one can say that in the twentieth century they are taken out of the ontological sphere and given a specific historical sense. This is due to the deep influence of historicism and the Vienna school of art history, both working along that line. It seems strange that so many are not aware of the stream of thought called 'historicism', which has become so influential in our century as to be almost omnipresent. It exalts the historical in the same way as rationalism exalts the rational and was first formulated in its present form by Dilthey at the end of the nineteenth century.[206] His central teaching concerned human, i.e. cultural, values. These were not unchangeable; quite to the contrary, they were the result of a historical development and thus historically determined. The categories of becoming and of change are therefore applied not only to history and development as such but also to non-historical modes of being.[207] Values and norms are then made historical with respect to not only their positive content and form but even their very existence.[208] Of course, this can easily lead to relativism, a problem widely discussed in Germany, especially after World War I, and most thoroughly by Troeltsch.[209] This type of historicism, put briefly, says that norms are bound to the times in which they function and change with the flow of history.

We may wonder how these historistic ideas found their way into the world of the arts. Aside from the general influences exerted by the work of Dilthey and his followers, we must think here in the first place of the influence of art historians. We must include, with emphasis, the attempts at popularization, whether on a small or a large scale: in no other field is so much being published in popular form as in the field of art history. But let us restrict ourselves to the main figures in the art-historical discipline. The first decades of the twentieth century show a decisive change of attitude, one directly related to corresponding trends in philosophy. There was a departure from concepts influenced by positivism, which assigned a decisive importance in the determination of style to such external factors as climate, social conditions, technique, etc.,[210] while art history often restricted itself to the observation and statement of historical facts.[211] Then came a swing to what the Germans call a *geistesgeschichtliche Methode* ('a method dealing with spiritual history').[212] Special mention should be made here of the Viennese school, which had and still has an important influence in the field of art history.[213] Dvorak formulated the thesis *Kunstgeschichte als Geistesgeschichte* ('art history as spiritual history'), and his work determined the direction of this school.[214] Dagobert Frey, in his memorial study on Dvorak, stated the latter's starting point concisely as follows: 'Art is a region of spiritual production where the creative mind expresses itself most directly in the totality of its intellectual, volitional and sensitive powers.'[215] To which he added that for Dvorak art did not constitute one of the many facets of the study of the history of culture, which he understood to be the history of the spirit, but for him art was the principal road to the study and understanding of that spirit because creative spirituality expresses itself very directly in the works of art handed down to us.[216]

Applied to contemporary art by later philosophers and art historians, this implies that art also renders a direct expression of the *Zeitgeist* ('spirit of the times')[217] which it, more than any other medium, makes comprehensible. And not only do artists, in Dvorak's view, express the spirit of their time but they also, because their place is among the leaders of humankind, contribute to the determination of the development of the entire spiritual and material culture of their time.[218] Applied once again to the contemporary situation, this can also mean that the artist is a prophet who reveals the future in his or her work. These conclusions are forced on the reader of any popular history of art, and it is in this form that the idea of the artist as a prophet is most widely held and most pernicious!

In our century revolutionary intellectual movements, some of them even of a pronounced anarchistic character,[219] have often first manifested themselves in art and, partly because of the tradition thus established, they still prefer to manifest themselves in that way.[220] This has given art an additional weight: it has become a weapon, a primary manifestation, a visible programme – in any case something new, revealing a concrete message, directed towards the future. All this is possible only within the framework of modern art, in a specific 'application' of the Romantic idea of the artist, but it requires the artist's being bound very closely, as prophet-priest, to the contemporary situation. Perhaps more clearly than by many arguments this idea is expressed in Sandberg's words:

> the period of repression and falsification in which we live
> does not ask us for an answer
> but shrieks for protest
>
> that protest, fierce and piercing in music
> penetrating and often enigmatic in book and play
> breaks loose cursing and seething in painting
> and in images shows destruction next to new budding life.[221]

This prophetic-interpretative function of art is welcomed in our times all the more positively because of the crisis in our entire vision of reality.[222]

After the 'unmasking of values' by the positivistic sciences in the preceding century – energetically continued in the twentieth century – came the 'unmasking' of the natural sciences themselves in the swing towards the primacy of autonomous humanism.[223]

The question may now be put whether art indeed satisfies these expectations or, to put it more precisely, whether it can satisfy them. One is continually struck, even now that modern art is already sixty years old (the Fauves were active in 1905, Picasso's *Les Demoiselles d'Avignon* dates from 1907), by the fact that so many people understand little of its content and means of expression.[224] It is still continually necessary to explain this art and to defend it against all kinds of attempts to make it suspect, as though it were nothing more than charlatanry. This distrust of modern art is very widespread.[225]

Now, it is inherent in the notion of the artist-prophet, as defined in our times that, just because they are prophets and ahead of their time, they cannot be understood. It is then our task to listen to them with respect and attempt to comprehend them. But, we ask, how can we listen if we do not understand? This is not an insolvable problem, say some, because there are critics to explain matters to us.[226] But do the critics always give the right explanation? And what guarantees their doing so? And if the critics do not agree, which of them is right? And, in such a case, is it not then the critics who are the prophets, or at least the priests, who must translate the incomprehensible Pythian message for us? If this is the case, modern art inspires just as much confidence as the Delphic oracles of antiquity. 'Criticism of art has become a kind of mantic, a prophetic art that prophesies by way of "signs".'[227]

There is a second question directly related to this one: which of the arts is the truly prophetic one? Great, creative art, it is said. But this answer leads only to new questions. Who is to determine what is truly great art? Those who are closely concerned with modern art know that it is unquestionably possible to reach some kind of agreement on this point – the masters can really be distinguished from the imitators, the hangers-on and the charlatans. But for that the criterion is never the prophetic content; rather, it is the artistic quality. The latter is never dependent on the degree of stylistic renewal or originality,[228] and conversely, the work of a person with prophetic insight may be third rate. In short, the notion of art as prophecy in no way helps us to understand the phenomenon 'art' or to approach the individual work of art. It closes rather than opens the path to real insight.

But let us return to the question of whether art can be prophecy. Let us imagine that we have a work of art before us concerning which there is general agreement both as to its high quality and the meaning of its content. In what respect, and why, is this work prophetic? After all nothing has been said yet about the content of the work, whether it has value or not, is new or not, and – put still more acutely – is true or not.[229]

But even if the idea expressed by the work of art is true and valuable, is the work then prophetic as well?

Even if we are right in calling the artist a prophet, why would he or she always be a true, and never a false, prophet? Infallibility would be possible only on the basis of the old *topos* that the artist is divinely inspired – but to accept this would raise Plotinus' theory to a kind of theology requiring absolute submission. We may approach this question critically not only because it is a product of Graeco-Roman antiquity but because also for our times the question remains: By just what god is art inspired? If it is the spirit of the times that art expresses so well, as is argued, then it is once again not only Ephesians 6:12[230] that prevents us from capitulating.

Even if we must accept that since the Second World War the leading artistic movements, the so-called avant-garde movements, gave (and still give) expression to a particular spirit, the ideas they expressed can still be discussed. We are forced to speak of ideas,[231] because if it were only a matter of autonomous-artistic expression[232] there would be little point in speaking of prophecy with a directive function in spiritual things. The question of the extent to which art is prophetic in our times becomes the more pressing just because art does not sound only one note, does not point in only one direction but many. And who is right?

May we indeed speak of a *Zeitgeist* in the sense that a period is a homogeneous unit? To go into this question would take us deep into theoretical history, problems of the demarcation of periods, historical synchronization or asynchronization, etc. Even without doing so, however, we may put it that in every historical period several movements exist at the same time, sometimes in conflict with each other, sometimes not, some more important than others and all differing both quantitatively and qualitatively. When we examine a period more closely, we see in the history of art too that a number of different directions exist at the same time. Naturally there are certain elements of unity as well, just as all the people of a country speak more or less the same language – but in the end what is decisive is not what language is spoken but what is said with that language.

This is certainly also true for the arts in our own [twentieth] century. Two main streams are to be distinguished. First, more or less traditional art, which even if it uses new means of visual communication does not break with the past and whose content is related to the experience and vision of reality of the average contemporary. Sometimes this art lacks genuine creative force, often it tends to be really bourgeois in the derogatory sense but, even if truly great artists are rarely found among these traditionalists, many of these works are worthy and show real human relevance. Secondly, there is modern art itself, which just because its stylistic and expressive means often represent such a radical break with the Western tradition remains difficult to understand for many of the artist's contemporaries. The view of life and the world expressed by this art is related to existentialist philosophy (even when it is older than that) or other irrationalistic and mystical-anarchistic thoughts. Consequently it reflects the deep spiritual crisis of our age arising from the scientific predominance of technology, which tends to rob people of their humanness, of their humanity. Here too we find great diversity in character, style, and aims; yet there is great unity, growing and becoming more influential every day, concerning the basic principle that our world has become absurd: that life has no ultimate meaning, in short that, as one Dutch poet has said so strikingly, 'beauty has burnt her face'.233 This art is, in a sense, anti-humanistic and certainly antichristian. Of course, we must realize that there are many who follow the great creative geniuses without understanding them, or adopt their inventions to produce works that go no deeper than shallow decoration. Nevertheless we must acknowledge that, in many ways, the great modern artists have developed new artistic possibilities that we cannot ignore except to our own disadvantage. We must also admit that their protest against some of the great evils of our times is not only genuine but sometimes right. Even if their solution or answer to the sad spiritual situation of today cannot be accepted, they are human and they do react to, or act in, a real and living situation.

A theory of culture can explain the hypothesis that the artist is a prophet: when an artist who creates new forms and expresses new ideas exerts an influence, that influence will be unmistakably evident in the subsequent period. But this proves only that art is not unimportant, and that it contributes to the spiritual atmosphere of a given period; it does not prove that the artist has prophesied, for that would be post facto reasoning. The artist is not a predecessor, not a prophet but rather a shaper of culture, a figure of historical significance.234 He or she is not a prophet but, at most, a preacher, one who bears witness to the ideas inherent in the movement to which he or she belongs.235

This last is very important. We do not demand that art be autonomous – we will return to this point later – and even less do we think that art was autonomous in the past. Quite the opposite; art (just as all other human activities) cannot do more than give expression to human vision, insight, perspicacity, an attitude towards life and towards humanity,236 although we should add that this is not the primary function of art. But if we acknowledge that the artist's subjectivity puts a stamp on her or his work, we may ask whether that is sufficient reason to say that she or he sees better, deeper and more sharply than the non-artist. Among the gifted artists are some with great insight, but there are also others possessed by highly disputable ideas.237 In short, the content of art is not above discussion. It is unfortunately true that an abysmally bad idea can be presented with great artistic ability and conviction.

Art as prophecy, that was our problem. It is remarkable that the formal study of aesthetics today not only does not take up or defend this thesis but seldom extends beyond the artist who expresses his or her feelings, his or her observations and experience: aesthetics, as a philosophical discipline, is concentrated almost entirely on the problems of the theory of expression, sometimes related to a theory of semantics or symbolism.[238] The term 'prophecy', not to mention 'divine inspiration', is seldom or never even mentioned. The starting point of contemporary aesthetics lies far from that of Plotinus and his school.

We may add that this has caused a specific and dangerous situation. We have, as it were, two theories of art at the same time today: one of them speaks of artists as *engagé*, directly tied to the present situation and directly reacting to it, protesting, preaching, trying desperately to reach their human fellows with a message of despair or of new possibilities; the other says that art is never more than beauty in line, colour and expression, fully human and general in scope, never with a specific message related to a specific (philosophical) approach to reality. Consequently, on the one hand artists, in line with their calling as prophet and priest of culture, with their blood and all their human strength, make works of art that cry out their message; and then, on the other hand, people come to stand in front of it and say how interesting it is as a new aesthetic experiment, how cultural and important it is, while ignoring the heart-breaking sob or shout contained in it. This is a dangerous situation; it means people are almost unaware that they are being preached at, and as a result the message can do its work without any critical appraisal on the viewers' part or it may cause them to become completely passive and, in their mystification, to turn away without seeing that the message works all the better when the underlying issues are not discussed. For the artists themselves this has created a truly horrible situation, one that gives an added impetus to the development of such new artforms as 'happenings'.[239]

Another problem to which the idea of the artist as interpreter of her or his times brings us concerns the meaning of older art, i.e. the art of all periods before our own. Do Greek, medieval, and seventeenth-century works of art still have something to say to us? Or can we value them only after we have first robbed them of their proper content and function and 'buried' them in a museum, as Malraux put it?[240] Of course, an attempt can be made to consider the great masters as prophets in the sense of seers of the timelessly divine, but this will be found to lead sooner to the falsification of history than to intensification of real spiritual insight.[241]

It is our opinion that the art of earlier times continues to play a role in our culture – and by this we mean more than as financial investment and similar factors. Were this not so, there would be far less point in following our profession as art historians.

It is very striking in connection with the thesis of the artist as prophet, and one of the strongest arguments against it, that in the science of the history of art, art is often related to cultural and intellectual history but never to prophecy. An occasional introduction drops a few 'profound' words in this direction,[242] but no trace of anything of the kind recurs in the treatment of the artists and the history of the arts. The continual contact with works of art, including works of lesser quality; the recognition of the importance of traditions, theories,[243] and social factors; the awareness that art is unquestionably related in many ways to contemporary events and intellectual movements – even though it only rarely leads them – the concentration on problems of style, composition, means of expression, form, and themes; the problems raised by the question of where the essential content and function of works of art in different periods are to be sought[244] – all these factors eliminate any need for a mystification of art into problematic prophecy. Admiration for the truly great works of art will in no way suffer.

Little by little the thought is occurring to us that it was perhaps a mistake when, in the eighteenth century, people began to equate painting too closely with poetry, and thus to see it primarily as an expression of spiritual values.[245] In literature the formulation and propagation of ideas is indeed to be expected. Throughout history new ideas have often first emerged in literature, which gave them much influence. But for the plastic arts the situation has been quite different. In the past they seldom attempted to achieve such influence, as the history of art clearly shows. Of course they sometimes did influence the minds and manners of the contemporaries, just by showing implicitly the meaning and implications of certain basic ideas or the relevancy of certain attitudes. Very often, in fact, new forms appeared in the plastic arts under the influence of ideas and standards which originated in philosophy and literature: the visual arts reflected current thought and ideas. But to speak of prophecy in connection with painting is an over-estimation of its task. The role of prophet is not well suited to the painter. The demand that artists express their times may, in fact, have contributed to bringing painting up the blind alley in which it now finds itself.[246]

This last paragraph may need some clarification. It may seem contradictory that on the one hand we have stated that art specifically has become a vehicle to express spiritual values, while on the other hand we have showed that this has led to the present abyss. Indeed there is a certain paradox in the way we must judge, for example, Picasso. He does portray the modern spirit very forcibly, and in that sense we must say that he expresses reality: his work does reflect in a very real way the spiritual situation of our times. But, having judged his work to be art, we must concede that it is often horrible and lacks beauty. And truth, real reality, as God created it, even if marred by sin, is not like that, and we may demand of a painting that it be a thing of beauty and a joy for ever. To avoid misunderstanding, we do not mean to say that art must be idealistic but that it should be beautiful, as for instance even a crucifixion by Grünewald is beautiful in its own way. The point we wish to make is that perhaps modern art is wrong in trying to depict the horrible plight of modern humanity, as it is not the task of the visual arts to philosophize or to preach. (We may add that it would be fruitful if advertising art and industrial design were incorporated into the study of twentieth-century art. This would show that other artistic attitudes are possible, even in our own times, different from those professed by the High Arts that again and again are playing the prophet.) In their intention to show the wrongness of the world in which we live, they make our world worse instead of better. They add to the ugliness, shabbiness and emptiness.

There is indeed a marked difference between the arts before or after the eighteenth century. Older art sought to function as art, to make something that provided in an adequate way for a certain need or fulfilled a certain task, whether religious or decorative. As the need or task was of course in line with the spirit of the age, and each artist quite naturally a child of his or her age, we, living in another time, can see and understand something of the ideas and spiritual values that belonged to the world of the artists and their patrons. If they 'preached', it was by implication, not explicitly willed, for art belonged to the human environment. Modern art, on the other hand, more often than not does not try to answer a need, making something of beauty and human value, but seeks primarily to prophesy. In this way art has become a kind of philosophy, something which is at any rate very intellectual. Sometimes art is even intended to be ugly or, as such, to draw near to the borderline between art and non-art. We must carefully consider these differences, as we are all influenced by the art-historical theories of the school of Dvorak which have overstressed those spiritual values – in the sense of overcharging *Weltanschauung* ('world view') – in a historistic way. These same theories engendered, when merged with the age-old idea of the artist as a prophet, the modern version of that idea, namely the artist as a visionary who interprets our times.

Is a painting or piece of sculpture robbed of its lustre when it contains no prophecy or may not be equated with literature? Note well that we have not said that this would make it inferior to literature. Where does its importance really lie? Is that to be determined by the history of art? In no sense. The history of art studies only one aspect of art, an aspect abstracted according to the nature of the discipline involved. But we know too that often enough a work of art becomes really understandable only after thorough study of its historical aspect. The rediscovery of the Mannerism of the sixteenth century, which first made it possible to properly evaluate the art of that period, serves as a good example of this. We must be able to 'read' a work of art to 'see' it adequately, and for this we must be able to understand the pictorial means used, and take all kinds of historical factors into account. To put it briefly, we can arrive at an understanding of the history of art only by looking at art and we can see a work of art only via the history of art. This need not alarm us. It only makes it clear that the work of the art historian can never be concluded, even if all kinds of biases are avoided. It is not, however, necessary to become pessimistic as if it will never be possible to say anything really true and meaningful about the artistic monuments of the past. Art is the result of human creativity, and the people of the past were just as human as we are today; in that sense their work is understandable to us, however much we must take into account all kinds of changes in attitudes, concepts and breadth of experience.

The meaning of a work of art is not determined by the history of art and even less so by a sociology of art or a consideration of the religious, cultural or psychological function of the work of art. For a work of art cannot be explained by any function in human and social life, even if that were a prophetic one. The study of such functions, however important it may be, always assumes the work of art and does not explain it.[247] The meaning of a work of art is never identical with its function; it can even change function without losing its content, as for example when a cult-image is placed in a museum.

A work of art does not acquire meaning because it fulfils some function in human life; a work of art has its own meaning, and not only does it have meaning but it *is* meaning.[248] It possesses all kinds of aspects which determine its concrete form and which we can analyse. But all these aspects presuppose that a work of art is in itself meaningful. We do not mean by this that a work of art is autonomous; quite the contrary. If it refuses to take its full place in human life, it loses its meaning. Nor does concentration on the aesthetic aspect, in art-historical terminology the stylistic aspect, help us to come closer to the proper meaning of the work. Pure artistic beauty alone does exist, for example in geometrical decorative design, but we ask more of a painting or piece of sculpture. Iconological and iconographic aspects, just as technical aspects inherent in the material used, and even the dimensions, all these things belong to the individuality of a work of art – and must do so, otherwise artistic integration would be lacking and something would be out of kilter. Works of art are bound to laws of structure, normative in character, however difficult they may be to formulate verbally. Without these specific norms we would not even be able to recognize a work of art in its own meaning.

A work of art is meaningful and yet not autonomous. This is so because it cannot find its meaning in itself. It is there because it belongs to creation and has been assigned its own meaningful place therein. Its very being points to the Norm-Giver; and for this reason it is not independent of the Second great Commandment – neighbourly love intrinsically determines the character of the work of art – and is therefore never merely an external, non-artistic prerequisite. Nor is art independent and 'free' of the first commandment: for a work of art this means that it has to fulfil its meaning, that it has to exist as meaning, taking its place in the fullness of human life as God intended in creating the artistic possibility.

These inherent qualities do not stand apart from aesthetic formal beauty, from artistic integrity, or from a sensible choice of subject matter. Quite to the contrary, it is in these things that they become apparent. That is why we have said that art not only has meaning, as though it could be said that it had some religious or human meaning apart from its aesthetic structure, but that it *is* meaning, is meaningful in the unity of its artistic reality. Here, it may be appropriate to speak of artistic truth as distinct from intellectual accuracy. We think rather of 'doing the truth'.[249] Works of art can be ethically indifferent – as for instance Picasso's paraphrases of works of old masters[250] – and yet, because they tarnish beauty, be basically unacceptable: they are not 'doing' the truth but serve the lie. 'To do the truth' is directly bound up with a striving towards optimal artistic quality for reasons of neighbourly love, with which a sense of responsibility is inextricably connected.

We may now ask: What is Christian art? It is clear that this term cannot mean only art with biblical or ecclesiastical subject matter. It is quite possible for a painting of a crucifixion, for example, to have an unbiblical content or even to be antichristian.[251] And it must be clear that the inherent Christian qualities are not bound to one specific style – just as a sermon can be preached in different languages without losing its integrity. Yet it may be true that one style is better suited to 'do the truth' than another – just as Christianity when it enters into the cultural life of people, alters their language and adds new elements to it, and may eliminate certain peculiarities. The real Christian quality cannot be found by looking for specific elements. In a way, just the opposite is the case. When things are in accordance with God's created possibilities and his will for his world, they are just 'normal'. When love reigns in a community, that community is not strange but healthy. Problems, strangeness, conflicts, tensions, etc. always arise only from sin and its results. In a way it is therefore perhaps even better to speak not of Christian art but of truthful art, art that is art in the fullness of the meaning as God intended it to be. Perhaps a still life of a man like Heda (who worked in the Netherlands in the early seventeenth century) is more intrinsically 'Christian' than a Crucifixion by El Greco.

Christian art is not to be defined as art made by a Christian. Christians can sin; they can make (even with the best of intensions) ugly, silly or shallow works of art. And a non-Christian can make beautiful and truthful ones. The criterion is the inherent truth of the work. This fact gives rise to another question: how can such truthful works of art come into being? The answer is that they can be made by artists who are fully human and true to their calling. This may happen anywhere and at any time, when people act out of their created humanness. As soon as sinful elements, or tendencies not in accord with God's will as laid down in his creation, enter into the production of the work of art, its integrity is challenged and 'strangeness', ugliness and mannerisms enter in.

Therefore true art, really human and really meaningful art is, in the period between the Fall, or better, Christ's ascension and his Return, more often than not the result of the fruits of true faith as they become part of a cultural reality: in this sense there is much Christianity in our European art of the past, even in works made by unbelievers. On the other hand we can understand from this why in our times, while Christianity has lost its leading cultural position and non-Christian tendencies have become paramount in the field of art, art has become problematic and strange – even to such an extent that many Christians no longer know how to create something intrinsically and humanly right without falling back into the shallow ways of expression borrowed from nineteenth-century naturalism (spiritually speaking akin to positivism and religious liberalism).[252]

But let us return to our main argument. God included in his creation the possibility of artistic work and allotted art a role in human life that is in itself meaningful. That is why it is just as impossible to ignore art or to exclude any aesthetic or artistic standard whatsoever as it is to overlook economic values or social or moral factors. The disregarding of any of these aspects of life leads to impoverishment or to chaos, lovelessness and, finally, to dehumanization. We can only guess at how intense the impoverishment of spiritual life becomes when art receives too little attention, but we should take great care not to underestimate it.

We do know, however, that in this present world the beauty, the artistic meaningfulness, the intrinsic value of art can never be fully realized. A single master work, a single complex insight, a temporary maturity in forms of living, that is all we may expect or experience. And this is why we can agree with Abraham Kuyper, the founder of the Free University, when he says in his own special way: 'Our being cannot be satisfied unless the thirst for beauty that we experience is quenched. That is why the child of God fights for beauty and holiness, because at Creation people were absolutely beautiful. The beautiful and the good for which Plato was searching will come about when the Lord returns.'[253]

Commitment in Art

Art[254] in our world is not like a blank sheet; it is, by tradition, loaded with content, with meaning that is more than 'reality artistically interpreted on a flat surface', meaning that it far exceeds its functions as a wall decoration, a visual statement and a personal expression.

A painting especially, even more than sculpture, comes to us as an icon charged with meaning that makes it transcend ornaments and decoration, however artistically valuable or beautiful they may be.

If we want to understand something of this tradition we must go far back into history. For this purpose it is adequate to begin with the Byzantine world or our Middle Ages, bypassing the question of how art in that time gained its high position. A painting in the Middle Ages was primarily the representation of the sacred. We recall Christ, exalted as Lord and Judge of the world. We recall the Saints and more especially the Madonna – the Virgin with Child. It is clear that the Madonna icon is never, and was never intended to be, a portrait or a historical painting in the sense that 'in the year X this could be seen in Bethlehem', and is even less a heavenly reality. The painting, or icon, represented the truth of an idea, of a supernatural Reality (with a capital R) that is of critical importance to us. The painting meant the Truth of Mary, her devotional, theological and soteriological position. In a certain sense in the Middle Ages she stood for the gospel as such, as Christ appeared all too exclusively as the powerful Judge of the world, if not to the theologian then certainly to the common person, for whom he became almost a kind of bogeyman.[255] A painting was thus far more than an illustration; it was Evangelical Truth become visible in a very deep sense. So actively present was the Truth for the worshipping spectator that, from this point of view, it is easy to understand why these paintings were approached rather hesitantly and sometimes considered capable of performing miracles. They were not worshipped (although this could conceivably have happened) but were certainly revered.[256] Thus we can easily understand an extraordinarily large richly-figured Baroque altar decoration that has at its centre a quite small and artistically undistinguished Madonna icon.[257] It was a typical Baroque artistic-figurative homage, an adequate framing for an icon, laden with religious portent.

Alongside these medieval representations of holiness (continued through the Baroque) we find paintings that depict the central holy events of Christianity in relation to the feast days of the church calendar such as the Annunciation, the Birth of Christ, the critical events of the Passion, the Resurrection and the Last Judgment. The repertory was prescribed. These paintings were not concerned primarily with the history of the event; they were expounding a dogma.

From the fifteenth century on, the repertory was considerably extended to include the lives of the saints and martyrs, for example.

During the Renaissance, mythology was given a place beside the Christian subjects. These Graeco-Roman myths were included not just because they were interesting or because they were such pleasing stories but also because they held relevance. In a kind of Neoplatonic, poetic 'theology' these (more or less) allegorically to be understood gods and their histories were considered to contain – one might almost say proclaim – deeply human, humanist, truths: Apollo, Jupiter, Mars, Minerva, Bacchus, each had his own quality and significance. Venus was revered above the others as the personification of Platonic 'Heavenly Love'[258] and as beauty and love as they are related to human life. Finally, the many illustrations of e.g. Ovid's *Metamorphoses* indicate that these themes had a deep significance – they meant far more than convenient starting points for artists to make their composition.[259] Art thus reflected current thought and mirrored people's beliefs and understanding of reality.

A new secular iconography arose, either in honour of the sovereign, praising him in his office, or to portray deep moral truths in an allegorical or emblematic way.[260] Although it is not possible to go into this exhaustively, we want to stress that in the sixteenth and seventeenth centuries art, particularly painting, even including still lifes, contains a much deeper meaning than one often suspects. Thus the painting remains a representation, if not of the Truth, then at least of a truth; it is far more than a thing, fit for a practical purpose or a simple decoration. In this way European painting continues an old tradition, giving the work of art added value or importance no matter whether it has a theological-devotional function or presents a more general statement of principles of human life.

The structure of the great European civilization of the Reformation, the Counter-Reformation and humanism was slowly but surely destroyed in the wake of the Enlightenment in the eighteenth and nineteenth centuries.

This was the result of a complete change in basic principles. Before that time a human being was a creature, standing in the midst of a created universe with other creatures in relation to the Creator, with life and world regulated by principles outside the human self. Now with the Enlightenment, human being as reasonable being was placed in the centre, and starting from one's own subjective perception of reality one had to create for oneself the basic principles on which to build one's life. So, for example, before the Enlightenment there was an eternal godly law that people should not steal; now after the Enlightenment – in this particular case reflected by Hobbes and later the French Encyclopedists – people themselves declared stealing unlawful and made a pledge in a social contract.

It is impossible at this point to go more at length into the thought of men like Descartes, Locke, Hume, Diderot and Kant who, with their friends, laid the foundations for a new world. Their work meant a real revolution, and it took two centuries before the culture was changed according to their view of life. They gave us the world in which we now live with all its problems and its deep spiritual crisis. The base of the crisis is that God has been dethroned – in the beginning almost silently, later more openly – and that people now have to build their own world rationalistically. History has shown by now what a world where God is dead really looks like.

We want to stress one aspect: before the Enlightenment, philosophy was concerned primarily with ontology – dealing with being; after that it became concerned with epistemology – how we as human beings can have any knowledge of any reality outside of ourselves, and how we can arrive at universal principles. The old principles and ideas were gone and people were left with what they could see, feel, touch, weigh and measure. One had to start from one's observations.

This revolution was not simply something taking place in a confined world of philosophers and intellectuals. Slowly but steadily the new principle conquered the world. Around 1800 it began to afflict art, which in the course of little more than a century came to realize the full consequences. Art, as a result, became a kind of philosophy, a kind of epistemology, an intellectual activity.[261] We have already dealt with this problem from another point of view in the first part. Painting now had to deal with the problem of how a painter, who would see only the particular and individual, could depict human truth, namely that which is general, more than just what the eye sees.

The first painter whose work reflected the basic change brought by the Enlightenment was Goya, rightly called the 'first modern painter'. His double portrayal of the clothed and the naked *Maya* is a comment on Giorgione's *Venus:* showing that the 'old' Venus had lost its meaning, Venus as a concept of love and beauty was dead, and all that was left was a woman who could be either clothed or naked. Manet in 1864 created a scandal with his *Olympia*, a work that makes clear that the concept of Venus had been radically destroyed, for a naked woman showing herself like this could not be anything other than a prostitute. Even before this, Courbet had caused a stir with his *Stonebreakers*, not because there is anything strange about stonebreakers but because the work by its proportions claimed equal standing with the truths earlier put forward in art. By understanding such a painting in the context of the tradition that art is fused with truth, one can appreciate the shocked reaction of the people in that time. What happened in and through this so-called 'Realism' was no more and no less than the demolition of the theme: the old values were dead, and nothing remained except the visibly and tangibly concrete.

The next step was taken by the Impressionists, particularly by Monet around 1885. Reality itself fell away, as it were, behind the paint, leaving only the impression of the sensual colour perception and the strict subjectivity of the onlooker. It is not so strange that at precisely this point Monet's companions dared go no further. Renoir and others began to make 'nice' pictures, but without much meaning or consequence. The public, realizing that great values were at stake, expressed violent indignation.

The profound endeavours of van Gogh, Seurat, Gauguin and Cézanne to restore human content to art, to restore contact with reality so that painting once again would be a representation of meaningful truth, can merely be mentioned. Their work did not endure. Humanity was too crippled by the positivist natural science of the nineteenth century for art to remain untouched, continuing as if there were nothing afoot, as if humanity were the same as before.

Even so, masterpieces proclaimed themselves from the walls of museums and were revered as creations of the human spirit, representations of deep human truths – icons of a (mostly) humanistically conceived culture. They maintained the life of the old traditions. Paradoxically, it was precisely this tradition of expecting more of a painting than only beauty or a reflection of nature that opened the way to modern art.

Modern art is based on the principle that the artist is pledged to formulate a deep human reality and to represent this in his or her work. In the same way as the old idea of the icon, which made the painting almost into an idol, might have overstressed the importance of art, art was now asked to give real insight into reality – art itself became a revelation. In 'The Artist as a Prophet?' we show one aspect of this overestimation of art; here we want only to point out that in our Western tradition there was a ready framework within which these new principles could function.

As the old concept of human being was dead, and humanity and their world seemed absurd, and it was possible to speak of the defeat of humanism, art now had to show these truths. One could say that the mere fact that painting was loaded with a quasi-religious or philosophical pretention made it possible for such horrifying things to be said, or rather, painted. In any other context such things would have been found unacceptable and rejected on grounds of inadequate artistic execution.

This new vision of human beings and the world – a result of the development starting with the Enlightenment and continuing through Romanticism and positivism – was first given expression in painting. It happened around 1911: the old view of people having positive contact with reality, a contact already loosened by Impressionism, was totally destroyed. Human being as an absurdity, estranged from the world, which was in itself chaotic, accidental and apparently contingent and hostile, became the painter's new preoccupation. Some artists, like Picasso, began to paint absurd humanity, while others, like Kandinsky, turned to abstraction. In this revolution, this violent destruction of so many established values, much that was deeply anchored in the reality of human life was torn down. A great part of the alarmed public found it unacceptable. Just as people had reacted violently at the beginning of Impressionism, so Kandinsky relates how his abstract paintings had to be cleaned every night at his exhibition in 1912 because the public had spat on his work.[262] The artist was committed and had a message. That much the public accepted and did not deny, but being themselves also committed, they retained the right to reject that message.

For several artists belonging to the circles of Picasso and Kandinsky these steps towards abstraction or absurdity were too great and the consequences too horrifying. We see that the ones who did 'stay behind', such as Derain, Delaunay and many others, returned to a more moderate and traditional style. Still others, such as Marcel Duchamp, immediately grasping the implications of what Picasso was doing, drove them to their uttermost consequences both in their work and in their life. This response led to Dadaism and later to the Surrealist movement.

To briefly recapitulate: a painting in our European civilization means far more than just a picture. It stands within a tradition, functioning in a framework that is already very old. The aura of holiness, Truth and prime significance still surrounds 'Art'. Many modern works would not be possible without this background. One can think of Yves Klein who painted just an even blue surface or of Fontana who exhibited a bare canvas with only a razor-slit in it. In a certain sense one could say that contemporary art, being an absurd statement about the absurdity of reality, is commenting on earlier art. It says: this stands on equal footing with the art before our times; this is the real truth, this is reality. That means there is a polemical element in modern art, something that is often called protest. As painting was once concerned with what is sacred and true, what is good and beautiful, the modern artist now appears and says: 'Look what it really IS, this truth, this goodness . . . it is nothing; it is absurd. Human being is dead, and so-called "humanity" is fiction.' On this basis we can understand why modern art is sometimes a direct comment on old paintings. Picasso's interpretation of works by Courbet, Manet and Velasquez,[263] and Bacon's whole series of portraits based on one work of Velasquez's come to mind.

One further remark before continuing: we must not think that this modern art cannot be questioned because it belongs to the uniqueness of our times and it is the way that twentieth-century people see the world. This historicistic[264] fatalism is a trap, as if we were caught in some cultural pattern and could view life in no other way. Fortunately 'real' reality does not change and does not depend on our understanding of it. It is not necessary to see reality as Picasso sees it, and there is far less reason to paint it as he does. That sense and meaning can be seen in our world is proved simply by the fact that another kind of art exists – that of Maillol, Rouault and so many others, as well as that done in such specialized branches of art as cartoon drawing, advertisement and applied art.

Thus we may not say that for Picasso and his followers – to briefly typify the modernist – there is no other possibility because they are bound by the uniqueness of our times. But neither can we say that they present, simply in a new way, the same old truths found in old art.

How is it that this idea has gained such wide recognition? People have come to believe that Picasso and his kind are doing nothing different from earlier art, but are just saying it with new pictorial means that are unfamiliar to us and which we still do not understand. If this is true, then there is hardly any reason to be alarmed. The origin of this current opinion is the problem with which we should now like to deal. To do this we must change the course of our approach and take an entirely different direction.

Let us next investigate how the spectator approaches a work of art. Before the eighteenth century people were very forthright in their reaction to a work of art, whether or not they found it beautiful. They criticized it on its merits. That was possible because both the artist and the public judged with the same criteria. Since the Enlightenment this has changed. Certain literary, philosophical and political groups took the consequences of the new radical subjectivism, and art made this visible. Art, and particularly painting, was the clearest protagonist of the avant-garde. The public, realizing that intrinsic truths were at stake in this artistic revolution, reacted sharply against the work of Courbet and Manet, and later against the Impressionists and still later against the definitive emergence of the modern vision of human being and the world in the works of Picasso, Kandinsky, the Dadaists and the Surrealists. But since the 1920s the violence of the protest has subsided. Were people going to acquiesce? Had they mellowed? Were they convinced of the truth of modernism? This might be true of a very small group. On the other hand, it is possible that people may have perceived that they could give no real answer to the problems raised, for they had come to accept the principle of the Enlightenment themselves.

Yet, the most important reason lies in the trend of criticism taken by exponents and defenders of modern art. The situation is, at present, such that a part of the public supports and, to a certain degree, understands modern art, and accepts it positively. On the other hand there is a considerably larger group that voices no opinion, that withholds all protest and accepts extremist modern art against its will, afraid to murmur a word against it. The writing on modern art and art criticism have created a kind of snobbishness whereby people accept the newest developments, sometimes with conviction but more often with resignation, lest they should be thought the less for not accepting it. That becomes obvious when we see the reaction against somebody who takes a critical position. But what seems to be even more dangerous is the reluctance of many to take up any position of commitment or to assume real involvement. People avoid the spiritual struggle; they flee from it because they are afraid of being confronted with the actual state of affairs in our Western culture.

But it has become increasingly difficult to see that really deep matters are at stake. People have undergone a kind of brainwashing to the effect that 'new' is acceptable by virtue of its being new. In the following paragraphs we shall go into the contributing factors, in which old traditions play a very specific part.

First of all we should like to give attention to aesthetics, the theory of beauty and art. It was first developed in Greece, where classical art was also conceived, and therefore it is connected with that art in every respect. The ideal for the artist was not to express subjectively any personal feeling and even less to make an existential statement concerning the human condition. The problems of the time, human inadequacies, failure or predicament – all such matters were excluded from art; the purpose of art was to reveal the ideal, beauty in its highest form. Where this beauty was to be found, and how the artist was to realize it, were the great questions that aesthetics sought to answer.

Later, very much later – for we are quickly travelling over great stretches of time – we find aesthetics still concerned with these matters. How could the artist create a beautiful work? It is possible, but how would the artist know beauty? In reassuming the ideas of Plato and Aristotle, sometimes even with a scholastic tinge, people built up theories which could elucidate a practical path for artists, putting in their hands an attainable ideal, and showing them how they could achieve it. The theory of art of the seventeenth-century classicist Bellori forms a final synthesis, in which all these elements are fused in a workable whole.[265]

But even those who did not share the classicist ideals of art and who thought that art had to depict daily life in its *schilderachtigheid* ('painterliness'), as in seventeenth-century Holland, said that art was meant to amuse and to give something of positive value.[266]

Aesthetics, in the philosophical sense of the word, was first conceived in the eighteenth century. The old notions returned, clothed in new raiment. The most important point for us is the theoretical distance: aesthetics became an abstract philosophical discipline, which hardly took into account real works of art. And not only that, but it was proposed that a disinterested observation of art, in search of abstract aesthetic qualities instead of content, was the aesthetic approach par excellence. For Kant, aesthetics pertained to the beauty (of nature and) of the successful work of art, which could be recognized and understood by the spectator as a work of genius, of which the values were unchangeable and universal.[267]

We must thoroughly realize that this humanistic approach to art from an aesthetically formulated distance was carried out totally without reference to the content, theme and concrete statement of a painting as such. In the ensuing period, aesthetics formulated many new questions, sometimes taking psychological and experimental approaches, but the attitude expressed by Kant remained and his thinking has had enormous influence right up to our own times. Aesthetics remained far away from real art. The result of this could be predicted. Morpurgo-Tagliabue could write in his comprehensive work on contemporary aesthetics: 'Contemporary aesthetics, in its numerous and methodically different forms, whether speculative, descriptive, experimental or historical . . . does not correspond in any single aspect to modern art.'[268]

Aesthetics is not concerned with the content of a work of art. It seeks formal problems, and even when it deals with expression or communication it does not question the content of the statement but primarily concerns itself with the grammar, the structure and the framework through which such expression is made possible.

Let us look at *The Journal of Aesthetics and Art Criticism* of May 1964–65. It contains an article entitled 'The Artist's Intentions'. In one of its conclusions it admits that works of art express emotion, but it does not go so far as to say that the emotions are those of the artist. There is an article on Abstract Expressionism which clearly states that these works are disturbing, yet it concludes that paintings of this school use a variable scale and posits the 'active and enlightened presence of the artist'. Other articles discuss the distinction between the sensual and the meaningful in aesthetics, between motivation and the creative arts. Then there are papers concerning the questions of why a falsification (forgery) is aesthetically unacceptable; whether poetry has a controlled content, and many other questions which in themselves are very important. But even when dealing with modern art – as in the case of the article on Abstract Expressionism – discussion of the content is avoided. The writers stay abstract in their investigations. Such a position can be justified to an extent, although the question arises whether this does not smack of escapism, of evasion of commitment. As humanists they hope that all people strive for the good and find in art nothing other than deep, humanly relevant ideas and feelings, although they often leave these unspecified.

This problem of aesthetics has been brought forward because it is related to the manner in which modern art is criticized today. The same distance, by which one's real feelings remain untouched, can be sensed in the remarks of the guides in the museums, even at the most extremely modern exhibitions. The only demand is for quality, and people busy themselves with the kind of pure aesthetic analysis we have just been discussing. Sometimes they even say that a work of art is nothing more than line and colour, composition and an undefined expression. The new art gives nothing more than a human message, conveyed by new means. Or people anchor themselves to the idea that artists are expressing their times, and when they live in different times their forms are different.[269] But all the while the sometimes obvious content is being ignored. And even when there is an attempt to discuss content, they make it subjective and say 'This is how things are seen by this person.' In any event, to question the truth of what is stated in art is taboo.

The effect of this attitude is strengthened as the public brings its own notions to art. The real laity, the less educated public, is not in the least a virgin sheet of paper. Old and tried traditions bear directly on the way they look at art. These traditions originate from earlier art theories, from the classical tradition we have dealt with before. The central concept is that noble ideas and beauty find expression in art. This concept is continually reaffirmed when people stand in admiration before the old masterpieces hanging in the museums.

In the nineteenth century this ideal was formulated as: 'The highest art is that which, taking for its means of expression line and colour descriptive of human form, should perhaps, more like music than poetry, suggest the highest emotions, sentiments and phases of thought as the outward manifestation of humanity.'[270] Such a statement is typically humanistic. This concept was coloured even more strongly by the Romantic notion that art is the expression of the soul of the artist, who in his or her feeling for beauty can create nothing but beauty. Art is the most individual expression of the most individual emotion, certainly, but then of an elect genius, whose greatness gives to his or her work universal human worth and truth.

People who enter museums of modern art with such a viewpoint can but be defenceless prey to the abstract aesthetic approach that is offered to them. They dare not expect anything else than that the artist, being good in the depth of her or his humanistic soul, is striving towards goodness and beauty. And should observers stand alone in front of modern art, they are amazed, for they cannot find the beauty they are seeking and on first sight feel they are being assaulted; but optimistic and firmly believing the beautiful spirit of artistic genius, they soon come to the conclusion that they do not understand, that the forms are too new, that they are of a past generation which still cannot see the beauty that is offered. Thus they flee an honest confrontation and rescue themselves and the art they are looking at by veiling it in idealistic humanist concepts without ever really verifying that.

This idea, that the observer is seeing something new of which the beauty and meaning as yet escapes her or him, may perhaps be attributed to the influence of studies of art history in which the real content is rarely discussed, certainly never critically. As a historical discipline, art history wants to attribute everything to historical causes and all kinds of factors, taking as its point of departure the human ability to create adequate forms. Very often people have limited themselves exclusively to questions relating purely to style and form or concentrated on language and grammar rather than on what is being said. Even if subject matter is dealt with, people still avoid a real discussion; in any case, they never pose the question of truth. Or, as one modern artist put it, 'The historians of art turn every desperate spiritual revolution into intellectual table-talk.'[271]

In relation to this we quote from a recent article on the Cobra artists (an avant-garde group from around 1950) published in connection with the exhibition held in 1966 at the Boymans-van Beuningen Museum in Rotterdam: 'The Cobra-group does not incline one to feel scandalized. Consciously intended to be shocking and anti-aesthetic, most Cobra-creations now have a remarkable refreshing and aesthetic effect. They have become what they were not intended to be – *objets d'art.*'[272]

To summarize, we see that there are two distinct ways of dealing with the art of our times. On the one hand there are artists who want to hurl their highly charged message into the world, to protest, to build a new anarchistic or antinomian culture. They tell us that the human condition is horrible. On the other hand there are the dispassionate spectators who will consider the painting only as an *objet d'art*, neutral, purely aesthetic, cultural, humane, contemporary and, as such, interesting, even fascinating, of better or lesser quality, but in a framework where the question of truth or the consideration of the effect modern art has on us ought never to be brought up.

The new situation, manifesting such a deep change in the public's attitude, was clearly summed up by Kandinsky in 1936, when he said: 'The times were hard, but heroic. We painted, the public spat. Today we paint and the public says: "Isn't that nice." This change does not mean that the times have become lighter for the artists.'[273]

Presently we can discern two streams of literature on modern art: that which flows from the pen of artists themselves or their supporters and friends, and that issuing from the art critics or historians who identify themselves with the public and who set themselves up us experts to convert the public to a dispassionate, aesthetic attitude.

As an example of the criticism coming from the side of the artists and their related surroundings, let us look at this short piece from the magazine *20ième Siècle*, the number from May 1964, called *Un siècle d'angoisse* ('A century of distress'). It should be observed that this issue does not deviate in principle from any of the others. There are articles about Edvard Munch and Max Ernst and this quotation is typical:

'Dissonance is the basic tone of Ernst's work, which is dark and full of anxiety, and I should say that anxiety is the foundation of his work.' Then there is an article that refers to Bacon with the description 'Bacon, the convulsive in which anguish suits the heroes',[274] and another one about Metcalf, a sculptor, of which it is said that 'He takes us over the precipice, and he makes works to shock us as the Dadaists did earlier.' There is an article concerning the destruction that has prevailed in our century, about the thinking that has resulted in nothingness, illustrated with works of de Chirico, Chagall, Kokoschka, Klee, Kandinsky, Matta, Miró, Fontana, Giacometti, Germaine Richier, Tanguy, Picasso, Hundertwasser and Vasarely. Still another article refers to *Roel d'Haese* or 'tamed anxiety'.

An exceptional person in this connection is Albrecht Fabri, a German art critic. He writes that the spirit of an artist lies in his reds, blues and greens.[275] This is to him not a way to aestheticism or neutral detachment. For reasons to be discussed we agree cordially with him, for otherwise a misunderstanding might arise. We most emphatically do not say that only the spiritual processes in the mind of the artist are important in the creation of a work of art and that the result does not matter. It is also decidedly not so that a work of art should illustrate a literary or philosophical concept. No, rather, the painter artistically concretizes concepts. She or he thinks with hand and brush, in terms of lines and colours and shapes, realized by the use of artistic media. In the quotations above it is not our intention, any more than it is that of the authors or of the artists mentioned, to discuss their ideas alongside or outside of their works. We wish to deal with the realization of those in their art. Therefore it is not contradictory to Fabri's proposition if elsewhere he says: 'Picasso is a kind of drill. What is left when he washes his brushes are ruins.'[276]

We should like to end this part of our discussion with a quotation from the great English painter, Francis Bacon:

> Also, man now realizes that he is an accident, that he is a completely futile being, that he has to play out the game without reason. I think that even when Velasquez was painting, even when Rembrandt was painting, they were still, whatever their attitude to life, slightly conditioned by certain types of religious possibilities, which man now, you could say, has had cancelled out for him. Man now can only attempt to beguile himself for a time, by prolonging his life – by buying a kind of immortality through the doctors. You see, painting has become – all art has become – a game by which man distracts himself. And you may say that it always has been like that, but now it's entirely a game. What is fascinating is that it's going to become much more difficult for the artist, because he must really deepen the game to be any good at all, so that he can make life a bit more exciting.[277]

In opposition to the manner of criticism that takes the artist with complete seriousness and does not strip his or her expression of content in order to concentrate exclusively on stylistic forms and techniques stands the aestheticizing criticism, the elegant writing on art that neutralizes everything into one huge universal human culture, so that finally the only criterion for art is quality. As example we quote a few passages from the text written by Paul Eluard for the Picasso exhibition recently held in Amsterdam (1967):

> Of the men that have left traces of their existence on earth, about whose existence cannot be spoken without realizing that they shall remain there, Picasso is one of the greatest. After having conquered the world, he has had the courage to turn it against himself, being sure, not of the victory, but of his strength to oppose it ... Apart from all established concepts concerning objective reality, he has restored the contact between the object and the observer, the one who thinks it, and he has been the one who has offered us, in the most daring and sublime way, the undetachable proofs of the existence of man and the world.

And further:

> Picasso has created fetishes, fetishes that have a life of their own. They are not only signs that contact men and the world, but, at the same time, signs in movement, a movement that makes them concrete. The geometrical figures, the cabbalistic signs such as male, female ... table, guitar, become for all men again males, females ... tables, guitars, more common than before as they are now intelligible, observable for the mind as well as for the senses. What has been called the magic of design and of colours, begins to penetrate, nourishingly, everything that surrounds us as well as ourselves.

The article ends: 'Indeed, this man kept the breakable key to the problem of reality in his hands. To him it meant to see the seeing, to deliver seeing, to attain clairvoyance. In this he has succeeded.'

We could quote many similar texts but this is enough. We should like to underline clearly that such treatment does not do justice to the artist. As a result artists often feel frustrated. They have something to say, have painted their canvas with their blood, so it is anything but neutral, anything but only humanly cultural – but their cry, their scream,[278] is politely attended to and then with pleasant words rendered ineffectual. That frustration can be expressed in still sharper cries, still clearer protests; who can say whether these increasingly violent expressions in our times are not induced by the public's passivity? Should we perhaps understand Picasso's heads from around the 1940s in this way? People had, in discussing Picasso, suggested that he reproduced reality in a new, non-Renaissance way, namely by picturing it from different angles – for example simultaneously showing a head both in profile and frontally. Demonstrably that is not what Picasso originally did. Critics discussed it in a too innocent and over-simplified way. In reaction, around 1940, Picasso 'showed them' what it would be like if he did as they had suggested . . . the result is the most horrifying he ever achieved. This same conflict between the artist and his public also ignited the initial 'happenings' in the fifties in New York. We can read about it in the last issue of *Randstad* and quote: 'Forty years of abrasion have made the human skin callous, and it is rather difficult today to arouse the old bourgeois. Since those days we have become accustomed to the idea, for example, that everything in a gallery with a lamp above it and a name beneath it, is art. This narrow-mindedness evidently enrages the artist.'[279]

We should like to draw our conclusions. If art is important, we should act accordingly. We personally are certain that art is more important now than before: It has always been important, in that it has always had a function in the world, but today it has become the religion of our times, something mystical, a revelation of the deepest reality but in an irrational way.[280] Modern art, in a very direct and special way, speaks of the same things as existentialist philosophy. It is antinomian or gnostic and often preaches an anarchistic mysticism.[281] Its expressions are often strange and ununderstandable at first encounter. In a way this is fortunate, for then at least a number of people might pass it by. On the other hand it is not so fortunate, for if people turn all laws upside down, beauty and the possibility of communication may suffer. But we must not deceive ourselves. The strange situation in which art says 'A' and the art critic says it means 'B' – a diluted, detached, euphemistic rendering of the actual message – does not make art impotent. This art communicates something, even if only that there is nothing beautiful or sensible to say. For the very reason that viewers are not on their guard, the influence of this art via an involuntary brainwashing can be great. People want to keep up with the times and are afraid to voice an opinion or take a stand against such art. In a sense we are being indoctrinated by an attitude of snobbery, in which the newest is pushed, published, propagated and prized by virtue of its novelty. This modern art has infiltrated every layer of communication, simply because so few take account of the actual message – so even if one does not like it, one must be 'cultural', and that is why . . .

Modern art has had an enormous effect on modern life. Statistics can show very little here, but the fact that pornography is now sold openly in shops, that drugs are used more than ever and are even recommended, the fact that people can go further than ever, beyond all boundaries in films and that the censors dare cut only a very little, the fact that anarchistic movements have grown in the last decade and the unmistakable fact that many young people see no meaning or colour left in life – do we really think that this happened all by itself? Is not the increasing rate of dechristianization a direct consequence of the fact that people who do know the gospel neglect to speak it in the proper place? In more than one expression of protest we can hear the despondent complaint that the church, those who call themselves Christians, have given no answer to these deep needs. One thinks of 'Eleanor Rigby', the song by the Beatles about a girl who is buried in the church, 'nobody was there, nobody was saved', and the refrain 'All these lonely people, where do they all come from?'

We must realize that the writer of this paper is not the only one concerned with the great influence of modern art on today's culture in general. The twentieth-century revolutionaries talk about it too, and are much aware of the importance of art in furthering their cause. In an article written by an American in the *International Times* it is claimed that the following revolutions have already occurred: the sexual revolution, the artistic revolution and the psychedelic revolution. I quote here what is said about the artistic revolution:

> Great subverter of the hollow society, mass your media – you are helpless before our skills. You don't know if we are parodying you or you are parodying us anymore. Beatles, Dylan, happenings, pop. Rock and roll great continent! The Box will destroy you! Our bodies are opening ... We will force you to support us – to support the artists who are digging your dark grave. Join us before it is too late. Do not die! There is life enough for everyone! When the mode of the music changes the walls of the city shake![282]

If we want to struggle today at a meaningful front, we must be aware of these issues. We must answer the questions posed by modern art and quash the lie, the spirit of anarchy, that it proclaims. But we are all too quickly bowled over by people who show us in such a clever way that the world is rotten and that they have every reason and right to protest. Perhaps as believers we should have protested much earlier that the church and Christianity have become bourgeois. But that we did not, does not excuse the antichristian message. This world is not rotten as such, and the evil in it should be called sin instead of human shortcomings. There is also a solution, in Jesus Christ, who came into this world to redeem it of all evil, the evil the modern artists curse. Far less than they could, could God tolerate it, for it has denatured his beautiful creation.[283]

We must be fully aware that the truth is at stake, the question of whether God's creation is good, whether life is beautiful and worth living, and whether evil is sin and a result of sin. It is a question of whether human life has value, whether our work has meaning and whether there is meaning outside God and Jesus Christ. It is no academic question to ask what the results are of overstepping the First and Second Commandments, refusing to acknowledge God, refusing to love our neighbours and dragging them through the mire because we do not recognize them in their humanness. No, these are not academic questions but living questions for today – as vital as they were yesterday and will be in the future. The answer, too, is not an academic one: we see it being worked out around us, in modern art and its effects, and it makes us more than wonder whether we are living in an apocalyptic age in which the lawless rule and possess the power of culture.

Where are we heading? What do we ourselves want? Is it not at least to realize in our own lives something of Philippians 4:8: 'Whenever you find anything true or honourable, righteous or pure, lovable or praiseworthy, or if "virtue" and "honour" have any meaning, then let your thoughts dwell there.' We must realize this in our own lives and then also in the world around us, for only in this way can happiness, freedom and openness exist, because only in this way can we really love our neighbour.

That is where we are heading in our discussions with the modern artist, whom we love, whom we want to save from despair and antinomianism (the consequences of which de Sade so ably demonstrated), whom we want to save from the supreme lie that both God and humanity are dead. Because we value the modern artist as a fellow human being whose work has effect and is not done randomly, senselessly and without meaning, we cannot ignore the really deep questions that lie at the root of her or his work.

Within the scope proposed by this article, we formulated our ideas, foremost in relation to the art of today: Pop Art, Zero, Op Art, Bacon, Matta, Lam, etc. If we plead for engaged attention and preoccupation with art it surely follows that we must honour what ought to be honoured and pledge ourselves to that which we value as beautiful and worthwhile. When artists make something fine and positive today, circumstances are against them; they stand alone and must swim against the tide. Let us then support them, so that their goodness is not lost in the mud. Let us help them in word and in practice as enthusiastic people who do not maintain a snobbish and even sinful detachment. Perhaps we formulated too much in the extreme, but nuances are possible only when we concentrate on concrete examples, on specific works of art.

Paul writes concerning things that are true, worthy, righteous, pure, lovable, harmonious, godly, praiseworthy.[284] Surely these principles do not by-pass reality. They are not old-fashioned and are far from being bourgeois. We as human beings cannot realize them in our own strength; they are too beautiful for that and we are too sinfully weak. But in Christ, in the renewed strength that he made accessible by his resurrection, they become possible, not only in our personal lives but also in our culture, in the widest sense. Therefore we plead for involvement in looking at art, involvement with modern art – involvement driven by the gospel, for it is the power of God for salvation and leads to life, renewal, freedom and love. In this way only can we be salt that retains its saltiness and take a meaningful place in this world. Human lives, in the deepest, fullest meaning of that word, are not cheap, and to pledge ourselves to their value is worth the trouble if we really love God and love our neighbours.

We must not be annoyed at our neighbours' involvement – it is no more than their right. We can praise them for their honesty, their daring to face the consequences. But the gospel remains a joyful message that involves rescuing lives, renewing life both here and now. Only by professing this message of life, also in the spiritual struggle of today, about which we cannot be complacent and to which there never is an easy solution, can we, both as artists and viewers, become real doers of the Word.

Appendix: Schematic Summary of the Artistic Revolution[285]

Protest
- against Victorian morals, which are bourgeois, groundless and without deeper justification.
    - Therefore: ➔ shocking behaviour; unkempt, careless in clothing; or harsh colours, miniskirts, etc.
- specifically against all codes in sexual matters.
    - Therefore: ➔ pornography as a means of undermining morals. A new morality (not just immorality) emerges that gives complete freedom in sexual affairs.
- against Christianity, being stronghold of bourgeois morality and mentality, and . . . (see 2 Thessalonians 2 and 2 Timothy 3).
- against all authority, seen as defending existing order that is unacceptably wrong. Especially against all 'paternalizing' in censorship, laws against drugs, etc. And against all bureaucracy, cold inhuman effectiveness, not fighting poverty enough on national and international level.
- against technocracy, seen as choking all humanness and freedom. Especially as economic values are placed higher than human worth and life (sex-exploitation in ads, health endangered by cars, noise of planes, etc.).
- but accepts technology insofar as it reduces work in mills and factories through automation and produces an affluent society.

Teaching
- mysticism of a nihilistic kind, today often in form of Indian religion (Buddhism, Zen Buddhism) (that teaches existentialism in a non-intellectualistic way). Protest against Christianity and Western world inherent to it.
- 'drop out' – don't work in this society, don't work for a career, money, etc., as these represent bourgeois values.
- 'tune in' – being one of the group, tending towards a kind of tribal way of living. New way of bohemianism. A new elite.
- 'turn on' – use drugs, either LSD or marijuana, as means of mystic experience, enlarging human realm of experience – being at the same time protest, etc.
- revolution – overthrow of this order, which has become 'impossible'. Is therefore sympathetic to all revolutions, and all movements against our Western system – Vietnam, race riots, guerrillas, etc.
- extreme left, but not communism, which is too much against freedom, too much technocratic and too legalistic.
- no war, peace everywhere.

Appendix: Schematic Summary of the Artistic Revolution 205

- freedom (see 2 Peter 2:19).
- an utopia, a better world – that will come automatically if 'this society' is done away with after the revolution.

Promoted by

- art movements – Dada, Surrealism, 'happenings', Theatre of the Absurd, modern film, modern (pornographic) writing, protest songs, rock music, modern music, etc. Much of that professed anarchistic in content.
- use of drugs, LSD etc.
- teaching of Eastern rites, etc.
- real situation in Western world: technocracy, bureaucracy in its negative effects, bourgeois mentality, Victorian repression of sex, Christian legalism and shallow preaching.
- modern means of communication (press, especially TV and radio). Just by showing all things going on from very near, and prominent people in their intimacy, they reinforce a detesting of the situation (mentioned in our last point above). Programmes etc. are made by journalists or radio- or TV editors (either sympathizing or more likely ignoring the real issues) that have to be 'creative' and 'up to date', meaning that (often unwittingly) they promote the 'latest', being a more way-out thing, further in the line of the revolutionary development. They have to follow the trend; that means that they speak according to the spirit of the age.
- the 'snobbery' of many people in leading positions, seeing modern art merely as a new (even if strange) movement, as 'culture' that must be promoted.
- the lack of any real foundation for morals and values – Christianity only paid lip service to, any other (religious or basic philosophical) ground for life missing (God-is-dead).
- the threat of nuclear war.
- social injustice, and specifically disorder in family life (broken homes, careless and love-less raising of children, egoistic living, etc.).
- activity: dances, gatherings, 'happenings', hippie lifestyle ('drop out' in practice).
- directed action: demonstrations, provocative behaviour, art-manifestations, papers and pamphlets.

Adhered to

- by young people, students, as well as lower-class people, primarily from urban centres.
- sympathy of many older people (under 40), without taking part in action.
- leaders (allegedly none, but in reality): artists, poets, etc., utopists, cultural philosophers and maybe (or easily) political agitators.

Result

- cultural revolution since the Second World War, with ever increasing force.
- revolution in morals and ethics.
- possible violent, open (political) revolution. Cf. R.H. Sanger, 'Is Insurrection Brewing in U.S.?', *U.S. News & World Report* (Dec 25, 1967) pp.32 ff.
- possible counteraction: bourgeois counter-revolution ('fascism').
- in each case in the end leading to dictatorship and a new (non-Christian) culture and society.

Part III

ARTICLES AND REVIEWS ON TWENTIETH-CENTURY ART AND ARTISTS

Articles on Artists and Art Streams

• New Art: Art Nouveau and Jugendstil[286]

Anyone who admitted ten years or so ago that he or she loved the art products made around the turn of the century was virtually assured of not being taken seriously and of being designated a person without taste. Now however the Gemeentemuseum in The Hague has devoted a large exhibition to Dutch 'New Art', better known as Jugendstil or Art Nouveau, while in Paris at the extensive exhibition 'Sources du XXième Siècle' also a tremendous department was set up with furniture and other applied arts products from the years between 1890 and 1910, the brief period in which this distinctive sort of art flourished.

Jugendstil, or whatever one chooses to call it, is indeed a remarkable phenomenon, which helps to account for the contradictory opinions, the fierce defence and the fierce attack both at the time and still today. This movement aimed above all else to find an artistic, beautiful and responsible form in which the materials used could also be done justice, for what we now call industrial or applied art, for furniture, tapestries, wallpaper, typography, in short for everything people make, with the exception of the fine arts. The origins of the movement lay in England, but in every country people applied the basic principles in their own way. So too here in The Netherlands.

This New Art is a typical transitional phenomenon. That is probably why it also could not last too long. On the one hand it was an effort to breathe new life into old forms by smothering them with ornamentation of a strange super-naturalistic and yet stylized character; on the other hand it was a search for new, logical forms suited to the thing, handy for use and at the same time beautiful and in agreement with the material. In this, Jugendstil ushered in the twentieth century – notice, for example, the ceramics of W.C. Brouwer. Various pieces of furniture that we see here make clear what the twentieth century must have learned from it: if we just eliminate a certain curl or recapitulative flourish, we see modern furniture materialize before our eyes.

Yet it remains remarkable that in spite of all the observations one can make here and even in spite of the realization that modern architecture in the Netherlands begins with Hendrick Berlage's Stock Exchange in Amsterdam, a 'New Art' product in its own right, it is nonetheless a past world that we encounter at the exhibition in The Hague. A beautiful world, a refined world, poetic, delicate, with some sober notes that, however, immediately had to be transposed into beauty again. Here people wanted to turn 'ordinary' things too into products of art. It is not only the intermediary character of this movement as a transitional phenomenon that caused its short longevity but, perhaps to a much greater degree, also its aestheticism, the desire to make everything beautiful, to lay poetry into everything. It soon made this art appear as antiquated, an exaggerated product, over-saturated with the atmosphere of an eccentric atelier, smelling too much of the rose perfume of the poet. A number of its wholesome concepts, however, have become firm basic formulas for all the furniture and applied art of the twentieth century: honesty in the use of materials, comprehensive form of the furniture, subordination of ornamentation to the whole, and simplicity and concentration.

Why should we not just stroll about this exposition simply to look around, to enjoy the beauty, which we recognize as a typical product of its time, in order to perhaps discover something that is really beautiful and valuable to us? And, after this visit, we shall discover how much there still is of all this in our environment today, whether as the original product or as its echoes in modern furniture or (and this is disagreeable) as all manner of commercial products.

• Whence do we come? What are we? Where do we go?[287]

Bunyan, the well-known late seventeenth-century Baptist preacher, may be best known, or perhaps we should say famous, for his book *Pilgrim's Progress*. The book is typical of his Puritan mindset, which could be characterized as Calvinist with Anabaptist leanings. Bunyan himself wrote a rather extensive poem defending his liberal use of allegory in the book and briefly summarizing the tenor of his work. From this poem stem these words:

> This book it chalketh out before thine eyes
> The man that seeks the everlasting prize:
> It shows you whence he comes, whither he goes.[288]

In 1831 Carlyle wrote his *Sartor Resartus* – which could be translated as 'the tailor retailored' – in which he tells somewhat mockingly of how Professor Teufelsdröckh has developed a philosophy of clothes, which he will try to explain to the British people. This Teufelsdröckh, who lives in Weissnichtwo (namely, in the Wahngasse), may be a complete scatterbrain but he nevertheless offers some important ideas. It is a sparkling book full of humour and friendly irony. In it Carlyle expresses his own views in an indirect way, as if hardly taking himself seriously, but in the end this approach helps him to make his point all the more convincingly. It became a very influential book, especially in later years when those who had become weary of all the positivistic scholarship and ideology were searching for a way to break out of the shackles of this oppressive, idealistic view of science. Undoubtedly Carlyle was deeply influenced by German idealism – the philosophy of freedom. It could be said that he managed to take this philosophy that is rather incomprehensible to the layman because of its technical jargon and make it understandable to the ordinary English public (and later also to the French public), albeit that he combined it with Neoplatonist ideas.

Everything, Carlyle believed, is merely a symbol for the divine, and all great men (including the great founders of religions, poets and politicians – in short, all geniuses) are the most direct revelation of the divine. Carlyle later developed these thoughts more extensively in his *On Heroes and Hero-Worship*. He states:

> The Universe is but one vast Symbol of God; nay, if thou will have it, what is man himself but a Symbol of God; is not all that he does symbolical; a revelation to Sense of the mystic god-given Force that is in him; a 'Gospel of Freedom', which he, the 'Messiah of Nature' preaches, as he can, by act and word?[289]

Indeed, freedom is the nucleus around which his whole philosophy revolves, despite all the interwoven theories that take a lot after Platonism. As he says in his own inimitable style and diction:

> Man's unhappiness, as I construe, comes of his greatness; it is because there is an Infinite in him, which with all his cunning he cannot quite bury under the Finite. Will the whole Finance Ministers and Upholsterers and Confectioners of modern Europe undertake, in joint-stock company, to make one Shoeblack HAPPY? They cannot accomplish it, above an hour or two; for the Shoeblack has a soul quite other than his Stomach and would require, if you consider it, for his permanent satisfaction and saturation, simply this allotment, no more, and no less: *God's infinite Universe altogether to himself*, therein to enjoy infinitely, and fill every wish as fast as it rose. [290]

These notions take Teufelsdröckh into a major crisis. We learn this through his autobiographical writings, a jumbled chaotic mess which Carlyle is able to access because of the intervention of the Geheimrath Heuschrecke – at least, this is how the book tells the tale. In reality these are Carlyle's own struggles, and this is his way of weaving his own autobiography into the story. It is certain, he states, that I exist, and that a short while ago I did not exist: 'but Whence? How? Whereto?' [291] And so he stands,

> shouting question after question into the Sibyl-cave of Destiny, and receiving no answer but an Echo. It is all a grim Desert, this once fair world of his: wherein is heard only the howling of wild beasts, or the shrieks of despairing, hate-filled men; and no Pillar of Cloud by day, and no Pillar of Fire by night, any longer guides the Pilgrim.[292]

Perhaps this is an allusion to Bunyan's book. But it is certainly also a reference to the Scriptures even though this man, who was raised as a Calvinist by simple but believing parents and who even studied theology at one point, had come to the point of rejecting all the Christian answers to these questions. 'To me the Universe was all void of Life, of Purpose, of Volition, even of Hostility: it was one huge, dead, immeasurable Steam-engine, rolling on, in its dead indifference, to grind me limb from limb.'[293] Thus even God's creation itself appears hostile to him, so that in a later passage he compares heaven and earth to the jaws of a voracious monster clamping down, ready to devour him. But this crisis, during which he negates virtually everything, is followed by a period in which he actually affirms this earthly existence and overcomes the crisis, or so it would appear. The solution he finds is a remarkable combination of faith in human freedom with the remnants of his Puritan-Christian upbringing. 'Our life is compassed round with Necessity; yet the meaning of Life itself is no other than Freedom, than Voluntary Force; thus have we a warfare; in the beginning, especially, a hard-fought battle. For the God-given mandate, Work thou in welldoing, lies mysteriously written, in Promethean, Prophetic Characters, in our hearts.'[294] It never allows us to rest until we have fulfilled our duty – this duty being that which he placed at the centre of his own life and proclaimed to be the task of all people: the duty of letting our lives become a visible, practiced Gospel of Freedom.

In the meantime, this fulfilment of duty and this creed of individual freedom do not help to answer the profound questions about the meaning of life. Rather, the opposite is true. Thus we can understand the quotation which comes later in the book, echoing the words Bunyan once wrote (and which Carlyle will have known well since he was an English boy raised in a Christian home): 'Thus, like some wild-flaming, wild-thundering train of Heaven's Artillery does this mysterious MANKIND thunder and flame, in long-drawn, quick succeeding grandeur, through the unknown Deep . . . But Whence? – O Heaven, Whither?' [295]

Indeed, any deeply thinking person (as Carlyle was) who deliberately rejects God's revelation in the Scriptures, who refuses to love the Lord but chooses individual freedom instead, will be confronted with unanswerable questions. The whole world becomes an 'unknown Deep', and the 'Whence? Whither?' will never be answered but will stand forever as a terrifying, excruciating unknown.

In 1864 Taine wrote *L'idéalisme anglais, Étude sur Carlyle* ('English idealism, a study of Carlyle'). Taine, a well-known art philosopher and essayist from the latter half of the nineteenth century is difficult to characterize. Undoubtedly he belongs to those who cherished a positivistic life and world view. He placed great emphasis on that which is rational, well reasoned and provable, and in his essays he stresses the 'natural' factors and the scientific method. He became especially famous for his sociological theories, in which he argued that all art is inextricably bound with the environment (also the natural surroundings) in which it is born. On the other hand, some of his statements point to a more idealistic and strongly subjective point of view; he was also (as was Carlyle, for that matter) a great admirer of Goethe. In his theory of art this becomes apparent from, among other things, the fact that besides race and environment he also accepts the *faculté maîtresse* as a determining factor for art – that is, a spiritual disposition which breaks through the causal determinism [296] apparent in the elements we mentioned earlier.

It is no surprise, then, that on the one hand he criticizes Carlyle for seeking the solution to his agonizing questions in spheres that can no longer be understood by reason. Taine himself preferred to be more 'logical' and sensible, holding on to the order and permanence of things. People should not, he felt, wander off into unknown backgrounds and depths; they should attempt rather, by means of scientifically proved facts, to develop a less *grüblerisch* ('brooding') but logical system. On the other hand, Taine deeply respected Carlyle and this book attests to his great interest in him. As a matter of fact, in his *Notes sur Paris, Vie et Opinions de M. Fredéric-Thomas Graindorge . . . publiées par H. Taine, son exécuteur testamentair* of 1867 he offers a typically French imitation of Carlyle's *Sartor Resartus*. We say 'typically French' because that Mr Graindorge, who plays a similar role in this book as Teufelsdröckh does in Carlyle's book, is certainly no profound and esoteric philosopher; rather he is portrayed as an amicable *bon vivant*, always making side remarks about the girls, the mistresses and the parties in Paris. Nevertheless, it was Taine's book that served to introduce Carlyle and his ideas to France. He quotes Carlyle extensively in the book, in lengthy passages translated into French; this allowed the French, most of whom could not read English, to become familiar with Carlyle's ideas. For our purposes it is most interesting that he translated Carlyle's 'Whence? Whither?' as 'Mais d'où venons-nous? O Dieu, où allons-nous?' This is really an inexact and inaccurate representation of Carlyle's thoughts, because Carlyle's 'Whither?' and 'Whence?' were intended to encompass the whole earth, the entire creation, whereas Taine's translation limits the question strictly to its human element.

At the end of the century we see the repercussions of the positivistic world view. People felt trapped by the natural sciences, which more and more threatened to control their lives and compromise their freedom. 'Is this not the time to react; is this not the time to chase the intruder (whom Verlaine calls the 'murderer of prayer') out of the house and, if it is still possible, to lock up the surging scholars in their own laboratories?'[297] says Aurier, one of the typical representatives of the new movement. In the realm of the visual arts there was also a reaction against realistic art, as people sought a more subjective form of human expression, detached from the outside world. This was a reaction against naturalism, which tried to depict the real world as precisely as possible, even taking into account the latest scientific theories about light, etc. Gauguin, the most important representative of the new movement, spoke of 'the detestable error of naturalism'.

We cannot go into much detail about the development of Gauguin's art, nor about the various influences on his work, influences which in his early years included especially the Japanese woodcuts, and in his later phases included the Borobudur sculptures, of which he possessed a series of photographs. But it is helpful to know that particularly the last-mentioned Hindu-Javanese art left its unmistakable mark on Gauguin's art, and specifically on the work we will discuss here. That painting is entitled *D'où venons-nous? Que sommes-nous? Où allons-nous?* ('Whence do we come? What are we? Whither do we go?') It was painted in 1897–1898 on the island of Tahiti, where Gauguin lived apart from a short interruption from 1891 until his death. The title uses the same expression we discussed earlier, but expands on it somewhat. We know that Gauguin was acquainted with Carlyle's work, because a portrait he painted ten years earlier of his friend the Dutchman Meyer de Haan shows a table with the book *Sartor Resartus* lying next to Milton's *Paradise Lost*. Gauguin probably knew some English, since in his younger years he was a seaman, but we can safely assume that he had read Taine's book about Carlyle, and that he will have greatly appreciated its translation of large fragments of Carlyle's writing. In choosing a title for his painting, he used Taine's translation. We should, however, not assume that he was consciously quoting Carlyle. More likely, he did not remember where he had read that quote, and perhaps even thought he had made it up himself. But we can certainly assume that Carlyle's thoughts, so beautifully expressed, made a deep impression on him. He must have recognized in them a kindred spirit. Also with regard to their theories concerning art and its symbolic character these two artists bore a strong resemblance. There are other points of similarity as well. We can safely surmise that, consciously or unconsciously, Gauguin's title is a reference to Carlyle's writings as translated by Taine. That also explains the inexactness of the translation; he simply adopted Taine's inaccurate rendition. It is remarkable to see this painting, now hanging in a museum in Boston in the USA, with the awkwardly worded title 'Whence come we? What are we? Whither do we go?'. The faulty formulation of the French translation is all the more strongly accentuated by its re-translation back into English.

In 1899 this painting was exhibited in Paris, and art critic André Fontainas remarked that the painting had no clear meaning and did not constitute any understandable allegory. Gauguin responded in a letter written in his typically captivating, telegrammatic style, and we wish to quote from it here because it is the best way to understand the spirit out of which this artwork was born. Don't forget to look at the painting itself as you read it.

> Here, near my hut, in complete silence, I dream of violent harmonies in the natural scents that intoxicate me. Delight elevated to times immemorial by I don't know what sacred horror that I suspect to be there. The distant past a scent of joy which I inhale in the present. Animal figures of statuesque rigidity: I don't know how ancient, elevated, religious in the rhythm of their gestures, in their rare immobility. The eyes that dream are blurred by an enigma that cannot be solved. And it is night – all is at rest. My eyes are closed to see without understanding the dream shooting past in the infinite space before me, and I experience the doleful march of my hopes.

He goes on to speak more specifically about the painting, responding to Fontainas's allegation that the work is incomprehensible:

> My dream will not let itself be comprehended, and it contains no allegory. As a musical poem it transcends every libretto. A quote from Mallarmé: 'Immaterial and lofty, the essence of a work is precisely in that which is not expressed; it is contained implicitly in the lines without colours or words, and it is not brought about in a material way ...' Turning back again to the work: the idol is not explained in a literary way, but is like a sculpture, also less animal-like as it connects itself in my dream in front of my hut with all of nature which reigns in our primitive soul: an imaginary comfort for our suffering caused by the indefinable and incomprehensible with respect to the mystery of our origin and our future ... When I awake, my work completed, I say to myself: Whence do we come? What are we? Whither do we go?[298]

Although we notice here in Gauguin some similarities to the experience of reality found in Carlyle, it evokes quite a different spirit. Gauguin does not speak of crisis or struggle. Where Carlyle recoiled and tried to flee, searching for certainty, for something solid, for the meaning of life, we find Gauguin in a kind of dream-like state, lost in the whole, plunged into the distant past. With Gauguin there is an experience of terror as well, but it is neutralized and softened by something that is beautiful and elevated and remote. It is here that Gauguin finds his comfort, although he admits that it is imaginary, a comfort in suffering, which is vague and poorly defined, and caused by the mystery of 'Whence? Whither?'

All his life Gauguin vehemently opposed rationalism. He fought against everything that would restrict freedom, against all rules and prejudices. He once wrote that the artist at his easel must be completely free, slave to neither nature nor neighbour, the past nor the future; always he must be nothing but himself. Gauguin realized too, however, that there are heights and depths to which we by ourselves have no access; and that in the depth of our souls we are bound. But Gauguin had many predecessors, and a long tradition preceded him. Because of that his pain is vague and undefined, more like a kind of dreamy poetry than that it really shakes up his world. There is mystery, yes, but it hardly arouses any sense of anxiety anymore. Was that because Gauguin did not have a Christian upbringing to 'overcome'? Had the mystery already become commonplace for him?

This artwork, then, is not really poignant, it does not touch us in the core of our being. Rather, it is like a quiet and nebulous poem, more dream than reality. Perhaps it is in the end just resignation – the old 'Oh well, that's just how life is' attitude – which is so often passed off as wisdom. The question mark is there, certainly, but that's just part of life; it actually is beautiful, elevated and mysterious. The dream of Gauguin is life in an indeterminable time in the past; a dream of ignorant beings living an animal-like existence. They may be aware that the world holds many unsolvable mysteries, but they retain something elevated, a beauty and solemnity of an ancient culture that is gone for good. A world that knows the questions, but the hurt is gone or almost gone.

In a letter to his old friend Morice, Gauguin explains his work in more detail:

> Whither do we go? Near to death an old woman. A strange bird finishes off the whole (at the left of the canvas). What are we? Our daily life (the figure in the foreground). Instinctive man wonders what it all means. Whence do we come? Source. Child (right). Communal life (the seated figures to the right). The bird concludes the poem as a comparison of the lower being with the more intelligent being in the big whole, which constitutes the problem indicated by the title. Behind a tree two dim figures (behind the seated figures on the right), dressed in somber colours, form a sad note beside the Tree of Knowledge (sad because of this knowledge), compared with simple souls in a virginal natural world which could be a paradise of human design, as they let themselves go in the joy of life.[299]

In the latter part of this quotation, we discover Gauguin's 'solution' – namely, that we are good and free as long as we remain unfettered by knowledge and science, which have destroyed the harmony that was part of humanity's primordial existence. (Gauguin's move to Tahiti to live among the natives was his attempt at living out these convictions.) Ultimately this painting is more of a testimony to the earthly paradise that could have been than to the disturbing questions in its title. The primitive, primeval and good is glorified, because that is where human being originated. But reason and science have spoiled all that; they have ripped freedom to shreds and have caused life to sour. The age-old questions voiced by Carlyle are given another twist here, and they become a testimony or a prophecy – albeit a *false* prophecy which suppresses the truth.

What about our own times? Modern people have learned that it is pointless to ask these questions. They have discovered that all previous generations 'called on their idealism and their well-tested theories of knowledge to make it possible to live peaceful, quiet lives amidst the mysterious riddle of horrors taking place right before their eyes'.[300] People want to maintain their personal freedom at any cost, and 'the one who is free not only refuses explanations, but he also guesses, with infallible intuition, that even the possibility of an explanation poses the greatest danger to his freedom.'[301] They want to maintain this freedom even though people are well aware that this means that their life, and everything else, becomes meaningless. We have simply been randomly thrown onto this earth without any 'Why' or 'Whither' . . . A deep anxiety has gripped our souls, a fear for our very existence, our lives. Now we say that anguish and despair will reveal to us who we are. We have come to realize what it means to live in a world without God. Or perhaps, trying to think more positively, we say that: 'Yes, the gods probably do exist, but they have not revealed themselves to us.'[302] Thus, all apparent splendour, all the seemingly profound solutions that people in their apostasy had found to rescue the meaning and purpose of life and the value of human being, all this has been debased. They have been forced to confront the truth – namely, that life without God is meaningless. But they are fixed in their intent, refusing to repent. They continue to suppress the truth in unrighteousness. The result is a deep crisis that becomes (as evidenced by Carlyle's writing) permanent, inalterable, and insolvable.

What about us? Brothers and sisters, you know where to find the answers to these questions, don't you? It is not that we know everything, or can understand everything. It is not that there are no more mysteries for us, mysteries such as why God chose to create the world and its inhabitants. But it is usually not out of escapism or superficiality that we hardly busy ourselves with trying to solve these mysteries. Rather, it is out of trust, the deep conviction that our Lord only does what is right, and that his work is never without purpose. We also realize that these questions are irreverent, and that he has revealed to us everything that we need to know. Moreover, we know that we have more to do than sit around trying to answer those kinds of questions. Each of us has a unique calling to do what our hands find to do. Walking in the ways of the Lord is never meaningless precisely because that is what he asks of us. 'The secret things belong to the Lord our God, but the things revealed belong to us and to our children forever, that we may follow all the words of this law' (Deuteronomy 29:29).

• Angst[303]

Angst – a profound sense of anxiety or dread – is the emotional undertone that accompanies life in our times. However hard we try to drown out our fears and cling desperately to the hope that human science eventually will build us a better world, we know deep in our hearts that this is an idle dream. We thought that science would succeed in giving us total control of our lives; instead it has presented us with problems and difficulties of such a magnitude that we can hardly even comprehend them. We certainly do not have the solutions. Yet we will understand our own times even better if we discern how science, which recognizes no boundaries whatsoever with respect to its realm of investigation, has undermined our faith in the idol of humanism, of human being as a moral and reasonable, free personality. We have started to glimpse the awesome depths and aspirations of the human heart, which we discovered to be a gaping abyss containing little of the goodness and beauty which it was thought to hold. Even humanistic freedom itself, on which basis human beings freely determine their own fortune and future, and recognize no law other than what they themselves had accepted in freedom, even that freedom often turned out to be fictitious and deeply problematic.

Filled with anxiety and despair, modern people move about in space and time. Having been randomly flung on to the earth at this particular time in history, all we can really be sure of is that we exist. But for what purpose? Why? Is not all human effort futile and absurd? Are we not just foolishly trying to find significance in things that are inherently meaningless? Truly, here we have become deeply aware of what it means to live in a world without God, drawing from that fact all its logical conclusions.

Existentialism, with its prophets of despair, has put this angst into words. But long before that it was already being expressed in art. Thus we can regard the lithograph *The scream*, made in 1895 by the Norwegian artist Munch, as a symbol of our times. The artist has not tried to reproduce the external world with the accuracy of artists who preceded him. On the contrary, as a forerunner of Expressionism, he aimed to give voice to his subjective feelings. It is difficult to describe this work of art, but viewers who take the time to let it penetrate their soul will certainly understand its content and meaning: the scream as an expression of human angst, while the most frightening thing about it is that the reason for the terror is unknown. We see heaven and earth churning around the man like hostile forces that threaten his very existence. The cry of angst is voiced as the man is fleeing – but he has nowhere to flee to, no hope for the future. Therefore it is an angst that grips the deepest centre of his heart, a chilly, hellish anxiety without any possible escape . . . unless he repents. But for a long time already people have 'unmasked' the Christian faith as a completely unfounded, subjective opinion against which they have hardened their hearts.[304]

What we are witnessing here is God moving about the earth in judgment, also by sending powerful delusions upon people.[305] We see them fainting with terror, apprehensive of what is coming upon the world.[306] People will seek prophets but will be unable to find them, for they have rejected every faith except faith in their own existence.[307] This is not only the case with the philosophers of despair themselves, the true nihilists,[308] but it is true of all modern people. For, though they may quake and tremble in anticipating these consequences, they have no reply since they have lost sight of the true foundation of the word of God and thus have no certainty about anything. They do not repent; they do not even recognize the punishing hand of the Lord![309]

• The art of the twentieth century[310]

Contemporary art, strange though that may sound, is very little known and understood today. Not only do the various modern artistic movements and schools of thought look like a chaotic hodge-podge to those who are not particularly well versed in them (and sometimes even to the experts), but frequently the works of art themselves are partially – or even completely – misunderstood. Many people write off modern art as being strange or bizarre, and they do not know what to make of it.

Fortunately this is not true of all contemporary art. We must not forget that there is enough reputable art created today which is understandable and enjoyable. Besides those artists and artistic movements committed to a continuous renewal of the revolution, there are many artists who have retained or are returning to a more moderate, normal style. This may be because they have had their fill of the bizarre or because they simply also have to make art that society sees as 'normal'. We are thinking here of portraits, for example, or illustrations or other genres that are more closely tied to everyday life. So there is also a large group of painters, and they may even be in the majority, who continue to work in the older, more naturalistic traditions. When people speak of modern art, however, they are usually not referring to the latter group but are thinking of Picasso and the Experimentals and of other trends and movements related to them.

Although we can point to numerous forerunners of modern art in the second half of the nineteenth century, and can show that it has deep roots in the eighteenth century, the actual revolution in the art world which led to what we call 'modern' art took place in the years between 1900 and 1920. Various different trends emerged during those years, but they all had one thing in common: *they broke with naturalism.* The task of art is not to imitate reality as it appears to us, these artists said, and true art does not depend on the artist depicting reality just the way it looks. And they were certainly right about that! The naturalism to which they were reacting was a fruit of the Renaissance and Western naturalistic art, which attempted to achieve its goal with the help of perspective, knowledge of anatomy and of the play of light and shadow, and even of certain theories about light.[311] This was undoubtedly closely tied to humanism, as we discussed in a previous article.[312] Modern art's departure from the dogma of naturalism is one of the few beneficial fruits of the modern stylistic developments, and we may be glad about the positive results of this, which we can see especially in the field of the applied arts (decorative sculpture, advertising graphics, illustrations, etc.).

Our goal here is to analyse the various tendencies and fundamental ideas that dominate modern art. In the first place, there is the *movement towards the absolute*.[313] These artists had no interest in depicting that which is temporary or passing, nor did they try to capture the external appearance of their subject matter. In this we see their rejection of all the naturalism of the previous centuries. Rather, these artists were in search of *absolute beauty*. The beauty in a work of art had to be dependent on the aesthetic qualities of the work itself, and not on what was being depicted. These artists sought to represent that which is enduring, the essence of reality outside of ourselves. One might say that in the first twenty years of the twentieth century all the artistic energy and talent was directed to a single goal: finding a form to capture the absolute. One musician even became intent on discovering absolute sound. There were artists who said that colour must be divorced from form so that colour can be accorded its own true meaning – i.e. the meaning that it has in itself, unrelated to its connection with anything else in the world.

These efforts led to 'abstract' or 'non-figurative' art, which depicted nothing one might recognize from the world around us. *Cubism* is one example of such art. The artist began by ignoring in the natural given anything that seemed arbitrary, incidental or individual – i.e. anything that distinguished it from other instances of the same kind – and sought instead to depict the geometric spatial forms[314] that make up its essence. In this way everything was reduced to cubes, pyramids, planes and spheres. During the years between 1905 and 1910, under the leadership of Picasso,[315] the natural givens became more and more unrecognizable, so that in 1910 some paintings were created which consisted of nothing but planes and cubes. The original point of departure (e.g. a few bottles with a guitar) was often just barely discernable. In the following years there were others, especially Mondrian, who took these principles to their most logical and extreme conclusion. It can truthfully be said of Mondrian that from about 1920 until his death he did not draw a single crooked line. His paintings generally consisted of a few straight black lines and one or more bright red, blue or yellow patches.

A painting created according to these kinds of principles can, of course, possess only one main property: the harmonious arrangement of line and colour. That was all these artists were looking for, as they were striving for 'absolute art'. When you follow these ideas to their natural conclusion, you naturally end up with a sterile, meaningless play of circles, squares and lines which, however well balanced they may be, are not capable of stirring up any thought or emotion. The Style group, which was named after the magazine *De Stijl* and of which Mondrian too was a member, also became deeply involved in the field of the applied arts, and this was an area where these ideas were more meaningful. The movement had a strong influence in the development of furniture design, interior decorating, typography,[316] etc. Our own country boasts several examples of architecture built according to these principles, the Gemeentemuseum in The Hague being one excellent example.

There were other groups which were more strongly influenced by Expressionism, a movement that also emerged between 1905 and 1910; these were the *Dadaists*, the *Abstract Expressionists*, or whatever other names they have been given. Their goal was to paint with utter spontaneity, in such a way that their thoughts did not interfere with the process. They wanted painting to become an almost unconscious activity, and the resulting work, they believed, would be an expression of a painter's deepest and most primal urges, as well as being in accordance with the 'harmonious laws of the universe', the 'soul of all humankind'. This time, instead of geometrically constructed compositions, we see wild, uninhibited, 'spontaneous' and uncontrolled forms. These artworks are sometimes difficult to distinguish from the doodles that people scribble absentmindedly on paper when listening to a lecture or talking on the telephone. The artists of this stream would welcome that comparison because it fits their theory beautifully, i.e. that art is an unrestrained expression of what lives in the artist's subconsciousness. Paul Klee, Kandinsky and Chagall are the most well-known representatives of this movement.

Such pantheistic thoughts, in which people seek the universal and in which the individual is just one expression of that, are very prevalent today. It is a kind of modern mysticism, vague and poorly defined, in which people are seeking some kind of totality, the all. Sometimes notions play a role that remind us of animism, in which everything, including that which is dead, is animated or inspired. We can see clearly here the influence of Eastern religions but cannot take the time to analyse that more thoroughly in this article.

After 1925 *Surrealism*, which is based on similar beliefs, originated out of this movement. In Surrealism too we find the depiction of archetypes,[317] the primal thoughts which are present in every person's psyche. But in this case the artists try to depict the archetypes by rendering as accurately as possible the dreams, the free-floating fantasies and images that live in the subconscious and which they perceive to be manifestations of the archetypes. In a very naturalistic way, sometimes even more precise than our seventeenth-century still-life painters, these artists attempted to portray the most bizarre and wildly fantastic monstrosities. It is no surprise that Freud, the famous psychologist who placed such strong emphasis on the sexual, had a major influence here. The images are sometimes highly erotic, to the point of being perverse. The thought-world from which Surrealism draws its ideas is sometimes strongly related to the ideas of existentialism, the modern philosophy or world view which declares all things to be futile. Life, people, human being, doing and striving – everything is meaningless. We will come back to this later.

The driving force behind this search for the absolute and this desire to freely express the deepest urges of the human soul – framed as these thoughts may be in pantheistic ideas – is always *the human longing for freedom*. Commentaries about the lives and works of modern artists keep coming back to this almost monotonous refrain: the search for the absolute freedom to express oneself. In the words of one of these artists: 'A sincere heart is truly free only when it has its own logic and reason.' Another declared that painted art must be as free from the surrounding world as music is. Everything hinges on the freedom of artists to entirely unfettered expression, unbounded by anything outside of themselves. Artists must be unconstrained by any law or norm, at liberty to give unrepressed and spontaneous expression to whatever lives in their souls. It is no surprise that such art can and does not contain much that is lovely, as we are 'incapable of doing any good and inclined to all evil unless we are born again by God's Spirit' (see question and answer 8 of the Heidelberg Catechism).

Another characteristic of modern art is the *strong emphasis on expression*. Expressionism even derives its name from this principle. Beauty, and everything else that until now determined the value of art, is deemed to be of no consequence; only the expressive power is what matters. Van Gogh was the great forerunner in this. On several occasions he formulated his ideas in similar words in his letters. By means of line and colour, which were understood in terms of their symbolic value, artists tried to give expression to human passions, conflicts and energy. Art tried to convey the soul and the power of nature and the human spirit, and we are frequently left with distorted and misshapen images, often painted in colours quite unlike anything we see in the real world. Anything goes, as long as it serves the goal of expressiveness. We said earlier that this idea – that art must do more than just depict and imitate nature – is the most wholesome element of the modern movement. By this I do not mean to say, however, that this movement was more wholesome than the naturalism of the nineteenth century to which it was reacting. Its fundamental principles, after all, represent a further stage of development in the revolution against God. This is something that we must never forget: that we are dealing here with a consistent and ever more persistent apostasy from God. In it we see the 'man of lawlessness' who selects his teachers according to the desires of his own heart, while dressing it up in all manner of profound sounding, beautiful language.

The most important basic element of modern art, connected with all we have just expounded, and that which reflects the most revolutionary forces of our times, is *primitivism*, or *an enmity against culture*. Already in the eighteenth century people claimed that primitive, barbarian people had a more pure human nature than eighteenth-century people. Humans were considered to be basically good, at least when free from all the 'fabricated', 'conventional' ideas and sentiments forced upon them by culture. But at that time this was still a theoretical idea only. (Those who propounded it, by the way, looked for the primitive humans they idealized in the works of Homer, etc.) It was not until the modern age that people began to work with this idea in all seriousness, and the influence of truly primitive art from black African culture, ancient Mexican art or prehistoric art, cannot be underestimated. Culture and all norms, which they prefer to call 'conventions' and 'customs' to strip them of their normative character, ruin human being, so they say. It follows that the artwork of the mentally ill and of children is greatly valued. As one writer states:

> When a normal painter stands before his work, he is unconsciously directed by his upbringing, the times in which he lives, and his environs, and therefore is often held back from really 'letting himself go'. A mentally-ill person, on the other hand, has absolutely no respect for humanity or for the things around him, and therefore 'dares' to let go like a child. The former, by nature of his illness, the latter, by nature of the absence of training (i.e. civilization), bring about creations which may be disorderly but are completely directed by spontaneity. Therefore they are more inclined to depict the naked truth honestly and purely, truth which we usually prefer to deny or hide. The artists of this time ... ask that we approximate the thought world of the child or the mentally-ill person, and that we break out of the comfortable boundaries of our traditions, presuppositions and conventions. They call on us to devote ourselves to the most pure, honest and unfettered plastic creation.[318]

Dadaism and Surrealism are the movements which have taken these deeply revolutionary ideas the most seriously and their art is the clearest expression of all the thoughts and all the goals of the modern artist. They certainly do not beat about the bush: 'We need to be lawless if we are to comprehend the new law'; 'We defend the case of the devil'; these and other statements have been made by the most fanatic and 'progressive' members of this group.[319] A quotation like the following will explain these concepts more clearly still:

> Surrealism is not a ready-made formula, not an actual theory, and not even an artistic position; rather, it is a world view, a way of life, an attitude of intellectual despair. One must see it within the framework of our

generation's struggle for a complete revolution ... of the search of this desperate generation which is only driven on by despair ... Revolutionary revolt against the status quo, against our rotten, degenerated civilization, against hardened 'make-believe' values ... against hypocrisy, rationalism and oppression, against slavery and the dying off of our deepest roots ... Surrealism is revolutionary, a rejection of all culture and society, whose hollowness and repulsiveness they have felt right down to their bones ... the rejection and ridicule of everything bourgeois society clings to: country, God, and reason, conscience, beauty as an end in itself, talent, poetic genius, artistry, yes, even the desire and will to live ... Surrealistic liberation leads to a liberation of desire ... a liberation of the deepest base and core of life itself, these are the things it attempts to extricate from the well-fortified walls of convention, culture and society.[320]

"They have become prey to a panic of thoughts, 'anxiety', 'despair', 'absurdity' are the words they use as a cover-up ... in Surrealism people try to organize the absurd ... they want to show that everything is absurd and internally disconnected. Ideas, logic, order, Truth, Reason – all of this they deliberately surrender to the nothingness of death – and as a result human life becomes sterile and absurd too.[321]

All of this is quite clear, however foolish and strange it may sound to our ears. And it certainly holds a kernel of truth, insofar as the Surrealists have seen that the humanistic world is empty and hollow and without a source of strength for the human heart. 'But they did not repent . . .' In these artistic movements people come to an *ultimate realization of apostasy;* they gain an understanding of what a world without God looks like. They draw the extreme conclusion, literally into absurdity, of the attitude to life that people in principle have subscribed to since the time of the Renaissance. It is striking that they talk so much about the absurd and claim that one only gets to know oneself through fear and anxiety. They recognize that life and the world are thoroughly meaningless and that, without God, everything truly becomes absurdity. Also many of our contemporaries, though they may not go as far as these pioneers, have no real defence against these ideas though they may lament that much 'goodness' and 'beauty' are nullified.

'Men will faint from terror, apprehensive of what is coming on the world . . .' (Luke 21) and 'men will flee to caves in the rocks and to holes in the ground from dread of the Lord and the splendour of his majesty, when he rises to shake the earth' (Isaiah 2). We had better keep this in mind when we see and recognize these signs of the times. Because these things do not happen by accident. 'God has placed people under a powerful delusion, so that they will obey the lie. The secret power of lawlessness is already at work . . . and it comes with every kind of deceptive evil' (2 Thessalonians). For there comes a time, says Paul in 2 Timothy, that men will turn away their ears from the truth, and will turn aside to myths. Realize this: there will be terrible times in the last days. People will be lovers of self, lovers of money, boastful, arrogant, revilers, disobedient to parents, ungrateful, unholy, without love, unforgiving, slanderous, without self-control, brutal, not lovers of good ... lovers of pleasure rather than lovers of God.

We are seeing these and similar prophecies being fulfilled in all their horror. Let us take heed! (Matthew 24).

• Pondering four modern drawings[322]

It has been said that modern art is over most people's heads, and that there is no real interaction between modern artists and their public. But when you visit manifestations of hyper-modern art, particularly where pieces are shown that were created by truly talented, master artists, you will have to come to the opposite conclusion. For the people wandering around at such exhibitions often have looks of despair on their faces and they often come up to me and ask how they should understand and interpret these works. Unlike kitsch or works without quality and meaning, modern art does not leave its viewers cold and untouched. Rather, it has the power to grip us profoundly and to inspire debate and study, questions and discussion. It incites us to try and understand the world and times in which we live. Hopefully it will also inspire us to reach for the Scriptures, not just as words of comfort but also to help shed light on our situation, to give us insight into the current maze of opinions and movements and (usually false) prophecies.

Contemplation of extreme modern works of art is one of the most direct and vigorous ways of being confronted with the problems of our times. It leads us to ask questions, but often it also leaves us literally speechless. Three times I have actually had the experience of seeing someone weep before one of these paintings. Modern art inspires us to debate and discuss, and to ask questions about its meaning. It compels us to try and comprehend the driving forces and powers which have inspired the works, whether they are spirits of good or evil. This leads us to more penetrating questions about issues such as the purpose of our existence, our work and our culture, and about the value of human life. People are longing for a prophet but there is no prophet,[323] and when all is said and done one is still left standing alone with these paintings. They hang there as witnesses to the fiasco of humanistic culture, witnesses to a society that is constantly ramming its head against the wall of God's created order. This is what happens when we take the humanistic point of view to its logical extreme that says human being is at the centre of the universe as its creator and ruler, and that God is nothing more than a projection of the human mind. At the same time science – which for the humanist takes the place of revelation (how could it be otherwise when you shut your eyes to God's revelation?) – has dug deeper and deeper to 'unmask' all false human values, only to discover that in the depths of the human soul a bottomless abyss full of horrors is to be found. This discovery, in turn, led to a crisis in humanism. The scientific endeavour which was expected to clarify and dissect everything, to explain everything on the basis of the laws of nature, has also proved to be a threat to human freedom, the humanist's greatest treasure. We are forced to ask: Do we really have any freedom? Is everything not predetermined? Thus, reality itself becomes an incomprehensible and hostile power, aimless and meaningless, holding us captive in this universe where we have been placed randomly.[324] The hallucinations of St Anthony, who tried to free himself from the material world in order to earn heaven on the basis of his own righteousness, and who willfully wanted to make everything religious, scorning all the statutes and ordinances of God – these are also the hallucinations of the modern person. Both are driven by the dream that it is possible for us in our own human freedom to create or earn a utopian future for ourselves, and both perceive God's creation and revelation with disdain. That is also why in the nineteenth century a man like Flaubert could come up with such a convincing, deeply-felt and well-considered portrayal of the mystical hermit in his *Temptation of St Anthony*.

The (modern) manifestation of human freedom – which of course can be realized in art much more consistently than elsewhere – is, therefore, likewise an expression of a shaken world view. This world view sees the earth as a place where everything is uncertain and accidental, in the deepest sense 'lawless', without purpose or connection, made up of particles flying around randomly. The laws of nature are the hands by which the enemy, nature, maintains its stranglehold on us.[325] Modern art is naturally one of the most effective ways to depict this despair, this anxiety, this angst concerning our own very existence and survival. It presents us with the hallucination of a threatening, hostile reality.

It is not often that we see this world view and all its implications clearly brought to light. Only the most talented people, the geniuses and the deepest minds can accomplish this to some certain degree. [326] Their efforts however will always fall short, because that which is sinful, satanic, and a denial of God and his creation will never be able to be fully realized in this dispensation; if it were possible, the consequence would be instant death and annihilation. But these are the forces that spur on much of the culture-forming activity in the twentieth century even though people are continually being forced to capitulate before the truth of God's created order. In this activity art has tended to take the place of science by revealing the world to us: art, the revealer of the nature and meaning of life!

Modern art, therefore, has sought in a more consistent and deliberate way than art has ever done before the themes and forms of expression fit to express the artists' perception of life and reality. Certainly today's artists are also capable of seeing beauty in a flower, or recognizing the charm of a beautiful woman or the richness of life in a village scene, but to them these things are non-essential because they do not reveal anything about the nature of reality to them. No, they choose to draw instead the oppressive vision of an exuberant monster in a dimly lit room with an open window, that lets in the cold and the moonlight.[327] Or they try to convey their view that everything is accidental and random by sketching a piece of seaweed that seems to take on the form of a rooster; both the rooster and the seaweed are thus declared to be haphazard revelations of reality, disorderly and unstructured.[328]

Of course, one might argue that the spider-like monster is just a fantasy, and that the artist really was not trying to make such a well thought-out statement. Concerning the second point, that may certainly be true. A work like this is not so much a matter of reasoning or philosophy as of feeling, a way of experiencing the world. Art tries, literally, to picture the things which philosophy tries to put into carefully thought-out words. Concerning the first point: of course it is true that this is a product of the artist's fantasy. But then the question becomes: how does someone arrive at such a fantasy, and why would he or she consider it relevant? For that matter, the 'spider theme' seems to be a recurring motif these days. Kafka, for example, wrote a book describing the experiences of a man who wakes up one morning to discover that he has turned into a huge insect. And insofar as the fantasy in the mentioned drawing is still somewhat amusing, it is only because either the artist has not been able to fully realize his hallucination or because we are truly dealing with nothing more than a playful fantasy. However, the fact that a fantasy can be expressed so freely and finds its way to such themes cannot really be understood without looking at the work of the impassioned predecessors of modern art. It is true too, of course, that sometimes an object like a block of wood can be transformed by our imagination into something quite different. But that just proves that these artists are always forced to come back to the infinitely rich created order, a creation which encompasses both this richness and playfulness of form and this ability to fantasize.

If one were to follow the history of art since the time of the Renaissance, and specifically its development during the nineteenth century, one would be struck by the fact that art became consistently more subjective. Increasingly a work of art is perceived as the expression of human creative activity, and the strictly personal 'signature' of the artist comes more and more into the foreground. Sketches are considered to be more important than the finished work of art, because they are seen as a more directly spontaneous release of the artist's creativity.[329] And especially in our century, when every tendency is taken to its furthest extreme, the main goal is the immediate expression of one's own feelings, subjectivity and subconscious, unfettered by any laws or norms (which people today prefer to call 'conventions'), unencumbered by the burden of centuries of cultural activity. Reason, which used to be excessively idolized, has now fallen into disrepute and is seen as the enemy of every truly creative act. This has led to great admiration for the art of children and the mentally ill, since neither are hindered by the baggage of tradition. In the extreme 'avant-garde' movement of the Experimentals, artists take pride in works that look as if they were painted by a four-year-old child. This is why there is so much talk about 'honesty', by which is meant only that which springs spontaneously from one's own subjectivity is genuine, while the artist who bows to anything outside him- or herself, any external norm, is being 'dishonest'. This also explains why there is a tendency to fall back on, or to be inspired by, so-called 'primitive' art. The assumption seems to be that primitive culture represents something primeval, fresh, an expression of 'unspoiled' human being – indeed a cardinal error! For in modern art the primitive is rather the end point of apostasy; though it is understandable that people today feel a kinship with the primitive, since it tends to have a similarly oppressive world view. Taking all of this into account, we can begin to comprehend a drawing like that of the 'jolly' social gathering of four gentlemen.[330] Notice the entirely dissolute, free 'handwriting' of the artist; notice the direct and careless expression; notice the 'honesty' of this drawing. The fact that its vision of humanity is not particularly friendly cannot be blamed, of course, on the artistic approach. Rather, it is a result of the rebellious spirit, of the perception that we live in a 'rotten' world where small-mindedness, egoism, social abuse and hypocrisy reign.

Regarding the last remark we want to make one more comment. Of course, it is true that to a large extent the world is really like that! It is true that within their deepest being, humans harbour chasms that hold few charms. It is true that reality, particularly in its most extreme technical disclosure, sooner reveals itself as a destroyer than as a slave of human power. Is it not true that modern technology, in the atom bomb, the television etc., is more inclined towards a destruction than a building up of culture? All of it is true: and these truths are found in our doctrinal confession as well, which goes even deeper when it says that human beings, by nature, are inclined to all manner of evil. The people around us still prefer to believe that human beings are basically good at heart, and that may even be one of the reasons why people have become so rebellious; this world would be so much better if only people would practise honesty and goodwill.

Without repentance there is no way out of this impasse. There is no point in tapping Picasso or his colleagues on the shoulder and saying: 'Come on, paint something pretty for a change – some friendly cattle and charming cottages and neighbourly people.' We would be asking them to lie. No, we will not find a wholesome world or healthy art or a positive world view until we repent, turn our hearts to the Lord of Hosts instead of to ourselves, accept the forgiveness of sins through Jesus Christ and turn from our sinful ways to walk again in the ways of God. If not, what can we expect other than the fulfilment of the Scriptures as we find it in 2 Timothy 3 and 4, for example? The only way to be liberated from hatred towards God and his creation is through repentance; that will clear the way back to positive cultural activity – even though we know that people are imperfect and incapable of sinlessness and perfection.

There is one more characteristic of modern art that needs to be mentioned. It already emerged to some extent in the drawing just discussed, in which the play of lines is almost as important as the image itself. We are talking about the fact that the artwork *as such* has been restored to its proper position. The naturalism of the previous century, which tried to depict only the outward appearance of things, without commentary, had forgotten that a work of art must also satisfy aesthetic criteria regarding composition, form, etc. In this century artists are rediscovering the unique criteria of composition and form which are required for a work of art. This was taken to its extreme in so-called 'collages', paintings in which artists put pieces of wood, newspaper, sandpaper, etc. together in order to emphasize the inherent value of the surface, the reality of the work of art in itself.[331] A more positive outcome of this emphasis was the nudge it gave to new 'monumental' sculpture, painting and stained glass (of which Mendez da Costa, among others, was such an eminent representative). Da Costa's work can be seen in the monument for Christiaan de Wet in the National Park the Hoge Veluwe, or in the Insurance Building opposite the Stock Exchange in Amsterdam. This art rediscovered stylization, which still allows the unique structure of the stylized image to remain intact. Much of the decorative sculpture created today shows evidence of this; we see it in the sculptures of the Stock Exchange building, as well as elsewhere in countless modern buildings.

The work of art itself – its composition, its artistic structure and its unique character, which may look quite different from the reality being depicted – is receiving attention once again. Now we are ready to understand a work of art like the drawing of those wolf-like creatures. [332] We see that the decorative interplay of lines and planes has been restored to its rightful place. The fact that it is such a cruel scene, and has echoes of the primitive art of the Scythians and Celts, is another matter and we have already discussed the reasons for this. A work like this cannot be understood naturalistically, but it has aesthetic significance and as such is not anti-normative. Let us never forget that the extreme naturalism of the nineteenth century, in its effort to imitate reality as faithfully as possible, could not be seen as 'Christian' either in its presuppositions or in its structure. It breathed a spirit of positivism, which holds that only that which we can see and touch is true and trustworthy.

At times today modern art seems hardly human; it seems barbaric. It is not normal but distorted and strange, and it twists the actual givens. Sometimes people say: 'Just give it a year or two and we will start to see this as normal and ordinary. We just have to get used to it.' And then they refer to the hackneyed example of van Gogh, who was not appreciated at first either. It is true that nineteenth-century people initially found van Gogh's art hard to stomach, but after they got used to it and became accustomed to the intense colours and the passionate expressive forms, they began to realize that his art was not so crazy at all – like coming into the sunshine after being in a dark room: their eyes had to get used to the light. But van Gogh's art still evidenced a 'normal' sense of reality. It left things in their proper places and viewed them with loving eyes. And so the example of van Gogh does not apply here. We also want to point out that abnormality, strangeness and distortion are part of the very essence of modern art; one can look at it positively or negatively but the intention is not that we get used to it, because the minute it becomes 'normal' it loses its power. It would have nothing left to say; its voice would become muted and its substance would simply evaporate.

Modern art does not tell stories or present little anecdotes. Its goal is to show something of the essence, the true substance of things – never the transitory externals, the outward appearance, but the core, the heart. That is why modern works of art cannot be explained by talking about the piece of nature that is depicted or the story that is portrayed. We will never be able to get used to it, despite a thousand essays on the topic. We will never be able to 'understand' it – in the sense of: 'Now I can also see the world in the way they do.' No, modern art can only be understood as the expression of a profound and primitive human urge to rebel against God and to hate his creation. It is an expression of despair and of our own deeply-felt sense of inadequacy, of the crisis of the humanistic spirit. Modern art reveals modern peoples as they collide with God's creation and is left with nothing but contradictions, nothing but the devastating activity of the forces they themselves have unleashed. But modern art is also a reaction to the previous century's art, which certainly had reached a dead end. Renewal was desperately needed. Unfortunately, apart from a few positive achievements (like stylization), we have not progressed any further than false prophecy and wails of despair.

The drawings discussed here were all taken from the journal *Zwart en Wit* [black and white], of which I recently received a sample issue. Every issue contains about 16 drawings; we chose a few typical ones for this article. But if you page through the magazine, you will find other kinds of artworks too, works which are more human and normal though they still carry the signature of the twentieth century. In the issue before me (no. 1 or 1951), for example, I see drawings of a woman's head, a figure study and a few landscapes that you would probably enjoy. We should not forget that not everything in our times has become distorted and upside down, and that there are many, regardless of their spiritual outlook, who still see things in a commonsense and normal way, who still have a wholesome way of looking at things, who still know the experience of joy, and who approach God's creation without animosity. Also, a bow long bent at last waxes weak: even an insurgent like Picasso created some very 'ordinary' drawings and paintings, showing that when he took a more sober view of things, they once again took on their familiar appearance. After all, nothing is more tiresome and, in the long run, more unbearable than always saying 'no', always rebelling, always living in tension with the world in which God has placed us.

• Surrealism[333]

The modern world is riddled with contradictions. These contradictions do not only define the struggle between various movements but they also evoke inner tensions in the soul of twentieth-century people, in whom all kinds of totally incompatible motives and thoughts exist side by side without any possibility of being synthesized or resolved in any way. On the one hand we see the urge to destroy the things of old; on the other hand there seems to be a taboo that requires museums to preserve at any cost all that is old. On the one hand there is the absolute individualism that scorns every restriction; on the other, the tendency to lose oneself in the crowd and to value only what is universal and general. On the one hand there is a desire to determine and calculate everything rationally – think of planned economy, etc.; on the other, the desire to be free to express one's individuality without inhibition, without interference from the powers of reason. On the one hand the dignity and value of people are spoken of with great reverence; on the other, every relationship is depersonalized and people are transformed into machines, whose productivity becomes simply a commodity while all higher 'values' are seen as emanating from sexual or other 'lower' passions. On the one hand there is an attempt to regulate and control all things; on the other, the profound conviction that reality is incoherent, unmanageable, chaotic and incalculable.

It is impossible to resolve these contradictions, which become all the more acute because proponents of the various groups become progressively hardened in their views. It is impossible because these contradictions are founded in the very condition of the heart of humanistic people, who desire both freedom and autonomy as well as complete control over nature: to be able to calculate, determine and explain everything. The former implies unpredictability, while the latter leads to a complete destruction of freedom. The deepest root of this is the fact that people in their hearts no longer recognize God, the Lord of lords: apostasy and the striving to be totally autonomous are the causes of this inner crisis.[334]

Modern art is the direct expression of this attitude to life. Never before in history have artists so consciously resolved to reveal that which lives in the human heart, exposing the modern world in all its distress, worry, crisis and tension. Their goal is to depict the depths of the human heart, and in so doing they have discovered that it is filled with misery, rebellion, perverseness and emptiness. Better said, they unintentionally have given us ample proof that the hearts of human beings are inclined to all evil. If modern art truly desires to reveal the modern, then we can conclude that this art is also a symptom of the modern world, a symptom that helps diagnose and clarify our culture's essence and character. Having said this, we will do well to remember that in the modern world, which is so riddled with contradictions and tensions, it will also be difficult to lump together all modern art. In art too we will discover inner contradictions and tensions, inconsistencies within the consistencies. Paradox may well be the best and only way to approach the modern, not because the inner contradictions as such are part of the created order but because people in their wilfulness have formed themselves and their world with such disharmony that paradoxes have emerged and become reality.

Keeping this in mind, the reader will understand that it is impossible to satisfactorily capture 'the essence of modern art' in one short article without resorting to hollow words and vague generalities. To do justice to this topic we must make very precise distinctions and avoid sweeping statements. For although we might succeed in making some profound-sounding declarations about the utterances of sinful people, we would, by placing everything 'in the light of eternity', be overlooking all the finer nuances. What is worse, we probably would have failed to understand the matter in all its depth. It is perhaps not so difficult to pronounce the fate of certain people on the Day of Judgment, but though this may give us knowledge of truth it does not give us wisdom. Therefore we will deal with the multitude of facets of modern art in a number of articles,[335] and we will do so in the light of the Scriptures so that we may truly understand what is happening and try to gain some wisdom and insight into these truly apocalyptic times. Those who have a deep knowledge of these matters have declared that these times are unique, without parallel in world history: that never before human wisdom has become so clearly transformed into folly; that never before people have so lost all sense of proportion, never before strayed so far from a sober view of reality, and that never before revolution has been so elevated to an abiding principle. Finally, that never before we have seen such a conscious and deliberate rebellion against God with the consequences thought through literally ad absurdum. The Devil has been given permission to roam free and, knowing that his time is short, he has established the kingdom of the Antichrist with its semblance of greatness and happiness, a kingdom which in reality constitutes nothing but chaos, foolishness and disharmony. This has led to the cultural crisis of today, which in turn has led to a flood of literature that analyses the times but succeed only in declaring despairingly how hopeless the situation is today. Such analyses are symptoms themselves, indications that God is bringing his judgment to the earth and has removed all certainty, so that in apprehension and terror people wonder what is coming upon the world (Luke 21:25–28).

In this article we will focus on Surrealism. It is a movement with roots reaching back to the late nineteenth century, though it took a definite shape only around 1925, building on the destructive forces unleashed by Dadaism, which originated during World War I. Since then, this movement has grown and is still gaining influence, particularly in the time since World War II. In order to be as concrete as possible and to avoid vague generalities based on information that will be unfamiliar to our readers, we will consider the example of one specific Surrealist painter. We will discuss Johfra, whose works were recently exhibited in The Hague. He is a painter about whom you are likely to hear more in the future.

Johfra (whose name is obviously a pseudonym) is a man with an inexhaustible imagination, capable of dreaming up all manner of frightening, hallucinatory-like images that seem to belong to an underworld rather than our own world. Even if we managed to interpret his paintings of dead roots infused with an insect-like quality as nothing but a morbid, demonic game, there are many other works which clearly have a deeper meaning. For many years we have demanded of art that it be a reflection of real life, a revelation of truth (so that art became, as it were, the religion and source of truth for unbelievers); well, now we are getting what we asked for. This art certainly succeeds in expressing what lives in modern hearts. As a symbol of our times it reveals to us something of the modern person who, by renouncing him, has truly lost God and has now descended into the realm of the demonic.

It will not surprise us, then, that the exhibition includes depictions of passages from Dante's *Inferno*, and in particular of the forest of Souls, souls transformed into trees. It is also in the light of this demonic urge to soil all that is beautiful that we can understand the parody of the *Venus* of Botticelli – a disgustingly fat woman in whom all beauty has been transformed into gross, dull vulgarity. Also Johfra's portraits in their incoherent arrangements reveal something of the nature of humanity and serve as an example of how modernity sees all things as unconnected. Yes, this art certainly plumbs the wretched depths of the human soul. Over the past century, in the name of science, the higher characteristics of humanity have been unmasked; human being has been stripped of all its splendour and left worthy only of loathing. Any humanistic faith in humankind can hardly be taken seriously. Here before our eyes, more clearly than perhaps ever before, we see a graphic illustration of the first section of the Heidelberg Catechism (the part that deals with human misery) and of the truth that we live on a cursed earth which, without the comfort and inspiration of the subsequent sections of the same Catechism, becomes a virtual hell on earth.

Does Johfra know anything about such things? Perhaps he does have some knowledge of them, since other works of his lead one to guess that he is Roman Catholic, or at least comes from a Catholic background. Does his *Ecce homo* not picture a person in an advanced state of deterioration and disintegration, sitting among ruins and incoherent monster-like creatures (symbolizing chaos), begging at the side of the road? Is this person waiting for the prophet who is not to be found (Ezekiel 7: 25) while, behind him and without his awareness, angels look down on him?

Then we have that remarkable painting – a kind of synthesis of the late medieval images of Christ in Purgatory[336] and the contemporary depictions of Appearances of Mary[337] – in which we see a solitary person sitting before a great portal in a forbidding rock, while a dragon hovers overhead and Christ appears in the foreground. The view of nature as a threatening reality, a surly, demonic, menacing force, can be found in earlier art as well. It is the consequence of the deification of nature, of trying to place it in submission to humankind so as to make it subservient to our longings and desires, in order to give free reign to our freedom. But reality constantly resists this effort, while nature (on the one hand because of her deification, and on the other hand because in order to deify her we have become alienated from her and have come to see her as a force outside of us) has become a diabolical power, cold, hard, and merciless.

Such a view can be found already in the time of the Romantics with Caspar David Friedrich, an artist with whom we will deal more a bit later. Friedrich also depicted humans as trivial and insignificant amidst the expansive landscape, as singular sparks of life in an immense creation (which, though it may be beautiful, is the realm of death) – small and lonely figures in a world of deathly loneliness and abandonment. But, as was the case with all the art that served as a prologue to modern art, this imagery was still fairly subdued and remained normal to a certain degree. In our times such images are carried to their most extreme conclusion. One painting by Johfra presents a savage scene of impenetrable and insurmountable rocks. Vultures fly around and perch on the rocks, foreboding symbols of death. In a passageway among the rocks a woman stands undressed, waiting. Is she expecting a lover with whom she can lose herself in love's sweet passions? That would seem absurd in such surroundings. Moreover, all activity that takes place here is meaningless anyway, for death lies in wait. Enjoyment of any kind is impossible in such a place, a landscape devoid of any beauty or fertility, any evidence of food or drink, any loveliness. Despair and death reign here and only they still have some real meaning. Nature is chaotic, lacking any architectural soundness; yet it is depicted with utmost refinement. Concerning the technical aspects of this painting there is little to criticize.

If one begins with the humanistic presupposition that only those things that can be understood and fathomed rationally have any purpose, then it follows that anything not humanly explicable or understandable must necessarily be seen as senseless and chaotic. This view, in which rationality is equated with meaning, follows logically when everything is seen from the viewpoint of the natural sciences. To those who see nature as a hard, invincible reality outside of themselves – an icy demonic power which perhaps can be understood one small piece at a time, but of which the whole is totally beyond our comprehension – the creation must look like chaos, a world in which various parts, though meaningful in themselves, are thrown together randomly in meaningless structurelessness. This can be clearly seen in Surrealist art. It is a common procedure among these artists to put together any number of incoherent parts for the purpose of prophesying about the meaninglessness of our structureless, chaotic world.

Do not think that this is all just playful fantasy. For it is based on the deep convictions of people who are drawing the ultimate conclusions of what it means to live without God, without a Creator. When people choose to turn from him, what can remain but chaos, a reality devoid of any purpose? We find similar convictions in modern literature. Just to give you a small example, this is one paragraph from a story that continues in this vein for four pages:

> Once upon a rozenzeit there was a girl named Zweegy-Weegy. What was her titulus? Souidji-Vouidji la bell' neigeuse. Duskmossily she fiddlefaddled her younghood away in a city named Sursumcorda – aussi nommée par certains géographes Surhommekoda – though of naught but her bloomhair and her gem on the trousième oueil which she had in the middle of her forehead, lived all by herself with herself through herself on the balcon of the eight étage in the rue Cunigunde ...[338]

The passage, with its mixture of French and English and riddled with blasphemous references, is impossible to translate. And in fact this is a relatively moderate quote; we could produce examples that are far more extreme. One could devote a whole study to this movement on the basis of various utterings in the journal from which we borrowed the above quote as to its profound connections with the past: deeply-rooted ties with gnosticism, with the Orphic mysteries, with heretical secret doctrines like those of the Albigensians and the Bogomil. But all this would prove only that this kind of service to the Devil – they themselves say 'In this way we defend the cause of the devil'[339] – is not a new phenomenon. In our modern times such views have just become more common: in the past these ideas were held by sects outside of mainstream culture; currently they represent one of the leading cultural movements. That is what makes the phenomenon so relevant – I would not call it interesting, it is too oppressive a movement, deeply affecting us all, for it threatens to revolutionize our entire cultural life. Therefore, let us not stop at the first part of the Heidelberg Catechism but also take into account the second and third parts. We must find our comfort in the way of Sunday 1 [of the Catechism], for then we will stand firm and will not need to fear. Jesus Christ has the power to save us from the grip of hell.

• Rouault [340]

Undoubtedly one must count it as one of the positive renewals brought about by modern art that it broke with the naturalistic notion that, in the art of painting, the effort must be made to render reality as exactly as possible. For while it is indeed the task of visual art to represent reality in a beautiful way, reality is more than its natural aspect, which was all that naturalism ever had an eye for, at least when it was consistent. No, art must not just render the visible, external, measurable and weighable. Far from it. It also can and should depict reality in its fullness.

In its fullness! Naturally artists who aspire to do so will never attain their goal for the simple reason that the created world, the full reality, is too wide and too rich even to be seen and apprehended in the fullness of its meaning, essence and diversity, let alone to be captured in a few images. The richness and depth of the oeuvre of an artist accordingly depends on her or his own richness and depth, the wisdom and depth of her or his insight, in short, of a person's wisdom.

And if modern art often falls short in this task, then that is not because of its starting point, its abandonment of naturalism in its all too consistent and far-reaching application; it is a result rather of its lack of wisdom, an absence of insight and sometimes of a living in tension with reality itself. Because of this the human element is all too often missing. In the search for the absolute, the lasting – by the lantern of one's own insight into life and one's own world view[341]– in the search for the suprahuman, people have all too often become stuck in the infrahuman: the geometric or the unconscious or the subconscious or the nought of pure colour and line.

One modern artist, however, who is indisputably one of the greatest of the twentieth century, cannot be reproached for this. In his work the full person speaks and the world is seen not as through a mathematical formula or microscope, not through the glasses of Freudian psychology or with a purely aesthetic measure, but with a sense of life finely attuned to the fullness of reality. The art of this French Roman Catholic painter is laden with a deep and rich meaningfulness that we all too frequently miss, alas, in the work of his contemporaries, who perhaps have equally great talents. We are referring to Georges Rouault who turned 80 in 1951 and who undoubtedly, alongside a number of his generation – Picasso, Matisse, Chagall and perhaps a few other contemporaries – has assured himself for ever of a firm place in the history of art of the first half of the twentieth century.

Born in 1871 in Paris, he became a student in the atelier of a glass painter in 1885. Here he also was able to handle pieces of medieval stained glass that must have made an indelible impression on him. In 1892 he went to the art academy, where he soon became a student of Gustave Moreau, a most remarkable artist whose work we cannot discuss here but who was undoubtedly a splendid pedagogue. Not only Rouault but also a host of youths who would eventually grow into well-known twentieth-century masters owed a great deal to his instruction. His death in 1898 came as a great blow to his favourite student who then, since Rouault's own family had moved elsewhere, was left behind in utter loneliness and in very difficult circumstances. Contact with important representatives of the Renouveau Catholique, a movement that wanted to blow new life into Roman Catholicism by focusing directly on everyday reality, then pointed him to a new direction. Yet when Rouault proceeded to engage the world of the day in his own manner, he again lost many friends, from this movement.

What did Rouault do? Following a stay in the mountains to recover from a serious illness, he returned to Paris and entered the circle of the Fauves.[342] Thus he stood in the midst of the new Expressionist movement which initiated the fierce reaction against the nineteenth century. They were characterized by an almost wild way of painting, the abandonment of every trace of naturalism, the application of very clear colours that often deviated from what the eye sees in nature and instead had symbolic significance. In general the members of this group never got much further than a sort of decorative art without much depth.

Rouault was one of them, to be sure. He too broke with naturalism, he too applied a fierce, virtually untethered 'handwriting' to his bluish aquatints, but his art was far from being superficially decorative. Fiercely and violently he vented his feelings about the world around him. He painted prostitutes, stately ladies, citizens and judges. Or rather, he painted Prostitution, the Middle Class and Justice. In doing so he lashed sin – these are no caricatures; they are biting satires. He shows the monstrous ugliness of it all. He paints evil, sin, as it had never been done before in history. If his works from this period are not beautiful it is because the reality he depicts is not beautiful. His works are loaded with meaning, with significance. Are they true? I believe so, insofar as such sin exists. Only on the basis of Rouault's Christian background is such a penetrating view to be understood, to be comprehended and . . . endorsed?

It is difficult to answer that last question. For spiritually speaking the monstrousness of sin is true and real – that in the first place – although perhaps concealed from the externally beholding eye.[343] Yet we – and by 'we' I mean not viewers in general but Calvinist viewers most particularly – somehow do not feel comfortable with these depictions of sin. Certainly, also because we do not like to be reminded of how deeply corrupted the world is in which we live; we would rather not think about that even if we sometimes have a lot to say about it. Yet it is also because a revolutionary sentiment surfaces here that we cannot share. For the satire acquires here an element of cursing that touches more than sin alone and, although the sin is shown, we miss not only the compassion but also the consciousness of solidarity in the guilt.[344] Especially the judges, and in them he touches on justice, are chastised for hypocrisy.

In this way Rouault unmasks, analyses and undermines conventions. The artist does not want to accept the world if it is like this. Respect, deference to established values, a spirit of forgiveness and an awareness of solidarity are alien to his art. Hence he is revolutionary through and through. And that is what makes us shudder here!

It is remarkable that we encounter this so often in Roman Catholic artists. They see this world through the eyes of their revolutionary contemporaries as consisting only of misery and dreariness. Yet they see it differently from the way in which unbelievers see it, for to them this is just one side of the coin; on the flipside they see the sacred, which stands elevated and beautiful alongside all this defilement and thoroughgoing, fundamental rottenness. And that is how Rouault too in this period paints the traditional biblical subjects, albeit always in his own way.

Then comes World War I, and after 1918 Rouault's art acquires another face. He has grown wiser and also deeper. The keen discernment remains and human misery continues to be his focus, but it is now ennobled by the *Miserere*, the 'Have mercy upon me, O God' of Psalm 51. Now he sets to work on the great series of engravings that engaged him till about 1927, but that were published only in 1948 in two volumes with fifty plates in each. Rouault was undoubtedly a great painter, who also made important stained-glass windows and ceramics, but we will not look any further at these and will concentrate our attention on *Miserere* – the title under which the engravings referred to above appeared – since they capture the heart, the core significance, of Rouault's work.

These technically most remarkable prints[345] together form a view of the world and life that bears witness to a profound wisdom. We are often reminded as we look at this work of Ecclesiastes, where we find the same penetrating view of human misery, limitedness and vanity. A deep melancholy permeates the whole, with perhaps too little of the 'It is finished!' to oppose it.

The significance of the prints lies undoubtedly in the way human truths and values are rendered artistically – precisely because of this they are difficult to describe. Yet the artistic quality, the deep authentic beauty of this work eludes comprehension if one does not consider the titles while viewing them: thus he writes under the portrait of a clown (and you need to have seen the deep melancholy of the clown portraits in order to know what Rouault makes of them): 'Do we not all wear a mask?' And under the image of a prostitute: 'A so-called woman of pleasure'. Often he also contrasts two images with each other; thus we find somewhere on the left page a lonely figure in a dead landscape and on the facing hand a crowned human head with the following texts under them, respectively: 'Are we not all convicts?' and 'While we believe ourselves to be kings'. You have to see that 'royal portrait' to know the meaning of this assertion: there is no majesty at all and we are subjected to the glare of a face bearing a predatory grin. Then there is a print of 65x50 cm with the poetic caption: 'It would be so sweet to love', juxtaposed with a print symbolizing the human struggle to survive. Infinite tenderness and poetry appear in the extremely concentrated simplicity of the former image, which is in black and white, as well as profound yearning – is it just a childish dream or is there hope of fulfilment? So here too we find melancholy, hardly utterable in words.

In the style we see how in an entirely distinctive way Rouault worked the influence of stained glass and perhaps also of Byzantine icons into something without equal in our century. Rouault is a solitary figure, without a predecessor and without students. Here we see how visual art may express much more than the flat naturalistic conception supposes, which demands copies of reality and halts at the external side of things. Here we have profound human wisdom represented in a deeply moving, beautiful way. Not 'illustrated literature' but genuine visual art!

Let us say no more. Our words fall short and perhaps leave what is most important unsaid. Rouault's art is not easy to approach. It demands thought and reflection. We hope in any case that you will try to increase your knowledge of his work at least through reproductions.

I would like to end with a citation – for Rouault also wrote, and not just about art but also poetic ruminations: 'Art is often a hidden source – or an oasis in the desert. We believe we have arrived because we know so much. All the while we forget, ignore, neglect the essential, that which always remains, namely the love for everything that lives, morning or evening, under the sky.'[346]

• This too is our times[347]

We Christians live with a sort of inferiority complex. It is certain that in our times many are saying farewell to the Christian faith; the Bible and all the traditions based on it are under attack. Christianity as a religion is highly valued as a way of thinking that people once espoused, in the past; but now it is really something of the past and of no importance given the problems we face today. It is as if these stoutly proclaimed words – who can help thinking of Malachi 3:13–16 and 2 Peter 3:3–4 – makes Christians timid, as if they dare not say, in rebuttal, that this is an arrogant lie. Perhaps they will dare to say so, and we hope they will, when things are said crudely and with direct bearing on the central truths and on the Truth, Jesus Christ. But when it concerns ways and principles in the societal or scientific field, then many who call themselves Christians lower their heads. Is it not true that in our times the Bible no longer shows the way and that the Lord is really far off, in any case far from the problems of today? How dare we assert that anarchism, or better and more sharply put, godlessness is the direct background for much that presents itself as avant-garde art? – sshhh, not so loudly, for then they might hear us and start to laugh: it is better to disguise this message a bit and to speak of an existentially tethered art, an art of protest against the badness of this world. Yes, the world is bad, if we construe the term in a biblical sense, but not in the gnostic-existentialist sense that this world is rotten in itself, that 'being' (*Sein*) is 'unto death' (*zum Tode*). God said that it was good, and it is sin that has caused the entire creation to groan and suffer the pains of childbirth and people to be weighed down under the curse. Yet the creation itself has not only remained open for the good and beautiful but evil and wickedness and sin and the curse have been overcome by Jesus Christ. Being need no longer be 'unto death'; it can be that only for a perverse and unbelieving generation [cf. Philippians 2:15] that regard the above as religious opinions, subjective only and without real consequences for today.

I am not going to preach. I call all this to mind only in order to make two things clear. The first is that when we discuss the art of our times we may do so quite happily and without fear, in a way that exposes the backgrounds. The world too knows these and does nothing to hide them – just read the introductions to exhibition catalogues of Amsterdam's Stedelijk Museum of Modern Art, for example. Art is not just 'beauty' or 'artistry' but is more than that: it is more human, deeper, connected with the fullness of being human. The second is that it is not necessary when we discuss the art of our times to regard as important only what the world regards as important. The revolutionary act, the destruction of value and values, the further realization of a view of reality in which God is absent (or at least believed to be so) and the proclamation of the meaninglessness of all things are not to be honoured as 'progress', and they cannot possibly be regarded as the only developments of cultural importance. The confrontation may be unavoidable for us, if we want to understand the leading currents of our time in order to keep ourselves unspotted from the world and in order to be able to help our neighbours by providing answers to their questions – is anyone more full of unanswered questions about life than the modern person? Questions stay unanswered in part because it is not deemed appropriate to refer to religion (following the suppression of sexuality in the previous century there has been in ours a suppression of religion, about which novels and theoretical studies are now obligated to say nothing). But it is even more important to acknowledge and support all the positive forces, and to honour as of inestimable worth the act of purity and the honest confession of the beauty of God's creation and of the all-important significance of real love, of God, of one's neighbour, and of the elect [people of God].

For this reason, in this article about the art of our times, I for once do not want to discuss modern art from Picasso to Appel or Matthieu. And that is not in order to raise an apologia in praise of tradition and to hail the work of many who still work along 'ordinary' lines as the *summum bonum*. Even less is it in order to unmask as decadent everything that deviates from the stylistic manners of the nineteenth century. Perhaps nineteenth-century naturalism as such was already decadent and destructive of meaning. Certainly we have no intention to summon you to find only seventeenth-century art great and beautiful – although it is and remains an unparalleled high point in the history of art and although this cannot be understood without reference to its basis in a Christian view of life. No, what we want to do is free ourselves from all kinds of preconceived opinions inspired by a misplaced inferiority complex, as if only the authentic modern tradition as alluded to above is meaningful and edifying while all the rest is culturally meaningless and without perspective.

We must be mindful that our work, insofar as it extends to the broad cultural plane – and it should, since our faith should be evident in our works – may not be aimed at preserving old, outworn forms; rather, it must be aimed at recognizing and appropriately honouring wholesome and lifelike expressions. We should aim at human activity that unfolds – or endeavours to unfold – in keeping with the norm of love and which genuinely tries to realize, in our day, what is good, fine and true in doctrine, practice and expression. Therefore I want to stand up for all that art which the museums all too seldom display of artists who do not belong to the revolutionary avant-garde. Let us enjoy it, seek it out, support it, focus our attention on it and with examples refute the tendentious contention that only current avant-garde art can offer a meaningful view of humanity, nature and the world.

In the process we could lift a great number of artists from forced isolation and help or even save lives that threaten to be broken – there are non-abstractionists who have reluctantly devoted themselves to the expressive abstraction of the most modern avant-garde, for otherwise no one would have shown any interest at all in them, and their work would have been consigned to a sterile vacuum, which is also the result of all those who have allowed themselves to be blinded by the effective propaganda of the prophets of modern art. There is a great deal more work like this than we often think that we should be able to find. And there are probably still a great many artists who eke out a poor and miserable existence in a forgotten little studio somewhere, forgotten because they bear witness to real love and real beauty. We could go on to speak of Veldhoen, Berserik, Schrofer (before he reverted to abstraction), Mari Andriessen, of so many lesser and greater talents. We must also consider that discovering new approaches – which from the standpoint of art history attracts the most attention – is not what is most important artistically; that is rather the creation of beautiful artworks loaded with a warm and positive appreciation of life. In our day the creation of something that is not revolutionary is perhaps already almost revolutionary; in any case it is an act that requires a great deal of energy.

We do wish however to discuss Rouault and in particular the series of etchings entitled *Miserere*. Georges Rouault was born in 1872. At the academy he was one of the best and favourite students of the exceptional artist Gustave Moreau. It is not clear precisely what motivated Moreau and still less exactly what he wanted to teach his students. Certainly his work was a reaction against the positivistically oriented schools of the late nineteenth century: his art is religious and mystical and totally oblivious to ordinary and everyday life. His sketches are sometimes made in a remarkably relaxed technique, virtually abstract and somewhat suggestive of the Abstract Expressionism of the period following World War II, yet without the same background and meaning. Besides that he also made large paintings in the tradition of the Salon painters, finely painted in a classical style; the subjects however are more Romantic and often feature all kinds of esoteric mystical allusions. Moreau's is not an easy art to place or to understand. Precisely what Rouault learned from him we do not know. Certainly he followed him during his student years, although Rouault's themes are more directly biblical in the Roman Catholic sense. Rouault always honoured Moreau as a great artist and great teacher.

When at the beginning of the twentieth century Rouault starts to find his own way, however, his art no longer bears any resemblance at all to that of Moreau. He comes under the influence of a militant Roman Catholic group that speaks and writes rather fanatically and extremely for the Church and against rationalism, against republicanism and much more. Léon Bloy was identified as their spiritual helmsman. Yet whether this movement recognized in Rouault a great and spiritually affinitive artist is the question. His art was certainly also influenced by the emergent Fauvism, of which his fellow student with Moreau, Matisse, was the acknowledged leader. Yet his art was neither traditionalistic nor Roman Catholic in the usual sense, and even less was it Fauvist, though it was fierce and not at all naturalistic. His watercolours from this period are in a muted bluish tint but do not in the least convey a calm impression. On the contrary, they are harsh caricatures in which all kinds of abuses are placed before us in a manner reminiscent of Daumier: judges who are inhuman monsters; prostitutes who allow us to see a great deal of their body but who are anything but attractive or even sensual, human monsters really; stately ladies who are uglier than sin in their haughty smugness. This is art that contains a harsh indictment but that chafes without evoking compassion; it shows sin without any reference to a solution or salvation. It is a hard art that – in contrast to the art of the Fauves which desired only to be friendly and as attractive as a tumultuous, exuberant dance of life – engages with the drama of sinful people but is still closer to Daumier in its revolutionary sentiment than to a genuine biblical outlook.

It was during the First World War that a change set in, a deepening. The openness to human beings and their sometimes so ugly baggage persists, but its leading theme is now the *Miserere*: 'Lord, have mercy on us'. In these years he began the series of etchings that would continue to engage him during the 1920s. Rouault worked slowly and was burdened with an excessive dose of self-criticism. He was not quickly satisfied. The etchings are not made in any orthodox technique: slowly he discovered a way of working that allowed him to realize his view. He personally called this series of etchings the centre of his art from which his entire life's work could be judged.

His paintings, among which are some of the most beautiful of our century, we will not discuss here. The attitude of the art world of our day is remarkably ambivalent. People honour Rouault as a great artist but seldom exhibit his work. To say they shun or ignore it would be going too far, but sometimes it seems that way. People simply do not know how to approach this art of a believer, a man who in his work witnesses to positive values, to human compassion, to love and sorrow, in short, to everything that the mainstream art in our [twentieth] century tramples upon as bourgeois and everything it would, like Nietzsche, want to pronounce dead. All the more reason for us to devote our full attention to it.

Rouault's art is human and communicates heart to heart. He does that in a language that is of our times, in a style that is unmistakably of our century, without for an instant yielding in his work to the spiritual content of existentialistic-anarchistic modern art. His art is the best evidence for the thesis that with the artistic language of our century one can express something besides disgust and meaninglessness. His art is human and therefore understandable. People can talk about it in a human way without having to resort to the esoteric jargon into which the art of recent decades so often beckons us – that difficult and highfalutin jargon by which people often try to rescue something that, culturally speaking, is of little value or to conceal their misgivings or to avoid a real discussion about the disturbing content. With Rouault that is not necessary. His work is subtle, rich in nuance, deep and fine. And at bottom not easy; but what great art is?

As a result of various tragic circumstances that we shall not rehearse now, the series of etchings brought together under the title *Miserere*, which features 58 prints, each of roughly 65x50 cm, was only published in 1948. First then No. 6: *Ne sommes-nous pas forçats?* ('Are we not all convicts?') – a profound characterization of our misery, to use the language of the Catechism. Human being in its pride, imagined highness, hardness and rebellion. No. 7, which forms a companion piece to No. 6, has as its title: *Nous croyant rois* ('While we believe ourselves to be king'). The piece suggests something of the satire of the prewar works and mocks human being as king but with deeper and richer content, and also with greater nuance. The series is not a cheerful one. On the contrary. Typical is No. 12, *Le dur métier de vivre* ('The hard struggle to exist'), that speaks for itself. One gains the impression that Rouault had too little eye for salvation, the victory over the Evil one whereby Christianity can be a religion of joy. 'Rejoice always' is a Scriptural word that points towards a genuine Christian lifestyle! Yet Rouault certainly did have an eye for the softer sides of life, for the wholesome and purifying effects of love, which if they may not always convey us to laughter nevertheless can lift us up above the suffering. We find that in what I think is the most beautiful print, No. 13, *Il serais si doux d'aimer* ('It would be so sweet to love'). The younger sister [or daughter?] turns full of expectation to the older sister [or mother?], a print full of anticipation of human depth and joy, to be found in love, even when it still often eludes us.

We could go on to discuss the stylistic features, how with the most restricted of means, as with restrained force, in a single stroke, in a single white passage, Rouault can express so much. We could discuss the carefully weighed composition that time and again allows full justice to be done to the theme, underscores it and evokes the desired tone. Yet these works do not invite that any more than do those of Rembrandt or Dürer.

A few prints of the series have woman as their theme. Also the prostitute, *La fille dite de joie* ('A so-called woman of pleasure') – telling title. Yet how much more compassionate, how much softer, with how much more pity and love of one's neighbour than in the watercolours from before 1914. We want to mention also No. 16, in which Rouault again gently and moved by inner commiseration does not mock but typifies (and with what profound Christian preaching): *Dame du Haut-Quartier croit prendre pour le Ciel place réservée* ('Upper-class woman thinks to have a reserved seat in heaven'). Finally we chose No. 29, a landscape: *Chantez Mâtines, le jour renaît* ('Watchdogs bark, the day is born again'). The sun rises but the land lies there ready for our heavy daily labour, the consequence of the curse. How effectively this heaviness and sombreness, more resigned than oppressive, is expressed in a few lines!

A couple of years ago Rouault died at a ripe old age. A rich life thereby came to an end. Perhaps he never penetrated to the Reformational *sola fide* ('by faith alone'), but the deep humanity of his art is certainly of authentic Christian origin. The effect is liberating and able to withstand every revolutionary, value-destroying attack of the Evil one. In this way Rouault's work is a testimony.

• Wholesome twentieth-century art[348]

During the two years that *Stijl* has been in existence, we have dealt with the subject of modern art several times.[349] In those articles our main emphasis was to show how modern art is a typical expression of the modern mind, and thus can serve as a sign of the times. As a result we often were forced to present its more negative sides. Nevertheless, there does exist modern art which has remained untouched by that deliberate and contrived prophecy of meaninglessness, nihilism, destruction and the crisis of certainty. Of course, besides the so-called 'modern art' there is much art created today in the spirit of premodern art. This 'movement' has no name; it is the 'ordinary' art, which we can only differentiate according to excellent and poor, art and kitsch and the various levels in between. However, the truth is that this more 'ordinary' art has often become too ordinary, since repetition without renewal has caused inspiration to shrivel up and die. That the majority of the art produced today is of this 'ordinary' kind is in itself a sign of the times, showing that the true modern art has not been accepted by the public, nor by the majority of artists themselves. But, and this we may criticize, this ordinary art movement is based on such a negative attitude, such an ostrich policy. Artists seem unable to work up the energy to keep breathing new life into living traditions; they prefer to stick with what is tried and true and have no defence against the powerful creative forces that have emerged in these modern times. Instead they choose to pass by with blinkers on, loudly reassuring us that 'Modern art is just a fraud; don't worry, it will pass!'

Fortunately, there is a third category of art: twentieth-century art which takes into full account the artistic renewals of our age, which remains thoroughly relevant to our times, to the real world in which we move, without indulging in a modernity that focuses only on the problematic. It could be classified as *wholesome* twentieth-century art. There are a number of artists in The Hague who, after years of abstract and Expressionist work, returned to 'normality' without trying to become epigones of a by now rather distant past. We could mention someone like Schrofer. Since 1924, under the strong influence of Mondrian, he made only abstract art, but around 1950 he suddenly emerged as an important portrait-painter.

We are thinking, too, of Berserik, who made his debut after World War II with an Expressionist style bursting with a personal power of expression. But (and we shall not go into excessive detail here) in 1951 he travelled to North Africa and there became aware of the great value of Dutch culture, realizing that one simply cannot deny that Holland is the land that produced Ruisdael, Vermeer, Potter, and countless other master artists. As a result he detached himself from Expressionism with its artistic but often contrived tensions, and began to paint in a 'normal' way. This does not mean that he returned to that poor imitation of nineteenth-century art which is often *labelled* as 'normal'; rather, he arrived at a living art which, leaving behind all prophetic aspirations, now paints our contemporary world – its stations and its harbours and, occasionally, its landscapes. He portrays people too, like the woman at her sewing machine in the kitchen; these occupy an important place in his oeuvre. Particularly special is Berserik's etching which was awarded the Jacob Maris Prize. It is a relatively recent work, based on a drawing he made as early as 1948. In it we see how the artist, once he is lovingly gripped by his theme, leaves Expressionism behind. It is one of the loveliest graphic works created in recent years, well-deserving of the prize that it was awarded.

The theme of this etching – mother-to-be – speaks for itself. How magnificently reality is presented in its fullness through the artist's wholesome, unaffected, unforced attitude to his subject. There is no sense of disgust – which is what we might expect of a modern artist – but also no unrealistic idealization or glorification of the subject. No, this is sober reality seen in its fullness, and that makes it a wholesome and excellent piece of art. It does not look like any work from the past, it is completely mid twentieth century. Yet it has no need for the complicated philosophical explanations that seem inevitably to accompany modern art as a necessary evil. We do not feel the need to 'enhance' this etching with a title like 'Hannah' or 'Rebecca', for it depicts a concrete contemporary scene, a scene which can also now bring joy to Israel, in more than one sense.

• Aad Veldhoen: contemporary wholesome art [350]

There are many people who think that no art is being produced nowadays that is worthy of the name. For their wall decorations they therefore resort to reproductions or to tasteless odd contrivances that no one enjoys and that are really only meant to fill an empty space on the wall.

Yet this is a serious misunderstanding. In the first place it is a good thing to become acquainted with modern art in order to find out what is going on in our times. Often people in our circle believe they have done enough once they have steeped themselves in social and economic and political matters, yet when one studies these apart from the general cultural background one will often miss the key to understanding the phenomena. To immerse oneself in modern art is to enter into a high-level 'conversation' with contemporary culture and its bearers – or at least it can be that, if one is willing to take the trouble. People shortchange themselves in many respects when they just leave 'art' aside (the quotation marks indicate the way it is often talked about in our circle, as if it were strange and unessential and of negligible importance).

However, I hope that here I have not confirmed the impression that modern art – I have in mind Picasso, Appel, etc. – is the only art being made in our times, or at least the only art of any importance. People are not all the same, and not every [Dutch] person is a member of the Labour Party or of the Communist or Roman Catholic or Anti-Revolutionary Party. The diversity one encounters in that realm also exists in the field of art. In this context I think of the very young painter and etcher Aad Veldhoen. He is an artist who in the short time he has been making etches, some two years, has mastered a staggering diversity of subjects and ways of treating the themes, also as to the technique. Without any hesitation I call him the most important artist of the youngest generation. I am all the more pleased to call attention to him because he does not only claim to have a love for reality but actually shows in his work a sharp eye for the unique and the beautiful, especially in the ordinary things around us. Without 'beautifying' or in some other way doing violence to the given reality, he is able to draw poetry even from a subject like the harbour with shipyards and factory chimneys at Ijmuiden. It is the lively naturalness – without resort to photographic copying, far from it – in his etchings that gives them so much to say to us. [See for example *Complete Works* 3, plate 8.] There is a fullness of human feelings and emotions in these artworks, without any maudlin sentimentality. They embody a rich human experience that teaches us to see and value reality anew, as it were, and to fathom its beauty.

I just wanted to introduce this artist to you as a sign that in our times there is something else to be found besides all the phenomena of crisis.

• Culture and revolution I [351]

Original publisher's introduction: H.R. Rookmaaker of the Free University of Amsterdam is an internationally known historian of culture. His latest book, *Modern Art and the Death of a Culture*, has just been published. In this essay he urgently invites further discussion of the relationship between culture and revolution.

It is already more than a century since Groen van Prinsterer wrote his famous *Unbelief and Revolution*.[352] At the heart of his message was this: make no mistake, the French Revolution is certainly now in the past, but the spirit of revolution is still very much alive, even among those who do not seem at all aggressive. The revolutionary spirit is the spirit of unbelief, of pushing God and his revealed way out of society to build instead a world of people's own (rationalistic) design.

Groen van Prinsterer wrote this shortly before the revolutions of 1848 and following. But perhaps today we can see more dearly than ever before how prophetic his writings were, and how we are actually living, constantly and increasingly, in the middle of a revolution.

With the Enlightenment of the eighteenth century – in which Groen van Prinsterer too saw the revolutionary spirit awakening – came a new philosophy and a new scientific attitude, rationalistic and founded in humanity itself. Through the propagation of these ideas, and under the pressure of unbelief, our world and our society were violently uprooted and changed. The results of this can be witnessed in our own times.

The first and most basic result is that a technocracy has arisen, so that almost all of reality – in principle everything – becomes subjected to the methods of the natural sciences. Not only in mathematics and physics, chemistry and biology, but also in psychology, economics and sociology – and indeed, in all other aspects of reality – the standard practice became the use of natural laws discovered through experiment and observation. By following these ideas and their outworking, people brought themselves into a position where they could govern reality.

Technology manifested itself in increasing mechanization, in the application of artificial techniques to control nature (e.g. with the use of artificial fertilizers) and the whole of socio-economic life, so that in fact the whole of life becomes scientifically planned. This has been done with great success, so that today people have reality under their thumb and we all enjoy the products of technology and the securities which a technocratic governing of human society has brought. A few 'nasty things' remain with us – the threat of war, poverty in underdeveloped areas, political instability in some countries – but we work hard at setting up a welfare state, an earthly paradise, a cleaned-up world. The revolution is seemingly successful.

I say 'seemingly' because in fact this technocracy brought, and brings, all sorts of problems with it. It is already many years since Aldous Huxley wrote his *Brave New World*, in which the world of the future became a sort of straitjacket, a nightmare. This nightmare of anxiety, of alienation, of loneliness, in fact the dehumanization which was the consequence of this *condition humaine* was articulated by the existentialists – this was the keynote of the 1950s. They showed how people have lost their freedom, how they, prisoners in their own world, without God, without purpose, without meaning, caught in one great machine in which all things operate scientifically, were really absurd and 'human' in name only.

Deep down in all this was a protest, a protest against life and its meaninglessness and purposelessness. It was not recognized that this was really the result of unbelief and revolution. On the contrary, God was accused of having plunged humankind into the mud of boredom and meaninglessness, while people at the same time believed that the world was like this because there was no God. In short, the revolution had led people into oppression, but the spirit of revolution remained very much alive and drove them on.

However, there had already been an earlier protest against this unbearable technocratic society, against this world in which human beings became reduced to cogs in a machine, numbers, prisoners within the system. That protest was to be found in art, which since the beginning of the century had been handling the themes of the absurdity of human being and of the world. Notice had been given of the fact that we are nothing but 'plastic people' and of our anguish in the face of the menacing demonic power that this evidently rationalistic world holds. God is dead, and humanity too. Where then are real truths to be found? What then is the meaning of life and work? Is there in fact any life before death?[353] These have been the questions and the message of modern art. Sandberg expressed it like this:

> the period of repression and falsification in which we live
> does not ask us for an answer
> but shrieks for protest
>
> that protest, fierce and piercing [raucous] in music
> penetrating and often enigmatic in book and play
> breaks loose cursing and seething in painting
> and in images shows destruction next to new budding life.[354]

Allen Ginsberg, a senior guru of the hippie movement, wrote a great poem more than ten years ago which began like this:

> I saw the best minds of my generation destroyed by madness,
>   starving hysterical naked ...
> who passed through universities with radiant cool eyes hallucinating
>   Arkansas and Blake-light tragedy among the scholars of war ...
> who were expelled from the academies for crazy & publishing
>   obscene odes on the windows of the skull, ...

Why? he asks in the second part:

> What sphinx of cement and aluminium bashed open their skulls
>   and ate up their brains and imagination?
> Moloch! Solitude! Filth! Ugliness! Ashcans and unobtainable
>   dollars! Children screaming under the stairways! Boys sobbing in
>   armies! Old men weeping in the parks!
> Moloch! Moloch! Nightmare of Moloch! Moloch the loveless!
>   Mental Moloch! Moloch the heavy judger of men! ...[355]

Such modern men certainly do not take things from a neutral standpoint! And we have not got to this point for no reason at all, for people have indeed been robbed of their humanity. Money, power, ruthless violence, demands for more and more sacrifices in its service – this is Moloch, the result of our technocracy. The Beatles put it differently in their record *Sergeant Pepper's Lonely Hearts Club Band* when they sing of love that's gone cold and people who have 'gained the world and lost their souls'.[356]

Indeed, this is clear, almost biblical language – protest against a degenerate world. Where could the answer and the solution lie? Should we not look for it in Christian faith? Look at the problem again: unbelief led to revolution, which itself led more and more to slavery under technocracy, dehumanization and the breakup of society. Lonely, anxious people, desperately searching for a meaning to their lives, for a today and a tomorrow, were the result. It is in this futile, questioning environment that the church should be best suited to proclaim the Answer. But it has not, and again we quote the Beatles, who sang a few years back in 'Eleanor Rigby' about the minister who sat darning his socks and did not care about 'all those lonely people . . . where do they all come from, all the lonely people?' Eleanor Rigby was buried in the church, the minister cleansed his hands as he walked from the grave, and 'no one was saved', not one of all those lonely people.[357]

Why is the church here in no position to give an answer? Is it not that it has become bourgeois, in fact riddled with bourgeois attitudes? The bourgeois Christian attitude may be said to be a sort of unbelieving religiosity. People acknowledge the basic tenets of Scripture and may even quote Bible texts but, not really knowing what it is to be committed to the sovereign Lord, they look for their securities here on earth; in fact, they have no real faith at all. This is not the first time in history that God's people have been bourgeois. Isaiah came up against it too.[358] And certainly the Enlightenment in the eighteenth century can in part be explained by the bourgeois church, even if there were certain openly unchristian elements already at work.

We have indeed spoken rather generally about the way Christianity has become bourgeois, but fortunately there are exceptions and one can still find genuine faith. But still we must not overlook the fact that some of the younger generation, whose revolutionary spirit we are discussing here, are from Christian homes, and that they are legitimately rebelling against that legalistic attitude whereby the reality of faith lies in being a supporter of rules and regulations. And we must also bear in mind that they find in the church a serious lack of any real purpose, a failure to meet the needs of this world, and that they often rightly complain that no real answers are given in Sunday school to the questions which are burning in their hearts. The world is collapsing around them and they sense it clearly enough to ask why sermons have so long ceased to have any relevance to reality; commandments become little more than threadbare traditions, truths that through continual repetition seem ready to fade out like empty slogans. What this generation wants, is inspired preaching that is backed up by real Christian living. But unfortunately this is lacking, as expressed in the words of Bob Dylan, the protest singer, when he sings about the 'good Samaritan' dressing to get ready for the 'show': 'for there's a carnival tonight on Desolation Row.'[359]

Yes, this 'Desolation Row' is the church – the bourgeois people – and there may be more of them outside than inside the church. They are the ones who strive for a peaceful and respectable existence, who steer clear of the difficult questions in life, but who want to enjoy life to the full; these are the people we can describe as 'normal', or as T.S. Eliot put it 'decent, godless people'. The younger generation is revolting against the emptiness, mediocrity, superficiality and meaninglessness of mere traditions, and against the lack of well-founded norms and values. It is a protest against a society in which the highest goal seems to be 'getting into the newspaper'. Many of the long hair styles, the unconventional clothes, the offhand manners, can be explained as a protest against bourgeois values of good taste and bourgeois security. This can go so far that today 'dropping out' is preached by the hippies in America and in Europe. So, they seem to say, let everyone strive towards a happy future, a great highway, a life with every comfort except for an occasional, unfortunate war. But, they warn, you can spend all you have and still derive no satisfaction from it, so surely the purpose of life does not lie there. Protest alone does not help: we must get into the action and show that bourgeois attitudes and values leave us stone cold.

Some of these things come out clearly in another song on the record by the Beatles in which they describe parents' reaction to their daughter's leaving home: 'we gave her most of our lives' . . . 'sacrificed most of our lives' . . . 'we gave her everything money can buy.' Yet she leaves home, 'after living alone for so many years'.[360]

Indeed, such young people can get nothing at home because the parents really have nothing to give. The old foundations have been undermined, but bourgeois people nevertheless want to hold on to a respectable and 'normal' life. But without real foundations the values with which they are concerned just lose their meaning.

This sort of bourgeois attitude has arisen before, as we have noted, and can be seen especially in the nineteenth century. There sprung up a terrific anxiety about all kinds of sexuality – 'nasty dirty sex'. It was as if people were afraid to think about this very human thing which, however, can become an animalistic act if the basis for human values is removed. This whole anxiety led to what has been called 'Victorian prudery', which eventually became the target for attack in the preaching of both literature and the fine arts to support modern views of sex. So strong was and is this attack that the result of it can rightly be labelled a 'sexual revolution'. This was a real element in art from the beginning of this century, from Jarry and Apollinaire to Dada and Surrealism, and might even be dubbed 'pan-eroticism'. Its greatest surge, however, has come in the last decade with a flood of nudity; in the treatments of the most intimate themes in films, poetry and prose; and in the preaching of 'free love'.[361] And of course what appears to be a vast increase in homosexuality is partly to be accounted for as a protest against Victorian bourgeois values.

All this did not spring up automatically. Here, for example, is an excerpt from 'In Defence of Obscenity', an article in an underground newspaper:

> Obscenity is an artificial concept, constructed by a trap-hatching dass of illiterate filthy dass mongers; by the bourgeois vultures of the Establishment who live by sucking the pecuniary asspus of the battered humanity emanating from the lower depths; by the monied gangsters who with visibly calculated intentions lurk to monopolize over this dark geyser called the lower class. I will indulge in Obscenity, for I will ruin & destroy all class-distinctions in Language.
>
> If speaking and writing in the total FREE LANGUAGE of the ENTIRE SOCIETY leads to the saintless labelled by the moneysuckers as 'depravity & corruption,' I WILL DEPRAVE & CORRUPT MAN TO SANITY.
>
> I'd go on defending Obscenity until I've forced the society to embrace the total vocabulary of MAN. I want POETRY to be given back to LIFE. CENSORSHIP IS AN OUTCOME OF THE COWARDICE WHICH NEITZSCHE CALLED MORALITY OF THE HERD.
>
> NOBODY CAN STOP THE FALL OF THIS CIVILIZATION: I PROPHESY...[362]

And this is not the only case of its kind. Different modern literary pornographers, such as Terry Southern and spokesmen for the ubiquitous *Playboy* philosophy, are understood to say that their intention is to undermine bourgeois values, to get rid of norms and to lead the way towards an anarchistic, lawless society.

Still another question claims our attention, namely the propaganda for a more and more widespread use of drugs. Many papers and magazines, from the pop music weeklies to the influential and international underground newspapers, propagate openly the obtaining and use of LSD, marijuana, and other illegal drugs. By its very nature this attitude is protest – doing precisely what is illegal and 'scandalous'. But the question we as Christians should be asking is: Why has the use of drugs become so prevalent in our society, especially among young people?

We have seen that through the development that led to technocracy, people have been dehumanized. They no longer have any real contact with others; people are basically lonely. They also no longer have any real contact with things, for anything other than the purely physical and technical must be sham and a façade.[363] Thus humanity is lost. People have bodies and yet have been trying for years to repress that, only to find the awareness of their physicality returning ever stronger. Everything more than the physical was only pure subjectivity, a projection of our imagination, something manufactured by us. Can these things be real then? Is there such a thing as love?[364] Is faith more than a psychological reflex? Is the striving towards economic security really anything more than the life urges that we share with animals? In fact, is it true that a human being is more than an animal or is this idea something people have conjured up through their facility for talking and thinking?

These people, alienated from their environments and even from themselves, nevertheless remain human in actuality, and can thus never be happy with the situation just described. Here lies a great part of the sorrow of our times. The crying out, the intense longing, the deep hungering after a real humanity, these all come through. But for them the way to Christianity is blocked, for it is associated with a bourgeois church, while the possibility of a biblical faith in the face of all the biblical criticism, a product too of the Enlightenment, is also precluded. We can begin to understand the use of drugs in this context, especially the drugs which 'expand the mind'. Through drugs people give themselves a psychedelic experience in which the world becomes something different, new worlds are discovered, contact is made and they become a part of the universe. Drugs are not only an escape out of technocracy, that all too prosaic reality with no real contact, but also a means of experiencing a supernatural world. They give us the sensation of seeing and feeling the lost, genuine humanity. Thus a transcendental view of things is again made possible, and a substitute religion is found. Sometimes, too, it syncretizes with Eastern religious thinking.

This is no mere caprice; we are in the midst of a psychedelic revolution. Again, a quotation from the underground press:

> The psychedelic revolution: This is our magic. With this we break open heads & new worlds emerge. Wd you believe? Break the patterns. Shatter the images! Down ikons! Tune in Turn On Drop Out. Fake games! Yr games are fake, boring Man was made. Man was made to change. No single thing abides. Flow with me.
>
> Fast flow the abiding tide.
>
> God in a bottle?
>
> But Lord they said you were everywhere.[365]

And in a more descriptive article in the same paper:

> The psychedelic generation with its distrust of all ideologies, with its deeply unauthoritarian and anarchistic impulses, with its practical knowledge of those social, cultural, personal games played (for pleasure or survival) by the surrounding robots is beginning to see thru such conflicts as the ones resulting from the industrialized turmoil of civilization. Expanding minds and bodies are demanding – sometimes violently, sometimes non-violently

but always with love – that the world they live in expand and mutate with them. How useless it is to judge these demands and this art according to moral, ethical or social 'values' which, for this generation, are worth nothing! The fact is that in Tokyo and Amsterdam, in Los Angeles and London, in Paris and Buenos Aires, in New York and Stockholm something is happening and, as Bob Dylan put it, 'You don't know what it is, do you Mr. Jones?'[366]

Technocracy, dehumanization, emptiness, the probes and protests of Art, the hippie movement with its drugs and sexual freedom – these phenomena affect all of us, even in our most secure enclaves. Revolution is their context and their necessary, if not sufficient, condition. But what about the future? What manifestations of the revolution will endure? What new forms of revolt will become evident? And, most of all, what impact may we expect from the dynamic power of the gospel?

• Culture and revolution II: we live in '1787'[367]

When Groen van Prinsterer demonstrated his profound insight by entitling his book *Unbelief and Revolution,* he meant that revolution since the Enlightenment has been more than a severe eruption of the oppressed against harsh rulers. The revolution is a mindset in which reality is revolutionized, torn from its joints, smashed to pieces. This mindset is directly connected with unbelief – people no longer desire to honour God, people desire to be at the helm themselves and to arrange things according to their own insights. The revolution began in the eighteenth century, not with any immediate violence but rather in the thinking and discussions of scholars. The period of the Enlightenment may seem from the standpoint of the history of philosophy to be a very difficult and at the same time most fascinating one, yet we lose a correct view of it if we fail to see that at that time, in those serene heads, it was unbelief that grew and revolution that was born. Now, more than two centuries later, the world has been altered to fit the pattern of their thought and their propositions have become our common property.

Their first dream, that of human beings ruling the world, became reality: it took the form of a technocracy, which Ginsberg has characterized as Moloch.[368] This dream turned out to be a nightmare. Their second dream – deeply in conflict with the first and yet directly connected with it – was that of human freedom. The more the attainment of this dream of freedom was frustrated by the realization of the first dream, the harder they dreamed it. That was understandable. People wanted to remain human, to be more than a machine, more than an animal. They pinned their hopes for humanity on this (humanistic) freedom.

Art in Romanticism was assigned the task of expressing human freedom and those typically human elements that eluded the natural sciences. Yet we see the rise somewhat later in the nineteenth century of a naturalistic art that is affinitive with positivism, the intellectual orientation that gives precedence to the natural sciences. Opposite to it however we see another art, which via Realism, Impressionism and Neo-Impressionism offered ever more strident opposition to the dominant stream. Especially at the beginning of the twentieth century people who worked in this direction set about unmasking technocracy with its demonically lethal, dehumanizing tendency to reduce human being and society to machines. In its own manner this art aimed to point the way towards human freedom and deeper levels of reality, a freedom and suprareality which were by their nature outside the scope of the rationalistic natural and social sciences. Art therefore emphasized the irrational and unutterable, and it was fiercely anti-naturalistic. That is the origin of modern art.[369]

Modern art[370] can at times seem strange, and it can in fact be strange and may sometimes wantonly trample on almost all beauty and artistry, but one can never reproach it for engaging our times without passion.[371] It is not that it is unable to make beauty, no, but it prefers not to, is unable to do so in a deep, spiritual sense, and so it screams at us:

> In these times what people have always called
> Beauty, beauty has burnt her face.
> She no longer comforts people
> She comforts larvae, reptiles,
> rats,
> But people she terrifies,
> Striking them with the awareness
> Of their being a breadcrumb on the skirt of the universe.[372]

Modern art has sometimes endeavoured to construct an intellectual and abstract fortress of transcendental beauty beyond this world (Mondrian), it has sometimes looked deeply into the pool of misery and anxiety and even criminality of the human soul (Surrealism), and it has sometimes attempted to restore people's human freedom through the abandonment of free creativity (Abstract Expressionism, Appel). Whatever the manner, it has always testified to the absurd, decadent, meaningless and alarming character of our technocratic world in protest and cursing. In the Dada movement this became an anarchistic programme in which artists were prepared to sacrifice all art for the sake of a new, 'free' world. Ultimately these people were out to win back the world, to restore purity, to reconquer a lost paradise.

There is one thing in my view that modern art did not understand: namely, that modern art itself did not offer a solution in and through its work but, instead, that it contributed to the unliveable and unbeautiful and terrifying character of our times. By its sometimes razor sharp analyses of the world in which we live, and even more by its deafening protest and the challenge inherent in that protest to 'go out and do something about it', modern art preached revolution. Its voice was heard. And it was understood. It is no coincidence that the Provo movement began in the same Amsterdam which was and is home to one of the finest museums of modern art in the world, and that the hippie movement established itself in San Francisco, where since the 1950s the 'beat generation' had lived and been exceptionally active.

But enough about that. For we wanted to show that we should not be surprised not only that there is a strong anarchistic movement today but also that all kinds of forms of modern art always play a great role with these groups: we have in mind the protest singers, rock (we have already cited something from the Beatles several times in order to make that clear), the happenings (which began in the artists' environment in New York), modern jazz, modern 'classical' music, literature and poetry, modern visual art and, last but not least, modern films.

What has changed in the last few years is that anarchy is now explicitly advocated and depicted. That actually has been the case for a long time already, but nowadays one has to keep one's eyes and ears shut not to notice it. As just one example we would like to quote here from the catalogue of a recent exhibition at the Stedelijk Museum of Modern Art in Amsterdam: 'They celebrate [the sculptures on exhibit]. One can only celebrate well at the cost of another. And it is at our cost, gentlemen, that this is happening. They kick us in the guts, our army, our morality; they pounce on our philosophy, they cast our country aside. Traitors all!'[373]

So we can say, to summarize, that today's revolutionary situation has been partly provoked and partly advanced by these extremely creative and active modern art movements and, furthermore, also by the propaganda for narcotics and the preaching of Oriental yoga. This is all connected with the lack of a genuinely believed, confessed and practised basis for values and norms, and it is connected with the reality of the world we live in backed by more than two centuries of revolutionary action. People revolt against this world because they have insight into how unfit it is to live in. Yet they think they can set everything right with an anarchist revolution – as if revolution could be cured by revolution. Some cherish the illusion that if only they could change the order of society, people would become better – as in the utopian Constant's Neo-Babylonian paradise.

The real threat of a nuclear war reinforces these tendencies and strengthens their hand; so too, and even more so, do modern means of communication and cultural politics. Modern means of communication as such are not bad or 'infected', but by constantly rubbing our noses 'in the facts' and showing political and other leaders close-up they strengthen our aversion to the situation. Moreover, radio, television and the press are served by journalists who are always out to show the latest developments – it is their job to be 'creative' and 'up to date' – which has an accelerating effect that propagates and supports, unintentionally – but sometimes intentionally – the movement consistent with the spirit of this age.

And cultural politics? People surely see that there is a crisis in cultural life, but they believe they can contribute towards a solution by helping the creative forces; at least, they feel, they are bringing something new. Precisely because they want neither to get involved in what is going on nor to form a judgment about it – as according to them art cannot be judged by moral standards – they unintentionally promote the revolutionary forces, which are precisely centred in the artistically creative circles. (To prevent any misunderstanding: we do not believe that art has been central in every era or that all creativity has found or finds its origin in revolution.)

This revolution, anarchistic in character, is borne by young people, often students, the future intelligentsia, from all levels of society. They have the sympathy of many older people – people who perhaps have conformed to middle-class expectations but who in their hearts believe the strident youth are correct. It is striking, for example, how positive the reports on the hippie movement have been in *Time*, for example.[374] They have no leaders, although poets, artists, philosophers of culture and utopians do show them the way.[375] Political agitators can easily take over the leadership if it fits their scheme, as has already happened during the racial conflicts in America this summer. We will say more about that later.

There is no organized movement but these people organize a great deal: an 'underground press' exists (*San Francisco Oracle*, *International Times* (London), *OZ* (London), *Witte Krant* (Amsterdam), etc. and there are many sympathizing publications from *Playboy* to *Hitkrant*); people managed to suggest in March in San Francisco that it would be a fine thing to hold 'Love-ins' all over Europe during the summer, and then they actually managed to hold them while tremendous propaganda was mounted via popular records. Thus the *International Times* was perceptive when it observed that 'Instinctively the new movement has a good grasp of McLuhan's theory of the media and exploits it to great advantage.'[376] And they also know how to make deliberate misuse of the lack of resistance from the establishment (the dominant groups in society) by holding up before them their own anarchistic basic position: 'permissiveness',[377] which accepts everything, never forbids anything and opposes 'paternalism', a term that comes out of this world of ideas.

We will now attempt to make all this somewhat more concrete by referring to a number of statements from the underground press and its satellites. The point is to make clear that they are thinking about revolution, and that they are conscious of their revolutionary activity. To sum it up in their own words: 'The new movement is slowly and light-heartedly building another society, international, without racial discrimination, with equal rights for all sexes, with peace and quiet; it works with a different concept of time and space; and the world of the future will probably have no clocks.'[378]

In an article in *Hitweek* on 'Anarchism as an Everyday Job' we read that 'A silent anarchistic revolution is taking place that manifests itself in, among other things, the question concerning the place of authority, even in the Roman Catholic Church.'[379] Under the title 'When the Mode of the Music Changes the Walls of the City Shake' an American student wrote about the revolution in the *Internationadl Times*.[380] And in *OZ* we read that

> Notwithstanding a disturbing tendency towards 'quietism', all hippies have *ipso facto* a political stance – an unyielding opposition to the 'establishment' that persists in calling them criminals because they use LSD and Marijuana, and that hates them because they like to sleep with nine in a room and three in a bed, evidently have free sex and a spirit free of conscience and believe they can raise healthy children in dirty clothes.[381]

In a special issue of the *Witte Krant*, which features the large headline 'Revolution' there is an article with the title 'Revolution is People Dancing in the Street'; in it we are told that that is what people did during the French Revolution.[382] In the *Village Voice* (New York) we read a call to young men from the middle class: 'To unite against the system, take up the arms of the rebels: the beard and the folksong, the poem and the noisy room, the alienation and the crisis of identity. Take up an inner rage that cannot be quenched, satisfactions that cannot be enjoyed, and pleasures that cannot be talked about. You have nothing to lose.'[383]

In an article in the *International Times* entitled 'Buddhism and the Coming Revolution', Gary Snyder, a leader of the hippies in San Francisco, writes that acting towards the true community of all that is (*sanha*) means to him the supporting of every cultural and economic revolution aimed at achieving a free, international and classless world. It means, he says, the use of means such as civil disobedience, severe criticism, protest, pacifism, voluntary poverty, and even violence if need be to check intolerant 'rednecks'. It means, furthermore, the supporting of every form of non-damaging individual behaviour, the defence of the right of the individual to use narcotics or practice cannibalism, polygamy, polyandry or homosexuality, worlds of behaviour that have long since been banished, so he says, from 'the Jewish-Capitalist-Christian-Marxist West'.[384]

There was a congress in London this summer entitled 'Dialectics in Liberation' that brought the revolutionaries together: Carmichael, Laing, Ginsberg, Goodman, Gerassi and the like. One can read about them in the issue of the *Witte Krant* that I have referred to, in which it is reported that they seem to be agreed concerning the need for (counter-) violence and hatred as the revolutionary starting point for the guerrillas.[385] Indeed it is striking how even in *Hitweek* (as in *OZ*) Black Power and Flower Power are seen as closely connected.[386]

What can we expect? The atmosphere is charged. Thus, for whatever reason, it could come to an eruption – to a real revolution, worldwide, beginning in the centres. Naturally, the hippies and so forth are just a small group. But there are many sympathizers – even in Christian circles.[387] All revolutions have been spearheaded by a small number of shock troops. Assume for a moment that they are successful: 'Long live anarchy, liberty, equality and fraternity!' We can read in the book by Groen van Prinsterer how in the shortest possible time a dictatorship will follow. One of its characteristics is certain: it will be fiercely anti-Christian. Or, if the revolution fails and 'bourgeois' forces get the reins in hand, then we will get a more or less fascist dictatorial regime – as one sees already in Greece and Argentina and as nearly happened in the United States (Goldwater). What must be done? Three things.

First, we shall have to see through the lies in all the writings from the angle of the hippies, or whatever we call them. Theoretically their position is vulnerable and full of contradictions, but in many respects it comes across as quite sympathetic. That is undoubtedly because they attack many things that are indeed indefensible. The problem is that their answer to the situation is not up to scratch and that they speak lies. Lies, because they are silent about the misery caused by rapidly spreading venereal diseases in their centres. Lies, because they keep silent about the many known cases of people under the influence of LSD or other narcotics who have committed murder or suicide.[388] A tragic case was reported in *Time* a few weeks ago. Narcotics, and all that goes with the use of them, belonged until recently to the underworld, the world of crime and corruption, of human wretchedness and spiritual ruin.[389] Now, suddenly, the same substances are supposed to save the world. We cannot help thinking of Peter 2:19: 'They promise them freedom, while they themselves are the slaves of depravity.' Lies because so many young lives have been thoroughly shattered. 'Drop out' sounds good and one can understand it. Yet the result is a group of vagabonds that have broken loose from their moorings and become addicted to sex and drugs. Such a life will inevitably take its toll. Already at the end of this summer there was a problem with keeping these young people under control. Yet even though that seems to have been done successfully, the next decade or so will find a large number of these people seeing a psychiatrist. And what about their children? It will take years, perhaps half a century, before the last traces are eradicated of the misery caused by the hippie life of one summer (if it is kept to that) in both America and Europe.

Furthermore, we read almost nowhere how it is possible for some to 'drop out' only because most of the rest of the world continues to work. The subject was raised at a panel in San Francisco in which Leary, Ginsberg, Snyder and Watts participated, but they dropped the question without answering it. In other words, they ultimately assume that a large majority of people will remain 'ordinary' and that the hippie life will exist as an alternative possibility, with a tribal connection.[390]

Second, after seeing through the lies we shall have to acquire an intellectual and spiritual understanding of these matters. We must recognize that in these events the words of the [biblical] prophets are being fulfilled. Paul presented a sharp portrait of people in the last days, speaking of 'the man of lawlessness' and 'men of depraved minds' (2 Thessalonians 2 and 2 Timothy 3). Let us recognize the signs of the times and notice that today lawlessness is being preached: 'Know that ALL is possible and ALL is permissible. No one will stop you.'[391]

Third, we must have a deep awareness that in all these things we are in a battle against spiritual wickedness, against the spirit of the age – Ephesians 6:12: 'For our struggle is not against flesh and blood, but against the rulers, against the authorities, against the powers of this dark world and against the spiritual forces of evil in the heavenly realms' – and that our political actions too should be guided accordingly. Prohibition or law enforcement will be of little help here and will in any case just be labelled as 'fascist' or 'bourgeois' and pour oil on the fire. We must resist all dehumanization, all technocracy that gives priority to economic efficiency and sacrifices human beings to Moloch. We shall have to be truly anti-revolutionary in the footsteps of Groen van Prinsterer. And finally, we may pray a great deal that God will give us reformation, a truly spiritual renewal. Return to the Lord. Pray that he will and can use us to show many people the way back to him. Anyone who thinks this is just a pious word tacked on at the end has understood little of the cultural situation.

Reflections on Modern Art

• Why modern art?[392]

1. Modern art's quest for human freedom

Modern art poses a remarkable problem. For in every period new currents appear that initially have to overcome a certain resistance because of their unusual forms and their being 'different'. After more or less contention, polemics and discussion, however, the new becomes ordinary, and finally after several newer currents have been resisted they have to surrender their place to what by then has become the new current, having become old-fashioned and antiquated themselves. This sketch of events implies that we are not speaking here of new directions that appear and remain without importance and influence. Yet the remarkable thing about today's so-called modern art, which has undoubtedly taken part in the general cultural development, is that even now, almost half a century after its inception, it still bears the name 'modern', it still is strange and it still arouses minds to conflict, debate and polemics.

Undoubtedly all this is due in part to the remarkable structure of the humanistic life and world view where two conflicting motives spring from the same root. On the one hand, humanists hope to control the world and, by means of technology and science, to build a paradise on earth. On the other hand, however, humanists are devoted to their personal freedom to do whatever their hearts desire. While in modern philosophy – in existentialism – and modern art, unconditional freedom is prominent, in our society in general it is nevertheless the first attitude that in fact has the powerful upper hand. Yes, this extreme commitment to human freedom in art and philosophy is precisely to be understood as a reaction to the hegemony of the tendency to regulate reality by means of science – planned economy, statistics, social psychology, etc. – in order to safeguard everyone's 'happiness'. For this impedes freedom and the right to decide matters for oneself. Yet as noted, the group committed to the control of reality by means of science holds the actual power, thanks in part to the fact that their promise of a utopia has made the masses, undoubtedly emancipated as a result of their work, follow their banner in socialism and communism. The masses continue to believe for the time being in the great future that can be constructed by means of technology and the economic and social sciences.

The movement that demands absolute freedom for human beings, disturbed by the perspective that everything will be regulated and sacrificed to the Moloch of an 'ideal' state, opposes all this in a fierce reaction. Nonetheless, both are rooted in the same belief in humankind and their value, their wisdom and insight to build a beautiful culture, without God and his word – both of which have been proclaimed by religious studies to be purely human creations. This freedom movement, which speaks mainly in philosophy and art, has grown into an elite current as a result of all this. In fact, since the Renaissance and Romanticism, both of which proceeded from the same standpoint, little has changed. Those too were elite schools that kept the people, the masses who could not touch these 'beautiful fruits of the human spirit', standing on the outside. In the same way the elite now looks down, although not in so many words, on the masses that 'do not understand' and are 'after all, a-cultural'.

So modern culture has become disconnected from the people and has accordingly become the uprooted culture of a clique, severed from normal life not only by existing outside of it but also by often reacting against it with all might. The elite does not concern itself with being understood or with being popular, in the good sense of the word. As a result a virtually unbridgeable gap has opened up between those who should be providing leadership in the fields of art and culture[393] and the people, who thanks to technology (radio, reproductions and inexpensive books) now are in an economic position to profit from that same art and culture. The people, having indeed become economically independent, have in turn become culturally uprooted: they stand outside the culture of the elite, who have thoroughly destroyed the old traditions and, while they have perhaps set up something in their place within their own ivory towers, have simply left the ruins they created outside. The radical break with tradition has for instance affected the folk song. Thus as a substitute for folk music we now see music dished up that has no connection with [today's] 'cultural' music: either superficial nonsense songs[394] or modern entertainment music. The latter is commercially exploited in what socialists will recognize as genuinely capitalistic ventures by the producers of the modern surrogate of folk music, by the conscienceless songwriters and publishers of Tin Pan Alley.[395] Meanwhile the people, uprooted and ever further removed from any appreciation of truly beautiful music, swallow these products based purely on sentimentality and poor taste.

In the visual arts the same situation prevails. The people do not understand contemporary art. Even if the elite were to come down off their throne to bring art to the people – some today are making a great effort to do so – then modern art still proceeds from assumptions that are entirely alien to the people and squarely opposed to the ideals they cherish. Those who are steeped in socialist slogans and who often lack the development to understand modern philosophy and literature lack the capacity to comprehend art that breathes existentialist freedom and builds on literary knowledge and assumptions.

And the people, cut off from leaders and guideposts in spite of all the activities of museums of modern art and the like, have to make do with the time-worn and worn-out, dull and meaningless 'art' that is sold in the frame-maker shops (O irony!), called 'oil paint on canvas'! This 'art', or rather kitsch, which is supplied by a painting industry attuned purely to the lack of taste in the uprooted public, apes soullessly the art of an earlier period, art with which the people are able to have some contact – namely art from a time when the leading artists were motivated by ideals affinitive to those that are now the ideals of the people, particularly the ideals of Impressionism. This art degenerates through an ever weaker extraction into kitsch, the art of the people. No wonder that modern art remains a problem and has not become popular.

Nevertheless, as you will observe, that does not yet answer the problem stated at the beginning of this article. For is it not so that a significant number of people who do not belong to the economically liberated masses also do not understand modern art? That also professors, statesmen, educated people must acknowledge their incapacity to understand it? On the other hand we could add in defence of modern art that there is indeed a certain core of truth in the assertion of the cultural elite that the all-regulating Moloch of the socialist ideal state destroys all individual freedom. For does it not nail down everything scientifically and statistically? Even if you choose freedom by camping during the summer, you are just a number, counted and processed by the 'statistical machine' as part of a percentage who 'choose that sort of vacation', categorized socio-psychologically as a certain type of person who reacts in a certain way to the regularity of everyday life. If everything you do is nothing but acting according to statistical laws, would you not then want to stand on your head? Spare yourself the effort, for culturally speaking the modern artists do exactly that, and as such they are also counted and classified.

But how can it be that even well-educated people still do not understand modern art? We should be mindful here that such people, including even professors etc., live from a humanistic orientation towards life that one could call 'liberal'. It is a type of humanism that stems from an earlier period, which rather meshes with Italian Renaissance art – art that accordingly forms the object of countless pilgrimages to the exalted beauties of Italy, of countless studies of Michelangelo, Raphael and so on. These kinds of art trips are like pilgrimages to the beautiful creations of our great humanity. Undoubtedly there are also artists who come from these groups. They are artists who produce 'understandable' art, often of high quality. Yet this too is usually only a continuation, though in an inspired and highly refined manner, of Impressionism and the school of The Hague, which was in vogue more than half a century ago (I have in mind P. Arntzenius of The Hague).

No, why these people do not understand modern art is because they ignore, consciously or subconsciously, the problems of the modern world and therefore are insensitive to its ideological contradictions. Also because modern art is often to be understood only with a view to the ideals of socialism and communism, to which it belongs as their dialectical opposite. 'Dialectical', since the modernist currents in philosophy and art, although they are founded on the same sort of humanistic starting point, are sharply opposed to the ideal of the socialistic state. Modern art and communism belong together – by far the preponderance of modern artists are leftist in orientation – and yet are strongly opposed to each other. Really, it is not an inconsistency that Picasso is a communist while the kind of art he makes is forbidden in Russia; nor is it an inconsistency that nothing is permitted there but weak extractions from older art, which in their eyes really should be condemned as bourgeois – the kind of art we call kitsch here in the West or, if it is on a somewhat higher level, the kind of art we call no more than a pale restatement of the art of the past. These are not inconsistencies but contradictions inherent in this ideological stance towards life.

And we Calvinists? We are often confused by it all and mostly incapable of choosing a position because the dilemma confronting us does not arise from our own wellsprings. Moreover, we are not important enough to be an influential factor. In earlier centuries we were a head and now we have become a tail.[396] Other fields aside, in the field of art things are definitely decided without us and, alas, often for us. We shall have to be prepared to make do to a certain extent with the art products of this world. Are there also Christians who are going along with the present decision making? That, happily, does not often occur, since Calvinists feel out of place there – though we fear that they often also tarry on the outside because they are totally immature and have become sterile in the artistic field (for reasons we hope to discuss some other time). Nevertheless, there is occasionally a prominent Calvinist who offers the best insight into the problems and backgrounds of the problems discussed here, perhaps precisely because of being a 'stranger' and an outsider. I have in mind Prof. S.U. Zuidema, undoubtedly the finest expert on existentialism in our country and perhaps beyond it.[397]

2. We can no longer paint 'historically'

Last time we saw how the spirit moving modern artists can only be understood as an urge for freedom in artistic formation, a freedom that is connected dialectically with the socialist ideal of controlling reality by means of natural science, statistics and planned economy. Now, the question that flows directly from this is whether it is the case that every artist who works in the modern idiom is oriented towards the political extreme left and driven by an inner urge to live out his or her own freedom. Certainly not all modern artists are communists, although most of them will no doubt be found to have socialist sympathies. At least, that will be the environment they move in and think in and their framing of the problem of life will be conditioned by it. The conscious and pronounced compulsion to be free, to live out one's own creative urge in an autonomous, irrational way bound by no laws and norms, will also not always make itself felt in the same measure or in the same way. Yet naturally it will be so that those who work in a modern way do not detest or oppose the spirit that speaks from the works of their leaders. With that however not everything has been said, and that is why I want to go into it more deeply.

What moves that great train of artists to follow their leaders down the path indicated by them? Financial advantage? Undoubtedly, at times, but do not forget that modern art has never yet guaranteed artists a good income. On the contrary, with the exception of the very best and most well known they have usually lived in difficult circumstances. A quirk of fashion then? Perhaps, at times, but if one wants to trace everything back to that, then one underestimates the seriousness and sense of dignity of these people. No, we probably come closest to the truth if we listen to a simple painter, who works in the modern way, whom I once asked about what moved him. He replied: 'Ah, sir, it is after all not possible anymore to paint historically.' Big problems form the background to this utterance. Of course, the terminology used is a little off the mark, yet it reveals that this man in his simplicity understood what was going on, even if he lacked the literateness to express himself well. 'It is not possible anymore to paint historically,' in other words, as the continuation made clear, 'I can no longer paint the way people painted fifty, a hundred, two hundred years ago.'

Yes, here we have a problem, not a theoretical problem but an existential problem, a problem that faces every creative artist: How can we express ourselves as twentieth-century people? What forms must we choose? We no longer live in the 'golden age' and thus it is no longer possible to paint as people did then. Leaving aside the entirely different spirit that moved people in those times, we need only think of the concatenation of factors that contribute to the shaping of art: the environment, the legacy of the immediate past, the struggle of the moment, the task and place ascribed to art. In other words, the factors that we sometimes sum up with the vague term 'the period in which the art arose' and that in part influence the purely artistic ideals. No, our century has its own present-day difficulties, its own social constellation and its own demands, and all of that asks for a new art belonging to our own times. Yet, what should it look like? As the great leading artists indicated? And if not, what then? How are we supposed to work if we may no longer paint 'historically'? is the question of artists who seek their own way. There is truly no easy answer.

Yet the problem lies even deeper. The science of art history was born in the period of Romanticism, and by now it has studied the art of the past for a century and a half. The results have been committed to books of various kinds, and in various ways – through guided tours and articles like this one, in popular books, through lectures and education – the results have formed and guided our view of the older art. In itself there is nothing wrong with that. Art history has showed how the art of any period is conditioned by the factors indicated above – and in doing so fulfilled its proper task. But, and here's the Romantic snake in the grass, art history has also showed how in every period artists were the great prophets who sensed in their artistically sensitive souls the issues of their time and revealed them to their less gifted contemporaries. Artists are ushered onto the stage as the leaders of humanity, as seers and prophets, guideposts for solving problems. There they are, the great 'saints' of the humanists: Raphael, Michelangelo, da Vinci, Dürer, El Greco and so forth. Art history has put them on a pedestal and conducted a process of canonization. And now, with these shining examples in mind, what can the modern artists do but with their sensitive artistic souls reveal us to ourselves, and depict the tensions and difficulties and miseries of our times? In this way modern art has been made into a series of painted reflections on the times, prophetic visions, revelations of what is hidden behind external appearances. If you then ask the simple soul alluded to above why he paints such an ugly fellow, his answer is: 'Ah, sir, we are no longer living in a beautiful, harmonious time like then, we cannot in the midst of the misery, the threat, the demise of human freedom, in the midst of a dead-end culture in which the bourgeois try frantically to salvage the last vestiges of worn-out norms, behind which only emptiness and smugness grin, certainly we cannot in the midst of today's social revolution paint sweet little cows and calves, nice scenes and lovely meadows – it is ugly to be sure, but it is true, for in it we reveal what lives in our times.' Would you like an example? I will quote something from the catalogue of an exhibition of works by a second-rate contemporary painter:

> Jan van Holthe was born in 1923 ... Cubism attracted him but under the influence of Nakache he abandoned this school and joined the Expressionists. He actualizes hatred, angst and despair pictorially ... He exhibits canvases with a sour colour and hallucinogenic rhythm ... The monstrous comes close to the low and reminds one of J. Rictus' verse: 'It is contemporary despair that whines.' In van Holthe's *Gevecht* ('Fight') two monsters in lugubrious violet colours stick out against a red sky. In this canvas but also in his *Dronkaard* ('Drunkard') he makes use of Picasso's inventions. Yet his *Gevangene* ('Prisoner') hands back our humanity with all its misery and despair.[398]

This is one example among many. Naturally they are not all alike. To the contrary. In general we can say that age, character, the circle the artist originates from and moves in and various other influences in addition to the artist's own talents determine the extent to which they follow the great masters, more moderately or more fiercely, more consistently or more reservedly.

One should say, however, that not all art falling outside of the categories of the great masters and kitsch is hereby typified. There is more to be said, for that 'I can no longer work historically' also has another side to it, which in its own turn will be found to have two aspects. In order to gain a grip on it we will again have to consult the past. In the last century there was a grand exhibition held each year in Paris by living French painters. It was called the Salon. What was shown there indicated what was *accepté*, for the living art of young renewers was usually rejected by the very conservative juries. And what did one see there? Well, the last offshoots of an art that had its beginnings in the Renaissance but that now lacked the spirit and the force to produce truly great creations. It was not so much a lack of talent as a lack of an ideal confessed with conviction, sufficient to breathe new life into the old forms, that makes these incredibly extensive exhibitions (one might have seen some five thousand paintings and sculptures there) demonstrations of the impotence to create something that was truly art. One saw many nude figures there, but the nude, once the highest goal of art, in which the old anthrocentric ideal of antiquity was renewed in humanistic form and which gained such unsurpassable form in Michelangelo's *David* at Florence or in the renowned *Venus* of Giorgione – this nude had degenerated into a sort of elevated kitsch, in which the public under the cover of enjoying art could indulge their erotic fantasies.

One also saw many history paintings there, a genre that with masters like Rubens, Poussin and David had reached great heights, inspired by the idea of representing lofty ideals in the deeds of noble personages. But by now it had degenerated into a photographic and not very artistic depiction of battles and events. Here too there was a powerlessness to show anything really gripping. And in this both humanity's shrinking belief in itself and the approaching crisis of humanism already announced themselves. Genre pieces such as our seventeenth-century masters had created in such abundance was also seen there: vapid, soulless anecdotes painted without much conviction. And so forth. And in all that, an evolving precision in imitating reality, registered with almost natural scientific objectivity but artistically without any value. It was truly no wonder that young, talented artists began to look for ways to break out of this impasse. Some of the élan and the rapidity with which at the beginning of the twentieth century the new anti-naturalistic art established itself can be accounted for in this way.

But suppose you attended the Salon and you looked carefully at ten or twenty paintings and then noticed, virtually subconsciously, that the given subject was chosen purely and only . . . yes, why? . . . in order to make something striking enough to be noticed in the midst of the thousands. If that was impossible through the apparent originality of a never previously exhibited subject, then perhaps it could be achieved through the dimensions or preferably through a combination of the two. And very soon you walked briskly through the halls looking for . . . a real painting, or at least a piece that was well painted. And in this way, almost unnoticeably, the artistic realization became more important than the subject that was depicted.

The elevation of the strictly artistic element, of form and the manner of realization, was advanced still further by the multiplicity of materials that art history made available, assisted in part by photography. For this brought an unprecedented wealth of art to light. By means of modern reproduction techniques art lovers were confronted with artworks from virtually all periods and peoples. From prehistoric cave art to the art of the great cathedrals, from African masks and the ancestor sculptures of Polynesia to the art of Byzantium, from Egyptian and Assyrian art to Giotto, the fifteenth-century Florentines and the Flemish Primitives, from Chinese art to art from one's own recent past. People could see all this and had to digest it. It could not but contribute to the downfall of the dogma of the superior splendour of naturalism. For people began to see that true beauty could be hidden in all these artistic expressions. And so the remarkable phenomenon of our times arose, that one can enjoy virtually all art and value the most conflicting forms of art all on their own merits.

It hardly needs pointing out that people were not all that interested in what was depicted in the artworks, for modern people do not really care about old gods and goddesses, ancestors or stories of saints – as they no longer believed in anything whatsoever. But what did fascinate them was the stylistic and artistic realization. Thus their attention was directed more and more to this aspect of art, which was at the expense of the content, the meaning of the work of art. There was an interplay of factors: the developments in contemporary art – which determine much more than we may realize how we approach art from the past – and the evolving study of art with its plethora of data. Each factor reinforced the other in the devaluation of the theme.

This is the reason why you will be struck by the lack of significance of the chosen subjects when you view an exhibition of modern art – leaving abstract and non-figurative art aside, to the rise of which all this will certainly have contributed as well. No, I have in mind here works that feature something we can recognize. Let's compare a seventeenth-century still life with a modern one. The seventeenth-century artists created a 'poem in paint' *about* the grapes, the glass, the silver plate; they sang their beauty, their sweetness to our eyes, while they stood in a direct connection with them as human beings. And with this paean of praise to the grapes it is likely that they meant to point further to the Creator of all things, since all glory belongs to him. Modern artists are not interested in grapes as such. To them they are irrelevant and meaningless. They might just as well have chosen something else. Certainly they too want to make a 'poem in paint', but *by means of* the grapes. These grapes, flowers, plates, people, houses, mountains and all the rest are only aids for making the poem. For the making of the poem is what it is all about. It is about the artistic realization. Hence the painting has no importance as a song about something else. It tells nothing, says nothing about what it depicts. If you want to know more about that you can better consult a travel guide, a physics text or an encyclopedia of biology, people will tell you. The painting has significance only as a work of art that was realized in an artistic way. The work of art accordingly contains its goal within itself. Subject matter is at most an aid to suggest something or perhaps only an occasion for painting. Yes, human beings have become blasé about the creation in which they have been placed. There is no longer anything that can fascinate or interest them. Everything has already been investigated, and seen, either in reality or in prints and photos. And these people, who have lost all real interest in the world outside themselves, in truth, God's creation, can now be fascinated only by a work of art in which the artistic means have become an end in itself.

And what is the reverse side of the picture we have tried to sketch here? It is that modern artists have to compete with the best of the best from all times and all lands and all peoples. It is not only their neighbour and colleague who is their companion and it is not only their contemporaries that they must surpass with the qualities of their own work. No, they must measure up to that entire imaginary museum[399] that all art lovers carry around with them in their memory. The modern beholder of art is cruel. If someone does something bearing even a remote resemblance to Bruegel, then he or she is compared to Bruegel and, if found wanting, rejected. Modern reproduction techniques make it possible for us to have masterpieces and museum pieces on our walls at home – but the modern painter has to compete with that and as a result often suffers economic shipwreck.

Yet the artist is familiar with that same imaginary museum. And to a great extent that is probably why we witness the passionate commitment of the entire artistic personality to finding a new twentieth-century style, for 'We can no longer paint historically'; the burden of the artistic legacy of all the generations that went before us rests upon our shoulders. And that weighs us down and confronts us with a virtually unbearable task not only economically but also artistically.

The questions we have discussed here can also be approached, however, from an entirely different direction, and that is what we will consider next.

3. The subjective creative act

We said previously that the average present-day artist follows more or less consistently, more or less pronouncedly, in a more passionate or more reserved manner, the leaders of modern art. We proceeded from the assumption that modern art is a remarkable art which 'people' cannot quite place, art that seems strange and, indeed, often is. It is a noteworthy fact that this school of art, or rather this style, now already fifty years old, is still called 'modern'. The term has gradually evolved into the name of a style comparable with terms like 'Baroque', 'Rococo', 'Impressionist' and so forth.

Yet if we return to the assertion of the first part of this article, to which we just alluded, then we have to say that it is not entirely correct. For a great deal of work has been made by very important artists of our century that by no means can be called monstrous, incomprehensible or ugly. I have in mind here the art of Rouault, many works by Matisse, Vlaminck, landscapes by German Expressionists such as Kirchner, Schmidt-Rottluf etc. 'Picasso' may have become a buzz word for everything modern, but his name certainly does not cover everything that is being made in our times. The type of art I have in mind, made in a modern style, distinguishes itself (if we would venture to give a general definition) from that of the preceding periods by its greater emphasis on the subjective creative act. Zola characterized Impressionist art as 'a corner of nature seen through the medium of a temperament',[400] a piece of nature viewed through the personality of the artist, which makes clear that already with the Impressionists, whose intention it was to represent nature as precisely as possible as one sees it, the subjective element played a role. Indeed in all humanistic art, objectivity and subjectivity play a role, the representation of nature on the one hand and the free act of creation on the other. These elements in actual fact exclude one another in their consequences, so that when the one is realized the other is felt to be short-changed. There is in this way an inner tension in the creative activity of the humanistic artists that is inherent in their attitude towards life, in which nature and freedom are dialectically connected – as we noticed in the part 1 above.

Well now, if with the Impressionists in the last quarter of the nineteenth century the balance was such that the emphasis still fell on the representation of nature, then since the turn of the century the accent has shifted to the subjective act of creation: to the *peinture*, the way of painting, the 'handwriting' of the artists, and the direct expression of their own creative urges and feelings. And so there are a great many works that have been made in our century right down to the present that depict reality in recognizable ways without distorting it, but that all the same bear the stamp of our times through the artists' very fluent way of working, a sketchiness due to an accentuation of the direct and the subjective. The artists shy away from a smooth finishing of a piece since that would damage precisely these elements. And the stress is not on an exact depiction of what is outside us but on the subjective realization of the work of art. Zola's definition is stood on its head so that one could characterize contemporary art as 'an artistic temperament that reveals itself by incorporating a piece of nature into the work of art'.

This is then moderate modern art, which alongside its loose directness and its subjective play with the givens of reality is characterized by the absence of a truly meaningful subject. Poems are made with the natural givens, as we said in part 2 of this article, but we should not forget that it is all about the poetizing as such and not about the real content of the 'poem'. This certainly is also caused by a fundamental relativism, with an absence of belief – not only in what the Bible proclaims but in anything at all. Is it nihilism? In a certain sense, yes. 'In a certain sense,' we say, for here we do not find a fiercely proclaimed, consciously confessed nihilism. This is not a deep-rooted denial of every value; it is rather an absence of anything at all that one might hold fast to or believe in. That is the reason why this art is relatively moderate. It does not consciously proceed from a life and world view and there is no contending for any 'truth'. On the other hand, it is precisely this 'ordinary' and 'just do it' quality, which of course can easily become superficial, that makes it possible to find attractive, enjoyable and acceptable art amongst the works of these contemporary artists. And there are many of these kinds of works around.

This interest in the subjective element in the act of artistic creation, in the 'handwriting' of the painter and in the strictly personal style, was the main factor conditioning critical reflection on art and the knowledge of art from the time of Romanticism. The given theme was not considered important. Cursory sketches in which the artists quickly noted down their ideas were sometimes even valued more highly than the completed and polished painting. Typical is for instance the interest in Rembrandt's sketches, sometimes cherished more than the completed drawings and the great paintings. This way of appraising art is not to be separated from the general development of art and tended from its side to reinforce the emphasis being laid on these subjective facets.

And this must have been fodder for those who, while drawing the consequences from the state of affairs that caused the birth of modern art, consistently and ferociously implemented the revolution that now took place even where it had to entail the overthrow of all established values. The true nihilists are artists who no longer believe in anything and do not want to bind themselves to anything. The only thing deemed important is the strictly personal indulgence of their urge to create, even if that would result in art that is no longer art but purely and only a 'psychogram', only 'handwriting' without content or form, disconnected from every norm or law, free from any rendering of nature, pure subjectivity in freedom.

This school manifested itself particularly after World War II in the group of the Experimentals, although there had been plenty of earlier forerunners and harbingers. It caught the limelight round about 1918 in Dadaism. Paul Klee was and is the front runner, Ouborg a leader, and Appel and Corneille important Dutch representatives of this truly international movement. Surrealism, as it manifested itself after 1924, grew out of Dadaism and was an attempt to underpin this aspiration with a system, a theory, an attempt to unite and set norms for the wild and lawless. The leader of this movement, André Breton, wrote about their method of working – automatism – that could bring to light profound individual tensions and resolve them to some extent. Automatism would convey us to the psychophysical field – and here the name of Freud is invoked – where there is a complete absence of tension and where there is freedom from all inhibitions generated by repression, a timeless situation in which external reality is replaced by a psychic reality that follows only the laws of lust or desire. But Surrealism was still too positive and in its results, still too 'literary' to satisfy some. As a result there was a renewed revolution aimed at driving it out of the avant-garde artistic arena.

In 1948 these Experimentals issued a Manifesto which I should like to have printed in its entirety here (but my co-editor would undoubtedly have frowned upon my co-opting so much space). Hence just a few citations. The Manifesto was written by Constant Nieuwenhuis:

> The culture of the individual together with the class society from which it arose faces demise, and its institutions, although still artificially maintained, present no further possibilities for the development of the activity of the creative fantasy and impede the free expression of human vitality ... Taking advantage of the general indolence, people try to suggest that there is a societal need for what is usually called beauty, and thereby they try at the same time to hinder the springing up from the vital feelings of a new feeling for beauty, in conflict with the old.
>
> Already after World War I the Dadaist movement attempted with violence to tear itself loose from this old ideal of beauty. Although this movement was forced to focus its activity more and more on the political struggle after the Dadaist artists had experienced that their struggle for freedom brought them into conflict with the laws on which society was based, the vital force that had been developed in this struggle also stimulated the birth of a new artistic consciousness. In 1924 the Surrealist Manifesto appeared ... But Breton's movement suffocates in its intellectualism ... because Surrealist art was an art of ideas and as such still burdened by the malady of the past class culture, while it failed to totally eliminate the conventions that this culture had called into life to maintain itself.

Notice that one never speaks of norms here but always of conventions, whereby they are demoted to human agreements.

> In this period of upheaval the creative artist can play no other role than that of a revolutionary, and he is obligated to destroy the last vestiges of an aesthetics that has become empty and bothersome, in order to arouse the creative instincts that still slumber in man unconsciously ... The creative thought does not consist of ideas and of forms that people might rather call coagulums of matter. It is rather a reaction to the encounter of the human spirit with the raw material, which suggests the forms and ideas to it. Every refinement of the form damages the material impact and thereby the suggestion that issues from it.

> A living art knows no distinction between beautiful and ugly because it poses no norms ... A new freedom arises that will enable man to express himself, as his instincts require.

> The artists from after World War II see themselves confronted by a world of décors and false façades with which every contact is broken and in which every belief is gone ... Their only salvation lies in a complete separation from the cultural rudiment in its totality (including modern negativism, Surrealism and existentialism).

Now, do not criticize me for failing to make enough critical comments. The revolutionary, lawless, God-denying character of all this is so clear that any further commentary seems superfluous. And certainly one may not regard it as just a pious little sermon if I go on to say that all this is really comprehensible only after one lays Scripture next to it. I want to mention two texts in this regard. The first, Proverbs 18:2 gives a sober and wise judgment of their way of working ['A fool finds no pleasure in understanding, but only in airing his own opinions']. And 2 Timothy 3:1–4 may justifiably be cited here and also needs no further comment ['But mark this: There will be terrible times in the last days. People will be lovers of themselves, lovers of money, boastful, proud, abusive, disobedient to their parents, ungrateful, unholy, without love, unforgiving, slanderous, without self-control, brutal, not lovers of the good, treacherous, rash, conceited, lovers of pleasure rather than lovers of God']. We fear that the situation in the world is now such that we see here the most powerful and influential movement of our times, even though there are still many who see the foolishness and danger of it all – yet they can offer little resistance to these rebels of the ongoing Western humanistic revolution and are often anxious and timid because their own ideals are being demolished.

Finally we will try to draw some conclusions and with that answer the question with which we set out at the beginning of this article.

4. Modern art as the art of crisis

The late Prof. Schilder once discussed a certain matter first under the title 'The difficulty of our subject' and then later under the title 'The easiness of our subject'. Alas, I do not believe we will be able to present such a second discussion. We could of course do so if we were prepared to let matters rest and give them a wide berth. However, anyone concerned to truly account for the times we live in and to truly understand from Scripture something of the apocalyptic times in which we have our task and place will not be able to avoid modern art. One does not need to have any particular love for it or to be one of those strange creatures who frequents museums to be regularly confronted by modern art and the issues it raises. One can make matters easy for oneself and simply ignore it all – but in that case one has to consciously avoid it, decide not to encounter it, and keep one's eyes shut wherever it is to be found. Naturally we do not come upon a work by Picasso or one of his circle every day. There is a great deal of that kind of work that we will never see unless we make the effort to look it up in a museum somewhere. Yet the spirit in which Picasso worked we meet every day. Every day art products connected with it are placed along our path in one way or another. Just think of modern billboard advertising.

Now if we consider again precisely what the problem is that we are about to discuss here, then we must say immediately that this time we will not be talking about the twentieth-century art that presents an understandable and directly apprehensible reality, different and realized with greater subjectivity than in the past but nonetheless differing only in nuance. Instead we will be concentrating our attention on the art that bears the style name 'modern art' – the art that is characterized by names like Picasso, Ouborg, and Dali. And the problem we will address is: Why do we have this type of art today? And, connected with that: What should our relationship be to this art?

Let us say first of all that this is not a question of beautiful or ugly. Many modern works confront us with problems, evoking all kinds of questions. We do not understand them and, disoriented, ask: What is that all about? while upon closer reflection we have to say that they are beautiful after all. Beautiful aesthetically, beautiful in colour and composition, and so on. This does not apply to the art of Ouborg, for there we no longer have any artistic pretension, inasmuch as he abandoned controlled artistic forming, the basis of all artistic activity. Yet we could think of some Picassos, of the exceptionally lovely works of Mondrian and the work of so many others that as aesthetic things are not necessarily ugly or repulsive. And that really goes without saying: if people in art regard the subject, the given as nothing, if people seek the meaning and significance of a painting strictly and only in the aesthetic aspect and thus devote all their attention to that, it would be most remarkable indeed if they did not succeed in realizing these abstract aesthetic qualities in a good way.

So it is by no means possible to dismiss all modern art as 'worthless' and without significance. It is one of the difficulties of our subject that we sometimes want to reject something and yet at the same time have to recognize its positive qualities, that it is in short impossible to just with a few words, even pious ones, shove this art aside. Modern art certainly also had its positive results, precisely in the field of aesthetic form, of style. We must remember too that in the last analysis any cultural forming whatsoever can only have abiding significance while giving a positive content to norms laid down by God in the creation order – all the rest is merely beating the air and tilting at windmills in a highly subjective way, estranged from reality, falsifying reality. Thus modern art has also positivized aesthetic norms – we need only think of modern architecture and of the style distinctive of modern utensils and implements. We hope to present another series of articles later devoted to this side of modernism.

Yet to eliminate all possibility of misunderstanding, I do not mean to assert that all modern art is beautiful, i.e. to be valued as artistically positive. Where modern artistic means – often acceptable means as such – express hatred and revulsion of this reality in which we live and blaspheme and mock God's creation – art in which the First and Second Commandments are very deliberately violated – there we will no longer be able to speak of beauty and loveliness. But with that we have come to the rebellion against God and his creation, a rebellion that renews and prolongs itself again and again. This is not formation according to a norm given in the creation order, for people voice their own highly subjective opinions – and with these they may infect and convince others, but no enduring style and no positive norm can be born of them.

Now, we could also approach modern art by way of saying – as often happens – that modern art is really nothing special; it is only a non-naturalistic kind of art and it is of course not a norm for art that it must be naturalistic. For naturalism is connected with the typically humanistic culture of recent centuries and, after all, in the course of history a great deal of beautiful work has been made that stylizes reality in a particular way, also deforms it in order to symbolically underscore one element in particular or to express a particular idea. Is modern art not of the same family as all primitive art, the art of all times and lands – Mexico, Peru, Africa, Ur of the Chaldees and our own Middle Ages with the magnificent Romanesque sculptures of, for example, Moissac and Vezelay? Indeed, with respect to one point there is an affinity, namely, that they all are non-naturalistic and thus symbolically depict something in a particular stylizing way. Granted. And to this we may add: the fact that we have the capacity to positively appreciate this art is also certainly connected with the developments in our own art. Yet we must make a distinction here. There is undoubtedly exotic art that is also strange and deformed – and it may even breathe the same sentiment as modern art: angst and hatred with relation to God's creation, hate and a lack of respect for people and other creatures. For instance the art of old Mexico and some African primitive art. Yet these cases, where the affinity lies deeper, are exceptions and the art of Peru and the greater part of the artistic products indicated above are quite different from that. And people who may feel queasy in a museum of modern art will experience direct contact with them: are there not after all many people who find French Romanesque art very beautiful, for example, but who cannot understand modern art? Besides, only a part of the phenomenon that is modern art can be compared with it. Abstract art – art that 'depicts nothing' and yet is not decoration but art in its own right – is something that has never occurred before, something unknown in any older or foreign culture. And this applies to the Ouborg-like Experimentalist expression of personal subjectivity as well.

Therefore modern art is hardly comparable with all other art, unless we limit ourselves to external appearances, ignore what is essential and thereby consciously distort matters. Modern art is different, although one may see some similarities with some products from the sixteenth and eighteenth and nineteenth centuries which sprung from the same humanistic culture. And we believe we can define what is at the heart of that difference as follows: modern art is the art of crisis.

In order to properly understand this we need to discern that modern art is the art of Western Christendom. Here, in Western Europe, God established his covenant and called generations to obey his word. But here too, very pronouncedly already at the end of the Middle Ages, came apostasy from the covenant. The Renaissance, par excellence, is the cultural product of that. Naturally, religion still retained its place – for making one feel good, something to attend to from time to time for the salvation of one's soul. Self-willed religion and worship persisted, to be sure – consider that initially virtually all Renaissance art was ecclesiastical or 'Christian' art. The beautiful façade of the sometimes magnificent Renaissance art conceals a tremendous crisis. The Lord surrendered these apostate generations to all kinds of spiritual delusions as the leaders were smitten with blindness.[401] And with all the self-willed religion and the total secularization of 'normal' life, as well as a total loss of respect for the word of the God of the covenant, ethics wavered as well. The church was not able to remain standing amidst these judgments and started to conduct a power politics of its own that was still Christian but only in pretension and name. In those times God sent judgment in the form of various epidemics and terrible wars – even allowing a part of European Christendom to fall into Turkish hands – and passed in judgment over the people who had angered him, people who, seeing, were blind and, hearing, deaf so that they left the Bible virtually unread. In those times God also heard the prayers of the righteous, the sheep that hungered and thirsted after his word, and he sent his servants, prophets like Luther and Calvin. In the Reformation people learned to prophesy again with the words of Deuteronomy

29:25–27 and the promises of Deuteronomy 30 were fulfilled. Then the crisis was broken and new life arose.

This crisis had found clear expression in art, in the Mannerism of the sixteenth century that was already a harbinger of modern art. Yet the renewal of life also appeared in art. Not only the generations that recognized the voice of their Master in the language of the Reformers, but also the rest of Europe in the Counter-Reformation enjoyed the blessing of the renewal of life that God gave when people sought his kingdom. God gave his restored covenant people 'showers of blessing' (Ezekiel 34:26): global dominion, a great blossoming of the sciences, wealth and welfare, beauty and much more. But they soon despised again the sword of the spirit, and the shield of faith degenerated into something useful for religious moments only. All that matters, after all, is that the soul should go to heaven, and religion is just there so that an encouraging word may be heard when appropriate, at Christmas and New Year, saying peace, peace, for the temple of the Lord is here. Yes, in this way the service of the word degenerated into the opiate of the people. And woe to those who refused to give this opium, Hendrik de Cock for instance![402] And so people neglected to struggle against the spiritual wickedness in the air and abandoned the task to which God had repeatedly called his people.

And let us not say that in the New Testament dispensation there are no longer any divine judgments. Read Matthew 7:19, 24–27 and Luke 14:34–35, and do not read them individualistically! Truly, in these times when people forgot to receive in thankfulness all the gifts of God – global dominion and the blossoming of the sciences, etc. – and prided themselves instead, in these times the Lord came with his divine judgments. He abandoned them to the spirit of the age. Seeing, they were blind and, hearing, they were deaf, no longer understanding the Scriptures. Their science often became foolishness and the fruit of science and economic blossoming – industry – often became a curse. Then, when our God could complain as in Ezekiel 16 about his people, yes, when he could reproach them even more since they had heard the word of God so purely and should have known that the risen Saviour reigns, then he continued with his divine judgments and sent a delusion upon those who had not accepted the love of the truth, so that they came to believe the lie. The lie states that humans can make a better world themselves if they change and invert the ordinances of God – in property rights, the sanctity of marriage, the love of truth, the inequality of people in rank and development and gender. And in continuing judgments he visited his people for the sins they had committed in exercising world dominion, he took away their colonies and summoned the coloured nations to fulfil his judgment upon his unfaithful children.

Truly, we live in times like those prophesied by Joel and like those we read about in Revelation. Just look around and see the apocalypse of our times in the ongoing infatuation and crisis and decay, in all the rumours of war and threats from unchristian world powers like Russia and China and Indonesia and even Egypt. See it and take note of it so that God does not have to complain as in Isaiah 42:24–25.

Now, do not say that I have started to preach and that this all has nothing to do with the problem we formulated in the title of this series. For modern art is at bottom only understandable as the art of the crisis of the Western world. The force of the communist or socialist error has turned the societal system into a straitjacket, and it is precisely the belief in it and the fear and anxiety caused by it that, dialectically, have evoked modern art – and with that we have returned again to where we began in part 1.

We must never forget that modern art is the fruit of an evil tree, namely, that of apostasy. Yet it seems that we sometimes fail to see the connection between the Scriptures and concrete reality and that we often do not or do not want to see the clear acts of God. How often do we not work, also in the church, without involving God, without taking him into account, as if everything is 'just' a question of human quarrelling and human striving? Yes, do we not sometimes reason 'piously' that God acts according to his counsel – as if it is some kind of fate – and not through his counsel, i.e. by living along with his children from moment to moment, for good or evil, reacting to prayer or cursing.[403] If that is so, and everyone may test his or her own actions against God's word, then we should quickly repent.

Paul writes in the continuation of the passage cited above from 2 Timothy that we should be sober [cf. 2 Timothy 3:14–17]. That means in the present context that we are not to treat every case the same. Appreciate what can be appreciated, enjoy what can be enjoyed, but reject and do not support anything that blasphemes God's name and disparages his creation, anything that despises what God has made good. And Paul continues: 'Endure hardship, do the work of an evangelist,' in other words simply do your task, be salt that salts, do not ignore these questions while trying to avoid the world but also do not forget to use the sword of the Spirit to fight against the spiritual powers in the air, so that you may keep ourselves free and unspotted by this world. The latter is certainly not the same as engaging in polemics on the basis of our principles – besides, in this field we have few or none of these as a result of virtually centuries of neglect. Yet we are to be ready at all times to give a reason for the hope that is in us . . .

'Be sober and watch' means in this matter also to watch the signs of the times. And in the emergency situation in which our Western culture finds itself it means crying to the Lord: 'Come quickly, yes come, Lord Jesus.'

• The function of visual art in our times[404]

Virtually all the speakers at this Symposium have connected the question of the function of art in our times with modern art, whereby they had in mind art from Picasso or Mondrian up to Dali and Karel Appel or from Sartre and Camus through Lucebert and Henry Miller. I have supposed that I must also comply with this restriction in my own contribution, notwithstanding the fact that the works of art left us by our forefathers have a quite specific and certainly not unimportant function in our times, into which we shall not go further here.

I quite agree with Prof. Hungerland's observation that it makes a great difference whether we interpret the question implied in the title of the Symposium as: 'What now is the actual function of art in our times?' or else understand it as: 'What now should the function of art in our times be?' Yet I am certain we can say something in response to the first question without falling into a formulation of wishes and expectations. We need only keep in mind that in the field of cultural development and current affairs no absolute pronouncements can be made. Thus in the course of the last few years I have been confronted a number of times with brand new drawings, works of art, or at least items that are meant to pass as such, that were fashioned in a style that every art historian would suppose had been abandoned three quarters of a century ago and was as dead as a doornail. I believe that if we just keep such possibilities in mind as well, we may be able to say something in general about the function of the visual arts – painting and sculpture – in the cultural system and, in short, explore the extent to which modern art has been and still is of significance in our times.

1. *Art finds forms.* While aiming to discover new facets of the experience of reality, whether emotional or intellectual, artists must find new artistic possibilities to express the new experiences. They will create new forms that will become typical for their style. In this way they will find new artistic formulas that will come to determine the visual language of their time, not only in art in the narrower sense but also with respect to the forms of the things that must fulfil their role, however modest, in everyday life.

Modern art has indeed profoundly affected the visual language of our day. And then we have in mind not only architecture – where Mondrian's influence and that of others are clearly discernible – and contemporary interiors with their furniture and so forth but also automobiles, trains, telephones and much more. In short, we can say that what people call 'industrial design' is nothing other than a very deliberate use of the new artistic forms. In this connection we can also mention fashion – think of printed textiles and the contemporary use of colour (that we include here for the sake of convenience with the language of artistic forms), typography, etc.

I believe this function of art is incredibly important. Someone once objected – in a conversation – to the display windows of a large department store. 'All they had done was steal ideas from Matisse,' so my acquaintance said. For myself I would rather speak in such a situation of a happy example of a positive influence by a living art on the 'artistic form language' in everyday life: Matisse helped to formulate a style that made it possible to do something like decorate department store windows in an artistically responsible way.

2. *Art defines the grammar and syntax of the iconic language that is used in 'visual communication', in the transmission of ideas by means of an image.* This too seems to me to be a very important function of visual art. Through it a visual language – what we call 'iconic' – is formed and continually renewed and enriched, or possibly sometimes impoverished. This iconic facet of the visual arts is very important for understanding art, since it is exclusively through the iconic that artists can make clear not only what it is that they want to say something about – a woman or a horse or a landscape – but also what they have to say about them. Through the forming of the iconic the rendering of ideas by means of images – 'visual communication' – is made possible.

This has become particularly clear in our times when we have an art that is no longer naturalistic. Modern art has discovered new ways of expressing ideas and emotions and relations between various matters. We all know how this language has not only influenced but also in large measure determined the visual communication of our times. I am thinking of posters, print advertising, the graphic presentation of statistics, even traffic signs – the designs of our traffic signals are based on ideas of De Stijl.[405] This all seems to me to be exceptionally important.

3. *Art helps people to gain contact with reality.* Such contact is indeed possible only when the structure of things, of entities given in our reality, is understood, seen, and when the mutual coherence of things is experienced. Now art has as a part of its task the opening of our eyes to all that is new around us, the new realities with which we are confronted. We may think here of modern traffic, railroad stations with their constellations of wiring up in the air, of steel constructions and machines, of modern cities, etc. Yet art will also have to help us to understand nature and humanity itself in their forms and identities which do no alter with time, to see and sense them ever afresh and anew.

The first task, of opening our eyes to the new forms and conglomerations of forms so that we can see and feel them in their relation to our everyday lives, is fulfilled to a certain degree by modern art. That is self-evident to some extent since modern art itself has contributed to defining these new forms. Yet there is more at stake here than I alluded to in point 1. Perhaps this can be made clear from the following examples: Delaunay's paintings of the Eiffel Tower and the cityscapes of Feininger, Stuart Davis, John Marin and others. And also from the work of Léger, the Futurists and the artists who work under their influence.

Nevertheless, perhaps modern art has fallen short in understanding and experiencing humanity and nature in a positive sense. These areas have been neglected too much in the search for new forms and new realms of experience. Perhaps this is one of the reasons for the rise of the twentieth-century crisis, connected to the fact that contemporary people have too little understanding of the world around them. The contact with this world is often broken, in part because art has failed to give them the key with which to understand the world in which they live and to experience it and move about in it without fear. This key has been removed, as it were, by the visual arts insofar as nature and human realities have ceased to serve as their themes.

This has all been made worse by the fact that many have lost touch with developments in art so that by now they understand neither its forms nor its language. As a result, art would no longer be able to offer them a key even if it still had one to offer. It occurs to me that this is an important aspect of the problems of our times – and not only for the artists themselves and the art critics.

Before proceeding any further I want to say something in order to avoid causing any misunderstanding. I have deliberately left unmentioned the very important function art has of being 'a joy for ever'. In contrast, I have simply presupposed the purely aesthetic factors, the questions concerning beauty and artistic level. Without the presence of true beauty and quality, art will never be able to fulfil its function. Only when people sense the new forms as being valuable can those forms be expected to influence a period's language of form. And art can only be a key to understanding reality when it is enjoyed, when people are prepared to make the effort to steep themselves in the work of art. And that will only happen when a work genuinely captivates people by its beauty. Only as 'a thing of beauty' and 'a joy for ever' can art fulfil its broader cultural task. This task meanwhile will never be the goal of artistic activity but rather a supplementary result.

4. Our fourth point is in part an aspect of what we have discussed under point 3, since it deals with a certain element of the reality with which art brings us into contact. *Art is an expression of a person's attitude towards life and, to a certain degree, a visual formulation of a life and world view.* Art is directly connected with that world view insofar as art will only depict those

matters that are considered relevant and important, and in the depiction those aspects will be emphasized that essentially constitute that relevance.

Now modern art is more clearly than any older artform an expression of a specific attitude towards life and the universe. The long-term influence of the principle of art for art's sake, which deprived art of a direct function in life, entailed this only ostensibly paradoxical consequence. One can typify some of the more recent currents as nihilistic iconoclasm: all vestiges of reality (captured in images) are destroyed and chaos, destruction, collapse, atomic explosions appear to determine the forms and compositions. Irrational myths appear again and again. What else would be the meaning of the title of a sculpture called *Sacrificial remains* (which does indeed cover the meaning of the piece)? We can also think in this connection of the later work of Braque. Extreme subjectivism is found in Tachism and such currents, in which the work of art gives expression to the desire to completely let oneself go, to be free from every law, to escape external reality and find absolute freedom. To such absolute freedom all structure and reality form a threat, a danger that must be overcome, at least ideologically. Modern art is in a large measure an expression of a new lifestyle and direction, a new look at reality, a new view of humankind and their place in this world. Revolutionary, irrational, existentialist and perhaps even Zen are the names by which one may indicate its content. Modern artists themselves and their kindred spirits emphasize these elements again and again, so there is really no reason to ignore this.

And now we come to the most important thing I want to say. If modern art brings us into contact not so much with the actual phenomena of today's world as it does with a modern life and world view – with a new way of thinking, acting and living – then the assertion that we must enjoy today's art simply because it is today's art is nothing short of pernicious.

In the first place we must not forget that a great deal of art is made today that is not modernistic in the sense we have just described but that expresses instead a more positive attitude towards reality – without being a pale echo of what has been said earlier or an academically vacuous repetition of forms that have become meaningless. A great deal that is of value is to be found between the extremes of Tachism and the Social Realism propagated in Russia. The art I have in mind here – I think for example of the work of the young etcher Veldhoen – is often neglected as a consequence of the politics of many museums of modern art that busy themselves exclusively with a certain avant-garde. As a result, many artists who in one way or another seek their inspiration in reality – one may think here of Willem Schrofer – are not given the honour they deserve as artists. One can compare this conduct with the way in which during the nineteenth century an entire generation of non-academic artists were denied recognition and positive acceptance, so that their development took place outside and separated from the realm of public art. We may perhaps even say – without snobbery and with an eye to what is actually going on today – that a possibility exists that a not unimportant part of the art of the last decade [the 1950s] is in fact also a sort of 'Salon art', a new sort of official academicism, a fashion. Even if we concede – must concede – that the best of the avant-garde artists (whatever that dangerous term 'avant-garde' may mean) produce an art that is truly deep and that flows from real spiritual forces. Modernistic art is an art that reflects (probably to a much higher percentage than is to be found in social reality) an attitude towards life that is found in the revolutionary and bohemian circles of our times, of which the beatniks are telling, albeit of a low level and extreme, representatives.

5. To come to our conclusion, art has, or can have, still a fifth function: *in discussing art we talk about the deepest and most important questions of human life, we talk about our life and world view and all that is directly connected with it.* Today that is perhaps clearer than ever before. Politics, theology and philosophy no longer determine as strongly as they used to the battlefield of the struggle for cultural power – which may help to explain the decline in interest in political questions (to limit ourselves to this terrain), together with the fact that politics tend to become strongly absorbed by technical policy matters.

We can understand those who say that a great deal of modern art is ugly and poor. We must not in the first place set out to convince them of the contrary but rather make clear to them the respect in which this art is important, originating as it does from spiritual sources and as such loaded with meaning: very often we will then discover that people's negative attitude arises from their having more insight into this art than they are aware of themselves, and that their refusal to put a positive value on this art derives from convictions diametrically opposed to the ones which modern art expresses.

Many people have something of an inferiority complex in the face of modern art – convinced they will never understand it, they do not see what moves these artists. They often try to compensate by affecting some sort of snobbism. However, it would be better to accept the spiritual and cultural struggle: everyone must take a stand, deciding what he or she finds beautiful and valuable or not, and having the courage to say so and to formulate and advance one's reasons for that.

Our attitude towards present-day art, for or against certain artistic expressions, helps determine the taste and conviction of the coming generation. If today only modernistic art would truly be valuable and culturally significant, then that would mean the battle is already lost by those who are not modern in that sense of the word, and that the revolution is already a fact. But if we are not modern and not borne in our own lives by such a life and world view, then let us take a stand and support what we do regard as positive and meaningful and fight to have it recognized – only of course if genuine artistic qualities are present. In this way we are of great help to our times.

Let us be frank. We must not abandon the spiritual struggle of our day saying that we do not understand modern art or that it is nothing but commercialism and charlatanism (in the manner of Prange's little book about the god Hai Hai). We must also not simply accept modern art as something that is inevitable simply because it is contemporary. Certainly it is contemporary, but it is not the only contemporary reality. Hence each of us must very consciously take a stand.

That seems to me to be the most important function in a cultural sense of art in our times: to instigate discussions whereby people will fight for a valuable art that reflects their own life and world view. This struggle constitutes one of the most important, perhaps the most important, frontlines in the spiritual arena. This is true for everyone, both those who stand behind modern art and those who do not. Those who support it must not try to intimidate others by ridiculing them as if they are not 'up to date' but must try rather to convince them of the positive qualities, not only in an artistic respect but also in a broader human sense.

A brief excursus may serve to make this matter clear. During many a guided tour past modern paintings one hears it said that people did not understand van Gogh in his time. The implication is that we should be careful not to embarrass ourselves by declining to accept these modern works of art positively, lest posterity judge us as we now judge van Gogh's contemporaries. Yet that is a dangerous position. At that time too people accepted some sorts of art and rejected others – perhaps our averse judgment of the work of Gustave Moreau, for example, is based on the standpoint taken by the same chap who disesteemed van Gogh. However that may be, we must not let our attitude be determined by the supposed judgment of a generation as yet unborn. We must, as I said, fight our fight honestly. If all of us simply nod our heads, it is likely that a future generation will judge us as the tour guide suggested. Yet if we adopt another, independently attained standpoint, it is possible that a future generation will praise us. Yet this should not be our motive – we carry on our struggle today, with an eye to the future, not to be honoured by the future but to serve it.

I do not believe I stand alone in asserting what I have just said and will close with a citation from an article in the *Journal of Aesthetics and Art Criticism*,[406] in which Henry David Aiken writes:

> Although it is next to impossible to say this in our times without fear to be misunderstood, it still remains true that art is neither politics nor morals, and that the lover of art has his own distinctive aesthetic obligations. Tolerance is essentially a moral, not a principle of taste. It demands that we respect the tastes of others; but it has no aesthetic corollary which requires that we make those tastes our own. Attention to the object, loyalty to one's own perceptions and emotions, and a willingness to enlarge one's experience for the sake of a richer, a more intense delight are, I submit, the only obligations to art itself which can be reasonably expected of any man.

• Form and content of modern art[407]

We saw in our previous article[408] that in the nineteenth century the theme as we are familiar with it in old art became ever less meaningful for an important group of artists until in fact only the motif was 'nameable': landscape, outdoor company, nude – instead of Bathsheba, Diana, etc. When they copied old paintings they often took just a detail, whereby the real thematic content was set more or less aside. We think here for example of van Gogh's copy of Rembrandt's *Resurrection of Lazarus* where we see only Lazarus and one of the subsidiary figures. Yet then, so we argued, the real content of the work of art is no longer found in the motif but rather in the way in which the motif is realized. Through the composition and the style a commentary is as it were given on the subject. This was already the case with the Impressionists but also with Cézanne, van Gogh and Gauguin. We could also mention Seurat, who painted different kinds of scenes rather than specific themes in the old sense, putting a distinctive meaning into them through his very tight classical composition and the play of light attained through his pointillist way of working.

In fact not very much changes in the twentieth century in this respect. In modern art too one seldom finds the representation of a theme. There is often a motif: landscape, still life, figure, fighting people, a couple, animal, etc. But it often has less significance than it did with the people of the late nineteenth century. It provides merely the occasion or at most the point of departure for the artistic act. The content of the work is expressed through the composition and/or style. Sometimes one can hardly speak of style in the way we generally use the term, namely, as a strictly personal handwriting or manner of working, and the content is rather contained in the composition. We see this to an extreme degree in Mondrian. With him there is no theme at all and no longer a motif either. The work of art is abstract or rather non-figurative and has as such indeed nothing to say. Whatever there is of content and meaning – and Mondrian speaks of depicting the absolute, which is no mean pretension – is given in the composition, in the way in which the few pictorial elements (black lines, primary colours red, blue, yellow, white and black) are arranged.

With another school, that of the Expressionists, the content of the work of art lies primarily in the style, in the strictly personal, emotional expression, through the way in which the means of expression are employed. With the German predecessors (for whom the term Expressionism became established) there is still usually a motif as the starting point. Yet very soon we see Kandinsky concentrate the complete content of the work of art in the style, the application of colour and line, while every nameable object (horse, tree, human form) is consciously avoided.

Different, but in this respect still very affinitive, is the work of Karel Appel. Also with him we very clearly have an explosive discharge of emotion that invests the style, the artistic script, with power and meaning and in this way forms the content of the work of art, while the motif is either entirely absent or else secondary.

Let us now review the entire development as we have explained it in this series of articles.[409] We began with medieval art and undertook to show that the proper content of the medieval works of art lay in the theme, even if it (a Bible story, for example) could be given a particular accent through the application of a particular formula, i.e. a traditional composition scheme. Theme and the particular composition thus determined the content of the work, independent of its stylistic realization, independent even in a certain sense of the artistic quality – although we would not want to suggest that the medievals were insensitive to the latter. In the seventeenth century the proper meaning of the work of art, the content, came to rest in the motif, a human given that determined the choice of the theme and in connection with which various formulas could be used. Also in this period the viewers of art said little about style, although they certainly knew something about differences of style. In the nineteenth century the emphasis shifted again, since the theme in fact vanished and the motif was no longer a bearer of meaning, although it did continue to play a role in the work of art. The real content came to lie in the style and composition. In the twentieth century the motif becomes even less significant and is not much more than an occasion for the work of art. In non-figurative art it vanishes altogether.

Reviewing the whole, we notice that far-reaching changes occurred. Two conclusions must be drawn from this – and for us this is the starting point of our investigations. In the first place we must conclude that it is not very meaningful to seek a generally valid answer to the question of what makes for meaning in a work of art, whether it is the form or the content or a combination of these two. Aesthetics has often addressed this problem, and the fact that no clear answer has emerged is undoubtedly traceable to the fact that the form–content relation (to use the old terminology, where today we would speak of style or composition in relation to theme) differs in the different periods. In the second place, we must conclude that in interpreting old works of art we must be very careful. Often one finds observed in reflections on art that although the artist chose this or that theme, the distinctive meaning of the artwork naturally must be sought in its stylistic-artistic realization. Well, that 'naturally' is a very dangerous word in this connection since there is nothing 'natural' here, while that word only means that in fact people are approaching the old art anachronistically from a twentieth-century standpoint. In this way often enough our insight into old art is obscured or the meaning of a particular work of art is even falsified – not purposely, mind you, but not for that reason any less incorrectly. There are examples enough, so those familiarizing themselves with reflections on art should be on guard.

In connection with the above, one more remark is in order. Namely, these considerations shed some light on why in various books about old art – I have in mind for example the publications of Skira – one finds depicted virtually exclusively just details of paintings, etc. Through this method of illustrating people modernize the work in question in a certain sense, by ignoring the theme so that only the motif is retained, or if people choose only small details, by allowing virtually exclusively the style to speak. This way of working too may be called a falsification of the work of art, which in this way is robbed of its proper meaning.

• Art or not art?[410]

A while ago I received a number of questions in response to what I had said in a lecture about modern art. I have left them unanswered far too long. Apologies. I will try to answer them now, without mentioning the names of the questioners, because I believe that many share these questions.

Is modern art really art and how are we to judge it? people ask me. First, what do people mean when they say 'modern art'? There is namely an art that does use a language of new forms, to be sure, different from before, but that wants to say very positive things and, in the context of our times, evinces a positive attitude towards our fellow humans and seeks to serve beauty. As an example I showed some of Rouault's work. There are some who look askance even at that – which is strange since via advertising and the like we come into contact with it every day and have no trouble with it. Indeed, precisely in modern industrial products, cars, washing machines, irons and much more there is a great deal of beauty to be discovered, a great deal of careful formation going on. For that we should be really grateful. Many people and talented artists are engaged in that. And in modern typography, in poster art for example, there are many things of beauty to be discovered. And if people look for it and open themselves to it, also in the so-called 'great' art.

That has to be said. Otherwise the story would be unjustifiably negative. Yet we know that is not what the question is really about, which focuses on the modern art of Picasso (in whose work, by the way, one can discover a great deal of beauty of the sort discussed above, beside the other sort), Bacon, Dubuffet, Pop Art, Op Art and so much more. Such art people do not find beautiful, sometimes rightly so, and then comes the question: Are we seeing it properly? Is it perhaps beautiful but we only fail to understand it? And if it is not beautiful or edifying, then why should we still have to call it art? In short, how are we to distinguish between what is valuable and what is not, and what are we to do with it?

Are there no charlatans, no sycophants who just go along in order to make a name? Are there no fiddlers and fumblers who simply cannot do any better? Of course there are. But that is nothing new. That has been so in every period. And that is really not so very difficult to distinguish, although we can sometimes be mistaken – to err is human. Yet obviously one who never went deeply into modern art cannot expect to be able to discern that directly. Art does require some effort – and it is well worth it! Every art that is of real importance, Michelangelo, Rembrandt or take your pick, does not 'yield' immediately but requires intensive consideration. Consideration that also pays off. Just as it is worth the effort to read one of Paul's Epistles slowly. If you dash through it you will certainly miss what is essential. Or you will misread it.

We may safely assume that the important modern painters are gifted, very able people who have often been willing to sacrifice their goods and blood – often literally suffering poverty – in order to make just that type of work. Because they could not do otherwise. Because they had seen certain problems in a very deep way. Of Bacon we know that he sometimes wept upon looking at one of his own works. Of Willem de Kooning we know that he is sometimes desperate because even when he wants to make something beautiful, something monstrous appears. For them this is simply the truth, unavoidably so – if they were to do things differently they would be liars. In short, the modern artists are often not happy with their work either. Yet even so, it is their message and they believe we should know it as well, and that we should not walk on oblivious to the real problems.

What can account for these problems? Not the artist as an individual who, as a sort of super sadist, is devoted to making all things ugly. Rather, it is the profound crisis of our times. A spiritual crisis. Everything has been, as it were, jolted from its foundations. It is the fruit of a development that has been under way now for almost two centuries, about which Groen van Prinsterer wrote already more than a century ago in his *Unbelief and Revolution*. People threw God out, and in doing so lost contact in the positive sense with the creation, with the good and the beautiful. Do you want to understand what is going on in our day? Read Romans 1 thoughtfully. Exactly in the light of modern art we can understand very deeply the truth of that chapter, the misery in which people have landed up because they will not acknowledge God. Modern people know that all this brings death with it – and death grins at us in ever so many ways from this modern art. Precisely because it is not just a few rare characters who act like that but because they are only rendering visible what is going on widely in our times, precisely for that reason we need to occupy ourselves with this art. For our task is on the one hand to keep ourselves from evil and on the other to help our fellow humans in distress. If as Christians we still want to mean something to the world in these times and make a positive contribution to the culture around us, then we must answer some profound and very serious questions. Questions with which this modern art confronts us. (That applies naturally just as much to literature and drama or film, but we will restrict ourselves here to visual art.)

One example. There is a true story about Picasso that goes like this: he had made a beautiful drawing, incredibly beautiful, and when it was finished he tore it up. When asked why he did that, he replied that something so beautiful could not exist in reality. Our world is not that beautiful. Think about it. Think about it in the light of the following too. Often when you ask modern people why nothing can be beautiful, why that could not be possible, they say: 'Ah, that's not on, just think of Vietnam, think of the misery in the world, hunger, sorrow, pain, trouble.' We need to be able to answer this before we can ask them for something beautiful. Can we then say that precisely because God too could not look upon this sorrow he sent Christ his Son to the world? The more we look at modern art, the more the central questions of the gospel are at stake.

But modern artists are not just people having 'spiritual' problems. No, they are engaged with the real problems of the present time – fruit of the intellectual revolution that began in the eighteenth century. Thus their work may often be understood as a desperate attempt to regain true humanity in a technocratic culture that has made humans into little cogs in the societal machine. In a world in which only atoms are genuine and real and all the rest is but a beautiful but incorrect dream. In particular, so they will say, it turns out to be untenable that there is a God who cares about this world. There are others who can only tell you, in deep sorrow, what has become of humanity – 'beauty has burnt her face' – and our view of human beings has been disfigured.

There is in modern art much raucous and impassioned protest, protest against a rotten world that dehumanizes humanity. Protest against the bourgeois way of life where people live comfortably but exert themselves only for social security, for money and for leisure time and suppose that they can live on undisturbed amidst the ruins of our Western culture. Live for status and tranquility. Yet it is a life without a basis, empty and hollow, in which morality degenerates into false moralizing. Against it rise the protests of the modern artists and, under their influence, of the Provos [a Dutch version of 1960s student revolt]. Modern art is by no means a marginal phenomenon but has rather a profound influence. Do we really think that it would be possible to violate and mock all values and norms and reality without that having its effect in the lives of thousands?

Indeed, modern art is a central phenomenon of our times: one can call it almost without exaggeration the religion of our times. Artists are elevated to cultural prophets who must reveal the meaning and substance of our world. Well now, to accomplish that they smash all apparent values and show human misery for what it is – yet they offer no new values in return nor do they indicate a way to be lifted out of the suffering. And how could they, inasmuch as they either do not know the Gospel or refuse to accept it. Because for our fellow humans God is really dead. For that reason the stench of his corpse hangs over Europe, Nietzsche wrote already a century ago! Should we not see that here we have to do with judgment, should we not prepare ourselves like Jeremiah to cry 'Woe unto you!' and call upon people to be converted? If we dismiss it all as nothing, that means we have nothing to answer in return. So we see that modern art has everything to do with us.

Consider Baruch in Jeremiah 45! What we can do, apart from witnessing, is to support and help those forces which are still around in our day and which are positive. In particular we have in mind here Christian artists who struggle to show something of the joy and peace that the gospel brings as a full reality of life, without however closing their eyes to the profound distress of our times. Often they work in isolation and we just let them muddle on. Many lose their faith, more or less cast out by the community of the church. Many get stuck and do not know how to make anything meaningful any more. The spiritual need amongst them is great, to say nothing about the material need.

An additional difficult point in all this is that we – the orthodox Christian community – have neglected art for many, many years. We thought it was a superfluous luxury. Do not misunderstand me: we do not need to complain that the indigent skipper or farmer who contributed his last dime to support the Free University did nothing for culture and art, but we do object to the fact that he and his pastor forbid one of his sons who had great talent to become an artist. If more Christians had become artists and if the community had supported their work, then perhaps today's art would have been different. And through that work, our world? To make a play on words: modern art is unsalted art that tells the truth in an unsalted way, because we were not the salt that salts. Really, art is no luxury. It is rather an assignment from God.

Are we doing something about it? There are some people working at it. They are few in number and have restricted means. We are thinking of the CCS, the Christian Cultural Study Centre[411] that seeks to address these matters, arouse insight and interest, bring artists out of their isolation, take care of young artists – there are many whose interest tilts towards art, which is encouraging. The CCS dreams of a training institute of our own where we want to wrestle with these sorts of problems and try to offer a positive answer in meaningful and beautiful art that is at the same time really contemporary.

I know that I have not answered all the questions. I just hope that I have been able to show you how difficult all this is, not because it is so difficult to understand but because we live in a world that is in difficulty, where the deepest and loftiest values are at stake. Cheap and easy answers are therefore no answers. Yet I hope too that you have understood that we Christians for the sake of our lives and also for the sake of the lives (in the deepest sense) of the following generation must really apply ourselves to all this. If not with visual art then with theatre, or whatever other artform. If we want to witness in our times then we must show that the biblical principle of life may indeed awaken creative forces. By only crying woe and lamentation we remain permanently behind the times and of no help to anyone.

Modern Art and Gnosticism

• Shestov[412]

We have spoken more than once about modern irrationalism. One of the most characteristic exponents of this school is certainly Leo Shestov, a Russian emigrant whose work has attracted considerable attention and who is regarded in a certain sense as one of the pilots of the twentieth century – as may be clear from the fact that people have found his work worth presenting to the public in Dutch translation in the form of an anthology entitled *Uren met Sjestow* [hours with Shestov].[413] It can be useful to read such books. It is one thing to read an organized exposition of the basic, central ideas of scholars – such as we endeavoured to present in an earlier article about philosophy[414] – and quite something else to read their own writings. For in that way, as apprehended from the mouth of the philosophers themselves, not structured abstractly according to the main ideas but expressed by full, thinking personalities replete with their manifold primary and secondary notions, it all sounds quite different. One then is better able to understand what moves these people and, beyond that, why they are read and became influential. One then comes to see how they are often able to hit the nail on the head in their thinking, how they can be brilliant, captivating and, for readers not equipped with the spiritual armour of God's word, compelling. One then soon understands that these people are not simply spouting forth nonsense – although it may seem so when we read only abstract discussions of their works – but that they are giving utterance to ideas and motives that well up from the depths of the human heart.

Beerling wrote an outstanding introduction to the selected fragments from Shestov in which he lets us see that:

> The only principle he respects is that there are no principles, the only norm he upholds is that of normlessness. Genuine philosophizing as he conceives it leads to the complete isolation of the individual. History, culture and politics provide no counterweight and are totally indifferent.[415]

For anyone who has devoted some attention to gnosticism by reading, for example, that lovely little book by Tunderman,[416] this has a familiar ring to it. And precisely because these notions are presented to us here in modern dress they are the more dangerous but at the same time the more understandable. Here now we sense the deep conviction that underlies them. For why does gnosticism disesteem principles and norms? Because 'Shestov fears nothing so much as the power that knowledge and the general principles inherent in it acquire over people.' A god that would be bound or that would bind himself to such rules is therefore a horror to him. 'Shestov's God is no rule but a quirk, a metaphysical incalculable, an absurdity.'[417] Just as William of Ockham once asserted that God is unpredictable and unfaithful and absolutely arbitrary.[418]

The fear to which we just alluded – which rendered it necessary to declare God a quirk – is powered by the urge to be completely free and unattached: 'the arbitrariness and unassailability of an individual standpoint'[419] is everything to him. Thus he also says that 'man himself must become God,' whereby he means to assert that the absolute lies in humanity itself, in the human free ego unattached to anything whatsoever, and that the campaign people wage to attain that absolute or to realize that freedom 'traverses abysses that constantly threaten to swallow up this absolute.'[420] These abysses are actually formed by nothing other than created reality itself, which in this way has become to him something strange and hostile since it threatens the autonomous I-ness that is intent upon installing itself where it does not belong and where it cannot be.

This irrationality is fed by the will, the deep motive in his heart to accept no ties to anything whatsoever, to be entirely free and self-determining. Hence the consequence to that is – and here we cite Shestov himself, from the foreword to one of his works:

> No guiding ideas, thus also no logical structure: the work crawls with inner contradictions, but that is exactly what I wanted ... to be a stranger, yes, the apotheosis of being a stranger.[421]

From his own mouth we hear once again how estranged Shestov is from God's creation – for the way in which he wants to be a stranger is quite different from that of the believer. A believer is no stranger to this earth, just a stranger amidst an apostate generation that will rule it until the Last Day when justice is restored! In Shestov however one is a stranger because one aspires to be tied to nothing:

> It is not by coincidence ... that they – the Shestovs – seek chaos and arbitrariness on our earth where science has discovered so much strict harmony and so much order; order and harmony suffocate them and they lose their breath in the atmosphere of nature and law ... They have reached some sort of truce with 'cause and effect', since external necessity forced them to do so. Yet if it were up to them they would long ago have torn mountains from their places and made rivers flow upstream ... It is only in the field of moral relationships, where their freedom is unrestricted apart from the abstract and illusory prescriptions of the moralists, that they have been allowed to celebrate their victory.[422]

Thus we land up here at what Tunderman called 'libertine gnosticism'.[423]

We could point out still more gnostic ideas and show that such notions that are at times considered antiquated are as alive as springtime, not because the old systems have such a resilient life but because they are founded upon a deep impulse of apostate humankind: to be free and self-determining, separate from God and from his creation, which people even come to detest. Yet we want to bring out still another consequence. Tunderman describes how on the grounds that everything 'lower' lacks meaning and is merely external, Sebastian Franck regards all 'desire-to-be-right' [the desire to win an argument and have others agree with one] as foolishness and as proof that people have not yet discovered true spirituality.[424] We find echoes of that in Shestov when he writes:

> It was not enough for man to be in possession of the truth. He wanted something else that seemed 'better' to him, namely, that his truth would be a truth for all. To be able to claim this he created the fiction that he did not make this truth himself but received it, signed, sealed and delivered, as it were, and then not from a being such as he is himself, a living and thus frail, changeable and whimsical being but from the hands of a being that neither knows nor desires change because it desires nothing at all and cares neither for itself nor anything else, that he acquired it through the mediation of that principle which teaches us that the sum of the angles of a triangle is equal to two right angles. But if the truth has such a remarkable and fully soulless being as its source, then human virtue comes down entirely to self-denial.[425]

In this citation we see how deep the foundations of modern scepticism can be. Here it is deemed senseless to struggle for the truth, and every truth is regarded as a 'truth-for-oneself' that is entirely subjective and valuable as such. This citation also teaches us to see that the rejection of all principles and [its resultant] opportunism can be very deeply founded indeed and have nothing to do in themselves with a lack of character or weakness.[426]

Is all this philosophy ultimately only disbanding, deceitful and absurd? No, there is one thing we can learn from this irrationalist, namely the failure of rationalism. Seldom has anyone perceived so keenly or laid bare so candidly the deepest roots of rationalism. He can teach us how disrespectful rationalism is when it absolutizes the laws God created and separates them from his act of creation, yes deifies them. Thus we read for example that a rationalist like Spinoza taught that the world consists of an infinitely great number of parts 'that move according to eternal laws having neither the possibility nor the right to alter in the slightest the order instituted apart from and in no wise for them. And God is in this respect no different in any way from people.'[427] Now, that is keenly perceived indeed, as is likewise the fact that human reason – 'that is the agency that definitively solves mathematical problems and teaches people to distinguish truth from falsehood in mathematics'[428] – enthrones itself and arrogantly asserts the right to be the judge of everything. Thus he writes – and nowhere, not even among believing thinkers, will one find it so sharply formulated:

That same Reason that presides over triangles and perpendiculars and that therefore supposes it has sovereign rights to distinguish truth from lies, that Reason that seeks not the best but the true philosophy, this Reason declares with innate self-assurance and in a tone brooking no contradiction that such a God – the God of the Bible – is not the most perfect of all beings and not even a perfect being and thus can be no God.[429]

And in this we can learn a tremendous amount from a man like Shestov, because his sworn enemy, rationalism, is our enemy too, an enemy of whose existence in our own ranks we are at times too little aware and from which we suffer all too often ourselves in the form of scholastic theology and in the form of a Christian 'science ideal' that teaches that a believing science must show the way and reveal the norms.

I would like to provide an example of this. In my paper published last year in *De Reformatie* I wrote that the Lord does not yet destroy his enemies but that he will do that in his own time.[430] Someone felt compelled to raise some objections against this: 'I find the word "destroy" unhappily chosen here. Destroy in the sense of "make an end to their existence" the Lord would never do.'[431] Now, at first glance that might sound right. It is consistently argued from the notion that there will be eternal punishment. However, that we may not reason in this way is clear from the fact that anyone who takes the trouble to look the matter up in a concordance finds that the term is used scores of times in precisely this sense in the Holy Scriptures, from Genesis 6:7 ['I will wipe mankind, whom I have created, from the face of the earth'] to Zechariah 12:9 ['I will set out to destroy all the nations that attack Jerusalem']. So we see that here again, undoubtedly unintentionally, how our ideas are placed above Scripture and our arguments prevail against God's word.[432]

But to return to Shestov. He may be in revolt against rationalism, he may despise, detest and disparage it, but basically it is maintained. It is consigned to a middle sphere, that of 'rationally comprehensible reality' where the 'iron laws of logic obtain'[433] – and although he means to transcend and squirm free of it in the name of his exquisitely individual freedom, still at bottom the lie of rationalism is not discovered and not genuinely opposed. We already saw that Shestov rebelled against reality – that he felt himself a stranger in it – and indeed he did so because he equated this reality with the artificial rationalistic order that people have made of it. He failed to see that the rationalists impoverish and level the wealth and fullness of God's creation through their general schemes and generally valid lines of argumentation. He failed to see that in rationalism it is humankind who in their science ascend the throne and play the lawgiver. That is also clear from his allusion to Tertullian's renowned pronouncement: 'The Son of God was crucified: I am not ashamed – because it is shameful. The Son of God died: it is credible – because it is preposterous. He was buried, and rose again: it is certain –

because it is impossible.'[434] With these statements Tertullian undertook to defend scriptural truths against Hellenistic science. In this way Tertullian had upheld them in the face of science, but not without first having bowed to science at another point in order to judge Scripture according to its wisdom. For there is much in Scripture that exceeds human insight and wisdom – but there is nothing preposterous in God's word and works (Job 1:22). There is much that is humanly impossible, but what is humanly impossible is possible for God. We must not first test God's word against worldly wisdom and norms in order thereafter to maintain it 'in spite of that'. No, the wisdom the Scriptures offer is not foolishness and we must listen to it believingly and bow before it.

Finally, Shestov may despise human reason but in the meantime he considers himself wise enough to subject the Scriptures to his judgment and to reject them. In the process he approvingly invokes his enemy Spinoza's assertion that the Bible contains a great deal of morality but that people will have to seek the truth elsewhere.[435] Thus we discover that in the end Shestov is just as arrogant and just as arbitrary as his rationalist opponents.

• Modern art and gnosticism: an open letter to Prof. Dr Jan Aler[436]

Dear Jan Aler,

When I was considering what topic would be suitable to write in this Festschrift, I received your excellent article, *Krise der Kunst – Kunst der Krise*,[437] as usual very well built up and superbly formulated, which set me thinking. I recognized some similarities with my own thinking,[438] and a question came to mind: Are we right? Indeed, with differences in emphasis and aims many have expressed comparable ideas on modern art and its crisis – a considerable literature can be amassed on this point, starting quite early [a list of titles for further reading appear in the endnotes[439]] and I should like to give one quotation just to make clear what we are really discussing. It is from Alfred Neumeyer in his book *The Search for Meaning in Modern Art*:[440]

> We must bear with and endure the monstrous horrors that attack us, for they mirror the specific dehumanization which has taken place in the twentieth century through technology, war and political actions. These bizarre, grotesque and monstrous elements also function as aesthetic play, as they have always done, except that, hitherto, the bizarre and the monstrous occupied only a subordinate place within a universal order that was based on religious or secular ethics.

Neumeyer, you and I and many others have written on modern art in this way, and have related it to the developments in thinking since the Enlightenment, the rise of technology, modern naturalistic science, and in general to people's changed understanding of their own place in the total universe.[441] But it has a specific danger, which is that we look at this development as inevitable, and something that, being historical, cannot be discussed. This, of course, would mean that we unwillingly and almost imperceptibly have accepted a naturalistic way of thinking about historic causality; this is the way the sciences think, a way of thinking, as we have shown, that is one of the factors that has brought humanity to their difficult and despairing dilemma. As a result we do not say but in fact take it for granted that people are completely moulded by historic circumstances and causalities, in short, that they are slaves of their historic situation.

This happens easily, because in the humanities a kind of historic thinking has reigned for a long time which assigns people a position in history that is almost preordained, and not very far from predetermined. I am thinking of the Hegelian approach which, through the influence of Burckhardt, has shaped much art-historical thinking – as Gombrich has analysed it – in such a deep, revealing way.[442] Often without explicit realization or argued acceptance the thinking of many scholars is still tinged with this kind of reasoning. And if we are not careful our studies often reinforce this deterministic understanding of history and of humankind's place in it. It is easy to make the mistake, when we go into the study of a certain aspect of history and its inherent development, of finding that the factual history with its own inherent logic shows that what happened was inevitable. History, being in the past, has become unchangeable and does show a historic logic: but this does not mean that at every moment responsible people did not also make real choices.[443] These free choices themselves worked into the whole fabric of historic cause and effect and produced the logic of the development as perceived *post factum*.

It is true that many no longer accept this type of absolutist thinking inherent in the Hegelian approach. Yes this does not mean that human free choice has been given a more appropriate place. As Hegelian history has been discarded for historicism *(Historismus)*, coming out of the school of Dilthey, history has become less pre-ordained and thinking more relativistic, yet in spite of this people are still caught in their own period with its own laws and ideas. Through the Viennese school of art history, and especially through the work of Dvorak – who became famous for his *Kunstgeschichte als Geistesgeschichte* – this new approach to history has had a great impact on art-historical studies.[444] This is especially important when we deal with modern art, as much modem art theory has fused the historicist's notions with the old concept of the artist as a prophet, leading to the modern idea that an artist has to be –

or rather, *is* – the interpreter of his or her own age.[445] This brings us back to our starting point: the question of whether artists are really tied so closely to their own period and must inevitably be exponents of their age in relationship to spiritual problems inherited from the past.

Of course, nobody can escape one's own historic time, and people's thoughts and actions have to be in relation to their historic situation if it is to be fruitful and relevant. But the great point is that people can act in freedom, and that they are creative in their reaction. In defining their answers they give form and shape to the situation, which is changed through it: the difference between physical causality and historic causality being exactly the fact that in the latter, apart from objective causes – which are themselves the results of chains of causality completely outside the realm of human historic causes, e.g. a flood or a drought – people have to choose in freedom which way to go.[446]

I do not want to blame you, my dear friend, for deliberately saying that modern people have come into their crisis because there was no way to avoid that crisis. If I did blame you, I would have to blame myself just as much. I only want to point out that our analysis of the course of history *post factum* tends to make clear the inherent historic logic that suggests an inevitability, even if we do not intend this.

But if we stress this point, the question forces itself on us: What really is modern art, and what is its relation to the historic situation as it has come about from the past thoughts and actions of people? Is modern art really *the* art of the twentieth century? If we say 'yes', we have pronounced a verdict against anybody who is not modern. If we say 'no', we can try to ask ourselves what modern art really is and what its position really is in our times.

We must be aware of the danger inherent in the suggestion that modern art is *the* art of the twentieth century,[447] and the danger that we, even if we are critical of its aims and its achievements, may actually reinforce this movement by stressing its inevitability, a movement that people simply have to accept if they do not want to be outsiders or people fighting for past values or standing as strangers in their own period. I really feel that art criticism and art history has actually helped the modern movement enormously, sometimes deliberately, sometimes unwillingly. If this is so, then the paradox would be true that we are talking about the modern movement as being inevitable just because we ourselves have helped it to become so by reinforcing its impact and cultural force.

If we ask ourselves what really is the art of our own times, it would not be easy to give an answer. We have to discern different streams, side by side, while the relationship between them is often hard to formulate and in some cases does not exist at all. I should like to point to the popular arts in which we have to include kitsch, but which at times in some entertainment films, such as those made by Walt Disney, can reach good quality. We could also mention as a typical phenomenon of our times that the arts from the past are alive for our estimation and interest, for example music from the seventeenth and eighteenth centuries, Shakespeare and, of course, visual arts from our European and even non-European past. We can call this 'necro' art.[448]

Next I should like to point to a wide stream of art that I want to distinguish from modern art proper and which I, for lack of a better name, call 'twentieth-century art'. I mean the broad stream of art, developing out of Impressionism and Post-Impressionism, that often shows expressionistic tendencies and as a whole can be defined by two facts: first, its content, which is human, realistic in the sense that its subject matter is taken from normal reality,[449] while second, stylistically speaking, there is a break with nineteenth-century naturalism and a new understanding emerges that art is a kind of language that works with lines and colours on the surface. To give some examples, we think of Matisse, the school of Paris between the two world wars, of Kokoschka, Rouault and Germans like Pechstein, Schmidt-Rottluff and other lesser artists, and in England artists like Spencer and Buckland Wright. So, generally speaking, this movement shows a renewal of stylistic means but does not search for as deep a break with the European tradition as modern art does. The public in general shows appreciation for, and has no difficulties in understanding, this new art. In fact, these artists have had a great influence on the style and language of posters and, to a certain extent, on popular art.

Modern art is in a different stream. To give some examples we can name Picasso, the Cubists, the artists from De Stijl, from Bauhaus, Neue Sachlichkeit and the Surrealists. This is the kind of art that has been discussed by Kandinsky in his *Über die Formfrage*[450] which points forward to great abstraction and extreme naturalism as the two possibilities for twentieth-century art.

Now modern art, on closer inspection, does show different tendencies; but we want to focus our attention on the fact that modern art speaks of the absurd, the irrational, of alienation and estrangement from reality. We can see these aspects in Picasso's Cubism, the Dada movement and the Surrealists as well as in many of the abstract or non-figurative artists. Yet we must keep open the possibility that what we are going to say does not apply to some groups or individual artists. But such detail would go beyond the scope of this letter.

I am happy to see that we seem in close agreement on this point. You refer in your lecture to the fact that this modern art is a movement, a kind of a sect – almost aside from the public – the art of a group of artists, museum people and art critics, in short, rather a subculture than twentieth-century culture as such. For precisely this reason we must hesitate to say that modern art *is* twentieth-century art *per se*. We should not be blinded by the fact that this stream is as strong as it is because of official support and the one-sided attention of art critics and art historians.

No doubt, my dear Aler, this modern movement I am speaking about is the same art you referred to in your lecture mentioned at the beginning – quite naturally you dealt mainly with literature, as I do with the visual arts, but I imagine you agree that for our present purposes this does not make a significant difference; just as the other twentieth-century art movements we mentioned above can also be found in literature and music as well as in the visual arts.

The problem is now to try to find the underlying spiritual meaning of this modern art. In this, I feel, I remain within the scope of your approach to art. If we were at great variance on this point this letter would not have been written.

You showed in your lecture that this modern art has deep roots in the past, going back at least to the time of Romanticism.[451] You pointed to Schopenhauer, Runge, Lautréamont-Ducasse (maybe you should first have mentioned de Sade), Jarry, while you cite in our century Kafka, Sartre, Camus, Godard, Lucebert, and of course also Marcel Duchamp, Tristan Tzara and André Breton.

In passing you use the words *Nihilismus, mythisch-gnostisch, Seinsverlassenheit, Seinsvergessenheit.* Since I am thinking in this same direction I was really struck by your use of them.[452] And I felt strengthened to go on investigating in this direction.

I feel that the word gnostic can be used as a key word. I think the basic study of Hans Jonas[453] on gnosticism, the powerful movement at the beginning of our era, can be of help. Jonas makes clear that the basic teaching of gnosticism is a dualism between god and the world, in which the gnostic god is completely and absolutely otherworldly, having no connection with this world, not even being its creator. The cosmos is made by lower demons, and in its centre is the earth, the deep dungeon where people are trapped by Fate. Humankind, being in some way related to god, are complete strangers to this world, and the only sensible thing is to look towards their redemption, their liberation from it. The way to reach this goal is through *gnosis,* knowledge. This thinking is defined by the opposition between the inevitability of people's being prisoners in this world and their freedom, their possibility to deliver themselves in one way or another.

It might be interesting to follow the influence of gnosticism in history, to trace its doctrines in medieval thought, in mysticism, in the Anabaptists, in Sebastian Franck[454] and through de Sade and so on into the nineteenth century and up to the present time when some of its doctrines can be found in the existentialists. We can leave open the problem whether there is a direct or indirect influence, or whether basic human questions lead to similar formulations.

Jonas stresses particularly the similarities between the existentialist thought of Heidegger and the gnostics. Yet he also shows great differences, in a chapter called 'Gnosticism, existentialism and nihilism':

in ancient gnosticism people were thrown (*geworfen*) into an alien, anti-god and therefore anti-human nature; but modern people, by contrast, are thrown into a completely indifferent nature, altogether the result of chance, without any meaning and without any possibility to deliver themselves or to be delivered or redeemed. As there are no gods anymore and human being is a product, through evolution, of nature itself, people are caught in nature. This nature is 'lower' than even the most pessimistic ancient gnostic believed and completely without any transcendence. There is some truth in the words of C.S. Lewis:

> At the outset, the universe appears packed with will, intelligence, life and positive qualities ... Man himself is akin to the gods. The advance of knowledge gradually empties this rich and genial universe: first of its gods, then of its colours, smells, sounds and tastes, finally of solidity itself as solidity was originally imagined. As these items are taken from the world, they are transferred to the subjective side of the account: classified as our sensations, thoughts, images or emotions. The Subject becomes gorged, inflated, at the expense of the Object. But the matter does not end there. The same method which has emptied the world now proceeds to empty ourselves ... We, who have personified all other things, turn out to be ourselves mere personifications ... And thus we arrive at a result uncommonly like zero.[455]

It can be rewarding to go rather deeper into the early history of modern thought as exemplified in modern art, and see what the nineteenth century shows us. Of course, this cannot be an exhaustive study, but rather a suggestive selection of a few quotations.

First we note from Carlyle, in his *Sartor Resartus* (1838): 'To me the universe was all void of Life, of Purpose, of Volition, even of Hostility: it was one huge, dead, immeasurable Steam-engine, rolling on, in its dead indifference, to grind me limb for limb.'[456] I prefer not to quote Nietzsche, with whom you are so conversant,[457] but I found a passage that is revealing and in our context quite interesting from G. Keller, in his *Der grüne Heinrich*. It deals with painting 'from which all that is concrete has been removed'. Such painting proves

> how logic and art proper first celebrate their most beautiful victory in unreality, in nothingness give birth to passions and gloom and conquer them. God created the world from nothing; it is a morbid abscess of nothingness, an expulsion of God from himself. The beautiful, the poetic lies in this, that from this material ulcer we allow ourselves to be absorbed again into nothingness.[458]

The shortest condensation of the whole biblical position – the gospel – could be said to be that God created the world and is interested in it; if God however is a complete stranger or probably non-existent, we come near to a gnostic position, as put into words by A.E. Housman: 'I, a stranger and afraid, in a world I never made.' Paul Klee's words in his diary are also interesting in this respect: 'the more horrible this world is, the more abstract art will be.'

The alienation from reality, felt to be ugly and inimical to humans, is clearly stated by Franz Marc:

> Already early on I experienced people as ugly – animals ... in them too I discovered so much that I felt to be appalling and ugly that my representations of them ... became increasingly more schematic, more abstract ... until I came at last to a full realization of the ugliness, the impurity of nature.[459]

One more quotation, this time from Apollinaire: 'Purity and unity do not have a place without the truth, which one cannot compare with reality because truth is reality itself outside all the natures that try to keep us in the fatal order where we are mere animals.'[460] We realize that he is speaking here about art.

We could go on quoting. But perhaps it would be more important to look. Is it clearer if we find traces of gnostic thought in the catalogue of a Rauschenberg exhibition than if we see his work itself? I am convinced that the work itself is clearer and more explicit. Words conceptualize, and are (or at least can be) clear in philosophy or discursive thought about art, but after all the art itself has to contain the message, or else the words do not mean anything – and if the words really say something about the art of the artist, why not turn to the works themselves? Of course the critic's writing is always second-hand, translating the artist's expression from his or her chosen medium into a verbal one. It becomes more important when the words come from a close friend of the artist, and sometimes even more so – not always – when artists themselves speak. Finally, however, the artist's work contains the message or it does not, regardless of the accompanying spoken or written words.

The last paragraph was just to say that the gnostic message can be seen in the work of Rauschenberg, Kienholz and so many other artists that are presented to us by, shall we say, the Stedelijk Museum in Amsterdam. Or it can be heard in the music of a Boulez, a Cage. Or seen in a film by a Buñuel, a Warhol or an Antonioni. In all this we are confronted with the message of 'no meaning', the ugliness and evil of reality, the inner silence – a world to which no god ever spoke or will speak. As Sartre expressed it: 'While God characterizes himself by radical absence, the effort to realize humanity like ours is continually renewed and continually ends in failure.'

Coming to a first conclusion we think that Jonas is right when he says that gnosticism and the modern movement have much in common. There is the idea of *Geworfen sein*,[461] the non-conformist mentality,[462] of ecstasy as a means to gain wisdom and knowledge[463] – as expressed in a modern-gnostic magazine that proclaims the hope to conquer nihilism by a new mysticism: 'a sinking into the stream of life', a 'hallucinated attitude before the object world'[464] – and last but not least libertinism, which was the distinguishing mark of modernism since de Sade and Nietzsche's *Umwertung aller Werte;* and nineteenth-century bohemianism, which accompanied the modern movement, especially Dada and Surrealism, till it has permeated our age with the new permissiveness.[465] Theologically speaking there is an affinity here with the attitude towards God expressed in the twentieth century by the phrase 'God is dead.'[466] In politics the gnostic tradition in history almost always has meant anarchism, a negative attitude towards a law-and-order society.[467] There is no need to argue that the modern movement is closely connected with anarchist ideals in politics – and many modern artists are active in this direction too, or are at least interested.

You speak in your paper of two facets of the modern movement: subject matter and formal qualities.[468] The distinction is certainly valid, yet one questions to what extent the two are closely tied together, in the sense that the formal qualities express the inherent meaning itself, that the form is the meaning. Of course you have noted this yourself.[469]

A very clear illustration of a gnostic alienation from reality as expressed through the formal qualities itself is to be found in Platschek's intelligent and deep analysis of the work of Wols: 'not only the protocol of painting but also the protocol of reality is renounced . . . the moment when that which is portrayed becomes a justification of coincidence and destruction, the image becomes the carrier of a new meaning, beyond the moment of its creation.'[470]

Yet I have two questions, which again are related to the issue of whether modern art is really expressing our age.

First, is it really true that the 'unbeautiful' form as such is related to our 'unbeautiful' times – as a Dutch poet has put it, that 'beauty has burnt her face'?[471] If we look back in time we find that many beautiful works of art were made in horrible periods of war, poverty, famine or the plague. It is possible to think of the times of war between Holland and Spain, when the battle was nearby, raging and devastating, during the second half of the sixteenth century: the agony and horror finds no direct expression in the arts of that period; even when the horrors of war are the very subject, as for example in a series of prints by Callot, he does not use stylistically ugly means. One can ask oneself if some prints of Goya do not for the first time in history exhibit explicit and deliberate ugliness – but this is a matter of debate.

Second, in what way were horrible subjects rendered in the past? For example Rubens' martyrdoms are painted with great virtuosity and they do not show a stylistic ugliness. Examples where ugliness in content and in style goes together are rare. An exceptional case is perhaps Grünewald's *Crucifixion* – but even here the issue is open to discussion. In the musical sphere a rare example can be found in the evocation of Hades in Monteverdi's *Orfeo,* with its unharmonic and chaotic sounds.

To return to modern art: sometimes, but certainly only in a minority of works, one finds horrible subjects depicted in a horrible way. More often than not the subject matter as such is almost neutral, while the stylistic means show all the incongruities imaginable. I am thinking of Picasso's girls on the beach of around 1930 – nudes in which the horrible is not in keeping with the subject, or rather, where the deformation tells its own tale because of the neutrality of the subject.

I should like to quote here from Hugo Ball – who in his *Das byzantinische Christentum* describes and quotes gnostic invocations. These are the last lines of one of his Dada poems:

> People die not only by mines and guns
> People are wiped out not only by grenades
> In my nights, monsters crush in on me
> That make me experience hell.[472]

Humankind are faced with great problems, and the past has left us with almost unbearable intellectual puzzles, which were sensed already in or even before the Romantic period but only now are courageously faced in their utmost consequences; there is no need to deny that Western civilization is on the eve of destruction – maybe from forces inside rather than from forces outside – yet the question remains whether modern art in its crisis, which you so clearly described, is really the only possible art for this age. It could even be questioned whether modern art as such has not done much to contribute to the crisis of our age, and whether this art itself is not the greatest promoter and agent of despair and destruction.

But however great the difficulties, however menacing the future, our attitude towards reality, humanity, values, and God himself can never be dictated by these circumstances. People – and artists are people, they are human beings – are responsible; and the despair comes from the inside and, as such, is spiritual, while nature and the structure of the world remain unchanged. People have to choose and be creative *also* in the position they take.

Modern art can be called the expression of a broad stream in our age, a religion without a liturgy – as Franz Marc said, 'paintings are the altarpieces of a future religion' – a movement whose influence we see growing every day. Modern art shows the insight of a neognostic upon our world. No historic fatalism, called historicism, need overtake us. If we take modern art for granted as the art of our age, we thus promote the teaching and preaching inherent in these works. Maybe it is time for those who honestly cannot call themselves modern in a gnostic sense, precisely because they want to be up to date, to protest against the protest of modern people, as this is more a gnostic protest against the created cosmos and the human world as such than against specific contemporary social or intellectual evils – even if such things, being only too real, are used as catalysts.

I once heard a moving, true story. A boy and a girl were sitting on a bench on the Left Bank of the Seine in Paris. They were students and pupils of Sartre. They wept real tears. Why? Because they loved each other. But love, so they were told, does not exist. It is only a façade for sexual urges. So they wept, because they felt something that could not be there.

Should we not be happy for those tears! For they prove that it is not the development of philosophy or science, not the historic period in which we live or the group that we belong to which decides what is true and real – the whole world and the whole of history cannot destroy the humanity of these students and their ability to love. And can we not see that they simply and only had to accept the reality of love, to look at each other and dry their tears? Would that not be a more responsible attitude?

Indeed, if they did, they would be able to love each other, even if that would mean a great effort to unlearn their teacher's lessons. Even if they had to search for a base to replace or rather to fill the empty hole left by their gnostic teachings. And even if that would mean new tears, tears for humankind, who have thrown away love and beauty.

To know that modern art, though truly of our times in the sense of being *in* this time, is yet not the only possible valid art, is in itself liberating; it means new responsibilities, and new tears.

Is modern art true?[473]

The art of the twentieth century is not identical with modern art. There is a great deal of art that is not 'modern' but yet of our times, and there are still many artists who paint portraits and landscapes, whether in a naturalistic style or in a typically twentieth-century way, that we could call expressionistic (Matisse for example). Modern art is no more than one current in our times, although it is a very influential one. That modern art is problematical may be clear. We want to try and show that modern art is not art with a certain style but rather art with a certain content.

The question is: What content is characteristic of modern art? There are two directions: the abstract and the absurd. The artists who follow the absurd direction say that as artists they must protest, must be critical and must be engaged. Politically speaking many of these artists are anarchists. They argue that art must be connected with its time, and many people are moved by their works since art does have something to say today. People then say the artist is a prophet, a seer and a critic of her or his own era.

If however we walk around a museum of modern art, we notice something quite strange, namely, that these people who say they must criticize their times do nothing of the kind. Consider as an example the head of a woman painted by Picasso. This head is strange and looks as if it is made of woven straw. What might Picasso thereby be criticizing? Is he saying that in 1938 the women were all mad? Or that the fashion of the day was so strange? Or is he perhaps not referring to specific women in 1938? Or perhaps not to 1938? Perhaps not even to women? Is he perhaps following the very old method of art and does he by means of this woman tell something about humanity and not about humanity alone but also about the world? Is he perhaps saying that the world is mad? But in that case this has nothing to do with today. One of Picasso's most famous pieces is *Guernica*. This painting is about the bombing of a little Spanish town. People say it is the most human painting he ever made. It is a strange painting, for when one stands in front of it there is no Spanish town to be seen. One sees misery and despair, but nothing specifically connected with the Spanish Civil War. Picasso was intensely engaged against Franco and the Nazis, but there is no swastika or Franco cross to be seen.

The question one can pose and that we want deal with is: Is modern art true? This should always be our question when we occupy ourselves with art: Is it true? Is modern art really true? And our answer is 'yes' and 'no'. First the 'yes'. This art speaks realistically about existentialist anxiety, about despair, about absurdity, meaninglessness, about values that have lost their value, about the emptiness of humans threatened by technology, about the decline and demise of humanism and all such things that are indeed found in our times. There are many people who regard our world in this way.

In order to clarify this I will give a few quotations, beginning with C.S. Lewis. He wrote a wonderful introduction to a book[474] in which he says that once upon a time, very long ago, there were nymphs in nature. These nymphs were goddesses of wellsprings and the trees were dryads and the planets were gods. But then knowledge set in and slowly emptied the world. First the gods were removed, then the colours, then smells and sounds and tastes until at last nothing was left. All the things that used to be outside of us we have internalized. These have now all become our observations, our feelings, our thoughts and our ideas. Outside of them there is nothing whatsoever. However, so he says, that is not the end of it, for now the subject – that is we – has become very great and outside that subject there is virtually nothing left. But now people turn the same method upon themselves, with the outcome that we who had personalized the entire world – who had given names to all things – turn out to be personifications ourselves. And when we get to the end, this turns out to be very much like zero. There is really nothing left.

And that is precisely what Wols talks about as well. Platschek, a German artist, has written an outstanding book about Wols.[475] He was one of Wols's students. He says that when you take a piece of paper and make some random marks on it and then look at it you always see something in it, for example a mountain; now destroy the mountain with your pencil and look again and you see a forest. So now destroy the forest. The clever thing about Wols is that he shows us all the stages. And they all lead to nothing, a zero point. What we see are coincidental forms, forms that point not only towards the art of painting but also towards reality itself. They tell us that reality is a coincidental nought. This art shows us the being of things, that there is utterly nothing. Because of that the art of painting becomes superfluous, but then reality too becomes superfluous, for reality is denied.

From the citations it may be clear that we also say 'no' in answer to the question of whether modern art is true. These things have nothing to do with our twentieth century. What Wols discusses are general matters. He tells us nothing about the nothing of Hitler, the nothing of Nixon, but he tells us about the nothing of the world. It is an interpretation, a view, an intellectual and spiritual attitude towards reality. It is a revolutionary activity in which values are destroyed. Why? Because these values have lost their value for modern people. Yet this is only a view; it is not reality itself. These people do not talk about concentration camps but about a negative experience of reality. Therefore we repeat: Is modern art true? And we answer: Yes, of course. But only as the expression of a group. And this group is a strong minority. We must never overestimate the strength of this minority. It is an expression of their intellectual and spiritual distress, of their alienation, their feeling of being sealed up in an alien world.

So, is modern art true? Yes, in this sense it is true. It belongs with this minority. But there are thousands of people who are not 'modern' in the way they regard the world. From this it is clear that people can look at the world differently. This touches upon an important question, namely: Are people prisoners of their time? If we live today, must we view our times as others do? Hegel claims that history transpires in various stages. Upon reading him one is in the first instance deeply impressed. Very soon however one discovers that a person is just a tiny cog in great historical drama. The historian and art historian Jacob Burckhardt wrote about the Renaissance as a historical necessity. This means that if you were an artist in 1440 you had to be a Renaissance artist. Transposed to today it means that if you are an artist in 1970 you must be a modern artist. But this is precisely the question. Are we really a captive of our times? We say 'no', for people are not imprisoned in history, people can choose their way in freedom. This does not mean that we can stand outside of our times, for we belong to our times, but we can say 'no' to particular ideas and views. We are free to advance answers and offer our own solutions. Human beings are more than reeds in the stream of history, the stream of time. We are free and we are human. We can say that a different approach is possible. Modern art is not inevitable and not necessary simply because these artists are alive today. That is a

Hegelian notion. Then we would be slaves of our times and imprisoned in it. How dismal and dreary that would be, and that is exactly how many modern people feel.

Modernism is a view that has its roots in history and is connected with the past and with many other matters. It did not arrive out of the blue, yet it is but one particular answer to the problems. One may then ask what problems it is an answer to, and what is its content? In other words, one can ask what is the solution that modern art tries to give to the real problems of today, and not just modern art but also modern theology and many other modern things. In our opinion it is the answer of neognosticism.

A year ago I read a book by Jonas. Jonas is a great expert on gnosticism. He was one of Heidegger's students. In the introduction to the book he writes that he discovered he understood gnosticism so well because he was a pupil of Heidegger. After spending twenty years studying gnosticism he went back and read Heidegger again, and to his surprise discovered that only now he could understand him well. At the end of Jonas's book there is a lengthy chapter about the similarity and difference between gnosticism and neognosticism.

We shall try to make this clear. What is gnosticism? Gnosticism is a religion based on various myths, which tell a complicated story. The content of these myths is that there is a good god and there is also an evil god. This evil god created the world. We people belong to the good god but we are imprisoned in the bad, evil world. Now, the trick is how to get out of this evil world to the good god. Yet we are imprisoned in the evil world. This is the crux of gnosticism: that the world is evil in its very essence, because it was created by a bad god, a negative god. The world is evil and therefore we can have no contact with it; we are estranged from it insofar as we are good. The old Gnostic religion may have been as great as Christianity. Also Paul (in Colossians 2) and John (1 John 2:18 f.) fought against gnosticism. They warned people not to go along with it. Gnosticism was a powerful movement. It was about separating oneself from the world. In the myths one has to fight against dragons and demons and all sorts of ghastly things. But today it is different, Jonas says. We too live in a bad world but there are no longer any demons. In the old myths one might perhaps have had to fight a dragon. That is horrifying and, most probably, one would have lost. Yet one understands the dragon: it is hostile to us. Today, however, we are imprisoned in a world which in five minutes' time may be smashed to smithereens by a comet. Why? Because some or another evil spirit is ill-disposed towards us? No, just because something collided with the earth. It has nothing to do with us. No one is hostile. Matter collides with other matter according to arbitrary laws.

With relation to these matters I found a statement from 1836 by Carlyle, an English philosopher. He says that for him the universe has been stripped of all life, of all meaning, of all will and even of all hostility. It is a tremendous, inanimate steamroller that rolls on and crushes us piece for piece and limb by limb. The cosmos is something entirely impersonal and that is the problem of our times. There is no longer a good god one can turn to. One wants to try and escape the bad world but can no longer even fight against demons for one is unconditionally imprisoned. We could provide citations about this from Nietzsche, who also belongs to this school, from Keller, from Housman, from Klee, from Franz Marc. Franz Marc is an early modern artist, the one who painted the blue horses. He writes that when he was young he found humans ugly and therefore set about painting beasts, but as he painted, so he says, he discovered that beasts are ugly, and so he took a look at the world and in that way discovered the ugliness, the filthiness of the world.

He speaks literally about the 'impurity' of the world. From then on he started to paint abstractly. Many more citations could be adduced from John Cage, Tinguely, Rauschenberg and Duchamp. But I would like to leave it with just one. This citation is from Ginsberg. Ginsberg was one of the leaders of the Hippies and perhaps he still is. In about 1950 he wrote a poem entitled 'Howl'. Last year he said about it in an interview that of course he had written that poem in the gnostic tradition. It is a long poem and we shall not cite all of it. It consists of three parts and in the last part every stanza begins with 'I'm with you in Rockland'. It is very clear that Rockland refers to a lunatic asylum and that the asylum is the world. We are all imprisoned in a lunatic asylum. Here is what Ginsberg writes:

> I'm with you in Rockland
>> where you scream in a straitjacket that you're losing the game of the actual ping-pong of the abyss
> I'm with you in Rockland
>> where you bang on the catatonic piano the soul is innocent and immortal it should never die ungodly in an armed madhouse
> I'm with you in Rockland
>> where fifty more shocks will never return your soul to its body again from its pilgrimage to a cross in the void

A 'pilgrimage to a cross in the void', that is human life according to Ginsberg. And it is a typically gnostic pronouncement. It is a view and a religion. And it is not a religion that just sings songs but it is an exceptionally aggressive one. It wants to change the world. It is a product of the crisis of our culture, but it also promotes this cultural crisis, it helps to produce it.

Our question now is: Is a different view possible? And then we say: Yes, it is. It is not necessary to be modern, for one must realize that the modern movement is just one movement, one sect, one view resulting from the banishing of God from this world. Nietzsche, who undoubtedly belongs with this current, has said 'God is dead'. He added: 'And we have killed him.' He also said that a stench hangs over Europe; and to this we could add: Can you smell it?

I would like to end with a story. It is a story of something that really happened. It took place in the mid-1950s on the Left Bank in Paris. Two students of Jean Paul Sartre's, a young man and a young woman, are sitting beside each other on a bench and they are weeping. Why are they weeping? Are they not permitted to go to bed together? Do they have an inconvenient papa or mama who would not approve of that? No, that is not the problem, for they have already had such experiences often enough. The problem is that they want to say to each other that they love each other. But they realize that if they do, one would think the other is just using a nice way, a nice façade, to say that he or she has a sexual urge and wants to go to bed with the other. But in fact they do not just want to go to bed with each other, they love each other. Yet they have no way to say so. This is a problem many young people have today.

Often when I tell this story people raise questions about it. They think it is a crazy story. This young man and young woman should just say: 'We love each other and who cares about Jean-Paul Sartre.' That would end the matter.

In a certain sense of course that is true. It is precisely as Christ has said: 'The kingdom of God is among you.' In that way the young man and young woman can say 'Love is here.' They do not need to go far to find it. Yet we should be careful what we are saying here. Let us suppose they say to each other: 'We love each other.' And then they go into the woods and make love. Immediately they will have a guilty conscience and think: 'Are we not kidding one another? Are we not just like rabbits? We talk about love but is it not just a nice façade?' Therefore they first need to have an answer or else they will have to live with this guilty conscience, with all the contemporary voices that deprive love of its meaning and drag it down. They need to have an answer to the huge question: Is there really such a thing as love? Does love have meaning?

That young man and young woman have to look the truth in the eye and say: 'Sartre was evidently wrong, for we love one another. We will go to Sartre and say to him that we have discovered that he is a liar. And that he deserves a punch in the nose.' But Sartre would then say: 'Don't you know that when I discussed these things I wept as well? That I had real tears in my eyes? But tell me, where does love come from? If you can show me that love is real then I will be grateful to you. But if you also have no answer, just leave me alone.' And we believe that Sartre is right, a cheap answer is not enough. And therefore, if we want to find the truth, we must begin somewhere else. And our answer is that we can never begin with human being, for if we do that then we end where modern people have ended, namely in nothing. Or, to put it in other words, in gnosticism.

But human being is more than history and we are free to leap out of the world. That is our creativity. How can we get hold of the truth? Only by beginning where we are meant to begin, namely by honouring God as the Creator. Only by saying to one another: 'We love one another. Thank you, Lord, we have received it from your hand.' Otherwise it does not work. Without a tremendous break with neognosticism – and with naturalism, which is directly connected with it – we will never be able to give an answer to modernism. Therefore we cannot say to a modern painter that he or she must paint a little like this and a little like that. No, we must give an answer to these questions. Just as in every other field, whether it be politics or theology or whatever, an answer must be given to the deepest questions that the modern person poses. Otherwise we walk around with a guilty conscience because we have found a cheap remedy. And then the other is right to say that Christianity is just a super aspirin, a sort of drug or opiate, a tranquilizing agent. We shall have to take hold of the truth and find the courage to go against the stream.

To repeat, the modern in art and elsewhere is a view, a standpoint, but we are free, and reality and we have not changed. We can choose a different standpoint, for we are not imprisoned. We are not little reeds in the stream of history. Or rather, we are little reeds in the stream of history but we are not compelled to go with the flow. We can resist the current. That could mean that you might be kicked, that you might sink, that you might be crushed, that you might not make it. That is possible. It is what we call martyrdom. We shall have to pray and work that many may have the courage to go against the stream. But we cannot do it alone. We need to be driven by a strong Motor if we are to go against the stream. If many people were to go against the stream, then the stream of history might even start to flow in a different direction.

• Do we need to be modern in order to be contemporary?[476]

A list of titles for further reading appears in the endnotes.[477]

It is self-evident that people, and certainly young people who are still seeking their way, will ask themselves how they can best use their talents. That is, in such a way that what they do will be meaningful in today's world. No one wants to be out of fashion, cutting into problems of the past, adhering to vanquished positions, for what we do must be incisive for our own times, for the world in which we now live. That is also why the question whether it is necessary to be modern is a question of life and death. It is posed by everyone who desires to choose and who must choose a way in a conscious manner. Scientists, theologians, and especially artists have difficulty with this because they are told that everything except the modern is outdated, old and no longer valid. That implies that one must be modern, on pain of standing outside one's own era. Many, however, have big questions about the modern and they regard it critically and distrustfully. Instinctively they have the insight that what is modern cannot be their way. And this dilemma can be heartrending.

This question, this cry of distress I have often heard from young artists who are still at the academy or in artistic training. We have wanted to try and find an answer. The result is here, in this contribution. Thus we shall look at the question with the artist in mind, yet we are convinced that the problems *mutatis mutandis* are similar for theologians and sociologists whose education and disposition require them to be creative, now or in the future, to point out new paths, to solve problems and to make decisions fraught at times with far-reaching consequences. For this people must be up to date. But must they then also be modern?

The term 'modern' has often meant and still today often means 'something contemporary', new and progressive. The word has the ring of newness and can as such be used positively or negatively. In the case of modern art, that is different. Here too the term originally meant something new and different, something one had to get used to, that the old guard simply could not, or preferred not, to follow. For various reasons this term has remained attached to this art. Perhaps because it was so difficult and took so long to become accustomed to it. For some the art of people like Picasso, Mondrian, Moore, Dali or Pop Art, Op Art, Dada and Surrealism and whatever else all these movements may be called is still foreign and new, even though it has now been around already for almost three quarters of a century. The word 'modern' has become a generic name. It has become an art-historical term like Baroque, Rococo, Mannerism and Gothic; remarkably these are all terms that originally had a negative ring and later acquired a neutral meaning.

When I pick up a book about modern art, by Arnason for example, then I find that the term is used in a neutral way and that it means little more than 'twentieth-century'. Yet that does not cover everyday usage, where a particular kind of art is named 'modern' and another kind of art, which is contemporary as well, is not. For the latter there is usually no name at all.

Modern art has unleashed a great debate, so the literature about it is extensive. There is also widespread confusion about this subject. If we choose to make a distinction between modern art as a particular movement and other contemporary movements, then that is also an attempt to bring some clarity to the debate. And that is necessary in order to answer the question – a question often evoked precisely because of the confusion and the debate – of what exactly the message of modern art is. Therefore we will begin by sketching the artistic life of our times in a few main lines.

The first thing that strikes us is that nowadays there is such a tremendous interest in old art. Just think of the exhibitions, books and, not to forget, museum visits. Of course one must add in connection with the last of these that many visits to museums are just made by tourists on their travels who, compelled by an old tradition – one is almost tempted to speak of a rite – saunter through all the museums with three stars. Yet happily there are also people who experience real pleasure in it and are truly enriched by it. The great interest in old art is however something typical of our times, of which the inception lies in the late eighteenth century, thus in the Age of Enlightenment, which in a deep and decisive way ushered in the new era at the end of which we now stand.

Besides this there is in our times also a very special phenomenon, namely popular art. This is something other than folk art and, as far as form and content are concerned, it is usually dependent on older art. The old art lives on in popular art – often simplified, made lighter, sometimes corrupted into clichés. Perhaps popular art is the folk art of the era of mass culture and commercialization, art produced for consumers, easily digestible and always with something new. Especially in music this has taken clear shape.

The reasons why people value and seek out old art again can be very diverse. It can be due to a sense of history, which has its roots in the nineteenth century, but it can also be an escape into something that seems relatively healthy and represents positive values. People feel safe in the presence of old art, of which the value has been assayed by the centuries and the content is familiar. Popular art is an uncomplicated echo of old art, a way in which it lives on as a wholesome cultural inheritance that, in a paradoxical way, is as alive as springtime. Or must we say that it appears alive but that in fact nothing is really happening? Perhaps popular art is safe to us, requiring no real participation and critical involvement, precisely because it presents us with fashions rather than essential renewals.

Sometimes – certainly not always – the interest in old art and usually the interest in popular art bespeaks a 'bourgeois' mentality. 'Bourgeois' is not the same as middle class. 'Bourgeois' indicates something else, namely a mentality. It stands for people who aspire to 'a normal human life', who want to live 'decently', have a career, attain a position and build up their security in money, prominence and a good name. They want to realize that normal human life, which is often legalistically maintained and which distrusts creativity, without a firm basis for the 'normality'. The old basis, Christian belief, has dropped away. Yet people live as if nothing has really changed. Life has become secularized but in a certain sense not yet pagan. Certainly people have not yet drawn or wanted to draw the ultimate conclusions implicit in the abandonment of the foundations of the Christian heritage. But our era is complex. This is called pluriform in the language of today, whereby the weakness of our culture, its disintegration, is elevated to a positive principle that easily leads to relativism. In any case, all kinds of spiritual movements have become entwined with one another. Therefore we will sometimes find a bourgeois escape from reality also in the art movements that we will discuss further on, but it would be much too easy to dismiss – as some have done – everything that is not modern (in the sense that we will formulate) as bourgeois or as escapism or even as dumb and stupid.

Art as visual language

It cannot be denied that in art, spiritual values are manifest and that there is also a close connection between the form in which people express themselves and the content that is communicated visually in that form. 'The medium is the message,' said McLuhan: the medium, the mode of expression itself, is already expression. Taking this into account we can say that visual art employs a visual language. We also encounter visual communication outside of visual art, of course. I have in mind maps, visually presented statistics, etc. Yet visual art is more than visual communication. There is also an element of beauty that is not merely communication in the sense just meant. Still, with a certain degree of simplification we can say that art is language. Various styles in the visual arts can be seen as different visual languages. One can express something with them. It is certain that one 'language' lends itself better to the expression of certain ideas than does another 'language'. Yet we can say that the various artistic languages that we are about to discuss can be used for the expression of all kinds of thoughts, beautiful and ugly, profound and superficial, poetic and prosaic, positive and negative, reflecting a great diversity in orientation and intention.

With all of this we want to make clear that reality is extraordinarily complex and that we should speak with far greater nuance than we are about to do by putting forward a proposition which is simplifying and schematic in the hope of producing some clarity: in our century there are three art styles, three ways of visual communication, three visual languages. There are three different manners in which twentieth-century people can express themselves visually. Modern art, as we shall eventually conclude, is not a style but is determined by the content.

These three visual languages, or styles, are naturalism, mannerism and the iconic style, and we all understand them simply because we are twentieth-century people. Of course not all visual language is equally clear – nor is the spoken word – but even so things can be rendered in visual art in such a way that they are 'readable' and something is made clear. Some matters can be expressed more effectively through spoken language and others are perhaps only communicable through visual images.

So we come to the first style or visual language: *naturalism*. Present-day naturalism is ultimately traceable to its origin in the fifteenth century, when the Renaissance and the Flemish Primitives discovered a new form of expression that can describe with great exactness what we (can) see. It is an art focused on visible reality. In the following centuries, through the High Renaissance, Baroque and Dutch seventeenth-century art, people wanted to express in art more than what can be seen. Various approaches were adopted. In a strict sense this art was therefore not naturalistic although it used primarily naturalistic means. Present-day naturalism finds its origin and form in the early nineteenth century. We think of Ingres, the academic, naturalistic Salon art that persisted long into the twentieth century – we can still see this naturalism almost everywhere. We only need to think of photography (and film). Yet we also see it in other places. We see it in the kitsch we can buy – maybe third- or even eighth-rate, but still art – and also in many good landscapes, still lifes and portraits that are still being made today. Do you want names? Hopper, Grant Wood, Andrew Wyeth – in America this movement is very strong – Paul Citroen, Chabot, Charley Toorop, Dik Ket, Jeanne Bieruma Oosting, and many others. Even Picasso has sometimes used this style, for instance in a few portraits, such as that of Stravinsky, for example. Beyond art in the narrower sense we find this style as a language of our times that we all understand in advertising, in illustrations for books and periodicals, etc. It really requires no explanation. We know all about it. Only a prejudiced art criticism has sometimes persuaded us that the age of naturalism is over. Indeed the percentage of great artists who avail themselves of this style has diminished. Yet that it is dead or out of date is untenable in view of everything we see around us.

The second style we want to discuss is *mannerism*. The term is derived from a sixteenth-century movement. Here too we observe that people proceed from the possibilities and attainments of naturalistic art, but here they start to play with it, distort it and introduce extra tension into it. We have in mind for example the work of a Modigliani and of a Pijke Koch and in England of Stanley Spencer, Hillier, Minton and many others. In America we have Benton, Stuart Curry and the like. In a certain sense this second style is a variant of the first.

The third style is totally different: the *iconic* style. Its origins go back to people like Gauguin. Here visual elements are indeed used as language with which to express something. Accordingly we do not find here the 'imitation' or 'copying' that in a certain sense characterizes naturalism. The artists that employ this style are extremely conscious of the fact that a painting is a flat surface, upon which with lines and colours they can express something, including what people cannot see. We call this the iconic style. While naturalism and mannerism are not new styles but prolongations of what one encounters earlier, the iconic style is new in a certain sense. As to its principles, at least, it is comparable with medieval art and a great deal of non-Western art.

Ideoplastic art, a German critic once called it.

Perhaps it will be clearer if we discuss some concrete examples. Matisse comes to mind in connection with the iconic style. Bright colours, sometimes with heavy outlines, deference to the surface, simplification in the drawing whereby details are not provided and shadows are omitted all characterize his art. Actually, all the Expressionists in Germany and the Fauves in France express themselves in an iconic visual language – or rather: their work is iconic visual language. I am reminded of a beautiful piece by Matisse. It is a cut out piece of blue paper pasted on another piece of paper; he made it while he was bedridden and named it *Femme-fleur*, the woman-flower or flower-woman. It is a visual poem that expresses something of the flowerliness of the young woman, something of the joy of life, something too of the erotic. I do not believe one will be able to find anyone in our times who has a problem with this little work, a wisp of a poem, a gem. The poetry is clear. The form is entirely flat and level and no details are provided. Yet we do not miss them.

Next to this Expressionist iconic work we also find a Cubist variant. In a certain sense Expressionism and Cubism are different visual languages, distinguishable from one another by their syntax yet both iconic in principle or, to put it differently, they are two different dialects within one language. I think here of Delaunay, whose *Eiffel Tower* of 1911 indeed renders reality in an entirely different way from what naturalism would have done, yet it is completely clear to us people of the twentieth century. Delaunay in his *Eiffel Tower* made a poem in honour of this tower which, thanks in part to its visual poetry, became a Parisian landmark. What he has to say about it is not strange, crazy, awkward or purposely distorted. He tells things in his own way. Therefore he can say other things than would have been possible with naturalism, while by the same token he cannot say some things that a naturalist would be able to express.

This style too has entered our age 100 per cent. Just consider the posters of Cassandre from the period immediately following the First World War. Anyone who looks around can multiply the examples. For us what is important is that we can immediately understand this visual communication. Thus we cannot criticize this style as such, because it is a language and as such only a means of expression. The question is rather what is said with it and how it is said.

Modern art

And so we come to modern art, the art that arose at the beginning of our century, about which there has been so much heated debate and which even now, some seventy years after its inception, is still controversial – even though in a certain sense it has won the argument, at least insofar as an important percentage of our contemporaries are concerned. In my book *Modern Art and the Death of a Culture* I have endeavoured to account for the significance and influence of this art. Thus we will not go into that here. All I want to do now is make clear what modern art is in distinction from other art in our times. *Modern art, we have already said, is not a style but is typified by a particular content.* It is eclectic in this sense, that in order to express itself it makes use of the various visual languages found in our times. Modern art can thus be naturalistic in style (e.g. Delvauz, Dali and other Surrealists) or manneristic (e.g. Escher, Max Ernst and others). Often it will make use of iconic stylistic devices as well (e.g. Picasso, in the period of his synthetic Cubism, or Henry Moore). Escher is a very well-known artist. It is significant that his work, which contains so many strange elements, appeals so strongly to our contemporaries. Modern art is not just for a small coterie of the initiated. Escher is very playful and says things in a soft and friendly way. Yet in order to see things this way there has to be a distance from reality. The familiar world picture – as people have seen and represented the world for centuries – must have been called into question and have lost its validity. The stylistic means he employs are those of naturalism or also often of mannerism.

When we look around in modern art we often encounter the motif of humankind imprisoned and hampered in their movements no matter how free they seem to be. We think here for example of Delvaux's *Echo* in which a nude woman wanders lonely through a great city full of magnificent, stately classical buildings. Yet although she can go anywhere, it is horrible to be so lost in a lonely world. The only thing that is left is her echo, her self repeated, an image of alienation, of being lost, of despair and hopelessness.

Naturalism and mannerism are the styles in which the Surrealists usually work. Salvador Dali, another artist who enjoyed great popularity, is very well known. During one period of his development he made a number of 'Christian' works, including his *Mystical Last Supper* and *Crucifixion of St John on the cross*. In both cases he did not follow the standard themes: the Lord's Supper or mass and the Crucifixion. In the crucifixion he follows a drawing by the sixteenth-century mystic San Juan de la Cruz and we see that the cross not only floats above the world but that it makes no contact with it at all either. In a strange, mannerist manner we view the cross from above, so that we do not see Christ's face. Most important, however, is that this Christ is not the Christ of biblical Christianity: the cross does not touch the earth, which is accordingly left behind without salvation. The Christ is perhaps only a vision. Perhaps he is really there – not suffering, for Christ's hands are not even nailed to the cross and both he and the cross remain symbols – but perhaps he has meaning only for those who are not of this world.

Picasso too had a Surrealist period during the early 1930s. At that time he drew the absurd human being in all its terrible ugliness. Often featured are 'women at the beach'. Joining a very long tradition, he uses the figure of the unclad woman as an allegory, as a metaphor, as a symbol for humanity. The woman – human being – has lost all that is human. Everything is there, to be sure, arms, legs, abdomen, head, breasts, but in a certain sense the only thing that is left is sex, and that too has lost its delightfulness. During these years art lovers and art critics began to discover Picasso and modern art, or at least they tried to take a positive approach to it and appreciate it. In Picasso's case they did so by citing Cubist theory and by acting as if his works were made in a new style but with an old and familiar content. That was a grave mistake, because in this way people rationalized away precisely what was essential: the strained relation with reality itself. Picasso himself was not at all happy about that. Towards the end of the 1930s he accordingly painted a series of 'head of a woman' paintings that were fashioned precisely according to the theories people were proclaiming. They are probably the most monstrous things Picasso ever made. Among them is one that depicts a woman's head as if it were made of straw, monstrous, but at the same time utilizing naturalistic means – the straw is clearly recognizable. We shall refer to this work again.

Modern art is far from neutral. Often we encounter harsh anti-Christian statements. Take Baj for example: the artist paints Adam and Eve in the way kitsch artists do or advertisement illustrators; he shows how kitsch, vacuous and commercialized Christianity has become and in the process depicts a 'God' in a way that one can only describe as blasphemous. Visual images do not bite but they certainly can be sharp, stabbing and painful. That is definitely his intention. To this we must add that Christians have sometimes contributed to the problem by using kitsch art on prayer cards and in Sunday school illustrations and evangelistic literature. Moreover, Christians have often neglected to address the problems of our times, so that Christianity has become for many an obsolete affair. We have often lost the connection with our times. Therefore Christians should not only be shocked but also ashamed by such a painting. We will have to learn from it.

Picasso also drew a Crucifixion in his Surrealist period. It became an acidic commentary on the Crucifixion. Mind you, not on the event at Golgotha but on the confession of Christians concerning it, a confession that is framed in a multiplicity of painted Crucifixions, including gripping ones by Rembrandt, Rubens, Riemenschneider, Cimabue and others. Picasso's drawing seems abstract at first glance, until we discover that the entire piece is composed of bones. The Crucifixion is dead; the Christian faith is dead, decayed, over! Perhaps this as well: it brought death with it. Naturally we must be mindful that Baj and Picasso come out of Southern Europe and produce a commentary on the Christianity they know. But let us not be too quick to say that it therefore does not touch us. In any case, such views are realities of our times.

There is of course a surfeit of pieces painted in an iconic style. Perhaps we must regard abstract art as an extreme use of this artistic language. However that may be, in this respect the modern movement gave birth to something new. Abstract, or rather non-figurative, art presents forms that are not recognizable depictions. Naturally in history a great deal of art has been produced that is non-figurative: ornamentation, the plinths for statuary, picture frames, vases, in short, many manifestations of what we call applied or industrial arts or crafts. Yet the abstract painting is different. It works in a medium that in our Western culture has always been the deepest bearer of ideas. When people produce an abstract interplay of forms instead of a Madonna, a Crucifixion, a portrait or even a still life, then that takes the place of these ideas. That is also how Kandinsky and Mondrian, the pioneers of abstract art, regarded it. They meant to render spiritual depth. And in doing so they shunned reality, the world around us.

To some extent one can understand non-figurative art as an extreme aestheticism: a work of art as only a matter of beauty. That can be connected with the fact that since the eighteenth century art has lost its function. Kant already defined art as something that has no practical significance. At the same time, however, in Romanticism people assigned art an exalted place as a kind of expression of the foundation of all being, as a revelation of the deepest and highest in which all contradictions are reconciled. In the moderns however there is also unmistakably a negative sense of reality, an avoidance of our everyday world. Sometimes, as in Mondrian, this amounts to the construction of an elevated and beautiful palace that depicts for us the (Platonically understood) Ideas at the edge of the abyss in which all the horrors abide that Surrealism, for example, presents to us.

A man like Jackson Pollock set out to destroy all (rational) meaning and significance. That is to say that for him art could only be true if it could show us the deepest meaning of things, and that was the complete absence of meaning. After searching a long time he found it in his 'drippings', with which he would later on exert great influence. These were pieces in which even the human handwriting was absent, because he simply poured the paint from the can onto the canvas. But even so, while he repeated this act his humanity and his artistic sensitivity surfaced all the same, so that in time he created beautiful patterns. Yet to him that was no pleasant surprise. To the contrary. Beauty as such has meaning, and this result disturbed him. Rightly so, for it shows that our reality and what is human cannot simply be dismissed and that they are an unavoidable reality. Later we see that he sets out to destroy this beauty again, which in actual fact fails. His demise came then in the form of suicide; at least, he died in a strange and unnecessary car accident.

Modern art is sometimes very intellectual. That is so even when it is completely irrational. That is perhaps a pseudo-paradox. Many of these modern works, certainly the abstract ones, may be characterized as marginal art phenomena. They are art that is hardly art, because people have so consistently pursued the disfigurement, the escape from and depreciation of reality itself, and not only the reality outside of art but also the reality of the art itself. By abandoning all norms, people lost art itself, and that, then, is again precisely art. Modern art is sometimes full of real paradoxes. Probably this is a result of the fact that people go to the furthest extremes in their non-acceptance of reality as created, as creation, but in order to express that they have to utilize the means this reality itself provides.

Modern works accordingly sometimes appear to be arguments in a debate more than works of art. In a certain sense they are a visual theology of nihilism. I think of the work of the highly intellectual artist Fontana, who in the early sixties broke through the surface of the painting. He cut the canvas with a razor or burned holes in it. Throughout the centuries it was on the canvas that things happened and were brought to expression. World views were portrayed on it, but the ground was always art in relation to reality, which was mirrored – subjectively – in it. Then Fontana broke through this ground and in so doing smashed the last reality itself. By breaking through the surface of the painting people penetrated into nothingness, where there is no longer any world. Remarkable but telling is his naming of some of these pieces: *The end of God.*

Modern art can also be naturalistic. Yet to preclude any misunderstanding, it is not only for strange, surrealistic representations that a naturalistic style is sometimes used. Particularly in recent years a new movement has come forward strongly that we can call Ultranaturalism. It usually involves large paintings that are painted very precisely, more accurately than a photograph. Indeed these artists often make use of photographs in their preliminary studies. Sometimes they gain inspiration from older works of art. The most ordinary everyday reality is depicted as neutrally or objectively as possible, to the finest detail. The remarkable thing is that when one studies and considers this art for its meaning, one has to conclude that this is abstract art as well. The abstract and the non-figurative do not, as it turns out, coincide. Mati Klarwein, an Austrian painter, made a piece in 1964 that he called *Abstract painting* while he used the forms of the Spanish landscape! It was one of the first works of this sort. When people make abstract works in which they play with forms that are meaningless in themselves, then in place of geometric shapes or brush strokes they may just as well make use of shapes borrowed from reality. That does not make any difference. That is possible of course on one condition only: that reality too means nothing. And reality means nothing if we present it as a 'fact' without any human interpretation. For reality is always fact plus meaning, as K.J. Popma has made clear. Yet reality is stripped of its reality when we only regard it as a source of light beams that strike our eyes. One can then even ask whether that reality is really there. [Howard] Kanowitz shows us that in his interesting and revealing work from 1970 (in Rotterdam's Boymans-van Beuningen Museum): what we think we see we do not see, even though we see it. The painting is a very naturalistic rendering of a number of pieces of paper pinned to the wall by which a game is played with reality itself: at first glance one seems to see a city through a window until one discovers that everything is just a painting after all – a painting within a painting. Most of the works from this school however employ images of a city, automobiles or people.

In passing I would therefore also say this: if we aspire to a new art that breaks through the modern and focuses once again on reality, then we must not simply turn to naturalism. We must seek for an art that offers a view of real reality, a reality that is more than mere factuality and one that is not foreign to us.

Modern art and our times

Art and religion have always been closely connected. As we have already observed, the Romantic mind in particular assigned art an exalted and profound task. Perhaps excessively so. However that may be, modern art is not decorative. Even where it is said to be art for art's sake it is more than mere art. It is an expression of an outlook, of a particular attitude to life, a religion. In a certain sense one may justifiably characterize great works of modern art as icons, as representations of what is central, the deepest and the highest. At one time that used to be the deity or the idol but now it is nothingness, the negativity. Sometimes it becomes simply demonic. Modern artworks hang in museums but they are really altarpieces in a nihilistic temple that will never be built. They hang in a museum for modern art, a sort of secularized, non-religious temple of a non-religious religion that believes in the non-existence of the divine. View it as a consummate paradox if you will. Yet it is also a tragic affair: modern people would so much like to find a firm basis, to find the way back to reality and humanity, to create a new myth. The moment they begin to do so, however, they realize that they are engaged in making gods for themselves. And so these are not gods. In a world that has been visited by Christianity, it is not easy to create a new paganism because the idols have been unmasked. Images look like idols. They are more than works of art but are devoid of a function because the religion that goes with them does not exist. The gods of this age are ease and comfort, money and sexuality. They are too vulgar and vacuous to become real gods. Yet they are certainly the beckoning spirits, albeit also often cynically unmasked in the many expressions of modern art that protest against the emptiness and the powerlessness to discover or create real gods, because people have whole-heartedly said farewell to the real God.

It may have become clear that modern art is not only a matter of a new style but also a matter of content. Before delving further into this it will be worthwhile to draw a conclusion from what we have noted so far.

There is a tremendous amount of confusion about modern art. It is our impression that this is fostered by the many – well-intended – introductions, explications, etc. For they invariably proceed from the assumption that the viewers do not understand the visual image and that it needs to be made clear to them that the image came about through the application of a new stylistic principle, a new way of forming that nevertheless expresses 'ordinary' things. We have asserted precisely the opposite, because we are of the opinion that twentieth-century people do understand contemporary artistic languages. People understand Matisse well, together with thousands of other artists whose works feature no modern content. And they also understand modern works. If the present-day beholders have questions, if they protest or feel ill at ease, it is not because they do not understand this art but because they understand it all too well and have some critical questions to raise about its outlook. Perhaps they literally do not want to believe their eyes: that people can think so negatively about reality. They become confused, however, when told that they do not understand this art while it is really 'ordinary'. Hence the wake-up call: believe your eyes!

The question then arises what this art does mean. Modern art shows us, to put it briefly, two things. Either it shows us people 'thrown' [cf. Heidegger] into this reality that they experience as a kind of prison or the artists construct another world in which they are themselves the god and creator, a world that has nothing to do with what we call 'reality'. They search for an autonomous art in which the autonomous person speaks. Thus we find next to each other pure abstraction in the non-figurative – in some cases, such as Mondrian, pure beauty – and the depictions of absurdity and negativity, of alienation from what is alien and hostile to us. In the latter we often find protest and political commitment, frequently with a streak of anarchism.

This art is based in the notion that artists have a task and are called to be prophets to clarify the times for their contemporaries and to be critics of the times in order to unmask at a very deep level the negativity of our world. Thus art is no longer art for art's sake – even if people often present it in the form of autonomous art – but is instead serving a deeper and more distant goal. Only in this way can the artist break through the impasse that has arisen because art has lost its function. In part we can understand this development as a fierce, desperate effort to give art meaning and significance again. What sensible person desires to make works that have no function, that are useless and at the same time often unmarketable? One can simply not live by permanent self-indulgence. For this point a solution has to be found if art is to be restored to health. But that too cannot arise from art itself. Modern artists are right when they say that to this end a renewal of society is needed. Or rather they are wrong, since it is not our society that must be altered – the art market, capitalism and such matters – but our culture in its totality. Cultural harmony must be restored.

We have now completed a brief tour of modern art. What did we see? Protests against the abuse of political prisoners? Against the exploitation of the poor? Against social injustice, housing shortages, political arguments? Once in a while we did encounter that, but remarkably enough we did not find it in truly modern art; when we find such an outlook it is expressed rather in one or another of the present-day art styles discussed above. Furthermore, 'real' artists usually do not want to be engaged so directly with everyday events. They leave that to the cartoonists, poster artists, and the like. No, when we look around we see little of our own times. Certainly we hear the scream of outrage, of frustration, anxiety, and the protest against absurdity. What is the significance of Picasso's *Head of a woman* that we alluded to above? Certainly he did not mean to say that in the 1930s, round about 1938, there was such an absurd fashion in straw? Also he is not venting hatred for woman. No, he is making an 'allegory'. He is concerned with humanity: humanity is absurd.

Here we may also mention Picasso's renowned work *Guernica*. The piece is one of the few important and modern artworks to have originated in direct relation to current political events. Picasso was inspired by the Falangist bombing of little Spanish villages during the Civil War. If we look closely at the work we see no Spanish village, no bombardment and no fascists. What we do see is the fear, the grief, the pain, the terror, the death of people and perhaps, in the bull, the persistence of Spain.

And if we look at the Abstract Expressionists, at the Op artists or at the new Ultranaturalists? We are struck again and again by the fact that our current socio-political reality has very little bearing on their work. Perhaps it is most to be found in the Pop artists. For they found their inspiration in their own times and by way of irony gave their critique of the banality and emptiness that have come to characterize our world. Yet here too it applies to a limited category of works only. Oldenburg's 'soft' typewriters are difficult to understand as a protest against the wage slavery of the secretaries. Indeed – and that is the other side – taboos are shattered in this modern art, bourgeois values attacked, destroyed or set aside and it is made clear that the old (optimistic) humanism is dead.

Therefore we come to the question: Does this modern art really depict our age? For all its societal commitment, is the cultural or socio-economic reality really the target? Once again, to preclude any possible misunderstanding, we are not talking about twentieth-century art in general but about art that has acquired the categorial name 'modern'.

Is modern art true?

Is modern art true? Our answer is 'yes'. It is an art that speaks of existentialist angst. It expresses despair, the feeling of absurdity, the inauthentic, the alienation and other matters about which so many have spoken in the twentieth century, most notably the existentialist philosophers and writers like Kafka and Camus. Modern art speaks about values that have lost their value, about humanity threatened by technology, about dehumanization, about the failure of humanism, and about the loss of the old consensus, a generally accepted positive awareness of norms and life. It is not difficult to illustrate this with a few quotations. Consider first William Barrett's well-known *Irrational Man* (1958), in which he portrays the spirit of the age. In the chapter on art he argues that modern art begins and also sometimes ends as a confession of spiritual poverty. That is its greatness and its triumph, he says, but it is also how it puts the cat amongst the bourgeois pigeons, since the last thing they want is to be reminded of that poverty. And further on he asserts that the moment humanity no longer lives with their face turned spontaneously towards God and the supernatural world, the artist too will come face to face with a flat and incomprehensible world.

C.S. Lewis is able to further clarify the matter in his foreword to Harding's *Hierarchy of Heaven and Earth*. In just a few beautifully crafted sentences, poetic as well as exact, he says that once the universe appeared packed with will, intelligence, life and positive qualities: every tree was a nymph and every planet a god. Human beings themselves were akin to the gods. But the advance of knowledge slowly robbed this rich and genial universe: first of its gods, then of its colours, smells, sounds and tastes, finally of solidity itself as solidity was originally imagined. All these items were taken away from the world and transferred to the subjective side of the account: they were classified as our sensations, our thoughts, our images and our emotions. In this way the subject became gorged, inflated at the expense of the object. But the matter did not end there. The same method, which has emptied the world, now proceeds to empty ourselves. We who had personified all other things turn out to be ourselves mere personifications and then we arrive at a result uncommonly like zero. While we were busy reducing the world to virtually nothing, we deceived ourselves with the fallacy that all these lost qualities received a safe depository in our own mind. But apparently our mind was not built for that. The subject is as empty as the object.

These notions of C.S. Lewis are reinforced by P.W. Bridgman, who in his *Philosophical Implications of Physics* (also cited by Barrett) writes about the development of science, that we are drawing ever nearer to the point where our inquiries must be stopped for good, not as a result of the construction of the world but because of our own construction. The world grows vague and escapes us because it becomes meaningless.

Most illuminating too is Platschek's analysis of Wols's art. Wols was a German artist who worked in Paris following World War II. His art is based on the observation that when a person draws a few random scratches, one can always identify something in them. Wols begins with such scratches and then destroys that picture, but it leads to the appearance of another picture, which he then also destroys and so on.

The genius of it is that when we look at one of his works we are conveyed past all the stages. They are figurations that can be read in various ways, depending on what one wants to read into them or put into them. About Wols's work Platschek comments that it touches the zero point that hides behind the accidental or uninspired form, a zero point whereby not only the art of painting but also the features of reality are rendered superfluous. The nonchalance with which what people generally call 'form giving' is handled, Platschek states, is no less than moving: every painting originates from the nothingness of spiritual matters, as Picasso too would declare, or more precisely from the nothingness of the things as such.[478]

Is modern art true? we asked. And we have said 'yes'; but we also say 'no'. The citations make it clear that this art has nothing to do with the twentieth-century situation as such. It is an interpretation. It is an outlook and not properly on our times but on reality as such. It arises from a spiritual attitude. One can also say that it is a revolutionary activity, in which values are torn down that have lost their value for modern people because they have lost sight of the foundations of reality. In short, modern art expresses a negative experience of reality as such.

Again, is modern art true? Does it reflect reality? Yes and no. Yes, as the expression of a group of people, a movement, a current. They form a minority but a strong minority. This art is an expression of their alienation, of their spiritual and intellectual despair, of their *Huis clos*, their 'closed doors'. In a certain sense there are many – many more than one would think at first glance – who feel things this way but who do not dare to accept the consequences in their own lives. They prefer to stay superficial and pretend the problems are not there. Yet we also passionately say 'no'. Reality is not like that. Is it not remarkable that there are so many, also amongst the artists, who do not want to see things that way? It is one of the remarkable problems of our times that precisely art, which claims to represent our times, seems so strange to so many. That it is not a question of getting more used to it, as is by now quite clear. After all, we are now living some seventy years after modern art has started; we are not looking at its forerunners.

Truth and historicism

There is another matter that requires consideration. When we ask questions about truth we must inevitably touch upon the question 'What is truth?' Truth is always subjective. It is a human position in relation to the reality surrounding us. What do we think about that reality? Truth appears when our insight and actions are correct, which means they are building up, going in the right direction, the good way. Christ spoke of himself being the Way and the Truth. He also spoke about doing the truth. Truth is dynamic. Truth is more than just ascertaining a static fact because reality is more than factuality: it exists only in the two-in-oneness of fact and meaning.

Since the nineteenth century there has been an important current in thought that we call historicism, which always relates truth to the times and to the world in which it obtains. Hegel, for example, speaks of different periods in world history. While examining his viewpoints we become aware that humans are no more than small wheels in a vast universal historical happening. They are totally and thoroughly conditioned by the situation meted out to them by suprapersonal and mighty events. Gombrich shows in his illuminating little book *In Search of Cultural History* how such notions have profoundly influenced art history and art itself, and he cites in this regard the extremely influential historian and art historian of the last century, Jacob Burckhardt, who speaks of the Renaissance as a world-historical necessity, a great universal happening. Historicism thus views human beings as entirely conditioned by history. Even the norms are tied to the times. That also means things cannot be otherwise than they are. It could not be otherwise, for example than that Botticelli was a great Renaissance artist, simply because that was the age in which he fulfilled a role. If he had made different choices he would have stood outside his times and thus have been of no importance.

If we apply such notions to our own time – one can hear and read them again and again where modern art is concerned – then we must of necessity be modern, simply because we live today. Anyone who as an artist makes anything that differs from modern art simply stands outside her or his times! And of course it is true: we live in *our* times and react to *our* situation. The question however is always how we are to react to it. We may also pose the question whether we do not in this way become victims of a line of reasoning that in fact makes a powerful current *the* current. For it could be – there are people who think so – that modern art is no more than an official and commercial art that lacks real creativity or, more accurately, has already lost it. Modern art was new and real in the first twenty-five years of our century. I do not subscribe to this view but I do want to leave open the possibility that somewhere in this world, still unknown to all of us, in an attic room or in the jungle, people are busy finding ways that will be decisive for the future. Later on we will see that they were the real renewers. If we were to meet them, would we have to criticize them with the observation that our times are different? But who determines what 'the times' are?

Certainly one must be aware of one's times in order to work meaningfully in them. Yet that by no means entails having to sacrifice oneself to the gods of this age or to surrender oneself to the spirit of the times. People are not prisoners of their times; they are free and responsible. They can accept the challenge to find new and better ways. They are not a wisp of straw, without a will, floating on the stream of history. People are free because they are human.

Therefore we do not say that modern art is inevitable; that 'it is the way things are, one cannot do otherwise.' Modern art is simply not identical with the art of our times. Any assertion that it is so is not only not true as a thesis and conviction; it is also not true when we simply open our eyes and look around. Modern art is the expression of one current or direction; it presents one view. Naturally its being what it is, is not arbitrary. We can investigate and identify the conditions, presuppositions and backgrounds that define it and trace its particular prehistory. It is a response to the demands of the time, but it is *one* possible response.

How then can we typify the message of modern art? We repeat, in order to make it very clear: the content is central, the *Aussage*, what these works mean. To arrive at this meaning modern art employs different styles. We must understand however that this art advances its message like all art in all times: in the unity of 'form and content', to put it in old-fashioned terms. It is precisely in the artistic form, in the way in which the given is treated and elaborated, that art manifests its meaning, its message. The theme is not enough to know what a work is about. An analysis of the form may bring us closer to the meaning of a work, but it can also miss what is essential. A work of art exists, after all, in the totality of all its aspects.

How can we characterize modern art's message? We would like to use the term 'neognosticism' in this connection.

Neognosticism

Gnosticism is a movement, differentiated in many ways, from the time of early Christianity. Although the church condemned gnosticism as a heresy and although there are many who regard gnosticism as essentially not Christian, there are others who view gnosticism as a sideline of early Christian thought which mixes biblical thought and all kinds of currents from the world outside of Judaism and Christianity.

We will not go into these questions here. Gnosticism is at bottom a mythologizing realm of thought. All kinds of strange gods, sometimes goddesses, demons and supraterrestrial creatures turn up in this doctrine. Furthermore – and that conditions its fundamental ideas – it holds that this world is bad and that it was created by a lesser or bad god. When gnosticism utilizes biblical terms, it may say for instance that this world was created by Yahweh and he did a poor job of it, but that there is a higher deity, Elohim. It is to him that we must turn to escape the dominion of the bad god. And we may do that by violating the laws of that god, so that we hear, for example, of the prohibition of marriage, and of fornication. We find, next to each other, a severe asceticism in order to escape this world and an extreme libertinism – because this world is bad after all, it is better to break all laws. (It would be interesting and important to find out the extent to which libertine sects through the centuries, including people like De Sade, have stood in a gnostic tradition.)

There is an anarchistic streak in gnosticism. It is connected with the fact that for adherents to this thinking, life is alien to this world since we still have a connection with the true, high god and are thus not at home in this world, the creation of the lower and bad deity. The issue then is our salvation: gnosis answers the question of how we are to get out of this world to the true, higher god.

Hans Jonas, one of the great authorities on gnosticism, makes a connection in his book *The Gnostic Religion* between this ancient gnosticism and the existentialism of our day. Whether or not a direct continuous tradition can be established, he notices a similar mentality and a similar world of ideas. At the same time it is important to observe that besides a great deal of agreement there are also great differences. Modern thought is with a few notable exceptions not given to mythologizing, and it is much more rationalistic. Nonetheless, Jonas states that it must be conceded from the outset that the denial of every objective norm for moral action in gnosticism and existentialism is developed at very different theoretical levels and also that antinomian gnosticism seems very primitive and naïve compared with the conceptual subtleties and historical argumentation of its modern counterpart. What was liquidated in the one case was the ethical heritage of a thousand-year-old ancient tradition; added in the other case was the legacy of a two thousand-year-old Western Christian metaphysics as background for the idea of a moral law. Nietzsche identified the root of the nihilistic situation, Jonas observes, with the words 'God is dead'. The sentence 'God is dead' meant, according to Jonas, that no effective force emanates from the suprasensual realm.[479] And a little further on the distinction is shown even more clearly, after it is again underscored that they are united by an extreme dualism between human beings and their metaphysical background, between the true god and this world, between humans for whom God is now dead, so that his existence must precede his essence, and the physical world external to us. Jonas accordingly goes on to observe that in addition a cardinal difference must not be ignored between gnostic dualism and existentialist dualism: the gnostic person is thrown into a hostile, anti-divine and thereby anti-human nature; the modern person, into an indifferent one, which means absolute emptiness, a truly bottomless abyss.[480]

A renowned formulation from the school of Valentinus, one of the most important gnostics, summarizes the content of gnosticism as follows: 'What makes us free is the knowledge of who we were and what we have become, where we were and what we have been thrown into, where we are speeding to and what we have been saved from, what birth is and what rebirth is.'[481] Here we see the same terminology used as in modern thought – freedom, 'thrownness' – but how much more radically and tentatively are they applied nowadays. And about salvation people no longer even dare to think.

The new gnosticism was born in the last century. Thus in Carlyle's *Sartor Resartus* (1836) we may read:

> To me the Universe was all void of Life, of Purpose, of Volition, even of Hostility: it was one huge, dead, immeasurable Steam-engine, rolling on, in its dead indifference, to grind me limb from limb. Thus must the bewildered Wanderer stand, as so many have done, shouting question after question into the Sibyl-Cave of Destiny, and receive no answer but an Echo. It is all a grim Desert, this fair world of his: wherein is heard only the howling of wild beasts, or the shrieks of despairing, hate-filled men; and no Pillar of Cloud by day, and no Pillar of Fire by night, any longer guides the Pilgrim. To such length has the spirit of Inquiry carried him.[482]

Indeed, neognosticism is rooted in Romanticism: it was born of an awareness that the new natural science in its direction and its view of reality, defined by the ideas of the Enlightenment and by the school of Descartes, Locke, Hume and the French Encyclopedists, threatens people and their humanity. This natural science taught that in nature everything is determined and that ultimately people too are natural beings. This impersonal, determined reality was a threat for humans, whose freedom and personality were at stake. As we see in Carlyle, that can easily lead to ideas bearing a resemblance to the old gnosticism. Then too people had felt imprisoned in an impersonal world, hostile to them, and then too salvation was regarded as possible only through a radical negation of this world, yet without a denial of its reality. Romanticism too essentially accepted the natural-scientific closed world without God as a power in his own right. People just tried to escape. The Romantic attitude towards life is conditioned by a strong pessimism that arises from an awareness that humankind and their cultural products are ultimately subject to the forces of nature – hence the relevance of such themes as death and the grave and ruins and 'horror stories' – and a strongly negative sense of reality, that appears next to and at times almost paradoxically united with a strong realism. People sought to save themselves, to restore or regain their dignity through art and in a bohemian lifestyle. In doing so they attempted to break through the restraints of manners and morals and experimented with various forms of mysticism and ancient heresies.

Gottfried Keller's 1854 novel *Der grüne Heinrich* is an example among many of how such a mentality seeks a form. In this book we come across the following statement, which is affinitive to gnosticism without following the doctrine precisely: 'God created the world from nothing; it is a morbid abscess of nothingness, an expulsion of God from himself. The beautiful, the poetic lies in this, that from this material ulcer we allow ourselves to be absorbed again into nothingness.' Remarkable but instructive is the fact that in the same book for the first time a painter makes an abstract painting, which is then highly praised by a spectator and hailed as the new way for the future.

Next in line is Nietzsche, who once stated poetically in *Thus Spake Zarathustra*: 'So I lie bound by myself, twisted, tormented by an everlasting torture and beaten by You, most cruel huntsman, You unfamiliar God.' We are not writing a history here and our citations are just illustrations. They are indicative of a climate, a mentality, a way of experiencing the world. We call this mood neognostic. Thus the poet Housman writes: 'I, a stranger and afraid, in a world I never made.'

The artist Paul Klee once wrote: 'The more horrible this world is (as is the case today), the more abstract art will be.' Most telling too is the comment of the young [First World War] casualty Franz Marc: 'Already early on I experienced people as ugly . . . animals too, (to which he had devoted himself in a grandiose series of paintings that included his well-known blue horses) also in them I discovered so much that is repulsive and ugly . . . as a result of which my art became increasingly schematic and more abstract.'[483]

We could let many more voices speak here. These might include Rimbaud and Lautréamont, who spoke of the manifestation of the mysterious and chaotic forces of a concrete and evil reality, the existentialists and others. We could invite you to a museum of modern art to look at the work of Tinguely, Rauschenberg, Marcel Duchamp or let you listen to the chaotic sounds of the music of John Cage, who gave his book about music the title *Silence*. We would rather end now however with a citation from the poem 'Howl', which was written in the mid-1950s by Ginsberg, who later became a leader of the Hippies in San Francisco. Ginsberg said in an interview that 'Howl' was written in the gnostic tradition. The poem consists of three parts. In the first part every stanza begins with the words 'I'm with you in Rockland'. And as we read we begin to understand that Rockland is this world and as such, a madhouse. The world, a madhouse:

> I'm with you in Rockland
>   where you scream in a straitjacket that you're losing the game of
>   the actual ping-pong of the abyss
> I'm with you in Rockland
>   where you bang on the catatonic piano the soul is innocent and
>   immortal it should never die ungodly in an armed madhouse
> I'm with you in Rockland
>   where fifty more shocks will never return your soul to its body
>   again from its pilgrimage to a cross in the void

Modern art in the world today

Modernism is more than a point of view. It is also a programme. In the Dada movement, in Surrealism, in Neo-Dada we encounter a fervent aggressiveness aimed at realizing this point of view, this understanding of reality. For the remarkable thing about people is that they not only have their interpretation of reality and a subjective insight, an own view of matters, but that they also want to have reality obey them, to change and reconstruct it in conformity with their insight. This is true not only for idealists and utopians but also for neognostics with their view of the meaninglessness and emptiness of our world. Their art gives a meaningless meaning to the meaningless.

Alford, one of the participants in the early Dada movement, later wrote about that. He said that after the self-assured rationalism of the nineteenth century there was an explosion of discovery, exploring what is outside and beyond the visible and rational in every field of the mind. This gradually led to the breakdown of all human, social and intellectual values that had seemed so firm until then. The consequence, Alford concluded, was demoralization, anti-logic, anti-determinism, anti-morality.[484]

Art is not just for artists. Art is a human activity and as such has an effect. Everything we do has some impact. If that were not so, the world would truly be worthless. Therefore it should not astonish us that this art in its more than half a century of passionate activity has influenced many people. The situation of the young generation around us has been shaped in part by it. The leftist Marxist mentality is also an attempt to escape out of this hopeless situation, this bad world, and to make a better one. Perhaps many are driven by despair.

Modern art is connected with a crisis in our culture, about which many have written. Modern art is an expression of it, to be sure, but also promotes it. Modern art does not open up the world but closes it off. It does not build up; it tears down. It does not disclose the positive possibilities but only the abysmal. It displays no beauty, just the hideous, even in what is beautiful. It does not strive for good, since all is evil. It preaches meaninglessness, since it is all the same.

Why is it that there are so many who cannot accept modern art? In all ages it has been the case that a new direction needed time to expand and gain influence, influence which then also had to be digested. Yet in our times there are still many who cannot or do not want to do this, even when they are active in contemporary art. Besides these people there are others who desperately try to appear modern; and there is a minority, albeit a strong minority, who really is modern. Yes, why is it that many in a museum or at an exhibition still view modern art, which by now might have become almost classic, as new and strange? Are the old values so strong and do they therefore vanish so slowly? Or are they not old values but rather real norms that reflect a true state of affairs? There is truly also a great deal that is old and mouldered in our world that is worth vanishing. We need not defend everything as if all were sacred ground. But do modern people not tend to throw out too much baby with the bathwater?

For people today, through the development of the sciences and the natural scientific methods, everything appear to be determined; human being seem nothing more than atoms without a will, compelled by laws

– economic laws, social laws, genetic laws, polemological[485] laws, pychological laws. People have become imprisoned in the world because like a King Midas we now touch everything with our rationalistic thinking, whereby it is rendered rationally transparent, but at the price of our human freedom. We live in a closed world.

The tragedy is that people blame Christianity for this. Two thousand years of Christianity are blamed for getting the world bogged down in a swamp, a swamp of social injustice, pollution, lust for power and wealth, greed and egoism, in short, in this entire dark situation. But could it not be the case that it is precisely the antichristian element in the Enlightenment with its rationalism, secularization and belief in the goodness of humanity that has landed us in the present crisis? It could be that the fight against the 'myth' of Christianity, as source of all the misery, only helps to clear away the ruins of ancient Christianity and its fruits. Then we retain even less; then we are literally given over to captivity by the heathen, to the chaos of the dictatorship of the proletariat, which in reality means the tyranny of a handful of power mongers who call themselves 'representatives of the people'. Russia is not an accidental outcome of a Marxist revolution but its logical consequence. Have we then not yet seen how correct Groen van Prinsterer was in his *Unbelief and Revolution,* which strikes us now, more than a century after it appeared, as prophecy?

Yet humans remain human. People cannot lose their humanity. That is the reason for the cry of despair and the wrestling to escape from the prison of this closed world. People endeavour to regain their freedom but do so in a neognostic, nihilistic way. It is a way that is destructive, more so as time passes by, and it is a way that is without real joy because love, beauty, dignity and also justice are missing.

Can something beautiful be made?
Is there an alternative? Is it possible in our day and age to make something beautiful, something meaningful? Has beauty not burnt her face, as a poet said? In 'Howl' Ginsberg inquired what sphinx of cement and aluminium had smashed open people's skulls and devoured their brains and imagination; he wrote of loneliness and ugliness and filth and went on to attack dollars and 'Moloch'.

Is it possible today to make something beautiful that has meaning, that is neither a flight from nor an avoidance of reality, that is also not just old and dilapidated, sentimental and traditionalistic, harking back to past glory and with no eye for the present day? Is it possible? A vital question for thousands of people. Also for us.

My answer is 'yes'. We need to realize that the modern movement is only one movement, one sect, one way of viewing things, and that even today it represents only a minority, albeit a strong minority. The modern movement is a religious movement, a religionless religion, a nihilistic sect that has created its idols for temples never meant to be built, which are built anyway, in the secular museums. In short, it is a movement full of paradoxes, the fundamental paradox being that people think they have lost their humanity and are in despair, yet would give everything just to be human again, because they cannot avoid the fact that they are human. Modernism is the result of setting God aside. 'God is dead', Nietzsche shrieked. 'And we have killed him,' he added. (Would the modernist theology that named itself after this shriek not itself exhibit gnostic characteristics?) Nietzsche continued: 'The stench of his corpse hangs over Europe.' Our question is: Do you smell it? The modern movement began with people's proclamation that they are autonomous and master of their own fate, their own god. In this they re-enacted the Fall in the superlative. The world thereby became a prison. That humanity is dead has even become a philosophical thesis and a palpable truth.

Naturally people still go about having fun. They eat, drink and even marry. They will never stop doing that. Yet for so many it is just the external side of life. After all, one has to live. Let us then eat and drink and be merry, for tomorrow we die. But we are already dead, unless . . .

I answered 'yes' to the question whether there is an alternative. To illustrate that I want to tell a story, one I have told many times in lectures and discussions. It is a true story. It happened in the 1950s in Paris along the Left Bank of the Seine. The main characters are students of Jean-Paul Sartre: a boy and a girl sitting together on a bench. They weep! Real tears! Why? Because they love each other. But why then weep? Because a Puritan mother or a Victorian father will not permit them to crawl into bed together? Well no, that is not the problem. They have had plenty of sexual experiences. They cry because that is not possible! Love does not exist, so they have been taught. Love is libido, horniness, if one chooses to put it in clearer, in less scientific terms. Love is a lovely façade for beautifying the animal, the merely carnal. Love is absurd and mere appearance . . .

The remarkable thing is that virtually every time I tell this story people ask me afterwards why the young people behaved so foolishly? After all, they loved each other. Yes, to be sure, is my reply, but then that is precisely the inner conflict, that they are human and truly love each other but that they have been taught and thus believe that love does not exist. Love has been unmasked and we have discovered the libido. Love is nothing other than a psychic experience that belongs to sexuality. The question here is one of truth. Truth must be able to pass the test of the confrontation with reality. The tears demonstrate that the modern naturalistic-existentialistic viewpoint, the fruit of a century-long démasqué – the writer Du Perron already spoke of it – is simply not true. We may be happy with their tears!

But is it then not love that they feel between them? They need only look at each other, embrace each other and say: 'Sartre is wrong, there is love, here, between you and me.' Yet, will they not always have the uncomfortable feeling that they are deceiving themselves and avoiding the truth and that what they have done is nothing other than what their parents and their parents' parents did? Namely, to put up a nice front, to decorate the hard reality, to hide from the truth, to escape? Can they love each other authentically? Is it really true and real?

Therefore they need only look at each other and embrace . . . but the crux lies in that 'need only'. It cannot be done that simply. Or it actually could be a bourgeois attitude seeking to lead a normal life, even in the absence of a basis for it, despite the fact that its foundations are in ruins and have sunk away into the fathomless depths of nothingness. It is a benefit of the modern movement that it has compelled us once again to account for the ground of these matters and not to casually ignore these problems and accept pseudo-answers.

The modern movement has also taught us, at least if we really want to learn anything from history, that the truth can never be found if we proceed from humanity, whether that be called our reason, our autonomy, our existence or our subjectivity. If we proceed from humanity, the outcome must be the ruination of the whole edifice of this world, simply because we are too small, too weak and too evil to carry that edifice. That edifice is ultimately the entirety of our cosmos, including the entire realm of human experience, the norms, values, humanity itself. That edifice is ultimately God's creation itself.

The truth can never be found if we begin with human being. Yet human being itself is more than the human situation and history. We have the freedom to give form again creatively to what are given in this creation as possibilities. Including love! But (and this 'but' must be written in capital letters), BUT that can only be so if we again begin by honouring the Creator as Creator and seek to accept love and beauty, yes, the entirety of reality from his hand and thank him for it. Without such a deep and decisive break with rationalism, which in the process of reasoning reduced reality to just the 'natural', atomic reality, to matter, and in this way descended into naturalism, without such a break from the neognosticism that grew from rationalism as an answer, we will never find the way out. In that case beauty will always walk with her face swathed in bandages and our love will always be as with rabbits and apes. 'Man' will always remain a naked ape [the allusion is to the book bearing that title], just as dumb and just as randy.

This is the spiritual struggle of our times. Our position is not determined – at least not only – by our situation. Life has meaning. We can lead meaningful lives and find beauty, justice and truth because we are human. Our struggle is therefore decisive.

Therefore, to come to a conclusion: *because* modernism in art and elsewhere is a point of view, a standpoint, and *because* people are free, essentially free and not slaves of their times, and *because* reality and humans are essentially unchanged but are still creatures of God, *therefore* there is an alternative. In that case however we must accept reality positively. No, even more, we shall have to regain reality. We have already lost so much. It will have to be rediscovered. It is accordingly senseless to be optimistic and think that 'accepting Christ' and 'being saved' and singing 'Hallelujah' is enough. Rebirth is certainly necessary. Songs of thanksgiving certainly also have their place. The prayer for God's help is indispensable. Yet proceeding from that foundation we shall also have to get to work. Perhaps it will take several generations to make up for lost time. To fully and properly rediscover the foundation – yes, I have in mind the foundation that can only be in Christ (1 Corinthians 3:10–15) – and once again to build on that. Even if the work is not only of precious stones, gold or silver but also always has straw mixed in with it, it will be less horrible and weak and absurd than the world built by the neognostics in the delusion that they are creating something grand while they are in reality just discovering the beginnings of hell.

People in our times, spoiled children living in the expectation of being gods, desire instant gratification: instant coffee, prefabricated cabinets, and life as an adventure but without dangers. Look at the travel bureau advertisements. The 'new generation' wants and intends to have all that. Thus they also hope through an instant revolution to acquire a better world, without understanding that smashing and destroying are easy but that building up and nurturing are hard work. It will only be possible through a great deal of effort and through thought, hard work and study, together with other people. And never without prayer. Without God's help it will not succeed. Only if we build on the firm foundation can something enduring arise.

Human beings are not reeds in the stream of history. We can and must swim against the current in order to avoid being swept away by the river into the abyss. Yet it is difficult. Some will allow themselves to be carried off by the flow. Some will be pulled into the depths by a whirlpool. Still others will be cast ashore and eliminated or trampled upon. Nevertheless, some will be able to overcome the current, albeit slowly. It is too difficult for us alone; hence we shall have to invoke God's help. If many join together the flow can be stopped or slowed. Perhaps too – that is our prayer, our hope and what we work for – the tide can even be turned by our common effort. That cannot be without effort or sacrifice. Yet we need not be slaves. Despair is also inappropriate, for God created not only the world but us as well – in his image and his likeness.

Reviews of Books on Modern Art

• J. Stellingwerff, Werkelijkheid en Grondmotief bij Vincent Willem van Gogh [reality and religious motive in Vincent Willem van Gogh][486]

Even in the sciences there is such a thing as fashion. Certain subjects or facets sometimes attract strong attention and are studied intensively by many while others remain in the background. At the moment the nineteenth century is the centre of interest in art history. Probably a reason for this is that people want to take a closer look at the origins of modern art and so have arrived at the forerunners. It is therefore not so surprising that an engineer from Delft interested in delving into a subject in art history would focus his attention on the late nineteenth century. Nor should the fact that van Gogh rather than a French master took Stellingwerff's interest surprise us when we know that this technician comes from the so-called 'new line', a movement represented by the journal *Polemius*, which used the term 'national' in its subtitle.

This 'school', which was a training ground for Stellingwerff, enabled him to bring out new facets particularly with regard to van Gogh's earlier period: the study of the nineteenth century as to the developments in the Dutch churches proved especially fruitful. On this point above all his dissertation is valuable and makes a real contribution to our knowledge of the person van Gogh. We therefore find it lamentable that we do not find more about that and that he did not devote his attention exclusively to it, namely to Vincent van Gogh in his Dutch period, when his contacts and conflicts with the church – and obviously also with artistic Holland – were the most intense. Now that the author has turned to investigating 'the whole van Gogh' it seems to us that at times some of that material is not developed as thoroughly as it might have been. It is more a biography of the person van Gogh, of the vicissitudes of his life and his insights, particularly with regard to religion, while analysis of his paintings is not done sufficient justice. For it is not enough to discuss the subjects of the paintings and the significance van Gogh himself attached to them; one must also investigate the visual language he employed and the way in which he handled the themes. Often it is only in this way that the meaning of a work will become clear.

Thus we may find ourselves in agreement with the explanation of the *Sower* by Millet and van Gogh respectively, while finding however that it is not made sufficiently clear to us how the Roman Catholic element in the former and the humanistic element in the latter can also be discerned in the paintings themselves. But perhaps we ask for too much. As a biography of van Gogh the dissertation already gives us enough, although I have to confess that sometimes the indications of the religious ground motive in its specific application to van Gogh remain too schematic, and in particular the dialectic, the inner tension between the two poles of nature and freedom (as exposited by Dooyeweerd, upon whom Stellingwerff wishes, after all, to base himself), is insufficiently clarified. Perhaps much of the tension in van Gogh's life and work can be accounted for in terms of the two contradictory demands he makes of himself: on the one hand to be as faithful as possible to the given reality, and on the other to express himself directly as freely as possible, to say things that no longer lie so much in the given material as in the mind of the artist himself. Both demands are religious in nature and therefore unavoidable for van Gogh as a human being.

In order to elucidate his view that the art of painting is also rooted in a ground motive, Stellingwerff discusses Rembrandt and Hugo van der Goes. Our criticism is the same here as with his treatment of van Gogh. The expositions that are meant to make clear to us what faith Rembrandt confessed, provide a splendid summary of the material and interpret it lucidly and in a manner virtually beyond challenge. Rembrandt's art, however, remains in the background.

For it is illuminating to see a statistical summary of the themes handled by an artist – here we see the engineer in action – yet ultimately the theme does not decide the meaning of the work, namely what the theme is made to say and proclaim. Stellingwerff has mentioned in passing the humanistic influences apparent in Rembrandt's earlier works. Yet we find it regrettable that he does not go into that more deeply, the more so because it leaves the conclusion insufficiently elucidated that not only was Rembrandt a child of God but also his work was defined by the ground motive of Creation, Fall and Redemption. And that is a pity because it diminishes somewhat the power of his thesis to convince the outsider, the humanist reader. By way of an aside, we would also have preferred to see Stellingwerff say something about the interpretation Wencelius gave in his very controversial book about Rembrandt and Calvin, about which [interpretation] Stellingwerff, given his own study, might have offered a clearer judgment than has been given until now.

In restricting himself to the more biographical aspect and in relegating to the background analytical concerns about composition and iconology there is, however, also gain. The human being that the artist ultimately always is, is done greater justice in this way, and so Stellingwerff was able to pluck the fruits of his having been formed in the 'new line' and of his theological study, to which he applied himself intensively in connection with the *Vrijmaking* [or 'Liberation', the separation of some of the Dutch Reformed churches in 1944], which was complemented later on by his study of the Philosophy of the Cosmonomic Idea. It is precisely these points, namely the biographical in connection with the religious, that are the strongest in this book.

Yet when the writer goes deeply into the analysis of a work of art, he fumbles in our opinion and the lack of years of familiarity with the material that an art historian would have, becomes clearly apparent. I have in mind here his analysis of the main work of Hugo van der Goes – of whose biography he gives a clear characterization to the extent that the sources allow. He approaches this work anachronistically, in a nineteenth-century manner – an approach or way of looking at things that naturally does not lead to misperceptions regarding van Gogh. But Hugo van der Goes did not conceive his painting as individualistically as the nineteenth-century painters did; he stands in a long tradition of the rendering of this particular theme. Stellingwerff has also not noticed that van der Goes is not portraying a particular moment, so that remarks like 'the baby has been washed but not yet wrapped in swaddling clothes' fail to do justice to the homiletic-theological import of this work. This painter was not so naïve as to think that Mary would have laid the newborn babe on the cold floor for adoration or to have done so in present-day clothes. Instead, here we have to do with a formula (comparable with the formulation of a dogma) that can be accurately traced to its origins. After the Black Death in the middle of the fourteenth century there was a period of intense reflection on religious life. Sometimes this led to mysticism, i.e. to the suppression of the elements borne by the nature motive (within the Roman Catholic nature-grace ground motive). Thus St Brigitte, a Swedish mystic living in Italy, had serious objections against an all too human representation of the birth, too earthly and natural and too little typified as 'incarnation of the Word'. Then she received a vision and saw how it should be done. In about 1370 Niccolo di Tommaso painted the birth for the first time in keeping with this vision.[487] And the work of Hugo van der Goes is in that tradition. It is actually no simple matter to indicate where in this scene nature plays a role, since the entire story – including the shepherds – is ascribed to the supernatural realm, to which after all the Bible is assigned as well. Nature appears rather in the way of painting, in the painstaking exactness, the naturalistic rendering of things, of Mary's cloak, the vase, the landscape, and so on, in fact of everything there is to be seen.

Fifteenth-century painting is extremely complex, full of inner contradictions and its study from an iconological standpoint, whereby questions of ground motive and its inner dialectic can be elucidated, has barely begun. Insofar as this particular chapter in Stellingwerff is concerned, we have the feeling that even if his analysis had been correct, he would rather have said something about this new Northern art in general than about Hugo van der Goes in particular.

But to conclude, we may see in this book a fruit of the 'new line' school, whose strength lies in the biographical-religious aspect, and we can honour the engineer who has mastered this humanities approach.

• H. Redeker, De Dagen der Artistieke Vertwijfeling [the days of artistic desperation][488]

Again and again, now in this way and then in that, we are confronted with the questions: 'What kind of times are we living in?' and 'What is the sense and background of all this activity?' We see that there is a revolution, yes, but 'Where is it coming from and where is it going, and why?' This applies particularly in the field of visual art, where people are at times robustly and sharply confronted with the problems. After all, in a painting we are faced in one glance with the painter's view of the world and we look, as it were, along with him or her. The directness by which art confronts us with this modernity has a much harsher impact than if we were to browse through a thick book or read a complex scholarly treatise, even if in the end they all say the same thing and reflect the same view of life.[489]

H. Redeker dared to tackle these difficult problems and to inquire after the meaning of the crisis and revolution in which we find ourselves. Redeker's book would already be interesting if for no other reason than that it was written by someone who himself stands in the midst of the turbulence and struggle of all that is 'modern', who presents himself as the spokesman, as it were, of the revolutionary mindset, who considers the way travelled and verbalizes its direction and purpose.

He supposes correctly that the crisis in art is part of a larger crisis in the whole of our culture – a crisis that at the same time is a revolution against the present situation, which was evoked by and arose in response to the centuries-long supremacy of rationalistic natural scientific thought. A multiplicity of human domains such as religion, sensuality, dreams, and also art, was rejected or consigned to the realm of the ostensibly make-believe, unreality and lies. The impoverishment and deformation that resulted from this have now evoked reactions – and initially art was assigned the task of being the revelation of all that was non-rational and had been repressed. Art – and Redeker correctly assesses the important place that art occupied in mental life – was made to be a revelation of all the malformed, senseless, repressed and corporeal, of the night-side of life and the spiritual *souterrain*, as Redeker puts it. Art working in this way, however, discovered the ground of the crisis and perceived that it could not be resolved other than by an entire and radical revolution of life itself. The revolution of art led to a crisis in art – art was not up to the too lofty task assigned to it, of being revelation, yes religion – and this crisis would only be solvable by a revolution of the world; for only then would art be capable of expressing what it is asked to, but cannot yet, express. The purpose of the revolution will be 'the union of spiritual and irrational elements in the fullness and genuineness of (human) existence'. Humankind themselves, in their general 'existential' totality should stand at the centre, not science or reason.

We see in this book how the personality ideal opposes the science ideal, which not only debased humanity but also endeavoured to dismiss the 'irrational' in human life as urges, and so forth. Due to the course of history it was exactly art – that was Romantically regarded as the expression of the free human personality – that was the first to revolt against the rationalistic world picture and to be hailed as the standard bearer of the revolution. One must not forget that the first artistic movements to seek new ways were already coming up in the years round about 1880, in Symbolism, while the revolution in art that called to life Abstract, Expressionist, Surrealist and other directions was already essentially completed by about 1910. Yet ultimately revolutionized art changed little about the world and humanity, so that the call for a total revolution soon made itself felt – a revolution, for that matter, which considered even the Marxist revolution as not radical enough, since Marxism too arises from rationalism.

Away with the science ideal! The theme resounds from many lines of this book as a kind of refrain. The whole person to the throne! The personality ideal rises in revolt. Yet it can only direct itself towards a marred and 'unmasked' personality . . . that is the ground of the crisis that reigns precisely in 'progressive' and cultural environments.

Redeker's study is instructive and illuminating, and helps us to understand better the meaning of many of the sounds we hear all about us. We cannot go into the details and parts of this book here, and we shall likewise resist the temptation to introduce the book to you more closely by citing passages from it. Suffice it to say that we find this volume so instructive because here we hear the voice of someone who is a 'modern' person himself, so that the modern ideals are shown to us so clearly and directly. Ultimately, however, the deepest grounds for the crisis and difficulties of our times are neither touched on nor seen: namely, the consistent apostasy from the Lord our God and the worshipping of human being. As a result of this, the course of events is sketched too much as unavoidable and necessary, without any unmasking of the false prophecy that determined its goal and direction.

Still, apart from these objections, it is a pity that Redeker has written such a difficult book, too difficult perhaps for those who are not at home in modern art and the modern humanities. On the other hand, it is perhaps just as well, since as a result the possible prophecy implicit in this book for the 'modern' person will not be entirely understood. Anyone however who takes the trouble to wrestle his or her way through the first fifty pages or so, and in that way becomes familiar with its typical jargon and somewhat obscure manner of expression, will be able to read the rest without difficulty and gain the benefits of doing so.

• J.M. Prange, De God Hai-hai en Rabarber, met het Kapmes door de Jungle der Moderne Kunst [the god Hai-Hai and rhubarb, with a machete through the jungle of modern art][490]

For many today modern art remains a strange puzzle, a pill difficult to swallow, an abracadabra phenomenon with no discernible way through it. Often I have noticed that people really do understand this art but do not trust their own judgment. When people think of art they think of eternal beauty, of something that they should be able to enjoy and that enriches their lives. It is questionable however whether this definition is good and correct, whether this demand may even be made, also with regard to old art. Certainly modern art does not satisfy it. Because of that people simply claim not to know what to do with this art. Yet perhaps they understand it after all, perhaps the negative, destructive, irrational and ugly are essential and real and belong to the meaning and significance of the work. Standing before an abstract work, some say, 'It is beautiful in colour but what am I supposed to see in it?' Well, perhaps it was the artist's intention to say nothing, to present just beautiful colours.

Proceeding from the pre-conceived idea about art mentioned above, people even when they do understand it simply abandon the field believing they do not, and so bar the way for themselves to gain a real understanding. And that is to their own detriment, if for no other reason than that when people do not try to understand the artistic and leading forces of the day they may perhaps later on simply accept the fruit of these forces without knowing what they have in front of them. People who do not want to listen to the spirit of the age must not be surprised if at a given moment they cannot understand and assess what is done by those who did listen. Whoever, in keeping with the word of the apostle, wants to fight against the spirit of the age, against the spiritual wickedness in the air, will have to listen to that spirit in order to get to know its programme, its content, its 'revelation'. Otherwise one will act like those political leaders who found [Egyptian President Gamel Abdel] Nasser such a nice fellow since they neglected to read his political programme and the formulation of his objectives.

Yet, however that may be, it is certainly difficult. For those listening for the first time it may seem as if someone is standing there speaking in Chinese. It may be important to learn Chinese, because only then will one be able to tell if the other is cursing or proclaiming the gospel, or speaking the truth or a lie. And learning a new language is not always an easy matter. Recently a number of little books have appeared that profess to be able to show us the way in this matter. There have been books that dealt with these things before which were, however, difficult to read and often expensive. But these ones are different – they are affordable and readable. Thus the path to learning the new language lies open. We want to discuss four of these little books here. Three of them at least are works we would really like you to own, and one of them we would urgently recommend.

Indeed, there is also one that we decidedly advise you against. It is a little book that has enjoyed great success, comparable with the sensation surrounding the van Meegeren case,[491] as the public likes to laugh in its sleeve at the fact that the great, the informed, the experts do not know what they are talking about either or, at least, can make mistakes, which brings them down to the public's own level. And this gives people a license to spout forth whatever nonsense comes to mind and to abandon all study and real research.

That little book is J.M. Prange's *De God Hai-Hai en rabarber*, which has the subtitle 'with a machete through the jungle of modern art'. Prange compares modern art to the god Hai-Hai and discusses the grandiloquence and the conjuring mumblings of the medicine men. And he, Prange, will now reveal the real meaning of their humbug. Although we would rather not write about this book – it is not pleasant to have to steep oneself in such rancorous and purely negative reflections – we shall do so after all because such important matters are dealt with here and the arguments presented may sometimes seem convincing to those who are strangers to the world of modern art.

The core of Prange's little book is to be found on page 8: 'Abstract painting . . . is a commercial enterprise.' He asserts here that all the modern painters who work that way are just chasing after cheap success and dear money. But he says still more. He contends (p.22) that museums today buy anything and everything that is served up under the banner of the modern and the abstract – and in a note he states explicitly that this art is thus the officially sanctioned art. He puts his finger on the fact that people appeal to the cases of Cézanne and van Gogh – who were also not honoured in their time – and out of fear of making the same mistake as their detractors people follow the latest trend, so that young art is glorified and becomes the official art. There is a lot of truth in this. In the last century the forerunners of the modern artists were excluded from the official Salon, unrecognized and ignored. They fought against the ruling majority, which however was no longer a creative force. But now this creative minority has become the ruling majority and everything must bend before its dogmas.

Certainly, in that assertion Prange is not incorrect. If he had gone on to write only against current museum policy, against today's official Salon, against the elevation to dogma of the principle of modernism, then we would have been happy to support him. But he gallops on. He indulges in an extensive argument about Pieneman, respected and renowned in his time, and insists that his case shows that no conclusions may be drawn from fame and the fact that something is called 'contemporary'. Again, we are somewhat in agreement with him. But then he goes further. If he does not want the vaunted abstraction, then we would think that he probably wants the disesteemed figurative art. Ah no, says Prange, I saw so much junk at expositions. Just as academic in character as the abstract works. We slowly come to understand that Prange is intent on rejecting everything that may not be called 100 per cent masterpieces, together with everything that today enjoys a whiff of renown and is seen and experienced as something great. He even says so in so many words (p.51). But is he not aware that he is pursuing a utopia, that there have been, yes must be more, mediocre artists in every age (must, indeed, because these artists, although probably not forerunners and shapers of style have at the very least a social task to fulfil – for example, by fulfilling the many commissions and requests of the time). What Prange really wants is that today there would be a Titian, a Rembrandt, a van Gogh and a Raphael, artists who paint in their ways. Yet one can only accept such geniuses with gratitude, not demand them, and the question is whether work such as theirs could have the same meaning and place today that it had in their own time. When one keeps in mind this implicitly expressed demand of Prange, one can go on to understand many of his pronouncements.

In the name of this utopia Prange proceeds to fight against anything and everything while losing all sense of proportion. He tilts at windmills, to be sure, but neglects the real fight that has to be fought. He jousts against windmills but does not even do so fairly. We want to provide a few examples. Triumphantly he announces that a proponent of modern art spoke about Mondrian's challengeable writings. Scornfully he repeats this several times in this book: such an artist, who as you say yourself writes challengeable things, should we now admire such a figure as great? But Prange forgets that people do not necessarily write nonsense and that they are not depreciating the following figures as artists when they say that the writings of Leonardo da Vinci, of Ingres, of Michelangelo, of Ghiberti, of Alberti, of any artist who ever took up the pen, are challengeable. For what human being ever wrote anything that was not challengeable?

Then he speaks mockingly of two professors who at some point had something good to say about photography. Such statements may perhaps serve to explain the success of the book but they betray a narrow mind – to put it mildly – that can tolerate no other opinion than its own. Let me say honestly that I am also not in agreement with the scholarly gentlemen in question, but that does not mean that they are stupid, still less that they have joined some sort of cheap swindling clan of money makers. And that is all in the context of a fulmination against the fact that in the Museum of Modern Art in New York there are also some technical products on display, steam kettles and vacuum cleaners and more. He seems to forget how necessary it was and is to introduce improvements in mass-produced articles precisely with respect to form giving. Can he not be grateful that in the twentieth century something has been achieved that towers above the utensils and implements that were made a century ago? Does he not forget that in the Rijksmuseum too there are jugs and plates and glasses and vases and chairs and tapestries and even a bed! As important representatives of a world that is gone, to be sure, but also as a testimony to the artistic mind of the artisans who made those objects. Prange loses all sense of proportion, as we said.

His writing is full of negative bad-mouthing. De Chirico was for years a leading figure in modern art. Then at a certain point there was an abrupt turnabout; he distanced himself from his older work and went back to painting in an old way. Yet it is poor work – so Prange cries – and, he adds, we also expected nothing better. But Prange forgets that he himself also once made lithographs that we cannot call anything but surrealistic, works that were also modern in their kind. Now what about that? I have not seen any examples of Prange's art in recent years. Must it too fall under the same odium he heaps upon de Chirico? Why does he not show us the way himself? After all, he is (or was?) an artist. Or must we take the abominable kitschy-kitschy cover on his little book as a warning to anyone having taste that Prange himself has become like that – is that perhaps an unsigned work of his? In any case, he thought it acceptable, for the second and third printings were furnished with the same piece of tastelessness.

Prange forgets still more. First he has tried to make us wary of everything that presents itself today as art. That would be moneymaking sponsored by an organization for the deception of many. Or it would be art like Pieneman's – the very fact that it is renowned and respected today shows that it is not great art, so Prange says. In this way there is, after he has also kicked around the simple, honest makers of 'ordinary' work, nothing left over. Hurrah! Now we have a license to go out and purchase for a pittance a piece at the picture framer's shop, an 'oil painting on canvas', such a really nice example of kitsch. Who could criticize us now? It may be nothing, but there is nothing better, nothing at all. Prange has said so. For there are a few good painters today, so he says – alas, not clarifying in what that 'good' might consist – but he may be happy that they are not respected and recognized. For that would only prove that they are nothing after all.

What Prange forgets is that besides the success of the fashionable painters in every period, the truly great ones also gained recognition. Prange cites Heine because in 1831 he wrote extolling Ary Scheffer. Yet one who reads what Heine said, soon discovers that he had his criticisms too and doubt about the man's stature – and that a few pages further on Heine is full of praise, virtually without restriction, for a painter who was not at all popular at the time, Delacroix. Indeed, Rembrandt was respected in his day and the so-called disesteem and tragedy are a nineteenth-century Romantic invention. Van Gogh? Even during his lifetime a fantastic laudatory article appeared written by Aurier, and if he had lived ten more years he would have become a world-famous figure during his lifetime. It takes time for people who do something entirely new to gain recognition. The biographies of all great figures testify to the struggle they go through to gain their place. That is not a bad thing, at least if we do not make a myth of it. Really, there have not been so many unappreciated geniuses in world history.

Why did we discuss all this so extensively? Because Prange supposes that besides all the great figures he also has to trash Picasso from beginning to end. But let us reflect on Picasso's case for a moment without even looking at his work. Is it possible that an artist upon his debut already gains admirers who respect him as a genius and who thereafter remain faithful to him, even when he changes his style and the nature of his work radically; is it possible that a man inspires and shows the way to thousands of youths – if it is empty and nothing? Indeed, the respected figures of the day like Pieneman received medallions and flattering reviews from the journalist of the week, but they did not fascinate those who know great art, they did not inspire, they did not renew – for the essence of their art was precisely the non-renewing and therefore generally understandable – and they did not alter the 'face of their century'. Among those who did do that however are Leonardo, Michelangelo, Raphael, Dürer, Rembrandt, Caravaggio, Carracci, Jan van Eyck, and so on. They were great figures who were honoured in their own time, renewers who sometimes in a brief period entirely changed the art of their day. Is it conceivable that an artist could continue to fascinate and inspire people of tremendous capacity as well as lesser personalities with his work for over fifty years (even if only to study the phenomenon that he is) if it were all nothing?

Prange criticizes, but it all comes down to Picasso's art not satisfying the criteria he has set down, namely to be like the art from Raphael to Velasquez and Rembrandt: 'It is all equally gawky and doltish,' so he writes. Yet measuring with the measure with which he measures, everything disappears except the greatest masters between 1500 and 1800. For in following his line we must perforce reject all Gothic sculpture, all stained-glass windows, all Romanesque art, all Egyptian art, all art of primitive peoples, in short all art not based on Renaissance ideals.

Prange also selected some plates – tendentiously, with comments in his familiar overweening tone: an unpleasant Picasso – as if he could be typified by just one work and rejected on the basis of it; a Braque that he compares incorrectly and then fails to do justice to in the presentation. Only in the case of the Kandinsky, however, do I really have to say that he is wrong: the work by Kandinsky is decidedly more attractive than the prehistoric horse.

But we will stop now. Apart from his indictment of failings and serious shortcomings in current museum policy with respect to modern art and apart from his recognition of the danger and reality of a present-day Salon art, of a majority that wants to impose its dogmas on others, there is little that remains. Too little. Yet the question remains what we are to do with Picasso and whether there may not be something we could read that would help us. The question remains who the god Hai-Hai is. Prange may suppose he has shown that this god does not exist, but one may fear that Hai-Hai is unmoved by all that and just continues to stand upon its pedestal. For what Prange did is mortally dangerous. He says to us: this god is not there, it is pure bluff, idle sputtering and empty raving. But for all that this god, the spirit of the century, *is* there to be sure, and force of error though it may be, this god is in any case a deeply spiritual reality that we cannot just frivolously kick aside. Those who really want to be engaged in today's spiritual struggle must take their opponent seriously. The god Hai-Hai may be a living Moloch, but if so we cannot avoid the conflict by rationalizing it away in Prange's footsteps.

Next time we shall see what others have written about these matters. Perhaps we shall then be able to see something of the spirit of our times in its true proportions and according to its true nature, and gain an understanding of modern art as its revelation.

• H. Sedlmayr, Die Revolution der modernen Kunst ('The revolution of modern art')[492]

We saw last time [in the first of our four reviews of recent books about modern art[493]] that J.M. Prange supposed he could, in a small, contemptuous book, unmask the god Hai-Hai, which is to say the spirit of the modern era, as non-existent. In that framework he also declared tremendously creative geniuses like Picasso to be charlatans, gold-diggers, bunglers and whatever. Indeed, Prange used a machete, rough and without nuance, more than the fine lancet of analysis. He failed to see that one may label the worship of the god Hai-Hai as an illegitimate, degrading idolatry of the worst kind, but that this deity nevertheless exists and endures as a power that one may not mentally dismiss without falsifying or even rendering impossible one's apprehension of today's world. Mortally dangerous, we called his theses, because he wants to lull good folks to sleep – 'it is there but is without significance' – whereby the spiritual struggle threatens to be entirely neglected. The result can only be that the god acquires more power over the spirits, as no resistance is offered.

Hence we must be happy with the opportunity to discuss another little book that delves much deeper in an effort to understand modern art and that sheds light on many aspects of the subject, which can only be to our benefit. Its writer concludes with the important thesis that it is by no means necessary for us to conform to the revolution in modern art and, further, with a brief summary in which he states that the spirit of modern art – Prange's god Hai-Hai – is destructive of all human value and threatens human being and culture with ruin. This man has in any case perceived the seriousness of the subject and has not walked past it with a laugh – Prange reports that he stood in front of Picasso's *Guernica* and laughed; he ought to have wept – and he has endeavoured to fathom the modern mind in its depth, the better to investigate and understand the abyss that is gaping ever more clearly before us.

We refer here to H. Sedlmayr's book *Die Revolution der modernen Kunst*. This is a volume in the so-called RoRo series, German pocketbooks about important problems and themes which in general have very good content (and are inexpensive). Light reading it is not, but here at least difficult material is not simplified into an unrecognizable caricature. On the other hand it is also not too difficult; it was not written for professionals.

The German art historian Sedlmayr has developed a method of his own for fathoming the art of a period. He namely looks for fundamental features, basic characteristics that make the phenomena transparent. Whether his method is really the right one for art history is not a question we shall try to answer here, but we can say that in this case this method leads to clarity. He identifies four essential characteristics of modernity in art: a desire for purity; art under the spell of geometry and technical construction; the absurd as a refuge for freedom; and the quest for the original, primal forces.

The first of these, the desire for purity, is indeed a motive that anyone who has looked into these matters must recognize as an important component. The issue is to make art pure art, to cleanse it of everything that is not art in the proper sense, of everything that cannot be understood in a purely aesthetic way. In painting we encounter this in so-called abstract art, i.e. art that has no subject. This occupies an extensive chapter in Sedlmayr and we shall not venture to relate it at length here. It shows us the results of a long development: in the Middle Ages art was often an ideogram, a sign for making a higher reality visible. With modern times naturalism set in, the effort to present things in the work of art as the eye sees them. But the deeper element endured: Giorgione's *Venus*, Michelangelo's *David*, a Rubens landscape, a biblical scene by Rembrandt, Vermeer's *Street in Delft* and Jan Steen's *St Nicholas morning*[494] involve infinitely more than showing a nude lady, a nude man, a piece of nature, a reconstructed photo of 'how it was', a detail of Delft or a party, respectively. With these subjects the artists addressed themes that in one way or another were close to their hearts and through which they wanted to express their view of reality, or at least a facet of it. A later era, above all the nineteenth century, rejected everything that could be called literary, everything that was a 'story', everything that Venus is, besides a naked lady, everything that made a landscape by Rubens something more than a registration of light rays cast by a piece of nature on one's retina. People now represented only what the eye could see, and the work of art meant nothing more than that. In part this happened in reaction against an official and decadent academic art that was virtually entirely preoccupied with the story, an art that forgot that art must be more than that to be art. The aesthetic aspect was forgotten by the academicians but declared to be everything by their opponents.

Our century follows next. Now the subject, too, is dropped. The principle persists that the work of art is exactly what it offers one to see, but now in a much more consistent form. The painting is no longer a 'landscape'; it is itself. 'Do not ask me what it represents,' said Mondrian to those who viewed his art. 'It represents exactly what you see,' black vertical and horizontal lines on a white surface. A modern abstract image means nothing, or rather it means itself, it is pure form that represents nothing but rests only in itself. The work of art is its own content, is itself the artistic reality – and no longer a representation, symbolization or depiction of something else. A remarkable development, to be sure. In the course of recent centuries the work of art has drawn ever closer to ordinary everyday visible reality, to reality as a camera registers it, in order in the end to become itself the reality. Such a development may serve to make clear that there are deeper forces at work in modern art than profit and impotence.

The second – art under the spell of geometry and technology – is in a certain sense an extension of the first. This too is a facet that at least in part defines modern art.

Sedlmayr's third point, the absurd, that found and finds form particularly in Surrealism, is indeed a remarkable and important phenomenon. It goes much deeper than the desire to make something crazy. The last basic principle, the quest for the primal forces that determine reality, is clear in Expressionism and likewise unmistakably present in many modern artists. They want to escape the trivial and the not particularly meaningful external side of things, go deeper and look behind the things for their ground. Thus this art, a clear example of which is the work of Paul Klee, often comes very close to mysticism: one flees from the hated and despised reality of individual things for the sake of apprehending the absolute, the enduring, that which rests in itself. People know they cannot accomplish that, so this work often breathes a certain melancholy, doubt or despair.

After this analysis of the various forms in which the modern mind manifests itself, Sedlmayr attempts to delve deeper, to see what is behind them, to penetrate to the why. And then he points to nihilism. It need not astonish us that the core of much that can be called 'modern' is to be found there. For people have rationalized away and have rejected the God of the Bible, but they cannot simply put any other gods in his place – for it is precisely the Bible that has taught them that other gods are only human inventions and creations. But God and the reality of his work, also in the creation – remember what Paul wrote about that at the beginning of his Epistle to the Romans – cannot be rationalized or explained away. Someone once remarked correctly that modern people live 'in the shadow of the non-existent God', which is why their nihilism is a crisis, a permanent revolution, rebellion. They live in a permanent fear of being deeply moved by something in reality – which always reminds us in some way or another of God as the Creator and Sustainer – or of losing their heart to something. People desire freedom severed from all ties and restrictions but can only discover that they are 'confined' in God's world.

Many modernist phenomena can be understood by seeing them as expressions of aestheticism, so Sedlmayr asserts correctly. Aestheticism is a matter of art being the highest value and having its meaning in itself. But art is thereby denatured into a non-committal game without content and without meaning: for every meaning or content would constitute a reference or an attachment again to something beyond art. Or art is seen as revelation. More often than not, however, people will show how they understand the reality in which they live – and then voice is given to all the hatred against God's creation, to all malaise and sense of being confined in this cosmos, to all hatred and revolt against anything that in any way can impede or bind human beings. Thus a great deal that is awful and ugly in modern art is a consequence of aestheticism, of glorifying art.

People sometimes seek in art the revelation of general, reality-defining basic principles. Art thereby sometimes loses its meaning as art and often its comprehensibility, namely when people seek to depict through it basic principles of reality without referring to anything concrete. For it is a fact that abstract concepts can never be grasped as such; they only exist as abstractions, which appear only when one divests concrete givens of their concrete characteristics. Therefore I must always use examples if I want to explain what love, hate, beauty, language, history or marriage is. All of these exist only in concretized form and cannot be separated from it. Abstract concepts cannot be defined apart from the reference to reality in the 'for example' or in the simple showing of things. Therefore it is also not true when the modernist says that he or she has liberated art from the story and can therefore now offer what is essential in visual form. For the nineteenth-century academic pieces may have presented stories, pure and simple; a *Street* by Vermeer or a *St Nicholas morning*[495] by Jan Steen offers us much more, even if the content of these works is never separable from what is shown. These last works one may compare to the 'for example' I just mentioned above: in and with these objects something of value is told us that can never be given in separation from them, for then I would either be saying nothing or else no one would be able to understand me.

We are digressing. What Sedlmayr wants to show, and we followed him in it, is this, that behind all modernist work there is a spirit that we may not ignore if we desire to understand what it is that modernism is an expression of and why it is what it is.

We want to conclude now with an example that may serve to make various matters somewhat clearer. I have in mind Karel Appel's art, which I would typify as nihilistic iconoclasm. Iconoclasm, which means literally the destruction of images, because by radically destroying, deforming and turning around everything that was once offered in the way of representations, views and images of reality, he at the same time destroys, knocks down and dishonours the values that were contained in them. With the image, the values contained in it went by the board. And it is nihilistic because the destruction is not aimed at things that had decayed and were due for renewal; rather, he distrusts every value or attachment to laws, norms, givens or attainments, while he no longer can or will believe in anything. If we keep this in mind, it can no longer surprise us that if anything recognizable appears from his brush, it is freaks, monsters and terrors. The view that we find amongst the deepest of this type of painters is often closely affinitive with gnosticism, which regards what is created, and the fact that it is created, as sinful, bad and inferior.

We can warmly recommend Sedlmayr's little book. Although there is a 'but' involved. It is our belief namely that this study does not sufficiently teach us to look, does not tell us enough about the origins and the grammar of that new language that is also an important aspect of modern art. The study is somewhat too one-sided in its focus on spiritual problems and, while everything that the author mentions is certainly true, it is also good to look a little further and inspect the other side of the coin. Sedlmayr is so fascinated by the countenance of the god Hai-Hai that he forgets to notice the people involved, neglects to listen to their song, neglects to listen in on their everyday conversations. Is it not an unmistakable fact that art is art and not philosophy or a life and world view, however much art may involve these as well? Therefore we shall return the next time with a brief discussion of two more little books about modern art.

- **R.W.D. Oxenaar, De Schildernkunst van Onze Tijd [the art of painting in our times], 1928 and W. Hess, Dokumente zum Verständnis der Modernen Malerei ('Documents toward the understaning of modern art')**[496]

A new style, a new current, in short, something new in history never begins by itself, out of the blue. It also never arises from a single principle, through a single circumstance or cause. Upon closer analysis of the aims, ideas, reasons, backgrounds, circumstances and conditioning factors one will always discover a number of causes – the prehistory of a new style or school is always complex. Every one of the contributing or co-determining causes that help to call the 'new' to life is indispensable, and every one of them has helped to give that 'new' its own face. If something new ever did arise under the influence of a single determining idea or circumstance, it will usually have been of little significance, quickly overtaken by other contemporary occurrences and soon forgotten as a failed experiment. It is precisely this multiplicity of causes and backgrounds that gives the 'new' its foundation and right to exist and energizes those forming it.

That is also the case with the modern in art. It is not only the spiritual factors that determined it, not only the crisis in modern thought, not only the negativism in the attitude towards the given reality. None of these factors would be sufficient in themselves to explain why the modern has turned out to look the way it does, now, as a historical reality. That is why Sedlmayr's analysis is not adequate to explain or understand modern art precisely with respect to its concrete artistic styles. He shows us exceptionally important facets but – and we shall return to this – a number of the points, at least, on which he bases his analysis apply equally to the Far East, and have done so for centuries, without having led there to anything that could be called 'modern art'.

Therefore it is indispensable for a good understanding of modern art that people explore at least to some extent its prehistory, the way that was travelled and that led to it. Outstandingly suited for this purpose is the little book by R.W.D. Oxenaar, *De schilderkunst van onze tijd*. Oxenaar provides a survey of painting since the middle of the nineteenth century and in that way gives us an insight into the historical developments that can in turn help to make certain facets of modern art clear to us.

An objection can, however, be raised against this method and certainly against its conclusions. The impression is established that there is one historical line, one line of development. Everything that does not lie in this line, that either clings to what used to lie in this line or simply goes in another way, is then either outdated or has no contact with its time or is simply of no importance. But that is untenable and leads to a kind of dictatorship of the historical development. Let us keep this in mind: what Oxenaar presents is one very particular line of development in one very particular (Parisian) environment alongside which many other lines, many other endeavours, many other possibilities exist that he leaves unmentioned. Thus we do not contest – details aside – his historical sketch, but we do challenge the conclusion implicit in it, namely that something can be meaningful only if it had its place along that line – with the imposed conclusion that only that has importance today which lies in the line of this particular historical development.

Given this notion, we can understand Oxenaar's statement that 'Floating along on the stream of time, one is at least able to recognize art where it arises and to digest it as a not fully describable yet self-evident complement of one's own personality.' We would call upon you however not to just float along on the stream of time but to take a stand in the turmoil of present-day events, to fight your fight at the place where you find yourself, to participate in the forming of what the future will bring. Do not accept everything on offer today as up to date but test, reject, accept, criticize and celebrate what you regard as meaningful, valuable or correct. If you are perhaps opposed to the modern in the sense of Karel Appel and his circle, fine – oppose it, but not without knowledge, not without having gone into the work itself – and see if elsewhere there may not be other contemporary work that you do find valuable, wholesome and good. Granted that not everyone is called to do this, but against a Prange-like attitude that 'Hai-Hai does not exist,' against the all too prevalent attitude in our circle that we should disengage here, I would like to show another possibility. I am not imposing a burden on you, for the Lord does not do that. And you do not have to go along with it full of qualms – nothing would be gained by that. To the contrary. But what I suggest is that there where your hand finds something to do, you not shy away from the struggle, not play peek-a-boo with your own times, not withdraw into an isolation that can turn out to be sterile, since in isolation we simply fail to fulfil the task given to us, namely to be salt that salts. And that is what we are if we do not become blinded by the glamour of reasoning that this would be exclusively the present, but keep an open eye for what the present may offer that is good and beautiful, as well as for what is ugly and not enjoyable.

One of the causes that led to the rise of modern art is undoubtedly the reprehensible nineteenth-century academic art with its emptiness, its commercialism, its shallow naturalism that offered nothing more than a simple or sometimes blatantly banal anecdote. In reaction people have thrown out everything that characterized it: the little story as content, naturalism as form. But with these things, which were rightly discarded, they also threw away the theme, which is so utterly indispensable for meaningful art. Furthermore, no guarantee at all was won that now no poor, no empty, no commercialized, no inartistic art could arise. On the contrary, I am only stating the obvious when I assert that today, precisely in the school of the so-called 'Tachists' who work in the line of Karel Appel or of those who came after him, a mass of work is being made that is in fact purely 'academic' work – that is, art according to a new dogma, the theory of modern art, on which the first and last word is that the work may feature no recognizable, 'ordinary' reality.

We have written all this because we believe that Oxenaar has not remained entirely free from a negative approach to the old art (the defining characteristic of which he sees, incorrectly I believe, as perspective), nor has he entirely avoided the opinion that every work that arises today in the new vein is self-evidently fraught with significance. Yet that does not detract from the fact that we value Oxenaar's little book. It is drawn, not unintelligently, from the major handbooks in the field. It is a very useful and not unoriginal summary of the prevalent view of history espoused by the adherents of modern art. Finally, it is a clear survey of a development that did indeed occur as he reports it, although he has looked too exclusively at a single line and seen far too one-sidedly only what is positive in it.

You can very well read this little book in combination with Sedlmayr's. More than once you will notice how Sedlmayr's interpretation serves to make clear the intellectual and spiritual foundations of the historical course of events, while Oxenaar's historical sketch serves to answer some of the 'how' and 'why' questions to which Sedlmayr devotes too little attention.

A criticism of Oxenaar's book is also that it remains too much a historical study. Oxenaar describes the way, Sedlmayr – undoubtedly at a higher level – shows us the backgrounds (and Prange just steers us further into the fog), but none of them offers interpretations of concrete, well-chosen examples. I am sorry to have to say that to the best of my knowledge nothing like that is available in an easily accessible little book. Perhaps one will be more likely to find it in a work devoted to a single painter such as Klee or Picasso or another great modern master. Yet we regard precisely such studies of one or a small number of works as indispensable to anyone who wants to learn to see and understand modern paintings. No one ever learned a language through a grammar book alone, even less through the study of linguistic principles or by digging into the history of a language. One really only learns a language by translating, by getting deeply into concrete works in which the language is spoken.

We did not appeal to the image of language at random. For every visual art is also a language, consisting not of sounds but of signs, of pictures, of lines and colours. It is certain that modern art is in many respects an entirely new visual language. It was developed for expressing a new content, new ideas. In language when a new idea or a new concept arises we must form new words for naming it. In art that goes even further, for there one expresses oneself not only by means of signs, themes or subjects but also by means of the manner in which subjects are depicted. One who believes that what is essential in reality lies in the utterly individual distinctiveness of things will when depicting them devote great attention to the details; while one who believes that all of that is really unimportant and who seeks the core of things in a general form, in a general concept, will set to work in a stylizing way of some sort. Thus in art a new life and world view will not only give occasion for new subjects, new themes and new motifs but also will express itself in a new style, a new manner of painting.

With this in mind, one can understand that people sought new forms in the twentieth century. The occasion lay in part in the vacuity and 'artlessness' of nineteenth-century academic art that makes a reaction against naturalism understandable, but the real cause lies much deeper, in the new spirit of the times – which, to indicate it briefly, we may perhaps typify with the word 'existentialism' (taking that word in the broad sense).

Oxenaar does not go into this side of the matter in any depth. Yet he too cannot ignore the question of content – anyone doing that would cut him- or herself off from any possibility of understanding the 'revolution of modern art'. He states for example: 'Religious and social circumstances demanded a new content through a new form . . . the steep path . . . towards a new contemporary mythology.' And in connection with the rise of abstract (non-figurative) art he writes:

> Reality seemed to lead a tarnished, torn existence under the coercion of colours and forms that were growing ever more independent. It clearly could not be long before renunciation of this now worthless connection with a fictive standard reality would follow, as the ultimate consequence ... and at the same time as the terminus of the rise of the internalization of art, of a purging of irrelevant components.

It may be clear that no one who loves reality, God's creation, can work for such a thing. One can hardly call that a 'fictive standard reality'. It is clear that here a yearning for radical freedom, separated from every attachment, form or norm is pioneering the way and moving the minds. It also shows the powerfulness of the aestheticism that Sedlmayr signalized.

In some respects this depreciation of reality, of 'nature', is what one also finds with the mystics of all times. And indeed in modern thought there are all manner of connections discernible with mystical and gnostic thought. Paul Klee's work, for example, may be typified as mystical.

This circumstance explains not only why there are various elements in modern art that are reminiscent of older European art – we think of Hieronymus Bosch, Grünewald, El Greco, Blake and the art from round about AD 1000 in the Rhineland (including a series of remarkable miniatures), each in its own right an example of art bearing a certain relation to mysticism – but also the similarity with certain currents in present-day Japan. For in Japan there has been a movement for several decades now that, proceeding from the old calligraphy (beautiful handwriting of Japanese hieroglyphs), has come to a new abstract art. This art is strongly rooted in Zen Buddhism, a particular form of mysticism that ultimately seeks the 'nothing' wherein all being is overcome. The idea of seeking the absolute and deepest meaning behind all phenomena in overcoming the connection with the world of here and now is pantheistic; and it is typically Buddhist to seek salvation in absorption into 'nothing'. Subjectively considered they are correct:

one who does not know (or want to know) God will ultimately find nothing, precisely there, in the place where God is. In Japan all this rests upon very old ideas and traditions. In our context it can therefore not be surprising that a number of leading American artists, Mark Tobey, Morris Graves and others – figures who among others represent an increasingly important American modern art – are strongly under the influence of Japanese Zen Buddhism. Tobey even spent some time in 1933 in a Japanese Buddhist monastery. One cannot speak here of just a Japanese influence but rather of a deep inner, spiritual affinity, which makes it understandable how Japanese ideas and forms can help Westerners find their way.

One objection we would raise against Oxenaar's exposé is that he tends to locate what is essential in the modern too much in abstract art, with Surrealism as a kind of dialectical and thereby equally accepted counter-pole. For we believe that there are more important schools, although it cannot be denied that in abstract art and Surrealism one can see the most powerful and consistent revolutionary facets of the modern school. That is of importance because in developing the modern style, people did indeed also form a new language, a new way of expression that in fact appears least clearly in the extreme directions (we shall see why shortly). To the extent that people rejected nineteenth-century naturalism, which had forgotten that art is a great deal more than the imitation of the visible, they discovered anew the essential elements belonging to the structure of visual art. In particular they rediscovered that art is not imitation, but that it can speak out in its own visual way, through a visual language, a language on a flat surface with colours and forms and lines.

In the beginning of this series of articles we used the example 'as if someone is standing there speaking in Chinese'. Now, one can never expect that a language would not adhere to the norms for language laid down in Creation. For if we were to violate the most important and fundamental norm for language, namely clarity, then we would simply not be able to understand one another any longer and language would have become a worthless instrument. And the Chinese language of our example can be a good language, but the person speaking it can use it to curse or to tell the truth. We will only be able to check that when we have learned to understand the language.

The same thing is true in some respects of modern art. Perhaps the modern language was formed in part in order to express a 'new mythology', but insofar as people were engaged in language-formative activity, they were making something that in itself could be valuable. And that is indeed the case. For contrary to what most people think, it is simply not true that modern art is always incomprehensible. Often the ostensible incomprehensibility arises from the insistence upon a particular demand – it must be beautiful and represent ordinary reality – which people suppose is fulfilled by the modern work. But as soon as people discern that that artwork is made in order to express a negative attitude towards reality, that artists have purposely sought the ugly and wished to do violence to reality (as being worthless) in order to express their hatred for the creation and the Creator, as soon as people discern that, the incomprehensibility vanishes and the matter becomes clear. Non-comprehension of modern art arises in most cases rather from a lack of understanding of the 'existentialist' idea expressed in it than from an inability to understand its visual language.

We shall explain directly why we put so much emphasis on this, but first we want to say that there is indeed much in the current of the most modern extreme art that no longer says anything – we noticed that earlier, namely in connection with art that is nothing more than forms (whether beautiful and spontaneous or not). Here we have the flight away from reality carried through most consistently. Here too is the noncommittal game, as a consequence of a limitless overestimation of the purely aesthetic, carried through to meaninglessness itself. The colours may still be beautiful and the new forms may be useful for decorative purposes as in fabric for curtains, printed textiles for ladies' clothing and more, but what is proper to visual art, namely that it says something to us, is lost.

At other times modern art deliberately violates the norm of clarity. In such cases the work of art does indeed have content, does have something to say, but the expression is ambivalent (having two possible meanings) or polyvalent (having many possible meanings). The intention then is that the viewer should enlarge on the play of forms and in this way give the work his or her own meaning. Irrationalistic nihilism certainly plays a part here: irrational in that people desire to recognize no norm or attachment whatever, nihilist in the avoidance of every certainty, of every clarity, of every conditionality (which would always presuppose the recognition of certain values).

But let us return to the new language that was formed as a result of the search for means to express a new vision of reality. This language has certainly caught on in the twentieth century and to a large extent determined its face. The new language – that we do not call modern because we usually use that term in connection with the new spirit of the age – confronts us in advertising leaflets, book illustration, in short, everywhere that clarity is required and the content as such cannot or may not be primarily ideological. The new language seems useful not only for the anti-gospel of radical apostasy, but also for saying other things that are very well comprehensible, as they are connected not with a nihilistic philosophy but with general human knowledge and experiences (general at least within the culture conditioned by the West). A visual language such as that used in comic strips like Donald Duck, the as such not naturalistically comprehensible manner of expression of modern posters and advertisements, brochures and book illustrations or book covers is undoubtedly connected with the visual language of modern art – namely with those occurrences of modern art that were not so extreme as to abolish their own intelligibility. Just look at the Picasso on the cover of Oxenaar's little book in order to understand what we mean, or at the drawn covers of pocketbooks and record sleeves (just there one may sometimes find extremely valuable examples of contemporary visual language). In short, anyone who wants to look for examples will not have to look far. We went into this aspect of our times extensively because it is not really done justice in any of the little books we have been reviewing. For while it is true that these graphic expressions are not art in the proper sense, which is to say in the sense of great art that has its own value and that can ultimately command a place in a museum, it is equally unmistakable that many of the products of this sort are of a high artistic quality. Finally we must say that there is also art proper that employs this new language (in a non-modern way). I have in mind Kokoschka, Piper, present-day (Roman Catholic) ecclesiastical art, and others.

Also done insufficient justice in all the little books mentioned is the fact that a great deal of work is being produced in the visual arts that can in no way be called 'modern' – that is, it does not use the new form-language – but it is still contemporary and up to date. An artist who works in this way is, for instance, Veldhoen. He is still a young artist who definitely produces living and original art although he does not speak the language of Picasso but that of Rembrandt, Berchem, Potter, Tiepolo, Fragonard, Goya. And it was not made clear enough – certainly not by Sedlmayr – that with the moderns not everything has to be always equally extreme. Among the less extreme art (as we already discussed) there is a great deal to be found that has something valuable to say, that is worth the effort, and that in and through the use of the new visual language is simply beautiful. I have in mind the work of Rouault, several of Picasso's works, Braque and so many others.

For those who would like to know more about the history of modern art we would like to mention the outstanding book by Werner Haftmann, *Malerei im 20. Jahrhundert*.[497] A second volume contains reproductions to accompany what is said in the first substantial volume. Here is a book that indeed goes deeply into matters and, without losing sight of the main lines, does full justice to the details. It is not my intention to review this book here – just consider this to be a commendatory announcement.

One little book remains for us to review. It is a little book we would be pleased to see all of you own: *Dokumente zum Vertständnis der modernen Malerei*,[498] by Walter Hess – in a RoRo edition that costs very little. It features excerpts from writings by many, and important, modern artists, preceded by short introductory sections. An objection could be that all the citations have been translated into German. Yet nowhere is such important material available to the layman, so carefully selected and so clearly grouped. Anyone who really wants to gain some insight into what moves and inspires modern artists, who wants to assay and know their follies and their wisdom and insight, may not miss this special little book. An extensive review of it is not feasible and a detailed critique not sensible, so we shall just leave it at that.

We hope that many will reserve a little corner in their bookcase for the last three books we have discussed – their cost is not an obstacle – and of course that those who do so will also read them. (The first little book we dealt with can better be left unread). They provide access to an important slice of the twentieth century, an important facet of our times that one can ignore only to one's own detriment, and possibly also to the detriment of others.

• W.L. Meijer, Kunst en Revolutie [art and revolution][498]

This book is in many respects affinitive with my *Modern Art and the Death of a Culture* and to that extent I can therefore be happy with it.

It strikes me at times as too schematic and somewhat in the vein of a schoolmaster, but what the writer says about art is sensible and he knows what he is talking about. To the extent that the book is informative, it is to the point. There are a number of well-chosen reproductions that help in understanding the text. The book is obviously written for the layperson and in that respect too the writer has been successful: the text is clear, and unnecessary expert terms have been avoided without inviting superficiality. This is popular science of the good sort.

While the book is clear and generally illuminating about art, it remains too vague about the second term, revolution. It is clear that the term 'revolution' is used by Groen van Prinsterer in his *Unbelief and Revolution*, but the writer does not bring that out. In that connection we must also say that the discussion of the Enlightenment – and with it of eighteenth-century art – is superficial and sometimes even incorrect. The eighteenth century is very difficult, complex and full of contradictions. And it goes without saying that all of it cannot be made clear in a few paragraphs. Yet whatever the difficulties, we must try to do justice to the people of that time. Especially when their agenda does not have our sympathy.

That is perhaps precisely where the crux of this book appears: it is written within a subculture, for Christians by a Christian, and within that specifically for a still much narrower circle. It does not attempt to convince others nor does it justify its own starting point. The reader, so it is understood, is not only in agreement with the starting point but also with much more, such as the meaning of revolution and so on.

That is also why several other writers about modern art such as Haftmann and Sedlmayr can be described on page 232 as opponents. With respect to the latter that certainly seems contestable to me – I can even imagine that some would want to locate Meijer and Sedlmayr quite close to one another. But to write and think from the antithesis in the sense of Kuyper does not mean that we call others 'opponents'. It is not just that we find that non-Christians should at least be seen as possible co-readers. We find Meijer's attitude difficult to accept because it expresses no humility or sense of one's own shortcomings. Modern art is an expression of extreme modernist thought, most radical to be sure, but matters would never have gone so far but for the Enlightenment, which was in part a consequence of the shortcomings of Christians with regard to philosophy and theology in the seventeenth century. Then in the further development, in the nineteenth century, Christians were generally absent and out of the picture. Christians were insufficiently salt that salts. For what is 'unsalted' as a result, we cannot reproach others – we better lament the present situation along with others, like Jeremiah does in Lamentations.

That brings us to the following: the despair, the cry of misery of the 'others', also of the 'opponents', or their resignation are barely noted if at all. That we Christians are in equal difficulty and also often no longer know the answers, and sometimes analyse matters incorrectly as well, is not the tone of this book. We would like to refer Meijer here to Zephaniah 2:3 or to Malachi 3:16 ff. (in its context). In a time of judgment one may do well to keep one's head down.

Whether there is indeed any direct connection I do not know – I suspect so – but this book is written too much in the line of Nordau and Sjeerp Anema (*Moderne kunst en ontaarding* [modern art and degeneration], 1924). And while it is much more to the point than especially Anema, it is still a half-truth – and therefore perhaps a lie – when Meijer writes: 'The artist rejects the wholesome forms of art in order to express himself in the iconography of the disturbed mind' (p.209), or a little further on, 'Picasso ... seeks the world of shadows and corruption' (p.216).

Finally, I would like to raise briefly another question, although it would carry us too far afield to go into it extensively. It is the question of whether art can be regarded as a metaphor for cultural historical developments, as it is here. Art is an expression of the mind and mentality of the artist and so indirectly of the spirit of the age, and it therefore can be used cautiously as a metaphor for the latter. Yet if one short-circuits this, strange pronouncements can be the result, as for example on page 164: 'Where a medieval preferred the triptych, the Symbolist of around AD 1900 chose a monotype (an unrepeatable print restricted to one image).' The metaphor is incorrect, what it means is challengeable, and from the standpoint of art history it is indefensible, while the reasons why certain artists in certain times (sometimes) did so have nothing to do with the intellectual and spiritual implications suggested here. In my book I spoke of the death of Venus – that was a poetic metaphor for a philosophical development that did indeed have cultural-historical implications – but Meijer says I thereby 'typified' developments. As I see it that is quite something else. Finally, we must ask ourselves whether one can base oneself so strongly on a single painting by Picasso as is done here. The piece, *Les Demoiselles d'Avignon*, is certainly loaded and unique from the standpoint of art history, yet one cannot infer everything from it.

But enough. There is something of a hyperbole in this book, something too much, something that has an extremist ring to it. It is written too much from the position of 'us' and 'them'. Nevertheless, it contains much that is valuable, and when all is said and done we expect that a future book, written after the rough edges have been worn off, will be better, such that one would also be able to give it as a gift to one's unbelieving neighbour.

Trouw Reviews of Expositions of Twentieth-Century Sculpture

• Rodin's life's work: Dante's humanism in bronze[500]

In 1880 Rodin the great French sculptor received the commission to make bronze doors for a new museum to be built in Paris. He began with a design that recalled similar works in Florence, but as the work progressed the piece grew into something that one can hardly any longer call a door and that certainly cannot be used as such. In fact, just as Beethoven composed a mass that can virtually no longer be called a mass, so here too the artist proceeded to realize his personal artistic vision without respect to all the architectonic and practical requirements. *The gates of hell* became Rodin's life's work, a grand project into which a myriad of figures and groups are gathered, inspired by Dante's *Inferno*.

It is as if we are standing before the gates of hell, which are however scarcely able to contain the lake of fire that rages behind them. Dante's figures of tormented souls enveloped in a formless mass of flames and molten lava appear before our eyes. *The thinker* sits pensively above this, with death and an impressive group of the damned behind him; and this entire grand vision, which as a whole is a portal and then again is not, is crowned by three spectres who call out to us that anyone who enters this gate must abandon every hope.

For virtually every figure in this mighty bronze work Rodin made a pre-study, which is a work of art in itself. One may ask whether it was really meaningful for him to do so, since the ultimate work confronts us as a grand vision in which all the details, and certainly all the passions expressed by these details, scarcely stand alone to speak for themselves but are gathered up into the whole. Yet it would be childish to criticize the master for this. For if one sees the exhibition at the Stedelijk Museum this summer, which besides the doors features some forty of these separate statues or groups, then the total impression created by all these independent sculptures is arguably more impressive than that evoked by the portal itself.

What a multiplicity of feelings and emotions, endless variations on the theme of human being, is rendered here. These are all more psychological, to be sure, and less existential than the most important work of Picasso displayed in the gallery upstairs, and undoubtedly more an expression of the humanist tradition that imbued the Western world from Dante's day to Rodin's.

In this work there is more cultivation, more refinement, greater nuance. Yet there is also certainly more glorification of humanity, no matter how much the portal as a whole depicts human beings in their downfall and suffering. Yet Picasso probably gives us more of the hell as it is already foreshadowing itself in today's world, more concretely and true to life. For the vision of hell seen through Rodin's gates is more that of the struggle of humanity against the elements, against the passions and against fate; it is more a vision of humankind in the infinitely varied facets of their dynamic inner feelings, as particles in a powerful cosmic drama, than it is a confrontation with real hell, the place of outer darkness.

A humanist hell, the epic of humankind in their struggle and failings, but also in their heroism and greatness – that is what we have in Rodin. In Picasso there is no struggle and no heroism, just awful suffering, the consequence of cruelty and senseless violence, the truth about this world under curse since the Fall; hell then, since people heed neither God nor commandment. In this way, the exhibition together of two great works of art having somewhat similar content compels us to compare them, while the differences between them illuminate the distinctive character of each.

• Henry Moore: creator of dynamic forms[501]

'The task of the sculptor is to change a lifeless block of stone into a composition that lives through its shapes, which in their spatial interplay in turn support one another or create contradictory tensions,' according to the sculptor Moore himself, whose work can now be viewed in the Stedelijk Museum in Amsterdam.

And this one sentence also typifies his work. Because he seeks to infuse his sculptures with dynamic vitality, but not a vitality that is grounded in what is represented, because even a resting figure, for example, is set in a very dynamic composition. He wants his works to be a direct expression of organic vitality: he wants to use natural forms, or rather, nature-forms, not by copying a particular given but through letting himself be inspired by the way in which nature creates forms as it can be observed in mountains and hills and rocks, seashells and pebbles. And this underlines another important aspect of Moore's aim: to make shapes that fit the material in which he works.

In this regard it is worth noting how his forms and conception completely change when he uses a different material: the soft suppleness of wood, for example, offers completely different possibilities to that offered by hard stone.

It is not playfulness that drives the sculptor to look for those universal shapes that speak to the subconscious of every one of us; no, it is a life and world view that sees the basis and meaning of everything in the organic and, also in the arts, seeks a form that corresponds to that.

There is no doubt that Moore is an outstandingly talented artist – his drawings, made during the Second World War in the underground shelters in London, immediately arrest one and bear witness to that but, alas, these are not shown. That he infuses his work with a dynamic tension of a purely aesthetic kind cannot altogether be denied – yet we may ask ourselves whether they are really beautiful, namely in the sense that they engage us in such a way that we are moved. After all, one's appreciation is not completely and exclusively a matter of abstract aesthetic factors but, and certainly in a contemporary work, one's own world view also plays a large part. Therefore we will never be able to reconcile ourselves with this revolutionary art with its subjectivistic hybrid deformations. We have already mentioned the inner tension between the serenity of the given and the dynamic motion of the sculpture – a tension that is not solved, so that we often have no peace with the strange way in which the 'subject' is dealt with, be it a reclining figure, a family or a woman with a child.

In closing we may well add a word of praise for the excellent way in which the exhibition has been arranged in the Amsterdam Stedelijk Museum of Modern Art: a difficult problem was solved in an exemplary manner.

• Henry Moore searches for a new kind of sculpture[502]

Complete control of mass, material and space

Sometimes we say of a painting that 'it doesn't rise above the paint', whereby we mean that the artist was unable to make us see past the medium itself – instead of seeing trees, grass and so on, we see only green and brown paint. The same kind of thing could be said about some sculptures. But the remarkable thing about the sculpture of Henry Moore is that in his work the material not only holds its value but is emphasized. The weight and the mass, the structure of the stone or wood or whatever, receive their own expressiveness and significance.

That is an important facet of Henry Moore's search for a new kind of sculpture – one that is really sculpture and not a semblance of reality. The image must remain an image, not becoming, as it were, the subject itself – which is what has sometimes threatened to be the case in the previous era. Initially Moore drew his inspiration mainly from early Mexican sculpture, which is also heavy and imposing but nevertheless has an expressiveness that makes all the later European art look sickly and frail.

After having in a similar way reinvested his material with its own natural weight, and after having giving his work a dynamically expressive power, he sets out to discover the possibilities for pure sculpture. The expression of an actual subject was largely lost, but the sculpture now received a life of its own, becoming a dynamic interplay of volume and space, yet in such a way that an inherent calm and unity was maintained. Moore explained it like this: 'For me a work must first of all have a vitality of its own. I don't mean a reflection of the vitality of life, movement, physical action, lively dancing figures etc.; I mean that a work can have a charged energy inside itself, an intense life of its own, independent of the thing it is meant to portray.'

The forms that Moore chose were, on the one hand (and this goes without saying when we understand his goals), determined by the nature of the material itself; on the other hand they were determined by something that rises above that. He selected his forms out of the organic world, out of 'dead nature' (i.e. nature as shaped by the actions of erosion, wind etc.) – forms that have been sculpted, as it were, by nature itself. Not that he depicts or reflects any specific subject but, rather, he creates forms the way nature does it, inventing something completely new, something we have not encountered before, almost as if it has been organically grown. The suggestion of the human form plays an important role in his work, but the point is not the actual depiction of a human figure; these forms have, along with the unique characteristics of the material, their own life and vital power. Moore hopes to have caught something of the essence of reality and of life in his creations. His intention is not to make pretty decorations or elegant shapes, nor to create beauty as such; he aims at something deeper, at an expression of the force of life itself, of nature in all its richness – in all of this, the determining factor for him is vitality.

Not lovely

And now, the sculptures themselves. Most people have difficulty evaluating this art properly. In our own time artists have taken the idea of pure art, art detached from its stated subject, to an extreme, but the public has not been willing to follow.

However, anyone willing to abandon the question of 'What is this supposed to mean?' will have to admit, when they view this work in the Boymans Museum, that we are indeed dealing with a great sculptor, one who is truly able to shape the material and the mass and the space artistically, and one who is able to transform them into pieces that have their own life and their own life force. These works may not always strike us as pleasant; certainly they are never pretty or sweet.

Whether Moore really does succeed in portraying the essence of life, and does not just produce what we could call super-decorations, is a question we should probably answer affirmatively. It seems to us that he is at his best when he stays closest to the natural given, as in some of his creations entitled *Family*: a man and woman seated together, holding a child. In these works with an almost hieratic expression he has truly created something that can serve as a symbol for general human worth and reality. Sometimes in these works he plays fast and loose with his 'people' and we get beings with heads that look like car parts or little stumps; because we see them that way (for, after all, it is impossible for one to detach oneself from the subject), they do not satisfy in the long run. Then we would prefer the completely unrecognizable pieces, for there our associations do not hinder us; or we would prefer the work in which the structure of the person as such is not affected but is rendered and represented (not imitated or copied) in a truly sculptural way.

In summary, it is very difficult to evaluate Moore's work in its entirety: sometimes it is acceptable, sometimes not; sometimes it is enjoyable and sometimes not; but we are always convinced of the great talent of this sculptor.

• Beautiful wood sculptures of high quality: Cor Wijker, spirited and convincing[503]

In the creation of a work of art there are two steps to be distinguished: the aesthetic conception, and its realization in the actual piece of art. Even though the two can never be separated, yet we can say that the latter – good technique – is nothing without a spirited conception; whereas good artistic ideas – even in the absence of skilled technical ability – can lead to results that can truly move and touch the viewer.

This is the case with Cor Wijker, the recently 'discovered' sculptor whose art is currently showing in the art gallery The Art of our Times on Prins Mauritsplein in The Hague. We do indeed notice shortcomings in terms of the technical skill of some of these pieces, shortcomings which sometimes prevented him from successfully giving expression to his vision. But why dwell on that? After all, this artist, who for so many years worked just for his own enjoyment, has a sharp eye and an exceptional instinct for composition, and the finished product is such that we hardly notice the 'mistakes'. Yes, the mistakes are erased, as it were, by the spirited, convincing power of the work.

We wish to point out the large woodcarving, *The shipwreck of the Drente,* as one of the most beautiful and successful of all his works. This relief depicts the energetic effort and strain involved in a rescue operation. We see the rescue boat trying to reach the scene of the disaster and all the bustling activity on the shore, while the raging sea and the strong wind are very convincingly depicted. But what strikes us most is the witty observation of all those frantically busy people. It takes real talent to depict these things successfully.

The other pieces are also worked as relief carvings in wood. The *Last Judgment* shows how those on Christ's right ascend to heaven, while those to his left, the doomed, are plunging downward. Although the whole is reminiscent of our folk art, that is just a fleeting association, for we are dealing here with a very personal vision.

The flood gave Wijker the opportunity to show groups of little figures in agitated motion: a very successful work in its details as well as in its totality.

However, the most striking work in our opinion is *The evacuation* of 1938. On first glance it appears to be inspired by the events of 1940–1945, but it turns out to have been based on similar events during the Spanish Civil War. This piece makes clear that we are dealing with an artist with superb imaginative power: this exodus of a few humble citizens has truly become a very moving work of art, convincing in its sober but certainly not pathetic portrayal of the scene.

We could make mention of more works – the *Four apocalyptic riders*, for example, or the *Storm at sea* (based on Matthew 8), or the *Entry into Jerusalem*.

Also his compositions that have very few figures manage to accomplish wonderful results. Consider for instance the remarkable, almost self-evident, extremely skilled depiction of the Nailing to the Cross. Also *Abraham's sacrifice* excels first of all because of its superb envisioning power, and also because of its convincing aesthetic rendering – perhaps one of the most successful large-figured reliefs.

The few weak points of a purely technical nature that you can find in Wijker's work are easily overlooked because of its extraordinary aesthetic qualities. Indeed, how could you trouble a 'Sunday-sculptor', who works just for his own enjoyment, with such nitpicking, especially when, on longer contemplation, the convincing power and content of this art win out over all.

These are wonderful, high-quality sculptures which we can enjoy without reservation – and, unfortunately, that does not happen very often these days.

• Italian art in Museumpark Rotterdam: an old tradition revived[504]

Italy can boast an unsurpassed tradition of sculpture, and it comes as no surprise that in the aftermath of the general decline that occurred in this field in the nineteenth century, this branch of the visual arts has come back into prominence again, demanding an important place of its own. In recent years we have grown accustomed to seeing large exhibitions of sculpture, made possible in part by the fact that the Netherlands too (for the first time in history, one might add) has a significant number of sculptors of international quality. Yet even for those who have grown blasé because of these great exhibitions and who are thus not easily satisfied, it will be quite an experience to visit the current exhibition of the work of seven leading Italian sculptors, brought together for the first time in the world on such a large scale in the Museum Park in Rotterdam (behind the Boymans Museum).

Italy has a great past in this field and happily in this tradition has kept faith with itself. Although it is difficult to capture in words, one senses the cultural tradition in virtually every sculpture, each work having been created with such great skill and artistry. These qualities surface strongly in Manzu in particular, an artist whose work, far from breaking with that of the preceding century, joins it directly. Still, almost indefinably, his sculptures are modern, present-day works. Who upon seeing Manzu's dancers will not be reminded of Degas, even though these sculptures are genuinely modern and do not hide their Italian origin. Manzu's extremely impressive cardinals' portraits, in all their concentrated simplicity, will certainly also not leave anyone unaffected. It may be considered a tremendous achievement that he is able to create something so 'nineteenth-century' in its intent and theme as that playing child or that relief of an artist drawing a model without giving us the feeling, even for a moment, that we are dealing with something that is old hat, but instead makes us feel that we are in the grip of something contemporary and alive.

Wholesome and comprehensible modernism

Mascherini is undoubtedly a sculptor of stature whose sculptures express a more pronounced feeling for modern form. The stylization in his figures, with their strong simplification and their 'spikiness', attests to this without creating a suggestion of something bizarre or strange; on the contrary, the naturalness of these sculptures requires no further comment and simply betrays the old culture from which they too arose.

Minguzzi is more outspoken in his modernism with his experiments in bronze and never previously attempted themes such as 'figure in forest' or 'dog in rushes', and modern too in his expression of the feeling of being confined with no way of escape. In his figures, which undeniably exude a special atmosphere and breathe the scent of a very remote past, we detect the influence of prehistoric sculpture – I have in mind the archaic Nuragic bronzes. This is work that one must perhaps allow to sink in for a while in order to be able to see and appreciate what is positive in it. Then the little goat in particular will prove worth the effort: this beast, which expresses the suffering of extreme exigency and drought, conveys us to barren uplands and brings us into contact with the type of misery that affects animals as well.

Equilio Greco stylizes in his figures, surrounded as they are by what the Italians would call *sfumato*, something that is veiled and dreamy, with softened outlines. His heads of women 'do' something to us, without our being able to utter in words precisely what it is about them that has arrrested us.

The prize discovery of this exhibition is Calvani, whose serene, simple art of portrait heads, in their mood and concentrated simplicity, recall Despiau. Naturally we can also not pass over the ever so sympathetic and never intrusive art of Lorenzo Pepe, a man who cares a great deal for our country, a love we can understand when we allow his portraits to speak to us, serene and unobtrusive as they are in expressing a modesty that is precisely the mantle of his greatness. To be honest, we have little feeling for Lardera's empty, decorative abstract iron sculpture that neither fascinates nor angers us.

• The language of statues – an exhibition in Sonsbeek Park, Arnhem[505]

An open-air exhibition of sculpture has been organized in the Sonsbeek Park in Arnhem. It is a real pleasure to view sculptures in such a setting – and in a sense it is a more appropriate venue than a hall in a museum. Each statue has much more opportunity to speak for itself, as each work is given ample space.

The works of mainly contemporary sculptors have been assembled here in a fairly large area. Although this is modern art, some of it ultra-modern, it is curious that we do not find any of those strangely outlandish works that have helped to make modern art so inaccessible to the public. Undoubtedly this is also because of the nature of the medium, which imposes a much clearer limitation and restraint than, for example, a painting does. But although one does not encounter many truly abstract works here, one might ask whether the torso (body without arms, legs or head) is not just as abstract, for although the form is borrowed from nature, it is nevertheless a part removed from the whole, devoid of meaning.

But even more so, the various unclothed male and female figures are, in themselves, actually just as empty of larger meaning or content. It would be interesting to research the origins of this theme in Greek antiquity (where it was certainly connected with religion and cult), and then to follow its further development and progress in the Hellenistic and Roman times. After disappearing for a while during the Middle Ages, it came into vogue again in connection with the emergence of the humanistic world and life view, once again influenced by ancient times. Since Renaissance times it has maintained its place as a favourite study for sculptors.

Naturally, in the course of its development, it lost its religious function and importance, though it cannot be thought of apart from the humanistic view of life. But still the [nude] sculpture, in a very different way now, can speak volumes.

I'm thinking here, for example, of the beautiful statue by Rik Wouters, which could be entitled 'Exuberance'. One does not need the title from the catalogue to decipher its meaning, for the piece clearly speaks for itself. There is also a portrait of a woman by Wouters, a Belgian sculptor and painter of the early twentieth century, which gives a beautiful characterization of the face of this woman. Especially typical is the effective way in which he gives an impressionistic touch to the bronze.

Moving along with our consideration of the pieces, we can, of course, only give a general overview.

Of D'Hont, we are especially struck by the woman's figure with a dove on her hand, so tender and charming. From Ittman we have a small bronze statue, which displays a curious mingling of African influences with Western tradition, as is seen for example in the carefully worked, realistic portrayal of the hands.

Theo van der Nahmer shows us a bronze dancing girl figure, which is extremely effective among the trees. How very different it is in its inspiration (more refined, if you will) from the Wouters figure, which would however come out as better in terms of quality or expressive power. We are also struck by the delicate seated female figure (a portrait?) by Gerarda Rueter.

Mari Andriessen, who would get the medal of honour among the Dutch contributors, presents a marvellous group in his *Concentration camp*. How successfully he manages to capture the central meaning with just these three figures. The piece needs no explanation at all; it speaks completely for itself.

Foreigners

Gargallo, the Spaniard working in France, has built his *Prophet* out of all kinds of pieces of iron. At first glance it may seem a bit odd, but on closer inspection the piece is very successful; he really does manage to express via this statue what the title states. Henry Moore, one of the most prominent British sculptors of our times, is represented by *Three draped figures*, which are beautifully displayed in the centre of a lawn. In reality they are so much more effective than when viewed from a photograph, in which their 'modern-ness' is given an all too great and disturbing emphasis.

Wotruba, an Austrian sculptor who is beginning to make a name for himself internationally, is very successful with his half-kneeling, half-reclining female figure. Minne, the Belgian; Despiau, the Frenchman; and Kolbe, the German, are all well known, and are represented here with very characteristic pieces. There is also a good work to be seen by Renoir, the painter, who in his later years could no longer wield his paintbrush and began to work with plastics.

Najade, by the Belgian Puvrez, is striking because of its beautiful lines and controlled composition. The famous sculptor Maillol is represented by the more famous *Isle de France*, a kind of figurehead of exceptionally high quality.

In a separate building, devoted to the smaller sculptures, there is also wonderful art to be seen. Of these we cannot resist pointing out the often spirited groups by Mendes da Costa. Not much needs to be said about Meunier's figures of labourers and we will end, then, with a few words about the work of Rodin, also exhibited here.

An emotional Rodin

In 1878, as the subject for a war memorial, Rodin created the group *La défence*, also sometimes called *L'Appel aux armes*. This emotional piece was strongly inspired by Rude's *Marseillaisse*, and it shows us an entirely different side of Rodin from what we see in his better known works. Although such work no longer appeals to contemporary tastes, when it is made by a master such a group can still be interesting and convincing. An exceptionally expressive figure is the so-called *Adam*, which Rodin conceived after becoming acquainted with the work of Michelangelo in Italy. Truly, the face resembles that of the Adam in the Sistine Chapel. The strong emotional inner life, also expressed in the very dynamic compositional style, points to the future. It helps us understand how Rodin can be called a forerunner of modern sculpture, while the refined portrayal of the muscles still fits with the previous Renaissance tradition. Later Rodin used this figure as one of the three crowned figures for his large *Porte d'Enfer*, in which he tried to portray Dante's inferno. It is a piece typically representative of his times and, we need to add, not at all modern in its denial of every truly decorative principle.

Next to a few other figures, the wonderful bearer of the key in the group *The citizens of Calais* naturally draws our attention. It is indeed a masterpiece.

Taken as a whole, we must say that there are a few masters we would have like to see added to this exhibition; but of course some limitations were needed and it is not always possible to make available everything one would like to see. A similar thought comes up with nearly every large exposition; and this one certainly does present many worthwhile and important works, so that it undoubtedly can be called a significant exposition. And it can help teach us Dutch folk how to see and admire sculpture.

• Beauty in stone: the statue as a symbol of our times[506]

This year again there is a large open-air exposition of sculpture in Sonsbeek Park. That is a double joy. In the first place because it could be said that in our times, in which foolishness and lack of structure dominate the arts, it is the art of sculpture that has retained most of the old, traditional values: here there is still a normal view of human being and the world, without a capitulation to the destructive tendency that we see, for example, in the painted arts, where the inclination is towards the sub-human and the chaotic, and away from all that is human, normal and structured. Here, in sculpture, we still find adherence to harmony and structure, and to human reality without hatred and aversion. That is why an exhibition like this is like an oasis of cultural health in the Western artworld, though even here the disease germs have begun their destructive work.

In the second place, it is a joy because we Dutch people in general have so little appreciation and feeling for sculpted art. Actually this is quite remarkable, considering that sculpture is flourishing in our times – our best artists are the sculptors. Another remarkable symptom, related to this, is our lack of language for describing sculpture. The Dutch language has a wealth of words for describing and explaining every nuance in a painting, but concerning sculpture we have little more to say than 'harmonious', 'beautiful', or 'ugly' – perhaps we add a few words like 'expressive', 'peaceful', 'light' or 'heavy' – but that's where it ends. That makes writing about sculpture difficult too. But by means of an exhibition like this, we can learn to understand something about sculpture. We can learn how to view it; and also, by taking a closer look at similar exhibitions, we will enrich our own language with the relevant terms.

But although sculpture, in relative terms, is the most wholesome of the arts – at least if we leave out architecture and interior decorating – that does not mean it is without its problems. This exhibition will also testify to that; here too art, in its attempt to free itself from all social connections, is impoverished. Here too art threatens to become sterile and meaningless. Is that not evident from the fact that more than 75 per cent of the exposition consists of female nudes? In themselves, they are often lovely, tasteful and harmonious, but they have no significance beyond that.

Undoubtedly the theme arose from a humanistic faith in humankind, partly because of the influence of the highly revered ancients. But all of that no longer drives the artist today. Due to a lack of meaningful assignments (and that has been the case for years and years already) and due to the lack of an inspiring thought, artists can come up with little else than this quite gratifying theme, which requires all their skill – but they are unable to give it any real meaning. This has also led to the emergence of the human torso as subject – a monumentalizing of the sketch, thus robbing the artist even more of the possibility of investing his or her work with meaning. All that is left are pure proportions and a refined spatial sense.

What happens if artists leave that path and abandon that tradition? Then we end up going from bad to worse. We fall back into prophecies of despair, like in Kneulman or in the *Ode to death and destruction* by Visser, whose *Dying horse* – simultaneously a horse that is dying and a piece of rust, ready for the trash – is a sinister symbol of our times. This is even more so because it clearly appeals to the world view of modern people.

Be that as it may, sculpture is an oasis of a view of life not yet estranged from reality. A sculptor like Maillol, undoubtedly the greatest of the contemporary artists, still retains in his art a peacefulness, a harmony, a 'truth' that, despite the limited subject matter, puts it amongst the best of our times.

• Biennale of modern sculpture in Middelheim Park, Antwerp[507]

Modern feeling finds expression in sculpture

The art of sculpture, much more so than the art of painting, is a restricted artform: the character of the material and the intended function of the product will limit the tendency for the artist to try anything too weird. The element of tradition also plays an important role here, partly because of the huge tradition of Greek and Renaissance sculpture. Finally, because of the nature of sculpture itself, the artist will not quickly be moved to whims and excesses; sculptors, after all, must construct, build up and lend reality to their work in a spatial sense. Thus their understanding of structure will, of course, be greater than that of their colleagues who are painters, who can fantasize freely and can give every being or object, however odd, a semblance of reality.

All these factors together contribute to the fact that, until recently, the sculpture of the twentieth century seldom followed the extremes of the painted arts. The great names of the century in this area are Maillol, Despiau and Wouters. They, together with the older Rodin and Bourdelle, provided greatly diverse but also very accessible and reality-bound art. However, in the past twenty years sculpture has taken quite a new direction, and we still have no better name for it than 'modern'. The results of these new efforts and experiments can now be seen, in a truly unique display, in the second large sculpture exhibition in Middelheim Park near Antwerp, a beautiful park very well suited to this purpose.

Healthy modernism

We must mention here that sculpted art seldom surrenders itself to direct expression of a modern world view in a way detached from its form. The sense of ruin and decay may show itself in the remarkable work by Wotruba; meaninglessness and emptiness may be demonstrated by the Dutchman Kneulman (in a style closely allied with painted art); the modern concept of irrationality may find expression in the stubborn shaping of form, as we see often in Zadkine and others; and finally, the modern can be found in those works that can perhaps best be described as 'fencing' or 'scaffolding'.

Scaffolds have something accidental and unformed about them. They have to do with construction but also with transience. They have something unsteady and tentative . . . all characteristics that appeal to modern people. We think here of those iron pieces in which the British seem to excel, in which the emotional content also becomes clear from the sloppy construction and the rust that has apparently already set in. This type of work may be represented in Antwerp too, but it does not determine the character of the exposition. It seems that, in the end, the concept of form still wins out with the sculptors.

Instead of the older notion of form put forth by the Graeco-Renaissance tradition, which was determined especially by the human form, we find now that forms that stem from the world of machines and technology play an important role. Or, to be more precise, we have to consider here the question of what came first – the chicken or the egg? For we find streamlined forms in art before they appeared in technology, and even the builder of a modern machine starts out with a certain feeling for proportions and forms. However it may be – let's say it is a matter of interaction – we find the modern concept of form in the sharply criss-crossed lines, in acute angles, and generally in straight lines and planes as we see expressed so well (in their essence, as it were) in the work of the Belgian Madeleine Forani that is shown at this exhibition. Besides the aforementioned characteristics we may point to the somewhat unarchitectonic construction of the whole. The pointed shape that protrudes so far militates against every Greek sense of proportion. And it may seem like a figure by Rodin, looking at a similar sculpture by Leinfellner, is clutching its head (it looks like those two sculptures have been purposely placed opposite one another) as if wondering where all this is leading to. Yet it is a fact that those forms belong to our technical world, and because they are pure form, and not direct expressions of a tortured world view, they can be enjoyable for every viewer.

Angular and streamlined

In the last example mentioned, we find also the streamlining that so often characterizes modern art. Typical of this, though not its best example, is the statue by Nadine Effront, a dolphin-like shape with a smoothly polished surface. Does not the association of this shape with that of a fighter-jet help convey the impression of speed? Would not that very technical object have been godparent to the birth of this creation? And then, speaking of the influence of machines, we could mention a common characteristic of modern sculpture: its openness. The works are not closed masses, but have breaks, or hollow insides, as it were. An artist who takes this concept to its extreme is the Italian Basadella, whose works are constructed of criss-crossing straight and crooked bars; they remind one of a failed machine, with just a hint of the scaffolding sense. What is also peculiar is that this work is in harmony with the lean-to made of pipes with zinc overlay in a real scaffolding form of construction. The harmony is accentuated by the fact that both are painted in the same red, yellow and white.

The sculpted figures sometimes participate in the modern angularity too. See that seated woman by Kurt Lehmann or the figures by Mascherini that fit well with the modern rooster-tail hairstyle. However, we seldom encounter anything really and intensely human here, which is typical for the entire art of our times. We could point to some deeply inspired works by Manzu – his portrait of a cardinal, for example – and to the work of the Dutch Mari Andriessen. And in the midst of this all, like an oasis of unproblematic calm, the purely decorative figural art of the Scandinavians may strike you as almost old-fashioned; but we certainly would not want to have missed them here.

• Sculptures in park in Groningen[508]

Sculpture as ornament
Sculptors are very limited in their means: they can choose to create a single figure or a closed group, without surroundings, without colour, with nothing but the natural beauty of the material they have chosen – that is all they have to work with. From what, then, does this artform derive its worth? What is the role it is asked to fulfil? In our opinion, sculpture must be sculpture, no more and no less than that. The more purely it is a sculpture, the better it is. We are not suggesting that sculpture is an end in itself in the sense that the beauty it presents must be supreme and all-encompassing. To say that would be to sin against the First Commandment and to lose sight of the unique, humble role of this artform.

A sculpture that truly fulfils its role becomes, in its pure beauty and harmony, an 'ornament of life', sometimes even in the very specific sense of serving as a decoration for a park or a bridge. It can also have the additional role of serving as a symbol or a sign, or as a token of grateful remembrance. But in all this, the sculpture has no further purpose than to be sculpture. Because, what answer would one receive if one were to question further, for example, the 'lovely' Pomona statue by van Hoorn or that mighty owl by Rädecker or the springlike freshness of the girls' figures by Dobbelman or van der Burgh? If you expect a profound discourse, more profound than the images themselves, or a philosophical treatise rather than talking about the figures themselves – in the vein of 'Did you notice this?' or 'Notice how lovely that is!' – then you will be sadly disappointed.

The nineteenth century was too eager to try to replicate nature; it was too fixed in a naturalistic way on the peculiar and individual elements to be able to develop a flourishing art of sculpture. For a sculpture, restricted to a single figure, requires concentration, stylizing and generalization in order for it to be true sculpture, to provide us with abiding beauty and a meaningful ornament. We rejoice that our country has shared in the universal blossoming of this art and can now boast, for the first time in its history, a group of important sculptors. The exposition showing in the Stadspark in Groningen is a worthy manifestation of that.

A sculpture is often nothing more than a figure in which natural representation and stylization (which allows it to be called art) are irrevocably bound together. Look at the African woman by Koning with the beautiful play of angular and gently rounded forms, in which it manifests its modernity. Or admire that beautiful tightly stylized ibex by Gra Rueb, so full of restrained power. And do not by-pass that beautifully unified group *Mother with child* by Wezelaar, infused with noble rest and concentrated simplicity. Such sculptures reveal their modernity in that sense of form that is so peculiar to our times.

The classic tradition and the nature of structuring a sculpture – often requiring months of labour, and therefore not conducive to temporary experiments – both play a beneficial role. That contemporary feeling for form that we already mentioned, evidenced by angular shapes, can be seen in its most concentrated form, detached from the figure, created as form for form's sake, in the wire plastics by Ittman. Also in *Laura* by van der Nahmer we see this mid twentieth-century characteristic, but in a different way. Here it is the charming lack of elegance, or the angular elegance (which we often encounter in the world of fashion) that strikes us.

A sculpture can, however, also be more than just a figure; it can attempt to express something, to say something. We can see that here in the defensive position of *Homo prudens* by Pauline Eecen, which says so much in a single gesture. And in that beautiful *Pull*, in which the hastening forward of the woman, and the looking backward of the child, in itself so common, have been frozen and monumentalized into a very impressive image – a concentrated symbol of unadorned simplicity. And the *Dockworker* by Mari Andriessen, that grand Amsterdam monument, needs no further praise.

As we have already noted, modern sculpture sometimes tries to make do without the givens of a recognizable natural form. Here, in these super-ornaments, material and form must reveal pure and balanced beauty in order to make a statement and to have lasting significance. The examples represented in this exposition miss that, except perhaps the work by Ittman that we mentioned. In his cube compositions, Visser may grip us for a moment; but on our return to Amsterdam, just outside of Zwolle, we saw a factory in the distance which consists of single bright concrete cubes and a high rounded cylinder, which held much greater and more concentrated beauty than what we saw in this exhibition. And we had better not say anything about the large concrete structure placed near the sheds holding the small sculptures; the only positive thing is that it says so little that we hardly noticed it and passed it by as a forgotten pedestal.

• Surprises in Arnhem: high-quality Dutch art[509]

The new county building in Gelderland has been completed and officially opened, replacing the one destroyed in the Second World War. Now the artists who participated in the decoration of this building (which consequently promises to become a worthy monument to modern Dutch art) have been invited to display their work in the Gemeentemuseum in Arnhem. Each of them is represented by five or six works, and because they are mainly sculptors this can almost be called an exposition of contemporary Dutch sculpture.

The selection of artists for the building was left to the advisor, Prof. Hammacher, who naturally made some personal choices. However, he was not one-sided in his selection. Indeed, this exhibition shows us once again that the Netherlands presently possesses a rich art in sculpture and is busy building up a tradition in this field. Fifty years ago an exposition of such high quality, with such a large number of sculptors represented, would have been unheard of.

When one walks through the halls, one is struck by the *Two Negroes* by Wezelaar, wonderful studies of the traits typical to this race, while his *Seated woman* is also striking. Krop's work is, we must confess, disappointing: his portrait of Vincent van Gogh does not have power of conviction and the *Sitting nude* of 1934 shows how the somewhat forced Expressionism of that time quickly loses its attraction. The fascinating little sculptures of women by Grosman are expressive without being Expressionist – especially the seated woman in her simplicity and strong characterization rises above a mere study. Fri Heil works in a rather timeless style typical of Western civilization and characterized by craftsmanship and appealing forms.

Everdine Henny makes small but impressive little figures, not without humour – yet they rise above the genre of caricature.

Couzijn and Gerarda Rueter each present very personal work. The latter is friendlier, more feminine, while the former – one of the few who dare to attempt to sculpt scenes of daily life – continually surprises us. Titus Leeser's large nude, despite all its good qualities, has remained too much of a study; not that we can fault him for a schematic handling of the material, but the work hardly rises above a model study and the figure is not invested with meaning or significance; conversely, it can also not be considered decorative.

Reyers' *Phoenix*, though done in plaster, speaks to us much more here than it does in the hall of the Arnhem station, where it is poorly lit and lost in the space and where 'moving patterns' from the shadows cast by the bars across the windows clash with the vibrant forms of the statue.

Kneulman shows us his sympathetic side in his *Child*, a work that proves how one can substantially invest a single figure with meaning without falling into the trap of being allegorical or symbolic or literary.

And in between all these sculptures we find paintings by Lex Horn which could almost be called traditional Expressionism, and graphic art by amongst others Elenbaas that for all its good qualities does not impress us.

Without exaggeration or trying to suggest that everything here is wonderful, we can nevertheless confidently state that this exposition, which has essentially combined a number of artists in a rather arbitrary way, yet shows a unity, though hard to define, which for posterity can be called 'mid twentieth-century Dutch art', and it is generally of high calibre. We may rightly be rather proud of it. It is fine to admire foreign art, but let's not, in typical Dutch fashion, assume that everything that comes from outside our borders is better and more important.

• John Rädecker, artist of great stature: sculpture as a portrayal of an exalted vision of life[510]

Rädecker is at the same time both the best known and the least recognized contemporary artist in Holland, one of the most famous but also most neglected masters of the chisel. Could it be that we Dutch people are afraid to value our own artists? Could it be that the publicity the French, for example, give to their own artists has been so effective that many know the work of Maillol (a master who may well be compared with Rädecker) better than the art of Rädecker, of whom we certainly have every right to be proud?

There are many books about Maillol, and anyone seeking information about him can find plenty, including lots of very unimportant facts. But about Rädecker there are just a few very modest illustrated works, maybe a paragraph in written histories of Dutch art – and that is all you will find about him in the literature. How is it possible that you will find works by Maillol in Sonsbeek, as well as works by Rodin, who is from a much older generation, while the great leader of Dutch sculpture, Mendez da Costa, as well as our greatest living sculptor (which Rädecker undoubtedly is) are not represented by even a single work?

Of our times?

These are questions to which we have no answers. Could one of the reasons be that Rädecker's art is no longer contemporary? Indeed, the more recent sculptors have travelled a very different route. Yet, important art keeps its value; and who could claim that Rodin or Maillol accurately represent the modern spirit? Could it be because Rädecker's art is so difficult, so elusive, so strange? We doubt it. While it may be true that it is difficult, even impossible to put into words the effect that Rädecker has on his viewers, that is true of Maillol as well.

Certainly, Rädecker was given the high honour of being asked to create the National Monument on the Dam Square in Amsterdam. And while much is being written about him in connection with the forthcoming unveiling of this sculpture, it cannot be said that he is really popular or appreciated or even very well known.

This is strange and incomprehensible and, as if to further emphasize this fact, some of our museums which possess beautiful samples of his work have taken very good care of them but have kept them away from public view.

Maybe it is because Rädecker's work is so un-Dutch. But that is really the case with all sculpture, for although the art of sculpture is flourishing it does not find resonance in the hearts of our people. Be that as it may, in Rädecker we have a true sculptor, not a man like Rodin who gives bronze a paintlike touch, not a man who endows his statues with an appealing poetic feeling of a more literary sort. No, Rädecker's works have a thoroughly sculpted plasticity, pure in form with infinitely sensitively modelled surfaces, while the qualities of the material in all its beauty are made subservient to the overall effect.

Simplification

Rädecker started his development at the beginning of this century with heavy, stark, simplified figures which were not uninfluenced by the developments in Paris but show a very individual response to them. His works of that time possess an expressiveness, a certain intensity of communication, that earn them a place within the Expressionist movement even though they contain no sense of distortion. Over the years he softened his expression more and more, so that it became steadily more poetic, more dreamlike, without ever becoming mushy or weak. On the contrary, his sculptures breathe a very distinct air of beauty, of artistry. They never become naturalistic, but every single oh-so-refined distortion, every stylizing and simplification, every nuanced elevation of the form is completely responsible and purposeful in this art, which really is poetry in stone. It is an expression of a vision, an interpretation of being touched by a certain aspect of reality. In this it is very different from Maillol. The latter gives form and formal beauty above all else; even a figure in wild motion like *The source* is finally more a study in form than an expression of motion as a representation of feelings or poetic stirrings. And in Rädecker it is precisely the expression, the atmosphere that his work breathes, which is calm and lacking any extreme vehemence. Rädecker also constructs his shapes in an architectonic way, but this is never an end in itself. Next to the classic quiet and objectivity of the Frenchman, Rädecker is romantic, more sensitive, more emotional, more subjective and more 'internal'. His main theme is the female figure, and in this he also reveals himself as a link in the tradition that started with the Greek artists and was renewed during the Renaissance. But, similar to Maillol, the point is not to portray the female body or 'nakedness'. With both these artists we see an idea turned into a form.

Rädecker's portrait sculptures continue to be very important, exactly because he offers more than a subtly balanced form. The powerful monumentality of the large bronze portrait of Toorop, the stark simplicity of that of Annie Fernhout, or the sensitive expressiveness of the portrait of his wife belong to the high points of this artform in the twentieth century. If we are asked to critique them, we might say that they betray more of Rädecker's own spirit than of the spirit of those he portrays.

National monument

Rädecker devoted the last years almost exclusively to the National Monument [on the Dam Square in Amsterdam], a work that is difficult to judge. The symbolic representation of the idea, in figures which are not allegorical but which still, by the feelings and associations they evoke, must somehow express the idea, show how this master, now 70 year old, reaches back to impressions of his youth – something that happens often with great masters in their old age. This symbolic approach surely is not contemporary, and we are curious whether the greatness of his imagination and the persuasiveness of the work will succeed in winning over contemporary people in such a way that this work will take a place in our hearts equal to that of, for example, the Zadkine monument in Rotterdam.

But aside from this monumental work, which we must wait to judge as to its ultimate effect, there is still so much more – so that we must call Rädecker one of the greatest artists that our country has produced in the first half of the twentieth century. He is a man of international stature whose extremely personal art will probably not gain great popularity but who certainly merits his place among the greats of this century. There is certainly no reason to place foreign artists above him because they are more French, more classical or more productive.

Notes to Volume 5

Part I: Modern Art and the Death of a Culture

1 Bob Dylan, 'Ballad of a thin man'.
2 Marcel Proust, *Maxims*.
3 See Duccio de Buoninsegna, *Madonna with Child and two angels* (1283–1284) tempera on wood, 89x60 cm (Museo dell' Opera del Duomo, Siena).
4 Peter Paul Rubens, *The martyrdom of St Livinus* (1633) oil on canvas, 455x347 cm (Musées Royaux des Beaux-Arts, Brussels).
5 Rembrandt van Rijn, *Christ on the road to Emmaus* (coll. Dr J. Winter, Vienna).
6 Jan van Goyen, *Approaching storm* (1646), see plate 1 in *Complete Works* 3.
7 Nicholas Poussin, *Landscape with the funeral of Phocion* (1648) oil on canvas, 114x175 cm (National Museum of Wales, Cardiff, on loan).
8 Jan Steen, *The feast of St Nicholas* [or *St Nicholas morning*] (1665–1668) oil on canvas, 82x70.5 cm (Rijksmuseum, Amsterdam:); see plate 2 in *Complete Works* 3.
9 Titian, *Venus and Music* (c.1477–1576) (Madrid, Prado).
10 Flaming Youth, *The Planets, Ark Two*.
11 *A Goodly Heritage* (London: Banner of Truth Trust, 1959) pp.53 ff.
12 F. Antal in his writings on Hogarth discusses this lack of a real English school of painting before Hogarth's time, apart from portraiture, and ascribes it to the strong influence of Puritanism in the cultural atmosphere.
13 Published in 1952.
14 See the helpful book by Basil Willey, *The Seventeenth Century Background* (Harmondsworth: Penguin Books, 1962), particularly the discussion of Glanville.
15 Deuteronomy 32:15.
16 See too R. Hooykaas, *Natural Law and Divine Miracle: The Principle of Uniformity in Geology, Biology and Theology* (Leiden, 1963) esp. pp.209 ff.
17 Cf H.J. Blackham (ed.), *Objections to Humanism* (Harmondsworth: Penguin Books, 1965) p.62.
18 Published in 1690.
19 Published in 1739 and 1748.
20 R.T. Clark and J.D. Bales, *Why Scientists Accept Evolution* (Grand Rapids, Michigan: Baker Book House, 1966).
21 I have discussed them in an essay 'The Artist as a Prophet?' (originally published by L'Abri Fellowship under the title *Art and the Public Today*, 1968); see in this volume, part II.
22 Paul Simon, 'Patterns'.
23 Francisco de Goya, *The dream of reason produces monsters* (Prado, Madrid).
24 Goya, *The execution of Spaniards by the French, 3 May 1808* (Prado, Madrid).
25 Goya, *The clothed Maya* (Prado, Madrid).
26 J.M. William Turner, *Rain, steam and speed* (London, National Gallery).

27 John Constable, *The haywain* (London, National Gallery).
28 Gustave Courbet, *The grain sifters* [winnowing girls] (1855) (Musée de Nantes, France).
29 Honoré Daumier, *The beautiful Narcissus* (1842) from the 'Ancient History' series, lithograph (Paris, Bibliotheque Nationale de France).
30 Quoted from J. Bronowski, *William Blake* (Harmondsworth: Pelican Books, 1954) p.131.
31 From an article on Blake by A. Blunt in the *Journal of the Warburg and Courtauld Institutes* VI (1943).
32 William Blake, *Songs of Innocence* (1789) (London: British Museum).
33 See Alexandre Cabanel, *Phèdre* (Montpellier, France, Musée Fabre).
34 Hendrik Leys, *Women praying at a crucifix near St James in Antwerp* (Antwerp Town Hall).
35 Antonion Ciseri, *Ecce homo* (1864) (Florence, Pitti Palace Museum).
36 Holman Hunt, *The shadow of death* (1870–1873) oil on canvas, 92.7x93 cm (Leeds City Art Galleries).
37 See, for an illustration of the theme of this chapter, J.H. Plumb, 'The Victorians Unbuttoned', *Horizon* (Autumn 1969).
38 Paul Simon, 'Flowers Never Bend'.
39 Pierre Auguste Renoir, *Le Moulin de la Galette* (1876) oil on canvas (Paris, Musée d'Orsay).
40 Claude Monet, *Quai du Louvre, Paris* (1867) oil on canvas (The Hague, Gemeentemuseum).
41 Monet, *Poplars at Giverny, sunrise* (1888) oil on canvas, 74x92.7 cm (New York, Museum of Modern Art, William B. Jaffe and Evelyn A.J. Hall collection).
42 Letter to Schuffenecker, 14 January 1885, translated freely. See my *Synthetist Art Theories* [in *Complete Works* 1, p.101] and the notes for a more precise translation. For the Tahitian painting dealt with below see *Complete Works* 1, pp.196 ff.
43 Paul Gauguin, *Vision after the sermon: Jacob wrestling with the Angel* (1888) oil on canvas, 73x92 cm (Edinburgh, National Gallery of Scotland)
44 *Raconteurs d'un Rapin* (1902). See also *Complete Works* 1, p.201 for an alternative translation.
45 George Seurat, *Le Chahut* (1889–1890) oil on canvas (Otterlo, the Netherlands, Kröller-Müller).
46 See for example a poster by William Bradley (1894).
47 From their opera *Patience* (1881).
48 See N. Pevsner, *Pioneers of Modern Design* (New York: Museum of Modern Art, 1949).
49 Leonard Cohen, 'Songs from a Room'.
50 Henri Matisse, *Luxe, Calme et Volupté* [luxury, calm and sensuality] (1904) 37x46", oil on canvas (Paris, private collection).
51 Matisse, *Jeanette III* (Jeanne Vaderin, 3rd state) (New York, Museum of Modern Art, Lillie P. Bliss bequest).
52 Wassily Kandinsky, *On the Spiritual in Art* (1912), ed. and transl. by Hilla Rebay (Solomon R. Guggenheim Foundation, 1946).
53 Ibid. See Wassily Kandinsky's woodcut from *Klänge* (1913).

54 H. Spiegelberg, *The Phenomenological Movement* (The Hague, 1960) p.79.

55 *Ideen zu einer reinen Phänomenologie und phänomenologischen Philosophie* (1913).

56 *The Eighteen Nineties* (Harmondsworth: Pelican Books, 1950, first published 1913). This excellent book deals with very much the same problems as I do here.

57 Pablo Picasso, *Les Demoiselles d'Avignon* (1907) oil on canvas (New York, Museum of Modern Art). Quoted from E.F. Fry, *Cubism* (London: Thames and Hudson, 1966), which gives many more quotations of contemporaries of Cubism.

58 Ibid.

59 Georges Braque, *Maisons a l'Estaque* (1908) 60x73 cm (Bern, Museum of Fine Arts, Hermann and Margrit Rupf foundation).

60 See Picasso's *Nude* (1909) and *Woman in an armchair* (1913) oil on canvas, 148x99 cm (New York, collection Mrs Victor W. Gantz).

61 Translation by S.W. Taylor, from the introduction to the catalogue of the Apollinaire Exhibition (London: Institute of Contemporary Arts, November 1968).

62 Quoted from Jaffé, *De Stijl* (Amsterdam) p.6.

63 Quoted in Fry, *Cubism*.

64 Robert Delaunay, *Eiffel Tower* (1910–1911) oil on canvas, 202x138.4 cm (Solomon R. Guggenheim Museum, New York).

65 For example, André Derain's *Two sisters* (Les Deux Soeurs) (Copenhagen, Royal Museum of fine Arts).

66 Marcel Duchamp (1912) *The king and queen surrounded by swift nudes* (*Le Roi et la reine entourés du nus vites*) oil on canvas, 114.9x128.3 cm (Philadelphia, Museum of Art, Louise and Walter Arensburg collection).

67 P.F. Sloan, 'The eve of destruction'.

68 Ephesians 6:12, J.B. Phillips's translation.

69 Franz Marc, *The fate of the animals: the trees show their rings, the animals their veins* (1913) oil on canvas (Basel, Kunsthalle).

70 'Und Alles Sein ist flammend Leid.'

71 Romans 8:18 ff.

72 See Paul Klee's *Twittering machine* (*Zwischer-Machine*) (1922) (New York, Museum of Modern Art).

73 In *Avant et Après*.

74 Wassily Kandinsky, *Im Blau* (1925) oil on canvas, 80x110 cm (Düsseldorf, Kunstsammlung Nordrhein-Westfalen).

75 Stuart Gilbery in *Transition* 22 (1933).

76 From *Ursonate* (Hanover: Merzverlag). This poem continues: 'Bemm bemm / bemm bemm / Bemm bemm / Bemm bemm // Tilla loola luula loola / Tilla loola luula loola / Tillla loola luula loola // Grimm glimm gnimm bimbimm / Grimm ... etc. etc.

77 See Giorgio de Chirico, *The disturbing muses* (*Les Muses Inquiétantes*) (1925) oil on canvas, 97x67 cm (Milan, Coll. G. Mattioli).

78 By Mati Klarwein (1963), reproduced in R.E.L. Masters and J. Houston, *Psychedelic Art* (London: Weidenfeld and Nicolson, 1968) plate 58.

79 Romans 8:19–22.

80 Isaiah 24:4–6, RSV.

81 Isaiah 5:25.

82 Psalm 14:1.

83 For example, his etching *L'Indicatif Présent* from *Poèmes de Luc Decaunes* (Paris, 1938).

84 Cf. H.P. Raleigh, 'Value and artistic alternative: Speculations on choice in modern art', *Journal of Aesthetics and Art Criticism* 27 (1969) pp.293 ff.

85 Georges Rouault, *Il serait si doux d'aimer* ('It would be so sweet to love') etching from *Misererè* series (1922–1927).

86 Karel Appel, 'Poeme Barbare'.

87 See, for instance, F. Eversole (ed.), *Christian Faith and the Contemporary Arts* (Nashville: Abingdon Press, 1962).

88 See Appel, litho in *Reflex*, journal of the Experimentals in Holland.

89 Catalogue of an exhibition in the Stedelijk Museum of Modern Art (Amsterdam, 1968).

90 *Neue Figurationen* (1959) p.79.

91 Arman, *The skeleton of Achilles* (Helsinki, Art Museum of Ateneum, Coll. Sara Hildén).

92 See Bacon's *Head* VI (London, Hayward Gallery), after Velasquez's portrait of Pope Innocent X.

93 Quoted from J. Russell, *Francis Bacon* (London: Methuen, 1965) p.1.

94 See Wesselman, *The great American nude 2* (New York, Museum of Modern Art).

95 See Warhol, *Campbell tomato soup can* (Paris, Galerie Denise René).

96 See Vasarely, *Composition* (Paris, Galerie Ileana Sonnabend).

97 No. 11–12, 1966. Some of the examples quoted below are also from this issue.

98 The lectures were published in a book under the title, *The Dialectics of Liberation* (Harmondsworth: Penguin Books, 1968).

99 E.g. see back cover of *Seed* magazine (Chicago, January 1968).

100 Rolling Stones, 'Street fighting man'.

101 See further A.T. van Leeuwen, *Christianity in World History* (London: Edinburgh House Press, 1964).

102 Issue of 20 December 1968.

103 In the catalogue of an exhibition held in 1967 at the Stedelijk Museum, Amsterdam.

104 Issue of 10 January 1969.

105 *International Times*, 27 February 1967.

106 *Irrational Man* (New York: Doubleday, 1962) p.244.

107 I have written about this at greater length in 'The Artist as a Prophet?', one of the two essays published in my *Art and the Public Today*. See in this volume, part II.

108 Abingdon Press, Nashville, 1962.

109 Vol. I, no. 7 (1967).

110 Quoted from *International Times*, 14 February 1969.

111 'Why Those Students are Protesting', *Time* (3 May 1968). See also B. Bettelheim, 'Obsolete Youth: Towards a Psychograph of Adolescent Rebellion', *Encounter* (September 1969).

112 From an article in *Seed* (Chicago underground press paper), 5 January 1968.
113 *International Times* (London, 14–17 February 1969).
114 F. Halliday, in the symposium 'Student Power', ed. A. Cockburn and R. Blackburn (Harmandsworth: Penguin Books, 1969).
115 In the issue of 28 March 1969.
116 'The Permissive Society', in the issue of 13 November 1967. Europe may be one step behind, but is little different.
117 Revelation 6:16; 9:20.
118 2 Thessalonians 2:9–11.
119 18 Revelation 6:12–14; Isaiah 57:17; Hosea 5:6.
120 Cf. Matthew 24:12.
121 Mahalia Jackson (Newport, 1958).
122 1 John 1:1; Hebrews 1:2.
123 Romans 7; 2 Peter 2: 19.
124 Galatians 5:23.
125 Cf. Romans 6.
126 Mark 7:21, 22.
127 Oscar Wilde dealt with this problem in his *Picture of Dorian Gray*.
128 Revelation 12:5.
129 See the section on surreality and Christian reality in chapter 6 of this part.
130 Exodus 31:3. 4.
131 See Romans 12:19' 1 Corinthians 5:13.
132 Matthew 15:1.
133 1 John 3: 21, 22.

Part II: Art and the Public Today

134 Huémoz-sur-Ollon, Switzerland: L'Abri Fellowship Foundation, 1969 (2nd edn).
135 Inaugural lecture by H.R.R. on assumption of the professorship in History of Art at the Free University at Amsterdam, 28 May1965.
136 Published in *Schrijftaal* II: *Kwadraatbladen* (1964).
137 Seymour Krim, *The Beats* (Conn., Greenwich, 1960) p.211 ff. Today Ted Joans is active in organizing happenings, see *Randstad* 13 (Amsterdam, 1966) p.229 ff.: 'Ted Joans, Happy Hip Happenings'.
138 Q. Horatius Flaccus, *Ars Poetica*, line 455. The whole section from line 453 up to line 476 is very interesting in relation to out atgument here; translation taken from H. Rushton Fairclough, *Horace, Satires, Epistles and Ars Poetica, with an English translation* (London, 1926).
139 Cf. O. Pöggeler, 'Dichtungstheorie und Toposforschung', *Jahrbuch für Aesthetik und Allgemeine Kunstwissenschaft* V (1960) pp.183 ff.
140 E.R. Curtius, *Europäische Litteratur und lateinisches Mittelalter* (Bern, 1948).
141 E. de Bruyne, *Geschiedenis van de Aesthetica I: De Griekse Oudheid* (Antwerp, 1952) p.100 passim; J. Lemeere, 'Les concepts du beau et de l'art dans la doctrine platonicienne', *Revue d'histoire de la philosophie et d'histoire générale*

de la civilisation VI (1938) pp.1 ff.; E. Kris & O. Kurz, Die Legende vom Künstler (Vienna, 1934) pp.51 passim.

[142] See previous note and F.B. Blanshard, Retreat from Likeness in the Theory of Painting (New York, 1949) pp.55 passim.

[143] B. Schweitzer, 'Der bildende Künstler und der Begriff des Künstlerischen in der Antike', Neue Heidelberger Jahrbücher N.F. (1924) pp.28–132, p.116; see also P.O. Kristeller, 'The Modern System of the Arts', Journal of the History of Ideas XII (1951) p.496–506.

[144] Schweitzer, 'Der bildende Künstler', p.117.

[145] Ibid. p.124 ff.; E. de Bruyne, Geschiedenis van de Aesthetica II: De Romeinse Oudheid (Antwerp, 1953) pp.232 ff.

[146] Kris & Kurz, Die Legende vom Künstler, p.53.

[147] See my article 'Two Kinds of Love and the "Carcer Terreno"', in Complete Works 4, p.73 – a study of the importance of the position of the four Michelangelo sculptures in an artificial grotto in the Boboli Garden – and the literature cited there.

[148] E. Panofsky, Idea, Ein Beitrag zur Begriffsgeschichte der älteren Kunsttheorie (Leipzig, 1924) pp.24 ff.; and Kris & Kurz, Die Legende vom Künstler, p.55.

[149] 'Die Renaissance gesteht dem bildenden Künstler die echte Begeisterung zu, der Künstler aber, der zum Griffel der Gottheit geworden ist, wird selbst als göttlich geehrt. Die Religion, zu deren Heilsgestalten er zählt, ist die "Geniereligion der Neuzeit."' Kris & Kurz, Die Legende vom Künstler, p.56.

[150] Cf. Kristeller, 'The Modern System of the Arts: A Study in the History of Aesthetics', p.514; N. Pevsner, Academies Past and Present (Cambridge, 1940) pp.33 ff.; R. & M. Wittkower, Born under Saturn: the Character and Conduct of Artists (London, 1963) pp.15 f. and passim.

[151] J. v. Schlosser, Die Kunstlitteratur: ein Handbuch zur Quellenkunde der neueren Kunstgeschichte (Vienna, 1924) pp.533 ff.; E.H. Gombrich, 'Icones Symbolicae: The Visual Image in Neo-platonic Thought', Journal of the Warburg and Courtauld Institutes XI (1948) pp.167 ff.; D.Mahon, Studies in Seicento Art and Art Theory (London, 1947); J.A. Emmens, 'Rembrandt en de Regels van de Kunst' (Utrecht, 1964, diss.); R.W.Lee, 'Ut Pictura Poesis: the Humanistic Theory of Painting', Art Bulletin XXII (1940) pp.197–269.

[152] B. Rogerson, 'The Art of Painting the Passions', Journal of the History of Ideas XIV (1953) pp.68–93.

[153] The term 'scientism' is used to denote the specific emphasis given to science, exalting it into a kind of revelation. Between science and scientism there is the same kind of difference as between rational and rationalism.

[154] W.Windelband, Lehrbuch der Geschichte der Philosophie (ed. H.Heimsoeth) (Tübingen, 1948) pp.471 ff.; H. Dooyeweerd, A New Critique of Theoretical Thought I (Amsterdam / Philadelphia, 1953) pp.385 ff.; P.O. Kristeller, 'The Modern System of the Arts: A Study in the History of Aesthetics II', Journal of the History of Ideas XIII (1952) pp.42 passim.

[155] Windelband, Lehrbuch der Geschichte der Philosophie, pp.512 ff.; Jean Gibelin, L'esthétique de Schelling d'après la Philosophie de l'art (Paris, 1933).

[156] M.Z. Shroder, Icarus: the Image of the Artist in French Romanticism (Cambridge, Mass, 1961); P. v. Tieghem, Le romantisme dans la littérature européenne (Paris, 1948) pp.355 ff., 359; cf. M.H. Abrams, The Mirror and the Lamp: Romantic Theory and the Critical Tradition (New York, 1953) p.192; cf. also V. Ehrlich, 'The conception of the Poet in Krasinski and the Romantic Myth of the

Artist', *Studies in Romanticism* I (1962) pp.193 ff.; concerning Carlyle's ideas in this, see my *Synthetist Art Theories*, in *Complete Works* 1, p.37.

157 'das höhere Seelenorgan der Menschheit'. B.Knauss, 'Das Kunstlerideal des Klassizismus und der Romantik', *Tübinger Forschungen zur Archaeologie und Kunstgeschichte* IV (Reutlingen, 1925) p.37; Abrams, *The Mirror and the Lamp*, pp.235 ff., p.176.

158 Donne-moi d'un poète, esprit, gloire, génie, / Tout, excepté pourtant l'enfantine manie / De tel, qui possédé de son docte travers, / Inepte et bête à tout ce qui n'est pas des vers, / Ridicule, jouet d'une verve inquiète, / A toute heure est poète et rien que poète.' Andre Chenier, *Oeuvres Complètes* (Paris: G. Walter ed., n.d.) p.457, cited in Knauss, 'Das Kunstlerideal des Klassizismus und der Romantik', p.12. Cf. Ehrlich, 'The conception of the Poet in Krasinski', pp.193 ff.

159 We use the Herford edition of 1948, introduced by G. Ehrhart; on Schiller see also Knauss, 'Das Kunstlerideal des Klassizismus und der Romantik', pp.60 ff.

160 Used in the original Greek meaning, i.e. inspired by the Daimon, the divine spirit.

161 'Den Stoff wird er von der Gegenwart nehmen, aber die Form von einer edleren Zeit, ja jenseits aller Zeit, von der absoluten unwandelbaren Einheit seines Wesens entlehnen. Hier aus dem Äther seiner dämonischen Natur rinnt die Quelle der Schönheit herab, unangesteckt von der Verderbnis der Geschlechter und Zeiten.' Schiller, *Über die ästhetische Erziehung des Menschen*, p.54.

162 'In der schamhaften Stille deines Gemüts erziehe die siegende Wahrheit, stelle sie aus dir heraus in die Schönheit, dass nicht blosz der Gedanke ihr huldige, sondern auch der Sinn ihre Erscheinung liebend ergreife.' Ibid. p.57.

163 Ibid., pp.157 ff.

164 A.J. Langbehn, *Rembrandt als Erzieher, von einem Deutschen* (Leipzig, 1891); B. Momme Nissen, *Der Rembrandtdeutsche Julius Langbehn* (Freiburg/Br.. 1926).

165 Th. Munro, *Education, its Philosophy and Psychology* (New York, 1956), p.296. On p.15 he defines 'the aims of aesthetic education'; H. Read, *Education through Art* (London, 1958, 4th edn; first printing 1941) – on pp.8 ff. he formulates 'the purpose of aesthetic education'.

166 Goethe wrote many times on the visual arts, e.g. in 1816 he wrote an essay on Ruisdael as poet. He made many drawings in his younger years and later developed a theory of colour. His influence on art theory has been important, especially through the work of R. Steiner, the theosophist. On Kandinsky, see S. Ringdom, 'Art in the Epoch of the Great Spiritual', *Journal of the Warburg and Courtauld Institutes* XXIX (1966) pp.391 ff.

167 Schiller, *Über die ästhetische Erziehung des Menschen*, p.55.

168 Cf. Knauss, 'Das Kunstlerideal des Klassizismus und der Romantik', p.56; also R.Benz & A. v. Schneider, *Die Kunst der deutschen Romantik* (München, 1939).

169 'Was du in deiner ewigen Seele empfunden, das ist auch ewig, . . . was du aus ihr geschöpft, das ist unvergänglich; hier muss die Kunst entspringen, wenn sie ewig sein soll . . . (wir stellen) Symbole unserer Gedanken über grosse Kraften der Welt dar.' H. Uhde-Bernays, *Künstler-Briefe über Kunst* (Frankfurt a/M, 1960) pp.135, 137.

170 R. Zeitler, *Klassizismus und Utopia* (Stockholm, 1957); cf. L. Venturi, *Histoire de la critique d'art* (trad. de l'italien) (Brussels, 1938) pp.240 ff.; G.J. Hoogewerff, *Verbeelding en Voorstelling, de ontwikkeling van het kunstbesef* (Amsterdam, 1944) pp.191 ff.

171 See my *Synthetist Art Theories*, in *Complete Works* 1, p.49.

172 *Koremon, Natur und Kunst in Gemälden, Bildhauereien, Gebäuden und Kupferstichen* (Leipzig, 1770); cited by Knauss, 'Das Kunstlerideal des Klassizismus und der Romantik', p.46.

173 Cited by Knauss, 'Das Kunstlerideal des Klassizismus und der Romantik', p.46, from F. von Alten, *Aus Tischbeins Leben und Briefwechsels* (Leipzig, 1872) p.330.

174 'keine Nutzbau, sondern ein Tempel, ein Kultbau sein'. Knauss, 'Das Kunstlerideal des Klassizismus und der Romantik', p.99; H. Sedlmayr, *Verlust der Mitte* (Salzburg, 1951, 5th edition) pp.31 ff.

175 Wittkower, *Born under Saturn*, pp.2 ff., 22 ff.

176 P.O. Kristeller, 'The Modern System of the Arts II', pp.44 passim.

177 Wittkower, *Born under Saturn*, p.12; Geraldine Pelles, *Arts, Artists and Society, Origins of a Modern Dilemma: Painting in England and France 1750–1850* (Englewood Cliffs,NJ, 1963); G. Pelles, 'The Image of the Artist', *Journal of Aesthetics and Art Criticism* XXI (1962) p.119 ff.; Knauss, 'Das Kunstlerideal des Klassizismus und der Romantik', p.36; also W. Hofmann, *Das irdische Paradies: Kunst im neunzehnten Jahrhundert* (München, 1960) pp.367 ff.

178 See my *Synthetist Art Theories:* 'Art as revelation', in *Complete Works* 1, especially pp.162 ff.

179 H.Bavinck, *Bilderdijk als denker en dichter* (Kampen, 1906) pp.150 ff.

180 'De kunst is het vermogen om dat schoone, die hoogere wereld aan de slechtere te opponeren, gelijk de kunstenaar met geoefende hand aan het ruwe marmeren blok een schoone gestalte weet te geven.' From unpublished notes taken during a lecture by Kuyper. His other publications on the fine arts are: *Het Calvinisme en de kunst* [Calvinism and art], rectoral speech 20 October 1888; 'Calvinism and Art', *Christian Thought* IX (New York, 1891/2) pp.259–282, 447–459 (this is a translation of the mentioned speech of 1888); *Calvinism, six Stone Lectures* (Amsterdam, 1899) p.189 ff.; *The antithesis between symbolism and revelation* (Amsterdam/Pretoria/Edinburgh, 1899), cf. my *Synthetist Art Theories*, in *Complete Works* 1, pp.163 ff.

181 Kuyper deals in his *Het werk van den Heiligen Geest* [the work of the Holy Spirit] (Amsterdam, 1888) with the inspiration by the Holy Spirit but does not confine this to artists. It concerns more a given talent than a direct inspiration, and it belongs to all ministry or craft; it is found primarily in the area of common grace. See pp.48, 53.

182 From several we cite here only: E.H. Palmer, *The Holy Spirit* (Grand Rapids, Mich., 1958) pp.38–39. Cf. also R.J. Dam, *Stoa en litteratuur bij het licht der Schrift* [Stoa and literature in the light of Scripture] (Goes, 1949) p.193.

183 'Dichters zijn profeten. Zij profeteren en getuigen van de heersende stromingen, welke de tijd beroeren.' Rudolf van Reest, *Dichterschap en Profetie* I [poetics and prophecy] (Goes, 1953) p.5.

184 Finley Eversole (ed.), *Christian Faith and the Contemporary Arts* (New York, 1962, 4th edn) p.12.

185 Cf. Karl Jaspers, *Die geistige Situation der Zeit* [the spiritual situation of our

time] (Berlin, 1953, 8th edn; 1931) pp.128 ff.

[186] 'Symbole zu schaffen die auf die Altäre der kommenden geistigen Religion gehören'. F. Marc, 'Die Wilden Deutschlands', *Der Blaue Reiter* (1912); cf. L. Flam, 'L'art, religion de l'homme moderne' (Amsterdam: The 5th International Congress for Aesthetics, 1964; lecture); also appearing in the acts of the same congress: U. Schöndorfer, 'Über das Verhältnis der Poesie zur Religion'; further G.W. Sommer, *Der Künstlerprophet* (München, 1922).

[187] G. Pelles, 'The Image of the Artist', *Journal of Aesthetics and Art Criticism* XXI (1962) pp.134–135.

[188] E.H. Gombrich, 'Metaphors of Value in Art', in *Meditations on a Hobby Horse, And Other Essays on the Theory of Art* (London, 1963) pp.12–30.

[189] E.g. J. Larrea, 'An Open Letter to Jacques Lipchitz', *College Art Journal* XIII (1954) pp.251 ff.

[190] J. Chaix-Ruy, 'Poésie et philosophie', *Revue d'esthétique* V (1952) pp.365 ff., an essay on the ideas of the poet Marcello-Fabri; D. Huisman, Esthetica (Utrecht: Spectrum, 1964) pp.104 f.; A. Fabri, Interview mit Sisyphos (Cologne, 1952) p.12; cf. also R. Blesh, *Modern Art USA: Men, Rebellion, Conquest* (New York, 1956) of which the subtitle is a citation from Eckhart.

[191] *Transition, An International Workshop for Orphic Creation* XXII (1933) passim; J. Alford, 'The Prophet and the Playboy: "Dada was not a farce"', College Art Journal XI (1952) pp.269 ff.

[192] E. Jolas, 'The Primal Personality', *Transition* XXII (1933) pp.78 ff.

[193] For Kandinsky in connection with theosophy and antroposophy, see the article cited in note 166 above by Ringdom, 'Art in the Epoch of the Great Spiritual'; for Mondrian, see H.L.C. Jaffé, *De Stijl: 1917–1931* (Amsterdam, 1956) especially pp.112 ff.

[194] B. Schierbeek, *De tuinen van Zen: over Zen-Boeddhisme en moderne kunst* [the gardens of Zen: on Zen Buddhism and modern art] (Amsterdam, 1959); Mark Tobey, 'Japanese Tradition and American Art', *College Art Journal* XVIII (1958) pp.20 ff. Compare also P. Metman, 'Schizophrenia or Initation', in *The New Morality* III (1963) pp.25–48, based on Buddhist mysticism.

[195] 'Un jour peut-être la sculpture-architecture de l'Atomium de Bruxelles signifiera à nos yeux le secret si redoutable de la pensée, l'analyse de la structure moléculaire de l'influx nerveux du cerveau. Ce jour-là nous nous apercevrons que la vision de Scheps avait anticipé l'incarnation plastique d'une qualité de l'intelligence associative et que cet architecte-géomètre avait songé à incarner l'Idee dans la terre des Hommes en reconstituant à partir de l'arbre sa dimension organique de relation.' Pierre Restany in the a brochure accompanying an exhibition of Scheps in Gallery 'J' (Paris, June 1964). Scheps makes structures of trunks of trees. Even if these words were written tongue-in-cheek they are to be considered symptomatic of the mystical-prophetic ideas of art. The Atomium is the central building, which was constructed to symbolize the Expo (world exposition) in Brussels in 1958.

[196] R.L. Shinn, 'The Artist as Prophet-Priest of Culture', in F. Eversole (ed.), *Christian Faith and the Contemporary Arts*, pp.72–80.

[197] Many articles can be cited, for example R. Rosenblum, introduction to the catalogue for the exhibition of Morris Louis (Amsterdam: Stedelijk Museum, 1965) cat. no. 373; L. Seitz, introduction to the exhibition of Hans Hofmann (Amsterdam: Stedelijk Museum, 1965) cat. no. 375.

198 Eg. C. Baudelaire, *Curiosités Esthétiques* (Paris, 1921) p.198 (at the end of the *Salon of 1846*); the same, *L'art romantique* (Paris n.d., 1st edn 1863) pp.54 ff. (about Constantin Guys, 'le peintre de la vie moderne'); cf. S. Dresden, 'Kritiek en Kunsttheorie bij Baudelaire', *Maatstaf* V (1957) pp.297 passim.

199 'L'histoire morale contemporaine'. Cf. E. Auerbach, *Mimesis, dargestellte Wirklichkeit in der abendländischen Litteratur* (Bern, 1896 / Gardencity, NY: Anchor Books, 1952 Engl. edn) chapter XVIII, p.437.

200 See my *Synthetist Art Theories*, especially the citation on p.5 in *Complete Works* 1.

201 G. Apollinaire, *Calligrammes* (Paris, 1945, 25th edn) pp.196 ff., the poem 'La jolie Rousse'; M. Adema, *Guillaume Apollinaire: le mal aimé* (Paris, 1952) p.234; C. Gray, *Cubist Aesthetic Theories* (Baltimore, 1961, 3rg edn) pp.110 ff.; W.Kandinsky, *Über das Geistige in der Kunst* (München, 1912, many re-editions and translations); Joshua C. Taylor, *Futurism* (New York: Museum of Modern Art, 1961).

202 See note 169 above.

203 *Curiosités Esthétiques*, pp.274–275 (the Salon of 1859 IV).

204 For example, Aaron Copland, 'The Creative Mind and the Interpretive Mind' (a chapter from his *Music and Imagination* (Cambridge, Mass., 1952), reprinted in F. Puma (ed.), *Seven Arts* (New York: Perma Pocket, 1953, 2nd edn) p.112. Cf. W. Hofmann, *Das irdische Paradies*, p.367.

205 'Jedes Kunstwerk ist Selbstdarstellung des Künstlers ... Die groszen Künstler .... bringen ihre eigene Grundhaltung mit.' 'Nicht der Künstler als Person, sondern die Urkräfte des Weltlebens sprechen durch ihn.' W. Baumeister, *Das Unbekannte in der Kunst* (Cologne: Dumont Dokumente, 1960, 2nd edn) pp.66, 69.

206 See P. Edwards (ed.), *The Encyclopedia of Philosophy* (New York, 1967): 'Historicism' and 'Dilthey'; E. Troeltsch, *Der Historismus und seine Probleme* (1922); J.P.A. Mekkes, 'Wilhelm Dilthey's Kritik der historischen Vernunft', *Philosophia Reformata* XX (1955) pp.7 ff. See also M. Rader, 'Art and History', *Journal of Aesthetics and Art Criticism* XXVI (1967) pp.157 ff.

207 M.C. Smit, *Historisme en Anti-historisme: Wetenschappelijke bijdragen aangeboden door leerlingen van Prof. Dr D.H.Th.Vollenhoven* (Potchefstroom: Franeker, 1951) p.153.

208 Mekkes, 'Wilhelm Dilthey's Kritik der historischen Vernunft', p.38.

209 See note 206 above.

210 For example, H. Taine, *Philosophie de l'art* I & II (Paris, 1924, nouvelle édition; 1st edn 1865).

211 W. Passarge, *Die Philosophie der Kunstgeschichte* (Berlin, 1930) pp.2 ff.; A. Springer is a typical example of this.

212 Passarge, *Die Philosophie der Kunstgeschichte*, pp.50 ff.; R. Hedicke, *Methodenlehre der Kunstgeschichte* (Strassburg, 1924) pp.132 ff.

213 Gombrich also comes from Vienna. Through him the Viennese School has had great influence, also on the work of the Warburg Institute, which in turn had significance for the development of present-day history of art in many ways.

214 Dagobert Frey, *Max Dvorak zum Gedächtnis: Max Dvorak Steilung in der Kunstgeschichte* (Vienna, 1922).

215 Ibid. p.13: 'Die Kunst (ist) ein Gebiet geistiger Produktion auf dem der schöpferische Geist am unmittelbarsten in der Totalität seiner

intellektuellen, voluntaristischen und gefühlsmäszigen Kräften bis in die dunkelsten halbbewuszten Regungen hinab zum Ausdruck gelangt.'

216 Ibid., pp.13 ff.

217 This idea is put forward by among others K. Jaspers, *Die geistige Situation der Zeit* (Berlin, 1953, 8th edn) pp.130 ff. (III, 2, about art); P. Tillich, *Christianity and the Existentialists* (ed. Michalson) p.138; idem., prefatory note in P. Selz, *New Images of Man* (New York: Museum of Modern Art, 1959) pp.9 ff.; see also Eversole, *Christian Faith and the Contemporary Arts*, pp.75 and passim; J. Dewey, see J. Rathner (ed.), *Intelligence in the Modern World: John Dewey's Philosophy* (New York, 1939) pp.997 ff.

218 Max Dvorak, *Über Greco und den Manierismus*, printed behind the commemorative article quoted in note 214 above, p.28.

219 'anarchism' here with a wider significance than political only; cf. W. Haftmann, *Malerei im 20. Jahrhundert* (München, 1954) p.247 (concerning the Dada movement); J.C. Taylor, *Futurism*, pp.9 ff.; cf. also E. Relgis, 'Lo Spirito del nostro tempo, gioco e sforzo – la letteratuta di domani, alcune puntualizzazioni', *Volontà, rivista anarchica mensile* XVI (1963) pp.228 ff.

220 Cf. Hans Redeker, *De dagen der artistieke vertwijfeling* (Amsterdam, 1950) especially sections 8 and 31.

221 'de periode van onderdrukking en vervalsing waarin wij leven / vraagt niet om ons antwoord / maar schreeuwt om protest / dat protest, fel en snerpend in de muziek / aangrijpend en dikwijls duister in boek en spel / breekt vloekend en bruisend los in de schilderkunst / en toont in beelden de ondergang naast het nieuw uitbottende leven.' W. Sandberg, 'De vitaliteit in de kunst', *Museumjournaal* V (1959) p.95. For many years Sandberg has been the director of the Stedelijk Museum in Amsterdam, which he has turned into one of the leading museums of modern art.

222 Cf. H. Read, *Philosophy of Modern Art* (New York, 1955, 2nd edn) p.8 ff.

223 Cf. my article 'Affluence, the Welfare State and Culture', in *Complete Works* 3, pp.339 ff.

224 K.W. Irwin, 'The Artist and the Problem of Communication', in F. Eversole (ed.), *Christian Faith and the Contemporary Arts*, p.63 ff. Many books have appeared that deal with modern art in a very critical way, often written in an emotional language. Among them R.W. Eichler, *Könner, Künstler, Scharlatane* (München, 1963); T.H. Robsjohn-Gibbins, *Mona Lisa's Moustache, a Dissection of Modern Art* (New York, 1948); H. Sedlmayr, *Der Tod des Lichtes: Übergangene Perspektive zur modernen Kunst* (Salzburg, 1964); H. Sedlmayr, *Verlust der Mitte: die bildende Kunst des 19. und 20 Jahrhundert als Symbol und Symptom der Zeit* (Salzburg, 1948).

225 Cf. J.F. Hartlaub, 'Das Unbehagen an der modernen Kunst', in *Fragen an die Kunst* (1962); H. Read, 'The Fate of Modern Painting', in *Philosophy of Modern Art*, p.53 ff.

226 E.g. Dewey. See Rathner (ed.), *Intelligence in the Modern World: John Dewey's Philosophy*, p.997.

227 Gertude von Schwarzenfeld, *Das neue Paris* (Hamburg, 1958) p. 58: 'Kunstkritik ist heute eine Art Mantik geworden, einer Seherkunst die aus "Zeichen" wahrsagt.'

228 Very often great artists are indeed opening new ways, but not only those that created new styles or pictorial means can be called great artists. There are many artists of great talent and artistic importance that have not achieved

works highly original in their stylistic, iconographical or iconological aspects. Originality cannot be used as a criterium for greatness or quality – even those artists that have been renewing forces have often repeated themselves in certain periods of their activity. Not every great work of art can be called a historic deed in its proper sense. Cf. my, 'The Constituent Factors of a Historical Deed' in *Complete Works* 3, part III. Cf. also J.W. Dixon, 'Fallacies and Heresies in Art Criticism', and D. Hare, 'The Myth of Originality in Contemporary Art', in *Art Journal* XXIV (1964/5) pp.143–150 esp. pp.139–142.

229 Important in this respect is a discussion concerning Picasso's Guernica, in J.J. Fisher, 'Expression Theory Re-Examined', *Revue Internationale de philosophie* XVI (1962) pp.64 ff.

230 'For ours is no struggle against enemies of flesh and blood, but against all the various powers of evil that hold sway in the darkness around us, against the spirits of wickedness on high.'

231 The lines by Sandberg quoted above ask of art a certain commitment, a statement of an idea that as such is not artistic. Cf. also Eversole (ed.), *Christian Faith and the Contemporary Arts*, pp.11 ff., pp.45 ff., pp.72 ff., pp.109 ff.

232 E.g. A. Fabri, 'Der Geist eines Malers sind seine Rots, seine Grüns, seine Blaus', in *Interview mit Sisyphos* (Cologne, 1952) p.7–10; C. Gray, *Cubist Aesthetic Theories*, p.114 ff. The comparison often made between music and painting is also typical. The question is whether it is right to say that music is abstract, as is almost always claimed in discussing it. I feel that more probably the theme in music must be compared with the theme in art. Much of the really modern music can therefore be called 'abstract', but not of the older music. The *topos* of autonomous art is new, and the idea of art for art's sake is one of its constituent factors.

233 Lucebert, 1952.

234 Such a reversal, which is not acceptable, is also made in F. Eversole (ed.), *Christian Faith and the Contemporary Arts*, p.49, where is stated that existentialism can be used to express the spirit of our age.

235 C. Rijnsdorp, *Aan de Driesprong* (Baarn, 1964) pp.99 ff., p.53. See also my article 'The Constituent Factors of a Historical Deed', in *Complete Works* 3, part III.

236 See my article 'The Constituent Factors of a Historical Deed' in *Complete Works* 3, pp.285 ff; and my 'Art and Entertainment' (*Kunst en Amusement*, 1962) in *Complete Works* 3, pp.43 ff.

237 Cf. Wittkower, *Born under Saturn*.

238 The theory of expression raises many problems resulting from its subjectivistic starting point. Also often confusion is raised by using the word 'expression' in two different ways, as 'something is expressed in a clear way' or 'artists express themselves'. These two meanings of the word cannot be equated in art theory. Because of the emphasis on the expression of the artist, often leading to a psychology of art, the debate concerning the structure, composition and specific qualities of beauty are often neglected. Some articles: *Revue internationale de Philosophie* XVI:1 (1962) is fully devoted to this problem; M. Rieser, 'The Semantic Theory of Art in America', *Journal of Aesthetics and Art Criticism* XV (1956) pp.12 ff.; Susanne K. Langer, *Feeling and Form* (London, 1953); E.H. Gombrich, 'Expression and Communication', in *Meditations on a Hobby Horse* (London, 1963) pp.56 ff.

239 Allen Kaprow, 'Happenings in New York', *Randstad* 11–12 (Amsterdam, 1966) pp.253, 259; J. Becker, W. Vostell, *Happenings, Fluxus, Pop Art, Nouveau Realisme* (Hamburg: Rowohlt, 1965). See also 'Commitment in Art' above.

240 A. Malreaux, *La métamorphose des dieux* (Paris, 1957).

241 We can cite W. Nigg, who wrote a book on the 'painters of the eternal' (*Maler des Ewigen*, 1951). His choice is in itself already open to discussion: Grünewald, Michelangelo, El Greco, Rembrandt. Why not Dürer, Raphael, Leonardo, Van Eyck and so on? Prophecy is a criterium that does not fit the pictorial arts.

242 E.g. G. Bazin, *Message de l'absolu* (Paris, 1964) p.8 (introduction); this book gives a history of art that was influenced by Malraux.

243 Here we could mention e.g. D. Mahon, *Studies in Seicento Art and Art Theory*; and more recently, J.A. Emmens, 'Rembrandt en de Regels van de Kunst' (Utrecht, 1964, diss.).

244 D. Frey, *Kunstwissenschaftliche Grundfragen* (Vienna, 1946); see also my lecture on 'The Changing Relation between Theme, Motif and Style', in *Complete Works* 4, pp.146 ff. (presented at the 21st International Congress of History of Arts, Bonn, 1964 and the 5th International Congress for Aesthetics, Amsterdam, 1964).

245 Literature, music and the visual arts are simply not directly comparable. See Kristeller, 'The Modern System of the Arts II', pp.45–46. Also, at universities the disciplines of art history, history of literature and history of music are not brought together in one department.

246 See my 'Commitment in Art' above, in this volume.

247 E.g. my article 'The Function of Visual Art in Our Time' (in this volume of the *Complete Works*, part III) in which this is implied. An article by Aler that appeared in the same book where my article was originally published, *De Functie van de Kunst van onze Tijd* [the function of art in our time] by J.M.M. Aler, deals much more directly with this problem, which shows once more how deep the difference is between literature and the visual arts.

248 H. Dooyeweerd, *A New Critique of Theoretical Thought* I (Amsterdam / Philadelphia, 1953) pp.60 passim. The aesthetic is not only found in the fine arts. Apart from beauty in nature there is also the beauty in utensils, industrial design,etc.

249 John 3:21.

250 See Henning Gran, 'Malergleden Personlig', *Kunsten Idag* 48 (1959) p.21 ff. (with a translation into English); J. Sabartes, *Picasso's Variations on Velasquez's painting 'The maids of honour'* (1959); M. Leiris, *Picasso et les Ménines de Velasquez* (Paris, 1959).

251 E.g. Picasso's *Crucifixions* (Amsterdam: Cat. Exp., 1967) nos.147,148; Dali's *Crucifixion of St John of the Cross*.

252 See my *Synthetist Art Theories*, in *Complete Works* 1, p.5 ff; also my 'Art and Entertainment' in *Complete Works* 3, pp.65 f.

253 'Onze ziel kan niet bevredigd zijn, wanneer de dorst naar het Schoone zich niet openbaart, niet bevredigd wordt. Daarom is het kind van God een strijder voor Schoonheid en Heiligheid, want bij de Schepping was de mens absoluut schoon. Het *kalonk agathon* waarnaar Plato zocht zal komen bij's Heeren Wederkomst.' From unpublished notes made by one of Kuyper's students while attending a lecture by him (ca. 1890).

254 In this article we speak mainly about the visual arts. Even if there are parallels, in literature, theatre and music, the situation may be somewhat different.

255 The twelfth-century tympanum of Autun Cathedral portrays the Last Judgment, and on the mandorla around Christ we read: 'Omnia dispono salus meritosque corona / quos scelus exercet me judice poena coercet'.

256 The Council of Trent formulated this difference emphatically, naturally to justify itself against the Reformation, which blamed the Roman Catholic Church for idolatry, and also to go against existing abuses.

257 We name here as an example Rubens's great altarpiece in Vallicella in Rome; cf. J. Müller Hofstede's article in the *Nederlands Kunsthistorisch Jaarboek* [Art-historical yearbook of the Netherlands], 1966.

258 We allude to that well-known painting by Titian, *Sacred and Profane Love*, in the Villa Borghese in Rome; cf. my article 'Two Kinds of Love and the "Carcer Terreno"', in *Complete Works* 4.

259 Cf. E.Wind, Pagan mysteries in fhe Renaissance, London; 1958

260 The study of the history of art is very busy with these problems at the moment. A comprehensive work does not exist yet.

261 In the etching *On Death, Part II: The Philosopher*, Max Klinger, a late nineteenth-century German sculptor, shows a modern man looking at the world, but in fact looking at himself in a mirror – expressing the far-reaching consequence of modern epistemology. The woman in the foreground is either 'mother nature', or 'the inspiring feminine principle'.

262 W. Kandinsky, *Essays über Kunst und Künstler*, ed. M. Bill (Teufen, 1955) p.188.

263 See the Catalogue for the 'Picasso' exhibition (Amsterdam, 1967) nos.105, 106, 121, 124, 175; and note 250 above.

264 See 'The Artist as a Prophet?', in this volume.

265 See R.W.Lee, 'Ut Pictora Poesis, the Humanist Theory of Painting', *Art Bulletin* XXII (1940) p.197 ff.; E.G. Holt, *A Documentary History of Art* II (Garden City, New York, 1958) p.93 ff.; D. Mahon, *Studies in Seicento Art and Art Theory* (London, 1947).

266 Cf. J.A. Emmens, 'Rembrandt en de Regels van de Kunst' (Utrecht, 1964, diss.) p.129.

267 See for example G.G. Gadamer, *Wahrheit und Methode* (Tübingen, 1960) p.54 passim.

268 E. Morpurgo-Tagliabue, *L'esthétique contemporaine* (Milan, 1960) p.164.

269 See in this volume, 'The Artist as a Prophet?'.

270 A quote from Watts, cited in the *Journal of the Warburg and Courtauld Institutes* XXIX (1966) p.366.

271 From the 'SPUR Manifesto 1960', quoted in *Randstad* 11–12 (1966) p.159.

272 J.A. Emmens and E. de Jongh, 'De kunsttheorie van Cobra', Simiolus I (1966) p.63. See also H. Rosenberg, *The Anxious Object: Art Today and its Audience* (New York, 1964).

273 W. Kandinsky, *Essays über Kunst und Künstler*, ed. M.Bill (Teufen, 1955) p.188.

274 'Bacon, le convulsif ou l'angoisse sied aux héros'.

275 A. Fabri, *Interview mit Sisyphos* (Cologne, 1952) p.9.

276 Ibid. p.29.

277 John Russell, *Francis Bacon* (London, 1964) p.1.

278 Here we could indicate the poem of Sandberg, quoted in note 221 above. See also: J.P. Hodin, 'The Aesthetics of Modern Art', *Journal of Aesthetics and Art Criticism* XXVI (1967) p.182.

279 E. Kendall, 'Pop Art, kunst zonder kunstenaars', *Randstad* 11–12 (1966) p.279–280. See in this issue also pp.253, 257, 132.

280 See my article 'Affluence, the Welfare State and Culture' in *Complete Works* 3, pp.339 ff.; also L. Flam, 'L'art religion de l'homme modern', a lecture given at the International Congress of Aesthetics (Amsterdam, 1964).

281 Read for example Elvin Clay, 'Een happening op Ibiza', in *Randstad* 11–12 (1966) pp.238 ff.

282 Tuli Kupferberg, in *The International Times* 9 (Feb. 27-Mar.12, 1967). See also the appendix at the end of this chapter – a schematic summary of the artistic revolution which I drew up in September 1967.

283 See my lecture on Buñuel's *Un Chien Andaloux*, entitled 'Art and Freedom', published in *The Creative Gift* and appearing in *Complete Works* 3, pp190 ff.

284 Reference again to Philippians 4:8, using the words of the King James Bible.

285 September, 1967.

Part III: Articles and Reviews on Twentieth-Century Art and Artists

286 Signaal 3,4 (1961) pp.7–8.

287 *Stijl* 2, 6 (1953) pp.168–177.

288 Taken from Bunyan's apology for his book.

289 *Sartor Resartus* (London, 1898) p.254; see also *Complete Works* 1, p.37 ff.

290 Ibid., p.221.

291 Ibid, p.68.

292 Ibid, p.193.

293 Ibid., p.196.

294 Ibid., p.215.

295 Ibid., p.306.

296 That is to say that everything is caught up in the law of cause and effect, everything determined by naturalistic factors that lie outside of a person.

297 G.A. Aurier: *Oeuvres Posthumes, avec notice de Rémy de Gourmont* (Paris, 1893) p.176.

298 'Ici, près de ma case, en plein silence, je rêve à des harmonies violentes dans les parfums naturels qui me grisent. Délice relevé de je ne sais quelle horreur sacrée que je devine vers l'immémorial. Autrefois, odeur de joie que je respire dans le présent. Figures animales d'une rigidité statuaire: je ne sais quoi d'ancien, d'auguste, religieux dans le rhythme de leur geste, dans leur immobilité rare. Dans les yeux qui rêvent, la surface trouble d'un énigme insondable. Et voilà le nuit – tout repose. Mes yeux se ferment pour *voir sans comprendre* le rêve dans l'espace infini qui fuit devant moi, et j'ai la sensation de la marche dolente de mes espérances ... Mon rêve ne se laisse pas saisir, ne comporte aucune allégorie; poème musicale, il se passa de libretto. Citation Mallarmé: "Par conséquent immatériel et supérieur,

l'essentiel dans une oeuvre consiste précisément dans ce qui n'est pas exprimé: il n'en est pas matériellement constitué" ... Reparlons du panneau: l'idole est là non comme une explication littéraire, mais comme une statue, moins animale aussi, faisant corps dans mon rêve , devant ma case, avec la nature entière, régnant en notre âme primitive, consolation imaginaire de nos souffrances en ce qu'elles comportent de vague et d'incompris devant le mystère de notre origine et notre avenir ... Au réveil, mon oeuvre terminée, je me dis, je dis: d'où venons-nous, que sommes-nous, où allons-nous?' M. Malingue: *Lettres de Gauguin à sa femme et ses amis* (Paris, 1946) p.286, Tahiti, March 1899.

299 'Où allons-nous? Près de la mort une vieille femme Un oiseau étrange stupide conclut Que sommes-nous? Existence journalière L'homme d'instinct se demande ce que tout cela veut dire. D'où venons-nous? Source Enfant La vie commune L'oiseau conclut le poème en comparaison de l'être inférieur vis-à-vis de l'être intelligent dans ce grand tout qui est le problème annoncé par le titre.'

300 Prof. Dr R.F. Beerling: *Uren met Sjestow*, p.38. See the article 'Shestov' in part III of this volume.

301 Ibid. p.134.

302 Heidegger, in his *Holzwege*.

303 *Stijl* 1, 2 (1952) pp.20–22.

304 Revelation 9:21.

305 1 Timothy 4:12; 2 Thessalonians 2:9–11; Psalm 81:13.

306 Luke 21:25, 26; Revelation 6:16, 17; Isaiah 2:21.

307 Ezekiel 7:26.

308 Nihilists are those who believe in nihil[=nill], i.e. nothing.

309 Isaiah 42:25; Jeremiah 2:29–30.

310 *Calvinistisch Jongelingsblad* 5, 13 (1950) pp.106–107 and 14, pp.112–113

311 I am referring to the Impressionists, who started to work around 1870.

312 See 'Art and Beauty in this World' in part I of *Complete Works* 4.

313 We will explain the different terms as much as possible in the text itself. To this end we will present the explanations and ideas employed by the 'moderns' themselves. It will become clear from the text when I render their and not my thoughts.

314 Geometric forms are those borrowed from the field of mathematics: cubes, spheres, pyramids, circles, straight lines, etc.

315 Picasso later moved on in other directions, but he remained the leader and pioneer of the revolution in modern art. We cannot go into his work in more detail here.

316 Their interest was particularly in the layout of the page – i.e. the arrangement of letters, the photographs, the graphic designs, etc.

317 Archetypes are the deepest and most primal basic urges or motivations that live in a person's subconscious, and they are also the expression of the 'soul' of all humanity. The term comes from the modern psychological theories of Freud, Jung and others which had a deep influence on the Surrealists.

318 Frans Boers: 'Naar aanleiding van kunstmanifestaties van krankzinnigen' [in response to the art manifestation of the mentally ill], *Kroniek van Kunst en Kultuur* (1946) p.220.

319 These quotations were taken from S. Anema, *Moderne kunst en ontaarding* (Kampen: Kok, 1926) pp.140, 141. We highly recommend this book even though we may not agree with the author on all points.

320 H. Redeker in *Het Woord* (1946) pp.422, 423.

321 Thus R. Huyghe in an article entitled 'De eeuw van het absurde', *Kroniek van Kunst en Kultuur* (1947) pp.84–87.

322 *Stijl* 1, 12 (1952) pp.282–290.

323 See Ezekiel 7:26 and Isaiah 42:25, Jeremiah 23:17, 18; 2 Thessalonians 2:11 and others.

324 Or *geworfen* ('thrown'), a term used by the modern existentialist philosopher Heidegger, which emphasizes the randomness of our arrival on earth.

325 This idea is voiced for instance in the novel that can teach us so much about modern people, namely Kafka's *The Trial*.

326 In the area of the visual arts we think here of people like Picasso, Zadkine, Kokoschka, Chagall, Klee.

327 Describing a drawing by Oey Tjeng Sit.

328 Describing a drawing by Ger Langeweg.

329 Many art lovers and critics, for instance, deem the sketch Constable made for his *Haywain* of more importance than the painting Constable himself considered as the finished work. Also the sketches by Rembrandt are often considered more essential for his artistry than his worked-out drawings and paintings.

330 Describing a drawing by Leo Schatz.

331 Picasso and Braque made works like this around 1910.

332 Describing another drawing by Ger Langeweg.

333 *Stijl* 1, 6 (1952) pp.118–125.

334 A short time ago a book was published which I now strongly recommend to anyone interested in these issues. It is one of the best works dealing with these problems that has appeared until now: H. Sedlmayr, *Verlust der Mitte, Die bildende Kunst des 19. und 20. Jahrhunderts als Symptom und Symbol der Zeit*, (Salzburg, 5th edition, 1951). This book describes and deals with these tensions and contradictions in great detail.

335 These articles appear in this volume as 'Pondering Four Modern Drawings'; 'Whence Do We Come? What Are We? Whither Do We Go?'; 'Modern Sculpture'; 'Wholesome Twentieth-Century Art'.

336 Between his burial and resurrection, Christ is said to have freed the souls of the Old Testament believers from purgatory, where they were waiting for him. Dürer was one of the artists to make a woodcut of this.

337 E.g. the Mary of Lourdes in many churches, particularly in France.

338 E. Jolas and G. Pelorson, 'Hysteriette of la Cosmosa', in *Transition* 22 (The Hague, February 1933).

339 Quoted from S. Anema: *Moderne Kunst en Ontaarding* (1926) p.141.

340 *Ruimte* 1, 3 (1954) pp.38–42.

341 See Matthew 6:23.

342 Literally the 'wild', called this way after a facetious remark of a critic in 1905 who called the hall where their submissions to the great Autumn Exhibition were hanging 'the cage of the wild'.

343 One could think here of Degas's and Toulouse-Lautrec's depictions of the life of prostitutes, although the latter sometimes pictured more than just the cold facts.

344 Compare this with the work of Jan Steen, who with all his moral teaching also displays a spirit of compassion and solidarity.

345 'Print' is the term used for every kind of graphic artwork. So these are not reproductions! We will not attempt to describe the complicated engraving and etching technique here.

346 Citation from *Kunsten Idag* 2 (1954).

347 *Sola Fide* 17, 3 (1964) pp.13–18.

348 *Stijl* 2, 12 (1953) pp.331–333.

349 See in this volume: 'Whence do we come? What are we? Where do we go?'; 'Angst'; 'Pondering Four Modern Drawings'; 'Surrealism'; and 'Modern Sculpture'.

350 *Calvinistisch Jongelingsblad* 13, 10 (1958) p.149.

351 *Christian Scholar's Review* 1, 2 (winter, 1971) pp132–140; also published in Dutch in *Opbouw* (1968) and in *Nederlandse Gedachten* (1967/8), and in English in Credo (1968).

352 Groen van Prinsterer, *Ongeloof en Revolutie* (Amsterdam: H. van Bottenburg, 1940).

353 E. Stark, 'On the New Left: Guerrillas under the Sun', *The Village Voice* (September 7, 1967) p.9.

354 W. Sandberg, 'De vitaliteit in de kunst' [vitality in art], *Museum Journaal* V (1959) p.95. [We have replaced the original translation here with the translation that is also to be found above in 'The Artist as a Prophet?'. The translation here originally read: 'The period of oppression and counterfeiting in which we / live, asks not for an answer but shrieks in protest / that protest, fierce and raucous in music, moving and often opaque in books and plays breaks loose cursing and hissing in painting and shows in art last gasps next to budding life.']

355 Allen Ginsberg, *Howl And Other Poems* (San Francisco: City Lights Books, 1959).

356 From 'Within you and without you', a song with an Indian-inspired accompaniment.

357 'Eleanor Rigby' from the LP record *Revolver* (late 1965).

358 See Isaiah 1:1 ff.

359 Bob Dylan, 'Desolation Row' from LP record *Highway 61 Revisited*.

360 From *Sergeant Pepper's Lonely Hearts Club Band* (1967).

361 See for example 'Anything Goes: Taboos in Twilight', *Newsweek* (13 November, 1967) pp.74–78.

362 As published in M.R. Choudhury, 'In Defence of Obscenity', *International Times* (16, 29 January, 1967) p.7.

363 See particularly the work of J.H. v.d. Berg, *Leven In Meervoud?* [living in the plural] (Nijkerk, 1964).

364 Interview with A. Klophuis, under the title 'Sex is Mono, Love is Stereo' in *Hitweek* (21 July, 1967).

365 T. Kupferberg, 'When the Mode of the Music changes the Walls of the City Shake', *International Times* (27 February–12 March 12, 1967) p.9.

366 Emile Henry, 'Sartre', *International Times* (27 February–12 March, 1967) p.9.

367 *Nederlandse Gedachten* (6 January 1968) pp.6–7, 'Culture and Revolution, Part 2: We Live in "1787"'; also published in *Opbouw* 12, 17 (1968) pp.130–132.

368 See note 354 above.

369 These thoughts are by no means exceptional or original. See for instance (one example among many) the chapter entitled 'De kunst en de westerse revolutie' [art and the Western revolution] in H. Redeker, *De dagen der artistieke vertwijfeling* (Amsterdam, 1950).

370 We use the term 'modern art' to designate the avant-garde, from Picasso to Appel, Vasarely and Rauschenberg. The term 'contemporary art' or 'twentieth-century art' we use to denote art that emanates a very different spirit, for instance by Rouault or Jan Sluyters, poster art, etc.

371 From a different angle I wrote about this in 'The Artist as a Prophet?', see above in this volume.

372 'In deze tijd heeft wat men altijd noemde / Schoonheid, schoonheid haar gezicht verbrand. / Zij troost niet meer de mensen / Zij troost de larven, de reptielen, / de ratten, / Maar de mens verschrikt zij / En treft hem met het besef / Een broodkruimel te zijn op de rok van het universum.' Lucebert (1952). [The expression 'beauty has burnt her face' may have been first used by Schierbeek.]

373 Introduction catalogue *Niki de Saint Phalle,* Catalogue 419 (Stedelijk Museum of Modern Art, August-October 1967). See also *Museum Journaal* 12, 7 (1967) in which the events of this summer are discussed.

374 See *Time* (7 July, 1967) pp.12 ff.; more elaborate and naturally sympathizing is *Playboy*, 'The new wave makers', pp.130 ff. About the Provos in the Netherlands there is also a special issue of *Lucerna* VI (June 1967) pp.239 ff. and a special Provo issue of *Delta* X, 3 (Autumn 1967).

375 See *Randstad* 11–12 (1966) which gives an extensive overview of the artistic activities and their backgrounds.

376 Tom McGrath, 'Hallucinations?', *International Times* (13 March, 1967) p.4. See also note 361 above.

377 Ibid.

378 Ibid.

379 Interview with Rudolf de Jong in *Hitweek* (27 April, 1967) p.5.

380 See note 364 above.

381 Warren Hinkles, 'What makes Hippies happen on the Psychedelic Bus', *OZ* 3 (April 1967) p.5.

382 H. Van Oortmerssen, 'Gesprek met Paul Goodman', *Witte Krant* 5 (Amsterdam, August 1967).

383 E. Stark, 'On the New Left: Guerillas Under the Sun', *The Village Voice* (7 September, 1967) p.9.

384 Gary Snyder, 'Buddhism and the Coming Revolution', *International Times* (February 13/26, 1967) p.9.

385 Editorial in *Witte Krant* (August 1967) entitled 'Revolution'. Also *Hitweek* wrote about this in their issue of 4 August, 1967.

386 *Hitweek* (4 August, 1967) p.2; *OZ* 7 (October 1967): 'Michael X and the Flower Children'.

387 See in *Christianity Today* XII (24 November, 1967) pp.192–193 the reports of

the meetings of the National Council of Churches, Detroit in October 1967.

388 Also in the special LSD issue of *Maatstaf* 10/11 (January/February 1967) we read just about nothing of all this.

389 David Wilkerson, *Twelve Angels from Hell* (Westwood, N.J., 1965) writes openly about this world – in the light of possible redemption.

390 *San Francisco Oracle* I, 7 (March 1967) p.14 passim.

391 Simon Vinkenoog, 'Loveletter', *Hitweek* 18 (August 1967) p.7. Also see his *Vogelvrij* (Amsterdam 1967), for example p.91: 'You are no slave! Authority does not exist ...'

392 The four parts of this article were published respectively in *Ruimte* 1, 6 (1954) pp.89–92; 11 (1955) pp.156–160; 12 (1955) pp.189–192; 15 (1955) pp.238–242.

393 We use the word 'culture' here in its usual sense: science, literature, etc.

394 In particular in the Dutch context I think of songs like 'Daar bij de molen' and 'Wij gaan nog niet naar huis'.

395 The name given to the hub of the entertainment publishers in New York.

396 Deuteronomy 28:13, 44.

397 See the volume of his writings in English translation entitled *Communication and Confrontation* (Toronto: Wedge, 1972).

398 An artist I have never heard about before.

399 *Musée imaginaire*, a term of Malraux, who devoted a book by this title to these problems.

400 'Un coin de la nature vu à travers un temperament.' See *Complete Works* 1, pp.12, 93.

401 See Groen van Prinsterer's writings on history and the revolution. Cf. my 'Culture and Revolution II', also in this volume.

402 One of the leaders of the *Afscheiding* (Secession) in 1834 of the *Gereformeerden* from the *Hervormde Kerk*. At the end of the nineteenth century the congregations of the *Afscheiding* partly joined the *Gereformeerde Kerken in Nederland* and partly evolved into the *Christelijk Gereformeerde Kerk*.

403 See the Heidelberg Catechism, Sunday 9 and 10.

404 In J.M.M. Aler, H. Hungerland & H.R. Rookmaaker, *De functie van de kunst in onze tijd* [the function of art in our time] (The Hague: Servire, 1962) pp.86–94.

405 See H.L.C. Jaffé, *De Stijl* 1917–1931 (Amsterdam, 1956), p.174.

406 See issue 9, 1 (1950) p.315.

407 *Ad Fontes* 13, 3 (1965): pp. 57–59.

408 See in *Complete Works* 4: 'Principles of Nineteenth-Century Art'.

409 Ibid. See 'About the Content of Works of Art', 'About the Content of Medieval Works of Art', 'The Art of the Fifteenth Century', 'Baroque Art', 'Theme, Style and Motif in the Sixteenth and Seventeenth Centuries', and 'Principles of Nineteenth-Century Art'.

410 *De Gereformeerde Vrouw* 25, 6 (1967) pp. 130–33.

411 For more about the CCS see *Complete Works* 4: 'The CCS, Towards a Christian Art Academy'; 'Art and We'; and 'The Influence of Art on Society'.

412 *Stijl* 3, 3 (1954) pp.82–86.

413 Prof. Dr. R.F. Beerling, introduction to *Uren met Sjestow* (Baarn: Hollandia, 1950). [English-language studies of Shestov's thought include James C.S. Wernham, *Two Russian Thinkers: An Essay in Berdyaev and Shestov* (Toronto: University of Toronto Press, 1968) and Andrius Valevicius, *Leo Shestov and His Times: Encounters with Brandes, Tolstoy, Dostoevsky, Chekhov, Ibsen, Nietzsche, and Husserl* (New York: P. Lang, 1993).]

414 See *Complete Works* 2: 'Philosophy of Unbelievers'.

415 Beerling, *Uren met Sjestow*, p.7.

416 J.W. Tunderman, *Marnix van St Aldegonde en de subjectivistische stromingen in de Nederlanden der 16e eeuw* (Goes: Oosterbaan & Le Cointre, 1941).

417 *Uren met Sjestow*, pp.8, 9.

418 See S.U. Zuidema, *De philosophie van Occam in zijn Commentaar op de Sententiën* (Hilversum: Schipper, 1936, diss. Free University) p.492 passim.

419 *Uren met Sjestow*, p.11.

420 Ibid. p.21.

421 Ibid. p.32.

422 Ibid. pp.94–95.

423 Tunderman, *Marnix van St Aldegonde*, p.60. See also the illuminating work by A. Janse, *Van idolen en schepselen* (1938) pp.46, 99.

424 Tunderman, *Marnix van St Aldegonde*, p.113.

425 *Uren met Sjestow*, p.57.

426 One encounters something of the same sort in Heidegger, who evinced a great affinity for gnosticism. See e.g. the essay by Prof. S.U. Zuidema, 'De dood bij Heidegger', in *Philosophia Reformata* 12 (1947) pp.49–66, especially pp.55–56.

427 *Uren met Sjestow*, p.51.

428 Ibid. p.52.

429 Ibid. p.54.

430 See *Complete Works* 3: 'Gird your Minds for Action and Keep Sober in the Spirit'.

431 19. J. Geelhoed, *Gereformeerd Studieblad* (January 1953) p.12.

432 Cf. also in this regard Tunderman's discussion of objectivism in *Marnix van St Aldegonde*, p.180.

433 *Uren met Sjestow*, p.7.

434 Ibid. p.58. 'Crucifixus est dei filius; non pudet, quia pudendum est. Et mortuus est dei filius; credibile prorsus est, quia ineptum est. Et sepultus resurrexit; certum est, quia impossibile.'

435 *Uren met Sjestow*, p.63.

436 *Zeitschrift für Ästhetik und allgemeine Kunst Wissenschaft* XVIII (Bonn: Bouvier Verlag Herbert Grundmann, 1973) pp.161–174.

437 Published in *Schopenhauer Jahrbuch* LI (1970) pp.50–73.

438 See *Modern Art and the Death of a Culture*, reproduced in part I of this volume.

439 Of course the following does not claim to be anything like a complete bibliography: T. Munro, 'The Failure Story: a Study of Contemporary Pessimism', Journal of Aesthetics and Art Criticism (JAAC) XVII (1958) pp.143 ff.; F. Lebel, *Notre art dement* (Paris, 1926); J. Alford, 'Problems of a Humanistic Art in a Mechanistic Culture', JAAC XX (1961) pp.37 ff.; A.

Gehlen, *Zeit-Bilder, zur Soziologie und Ästhetik der modernen Malerei* (Bonn, 1960); Heisenberg, Heidegger et al., *Die Kunste im technischen Zeitalter* (Bayerische Akademie d. schönen Künste (München, 1956); B. Rey, *Contre l'Art abstrait* (Paris, 1957); C.I. Glicksberg, 'Depersonalization in the Modern Drama', *The Personalist* XXXIX, 2 (Los Angeles, 1958); A. Gowans: 'A-humanism, Primitivism and the Art of the Future', *College Art Journal* XI (1952); H. Beenken, 'Die Krise der Malerei', *Deutsche Vierteljahrsschrift für Literaturwissenschaft und Geistesgeschichte* XI (1933) p.421; G. Boas, 'Il faut etre de son temps', *JAAC* I (1941) pp.52–65; R. Arnheim, 'Form and the Consumer', *College Art Journal* XIX (1959) pp.2 ff.; W. Hess, 'Die grosse Abstraktion und die grossse Realistik', *Jb. f. Ästhetik und allgem. Kunstwissenschaft* V (1960) pp.7 ff.; R.W. Eichler, *Der gesteuerte Kunstverfall* (München, 1965); S. Rudolph, *Die Krise der Kunst in Künstlerbriefen* (Lorch, 1948); M.P. Maass, *Das Apokalyptischie in der modernen Kunst* (München, 1965); Stuart Barton Babbage, *The Mark of Cain* (Grand Rapids: Eerdmans, 1966); J.F. Hartlaub, 'Das Unbehagen an der modernen Kunst', in *Fragen an die Kunst* (1952) pp.3 ff.; W. Barrett, *The Testimony of Modern Art*, in his *Irrational Man* (Garden City, N.Y., 1962, 2nd edn) pp.42–69; R.C. Kwant, *De Stemmen van de Stilte: Merleau-Ponty's Analyse van de Schilderkunst* (Hilversum, 1966); H. Redeker, *De dagen der artistieke vertwijfeling* (Amsterdam, 1950); H. Rosenberg, *The Anxious Object: Art Today and its Audience* (New York, 1964); Ortega y Gasset, *The Dehumanization of the Arts and Other Writings* (Princeton, 1948; originally 1925); T. H. Robsjohn-Gibbins, *Mona Lisa's Moustache: A Dissection of Modern Art* (New York, 1948); W. Sypher, *Loss of the Self in Modern Literature and Art* (New York, 1962); J. Gimpel, *Contre l'art et les artistes* (Paris, 1968); E. Gilson, 'The significance of modern painting', in *Painting and Reality* (London, 1957) ch. IX; F. Marker, *Lebensgefühl und Weltgefühl – Einführung in die Gegenwart und ihre Kunst* (München, 1920); M. Raymond, *From Baudelaire to Surrealism* (New York, 1949); M. Praz, *The Romantic Agony* (London, 1960, 2nd edn, originally 1933); *Un siècle d'angoisse*. Special issue of *XXe Siècle, N.S.* XXVI (23 May, 1964); J.P. Hodin, 'The Aesthetics of Modern Art', *JAAC* XXVI (1967) pp.181 ff.; H. Frank: *Die das Neue nicht fürchten* (Manager der Kunst) (Düsseldorf, 1964); R. McMullen, *Art, Affluence and Alienation* (London, 1968); N.V. Hoist, *Moderne Kunst und sichtbare Welt* (Berlin, 1957); H. Sedlmayr, *Die Revolution der modernen Kunst* (Hamburg, 1955); Herbert Read, *The Philosophy of Modern Art* (New York, 1955, 3rd edn).

[440] Englewood Cliffs, N.J., 1964, p.132. The book is a translation from the German, *Die Kunst unserer Zeit: Versuch einer Deutung* (Stuttgart, 1961).

[441] Apart from the literature mentioned under note 371, see also L. Mumford, 'The Pentagon of Power', *Horizon* XII, 4 (1970) pp.5–20.

[442] E.H. Gombrich, *In Search of Cultural History* (Oxford, 1969).

[443] See also H. Dooyeweerd, *A New Critique of Theoretical Thought* (Amsterdam, 1955, in translation) pp.229 ff., on causality in history.

[444] J. Klapwijk, *Tussen historisme en relativisme* (Assen, 1970), with an extensive summary in German.

[445] See 'The Artist as Prophet?' in part II of this volume.

[446] See 'The Constituent Factors of a Historical Deed' in part III of *Complete Works* 3.

[447] See my 'Commitment in Art' in part II of this volume.

[448] I am indebted for this term to McMullen, see note 438 above. One can also mention here Malraux's *Musée imaginaire*.

449 Of course symbolism is also living on in our century, at least up to c.1930 or1940; we think of der Kinderen, Toorop, Orozco, but this is certainly not the main stream.

450 in *Der blaue Reiter* (1912) p.74 ff.

451 Interesting in this connection: K. Lankheit, 'Die Frühromantik und die Grundlagen der gegenstandslosen Malerei', *Neue Heidelberger Jahrbücher* N.F. (1951) pp.55–90; H. Beenken, and M. Praz, for both see note 438.

452 You also used these terms in your 'De functie van de litteratuur', in J.M.M. Aler, *De functie van de kunst in onze tild* (Den Haag, 1962) pp.8–50, e.g. on p.45.

453 H. Jonas, *The Gnostic Religion* (Boston, 1963, 2nd edn). See also S. Pétrement, *Le dualisme chez Platon, les gnostiques et les manichéens* (Paris, 1947).

454 See J.W. Tunderman, *Marnix van St Aldegonde*, pp.105 f., pp.143 f.

455 From preface to D. E. Harding, *Hierarchy of Heaven and Earth*.

456 In the London edition of 1898, p.196.

457 For Nietzsche's relation to gnosticism see Jonas, *The Gnostic Religion*, pp.349 ff.

458 'wie Logik und Kunstgerechtigkeit erst im Wesenlosen ihre schönsten Siege feiern, im Nichts sich Leidenschaften und Verfinsterungen gebaren und überwinden. Aus Nichts hat Gott die Welt geschaffen, sie ist ein krankhafter Abszess des Nichts, ein Abfall Gottes von sich selbst. Das Schöne, das Poetische besteht eben darin, dass wir uns an diesem materiellen Geschwür wieder ins Nichts resorbieren.' Quoted in N. v. Holst, *Moderne Kunst und sichtbare Welt* (Berlin, 1957) p.17.

459 F. Marc, *Briefe, Aufzeichnungen und Aphorismen* (Berlin, 1920).

460 G. Apollinaire, *Les Peintres cubistes* (Geneva, 1950) p.11.

461 Jonas, *The Gnostic Religion*, p.83; see note 146 above.

462 Ibid. p.59.

463 Ibid. p.309.

464 E. Jolas, 'The Primal Personality', *Transition* 22 (1933) pp.78–83 (quotation on p.82).

465 Jonas, *The Gnostic Religion*, pp.64, 296 ff.

466 Ibid., p.360.

467 Ibid., pp.296, 298, 301.

468 Ibid. p.54.

469 Ibid. p.72.

470 H. Platschek, *Neue Figurationen* (München, 1959) pp.80,81.

471 Quoted in *Transition*, p.83 – see note 371 above.

472 H. Ball, 'Ich liebte nicht die Totenkopfhusaren', quoted in *DU* XXVI (September 1966) p.721.

473 *Opbouw* 16, 36 (1972): pp. 278–80. Text of a lecture held in February 1972 for the *Gereformeerde Studieclub* [Reformed studygroup] in Rijswijk, the Netherlands. This lecture Rookmaaker later extended into an article, which is the next article in this volume, entitled 'Do we Need to be Modern in order to be Contemporary?'

474 Foreword by C.S. Lewis to *Hierarchy of Heaven and Earth* by Harding.

475 Platschek, *Nieuwe figuratieve kunst?* (translated from German into Dutch by H.

476 B. Goudzwaard, H. van Riessen, H.R. Rookmaaker, J. van der Hoeven, *Macht en onmacht van de twintigste eeuw* (Amsterdam: Buijten en Schipperheijn, 1974) pp.69–111.

477 Bibliography: H.H. Arnason, *The History of Modern Art* (London: Thames & Hudson, 1969). Especially recommended for the illustrations; M. Jean and A. Mezei, *Genèse de la pensée moderne* (Paris, 1950); H.R. Rookmaaker, *Art and the Public Today* (L'Abri Fellowship, 1968) see in part II of this volume; H.R. Rookmaaker, *Gauguin and Nineteenth-Century Art Theory* (Amsterdam: Swets & Zeitlinger, 1972, 2nd edn) see in part I of *Complete Works* 1; H.R. Rookmaaker, *Modern Art and the Death of a Culture* (London, 1972, 3rd edn) see in part I of this volume; H.R. Rookmaaker, 'Modern Art and Gnosticism. An Open Letter to Prof. Dr Jan Aler', *Zeitschrift für Äesthetik und Allgemeine Kunstwissenschaft* 18 (1973) pp.162–174, see above in this volume; E. Rosenthal, *The Changing Concept of Reality in Art* (New York, 1962); F.A. Schaeffer, *Death in the City* (IVP, 1969); A.C. Zijderveld, *De abstracte samenleving, een cultuur-kritische studie van onze tijd* (Meppel, 1970), see for a discussion of gnosticism pp.122–130.

478 H. Platschek, *Nieuwe figuratieve kunst?* (a Dutch translation from the German by H. Redeker, 1960).

479 Jonas, *The Gnostic Religion* (1963) pp.359–360.

480 Ibid. p.368.

481 Ibid. p.362.

482 London, 1898, pp.192–193.

483 Cited from W. Hess, *Dokumente zum Verständnis der Malerei* (Hamburg, 1956) p.79.

484 See J. Alford, 'The Prophet and the Playboy: Dada Was Not a Farce', *College Art Journal* 11 (1952) pp.269 ff.).

485 ['polemological' is de Certeau's coinage for 'conflicts covered up with words'].

486 Published by Swets & Zeitlinger, Amsterdam, 1959. This review appeared in *Lucerna* 2 (1960): pp. 332–335.

487 See Millard Meiss, *Painting in Florence and Siena after the Black Death* (Princeton, 1951) p.149 and note 43; F. Antal, *Florentine Painting and its Social Background* (1948) p.198 ff. and ill.54; H. Cornell, *The Iconography of the Nativity of Christ* (Uppsala, 1924).

488 Published by De Bezige Bij, Amsterdam, 1950. This review appeared in *Correspondentiebladen van de Vereniging voor Calvinistische Wijsbegeerte* 15 (December 1951) pp. 16–17.

489 I had the opportunity to discuss these matters, including the theological context, with Revd F.A. Schaeffer. See his 'The New Modernism', an address presented to the International Council of Christian Churches (ICCC), second plenary congress in Geneva in August 1950.

490 Published by J. Heynis Tzn, Zaandijk, 1957. This review appeared in In *Opbouw* 2, 37 (1959): pp. 294–295. This is the first article in a series of four reviews. The other reviews, also in this volume, deal with books by Sedlmayr, Oxenaar and Hess.

491 Van Meegeren was a renowned forger. See *Complete Works* 1: 'Van Meegeren: Genius Forger and Decadent Artist'.

492 Published by Rohwalt Verlag, Hamburg, 1957. This review appeared in In Opbouw 2, 39 (1959): pp. 309–310. This is the second in a series of four related reviews.

493 To this series also belong the reviews of books by J.M. Prange, R.W.D. Oxenaar and W. Hess (see elsewhere in this volume).

494 See *Complete Works* 3, plate 2.

495 Ibid.

496 Combined here are the third and fourth articles in a series of four related book reviews. The first two articles, on books by J.M. Prange and H. Sedlmayr, appear separately above.These third and fourth articles both deal with Oxenaar's book, while the fourth article ends with a brief two-paragraph commendatory review of the book by Hess. Oxenaar's book was published by De Haan/Phoenix Pocket, Utrecht, 1958; the Hess book was published by Rohwolts Verlag, Munich, 1957; and the 2-volume book by Haftmann also mentioned here was published in 1954 by Prestel Verlag, Munich. The reviews appeared in *Opbouw* 2, 41 (1959) pp.325–326 and *Opbouw* 2, 42 (1959) pp.333–334.

497 München, Prestel Verlag, 1954.

498 München, Rohwolts Verlag, n.d.

499 Published by Oosterbaan & Le Cointre, Goes, 1976. This review appeared in *Beweging* 41, 2 (1977) p.25.

500 *Trouw*, no date.

501 *Trouw*, 21 January 1950.

502 *Trouw*, 20 June 1953.

503 *Trouw*, 21 Feb 1950

504 *Trouw*, 28 June 1954.

505 *Trouw*, no date.

506 *Trouw*, 8 July 1952.

507 *Trouw*, 27 Aug, 1953.

508 *Trouw*, 6 July 1954.

509 *Trouw*, no date.

510 *Trouw*, 8 October 1955.

www.ingramcontent.com/pod-product-compliance
Lightning Source LLC
Chambersburg PA
CBHW031604210526
45464CB00004B/1423